# ACCEPTANCE OF MEDIOCRITY

*An Autobiography*

*By*

# DAVID E. PULLMANN

*Edited by*

*Ruth Pullmann Riedel*

*Sharlyn Roehl Pullmann*

Cover photo: Overlooking Chesapeake Bay at Blackwalnut Point

Order this book online at www.trafford.com
or email orders@trafford.com

Most Trafford titles are also available at major online book retailers.

Printed in Victoria, BC, Canada.

ISBN: 978-1-4269-3091-1

*Our mission is to efficiently provide the world's finest, most comprehensive book publishing
service, enabling every author to experience success. To find out how to publish your book, your
way, and have it available worldwide, visit us online at www.trafford.com*

*Trafford rev. 5/21/2010*

 www.trafford.com

**North America & international**
toll-free: 1 888 232 4444 (USA & Canada)
phone: 250 383 6864 ♦ fax: 812 355 4082

# Contents

# *Preface*

*It was never my intention to write this book (some readers might say I never should have), until I read my father's autobiography,* <u>Putting Out the Fleece</u> *(Trafford, 2004). Many of the events in that account were already familiar first-hand to those of us in the family who knew him well, but it also contained private thoughts of the author that none of us would ever have known. However, its real value is the legacy it leaves to the generations that come after him, who not only could know none of the events first-hand, but will be able to catch a glimpse into the mind of a forebear they will never meet.*

*Ever the opportunist, my father had the notion that he could make money selling copies of his book. No, I told him, this was known in the trade as vanity fare, and would never have a wide market outside the family. He disagreed. "It has already saved a life," he said softly. Saved a life! How? Well, as one of the ladies at his assisted living facility was pouring out a tale of woe one evening, he went back to his room to retrieve his longhand original for her, the only version he had while other members of the family were handling the editing and publication process for him. When she returned it the next day she said she had gone home very depressed after they talked and was contemplating suicide when she picked up his manuscript. For her it was an apocalypse.*

*By the grace of God, my father kept his faculties until the very end and continued to draft the events of his life until he decided to publish them shortly before his death. On the other hand, I am beginning this project as I start into retirement, not knowing how many years lie ahead for me, what ailments might beset me or what the state of my mind might be later. I have often thought that I was born at the best possible moment in history, because I am a witness to so many singular and unprecedented events that those born as recently as two hundred years earlier could not possibly have imagined, including the first time that a human was able to leave this planet and return to it! These are truly the Golden Years for me, as I enjoy tremendous blessings from the Lord too numerous to list, not the least of which is a clear memory of the events of years gone by. Hopefully, I will finish the project while there is still a part of the story left to tell, but that is the point. I wanted to leave you a progress report, in case I am unexpectedly taken away in body, mind or spirit. Because some material may benefit those with a genealogical bent or an interest in folk archive some day, I have consciously chosen to include a few details of the kind my father had the good sense to leave out. Of course, I assume that such insertions will not render an otherwise good story obscured by meaningless drivel. I apologize to you in advance if I have miscalculated that risk.*

*Many have said, when they reach this point in their lives, that they have no regrets—if they had it to do over again, they would do it all again the same way. Would that I could make such a statement. No, sadly, I have many, many regrets. Suppose God were to give us two chances at life, the second time equipped with everything we learned the first time through so we could avoid all those mistakes we made. Would we make it through without a whole new set of mistakes? The good news is that we do have two chances at life. Even better, the second one is guaranteed to be mistake free. Best of all, through trust in our Savior, all of those mistakes we made the first time around are forgotten—by everyone, including God.*

*One of my professors in graduate school dedicated his book to his wife, without whose valuable assistance and devotion, he says, the book would have been completed long ago. I dedicate my book to those of you who are reading this after I am gone. I am waiting to meet you. "Be thou faithful unto death, and I will give thee a crown of life" (Rev. 2:10). If you believe this, I will see you soon.*

# Early Bird

"**M**ommy, remember when I was born?"

"Of course, dear, I was there. I'm sure I told you about it."

"But I *remember* it." The four-year-old then astonishes her mother with graphic detail of her own birth—emerging from a dark tunnel into the light, hearing shrieks, being touched for the first time, and then soaking up the soothing tones of a familiar voice, now strangely unmuffled.

What is the earliest memory you have? Are you one of those who can remember back to when you were born? I can make no such claims. For me, the earliest memory I have is a water fountain. Not a drinking fountain, but a bubbling, splashing display in the city park. What is equally vivid in memory, however, was the longing to see it again after we left. In the eye of an infant, that must have been something impressive to see, but we never went back, and I never saw it again. The *anticipation* of seeing it once more was itself a memory that burned itself into my consciousness.

Readers who know me personally are aware that an incident like this is apt to elicit an anecdote or episode from personal experience of which it reminds me. When retail giant K-Mart filed for bankruptcy under chapter 11 of the Bankruptcy Act a few years ago, we made the conscious decision to give them some business to support their effort to remain afloat. While shopping in the store for some furnishings that we wanted from their Martha Stewart collection, I stopped one red-vested clerk to ask whether he could direct me to the water fountain. He looked at me as if I had just stepped off the moon. I was just beginning to realize that he did not speak English as he motioned toward another Red Coat down the aisle who was stocking shelves. This fellow studied my lips carefully, so I formed the words WAT - ER FOUN - TAIN very deliberately for him. He processed that for a few seconds, then, eyes suddenly brightening, he pointed outside and said, "Oh … Oh. You go to gah-den shop." I remember thinking, "K-Mart, you deserve to go out of business."

That water fountain of my infancy was almost certainly somewhere in Detroit, where I was born Friday August 11, 1944, the oldest of the six children of Elmer and Martha (née Gimbel) Pullmann. My father was in the Navy there, attending the Packard Marine Engine School for specialized training on PT boats. We were in Detroit only until I was about a year old, and the only other conscious memory I have of that first year is the façade of the huge church we attended. In that vignette my mother is talking with some other ladies on the sidewalk, while I am captivated by the stained glass windows in its massive concrete walls.

My father left the Navy in late 1945, and, as he relates in his autobiography, we journeyed by car to Colorado about that time, accompanied by my grandfather, George Pullmann. He does not mention in that account that we ever went to Royal Gorge, but I seem to have a memory that we were there. I am not sure what age children develop a fear of height, but in my mental video of this event, I am being held tightly by someone as I peer over the edge to see some railroad tracks an incredibly long distance far, far below at the bottom of a narrow canyon. We would never have had any other opportunity to be in that part of the country for many years after. As with the water fountain, the expectation of seeing that again was as powerful as the initial experience and has persisted in my brain cells ever since.

The next scene locked in memory takes us near Westgate, Iowa, where we lived for a time in the home of my grandmother's sister, Selma Reinking. Since I was not yet two, I cannot say I have a conscious memory of their farm, located somewhere northwest of Westgate, but while we were there, my brother Ralph was born (May 23, 1946). I do not actually remember living with the Reinkings either, but I have a hazy picture of their daughter Wilma, perhaps just a teenager at the time, giving me raisins while I sat on the potty. I have a little clearer recollection of her merciless teasing, holding something I wanted just out of reach until my frustrated caterwauling brought my unamused mother running to the rescue.

Although we kids were never aware of it at the time, life was tough for my parents after my father left the Navy. He describes in his book how his employers at Bender Chevrolet misunderstood a government reimbursement program. As the months dragged on, the expectation of matching funds never came, leaving him $75 a month to raise his family of four. The Lord always provides, however, and besides the gracious help of friends in the community, it so happens that Iowa has many rivers well stocked with carp and bullheads, ample rainfall, and some of the most fertile soil in the world. Everyone had a garden, and after having our fill of its produce throughout the season, much of the remainder was canned for the winter. Still true today, many fruits and vegetables grew wild along the rivers and roadways, and my parents took full advantage of this bounty. Apples, plums, chokecherries, and ground cherries were in abundance, but also asparagus. While my parents picked it alongside the road one summer, I was the toddler "guarding" the bushel basket in the back seat of the car, and I remember eating so much of it raw right from the basket, that to this day I cannot stand asparagus.

Wild ring-necked pheasants were also plentiful in Iowa. It was very common to see them gliding across the road as we drove through the country, and an occasional windshield was smashed by one that procrastinated its takeoff or misjudged the closure rate of a pickup streaking toward it. My father was not a hunter, but once in a while around Thanksgiving season, someone would shoot an extra pheasant or two and give them to us. I can even remember once biting into a shotgun pellet that had buried itself so deeply into the meat that it remained hidden from the cook during cleaning. Pheasants nest on the ground, and as a kid I once ran across a clutch from which the poor hen had fled. I had never seen eggs that were speckled and multi-colored in the same nest, some gray, and some pale yellow, blue or pinkish.

Westgate was home to the Benders, the family of my paternal grandmother Hilda. The oldest girl in her family, she had long ago moved from there, but several of her siblings still lived in and around town: Emil, Martin, Frieda, Selma, and Erwin. Arrival into the affection and emotional support of family should have been a fortuitous environment for a young couple with little kids starting out, but my parents were greeted with indifference and even more than a little antagonism. All of this was transparent to us children, however, so we did not appreciate the urgency of my mother's pleas for our best behavior whenever we were invited somewhere.

I can still remember some of our visits to Aunt Frieda's house in the southwest corner of town. It was the first time Ralph had seen a house where you could leave a room through one doorway and come back through another doorway to the starting point. I can still picture him making the circuit saying, "Hey, it leaks." Of course, that initiated a game that the rest of the troop had to imitate until our embarrassed mother called a halt. Outside in the yard was an arbor of Concord grapes, which we were allowed to taste. I think it was my first exposure to them and quickly discovered that the outside skin was tart and the slimy inside full of seeds. Best way to eat them, I concluded, was to squeeze the skin until it burst, squirt out the pulp without having to touch it, throw away the skin and either swallow the rest whole or spit out the seeds. I know, what a way to waste a perfectly good grape, huh?

Aunt Frieda was known around town for her dandelion wine. From the sweet Mogen David Concord grape wine my father occasionally allowed us to taste, I thought I knew all about wine. So I was not prepared for the bitter treacle I sampled when she offered a little of her concoction to me. I could not understand how my father could accept the jar of that stuff she sent home with us.

Her house was actually owned by her brother Emil, who tragically lost his wife after she gave birth to their daughter Louise. Unmarried Frieda offered to move in with him to help with housekeeping and child-raising. This was not an ideal situation for either her or Louise, however, which led to a rather turbulent existence for both of them. Sadly, Louise was killed in the prime of her life in a collision with a train. In an exchange of correspondence with his cousin Mary Wunderlich, Nathan Bender (a cousin whom I will shortly identify further) recalls the morning of October 12, 1970: "I was home on military leave, preparing to go to Germany on the day Louise was killed at the train crossing in front of our property. I drove uptown to the front of the train, and there she was, still in the car, and dead. Had shivers from the sight." Mary responds, "That morning she had one of her screaming fits. My dad had just come home from downtown when he heard all of this and watched as she spun gravel tearing out of the driveway. He said to himself, 'Louise, Louise …,' and as he turned to go up the steps to the kitchen, he heard the train whistle and he knew. He said he never went into the house but went down to Grandma Reinking's (she lived right there by the tracks) and saw the train stopped. Aunt Emma and Uncle Ed Berghoeffer were at Grandma's and he stopped and asked Ed to go with him, and they saw her dead, still sitting in the car (hands on the wheel, I think)."

Emil was the blacksmith in town, and since his shop was one or two doors away from the Chevrolet garage where my father worked, I have a clear picture of him. Emil was already an old man in those years, and I can still see his stooped, stout frame trudging slowly home for lunch when the noon whistle in town would blow, and again at six when the whistle would mark the end of his long hard day. Most remarkable in my memory of him, however, was the size of his fingers. I would estimate that his thumb was almost three inches in diameter. Although I never saw him do this, my father said that after many years in the shop, his fingers became so calloused that he could pluck a bar of iron glowing nearly white-hot straight out of the forge bare-handed and nudge it over to the anvil. Then after beating it a few times with his hammer, he would fling it still cherry-red into the water tank, instantly boiling the surface with a sharp hiss.

Uncle Emil was a gentle old fellow who always had time for kids. One of the kindest of men, he was also one of the slowest—gauged by either physical or mental alacrity. I can remember one time when his sister Selma, who with her husband Will had moved off the farm into a house across the street from Emil, invited all of us over for the evening. Some of us were old enough to join the grown-ups for cards, and she introduced us to a fun new game called Crazy Eight. Another card game that could include the kids was called Pig. When a certain card is laid, play stops immediately and everyone places his index finger alongside his nose. The last to do so is the Pig. Every time, sometimes as long as a minute or so after play had stopped, poor Emil was the last to realize what was happening and looked slowly around the table to see befingered faces grinning at him. The whole table then erupted in laughter as, too late, he quickly put his finger up too.

Uncle Erwin was the youngest of the Benders, but also the tallest. Older brother Martin was quite tall himself, but little Erwin topped out at six feet, seven inches. My parents often related an anecdote where Erwin once became weary of being asked how the weather was at his altitude. When a rather rotund man asked him whether it was raining up there, Erwin replied, "If you were rolled out as flat as you should be, you could find out if it was raining on Mount Whitney." Since Erwin was so much younger than his sister Hilda, he and my father were roughly contemporary, seeming to me that they were of the same generation. In fact, his youngest son Tom (who, incidentally, eventually grew to seven feet tall) was in my class in school, and the next older boy Nathan (who reached a mere six-eight) was only one grade ahead of us.

Martin and Erwin were the owners of Bender Chevrolet, my father's employer. The difference in the ages of the two brothers caused more sparks than sparkle, however, and the mutual lack of respect between them eventually took its toll upon the business, as well—and upon their employees. Here, joining their team, was a bright young protégé with credentials from the United States Navy, one of the most prestigious of mechanics schools, using the most sophisticated equipment, in the world, and the best response they could offer was a guffaw from one and a hrumpf from the other. It seems that generosity and compassion were not in their souls. Perhaps because of the wariness focused on each other, they failed to recognize that their most important assets were right in front of them. Throughout his life my father could scarcely express his disgust for this period in his life, when he most needed the support, empathy and encouragement that he expected from these family members but failed to get.

We were members of St. Peter's Lutheran Church in town. Of course. It was the only church in town. In fact, virtually everyone in tiny Westgate was Lutheran and *ipso facto* a member of St. Peter's. One notable exception was Eddy Schwartz, a self-professed atheist who worked as a mechanic at the shop with my father and who refused to heed my father's entreaties for his soul. He also failed to heed my father's warnings about crawling underneath a car supported by only a floor jack. One night as he was working alone in the garage, his wife became worried when he did not return home and found him crushed to death by a car that fell with no warning when the jack failed.

It was at St. Peter's that we met a family that would change our lives for many years. Arnold and Arvilla Klammer, slightly older than my parents, had a farm two miles northeast of town. The Klammers were long-time residents of the community and familiar with the cliquishness of small-town Westgate. Arvilla was a Norwegian farm girl from the Gulbranson clan in South Dakota and was already fully aware of the high standards of acceptance set for an outsider who marries a local boy. My mother could identify immediately. Living with the relatives of her husband was like being mounted as a specimen under the microscope. They were not so easily convinced that such a gorgeous Venus from the backwaters of South Dakota could be good for their nephew. Surely someone that attractive must have loose morals, and they were determined to uncover them.

The Lord not only provided this wonderful Klammer family for empathy, but He was now going to open the door, literally, leading out from an overcrowded Reinking household that was building up steam. Klammers had an old hired man named Jim living in a tiny tenant house next to the primary residence on their farm. Sometimes Jim chomped away on a wad of his chewin' tabacka, but I watched in fascination as he rolled a cigarette. He would pull out a little square of white paper from his shirt pocket, then reach back for the red metal can of Velvet in his hind pocket. After he sprinkled out a small pile of tobacco, he would lick along the edge of the paper in his shaky hands, form a lumpy cylinder and light up. After a time Jim either died or moved on, not sure which, but the little house became vacant and Klammers offered us the use of it for a while to escape the scrutiny and pressures found under the noses of officious relatives.

I never asked my father what they charged for rent, but I suspect they offered the use of the "Little House," as my parents called it for years afterward, in exchange for whatever assistance we could give them on the farm. I was about four when we left that house, but I still have a rather clear picture of it. Visualize a square with a line dividing it into two sections, one two-thirds and the other one-third of the area. Now bisect the smaller section to form two subsections. This was the floor plan—three rooms. One of these two smaller subsections was the "master bedroom," and the other subsection was the kitchen. There was only one door, which opened upon the tiny kitchen. There was no indoor plumbing, but next to the sink was a hand pump for extracting fresh drinking water from the ground. It was cozy, warm and out of the elements. Most of all, it was private.

For me, one event stands out from this period on the farm. When a second child is born into the family, a new dynamic is set in motion that has far-reaching effects. The older child has to face the painful realization that his contract has just been renegotiated. His share of the attention has suddenly fallen from 100% to less than half, thanks to this new interloper. Where did this uninvited jaybird come from anyway? After Ralph came along, I apparently became so jealous one day when he was a toddler, that I whacked him hard enough with the rubber wheels of a toy tractor that I drew blood. I suppose it is safe to say that had an immediate effect to restore the balance of attention for the moment, but probably not the sort that would make me feel better for it. Incidentally, things are not so easy for Number Two either. In the shadow of One, smaller and weaker, always a follower, Two builds up such resentment to his place in the order that psychologists have a name for the condition: Number-Two-Child Syndrome. Worse, when Three comes along, another new profile emerges—Middle-Child Syndrome—having neither the privileges of the eldest nor the attention of the youngest. That is also when One, now suddenly responsible for whatever happens, begins to hear, "You're the oldest, you should have known better." It was while we lived in the Little House that child number three, Donald, was born (March 1, 1948).

Other memories at the Little House are fleeting: once when my grandmother, Emelia Gimbel, stayed for a while; once when my father had stepped on a rusty nail which pierced his shoe and while using a cane still managed to carry us through the snow to the car; once when an unwelcome visitor interested in my mother came knocking on the door; and once when I was reading the letters on the cereal box at breakfast and insisted that E was a "miket" and F was a "broken miket." My parents never could explain where I got that from.

# Kindergarten

**W**hich reminds me of a story, supposedly true. Somewhere in California is a community with a high influx of Hippies from the 1960's who are now in their second and third generations. The teachers in the local schools are quite familiar with their iconoclastic way and are no longer shocked or bemused by given names like Lotus, Farthing, Darlacious, and so on. The principal had sent letters to the homes requesting that the kindergarten kids come the first day wearing a nametag, so no one was taken aback when one of the students stepped off the bus with a tag reading Fruit Stand. Throughout the day Fruit Stand did not seem to be responding well when he was addressed, but the teachers attributed this to first-day shyness. At the end of the day, the staff was sorting the class according to the bus they would need to board. To assist in this process they had asked the mothers to write on the back of the nametag the place where the child would need to be dropped off. When they turned Fruit Stand's nametag over, it read Anthony.

By the time I was ready for school, my father had left Bender Chevrolet in Westgate for Foss and Rueber, a farm implement dealership in Maynard, a town about six miles east, only slightly larger but perhaps a little more progressive than Westgate. He bought an acre of land on the northeast corner of town and started to construct a house on it. When he got the basement built, he decided to cover it over with tarpaper and roofing cement to keep out the elements, so we could leave the Little House and move into it. Not only did this save him the six-mile commute each day, but also he was now close enough that he could actually slip home for lunch.

While he had every intention of erecting the next story on top of the basement when time and funds permitted, we would be living underground for a year or two. I do not recall the move itself, but it was not because of any rancor between us and the Klammers. On the contrary, the friendship deepened, and it was while my parents were tending to chores on their farm, once when they were away, that my sister Ruth was born (November 27, 1949) in their house. I can distinctly recall two sets of visitors while we were living in the basement. First were Margaret Stainbrook (my mother's sister) and her husband Gilbert, and they brought with them a novelty few people had in those days—a movie camera. Uncle Gilbert wanted action and told us to jump, so the old black-and-white home movies he shot still show toddler Donny standing there gawking in bewilderment at two older jackrabbits outside the front door of the basement. The second visitors were George and Hilda Pullmann, my grandparents. Their visits were rare for a variety of reasons (I can remember only one other), but this time they brought candy, a teeth-rotting treat my mother seldom allowed, so I am sure she was enthralled when Grandma pulled out those bags.

In order to pay off the construction debts they had accrued, my parents decided to raise some chickens on their property and sell them door-to-door dressed and ready to roast (imagine what the Health Department would have to say about *that* today). I can still see those thousand or so cute yellow fluff balls when they arrived, but how ugly they became in a few weeks when feathers started to sprout. It was also morbidly amusing to watch headless white birds flapping around the yard. Not so amusing was the operation to boil off the feathers, the burning-hair stench of the flame to singe off pinfeathers, or the gag-inducing offal carried away in pails to the back woods for burial. When every house in town had been canvassed for a sale, many an unsold chicken was still in the house, wrapped in butcher paper and looking for a roaster. Piling little kids into the car, my undaunted mother headed for towns around, walking through neighborhoods of Westgate, Oelwein, and Sumner until Hoover's campaign pledge to put a chicken in every pot was fulfilled.

Unlike Westgate, which had a small public school for elementary grades, Maynard had a large public school, K through 12. It was located on the south edge of town, but this was close enough for me to walk back and forth each day. I started all-day kindergarten there in the fall of 1949. Although I cannot recall much from that school year, snatches of it are quite clear. Each afternoon we went out into the hallway to retrieve our cots for a one-hour nap. I doubt if I had taken a nap since I was about two, even if then, so my hour was spent fidgeting and watching that big clock on the wall that had no second hand. I had never seen a clock that appeared to do nothing at all for a while, then suddenly jump ahead its next minute, so I just stared in fascination, anticipating when it would click its next move. After nap it was time to put our shoes back on and take our cots back outside the classroom. I could tie my shoes by myself, but some of my classmates needed assistance from the teacher, Jacquelyn Rowland, or one of the aides. I suppose I noticed the attention this afforded, so one day I pretended I could not remember how. The aide saw through my ploy immediately and insisted that I not only get busy tying my own shoes, but also help her with anyone else who asked.

Northeast Iowa is rich in limestone deposits, so chalky white gravel mined locally covered the roads everywhere around us. This finely ground stone was spread on the playground at our school also, but a pebble of quartz was occasionally sprinkled in the mix. The first time I saw one, I was sure I had found a diamond. Carefully wrapping my fist around my precious gem, I ran to the teacher supervising the playground to share my enthusiasm. Instead of proclaiming my discovery far and wide as I expected, however, she gave me a perfunctory "that's very nice" and sent me back to play. But then I saw another one, and oh, there's another one too, and …. Soon I understood. I had not noticed it earlier, but now it seemed there were sparkles all over the place.

School was a new experience for me, and I thought I understood it when I discovered other kids my age were there too. So who were these angry men who burst out of the school building toward me one day when I was standing on the sidewalk? They were huge—and they were yelling battle cries as they pulled those odd-looking cages over their heads. Their shoes made clicking sounds on the concrete as they rushed toward me, and I did not understand why the school had sent them out to trample me. But as I cowered on top of my lunchbox, some tromped past and others bounded right over me, continuing on to the football field nearby. I had no idea what that was all about.

There are only three names I can remember from my kindergarten class, but I can pull up in my mind the face of only two—Steven Kaune and Joanie Bachman. Somewhere recently I ran across a tiny wallet photo of Steven, or I probably would not have remembered what he looked like. He invited me to his birthday party when he turned six, and I vaguely recall my mother driving me to his house on the east edge of town for it, but not much else. Then there was one Nancy Guritz, who came to our basement home once to play. As she got ready to leave, she wanted me to accompany her back to her house to see her newborn kittens. My mother said no, but with a little wheedling, I got permission to walk with her as far as the bridge over the little stream that ran through Maynard.

When we got to the bridge, Nancy convinced me that if we ran fast enough, I could get back home soon enough that my mother would never know. She miscalculated. My mother was waiting for me when I walked in the door at home, demanding to know why I had disobeyed. I was dumfounded. How could she know? Well, for one thing the distance to Nancy's house was greater than she led me to believe. Then when we got there, I had intended to take just a quick look and leave, but because the kittens were so cute, I must have lost track of time. Meanwhile, my mother started worrying and, unbeknownst to me, had actually walked down to the bridge. Not finding me in sight, she really started to fear that I had fallen into the water. However, now that I stood before her, that worry quickly melted away, and I can still feel the walloping I got from a wooden dowel she used for a curtain rod. From that moment on the name Guritz was a bad word in our house. It did not help matters that Nancy had two older sisters already in high school, one of whom later "got into trouble," a euphemism used to avoid the taboo subject of an unwed pregnancy.

There is a reason I can remember Joanie Bachman so well. First, my father and her father Ernest were very good friends, and we visited them occasionally at their farmhouse about four miles northwest of town. Her brother Dick and sister Ann, as older siblings usually do, just ignored us little kids when we came over. Since I was not interested in doing Joanie's "girl stuff," and her younger brother Kevin was just a little kid, these visits were pretty boring for me. One day, however, her parents were at our house to talk to my parents, and I was summoned onto the carpet. I was being called to task for allegedly (that was not their word) telling Joanie one day on the playground that if she came to school the next day I was going to beat her up. It is possible that my memory is selective, but I still protest my innocence. I honestly believe I never said any such thing and contend to this day that she had me mixed up with someone else. For Joanie, however, it did not matter. She was so traumatized that her parents withdrew her from school and had her repeat kindergarten the next year.

We lived next door to Arvid Odekirk, a blind man who had in his house a loom that he used to earn his living making rugs. I was in the grocery store one day when he came in, and in my memory I see him turning toward us when my father said hello to him. Usually he kept his eyelids closed, but in this vignette I see him opening them a slit as he responded to our greeting. I remember thinking, boy, if I was ever blind, I would just *force* my eyes open. Wonder why he does not just do that, and then he could *see*.

I see that you have not already flung this narrative across the room out of boredom, so perhaps you will indulge me the opportunity to relate three other scenes in memory from our years in the basement home. First was the stray kitten my father, who hated cats, tolerated us to keep for a time. Unfortunately (for the kitten, not for my father), it was run over by a car one day, but my parents were too late in preventing me from running upstairs to witness its gruesome demise. For weeks I could not stop talking about those eyes grotesquely bulging from the carcass or get the picture of it out of my mind.

Almost as macabre as the flattened kitten was the fate of the large snapping turtle my father pulled out of the river nearby. When I first saw this monstrous reptile, the only thing visible was the shell, and I thought it was dead. But my father fashioned a loop from a piece of number nine wire and poked it menacingly into one end of the shell. In a flash a head shot out and grabbed it, then five other appendages brought the creature suddenly to life. My parents grew up during the Depression era, and one of the lessons they carried around with them was that nothing gets wasted. Here before us was some of the Lord's bounty, so my father reached back for his hatchet and off came the head. My mother talked for years after that about the meat from this turtle that still quivered in the frying pan.

It was while we lived in the basement that I and one or two of my siblings contracted measles. While I am not sure of the opinions of medical science on the subject today, it was widely believed in those days that children with measles who were exposed to direct sunlight were at risk of weakened eyesight or even blindness. As a result I can still remember itching for three weeks in a basement bedroom darkened by a blanket over the windows.

The house of the kindergarten teacher was about halfway between our house and the school. One of my mother's dreams in life was to play the piano, and she was determined to fulfill it vicariously through me. So it was that once a week, clutching some coins, I walked over to Mrs. Rowland's house for a piano lesson, en route to my mother's ambition that I would one day be a concert pianist. As I look back over my life, I can often see that God had a plan for me, even at those times when I was protesting most strenuously to the contrary. As we will see, these piano lessons were some seeds He was planting.

# Station Master

We were not in the basement house very long before it was time to move again. Two of my father's principles that I heard him express many times were: One, never rent your house if you can own it and two, there is more money to be made as a business owner than as one of its employees. He was always on the alert for a business venture, any chance to make money. His first opportunity for entrepreneurship finally came along for him about 1950 when the gas station across the street from Foss and Rueber in town was selling out. This would be ideal for him. He would have his own shop to work on cars, *and* it came with living quarters attached to the rear of the station. No commute, no separate mortgage on a house. He saw it as a perfect situation. While it meant that the basement house he had dreamed of completing would have to be sold unfinished, he needed the down payment for the station.

My mother never questioned whether this was a good idea or not. Instead, she was very supportive, and together my parents ran the station as a team. They did not quarrel often, but finances were always tight, and my mother had repeatedly insisted that she find a job to help with expenses. My father had always been adamant. But now she had her chance. She could pump gas, wash windshields, run to a neighboring town for parts, and a thousand other self-appointed duties she took on with enthusiasm. However, soon after my sister Deanna came along (February 27, 1952), her work around the station came to an unexpected halt.

We had been buying produce, especially milk and eggs, directly from local farmers, because their prices were usually below retail, and we never questioned the quality of it. Occasionally, we would find a little blood in an egg, but this could easily be scooped away without losing the rest. One day, when my father's friend Ernie Bachman was in the station, my mother offered him a glass of milk. He took one sip and said, "You need to get this milk tested. I think that cow has brucellosis." He was right. We had not taken the precaution to pasteurize the milk, and my mother contracted Malta fever from it. Grandma Gimbel came to live with us for a time while my mother gradually recovered, but at the age of seven I had to pitch in with meals and housework for the next year or so.

That did not mean there was no time for play. Although I do not remember who it was that presented me with a jackknife when I was six years old (it was not my mother), I was told I was not allowed to have it until I was seven. I can still see myself under the tree in the back yard on the day of my seventh birthday, when I finally got to have my jackknife. Now, what sort of mischief can a boy of seven do with a jackknife, do you suppose? Along the fence was an orchard of plum trees belonging to the neighbor to the west. Climbing on or over the fence was forbidden, but no one said anything about carving in the trunks of those trees that I could reach from where I was, did they? I do not think that this was ever discovered while I was within reach, but I can fairly safely predict what would have happened if it had been.

The back yard also had two small tool sheds, which became a jungle gym for me. I am quite sure there was no prohibition against climbing onto the roof, right? One day it seems I had the inspiration that I could fly. Oh, I knew no one had ever done it, but I convinced myself that the reason for this was that no one had ever really tried hard enough. I would be famous. The man from the radio station would be interviewing this kid who figured out how to do it. Had I not watched the birds? I just knew it would work. So I launched from the roof, flapping as furiously as possible. Hmm, what happened? I was sure I had done it according to the formula I had in my mind. Well, maybe not. Better try again. It is a wonder I did not break my leg with the first attempt, and now I was going to give it a second. This time I was sure I had put everything from deep within the wells of my reserve into it, but the result was the same. Something far down inside told me this plan did not have a really good chance for success, but even though I was reluctant to acknowledge my aerodynamic theory had any flaws, I decided to give it up.

For Christmas one year I got my first bicycle. I cannot remember wanting one, but my parents regarded this as a requisite of childhood. Willy-nilly, every kid must learn to ride, an imperative ranking up there with table manners or learning to swim. Some kids got to start out with training wheels, but they cost extra, so we had to learn without them, the same way my father and his generation did. The first few sorties were done with his coaching as he ran along beside, but after that it was a very steep elbow-skinning, knee-bruising, hand-scraping, fender-denting learning curve.

After using this same method for my own children years later, I discovered that running along beside that bike until the kid gets the hang of it is quite a workout extending over several days. There is an easier way. First of all, I do not believe in training wheels. I am convinced they do not help the child learn to ride a *bicycle*. If your child is not ready for the two-wheeler, buy a tricycle. If you have the training wheels on, let the child help you ceremoniously remove them. Then when both you and the child are ready, teach helmet, helmet, helmet from the beginning. I do not recommend knee and elbow pads, first because abrasions are usually not life-threatening or permanently defacing but also because your child's friends will snicker at them, and you do not want your little fledgling flinging off the helmet along with the pads. Next, find a smooth, level stretch of pavement. Then, with both parents positioned about ten feet apart, one gives the little rider a gentle push to the other. Back and forth he goes from that short distance until he learns to *turn in the direction that the bicycle tips*. When you see that first smile of confidence, step back one pace and try it from that distance. The job can be done in one afternoon.

A broom works great, by the way, for teaching your child to roller skate. Grasp the broom end firmly and extend the handle horizontally to your little first-timer. The youngster will be able to hang on to it for the steepest segment of the learning curve, while you walk alongside giving physical and psychological support. Eventually the initial walking-on-skates transitions to gliding-on-skates. Soon thereafter you will notice that you are supporting less and less of the weight, as the neophyte glider gains confidence. When you find that you need to trot along just to keep up, it is time to strap on your own skates for a *pas de deux* with your protégé. Better yet, just release your grip and let the little roller-skater carry the broom along the asphalt alone. After a few days the newly minted skater will fling the broom aside and take off on wings a-foot.

In his book my father tells the account of my surreptitiously draining the residue from soda pop bottles left behind by the customers at the station. I could easily avoid the ones used to extinguish a cigarette, but he describes how it was not so easy for me to distinguish at a glance orange pop or cream soda from gasoline. There was a part of that story I never told him. Next door, immediately to the east of the station was a lumberyard, which had an elevated floor held up by posts. From our back yard it was possible to crawl around underneath that floor among those posts, but the prospect of exploring that darkness (and what if the building fell on me?) was always so scary that I never did it. When I realized that I just drank some gasoline, however, I was sure I was going to die right away and curled up far under that lumberyard floor to wait for the end. After nothing happened for a few minutes, I considered maybe I still had a chance to live if I went inside and 'fessed up.

I can remember a few of the customers who came into the station. First was the fellow who joshed with little Ruthie and called her Dirty Face. He was genuinely disappointed if he came in and did not get to see Dirty Face. Then there was the dear old man who, to pay for his gas, pulled nickels and pennies one by one with his shaky fingers from a little leather coin purse until it was empty. He nearly cried when he saw it was not enough. My father told him it was okay. One day my mother was telling two young construction workers in the station paying for their gas that I could play the piano. They wanted me to play something for them and asked what piece I knew. I told them it was by some guy named Mozart, except that a seven-year-old does not know it is not pronounced Moh-zert. I went to the back where the piano was, played my little concert for them and then came beaming back up front expecting some praise or applause. They were gone.

The only instance, other than the one I related earlier at the basement home, where my Grandpa and Grandma Pullmann came together to visit us was when we lived in the station. We gathered together up front one night after business hours for family devotions led by my grandfather, and then he spent a little time playing with us. His favorite game was to pretend to throw a small ball across the room, then quickly hide it in his armpit. When the kids came back to him empty-handed, he would put on his most innocent face, pretend to sympathize and send them off to look again. Or he would produce it and say he had found it, and then pretend to fling it again. I was old enough by this time to see through his sham, and while the younger kids went running off to see where he had thrown it, I was digging around under his enormous arm for its real location. He, of course, denied it was there, and turned it into an elaborate shell game trying to keep me guessing where he put it.

Later, he pulled off one of little Ruthie's socks and tickled her foot in a manner in which his grandfather probably did to him. As he drew his finger slowly across her sole, he intoned "elsen", then slowly again with the word "schmelsen", once more with the finger as he slowly drew out the word "tief," then with a light tap he said "klopf." After a short expectant pause, he then broke loose with a gleeful "gitchy, gitchy, gitchy," wiggling all of his fingers on the bottom of her foot. The rest of us wanted our turns too. I did not know it at the time, but that would be the last time I saw him alive.

My grandfather's game reminds me of the one my mother learned from her German parents and often played with little children. Using her hand as the mouse, she intoned mysteriously, "Die Maus, sie kommt, die Maus, sie kommt, die Maus, sie kommt …," as the "mouse" inched closer and closer to the toddler. Then with the youngster's attention fully engaged, watching expectantly to see what would happen to the mouse, my mother made it jump quickly to tickle the child's neck, as she said excitedly, "Sie beißt, sie beißt, sie beißt …."

My father's youngest brother Paul came to live with us for a short time while we lived at the station. He was coming of age and hoping older brother Elmer might help him make his mark on the world by teaching him a little about auto repair. Uncle Paul squeezed into the boys room with us in our crowded quarters in the back, and at first he was the older brother I never had. He liked to roughhouse with us, but eventually his play took on a sadistic bent. I am extremely ticklish under the arms, and he took fiendish delight in continuing to tickle us long after we screamed for him to stop. One day my mother had to pull him off when he covered my face with a pillow to silence these protests, not realizing or not caring about the consequences. Either way, my mother did not have time to follow another juvenile around and invited him to leave. He found a job in Waterloo, and I recall a couple of visits at his apartment in nearby Cedar Falls.

Some boys go through a phase characterized by two behaviors: first, the irresistible impulse to jump up and touch something just out of reach and second, a compulsion to play toss-and-catch with anything that comes to hand. A pediatric specialist would probably say these are essential exercises in the development of motor skills, but the parent who washes the finger marks from the top of the doorframe or sweeps up the pieces of the cereal bowl or ashtray would disagree. It seems I had a particularly serious case of this affliction. One day when I was twirling a claw hammer out in the back yard, I missed the handle on the way down. The claws came down squarely into the back side of my right thumb. Since there was not much blood and I feared the disciplinary consequences, I was able to conceal the incident from my mother. A kid is always getting scratched up, she probably thought, and so never found out what really happened. I still have the scars to this day.

Our true friends the Klammers were a godsend. When my mother got sick from Malta fever, complicated by the aftereffects of Deanna's birth, Arvilla made the drive over to Maynard quite often, offering bedside care, comfort, and whatever assistance we needed. This was not easy for her, because she had a household of her own to run. Lavonne (the only girl, often called simply Sister by the family) was about three years older than I. Second oldest, Arnold, Jr., who somehow acquired the sobriquet Happy, was about a year older than I, and then came Larry Dean, about a year younger. These two boys became my very best friends in the world, and I can make the remarkable claim that I do not recall a single time that we did not get along—not a single argument, altercation or fistfight. The youngest was Russell, a year younger than Ralph, so together with Donny, the three of them became fast friends too—we the older threesome, they the younger.

Happy was the leader of our trio, and over the years we explored every corner of their farm. Sometimes it was moving stealthily through the windbreak hoping to see a deer, running barefoot between the rows of corn or freezing in place to hear the rustle of growth on a windless day, tiptoeing gingerly across the rickety loft of the machine shed, or just observing the castration operation on piglets squealing in protest. And then there was the unforgettable fun of romping in the haymow—in my case, just once. We were jumping from great heights into soft mounds and burrowing into elaborate tunnels one day shortly before my mother called us to go home. When I emerged from the barn, she almost fainted. I was coughing, choking, wheezing, and sneezing, tears streaming from my eyes, and my face was puffed out like a pumpkin. Arvilla was horrified. Nobody knew quite what to do. I was having a serious allergic reaction to the dust in the hay, but it was the first time any of us knew about it. My mother simply said, "Get in the car."

Farms around there had a variety of domestic animals, but theirs had only cows, chickens and hogs, as I recall. Everyone had to help, so all the kids had chores appropriate to their sizes and abilities. Carrying a heavy pail of water for the chickens was easier for two kids, so on some days my hand was next to Larry Dean's on the handle. Since we did not live on a farm, this was an interesting educational experience for me. Much can be learned about human nature by observing a flock of chickens. A pullet discovers a worm, but instead of seeking a secluded corner to enjoy its morsel, it trots into the midst of the flock to show off its find. Soon five others give chase until one of them steals it away and quickly gulps it down. Off to one side, looking foolish and forlorn, stands one now stripped of its prize. I seem to remember a certain king Hezekiah who had a similar experience when some Babylonian officials came to call. The floor of the chicken house was a sea of feathery white, and as we walked through it, most of the birds squeezed together to allow us to pass. However, I noticed that occasionally one would squat stubbornly close to the ground and refuse to budge, even when we tried to kick it out of the way. Does that sound like anyone you know? Over there was one in every flock with bloody scabs on its head instead of feathers, and patches of bare skin elsewhere on its body. I was to learn the meaning of the term hen-pecked. Not sure what instinct drives this behavior, but every chicken passing by pecks at this pitiful victim until it dies. Now that I think about it, humans do this too.

One of Happy's jobs was to haul silage for the cows. For those of you uninitiated to farm life, silage is chopped corn fodder that is stored inside those cylindrical structures we see on every farm in the Midwest. Over time it begins to ferment in its own juices, and without proper ventilation, the toxic gasses generated in this process have been known to overcome anyone who gets trapped inside or exposed to them for an extended period of time. Maybe I should not admit this, but I rather like the smell of the silage, so it was enjoyable for me to pitch in, literally, with a fork to help load that wheelbarrow. Spreading it in the manger was another matter. The cows were each clamped into a stanchion, yet the intimidation of that enormous head staring at me inches away required a great deal of courage I was not sure I had. It was always a relief when that part of the job was finished.

I found out what the chores were really like one time when the Klammers were away in South Dakota for a few days. My parents agreed to watch the farm for them, and my father thought I was old enough to learn how to drive their Ford tractor. He was explaining that there were five controls. The steering wheel was easy, but then there was this gear shift, two pedals and a knob. Press on the left pedal, set the gear lever to N and turn the key, he told me. I grinned when the engine came to life. This was going to be fun. You need to press on the left pedal again and move the gear lever to 1. Now let up on the pedal slowly. No, I said s-l-o-w-l-y. Okay, let's try it once more. I chuckled when the machine started to move. Pushing the pedal down again made it stop. Oh, I get it. But wait, if I can stop it just by pressing this pedal, why are you telling me I press the right pedal to stop? And if I can push the knob to go faster, why do I need to use the left pedal again to move the gear lever to 2 to go faster? This is too confusing. Besides I cannot reach the pedals without sliding off the seat. Maybe I'll just haul some water for the chickens ....

Parents were, and still are, urged to sit down with their children at the appropriate moment to teach them the facts of life. Such was not the case for me. When we drove along and would see a bull mounting a cow, we would ask my mother why they did that. This should have been the right opportunity for the Talk, but all my flustered mother could blurt out was something about, well, that's just how they play. It was Happy who knew all about birds and bees, and one day he was explaining things to me.

Larry Dean was nodding assent to everything he said. I listened with fascination, but when he tried to say my own parents did this, I just stared at him, incredulous. When he started to smirk, I just knew he must be telling a big fib. I was quite sure I would have known about anything as bizarre as what he was describing, and after all, I had never seen them engaged in any such activity. I can still hear Happy howling with laughter at my naïveté.

This reminds me of a story, but you need to be warned in advance that it is slightly risqué, so that you may skip over this paragraph if you do not want to hear it. A zebra escapes from the zoo and finds itself wandering around on a farm, never having seen such animals before. When it encounters a chicken on the barnyard, it asks, "What do you do around here?" "Why, I keep the farmer supplied with eggs, of course," it replied. Scampering down the lane, the zebra finds a cow and asks, "What do you do around here?" "Why, I keep the farmer supplied with milk, of course," said the cow. Leaping over the fence into the pasture, the zebra encounters a bull. "What do you do around here?" it asked. The bull leers at the zebra, passing its eyes lustily over its body and says, "Take off those pajamas and I'll show you." Oh, I see you were tantalized into reading this anyway, even though you told yourself you really should not.

This is not meant to sound uppity, but the atmosphere in the Klammer home was a little coarser than in ours. For one thing, my parents never touched tobacco and rarely any potent potables, but Arnie and Arvilla both smoked and were known to imbibe a little. My parents never used foul language (aside from an assortment of euphemisms), but we heard plenty of salt and pepper around their house. Oddly, none of it rubbed off on us, however, most likely because my mother was not afraid to wash dirty mouths with soap. This reminds me of the story of a woman who called the phone company to complain about cursing from two of their employees working on the wires in her back yard. When the supervisor called them in for an explanation, one of the men said, "Well, as Clarence climbed up the pole, some tools fell out of his bag and hit me on the head. So all I said was, 'Why Clarence, you really must learn to be more careful,' that's all." My parents were not dancers, but Arnie and Arvilla were fond of attending these social events with their good friends Roberta and Kenny Winegar. I cannot hear that name without thinking of the gruesome accident suffered by Kenny one day, in which a roll of fence wire recoiled on him, putting out his eye.

As if running a farm and raising four kids were not enough, Klammers were caring for an elderly aunt in their home, as well. I do not remember how she was related to Arvilla, but most of the time she remained locked in an upstairs room. We were seated at the table for dinner with them once when feeble Aunt Inga was helped down the steps to the table. It was my first experience with someone that old and demented. She never made eye contact or acknowledged anyone at the table, but babbled away incoherently throughout the meal. I can still see her pour her entire cup of coffee into her plate, then nervously stir it into the mashed potatoes. After staring at that for a long time, she would turn slowly toward Arvilla and murmur she was not hungry. Neither was I.

I was always grateful I was not one of Arvilla's kids. I can still hear her yell up through the heat register, "Everybody up. Get up, get up. Let me hear your feet hit the floor!" Hers was not an easy lot, and she had a stern disposition she felt was needed to maintain an even keel. The razor strap was always handy behind the bathroom door, and she did not hesitate to use it. Larry Dean once told me they stuffed a chunk of plaster into each hind pocket to absorb the blow, but Happy got caught, and then he really got whipped. That strap was never necessary on me, because the disciplinary standards of my parents were matched by hers. One word to them would have been sufficient. As far as I know, her punishments were not savage, but I still think burning the fingers of a kid caught playing with matches goes beyond the pale.

Corporal punishment was the norm, even in the schools. Both of my parents were brought up in the German tradition of strict discipline and unquestioned obedience to authority. My father relates an incident where his father whipped him with a branch from a plum tree. A plum tree has *thorns*. I never knew my mother's father, Emanuel Gimbel, who died when she was seven, but according to a description of him from my uncle Ed (my mother's oldest brother), his death was in some ways a blessing to the family. A man with an evil disposition and a violent temper, he would beat some of the animals until he broke the skin, and even once fractured the back of a sow with a two-by-four. His fierce demeanor was directed at the kids too, and discipline was dispensed with fire-breathing wrath.

I do not believe this is what God meant when he says in Proverbs 13 that one who spares the rod hates his son. That passage is not advocating a merciless beating. In the rest of the sentence, He says the discipline should be based on *love* for the son. In the real world of parenthood, however, children do not come with a user manual, set of instructions and a warranty. Parents tend to raise kids the way they were raised, employing methods and expressions that were used on them. I can still hear my parents say, "Now you stop that bawling or I'm going to give you something to cry *about*." Or this one, "If you can't hear, then you're going to have to *feel*." Or, "When we get home, you're getting the *stick*." This is not meant to be critical of them, and I honestly believe their intentions were pure, but as a parent who used these same techniques myself, I look back with deep sorrow and regret acknowledging that they simply do not work. On the contrary, they engender a catalog of undesirable side effects. In my own case, for example, those welts on the back of my legs produced in me a measure of life-long hypercriticism, hypersensitivity to criticism and deep-seated resentment of authority of all kinds.

Kids can truly bring a parent to despair, and at the breaking point the urge to respond with a slap or ear-boxing is all but impossible to resist. The appeal of a good spanking for the parent is that it is such a handy expedient (pun intended) and requires no creativity, so it is sure to be overused. But often the offense does not even rise to the level where such a response is appropriate. Swiping a cookie is not on the same level as assaulting a teacher. If there is one piece of advice I would have for young parents, it is this: Discipline in love, not in anger. Still, this is much easier to say than do. This does not mean I advocate the outlawing of corporal punishment, as some countries already have (including, ironically, Germany), but the paddle should be placed out of sight on the bottom shelf for use as a last resort, when ingenuity fails to produce results. Yet, age appropriate and offense appropriate, I think it has its place, yes, even in the schools.

Family size matters too. A small family is more easily managed than a large one. I would not trade my siblings for all the gold in Fort Knox (well, actually, now that I think about that …), but six children put tremendous pressures on my parents. I submit that six was too many for *them* to prepare for life and due to size alone was not done correctly without compromise and consequence. I will be telling you later about our own children, but we noticed that the difference between one child and two was like the difference between a pencil tap on the forehead and a blow to the toe with a mallet. The difference between two and three was more like being backed over by a forklift. One mother of four from our church described it as trying to nail Jello to a tree.

# Elementary, You See

**M**aynard had a Lutheran church in town, but it belonged to the American Lutheran synod, so we were still members of St. Peter's in Westgate and made the six-mile trek every Sunday. For those of you unfamiliar with these synodical partitions within Lutheranism, I should perhaps explain that they often represented barriers almost as forbidding as divisions between denominations. Even today this is true, but a generation or two ago passions were aroused to such an extent that when my parents were married in an American Lutheran church, my father's parents, members of the Missouri Synod, considered it a violation of conscience to attend the wedding. Although Westgate had only a small public school, it had something Maynard did not—a parochial school. Now that I was a rising first-grader, my godly parents wanted me to have a Christian education. My grandfather George was a Lutheran pastor, and all the children in that family got a solid foundation in the catechism and principles of Scripture, despite the fact that his long hours earning a living to keep a growing family intact left little time for this for his own children.

On at least one occasion his sacrifice was not only the expenditure of time but also the risk of his own life. In the pioneering years of his ministry in western South Dakota, George served the needs of a congregation composed largely of first- or second-generation German-Russian immigrants, who mastered only enough English to buy and trade. Since the nation was in conflict with the ideology of Germany at the time, a mob of the local citizenry approached him one day with hostility, demanding explanation. "I was not aware that our country was at war with the German language," he countered. When they insinuated that perhaps his command of English was not good enough to conduct his religious services in any language except German, he responded in perfect English, "Since you know English so well, can you tell me what 'sanctification' means—or what about 'justification'?" They were at a loss for words until the editor of the newspaper launched a volley with the quote that "there is a young preacher, preaching German, he should be hung on the first telephone pole." A few days later, as George was teaching school, a bullet whistled through an open window of the classroom. After New Year of 1919, the mob, jealous of the increasing number of students flocking to his meetinghouse, forced the school to close.

In Germany my great-grandfather Friedrich Püllmann too was a deeply devout Lutheran, and probably his father August before him. How far back did it go? Where did this belief in a Savior from sin come from? We do not yet have the biological genealogy back beyond the eighteenth century, but we do know that it was St. Paul who introduced his first-hand account of the Gospel to Europe, and it is quite possible that we can, in fact, trace our spiritual genealogy to *him*. Conrad Meese, who grew up in the household of the Püllmanns, relates an event from the life of Friedrich where he credits the grace of God for sparing his life. One night he dreamed that he was in the haymow of his barn when a fire broke out between where he was and the ladder to the ground, the only way out. Frantic to escape, he discovered a trap door he had never known was there beneath his feet and was able to jump to safety. A few days later this exact scenario played out for real.

I think Lavonne and Happy may have started out at St. Peter's Lutheran School, but by the time I arrived for first grade, they were no longer there. The Klammer parents had had some sort of falling out with the school, the church, or the congregation (not sure what it was about), so they pulled out and sent their kids to the public school situated across the street to the east. My mother now became the daily shuttle to Westgate every morning. Paved Highway 150 west from Maynard makes a sharp turn to the south a mile west of town, so we always continued straight ahead the remaining five miles on a gravel road to school. I can still hear my mother complain about the condition of that road—when are they going to put more gravel on this piece? is the road grader ever going to fix these washboards? how deep are they going to allow these potholes to *get* anyway? and so on. It is nothing short of a minor miracle that she was even able to get five kids out the door for school each day at all, and still manage the preschoolers at home until it was time to head back over to pick us up.

On one occasion when she was not waiting outside to pick me up after school, I acknowledged the Klammers as they were walking home—a mile east and then a mile north from town. It was a nice spring day, so they called to me to walk along with them. When I told them I was supposed to wait at school until my mother came, they persuaded me to walk the first mile and wait for her there. They reasoned that she had to come right past us anyway all along that route and could easily stop for me. As we walked along, Lavonne was talking about how it was possible to get a free ride from someone who came along. She said the way you do it is to put your thumb in the air and the car would stop. When we got to the intersection, they waved goodbye, turned north and continued toward home.

A few minutes later I saw a vehicle coming. As it got closer, I saw that it was a school bus heading east, back to Maynard. Not really believing what Lavonne had said would work, I nevertheless found myself sticking my thumb up. To my amazement, the driver slammed on the brakes and told me to get aboard. The bus then dropped me off at the station where I lived! When I walked in the door, my startled mother had not yet left for Westgate, so I expected to be praised for saving her the trip—and I was sure I would also get kudos for my brilliant resourcefulness. Instead, she was furious. I could not understand why.

On the drive home one day, we witnessed a horrific accident at the stop sign for Highway 150 within a mile from home. A car coming from the south tried to round the curve to the east, lost control and tumbled over two or three times. Unlike most of the fatalities on this dangerous curve, the car in this accident rolled to the inside of the curve (not sure how that could be, but I can still see it happening that way). First on the scene, my mother ordered us to stay in the car and rushed over to offer help. Soon she ran back, and we rode in silence at a fast gallop into town to send the fire truck and a doctor out to the site. Such things were not discussed with children, however, so I never found out what happened to those victims, or even how many of them there were. Having seen that at such a young age, I assumed it was commonplace to see accidents, but aside from a fender-bender in which I was involved, I have never actually witnessed one since.

St. Peter's School was a two-room facility, divided into the Little Room (grades K-4) and the Big Room (grades 5-8), with one teacher for each room. My first grade teacher when I started in the fall of 1950 was Mabel Timm, who met my mother's brother John Gimbel one Sunday when she was invited over for dinner, and in June 1952 they were married. She was also my teacher in second grade, and I suppose her relationship to our family put both of us in an awkward position at school—she sensitive to any appearance of having a teacher's pet and I sensitive to details of my deportment that surely must be too conveniently getting back to my parents. By this second year with her, younger brother Ralph started kindergarten, so she had both of us in her schoolroom. When they selected him to be their ring bearer in the wedding, I was hurt. Although I never said anything explicitly, they knew my disappointment and made a special effort to smooth it over. Of course it made sense. I was almost eight years old, certainly no longer cute. Ralph was the perfect choice, even though I could not comprehend that at the time. As compensation, they honored me as one of the godparents of their youngest son Paul, born several years later.

Although each of the two Rooms of the school was in a sense a single class, the different grades of the students were distinguished. In my first grade class there were six of us, and again in the second, but my attention was gravitating toward one in particular, a cute little girl named Dianne Hoehne. Unfortunately for me, all my puppy love overtures went unrequited. Worse, she feigned affection for Rollin Stedman instead and was quite demonstrative about it, putting her arm around him and telling everyone in my presence he was her boyfriend. She had discovered a little button labeled Jealousy and was having a delightful time pushing it. It did not matter whether the relationship with Rollin was reciprocal or not, because she had invented a sport where she could control the game *and* invent the rules as it progressed. One day another classmate, Dianne's good friend Theresa Bartels, wanted to borrow my eraser, which I was refusing to hand over. The girls huddled together whispering, then Dianne demurely asked if she could borrow my eraser. Even though I saw through the deception immediately, I was trapped in my inability to refuse anything Dianne might ask and held out the eraser. Dianne snatched it away and, with an evil smirk, immediately handed it to Theresa. Oh, the wiles of the female of the species are honed at a tender age.

Theresa was dropped off at school each day by her father, and I can still see the cans of milk he brought into town with him to be left at the creamery. I suppose the reason this has stayed in memory so clearly is that he carried these cans on an unusual trailer. It hooked directly onto the bumper and had only one wheel, which swiveled as the car turned a corner. The other two members of my class were Carol Bartz and Tommy Bender. Carol gets the award for Most Noble Character. Children are cruel, and someone (not I) at recess one day started the chant "Carol stinks." Unremitting, the whole school picked up the chorus and sang it day after day. I get the award for Least Noble Character, for I not only did not rally to her defense, but probably took up the mantra myself. Poor Carol, however, the absolute paradigm of Christian restraint, gave no outward sign that these pitiless darts affected her. Without any attempt at verbal or physical retribution, she stoically thrust out her jaw and resolutely faced her tormentors. Wow. I know I could not do that. What a scintillating model of Christ, exactly what the school was trying to instill in each of us.

Tommy was my cousin, well, actually once removed. Erwin, his father, had two children from his first marriage, James and Emily, who remained close friends with my parents throughout their lives. Some time before we came on the scene, a young lady named Dorothy Braatz became a teacher at St. Peter's, and James married her. Late in life, after Erwin's first wife died, he remarried, and Reuben,

Nathan and Thomas were born to them. Erwin and Lena were both of German extraction, so the English that Tommy spoke at school had a tinge of their accent. According to the rule to leave the room for the restroom, we had to write our names on the blackboard. One day I wrote my name as Davit, and when I returned to erase it, Hubert Firnhaber, our third grade teacher, said, "Oh, I see you have a new name." I said no, but that was how Tommy said it.

Already in those early grades Tommy was a full head and shoulders above all of us in our class, but he had the most gentle disposition and never took advantage of his size to intimidate anyone. He and I were good friends, despite the great difference in our sizes. His mother believed that every scratch or cut had to be daubed with a disinfectant he called Mercurochrome, probably a brand name. Whenever we visited their home, I recognized the aroma of that Mercurochrome the instant we stepped inside the door. Besides its distinctive medicinal smell, this potion had a bright red-orange color, so Tommy bore his tiger stripes to school quite often. Their family, a little more well to do than ours, was one of the first to acquire what every kid would quickly come to covet—a television set. His conversation was peppered with remarks about this or that he had seen on TV last night, especially some character named Jackie Gleason.

Television discovered the attraction that sports held for its spectators early in its history, and it seems Tommy watched all of them. He knew all of the players of the Milwaukee Braves and showed me the picture card of some guy named Hank Aaron or Joe Torre or Eddy Matthews that he got from packs of bubblegum he bought. One of the games we played at recess was called Keepaway, in which one team tried to keep the ball away from the other. We could pass or kick it to a teammate or just run all over the playground with it, anything to keep it away from the opponent. No one could catch me, and I could always steal the ball from the other team with my quickness. I loved this game. Then one day on the cement court with those hoops at each end, the big kids organized a new game of Keepaway, and Tommy and I joined in. But whenever I would try to run around with the ball, everyone would start yelling that I was "traveling." Tommy took me aside to explain that this game was called Basketball, not Keepaway, and said that if I wanted to run with the ball, I had to bounce it. Well, *that* surely took the fun out of it.

When I got to the Big Room, we played this game of basketball quite a bit, and I started to like it. There were Lutheran schools in Readlyn, Klinger, and other neighboring towns around, so the schools decided to organize some friendly basketball competitions among them. All of our practicing was done outside, so I assumed that basketball was an outdoor sport. Fall and winter in Iowa get quite cold, so we were on the court with coats, boots and gloves. But Tommy was telling me that when we got to the big basketball court in Waterloo, it would be indoors. Indoors? But won't the ball hit the ceiling all the time? I really thought he must be crazy when he said we would play in shorts and a tee shirt and wear shoes made out of canvas cloth.

I do not remember how well we played at the gymnasium in Waterloo, but on the way home, we always got to stop for a hamburger at the restaurant just before the turn from Highway 63 onto Highway 3 east. At home our tight budget forced my mother to economize with everything. To stretch a package of hamburger, she would mix in liberal amounts of oatmeal, eggs, bread crusts, stale crumbs, a little milk and ground vegetables, which were all cheaper than the meat. There was no food value in ketchup, so this was a luxury we could never afford. She had no time to make pickles, and buying them in a jar from the store was out of the question. So one taste of that pure-meat hamburger from Café 63, with slices of dill pickle and real ketchup on a fresh, store-bought bun, was a little piece of heaven. I really wanted two, but the restaurant charged the outrageous price of 25 cents for them, and my parents really could not afford even the precious quarter I had tucked into my mitten. I saved up my allowance, and on the last day of the season I felt like the king of Siam when I could give the waitress my order for *two* of those scrumptious burgers.

A hot lunch program might have been possible at school, because the church basement, which had a kitchen, was connected to the school basement by a tunnel. Since this would have been a major undertaking, however, everyone carried a lunch pail. Mine usually held a sliced bologna or jelly sandwich (but without peanut butter, for that was too expensive), an apple and a screw-top jar of milk sealed with waxed paper. One day Gayle Tellin unwrapped his sandwich, and I saw it was spread with ketchup. His mother probably ran out of lunchmeat, sandwich spread and ideas all at the same time, so just told him to squirt on whatever he could find in the refrigerator and run to the car. But I remember thinking, you lucky duck, you get ketchup. I would gladly have traded.

I do not remember when it started, but I came to detest that mayonnaise jar filled with milk. Mine was not a lactose intolerance, just a taste and texture intolerance of milk. When the school adopted a milk program to stock the refrigerator in the storage room with half-pint cartons, my parents signed up. As it seems my mother suffered from some delusion that chocolate milk rots teeth, they expected me to drink the white. I really did try, but when my allotment of milk was barely diminished at the end of the month, they really laid a guilt trip on me to get with the program. But when I went through the second month gagging with each gulp, Mr. Firnhaber appealed for them to give it up. Thankfully, they did.

Every spring the Lutheran schools got together again for what they called Field Day—games, prizes, ice cream, hotdogs, and clean fun. When thirty or so kids lined up for a race, I knew that blue ribbon was mine. Everyone knew I was the fastest runner at school. Out of the corner of my eye, I thought I saw a half dozen kids that were keeping up with me. Nah, can't be. As we crossed the finish line, I looked left and right to see four or five runners already there. Oh, well maybe they had not actually been in the race, no I bet they were already down at the end to cheer on their friends. But then I could see that the teachers were handing three of them ribbons. That was quite a blow to my ego to realize I was not only not the best, but not even *third* best.

Small for my age, I was always a ready target for bullies all through school. Adjacent to the parsonage was a pasture with a flock of sheep, and Burton Hoehne, Dianne's older brother, loved to throw me over the fence and then stand there to prevent my climbing out, just because he knew I was terrified of them. One year a new kid named Billy Gumm joined the school, and from the first day he started picking on me. Although a grade behind me, he was a husky loudmouth, and his heckling was relentless day after day, both inside the classroom and out on the playground. Something snapped one day after I reached my boiling point, when I took him down and sat on his neck. I had never fought back before, and my classmates could scarcely believe their eyes. Suddenly I was transformed into someone not to be messed with, and I never had any problem with Billy or any of his friends after that.

I was experiencing a growing sense of foreboding as the end of fourth grade approached. I would be entering the Big Room, taught by stern-faced Mr. Suhr. I had never seen him smile. Still, I never heard of anyone who was carried out of his classroom dead. If I were to submit an article to the My Most Unforgettable Character department of the *Reader's Digest*, the subject of it would be Henry

Suhr. He was the consummate professional and one of the best teachers I ever had. He would brook no nonsense, and although I never saw him actually paddle or slap anyone in the room, he had this peculiar method of flicking his fingers against the back of the head of someone who displeased him. One look from those piercing eyes would melt tungsten. Then came the unassailable voice of reason as he laid open the offense before the entire classroom.

Mr. Suhr had a deep fondness for students who loved school, and I loved school. He was a Renaissance man, and I soaked up everything he taught—mixed fractions, the sol-fa method of singing, systems of the human body, diagramming sentences, the rapture of travel to distant lands. He was very influential, and many of his admonitions stayed with me for life. His generation was anti-Catholic, to the point that anyone who intermarried would be forever and irreversibly ostracized from family, friends, community, and, yes, even the church. This bias was so deeply instilled in us that for several years to come I bristled at any encounter with someone Catholic, almost as if exposed to some loathsome disease. He had also spent some time in Chicago and knew about something of which Iowa kids had never heard—drugs. He warned us not to be a Dopey Dick. It was years before I realized he had been saying dope addict.

In our multi-grade classroom, Mr. Suhr conducted a lesson with one of the grades up front while the rest of the students were supposed to be at work at their desks. One of the chief advantages of this arrangement is the principle that younger students get a preview of the material coming up next and older students get a review of the material when it is presented to the lower grades. Sometimes when he asked the older kids a question, no one would answer, and I could not resist raising my hand from my desk in the back. He just winked and motioned for me to get back to my own business.

In addition to his duties in school, Mr. Suhr was an accomplished musician and took his place on the organ bench each Sunday morning. Since many of his generation and the ones still alive from the previous generation were more comfortable with German than with English, he needed to be on hand for both services and work from multiple hymnals. He was also a gifted artist and once rendered a pencil drawing of the church and school that was so detailed it showed every brick on the building. I believe it could have passed for a photograph. Unfortunately, his attempts to develop an artistic bent in me were fruitless, the inevitable result where talent is totally lacking.

Henry Suhr was also widely known for his beautiful, flowing handwriting and was determined to teach this to his students. He insisted that the proper technique was to move the entire hand and had us practice alternating rows of coils and jagged seismograms to get the feel of it. My cramped handwriting style was far less flamboyant and best suited my comfort level when the heel of my hand was anchored in a way that the fingers did the work, so I never did learn his. Ballpoint pens had been invented by this time, but they were notoriously unreliable, either skipping or blotching or both. Adults carried fountain pens, but in school we used a steel-tip pen that was dipped into a bottle of ink found in the custom-cut hole in each desk. There was a pen, and then there was ink. Richard Decker found out one day that proper terminology for our equipment was fastidiously expected when he said he could not find his ink pen. "Ink pen?" scorned Mr. Suhr, "as opposed to what? a mud pen? a pig pen?"

Art and music routinely involved the whole classroom, but one day Mr. Suhr organized a spelling bee. Everyone was lined up at the front of the room. Starting at one end, he moved down the row, asking his words to spell. If someone missed a word, the one next in line got the same word and got to move up if he spelled it correctly. The last one at the end of the row was eliminated. As the contest continued, I worked my way up to second place, but I could not unseat Patty Potratz, who to my consternation spelled everything correctly. Then unexpectedly, when she, Velda Poock and I were the only ones standing, I got my chance. Astoundingly, Patty missed on the word rhubarb, and I got to move into first place! Then Velda dropped out, but before I could ascend the throne, I became too excited and broke a rule. According to the rules, the word had to be pronounced first, then spelled. When I got the word brittle, of course I could spell it, so I started to blurt out the letters, b-r-i, oh, I mean, brittle, b-r-i …. Red-faced, I had quickly tried to cover my mistake by pronouncing it *after* I had started to spell. Too late. Despite my tears and protests that I had, after all, not misspelled any words, Patty's friends started to chant her name, and she was declared the winner.

I do not remember what the girls did at recess, but the boys usually went down the street a half block to the public park to play softball or football. Many parents considered that a baseball more dangerous than a softball, so it was usually a softball game that was organized. One day, however, when I was throwing a baseball with Nathan Bender, someone called to him, and he looked away just as I released the ball. When I yelled "Nathan!" he turned his head back around, thwock, just as the ball hit him squarely in the forehead. Because Nathan would later go on to earn a Ph.D. in psychology, I take full credit for all the sense that baseball knocked into him.

All the boys admired Gene Fitz because he was the only one who could throw a gravel stone clear over the church steeple. George Steinbronn and Jerry Meyer were the two upper classmen I most admired, and their status always made them the captains for choosing up sides for football. George was my hero, the strongest person I knew, and he took up for me quite often. Since I was always the last player chosen, I always hoped for an even number, so I would end up on George's team. Usually I avoided tackling anybody, because it looked like that might really be painful. One day Higgins was barreling straight at me, and I wondered if perhaps I might be wrong about how it would feel to try to stop him. He smacked into me at full gallop, and I will never understand how that titanic collision did not break my clavicle.

Many children today are not assigned duties at home. Because of broken homes, working spouses, and crowded schedules, chaos reigns supreme and parents find it more expedient to handle chores themselves than to delegate. Sometimes doting parents seem to have the convoluted notion that they should do as much for their children as they can, even to include their homework. Such was not the case for us. Every farm kid had chores, we "town" kids had ours, and these assignments extended to school, as well. At the end of each day a strange substance called sweeping compound was sprinkled liberally all over the floor between the rows of desks, and it was someone's turn to sweep up. Others had to wash the blackboard and take the erasers outside to pound the chalk out of them—not against the brick, please. The school was heated by a huge coal furnace in the cellar, and after the coal burned, it left behind chunky mineral material called clinkers, in addition to the ash. Tommy and I drew the duty one day to carry a tub of this ash through the snow 100 yards away over to Mr. Knief's garden (not sure what the fertilizer value of ash is). When Mr. Suhr noticed that the tub was at the tippy tip of my weight limit, that job was assigned to big boys or dads after that.

When we arrived at school one fall day, we were greeted by a substitute teacher, Marthabelle Rueber. Henry Suhr had taken ill, never to be my teacher again. Such things were not discussed with children, so I never found out what his malady was. I do know it was not terminal, because as an adult, years later, I stopped at his house when we were passing through Westgate. His wife met us at the door, and told us he was at a meeting down at the fire station. That was 1970 and would have been the last time I saw him. A prince of a man, he died of pancreatic cancer soon after.

The congregation placed an emergency call to Concordia Lutheran Teachers College in Seward, Nebraska, for a permanent replacement. Since all of last year's graduates had already received calls, they sent their most prominent senior to finish out the year for us, a young man named Robert Rikkels. Rikkels was diametrical to Henry Suhr in every respect. For one thing, he did not think it was distasteful to show off his basketball prowess against us at recess, still wearing his dress shoes. To maintain order, he resorted to the paddle quite a bit, especially on the bigger boys. The class sat totally silent as we listened to the crack of his board of education coming from the storage room just off the hallway. That was followed by a sober face that emerged from the closet—except for Reuben Bender, who usually came out grinning or cracking a smile. If I were Rikkels, I should have been more circumspect about taking on Reuben, who was taller and considerably stronger, and who outweighed Rikkels by perhaps thirty pounds. I never received a paddling from him, but I know that if I had, I would have another one coming at home. I remember once when my class was asked to name the attributes of God, I misspoke and said He was graceful. Mr. Rikkels glided around the room in his best ballerina imitation and then said, "You mean like this?" There were titters of laughter, but I was neither amused nor impressed. I know Mr. Suhr would never have humiliated me like that.

# West Gate to What?

**A**fter a couple of years running the Mobil station, my father was offered a job working at the same Chevrolet garage where he had started out, except that it now had a new owner, Warren Rueber. Leaving the station also meant leaving our home in Maynard, so we were moving to Westgate (the town is actually named for an early settler from the time of the Civil War, one Sylvester S. Westgate, not for the west entrance to Maynard—or heaven). On short notice my parents managed to find a dilapidated old farmhouse for rent about a mile and a half southeast of Westgate in the fall of 1952, where we suffered through one of the coldest winters of our lives.

The house had a large parlor with an Ivanhoe stove, and in the ceilings of this room were iron grates to allow the heat from here to reach the rooms above. However, the house was so poorly insulated that it made little sense to expend the enormous amount of fuel that would have been required to heat it. Not just the windows were drafty, but the walls too, and through many chinks we could see light to the outside. Instead, we closed the doors to all the rooms and huddled together in the kitchen, which had a huge cast-iron range. The kitchen, however, was not our sleeping quarters. No, the unheated upstairs had rooms for a couple of beds, and one of them held three boys dressed in flannel pajamas and buried under thick quilts. It was always such a delight to crawl out from this little igloo to get dressed each morning. No one dawdled. Ralph was now in kindergarten, so he and I crisply pulled on our overalls and walked to the school on the east end of town. On days without the risk that our faces would be frozen into a permanent grimace, we could ride our bicycles.

There is a reason I can recall one occasion on which the parlor was heated and used. My mother had organized a quilting bee one fall day, and several of the ladies from the church had come to our house to work together on this project. Late in the afternoon Arvilla came bursting into the house with a bombshell. Myra Trotter had been killed in a car accident. She and her husband were traveling down a country road when a car driven by some hunters from some distant town broadsided their car on the passenger side, killing Myra instantly. The oldest of their children was Ricky, a schoolmate a year or two younger than I.

Accidents of this kind were not uncommon. Iowa has many limestone gravel roads laid out along a grid pattern, with most of the intersections unmarked. A car traveling at a high rate of speed on a crossroad often revealed its presence by the white cloud of dust trailing behind it. Drivers learned early on that if that plume stayed in the same position in the windshield, the two cars were on a collision course. Unfortunately, this often stoked the primordial human urge to compete, as each driver tried to beat his "opponent" to the intersection. By late summer or fall the corn has grown to heights approaching twenty feet or so, making the roadways virtual canyons. The telltale plume cannot be seen, especially following a rain, and blind intersections claimed the lives of many of the unwary or uncautious.

Our house had no indoor plumbing, so one of my jobs was to keep the white enamel pail full of fresh water from the pump out in the yard. The pail held a small dipper for extracting drinking water and was kept covered with a lid. By morning, when the fire in the range had died down or gone out, a coating of ice would form on the surface of the water. One of my other jobs was to keep the speckled blue enamel bucket empty. Even with the lid on, it triggered my gag reflex as I lugged it across the snow to the outhouse (this particular privy was a deluxe model sometimes dubbed a two-holer for its capacity to accommodate two lucky users at once). We tried to make sure this blue bucket and the white one were never interchanged.

Enamel was the ceramic coating over many iron or steel utensils before plastic became widely available. These buckets, pails, dippers, pots and pans, even tables and furniture, were easily chipped, however, and without the protective enamel coating, the thin metal underneath would puncture or quickly rust through and cause whatever liquid the container held to leak. Sometimes a pinhole would be undetectable, so one was prudent to inspect carefully, especially when the container *must* not leak—like the chamber pot, for example.

Another of my jobs was to bring in a supply of corncobs from the shed outside. If you are not from corn country, you are probably most familiar with the moist white cob that remains after eating sweet corn. Sweet corn is picked when the kernels are the juiciest, but field corn is left until the grain has ripened thoroughly and is quite hard and dry. Incidentally, I urge you never to make the mistake of picking field corn when it is juicy and serve it as sweet corn, as my mother inadvertently did once. After the field corn has been shelled, or stripped of its kernels, the red-brown cob that remains has many uses. Ground up, it becomes chicken feed. The dry porous fiber produces a furious flame in a pot-bellied stove, and when no toilet paper is available in the outhouse or the woods, it can substitute for, ahem, that too. In fact, a farmhouse might have a whimsical decoration on the wall in the bathroom—three small cobs, one white and two red, encased in glass, bearing the following instructions: "First use the red cob, then the white one to see if you need another red one."

The farmhouse was situated at the end of a long lane, and directly across the gravel road from the entrance was the Tate farm. I can remember trudging down the lane through the snow at milking time with a galvanized bucket and some money to buy milk from them. Not sure, but I think Mrs. Tate might have been a widow running the farm with her adolescent son. In any case this teenaged son always took pity on me and carried the pail home for me.

My littlest sister Deanna was just learning to walk when we lived in this farmhouse, and I remember she was just about the cutest thing I could imagine. I loved her dearly. So why did I sneak up behind her and say "Boo!" one day when she was just practicing standing there without hanging on to anything? Brotherly love, I guess, but she started wailing instantly and was so startled that she piddled a little puddle right there on the floor. My mother made me not only change her outfit, but clean up the mess too.

Poor old Aunt Frieda had never heard of anyone named Deanna and could not get it right. She would ask my mother every time what the little girl's name was. Deanna. You mean Diane? No, Deanna. Diana? No, Deanna. DeanAnne? No, Deanna. Ohh…. Another black mark against my mother, this one for coming up with a name like that to hang on a kid. Arvilla's friend Mardelle occasionally visited at the Klammer farm when we lived at the Little House, and my mother liked her instantly. It was her Southern drawl that drew Mom in, and she laughed at everything Mardelle said, often for no reason other than the way she turned a phrase. So Mardelle was an obvious choice for her when it came time to select Deanna's middle name.

My father was determined not to spend another winter in that house. When Chris Decker from our congregation was settling his mother's estate, they came to terms on her old fixer-upper right in town. For the first time we were actually living in the town of Westgate, within easy reach of everything we needed to access. My father was a block from the garage and could even walk home for lunch, the kids could walk or bike to school and home for lunch, there were three grocery stores within walking distance, church activities were a walk away, and on the advantages went. Of utmost importance to my parents, they were now homeowners again and freed from throwing money to a landlord.

The house needed work, but my father saw this as an opportunity to remodel. The good news was that we could live in it throughout the construction. It had a furnace that was barely functional, no indoor toilet, and a dirt-floor cellar under part of the structure and crawl space under the rest. By pulling down a huge tree near the west end of the house, he could build an extension that would include indoor plumbing and a full kitchen. For weeks he dug and chopped at the roots of that tree and one day the tow truck from the garage backed in from the street and ka-whump, the towering maple came crashing down.

His plan was to remove the old stone foundation and completely rebuild it with cement block enclosing a full basement. This meant that half the structure would be supported temporarily on jackposts while the excavation progressed. When the first half was securely resting on the new foundation, the process could then be repeated for the other half. Just when the project was at its most precarious point, where nothing was holding up the west half of the building but those jackposts, a thunderstorm came up during the night that threatened to wash them out. The room for the boys was directly over this cavern. We were awakened by my parents, and all of us gathered at the east end to pray. As my father relates in his memoirs, our prayers were answered, when rain poured on farms all around Westgate, but miraculously none fell in town.

He added on a brand new modern kitchen, installed an indoor bathroom, replaced the wheezing old coal furnace with a new oil-burning floor furnace, ripped off the rotting front porch, substituted a fashionable picture window for the existing row of double-hung ones, and nailed in oak flooring. When the plasterers finished up, Arvilla came into town to check on our progress. After taking one step inside, she said, "You can't live here in these fumes. You're going to move in with us until this stuff dries." So our family of seven squeezed in for several days with her six—no wait, eight. They had just been blessed with twin girls, Janeen and Janell.

For a short period of time after I began piano lessons with Mrs. Rowland, my mother sent me to a music teacher closer to the station where we lived. The only thing I remember about her was the pungent, almost nauseating, aroma of the tomato sauce she was canning one summer day when I arrived for a lesson. After we left Maynard, my mother tried to make the commute back to this lady's house to continue my piano lessons, but they really preferred to have somebody right in Westgate, if possible. No one was up to their standards, but they found a teacher named Lulu Duffield in West Union, about twenty-five miles away. Since the cost to drive that distance for one piano lesson would have been prohibitive, my parents worked out a deal with her. She could use our piano and our house as her studio and draw in as many students as she wished. They offered her room and board for two days each week in exchange for free lessons for me and other family members. Such a deal.

My parents talked for years about this experience having old Mrs. Duffield in the house. My father always remembered how quickly her dash to the outhouse was in the winter, but how long she dallied in the bathroom once the facilities were indoors. My mother, on the other hand, always remembered how she always left something on her plate (forbidden for us), and it drove her crazy wondering whether this was some rule of etiquette or this lady just did not appreciate her cooking. Mrs. Duffield was affiliated with the Sherwood Music School and persuaded my parents to sign up for their correspondence program. The School offered packets of graduated etudes, studies and compositions in classical music, lessons in history and theory, periodic testing, and, for those who progressed through to the certificate of completion, a scholarship to their campus in Chicago. Sounded good. As the years went by I worked my way through their program and after a while started to consider myself a pretty good piano player. It seemed that I had an aptitude for music, and I even discovered that I had what I would later learn was termed perfect pitch, the ability to recognize and identify a particular pitch from memory.

Some of you may remember that before electronic recording devices were invented, music performances could be preserved on rolls of paper. A special piano used by the performer cut perforations in the paper corresponding to the notes played. The manufacturer then sold both player pianos and these piano rolls to the public for playing back the rendition. Such a piano was more expensive, of course, and, as anyone who fell victim to a request to move one could attest, considerably heavier than an ordinary piano, but the piano we had in the living room was such a limited edition instrument. Sometimes on a Sunday afternoon my father would have enough energy to operate the foot pedals for an hour or so, forcing the roll through the mechanism pneumatically, while we watched in fascination as the keys danced magically as if by invisible fingers and listened in awe to a melodious rhapsody of *Old Black Joe* or *My Old Kentucky Home*. To enhance the aural experience, the manufacturer would sometimes embellish the original with additional slits in the paper to generate simultaneous counterpoint, trills or melismatic passages in a register that would have been impossible for any single player to perform when the master was cut. This was such a delightful experience for me that I was determined not only to play like that one day, but to write my own music just like it. Would that such a fancy came to fruition.

When a congregation has a parochial school, the members tend to assume that a Sunday school is not necessary. However, this short-sighted position overlooks three groups: those children in the congregation who do not attend the school, those who do but need the review, and everyone else, *including* the adults. My parents took notice of this deficiency at St. Peter's and were determined to correct it. They encountered mostly apathy, but found real support from two quarters. One was the family of Bob Rueber, a generation older than my parents, whose farm a couple miles east of Westgate we visited quite often during this period. Bob would become the first superintendent of the new Sunday school. What should be uppermost in my memory about them was the devotion and affection they extended to my parents for the rest of their lives, but, sorry to say, I cannot think about them without seeing Zaida Rueber in her calico bonnet held secure by a hair net. She probably had alopecia, the treatment for which caused her to go completely bald, but before she was fitted for a wig, she always reminded me of Martha Custis. It was on their yard that I first experienced what it is like to have the wind knocked out of me. While climbing one of their trees, I grabbed hold of a limb about fifteen feet above the ground that was too small and too dead to support fifty pounds. As I stumbled around unable to draw a breath, I was quite sure I would be dead in a few minutes.

Another staunch supporter was the family of John Yelden, whose farm was about half way between Westgate and Maynard. I remember a few visits to their place with my parents, but on one occasion they filled in for my mother when she was unable to pick me up from school. Their youngest daughter was a few years older than I, but she did her best to entertain me in her room while her father and older brothers finished the chores. When they drove me home, Mr. Yelden did something I had never seen anyone do before. As we started out, the passenger door of the car was open, but instead of getting out to close it, he simply accelerated and the door slammed shut on its own. It was a science lesson about inertia, but I only noticed what a neat trick it was.

Years later, as an adult, I faced a similar situation regarding Sunday school when we transferred into a new congregation. Although attitudes toward the Sunday school by the students of the parochial school and their parents were identical to what I remembered from Westgate, we took issue with a different problem. Before now I had never heard of a congregation that shut down Sunday school for the summer, especially when they had purchased a complete set of materials from the publisher that included the fourth quarter. In the fall I introduced a measure before the voters to continue classes through the summer, using these materials. Ironically, the superintendent was opposed, on the grounds that he did not want his boys, in his exact words, "to get too much religion." When the measure was defeated, I began lobbying for next year. This time Stan Sacha, who had been appointed as the new superintendent, stood up with me, leading off with his pitch that starving our children of their spiritual growth for three months was as reprehensible as forcing them to fast all summer. However, though the vote was favorable, the former superintendent and other "pillars" of the congregation boycotted our classes. When the teachers announced they were refusing to continue, I told them that we had already lined up teachers and actually preferred that they take the summer off. Even Christ himself needed a break from teaching, alone, away from the crowds, from time to time, I pointed out. At the beginning of the next teachers meeting, one of the stalwarts turned to me and, knowing that I had instigated the new program, demanded to know, "Whose idea was this, anyway?" "Well, I think it was God's," I told her softly.

Because of their work with the Sunday school, my parents were delegates of the congregation one year to a convention in Houston, which extended for several days. They sent the two girls to stay with my father's sister and family in Nebraska, while Ralph, Donny and I went to stay with his brother Martin, a pastor living with his family of four children in Kinsley, Kansas. Kinsley, by the way, boasts the distinction of being the exact center of the continental United States. Uncle Martin made the mistake of letting me see him hand over to Jerelyn, Raymond and Freddy, my cousins, their allowances one day. He had a difficult time explaining to me that I was not entitled to an allowance from him. As consolation, he sent us down to the matinee to see *Huckleberry Finn*. It was supposed to be a comedy, but for some reason I saw something poignant in it and started bawling. Poor Jerelyn was trying to get something out of the movie and attempted to shush me up, but when that failed, she was so embarrassed that she eventually took us all out of there and back home. Maybe a touch of homesickness mixed in with all the other emotions of this strange experience, but I really cannot say for sure what set me off so.

When my parents returned, my father had brought a load of watermelons from Texas back with them, and we set up a roadside stand to sell them for fifty cents apiece. When he wanted to divide up the profits among all the children, I piped up to say that Jerelyn, Ray and Freddy, who already get an allowance, should not get any of the proceeds. My father disagreed and apportioned an equal share for each of them. The Arkansas River runs right through Kinsley, and we all put on swimsuits to splash around in the water one day. The river is so shallow at this point in its flow that we could easily see huge carp in the stream and caught as many as we wanted with our bare hands.

When the Sunday school program got underway, it was my father who happened to be the teacher of my age group, and I still see our class sitting there in the furnace room in the basement. Because of the severity of some dental problems, he had to be fitted for dentures at a very young age. As he valiantly tried to teach his class one Sunday while he was waiting for them to be made, I was so embarrassed by those bare gums that I recall wishing no one knew he was my dad. I know, I know, I even knew at the time how shameful that was, but I was unable to disguise my feeling. Uncle Erwin taught the older kids, and when I got to his class, he pulled out a pack of quiz cards he had bought. I knew my Bible history so well that no one else got a chance to answer any of his questions, and I later overheard him telling my father about that. I am not sure which of us was prouder.

When we had our first Christmas Eve program, I was standing next to Larry Dean holding up one of the alternating red and green letters of the word CHRISTMAS cut from construction paper. It was an acrostic, where each letter represented a word, and each child in the row recited a piece based on that word. When we got home after these Christmas programs, we were always surprised to see all of the Christmas presents already under the tree. For years I could never figure out how this happened. They were not there when we left, but as we walked into the house afterward there they were. I might have been an adult already before I realized how my parents pulled this off—they sent all the kids to the car, and before they left the house themselves quickly set out the pre-wrapped gifts.

One year I got a BB gun for Christmas. To this day I am a little surprised that my parents would let me have such a thing, especially in town, but they laid down some laws, and I never hurt anyone or shot out any windows with it. After a little practice shooting at cans and bottles, I became quite accurate with it. I was enjoined from shooting any songbirds, including robins, cardinals, or gold finches, but there are several birds that are considered pests by every farmer in Iowa. Sparrows and pigeons steal grain from bins and granaries, but crows are the master thieves. I once saw them peck through the screen of my neighbor's house to reach the tomatoes she had ripening on her windowsill. They will filch grain from anywhere, even following behind the corn planter to dig up the seed. These were fair game, and I shot so many sparrows that word got around in the sparrow community that our house was dangerous, and after a time my quarry dried up, so I took my gun along the next time we went to Uncle John's farm. I had fun one time shooting straight up in the air in such a way that I could hear the BB land on the galvanized metal roof of the building next door, then catch it as it rolled down over the edge and load it back into the gun.

If you are squeamish, do not read this paragraph. Across the street from us lived a family named Ohl, and every night dozens of pigeons would roost in the loft of their vacant machine shed. One time my father and I got permission from them (the Ohls, not the pigeons) to climb into their loft during the night with flashlights to catch them (the pigeons, not the Ohls). If we were to turn on the lights, the birds would fly all over the building, but if we shined the flashlight directly into their eyes, they were momentarily blinded. So here we were at eye level with them and snatched as many of the sleepy pigeons as we wanted and stuffed them into the gunnysacks we brought along. The next day my mother pulled out each bird, and with a quick jerk, snapped off the head, held it by the feet until it stopped dripping, cleaned it and dropped it into the roaster. The meat was good, but there was not much of it on all those little bones, so we never went through this exercise again. Oh, I see you read it anyway. Well, I knew you would be overcome by curiosity.

When my parents had a meeting in the evening at church, they had a variety of solutions for the babysitting of us, none of which included hiring someone. When they considered I was old enough, they simply put us all to bed and drove off. With no telephone, I can still remember lying awake worrying and worrying that they might never come back, so it was with great relief that I heard the car drive back into the driveway. One time they had Mrs. Duffield watch us, but we gave her such a merry chase that she never agreed to do that again. We three boys were all together in the same bed, and if we bounced around too hard, the bedspring would collapse inside the frame and hit the floor with a thud. Once we also knocked over the chamber pot in the process, spilling its delectable contents on the frayed old Persian rug left in the house by Mrs. Decker. Mrs. Duffield came running in and switched on the light, just in time to see Ralph jump naked onto the mattress to get his pajamas. She simply moaned, switched off the light, closed the door and left.

Sometimes they dropped us off at the home of someone, anyone, who would agree to watch us for the evening and bed us down when it got late. On at least one such occasion, that lucky person was Grandma Klammer. Fred and Martha Klammer were Arnie's parents, who lived near the center of town with their unmarried daughter Norma. Fred had suffered an accident in his twenties when his mitten caught in a corn shredder and drew in his hand and forearm. The hook he had in place of a hand was something a kid never forgets. Their house was boring except for the stereoscope they allowed us to squabble over whenever we visited. With it we could look through their shoebox collection of double-image photos, which, when focused properly, made them appear starkly three-dimensional. The collection was quite a travelogue of famous places and sights we had never seen or heard of—Yosemite Falls, Old Faithful, General Sherman sequoia with a car passing through its base, Mount Rushmore, and so on. I was forever grateful to Grandma Klammer for the white lie she always told my mother when my parents returned and asked whether we had misbehaved. Having raised two boys and two girls herself, Grandma knew the score and would always say, "They were fine."

One day a baby girl named Marlys came to live at Grandma Klammer's house. When I asked where she came from, my mother simply said, "Well, Norma was naughty." It was the only explanation I was going to get, but I did not know what it meant. Norma worked as a newspaper correspondent in Oelwein and ostensibly socialized with some of the men she met in town. An unwed pregnancy was met with such severe social disgrace in this generation that sometimes a young lady who found herself in such a condition was forced into hiding in the house for several months, until a midwife or doctor could discreetly slip into the house for the delivery and spirit the infant away to an agency without arousing suspicion. In some cases the girl was sent to live with a distant relative until the birth, and then would leave the baby to be raised by the relatives there, all the time praying that word did not leak out. When Marlys became the third child born to Norma without a husband, the relatives insisted this time she raise the daughter herself.

Tragedy almost struck Happy one day at the hands of his grandmother. He had walked to her house after school, and she noticed that he had a cough, so she spooned out a dose of cough syrup for him from her medicine cabinet. After Arvilla picked him up, he seemed lethargic, but when he became almost comatose, she picked up the telephone. Grandma discovered to her horror that the bottle she thought was cough medicine was ant poison. They raced to the hospital, where doctors pumped his stomach and treated him for ingestion of arsenic. All of us prayed, no one harder than I, that God would not let my best friend Happy die. The doctors were not sure he would pull through, but after a harrowing night, he finally started to come around in a day or two. It would be several months before anyone could be sure what the long-term effects were, but there was a good possibility he would be blind in one eye. When I saw Happy fifty years later, I asked him about this. There were no residual problems, and he told me what saved his life was that the systems of his body reacted so severely that they were shocked into shutting down until the treatments the doctors were giving him could take effect. I prefer to believe there was an additional reason.

# The Rest of Westgate

Around Christmas time in 1954, my parents received the news that my grandfather, George Pullmann, who was by then pastor of a congregation in Friona, Texas, had had a heart attack. I was quite surprised that my father makes no mention of this in his autobiography, because he sincerely held his father in the highest esteem. "Now there was a good man," I heard him say more than once. Since the details of his final days might be of interest or significance to posterity, I will pass along the following account from my grandmother. On December 21 he first took sick with heart trouble, but after treatment he felt quite well for two days. Then on Friday the 24th he had another attack. Thinking this one would also pass, he waited with treatment and made plans for his Christmas Eve service. When he did not recover on his own, my grandmother notified one of the elders, who took him to the hospital. There he was diagnosed with "acute coronary deficiency" and placed under an oxygen tent, without much hope for survival.

Not wanting to spoil the Christmas of her children, my grandmother waited until Saturday evening to call Martin in Kinsley, Kansas. Martin departed immediately for Texas and arrived around 1:30 a.m. The next day Martin's brother Carl and sister Frieda and their families arrived and stayed until Thursday the 30th. Frieda and her eight-year-old daughter Sharon stayed on for two weeks more, visiting the very sick patient twice a day until about January 4, when he seemed to be doing well and was discharged. My parents left us with Klammers and drove down with Uncle Paul, my father's sister Ellen and her three children on Monday the 10th. Expecting to see my grandfather resting comfortably in bed, they were all astonished that the indomitable patient met them at the door. Since the country parish was about twenty-two miles from town, the adult children of the family made the determination that their father needed to be closer to medical facilities and at least one family member. Martin suggested they transport him to Kinsley.

The entire party started for Kansas on Wednesday the 12th, and stopped about midway to rest at the home of a colleague, Pastor Fredricksen, in Woodward, Oklahoma. When they tried to continue from there, Grandpa had a relapse which forced them to return after only a few miles. The doctors there prescribed a sleeping pill, and while my parents stayed overnight with him in Woodward, the rest of the party went on to Kinsley to arrange quarters for George and Hilda. The elderly pair settled into a house about a block away from Martin and began life at a pace much less frenzied than the one they had just left at their congregation in Texas. Always accustomed to running at full throttle, George Pullmann was only now beginning to realize that the Lord might, after all, be able to get along without him.

At first he had continuous chest pains, but gradually they seemed to move to his left leg. On Tuesday, the night of the 18th, he tried to sleep in his own bed, but early the next morning he was cold and climbed into my grandmother's bed with her. When she commented that he felt cold, he said, "Yes I know, maybe I am getting the flu." These were his last words. He reached out his arm and it fell limp on Grandma. When she heard what she describes as a death rattle, she knew he was gone. He had been pastor at a rural parish called Golgotha near Wausa, Nebraska for about half of his ministry, and his body was shipped by train for burial there. Reinhold and Frieda Kumm (my father's sister) were running a farm not far from there, so our whole family packed into the car and drove to stay with them for the funeral, which took place on January 25.

Their three children, Judy, Allen and Sharon Kumm, were the cousins closest in age to me. We did not get a chance to see them very often, so it was always a special treat when we got together. Since I was only ten years old and was not really very close to my grandfather anyway, I was more excited about getting to visit Allen than mournful about our loss. Little Donny, who was only six and could not appreciate the gravity of the moment either, decided he would dramatize how it happened when he saw Grandpa laid out in the coffin at the visitation. Clutching his chest, he fell to the floor and pretended to be dead. Grandma shrieked and nearly fainted. She was not much amused when Donny stood up smiling. My mother led him away by the ears.

Allen and his sisters attended the parochial school in nearby Plainview, and their parents saw no reason why they should miss school that entire week. We went with them. Since we were missing school back home for a week, my parents thought it would be a good idea to be learning something here. Unfortunately, no one ever told me that it was proper etiquette for the visitor to keep his mouth shut, so I was the smarty-pants that was always raising his hand to answer the questions no one else knew. I preferred to think they were just too slow to answer. Allen and Judy never did forgive me for that.

A few months after that, when Fred Klammer died, Happy and Larry Dean were the ones losing their grandfather. According to custom at St. Peter's, the bell in the steeple pealed rapidly to celebrate the passing of a soul to heaven, and then after a pause, the bell tolled slowly, once for each year of the decedent's life. This time the bell tolled 79 times. On the day of a funeral, activities at the parochial school were usually curtailed or suspended, but we would not have been there in any case out of respect for our friends, the Klammers. Shamefully, however, Arvilla came out to the car to drive some of us over from the house in town to the service and found Happy and me sitting on the back seat playing cards while we waited. We got two sermons that day, and when hers was finished, we were ordered to think about what she said as we *walked* over to the church for the second one.

Even that did not sink to the level reached by Burton Hoehne and Larry Sabin one Sunday. Sitting in the front pew almost literally under the nose of Pastor Schultz high above in his pulpit, they were playing cards during the sermon. I suppose they assumed that from his lofty position, he would look out over the congregation beyond where they were and not see them. They were mistaken. He did not address them directly, but stopped in mid-sentence and just stared at them for a long time before resuming his sermon. Two red-eared boys put away the cards and sheepishly turned to face the front. The rest of the congregation was not sure what was happening. Did he lose his train of thought? Was he having a heart attack? Those who had nodded off were now wide awake. This was the talk of the town all the next day, when the grapevine had Reverend Schultz interrupting his sermon for a minute or two, no I bet it was five minutes, no at least ten. Word eventually got back to the parsonage. That evening he called the elders and some other leaders of the congregation, including my father, into his study. He had a surprise for them. His high-tech equipment included a wire recorder (using wire, not vinyl tape), and he had recorded the service. The silent gap was nineteen seconds.

Otto Schultz was probably in his sixties, and in cold weather I can picture his chubby face laced with those tiny bright red blood vessels often characterized by someone with high blood pressure and carrying some extra weight. In addition to his spiritual flock, he kept real sheep in the small pasture adjacent to the church property, perhaps as a metaphorical reminder to himself of his ponderous responsibilities. The parking area was situated between the church and school to the east and the parsonage acreage to the west. By the time we were members, everyone parked their cars in this lot, but along the boundary with the parsonage still remained the metal piping used for hitching posts in the bygone days when the members came in horse-drawn buggies.

I was sitting in church one Sunday when for some reason I thought of Burton Hoehne and how funny his name would be if it were Button instead. I was having difficulty suppressing a chuckle. The warm smile inside became a smile on my face and then before I knew what was happening out came a chortle through my nose I could not prevent. My father sitting next to me swatted my leg with the back of his hand, and for a time I was able to concentrate on the sermon. Then that ridiculous name popped back into my head again and I really had to fight the urge to laugh aloud all over again. It welled up inside until I could control it no longer and it just came to the surface with a disruptive snort. This time my father pinched the inside of my leg so hard I really had to choke back the urge to let out a yelp. It worked only to a point. I was no longer thinking about Button Hoehne, but my focus was on nursing my wounded leg, not the sermon.

Our house in Westgate was next door to a kind of general store run by a man named Martin Schwartz. Everyone called him Moose because he also ran a kind of men's club at the northwest edge of town that he called the Moose Club. Westgate had a tavern on the main street, but the Moose Club offered a little more than just a glass of whiskey or a bottle of Hamm's. You would join the Club if you wanted to see movies. Yes, that kind. One night Moose put on a special program of cartoons for the kids, and my parents allowed us to go. When the cartoons were finished, he announced that the show was over, and all the children should clear the building. But he did not allow enough time for families to leave before one of his X-rated films started up, showing pearl divers in Japan. My mother was furious, as she hustled us out of there. It was the first time I remember seeing a bare naked lady.

We had a kind of uneasy truce with Moose—he wary of the house of rascals next to his business and my mother wary of the dirty old man next to her home. For the most part he tolerated us well, despite the inevitable nuisance we represented whenever school was out. One time when we were hanging around the sidewalk out front, he came out with a box of Clark bars that must not have sold since about 1879. We rushed home excitedly to show my mother what we got, but when she tore off the wrapper of the first one, she found it full of worms. I do not think his esteem could plummet further in her eyes, but after she threw that box into the trash, we were never allowed to accept anything from him again after that.

I do remember asking Moose once whether he could help me make a little mirror as a Mother's Day present. We had a can of silver paint in the basement, and my idea was to spread some of it on one side of a piece of glass and, voilà, a beautiful mirror would result. Moose took a scrap piece of window glass, freehanded a circle with his glass cutter, and, as he handed it to me, soberly informed me that would be ten dollars. When he elicited the shocked look from me that he expected, he flashed his grin with several teeth missing and told me I could take it home. Of course, the finished product was a piece of junk, but I think my mother appreciated the sentiment anyway. I asked my mother why there was Father's Day and Mother's Day but not Kids' Day. "*Kids'* Day! Kids' Day?" she bellowed, "*every day is kids' day.*"

Moose would sponsor a fish and doughnut fry in the basement of his general store occasionally. Both were probably steeped in the same hot lard, but it was all scrumptious. As I was eating my doughnut, the lady across the table from me told me I was supposed to save the hole for her. So I ate all around the edge, leaving a thin circle of the breading from the middle, and presented that to her. At first she looked puzzled and forgot why I would be offering it to her, but then with a matronly pat on the head, she said it would be okay for me to finish it. People came from towns around to these feasts, so I do not know who she was. I hated to think she was a classmate's mother who might describe me and relate her tale about that gullible boy so easily duped who sat at the same table with her.

One day I asked my mother why I never got to have a birthday party, like the other kids at school. She said when I turned ten, I could have a party, so we invited the Klammers, kids from my class, Jackie Ohl and his sisters from across the street, and with my own brothers and sisters, I had a nice party. Some of the kids at school had also been telling me they got an allowance—money just *given* to them by their parents. When I had approached my parents about this, they said that when I reached age ten, they could give me a nickel each week if I did not neglect my duties. The only money I ever got before this was a gift from my generous godparents, especially my great-uncle Hans Puellmann (my grandfather George's youngest brother), who always remembered me on my birthday. I noticed from time to time that when my mother needed money she would pull out her checkbook and write a check, so I asked her how I could get a checkbook. I never saw her put any money in, so I assumed the bank was like the golden goose, where you could get as much as you wanted, as long as you had one of those special books. Nevertheless, to her credit, she thought this would be a good experience for me and set up a checking account for me at the bank in town, explained the harsh reality that I had to put money *in*, and showed me how to write a check. Then *she* kept the checkbook.

Since we did not have a TV, the library in town became one of my favorite places. Old Mr. Bruns was the man in our congregation who had lost a leg in WWI, and whenever he went up to communion on his crutches, I would always notice that crumpled up pants leg and wonder how he kept it from falling down and dragging on the ground. When he died, his widow became the librarian. Mrs. Bruns was probably kind to everyone, but she was especially good with children and loved to see me come into her "store." She knew the books I liked and always steered me to good ones I would not have explored otherwise. I read all of the Hardy Boys mystery books, and she got almost as excited as I when the newest in the series was published and came into the library. My mother had a surprisingly comprehensive overview of literature, given her limited years of schooling, and would recommend a title once in a while, but for some reason I could not be drawn into the exploits of the Bobbsey Twins or *Five Little Peppers and How They Grew*. Books of jokes and riddles were among my favorites, and I am continually hearing some version or other of many of those old jokes still making the circuit today.

Parents today are vexed by the plethora of negative effects on their children—the ubiquitous violence in video arcades and computer games, enticements on the internet, lasciviousness by wire or wireless media, and the like. But the influence of books can be just as powerful. I was totally swept up by Frank and Joe Hardy, and had the idea that Ralph and I could be just like them, with their secret signals, hidden passageways, and clever schemes. All we needed was a mystery to solve and some clues. My good friend we will call Randolph, on the other hand, gravitated toward the science fiction genre when he went to the library, which opened his mind to the realm of other-worldly possibilities. To him these became *probabilities*, which, I believe, ultimately led him to question his faith in Christianity and contributed to his decision one day to give it up.

I would sometimes read about a kid who could earn money by delivering newspapers on his bicycle. Westgate did not have a newspaper, and there were not many other opportunities for someone my age to make money. Whenever it would snow, Mrs. Mullins would give me fifteen cents to shovel her walk, but I was not very good at marketing this enterprise to many others. Almost everyone in town mowed their lawns with a push mower, a kind of miniature reaper with a reel that would sweep the blades of grass back against a horizontal blade as the machine was pushed forward. When a version of this reel type mower appeared with a gasoline engine, my entrepreneurial father got the idea that we could buy one on credit and pay it off by mowing lawns around town. Then, once it was paid off, the fees we charged would be all profit. It was self-propelled, but it was too heavy to be pushed very far without the engine running. That meant my mother would need to load it into the car and drive me over to the customer's house and wait while I finished mowing. Besides the extra overhead and the fact that she and I together could barely handle the loading, this was too much down time for her. Worse, the reel design did not work very well in tall grass, so each swath left a trail of dandelion stems and timothy grass still defiantly waving unmowed in the breeze. A different design, using the whirling blade most common today, was also making its debut about this time, and became very popular almost overnight. Every time my father would pass a yard where some potential customer was using one, he would utter a mild expletive under his breath and denigrate another one of those "whirligig" mowers that was literally cutting into our business. I do not remember what became of that power mower of ours, but his marketing idea sputtered.

Because the roof of Moose's building adjacent to our yard was metal, my parents collected the fresh unmineralized rainwater that trickled off it into an old oak barrel. This bounty could serve a number of purposes, including irrigation of the garden during dry spells—a task that fell to me. One day when I pulled out a bucketful of this supposedly pure liquid, I was surprised to see the water teeming with hundreds of cute little wriggly swimmers. With typical pre-teen logic I reasoned that perhaps birds had somehow dropped baby fish into the barrel. It would be many years before I made the correlation between those "fingerlings" and the mosquito welts we usually bore throughout the summer. Moose lived in a small house near the back of his general store and had a housekeeper living with him named Nettie Rueber. Nettie was an eccentric old woman who asked me one day to use her sickle to cut some weeds out behind the house along the railroad tracks. When I finished, she invited me in and paid me with some Indian head pennies that she scooped from a galvanized bucket. The last Indian head pennies were minted in 1908, so I am quite sure in retrospect that her hoard in that pail was worth a fortune. Alas, I had no idea at the time about such things and mindlessly spent them. Nettie died a short time later, and for many years I wondered what became of that trove of pennies and whether poor Nettie ever had any sense of the value of it.

I really hit the big time when my father arranged to have me work down at the garage for Warren Rueber. Warren would pay me twenty-five cents a week to empty the wastebaskets, burn the trash, wash the windows, stock parts on the shelves, and other odd jobs after school. Twenty-five cents a week! That was far more than my allowance. I would be rich. As it turns out, it was more than a job. When I started, I did not know it would be an invaluable window into the world of my father—the customers he encountered, the contortions he endured to effect a repair, the parts and tools that were his stock in trade, and the variety of skills and equipment required to do his job. I also found out I was not a good employee. It was much more fun to see how high a valve spring would bounce on the pavement behind the building than to wipe grime off of windows.

When we lived in Maynard, my mother had discovered that prices were better at the fancy new supermarket in Oelwein than they were at the stores in town. We had three grocery stores in Westgate—the most popular one run by the son of Pastor Schultz, the grocery-hardware store run by the Plattes, and the little grocery-pharmacy run by eccentric old Mr. Komroffsky—but she usually made the twelve-mile trek to the "big city" to load up the car with her bargains. If we ran out of some individual item, however, she would send one of us down the street to pick it up. One day she needed sanitary napkins, and thought one of us kids could run down to pick up a package of them for her. However, she had noticed Mose Buesing, often seen unshaven and stumbling in midday with his bottle, hanging around on the street earlier, so she sent both Ralph and me together to pick them up for her. Although she was quite specific about what we should ask for, we were not versed in such delicate matters and brought home a package of table napkins. I could not understand her disgust when she said, "Never mind, I'll get them myself."

Having joined the Navy without knowing how to swim, my father was determined that we get lessons. In basic training the petty officer had told the recruits that they were not necessarily expected to save someone else, but each of them was expected to learn how to save himself. Anyone can doggie paddle, he barked, and no one had better make him throw a buoy or jump into the water. With that they were thrown into the water, literally to sink or swim. My father could claw his way vigorously forward in the water but never progressed beyond that fundamental level his whole life. Oelwein was the closest place with a swimming pool, and carpools were set up to drive Westgate kids over there for swimming lessons. Teenage instructors did their best to demonstrate the crawl, back and side strokes to us, where to breathe in and exhale, how to kick efficiently, but I was the skinny little kid who just sat on the edge shivering.

One day the class was ordered down to the deep end, where the lifeguard threw a penny into the water near the number ten painted on the side. Everyone was expected to swim down and retrieve it. Despite the jeers of my classmates, I refused even to get into the water at this scary end of the pool. When two of the teachers took me by force and dropped me in, I clung to the side screaming. After a time I thought I might convince them that I was swimming along the side, paddling water with my free arm but holding on with the other. No one was fooled, and the scoffing continued even in the car all the way back to Westgate. Warren Rueber heard about it and started calling me Ten Foot. Worst of all, my parents did not get much return on the cost of those swim lessons.

My mother always had chores lined up for us. We canned peaches every season, and she put us to work peeling them while she sliced them off the pit. I can still hear her disgusted cry, "Oh no, a whole bushel of *clings*!" As I soon learned, the flesh of some varieties of peach pries away from the seed cleanly, while for others it adheres tenaciously, not only requiring the extra time and effort to scrape the pit but *wasting* the innermost layer that could not be salvaged. She kept a huge garden, so we helped pick peas, green beans, and corn and put them up in the chest freezer some men unloaded into our living room one day. Tomatoes were peeled and canned whole or pressed through a colander into juice. She had a pressure cooker, and it is quite possible that the hundreds of Mason jars we stocked every year in our basement kept that company in business. One day in winter she had a piecrust in the oven and asked me to pull it out and turn off the stove at a certain time while she ran an errand. Busily involved in my own projects, I completely forgot about that little obligation until I smelled something burning from the direction of the kitchen. The crust was totally black and unfurling such smoke that I dashed out the door with it and threw it into a snow bank. When my mother returned, she found that she not only did not have a piecrust, but her nice Pyrex pie plate had been thermal-shocked into several pieces. As she went for her paddle, I can still hear her demanding to know what was so "all-fired important" that it took precedence over what she had asked me to do.

The back yard had a huge raspberry patch, and early one spring I was tasked with pruning it. "How do I know which runners to break off?" I asked. "Just the dried ones," my mother said, "like this one, and that one there, you see?" But I did not really understand. They all looked dried to me. After trying to handle the thorns for a while barehanded, I decided to get a saw from the basement. There, that works much better. In about an hour, my mother came out to check on me and was aghast to see that I had hacked a quarter of her patch to pieces. I recognized the tune, and some of the words to the song that came next—it started something like, "Get out of here before I tan your breeches …."

After my grandfather died, the ten children of my grandmother wanted her to spend a month with each of them in rotation. It was the first summer after the funeral when she arrived at our house. As she was helping us in the kitchen to can peaches, I made the mistake of asking her some tactless question about whether she misses Grandpa. She immediately burst into tears and blubbered out something about "You children don't understand …." With a withering look at me, Mom told us all to go outside and play for a while.

Whenever Grandma Gimbel came to visit, she and my mother would chatter away in German, first because it was easier for my grandmother, but also because they could discuss things little ears were not supposed to hear. No one more gentle has ever been born than Emelia Gimbel, and the peace she brought with her when she arrived palpably softened the edginess of the entire household, especially my mother. When she came to visit, it was not just to sit around, so she was always busy folding laundry, peeling potatoes or "vashing dishes." When she had difficulty threading a needle for sewing on patches, I was always flattered that she came to me for help with it. Uncle John lived about fifteen miles away, and when he would stop by for a visit, it became a three-way German conversation. One day, as I was sitting on the basement steps just off the kitchen, I overheard my mother say something to John, and all of them laughed. I wrote down what I heard, to find out later what was so funny. When I asked her a few days later what "bist du ein Esel?" [are you an ass?] means, she demanded to know where I heard that. When I replied, "I heard *you* say that to Uncle John," she said, "Well, it just means, 'are you a donkey?'"

John lived in the country near Randalia, northeast of Westgate, and later a short distance away from there near Fayette. Whenever we visited them at Randalia, Ralph and I got to load our bicycles along and ride on the gravel roads all over around their farm. A simple pleasure, but we pedaled miles away on those bikes and back. The Fayette area is very hilly, so winter was the time to head over to his farm on a Sunday afternoon. He had the perfect hill, grassy and free of trees and brush, about a half mile long, with a stream at the bottom. It was quite a thrill to belly flop on a sled, streak down the slope at twenty miles per hour and still glide for another 100 yards on the frozen stream. Of course, the walk back up the hill took half an hour, but that too was a good prescription for staying warm. My father bought a toboggan one year, and now five or six passengers could galumph down together. When it got dark, we loaded up the snow vehicles, went inside and cranked up a batch of homemade ice cream. Too bad those Sundays had to end.

Before my Uncle John and Aunt Mabel had any children, we had spent so much time at their place that one day my parents asked me if I might like to stay overnight with them. My mother dropped me off one morning, and I spent the day shadowing John around the farm as he did his chores. I had never been to the grain elevator before, but we drove into town to load one of his wagons with corn. He even bought me a candy bar, a treat I never got at home. When we returned to the farm, some of his cows were munching weeds out along the roadway. After we got them herded back behind the fence, he looked at me and told me I had left the gate unlatched. It was not so much what he said, but the way he said, "Ya left it unlocked, din ya? Ya did, *din ya*?" I tried to choke back a sob, but that night at supper, it all came bubbling to the surface, and they realized we were heading back to Westgate yet that night.

We were visiting the Steinbronn farm one day, when schoolmate George saw me admiring his beautiful shiny bright red bicycle. After he had me try it out, he told me that he hardly ever rode it and asked if I wanted to buy it for twenty-five dollars. My bicycle at home was ready to be passed down to Donny anyway, so my mother heartily approved. I had more than enough money in my checking account, but the transaction with George took a little detour. We were in Oelwein a few days later, when I walked past a sporting goods store displaying the best softball glove I had ever seen. It cost ten dollars, the most expensive piece of leather in the store, but I just had to have it, and before I knew what was happening, I was writing out a check. Ten dollars in those days had the buying power of perhaps two or three hundred today, and my mother was livid when I showed her what I bought. What about the bike—the *bike*, remember? Well, I had actually considered that already, but the two purchases together would take my bank account down to zero. That was really her point. Just because you have some money does not mean you should spend yourself to zero and then have no reserve. All the kids at school envied my glove, and all the kids in the neighborhood envied my bicycle, and I proudly took both of these items, as well as my mother's lesson about spending, into adulthood.

Ralph and I got so we hated Saturdays and tried to come up with one scheme or another to get out of the house. For one thing, this was bath day, but my mother also had five kids underfoot without relief all day and was usually in a foul humor. But we could never quite understand why. Saturday was also laundry day, or at least one of the laundry days, at our house. Washing machines of that time did not have the spin cycle that every machine has today. Instead, the soaking wet heavy wash was lugged out of the tub and run through a wringer to squeeze out as much rinse water as possible. The more modern machines had electric wringers, but ours had a hand crank. Guess whose job it was to turn that crank and hang those heavy coveralls on the clothesline in the back yard? As it turns out, it was also a science lesson. I always wondered how the laundry could be clipped to the line in subzero temperatures in the morning before school and be dry that afternoon, when the temperatures never got above freezing all day. It was years later that I learned about the process of sublimation, where ice passes directly into a vapor without ever becoming liquid.

One of my favorite escapes during clement weather was roller skating. The sidewalk extended from the Shell station at the top of the hill all the way down to the creamery run by Raymond Nus at the north edge of town. This Shell station, directly across the street from the Chevrolet garage, was run by

Augie Potratz. The first time I ever saw television was the one he had running inside his station. For some reason the screen was covered with a sheet of transparent multi-colored plastic. I had heard about color television, so I thought this was how they did it, but I had seen color movies too and did not think this was working very well for coloring television. Augie's wife had a naturally squinty appearance, as if she had just sucked on a lemon. Once when I squinted my eyes and said I was Millie Potratz, my mother laughed so hard she had to run to the bathroom.

The Nus family at the north end of the street had four girls capriciously named Joan, Janet, Jane and Jean, all of whom were at St. Peter's with me but none of whom were in my class. Ricky Trotter, who now had a stepmother after he lost his mother in that car accident, lived across the street from them. I would see him and tomboy Jean Nus tromping around all over together, especially along the railroad tracks that ran beside the creamery. I got pretty good at skating, but the rough surface of the concrete took its toll on the wheels of my skates. They eventually split open, and the ball bearings tumbled out. Fortunately, if I took my skates into Platte's hardware store, they would put on a new wheel for me. I do not know whether I was the only customer for those wheels, but they charged me forty cents, and I do know quite a bit of my allowance money went for those repairs.

My father, like his father before him, *loved* to travel, and was always working out in his mind an itinerary to somewhere. In the summer of 1956 he traded in our car for a 1950 wood-panel station wagon, bought a tent big enough for our family and planned a trip to Washington state to see my mother's oldest brother, Ed Gimbel. Uncle Ed had bought a motorcycle and left South Dakota perhaps twenty years earlier to work the apple orchards in eastern Washington. After a time, he married and put down roots out there, never to return. Occasionally he would ship some of the produce from his orchards to us, and we would marvel at apples almost as big as melons.

As if our family, suitcases and camping gear were not already a carload, he invited my grandmother and Aunt Sarah (my mother's unmarried youngest sister) to ride along. Whenever we ran out of relatives to put us up overnight, we would pitch the tent in a park or anywhere else wide enough to accommodate it. The seats in the station wagon folded down, so Grandma and Sarah bedded down inside the car, while the rest of us found our places inside the tent. We drove until exhausted one night and, for lack of a better choice, camped in a wide ditch next to the highway. However, we did not realize when the tent was set up in the dark, that it lay a few feet away from some railroad tracks. Every hour the freight train came clattering through, shaking the ground, sweeping its light over us, and shrieking its mournful whistle. At daybreak my parents were still exhausted, having gotten very little sleep. Everyone was complaining about all that commotion during the night. Donny and I did not know what they were talking about. We had slept through it all and never heard a thing.

After we left Mount Rushmore, one of our campsites was in Yellowstone, and even though it was August, we were not prepared for temperatures to dip below freezing overnight. This time Donny and I woke up. I bet no one back in Iowa could see their breath that morning while they got dressed, nor would they eat their breakfast outside at a picnic table with frost on it. My father's brother Al was a pastor at tiny Eureka, Montana, about nine miles from the Canadian border, so we hoped to make it there by nightfall. Iowa rivers are always muddy, so peering more than an inch or so through the murk is impossible, but here were lakes with crystal clear glacial water that allowed us see to the bottom.

The radiator of our heavily laden old station wagon boiled over several times as we tried to cross the elevations of Montana and Idaho, but after a couple more days we coasted into Waterville, Washington, where I met my cousins Lois, Judy and Mary for the first time. Little Mary and Deanna were about the same age and looked so much alike that everyone in town thought they were twins. The Gimbels took us for a dip in nearby Lake Chelan, one of the deepest lakes in the world. Must be one of the coldest too—that water was *freezing*. Judy is a year older than I and was having fun teasing me throughout our visit, so she thought it was all in good sport to push me off the end of the pier into that liquid nitrogen and then cannonball right beside me as I bobbed up for air. They had a TV set in the house, but the only thing on it was the Republican national convention the whole time we were there, and I was not much impressed by that. I can also remember the washing machine they had running one morning as we sat at breakfast, making such a racket that Uncle Ed said, "I wish someone would steal that machine."

Perhaps some time around the Gay Nineties, when it was fashionable to stage vaudeville, operettas, even full operas, Westgate had built an opera house not far from the central business district. By the time we arrived in town, it was an unheated warehouse, storing stacks of tires, auto parts, school desks, and piles of junk. Someone had mounted a basketball hoop in there too, so sometimes we would slip in through an unlocked door, clear the floor a little and, our breath visible with every huff, play some one-on-one or Horse. One year the community decided to revive the old building and put on a stage presentation. Mr. Rikkels said he could play the saw, so, true to his word, he appeared on stage with a violin bow and scraped out *Swannee River* on a carpenter's saw. One group put on blackface and worked up a minstrel program. My mother took a part in a play, and for years, whenever it seemed appropriate to her, we heard one line from it that stuck in her head, "Is you *is* or is you *ain't*?"

A show like this would probably be judged racially insensitive today, but we were never raised to be prejudiced against black people. The simple fact was that we never came into contact with any. My father rarely traveled as part of his job, but on one occasion, he had a meeting in Des Moines and took the family with him for the day. While he was attending his seminar, my mother took us to the top of the capitol building, from where we were amazed by the tiny size of the people and cars below, to the radio station, where we were actually interviewed on the air, and to a big department store, where we saw an escalator for the first time. It was not only the first time we saw our capital, but the first time I could remember seeing blacks. Each time we saw one, Ralph and I thought it was something special and kept a tally, until it got up over a hundred by the time we returned home.

It was not uncommon for someone who grew up in rural South Dakota during the Depression years to assign raw survival priority over acquiring an education. Therefore, it was not unusual that my mother never had the chance to finish high school. This troubled her to the point that she enrolled in some correspondence courses to chip away at a high school equivalency. I am not sure she ever completed this program, but her ulterior motive was to make herself marketable enough to find a job. One of the courses she took was touch typing, and while she was practicing on an old Smith-Corona we purchased, she insisted that I learn it along with her. Eventually I became an expert typist, one of the most important skills I ever learned. Many schools today do not include office practice or keyboard skills in the curriculum at any level, and I think that is a serious mistake. In a world dominated by computer interaction, the QWERTY keyboard is ubiquitous, and I remain convinced that a thorough familiarity with it without having to look down is absolutely indispensable.

Moose's general store was the property to the south of our house. The house on the north had a large white barn in the back yard, which might have been used as some kind of shop or repair business for a short time when we first moved into our house in Westgate, not sure. Most of those years, however, the house was vacant, so we freely ran around on the yard, and I think my parents even got permission to use part of the land to expand their garden for a time. When I got to seventh grade at St. Peter's, we had a new classmate. Larry Gordon started school there that fall, and he and his family had moved into that vacant house next door to us. His younger brother Lyle was about Ralph's age, so whether they liked it or not, both of them had instant playmates. Larry was not much taller than I, but considerably more stocky, so one day on a whim I challenged him to race me out on the street. I could not believe he had won so handily, so I launched into self-assessment. I know, it must be these old tennis shoes. No, wait, I don't think I was really running my fastest. Let's do it again, I bet you won't beat me going back up to the starting point. He won again. I was crushed. How could this happen? It took me a long time to accept the obvious fact he was a faster runner.

My mother made friends with Larry's mother Irene, and one day, when she found out we did not have television, she made the mistake of inviting Ralph and me to watch *Lassie* with her boys on their TV. Mr. Gordon came home from work tired and hungry a few minutes after six o'clock to find neighbor boys in his house, but we did not pick up on his cues that we were not welcome. The next Saturday at 5:30 Ralph and I knocked on their door again. Mrs. Gordon seemed oddly distant when she greeted us, but icily ushered us in. This time when Mr. Gordon came home growling, the next program, *Soldiers of Fortune*, was just coming on. Without saying a word, he stomped into the room, switched off the television, stood in front of it and just glared at us. We got the message this time and never came over again.

More and more families around us were getting these television sets, including Klammers, but my parents could still not afford one. As consolation, my father would announce in a rare moment we were going to the theater in Sumner to see a movie. Each month we would get a mailing of the upcoming attractions they featured, and my mother would occasionally look them over and compare the choices to the pennies in her piggy bank. They hardly ever matched up. Two that always caught her eye were the varied adventures of Pa and Ma Kettle on one hand and the varied hijinxes of Abbott and Costello on the other. This was stimulating fare for us, and we squealed with excitement at the mere prospect of seeing them.

One day when I came home from school, Ruth came running out with the astonishing news that we had a television. No way. This could not be true. But when I ran inside, there was a console TV, a used model, but a real TV sitting there. This launched a whole new set of rules in the house. Not just when we could watch, but what—and the *volume* at which it played. Anything with shooting was forbidden, so Roy Rogers and all those westerns were out. Variety shows and sports were allowed, but boring, so for us it was primarily Disney, Lassie, Rin Tin Tin and cartoons. If we happened to be watching something questionable that my mother overheard from the next room or that seemed the slightest bit doubtful as she walked past the screen, she would curtly say, "Oh, turn it off." At Klammers the rules were a little different, so we could watch Gene Autry and the Lone Ranger. But I could never understand what was so funny when Lavonne doubled over laughing at the foils of these guys Bret and Bart Maverick. Their shenanigans were a little out of reach for me, but she understood their subtle humor completely.

# West of Westgate

When my father was sidelined by a hernia in 1956, he changed careers from using tools to selling them. The Mac Tools company gave him a territory in northwest Iowa, so he slept in his truck during the week and tried to slip home to northeast Iowa on weekends. Mechanics worked on Saturdays too, and since Iowa is over 300 miles wide, his new job situation began to exact a toll from all of us. One of the towns on his route was Aurelia, and while passing through one day, he noticed a basement home for sale right along busy State Highway 7.

The timing for my parents to buy one house and sell another must have forced them to take quick action, but it was devastating for me. We were about six weeks from the end of my seventh grade year when we were ripped away from Westgate. I would not even be able to finish out the year at St. Peter's. The comfort and familiarity of life as I knew it, the security of friends at school and especially my good friends Happy and Larry Dean were all gone, and in the blink of an eye we were swept out of there and back into a basement home again.

Aurelia was perhaps ten times the size of Westgate, with a variety of churches, many more businesses, civic activities, and recreational facilities. Most significantly for us, it had no parochial school, so I would be attending public school for the first time since kindergarten. Arlene Aldred, the principal, was explaining to me and my mother during enrollment that I was going to love it here. I would be in junior high, and they were just starting into something called track and field season. I had heard of track and field but had no idea what it was. This big cannonball called the shot put was far too heavy to lift, much less throw, I was not strong enough to fling the discus or javelin very far, and the pole vault seemed to require skills I did not have. I soon found out too that many of the other boys were faster runners than I, so the 100 yard dash and even the 220 were not for me, but the coach thought I might be able to do the 440, a quarter mile, one complete lap around the track. It did not take me long to discover that distance was too far to sprint, so at the first track meet I expected the other runners to take a rather leisurely pace around the track. From the crack of the gun they were off like antelopes, and I gasped in disbelief that they could actually run wide open all the way around. I tried to keep up, but had nowhere near the stamina to stay with the herd. I found out how it felt to finish last.

At Westgate I was always a top student, so I expected I could readily establish my *academic* identity here at this school, at least. Despite his best efforts, Mr. Suhr had not prepared me for this. Here I had a different teacher specializing in each subject. Bible history was one thing, but world history was another, and I had never learned anything about it. I knew all of my state capitals, but these kids knew their *world* capitals, cities and countries I had never heard of. What is social studies, and who are these guys Patrick Henry and John Jay everybody else already seems to know all about? One kid doodled a swastika on his orange workbook, but with no sense of what it meant, I copied him and drew one on mine too. I knew my grammar, but they knew literature. I thought I had a good grasp of science, but here we had a real laboratory with sinks, compounds and natural gas and were assumed to know how to conduct an experiment using the scientific method. What is *that*? Ah, now math is one subject where I can hold my own, but when I was asked to compute the area of a trapezoid or the circumference of a circle, I did not know how. What is pi, anyway? We even had shop, a woodworking class in which we made walnut bookends, but every time I showed my project to the teacher for approval, he sent me back to sand it some more. One day when I had my head on the desk sobbing, Aldred tried to offer me some comfort, but I could not even begin to tell her what was wrong.

Those final six weeks of seventh grade seemed like a whole school year for me, but at last they were over, and the summer to follow would turn out to be one of the best experiences of my life. The municipal swimming pool was adjacent to our house, and my father paid what was for us an astronomical sum—eighteen dollars for a season pass for the whole family. It was worth every penny. We were in that pool every day (unless they closed it for lightning), and the fee included swim lessons. Finally I was able to accomplish what those poor frustrated lifeguards at Oelwein struggled in vain to teach me. I started to make a little progress, and eventually I was able to achieve a junior lifeguard certificate. You would not want to be the poor schnook who needed *me* to jump in to save you, however.

Ralph and I discovered somehow that the grocery store down the street would give back a deposit for returned soda pop bottles. Five cents. Wow, we had struck gold. We got on our bikes and cruised all over town looking for them. At first we found glass Coke, RC and 7-Up bottles lying everywhere—discarded in the park, rolled into alleys, standing behind buildings, thrown from cars out along the highway. When we started rummaging through trashcans, we suddenly got an inspiration. The city dump. Of course. There had to be hundreds of them there. At first, the cashier routinely opened up the cash box to pull out deposit money each time, no questions asked. As the volume increased, however, the owners started to roll their eyes and asked us where we were getting all those bottles. One day when we brought in a few caked with mud inside and out, the lady refused them and told us not to bring any more in. It was okay. We were running out of places to look for them by then anyway.

Mr. Thevenin ran the hardware store in town and was also the coach of the Aurelia Little League. He discovered that I could pitch, and since none of his other players could throw as hard or as accurately, I became his pitcher, and we started to win some games. I had never played at night before, but in one tournament game we were out there under the lights. It was not often that I had to deal with base runners, but here I found myself with a man on first. No one had ever told me how to hold a runner on base, so one of the dads came out to ask me if I knew how to stretch. Stretch? Of course, I can stretch. No, this was a baseball term, he said, and showed me right there in front of all those spectators how to wind up, then watch to see what the runner was going to do before throwing the pitch. It affected my whole timing, rhythm and accuracy, and we lost the game.

I was using that glove I had bought a couple of years earlier in Oelwein, and I got to be a good fielder with it. My teammates admired it too, and whenever I was not using it, someone was always asking to borrow that baseball glove that had a pocket big enough for a softball. Hitting was a problem for me, however, and I usually struck out. It was a few years afterwards, far too late, that I figured out why. I had always subscribed to a theory to use a heavy bat, putting plenty of wood behind the ball to carry it farther. While this is probably a valid assumption, it assumes that the batter has the strength to get the bat around in time to meet a fast pitch. The bat I selected was always too much for me to handle, and I could never get it around in time to give the ball a ride. I had it all wrong, and I blame those coaches to this day for not pointing that out to me. Instead of swinging for the fence all the time, as I was doing, I could have been poking out singles with a lighter bat.

Since I got onto base so infrequently, I was a poor base runner. One time I got to first base by some fluke or other, when what to my wandering eyes should appear but my father sitting in the stands. He *never* came to my games. However, I did not hold that against him, because I understood this was something more important to me than to him and that he was busy earning a living. But there he was, and I suppose it spurred me to show off. First thing I did was to steal second. Then, even though the third base coach put both hands on his head in disbelief, I managed to steal third. Now I was really confident. I just knew I could steal home. No, the base coach said, no, don't try it, no, don't go, no, no, nooooo …. Too late. Like an imbecile, I disregarded him and sprinted in anyway. "Out!" hollered the home plate umpire. My father was proud just to watch me play, and I was proud that he came. He might even have done the same thing himself, he told me. One day Mr. Thevenin came to me to ask me when my birthday was. Little League rules limited players to age twelve. At first, he was worried that he might already have broken this rule, but we were both sad when a few days later, I became a teenager, and my Little League days were over. Not long after that, so was the summer, and we were moving again.

One of the towns on my father's sales route was Sutherland, a small town about twenty-five miles north of Aurelia. On one of his calls to the Brookfield Chevrolet and Implement shop, he was observing a repair and offered advice on a certain procedure the mechanic there was attempting. The owner, Beryl Brookfield, was impressed, and the next time my father came through Sutherland offered him a job there as a mechanic. Although Mac Tools was giving him a good living, the world of a traveling salesman was not very conducive to family life, and my father decided to accept Brookfield's offer.

The family that bought our basement home in Aurelia had a large family like ours, and either the day they came over to look at it or the day of settlement, the whole family came in. Their children were approximately our ages, so we were watching some TV with them, showing some of our toys, and playing games, while the adults talked business. At one point I started to pound out something on the piano. Their father went berserk. He came storming into the back room where the piano was and bellowed for me to stop. No one had ever been anything but polite when I played, so I thought he was just putting on an act and kept playing. Then, as he banged his fist on top of the piano, the veins in his neck stuck out, and with wild hair and beet-red face, he thundered, "Stop that! Stop it, I said! Stop it!" My parents were shocked and quietly led me away from the piano and from him. I had never been close to an alcoholic before, but from the vantage point of time years later, I look back on that incident and recognize what was almost certainly the ravages of alcoholism and violence.

In real life, society has developed an intensified intolerance of alcohol abuse, as evidenced by a decrease in acceptable blood alcohol levels while driving and a continuing increase in penalties. In fable, however, we continue to be amused by the lighter side of alcoholism, the tipsy character in movies, skits, and anecdotes. One such story passed around through my father's family actually begins with Limburger cheese. Limburger is a soft cheese from Belgium that is so sharp that it smells and tastes rotten to someone who has not acquired a taste for it.

Limburger on crackers was a favorite on New Year's Eve in my grandfather's family, and it usually prompted someone to recall the fellow who was fond of visiting the pub after work. When his wife tired of his stumbling home late and inebriated time after time, she told him the next night it happens, she would lock him out of the house. All went well for a while, until one night when he forgot and met his friends at the alehouse. Too late, he remembered his wife's warning. When he told the bartender about his problem, the bartender produced a package of Limburger and assured him that the wife would never be able to smell any alcohol if he ate some of this cheese. When he got home and found the door bolted, he knocked on the door. "Is that you, Harvey?" came the wife's voice from the other side. "Yes, open up." "Blow your breath through the keyhole." When she got a whiff of that Limburger-laden wind wafting through the keyhole, there was a pause, and then the voice continued, "Harvey, I said blow your *breath* through the keyhole."

In another version, the long-suffering wife decides to teach her husband a lesson the next time he comes home after a late-nighter. When he staggers toward home, she jumps out from behind a tree shrieking eerily, dressed in a devil costume with tail, horns, and trident. The startled husband stops in his tracks and says, "Who are you?" "Why, I'm the devil, and I am coming for *you*." Still swaying, the husband stares for a long time, trying to focus his bleary eyes, then wags his finger and says, "I shink I married your sishter."

I beg your indulgence for one more. An Irish wrestler was so strong that he easily defeated all his opponents and was making the circuit as an undefeated champion. His friends and supporters, however, were concerned about his frequent binges and warned him this would affect his prowess in the ring. He ignored their advice and, if anything, increased his consumption. After one match he was out all night at the pub and left at dawn with his friends. Their route home took them across an open field with a bull. When the bull charged, the wrestler took it by the horns and flung it to the ground, and then when it got to its feet, he flung it again. After several minutes of this, the bull had enough and trotted off. The wrestler turned to his friends and said, "I think you might be right about the booze. I couldn't even get that maniac off his bicycle."

Sutherland lays claim to fame with a footnote in history. In the Waterman Township cemetery on the east edge of town is the marker for James P. Martin, the last surviving Civil War veteran, who died at age 101 on September 20, 1949, in his home a few miles away. Our first house in Sutherland was an old two-story structure west across the street from the school playground and ball fields. It was an ideal location for all of us to be able to walk to school every day, even for Deanna, who was starting kindergarten that year. My father was about the same distance from the shop as he was in Maynard and could walk from home if my mother needed the car. The house next door to the south was occupied by Bill and Bonnie Burns, who had two little girls, perhaps even younger than Deanna. I can still hear in my mind the shifting sound of the automatic transmission of their 1954 Chevrolet convertible as Bill drove past our house late at night or early morning, as I lay in bed. According to Helene Drefke, leader of the youth Bible class at our church, Bonnie could have been the poster girl for Mr. Suhr's anti-Catholic campaign in Westgate. She had been Lutheran and converted when she married Bill, pledging that their children too would be raised in the Catholic faith, thereby giving her family the opportunity to write all of them off.

Two doors away from the Burns house was the estate of Gaylord Shumway. In the years before we moved to Sutherland, Shumway ran the law firm in town, but by the time we arrived, his widow was living as a recluse in the big house. She was already quite elderly by then, and unable to keep up with the weeds and brush that were overtaking the expansive yard. One day a man knocked on our door and asked if he could hire me for some help cleaning up the place. The widow had died, and he was the heir. I learned from that experience that I never again want to scrape peeling paint, as day after day we tried to prepare his mansion for a badly needed new coat. As we were carrying boxes of junk out of the attic one day, we came across an old single-barrel shotgun, and he offered it to me for a dollar. I was not sure what my parents would say, but I was not going to tell him that. When my father saw it, he looked down the barrel and told me to get to work honing the rust out of it. Was that a yes? We got some gun oil, and I swabbed that barrel for several days until we could no longer see any pitting against the light. One of my brothers had custody of that gun for many years, but I found out recently his landlord erroneously auctioned it off. But as far as I know, wherever it is, it can probably still rid the garden of a rabbit or squirrel.

Our neighbor to the north was Harold Gillespie, whose wife Corrine was someone to whom my mother could relate. Harold's elderly mother lived in town and had never really approved of the girl he had picked out. To Corrine it seemed that her mother-in-law made Harold dance around like a marionette, so whenever he got a call from his mother to make a repair or mow the yard, Corrine would come over to commiserate with my mother until she saw him drive back into the driveway.

The back yard was big enough for the obligatory garden my mother always planted, and it still left plenty of lawn for the sport of the Pullmanns—croquet. My grandfather was an expert and, according to my father, never lost a game. He passed the game on to his offspring, and my father himself became an expert. He cut no one any slack when he played either, and I cannot remember beating him until he was eighty years old. Unlike games using cards or dice, which usually involve a certain element of luck, croquet is almost entirely a game of skill. Masterful as the touch of his stroke was, however, his phenomenal memory of the sequence of events during play was nothing short of legendary. Time after time, in games of up to six players, he would have such a commanding overview of the match that he would describe in exact detail what a player did at which arch to which ball, and I still marvel when I think of his uncanny verbal instant replay. "No, wait a minute, you are dead on that ball," he would say. "Don't you remember, you hit the blue ball and then missed your arch."

One day I noticed a little mound of dirt in one corner of the croquet court we had set up in the yard. Later in the week a second mound appeared. Gophers. It is not possible to drive very far through the Iowa countryside without seeing at least one of these little striped rodents scurrying across the road or scampering alongside in the ditches. Besides the tunnels they dig everywhere and the pock marks that litter the earth with their entrances, the little thieves steal grain. They are a scourge on every farmer, but, like rats, hard to eradicate. As I watched from the window, a little earless head appeared in the center of one of the mounds and, like a furry periscope, just as quickly popped back beneath the surface. I grabbed my BB gun and tiptoed softly to the edge of the mound, pointed it at the top of the entrance and waited. In about fifteen long minutes I heard a little squeak and then saw a little nose. I pulled the trigger, and when nothing happened, I thought I had missed it. About three seconds later, a little furry ball shot out of the hole and hopped all over the yard like a miniature pogo stick. In a few seconds it stopped moving. Usually, when you see one, you have at least two, but after I filled in the holes, we had no more problems with gophers.

When I started eighth grade, I was once again in a new school. Like it or not, the new kid is on trial, where the prosecutors, judges, and jury are all his classmates. One of the first times I reported for

PE, Harry Rahbusch was the one interrogating the prisoner, while the whole locker room was listening to my responses. When they heard me say I had been on the track team from rival Aurelia, they wanted to know which track meets I had participated in. Alta? yes. Storm Lake? yes. The Pa-Su-Sa? uh, I think so. It was a trick question, and I fell into his trap. The Pa-Su-Sa was an annual track event involving only three high schools, Paullina, Sutherland, and Sanborn, and they had caught me lying to impress them.

The school building we were in had once been a K-12 facility like the one at Maynard, but Sutherland had just built a brand new high school on the south edge of town, so my class was in the last year in this K-8 elementary school. Courses were taught by a subject specialist as I had found at Aurelia, but this time I was not at the disadvantage of starting at the end of a school year. One of the teachers, Neva Camery, taught English but also ran a dress and millinery shop in town with her sisters. Though it was a year of catching up for me, I found myself woefully lacking in certain areas, particularly social studies and literature, and I found myself seriously wondering if I would be able to make it through high school without flunking out. Nevertheless, I had a keen interest in the physical sciences, math, and music, and thought these might be enough to sustain me.

The principal of the elementary school was Clarence Sutter, a Mennonite, who boldly one day took an initiative that today would probably be considered unethical or perhaps illegal. Whether it was through his church or on his own volition, he arranged for several of the best singers in school to accompany him seventy miles away to Sioux City to sing at a mission for the homeless there. He had enough room for five or six of us in his big Buick, so we packed in for the long drive over there. It was a new experience for me to see life on Skid Row, the seediness of the streets, unshaven bums dressed in rags, bottles empty or broken strewn everywhere, and the stench of urine permeating the air. Sutter was a beacon of light for these people, conducting the service as a lay minister, and relying on the choir he brought with him to lead the singing. When we got home, he made some overtures about doing this again some time, but either my parents stepped in to prevent that or his own discretion dictated this well-intentioned endeavor was fraught with pitfalls and was probably not a good idea.

On Saturdays the American Legion hall in town emptied its expansive floor of all the chairs and opened its doors to the public as a skating rink. Admission was free, but if your skates were not acceptable, you would need to rent theirs. The skates I used in Westgate were the kind with clamps that could attach to any street shoe and be tightened with a special key. But they had steel wheels and were not allowed on the shiny wood floor here in the Legion hall. Neoprene had not yet come along, but I could rent clamp-on skates with wooden wheels for ten cents. I had never seen shoe skates before, but here I could also rent a special shoe with the wooden wheels already attached for twenty-five cents.

Skating rinks, as perhaps some of you may not know, specify a variety of groups that are allowed on the floor during a particular segment—couples only, girls only, backward skating only, and so on. When the announcer proclaimed "triples only," two of my classmates, Ruth Rahbusch and Lana Frank, skated up and asked if I would join them. Ruth was the youngest of the large Rahbusch family of six-footers and weighed perhaps 180 pounds herself. Although Lana was not overweight or unattractive, she was still bigger than I, so I found myself blurting out, "No, I would rather skate with someone my own size." Now, can you think of a better way for the new kid in town to make friends than with a greeting like that? On Monday what I had said was all over school, and it was never forgiven or forgotten. For years I have wished I could go back to that moment with a do-over in hand.

The invention of the transistor led to an explosion of radios in the hands of teenagers, and the number of popular singers seemed to explode onto the airwaves to fill them. From the extensive pool of talents like Sandra Dee, Frankie Valli, Ricky Nelson, Nat King Cole and hundreds of the same ilk, one emerged as the biggest idol of all—Elvis. The first question a new kid in school was asked was his impression of Elvis, and a great deal of social standing hung on the answer. This was a very different sound from *Lavender Blue, How Much is That Doggie in the Window?*, or *Dear Hearts and Gentle People* that we always heard on the radio at home. I did not like it. As a sappy sentimentalist, I suppose I could tolerate *Falling in Love with You* or *Love Me Tender*, but when the music came from the hips instead of the lips, I turned away. This was not music; it crossed the line into burlesque. Of course, anyone like that was immediately branded as a square, but I never rounded my corners.

Sutherland had four churches in town, Catholic, Methodist, Church of Christ, and, of course, the one we joined, Bethel Lutheran. I had finished nearly one year of confirmation classes in Westgate, with some overlap in Aurelia, but the final year of instruction at Bethel was spent with several of my school classmates: Lana Frank, Marilyn Hillmer, Richard Jalas, Kenneth King, Nancy Pingel, Carol Waggoner, and Ronald Wittrock. The pastor, Fred Elze, was perhaps in his mid-sixties and had difficulty pronouncing names. It was difficult to keep from snickering during the prayer for someone, because he would slur over the name or turn it into a parody. As many times as he would refer to Ronald Wittrock, it always came out Rollin. I do not remember how badly he clobbered the name Jungjohann.

Pastor Elze also had an infectious laugh, which my father liked to imitate. At a Walther League (a kind of Lutheran youth fraternity) meeting one night, we played a game called Quaker Session, in which the leader would say, "The Quaker meeting is now in session. No talking, no laughing, no chewing gum." The ones who broke the rule dropped out of the game and employed every means at their disposal to induce those still playing to make a sound or smile. As more and more players were eliminated, we all tried everything to make Pastor Elze crack, but his stone face was immutable. When he finally emerged as the winner, he gave us his trademark boisterous laugh, and the rest of us not only joined in his merriment but marveled at his incredible self-control.

Finally, Palm Sunday, 1958 (March 30, I think) was Confirmation Day. If you are not familiar with this rite in the Lutheran Church, it is perhaps roughly equivalent to a bar mitzvah, a kind of official rite of passage into adulthood, at least with regard to certain privileges within the church. My mother made many of our clothes, but this time I wore my first new suit, a blue one bought specially for these festivities. Gifts came in from relatives, including a personalized hymnal and the concordance Bible I still treasure today. Best of all, our friends the Klammers made the trip all the way from Westgate. When little Janeen was asked what the occasion was, she replied that they had come for David's funeral. Fortunately, she was not a prophetess.

This does remind me of an old story. A couple in Minnesota decided to break away from the frigid temperatures in Duluth one winter for a few days in Florida. Since the wife had some business to finish up, the plan was for the husband to fly down first, then she would join him the next day. After the husband checked into the hotel, he decided to send her an email. However, his message was misaddressed and went to a woman in Houston who was just returning from her husband's funeral. When the widow turned on her computer to check messages, she shrieked and collapsed. Hearing the commotion, the adult children came running in from the next room to see what was wrong and found the following message on the screen: "My dear wife, I know you are a little surprised to hear from me, but there was a computer set up in my room when I arrived, so I decided to send you a message. I just wanted you to know that I arrived safely and that everything is ready for your arrival tomorrow. Your loving husband. P.S. It sure is hot down here."

The funeral director in town was also a member of our church. His son, Steve Baumgarten, asked me one day in school if I had any change in my pocket. He had discovered numismatics and was on a continual quest to look through everyone's coins for any he needed in his collection. One day he found a 1914D penny while looking through Wayne Fuhrman's coin purse, a rare coin worth perhaps thirty dollars in those days. Eventually, he got me interested too, and I filled most of the template coin books for Lincoln pennies, buffalo and Jefferson nickels, Mercury and Roosevelt dimes right out of circulation. Ever optimistic, I was sure I would one day find a 1909S-VDB penny, but even though there were still many buffalo nickels, wheat ears pennies, and even an occasional Indian head still in circulation in those days, a Victor D. Brennan (the designer of the Lincoln cent) was far too much to hope for. I made a rule for myself that I would not buy from or sell to any dealers, being content with whatever I could find in circulation. Although it was a passing fancy, I still have my collection, and while I did run across one or two with mintmarks, I doubt that it is really worth anything. Wayne Fuhrman, incidentally, was the younger brother of Janet, one of my classmates from whom I learned recently of his gruesome demise. While working inside a grain elevator, he was somehow snagged by the augur at the base of it. By the time his rescuers shut it down and reversed the augur, it had torn up his body to such an extent that he quickly succumbed to massive hemorrhaging.

As a youth my father had discovered the art of pulling fish from the streams and ponds around him and was determined to pass along his secrets to his sons. However, whenever he filled a soup can with night crawlers from the garden and dragged us off to the river, the only thing we wanted to do was jump into it. Fishing is boring, but therein lies one of the most important lessons he was trying to teach us—patience. Life is not about instant gratification, he would say. Moreover, besides the fact that fish are not coming anywhere near a lure where boys are splashing about, rivers are dangerous for swimming. First, there are the submerged logs and other debris to snag and drown a young underwater explorer, then are the unpredictable currents that could pull the unsuspecting below the surface, the sharp edges of the glass, machinery and implements that get dumped into the water, and any number of other hazards. Usually my father would tolerate this for a while, but then he would insist that we sit there next to him with a fish pole.

Ralph was the champion fisherman in the family. One time we heard him shouting from a sand bar out of sight around a bend. Fearing he had hurt himself badly, we all ran over to his location and found him proudly standing next to a huge carp that he had pulled from the water. When, after many subsequent attempts, I finally caught one almost equal to his, he took it to the next level. We were in Uncle Phil's boat on a lake in Minnesota on our way out to the deep water, when Ralph decided to drag his pole through the water while we rode along. A five-pound northern pike grabbed his sparkling lure and plunged into the deep with it. After my father and his sister's husband Phil helped him reel it in, we decided the water right here might be just fine. At the river one day, my father was having good luck catching bullheads, and as he added each one to his stringer, he lowered it back into the river to keep them alive and fresh. The next time he pulled it from the water, however, he found only the heads were left. Curious, he dropped his line next to the shore to see what monster fish might be eating his bullheads, when the bobber disappeared almost immediately. It was a small snapping turtle.

Sutherland was only about 100 miles from Sioux Falls, where Grandma Gimbel lived with still unmarried Aunt Sarah, so we made the drive over a weekend to South Dakota quite often. Grandma grew cucumbers in her garden and made the most delicious dill pickles from them that I ever tasted. Even Vlasic cannot make them taste that good. My own mother tried one year to make them using Grandma's recipe, but they were just not the same. Whenever Grandma would send a jar or two of them home with us, my mother had to watch me carefully to make sure I did not hoard them in a place where I was the only one who could sneak one.

My grandmother's house on 1116 N. Elmwood Street was only a couple of blocks away from Margaret and Gilbert Stainbrook over on Holly. Uncle Gilbert had built a little tractor, using a lawnmower engine and a transmission from an old pickup. Since his kids, Robert and Bonnie, were still a little bit young to ride around on it without supervision, Ralph and I loved these visits to Sioux Falls because we got a chance to drive this little home-made tractor back and forth all afternoon along a long gravel road near their house. One day when my father drove the car back from Stainbrooks to Grandma's house, he parked in front of her house facing south in the north-bound lane, against traffic as he might have done in Sutherland without a second thought. About a half hour later, a police officer knocked on the door. "Are you the owner of this car at the curb with the Iowa license plates?" he asked my father. "I just wanted you to know that we drive on the *right* in South Dakota. I will be back this way in about fifteen minutes, and if I still see it parked this way, I will put a ticket on it."

Stainbrooks lived very close to the municipal airport, and one day when we were driving past, my eyes popped out watching the landing of the biggest airplane I had ever seen. It had this word Braniff on the side, and I could scarcely believe that a machine that huge could fly. Occasionally a small airplane would fly over our house, but they were nowhere near this size, especially as seen from the ground far below. My father had once talked a stranger, who landed on his private strip near where we were fishing, into giving Ralph and me a ride, but even that one (perhaps a Luscomb or Cessna 140) was a dwarf compared to this one. From what I can remember, it was probably a DC-3 or Constellation, but I had no idea an airplane of these dimensions could exist, much less actually fly.

The impact of this behemoth aircraft that left me awestruck reminds me of a similar experience with my nephew years later. Lion Country Safari was a game preserve in Florida with lions, antelopes, zebras and other wild animals roaming freely, which allowed visitors to drive through in their cars to see these creatures in a simulation of their natural environment. Little Jonathan, about eighteen months old, was standing on the front seat with his thumb in his mouth, looking idly to the left at a herd of wildebeest, then to the right at some lions a few feet away outside the window, not particularly impressed with anything he saw on our slow grind along the winding path. When we came around a curve, however, we suddenly encountered eight or ten elephants in a herd a short distance away. Jonathan could not believe his eyes. His thumb came out, he pointed to the mountains of gray filling the window, and exclaimed, "Doggggggie. *Big* doggggie." Then, with excitement so intense the veins in his neck stuck out, he shouted passionately again and again, "Biiiiiig, *biiiiiiiig* doggggggie." He did not yet know the word for elephant, but his description left no doubt.

Pizza pie probably made its first debut in New York, but the first time I ever tasted it was when we were in Sutherland. I loved it from the first bite and craved its flavor and texture so much that I frequently bought a Chef Boyardee kit and baked it in our oven at home. My mother took notice of this and decided she did not need a kit. She could make it in her own kitchen, using her own ingredients, for far less cost than that box in the store. My parents were the youth counselors at the church, so one night Mom brought her pizza along as a snack to our meeting. But it did not look like pizza. She assumed the sauce she saw on the ones I made was nothing but ketchup, so her long-standing aversion to anything as unwholesome as ketchup was awakened, and she either substituted a can of tomato soup or simply left it out. We never used spices like oregano, anise, cumin or rosemary, so she left those out too. Surely Velveeta ought to be just as good as mozzarella, so that went on her pizza instead. No one would touch it, until Delmar Jalas worked up the courage to give it a try. My mother's smile faded to a scowl when, after one bite, he ran to the wastebasket to spit it out.

When the congregation sent my parents to a youth workers conference in the Black Hills for two weeks one summer, they arranged for my mother's brother Sam Gimbel to take care of Ruth and Deanna and her sister Lorene Engel to take care of us three boys. Uncle Sam and Aunt Hilda and five children lived on a farm about five miles away from Uncle George and Aunt Lorene and five children on their farm in central South Dakota. Since we rarely saw these cousins, I was not sure what to expect. Those two weeks turned out to be the highlight of the summer. George's nephew, Mike Engel, an older teen from town that we quickly idolized, led us through the gopher chase, which began with several gallons of water until the drenched creature came staggering out of its burrow gasping for air. It was the first time I ever rode a horse—and the first time I fell off. I learned also that geese are not intimidated by skinny little teenagers and will give chase, hissing with their necks forward and wings spread seven feet across. Cousin Betty discovered that their swimming hole had leeches, when she emerged with slimy black creatures attached to her feet and legs. Then we all noticed we were covered with them. One of the boys even had one, uh, well, maybe we should not mention that one.

After the first week, we traded households. Whereas Uncle George had three daughters closest to my age, Uncle Sam had boys, so in the second week, I was running around all over the farm with Gerald and DeWayne. Instead of the swimming hole, we dipped in the frigid water of the cow tank. Gerald had firecrackers and showed me how to shoot a tin can high into the air. If you punch a small hole in the side of the can to insert a firecracker, then invert the can in a shallow pan of water, the force of the explosion combines with the hydraulics in the pan and rockets the can upward like a little silver missile. The apprehension I had at the start of the two weeks was gone, and we wanted to stay longer.

One of the techniques taught at my parents' conference was direct involvement—participation from the youth group members themselves. Community singing might work, but when the singing is combined with actions, even teenagers start to break out of their cocoons. My parents drew upon material from their own youth to try this out on us. First was the song of an immigrant school kid telling his parents in mock-German what the body parts are called:

Was ist das hier?
Das ist mein schvet-boxer, O mama dear.
Schvet-boxer, schvet-boxer, nicker nicker nicker nock.
Das vot I larn in der schu-le.

Was ist das hier?
Das ist mein bread basket, O mama dear.
Bread basket, schvet-boxer, nicker nicker nicker nock.
Das vot I larn in der schu-le.

The schvet-boxer is accompanied by a rap of the knuckles on the head, the bread basket by a rub of the tummy, and each of the other body parts in turn by an indication or action appropriate to what is referenced: the girl-crusher (flexing both arm muscles), the nose-blower (careful with that one), and so on. As the list gets longer, the speed of the song increases, and the actions accelerate as everyone tries to keep up: toe-stubber, knee-jerker, girl-crusher, chin-chopper, meal-masher, nose-blower, eye-spyer, ear-muffer, bread basket, schvet-boxer, nicker nicker nicker nock in succession.

A second song my parents foisted upon the captive (but probably not captivated) youth group at Bethel was actually passed down to us through my grandfather, but beyond that its origin is obscure. It concerns an eccentric sausage maker named Dunderbach who grinds up small creatures, including neighborhood dogs and cats, into his sausage. There are probably more verses than any of us in the family can recall, but the following excerpts will furnish a sample how the yarn is spun:

One fine day a little boy did walk into the store.
He bought a pound of sausage links and laid them on the floor.
Now while the boy was waiting there, he whistled up a tune.
The sausages, they stood, they barked, they danced around the room!

Chorus:
O Dunderbach, O Dunderbach, how could you be so mean?
Some day you will be sorry you invented that machine.
Those dogs and cats and long-tailed rats, no more will they be seen,
For they were ground to sausage meat in Dunderbach's machine.

One day when he was working, the machine it would not go.
So Dunderbach, he climbed inside to see what made it so.
His wife, she came into the store, from shopping in the street.
She grabbed the crank, gave it a yank, and Dunderbach was meat!

O Dunderbach, O Dunderbach ….

The organist and choir director at Bethel, Helene Drefke, also had a second-floor studio on the main street in town for giving piano lessons. Although my mother insisted I continue to practice after we left Westgate, it was perhaps a year or more since I had taken any instruction. For a number of reasons, my sessions with Mrs. Drefke were sporadic. Foremost among them, I suppose, was that I was a teenager. That probably says it all, but in fairness there was a growing number of competing interests that were occupying my attention. If I really had to be honest though, I would have to say I thought I was so good that she was not able to teach me anything new. Mrs. Drefke always wanted me in her recital each spring, however, so I guess she was willing to tolerate this outrageously capricious behavior as she sat in her studio each week wondering if I was going to show up or not.

As summer approached, Lorin Brookfield, the younger son of my father's boss, was starting a job at Rog & Bob's IGA store in town. He was giving up his lawn mowing enterprise and asked if I wanted to take it over. My father made a deal for his equipment, and I stepped into this ready-made business opportunity right away. Since my customers were scattered all over town, I slung the gas can over the handle bar of my bike, rode with one hand and towed the mower with the other from one yard to another. Small yards were fifty cents, but Segelkes paid me two dollars for their two-hour acreage a half mile outside of town along Highway 10. As a bonus, they even loaded my mower into their car, so I would not have to transport it along the busy highway. I added a few customers to the ones Lorin left me, and before long I was in demand throughout the season. One day as I was pulling my mower along from my bicycle, a dog chased me down the street, snapping at my feet as I pedaled. When this happened a second time, I decided I would teach him a lesson. As it turns out, I became the tutee of the lesson. Richard Metz suggested I fill my water pistol with gasoline and give the dog a squirt in the face next time he chased me. However, I did not realize what a powerful solvent gasoline is until it dissolved my plastic water pistol into a worthless lump. I had to relearn this tough lesson several years later when I ran out of gas. The gallon can I carried had no spout, so I asked the restaurant across the street for a styrofoam cup, with which I intended to fill the thirsty tank with cup-size sips. The instant the first drop of gasoline touched the plastic, the little cup melted completely away in my hand. My only recourse was a makeshift funnel from a rolled-up newspaper, but I did not notice that the car ran any better from all the newsprint dissolved into the fuel.

I do not see the racks of comic books for sale in stores today that we had available everywhere when I was in school. I did not buy many of them, but I had a few favorites—not adventurous medieval knights in armor, outer space cadets or commando battles that kids today seem to relish, but Donald Duck, Pluto and Gyro Gearloose. On the back pages of all of them, however, were display ads for all sorts of intriguing gadgets a kid might want. Everyone remembers the skinny kid who gets sand kicked in his face by the beach bully, and then comes back after graduation from the Charles Atlas program to pound the bully into the sand. I was not interested in looking like Atlas, but without my mother's knowledge and certainly without her approval, I sent away for a jiu-jitsu course that I thought might teach me a few moves that no one would know I had.

When the course arrived in the mail, I read through several pages of the first booklet in the six-volume series, and then persuaded Ralph to walk through some of the maneuvers with me. Poor Ralph got flipped onto his back and, when he landed, bumped his head on the foundation of the house. My mother was not at home, and we still did not have a telephone, so when I saw the back of his head bleeding, I jumped onto my bike and raced for the shop to tell my father. At the end of the street lived Mike Steurmann, the neighborhood bully, and as I tore pell-mell down the sidewalk, he blocked my path and made me stop. He had no sympathy when I pleaded that my brother was hurt and needed help, taunting that I was just saying that to make him let me go. Finally, I broke free, and my father raced home to take Ralph to Doc Dahlbo in town. Ralph's injuries were not serious, but the doctor could not get him to swallow a pill, probably an antibiotic. After several unsuccessful tries, Ralph coughed it out, and the pill flew across the room, striking the opposite wall. "All right," said the doc, "we'll have to do it another way. Roll over." Despite my concern for the injury I had caused, I could scarcely contain a certain sadistic glee that it was not me getting that needle in the butt. My mother confiscated the jiu-jitsu course, and I did not get it back until I was an adult.

I spotted an ad one day that I knew my mother would approve—a course in piano tuning. This would not only save them money on tuning our own piano, but I could make money tuning others. It arrived in the mail in a little box containing a tuning wrench, some rubber wedges, a strip of red felt and a small plastic tube that produced a tone like a duck call. Fortunately, these items were accompanied by a booklet that explained how they were to be applied to the tuning pins and strings of a piano. Unfortunately, the booklet also tried to explain how to tune pianos. I did not understand it. The duck call was pitched to A-440, the A just below middle C, and I learned that everything was tuned to that. Fine. Now tune the next octave and set the pin. Okay, got that. Next, go up a fifth and listen for the wow-wow-wow to be sure it is in tune, the directions said. What does that mean? When I got finished, the piano was in worse tune than when I started. I decided to work on the old piano over at the church. I knew I could not make that one worse. I seemed to be making improvements until I heard a snap. Uh-oh, what was that? Then I noticed a broken string waving slowly at me. Oh well, each of the trebles has three strings, so no problem, this one will just have one from now on, I told myself. When I went on, there was another snap, then another …. I decided piano tuning was not for me. The kit still sits up in the attic untouched to this day.

When plastic was invented, there was an explosion of items that could be made from this wonderful new substance. There was a company called Wham-O that advertised all sorts of playthings not generally available at our local variety store—fake vomit, kits for doing magic tricks, ventriloquist lessons, and, of course, the rubber whoopee cushion designed to embarrass the unsuspecting from beneath a sofa pillow. My eye fell on the ad for a hard plastic boomerang. Would *that* be cool if it really worked. The wide-open field of the school across the street from us was perfect for trying it out when it arrived in the mail. With a little practice, I could get it to return with a crisp whuh, whuh, whuh, right back to where I was standing. Then one day it hit the guy wire of a light pole and chipped a small piece off one end. With some judicious filing, I got it flying again, but it was no longer as consistently accurate as before.

One day when I was trying to relearn the proper throwing technique, little toddler Jimmy Haht wandered from his back yard next door onto the field just as it left my hand. As my missile made its grand arc, I watched in horror as it curved straight for Jimmy. He was too far away for me to rescue him in time, so all I could do was brace myself for the inevitable disaster unfolding before my eyes. However, as the whirling blade reached him, one leg of the L-shaped weapon passed *behind* his head, as the other leg of it was at the same moment *beside* his head, and it spun harmlessly past. Innocent little Jimmy had no idea how narrowly he had just averted decapitation and continued to toddle over to where I was standing, unaware that while his diaper was dry, mine was not.

On a visit to Sutherland almost fifty years later, I wanted to drive through the cemetery to see how many names I might recognize. When I stopped to talk with the caretaker, Greg Bina, he motioned to a grave a short distance away and said, "Yup, that's my son right over there. Died in a fire." Then I drove into town to check out familiar landmarks, including the house where we had lived. I could not find it. At first I thought I was disoriented. It was as if the Bill Burns house and the Harold Gillespie house were now pushed together side by side, and ours had disappeared. There was a man working on his pickup in the driveway at the Gillespie house, so I decided to ask him about this. It was none other than Jimmie Haht, who now owned that house—directly across the street from the one where he had been that toddler years before. When I asked him what happened to the house next door, he said it had burned down when a young man living there apparently fell asleep with a cigarette. His name was Scott Bina.

# Moving Higher

As high school approached, I found out we would soon be moving again—but not to a different town this time. My parents bought four acres along Highway 10 on the southeast corner of Sutherland and were planning to build a house. For my father this was probably a mulligan for the project he had started in Maynard some ten years earlier. It turned out to be a beautiful home, the first brand new full-sized house we ever had. Next door to the east was the home of Clarence Jungjohann, one of the tavern owners in town, whose youngest son Keith was my perennial nemesis throughout school. For me, it was extremely important that we were staying in Sutherland. When a child is uprooted from one elementary school and replanted in another, the psychological trauma is palpable, but the pre-adolescent persona is sufficiently resilient to absorb the impact. I submit that the same is not true at the high school level. The years that begin at puberty are so formative that disruptions can be damaging, if not devastating. We see case histories of this damage recurring again and again, particularly in the adolescents of military families who are forced to move during the most fragile period in their lives.

The high school years are for many people the richest in memory, whether positive or negative. For some, they were the glory years, for some they were traumatic, but for most they were simply the most important. In many cases it is the beginning of a long journey to establish an identity, the opportunity, the obligation, to discover who we are. Some are so self-assured that the process is simple and short, while others are plagued with such self-doubt that the goal is never within reach. In my case, the high school years formed a bond to the location in which I was growing up. Whenever anyone asks me where I grew up, I always say Iowa. If the next question is *where*, I think of Sutherland without any hesitation, despite the relatively short time I actually lived there.

My father had plans for his four acres that went beyond building a house. He turned over in his mind a number of options for cashing it in on some kind of enterprise. Since we were along a busy highway, he was sure there must be a bonanza waiting to fall into his lap. Dreams of a miniature golf course, a croquet park, or even a drive-in theater were already on the long list of possibilities he was considering. In the meantime the three and a half acres not needed for the house and garden were leased out to a nearby farmer for growing a little extra corn. Beyond the property line away from the highway was an idyllic meadow that made the perfect place for boys to explore the stream—or to give that reconditioned shotgun its first firing. Two blocks to the west of us was a parcel of perhaps five acres along the highway that my father called the Ohlhausen property. He put down an option to buy it, with an eye toward a Dairy Queen store, a gas station to compete with Herb Hillmer's Texaco that was doing so well along Highway 10, or even his own auto repair business. The timing was not right, however, so his option lapsed, and he continued to plod along with Beryl Brookfield.

For the first time, we finally had a telephone some time after we moved into our new home. Today we are so private about our individual phones and the numbers at which we can be reached that many have forgotten a system based on the party line, where the telephone company installed essentially one wire serving multiple homes on a circuit. When Klammers first got their telephone, the pattern of rings determined when a caller was trying to reach them. One short and two long ring tones was for them, but one long and two shorts was for Trahns down the road. The caller turned a crank to initiate the ring tone and so controlled the duration of it. The earpiece was attached to a flexible cord, but the mouthpiece was fixed to the box high on the wall, intentionally placed out of the reach of children. By the time we got our phone in Sutherland, telephones had changed considerably, so ours had the transmitter and receiver together on one instrument, and instead of a crank to initiate longs and shorts, it had a dial to select the digits of the recipient's number—in our case 247.

On a party line anyone who picked up the phone could eavesdrop on the private conversation intended for only the *two* parties, so everyone learned to be very guarded in what they said. Judy Wittrock refused one time when I called to ask her out, and the next day everyone at school knew about it. Those listening in were called rubberneckers from the way they craned their necks close to the receiver to catch every word. Each person who picked up, however, shunted electrical energy away from the circuit, and often the signal was weakened to the point where no one could hear anything. Arvilla was once trying to receive an emergency call and yelled to all the rubberneckers to get off the line so she could hear the urgent message. Of course, it was precisely that type of call that made everyone want to listen in all the more. Central to all of the circuits was a switchboard, controlled by an operator who could be reached by turning the crank for one long tone, or, in our case, by selecting zero on the dial. To reach someone who was not on your party line, you would need to place your call through the switchboard. The operator could listen in on any call on any circuit and was, as expected, often the biggest gossip in town.

Hazing of incoming freshmen has probably been outlawed in most school systems by now, but when I started high school, freshman initiation was a privilege bestowed upon the seniors. The senior assigned to me on Freshman Initiation Day was Ronnie "Corky" Thompson, who decreed that I would report for my first day wearing a diaper and carrying a baby bottle. I was also to carry his books between classes, polish his shoes, fetch his lunch from the cafeteria, and just about anything else he requested all day. By the time I was a senior, however, a new administration was in place (more on that later), and these rites of initiation were thankfully gone.

The high school curriculum in those days had a certain gender bias that would probably not be allowed today. For freshmen there were no elective courses, so all the boys were required to take shop, learning how to use the tools of a builder, while all the girls were required to take home economics, learning how to use the tools of the kitchen. Almost as a gag, the roles were reversed one day, when all the boys were sent down to the home ec room to make cookies, while the girls reported to the shop to cut their initials from plywood. Typing was a required course for all students, but only the girls could advance into office practice because the duties of a secretary would always be carried out by women. This was a slight problem for me, because I was looking ahead to college, in which I felt shorthand could be a useful skill for taking notes. Surreptitiously, I sent away for a Gregg shorthand text, simplified version, and learned it on my own. When I started using it in school for taking notes, however, my secret leaked out, and I was branded as "one of *them*." I did not care.

Shop class was more than just hands-on experience with power tools. We spent a good deal of time learning mechanical drawing—conceptualizing a three-dimensional object from different perspectives to represent it on paper. One day when I came into the classroom to work on my project, the paper on my drawing board was torn and smeared with red, yellow and black streaks. Keith Jungjohann and Rick Moore had been in there after hours and decided to swat flies with a T square. For some reason they chose my drawing to wipe off their instrument after each success. The punishment handed out to them was to redo my sketch and restore it to the way it was before. Right. Their apology reminded me of the admonishment given by a parent who says, "Now go kiss and make up." You can make the child do it, but you cannot really make them feel sorry. Keith was the class bully, and like all bullies, always picked on someone smaller and weaker. He was not very big himself, but wiry and lightning fast whenever he would fight. One day in gym class, he made the mistake of trying to push around Ronny Wittrock, who stood up to him and pushed his nose into the hardwood. Ron was my hero that day.

My favorite tool in the shop by a wide margin was the lathe. I was fascinated by the way it would twirl a lump of wood that could be chiseled and shaped into a useful object. For weeks I whirled anything in my hand just to watch how it would appear on the lathe. I just had to have one. When I showed my father the Craftsman machine in the Sears catalog I wanted to buy, he tried to talk me out of it. But when he saw my droopy look and thought about worse things I could be asking for, he told me to order it. When the shipment arrived, the box had only the lathe itself, and I realized I would need to build the bench on which to mount it. It came without a motor too, but my father told me to go ask Mr. Perry at the Gamble's store whether he had any old washing machine motors lying around. My father welded the motor mount to a hinge and showed me how to design it so that the belt would stay tight, and before long I was able to start making chips fly all over our basement. I made a wooden bowl for my mother, mallet heads, even a croquet ball—which turned out to be useless because it was not perfectly spherical. I still have that lathe, and it was only about three years ago that Mr. Perry's old motor finally burned out.

When I asked my mother whether I could try out for the football team, she said, "No, I want you to keep your teeth." I was not built for football anyway, and I was greatly relieved that I could blame her when anyone would ask about it. One of my best friends was Dennis Williams, the only child of one of the tavern owners in town, and while I was too small for most sports, he was, well, too large. This reminds me of a man I saw recently at the IHOP restaurant, weighing at least four hundred pounds and wearing a T-shirt that read, "Anorexia Survivor." When I watch those nature programs on TV showing elephants running, they still remind me of Dennis. He had surprising speed, however (so do elephants), and probably could have played football, but he was content to be the equipment manager, and I became his assistant. I was not really built for basketball either but decided to try out for the team anyway. Of course, that did not work out at all as a freshman, but the intramural version of the game was more fun anyway, because here I was playing, not warming the bench that the varsity team would have reserved for me.

When track season came around, Dennis and I each found a niche. I had already discovered that competition among the sprinters was beyond my ability, so I settled more comfortably into the distance running events. For me, 2:12 for the half mile was not a bad time, even if it would never challenge any records. I took advantage of the fact that the long distances were not the high profile events, so while the really good hot-shot athletes were knocking each other out on the sprinting events, I was at the top of the dregs that were left to run the races no one cared about. A blue ribbon is a blue ribbon, and in my view, mine for the mile was just as good as the one Bob Schultz got for the 100 yard dash. Dennis discovered too that while all the lithe athletes competed in glamour field events like the pole vault, where spectators flocked, he could fling the shotput or discus across the chalk for a ribbon because no one else wanted to be entered into an event with such a low profile.

After my freshman year, there was a major shakeup within the school system at Sutherland. I do not remember whether an election replaced the school board with all new members or the incumbents had had enough with the current administration, but the entire high school staff was given its walking papers, from the superintendent on down to the art department. Irvin Struve, whose daughter Rebecca was in my class, was the chairman of the board, and he brought in a new superintendent from Burt, Iowa, named Russell Castor. Castor ran his program with an iron fist, yet he had a rippling sense of humor and a rapier quip for anyone who dared to challenge him. I liked him. Soon after he arrived, he was walking across the parking lot one day when a car driven by one of the football players sped around the corner of the building and nearly ran over him. The next day he called an assembly of all the boys—not the girls, the boys. "It's a good thing I am as agile as I am for a man my age," he said, "or I wouldn't be here today. One of you came around the corner of the school like a ruptured duck yesterday and nearly clobbered me. If that ever happens again, I will put up a chain and post Mr. Culbertson there to keep everyone out." He had brought Keith Culbertson along with him as his principal, and these two men, who had worked together as a team for several years, had each other's total support and saw everything eye to eye in perfect harmony. On a recent visit with Castor, still with a sparkle in his eye at age eighty-nine, he was telling me that Culbertson came from a dirt-poor family and struggled through school to earn his teacher certificate. When he applied for his first teaching assignment in Castor's district, he was in a borrowed suit that was too small for him, with the legs of the pants several inches above the ankle. Yet there was something about him that impressed Castor, who hired him on the spot and coached him through further training to achieve his principal credentials. I can think of only two who survived from the old regime. One was Willie Roemmich, a favorite son in Sutherland, formerly the teacher of freshman algebra, but who now found himself promoted to principal of the elementary school. The other was Kenneth Hoyne, with a well deserved reputation for excellence and well established respect as band director and advanced algebra teacher.

Although my summers were quite busy, I found time to join the high school baseball team. Dick Kummerfeld was a better pitcher than I, so I found a place on the team at third base. Dick's father was Leroy "Que" Kummerfeld, but I do not remember whether he was a billiards champion or how this particular handle attached itself to him. He had apparently been a very good pitcher himself in his youth and appointed himself Dick's mentor. Our coach, Mr. Roemmich, got the frivolous idea one day to allow us to see how well Que and some of the other dads could actually play. He staged a benefit game between our team and the adults. We found out that Que could still pitch—screwballs, sliders, curves and change-ups that I had never seen before. Mr. Castor smashed a ground ball to me at third base so hard that it was off his bat and into my glove almost simultaneously. I had no idea a baseball could be hit that hard. Neither did the coach and some of the dads, as they tried to hide a smirk when it nearly knocked me down. I had my usual problems hitting, but it was about this time that I discovered an additional reason—not an excuse, but a legitimate cause. Ralph was wearing glasses, and one day on a whim I put them on. I could not believe how much clearer everything was. My vision had been perfect in eighth grade, when everyone at school was last tested, but when I told my mother about this, we were headed for the optometrist in Sioux City.

Band was an entirely different musical direction from the one my parents had in mind for me. For one thing, no band instrument had the universal appeal of the piano. Every home, every church, every school had a piano, but not a trombone, clarinet or tympani. Keyboard skills were always useful serving the church, but the same could not be said for the snare drum or sousaphone. Then there was the cost of lessons and instrument rental and … well no, thanks, said my mother, we will stay with the piano. But I could still be of use to Mr. Hoyne when it came time for music contest each spring, as accompanist for one or more of the instrumental ensembles he put together. He was amazingly effective with these teenage musicians and brought home a Division I concert band award year after year.

I needed his help with the piece I chose for the music contest one year. Chopin's *Fantasie Impromptu* begins with a passage with four against three, a device I had never seen before, and has a middle section with three against two. He told me that to attempt it mechanically was like trying to pat my head and rub my stomach at the same time. Do it *musically* instead, he advised, each hand singing its part separately but not allowing it to compare what the other was doing. I followed his suggestion, and soon I discovered that I could actually play the piece. One day Hoyne handed me some music, and I could not believe what I was seeing. It was an exact copy of some sheets I had given back to him the day before, including comments and markings *in my own handwriting*. It was on ordinary paper, not photo stock, so how could he reproduce this *exactly*? I later found out that the front office had acquired an amazing new machine manufactured by Xerox that in only about five minutes could make a copy of any page fed into it.

Glee club was a requirement, for boys and girls separately, but mixed chorus was an extracurricular activity. I developed such a good voice that Virginia Ross, the choral director, often told me she wished I were twins. Tenors are always harder to come by in choirs than baritones and basses, so I was in demand for many of her vocal ensembles. Most of these madrigals, quartets and other small groups were set up for the annual music contest. This "contest" was not a competition where performers are eliminated by comparison to each other, but an opportunity to prepare and perform a piece before three judges (none of them Simon Cowell, thankfully), who would critique the rendition and assign a I, II or III rating. Although I entered the piano competition each year, I was able to work up the courage to enter a vocal solo only once, selecting *The Lord's Prayer* by Mallotte, a tired old warhorse sung at every wedding and funeral of that time. Hackneyed as it is, I still love that piece today. Even though I was very nervous on the day of the performance, I pulled it together enough to get a Division I rating.

One year Iowa announced an All-State Chorus, in which the best singers from all over the state would compete for the honor to participate in a mass choir. The schools received copies of the choral arrangements, and their music departments were to organize mixed quartets of their singers to audition at regional competitions. Johanna Jordan was one of the best sopranos (also one of the most statuesque beauties) in school, and she wanted me to join her quartet. Instead, I was matched up with Vicky Rausch, a rather rotund girl with a breathy voice, as the soprano of our quartet. Together with my good friend Joel Mugge as our bass and Judy Hagge, a homespun, ditsy sophomore as our alto, I did not think we had much of a chance. We did not even look like a quartet, much less sound like one. However, the audition was not a beauty contest, and when our turn came, we blended together perfectly. It was an opportunity to be remembered for a lifetime, as we were on our way to Des Moines, joining 800 other voices in a thunderous performance. Although some schools were represented by more than one quartet, we were the only one from ours.

While shop was still a requirement in the curriculum of the new administration, the mechanical drawing program had been eliminated. One day when I found myself in the part of the building where the drawing boards had once been set up, I noticed Mr. Castor and one or two of the faculty in there playing a game I had never seen before—table tennis, sometimes dubbed ping pong. I was immediately captivated, watching these experts volley that celluloid ball, now softly, now along the very edge of the table, now with back spin, now with a clearly visible curved path, and then smashed so hard it surely must split open. But wait, the opponent was able to return that forehand smash and the next one and still win the point with one of his own. This was the game for me. Size did not matter. I had the quickness, agility, and reflexes that the game demands, and I observed everything those experts did, including their trick serves, fake moves and the all-important technique for holding the paddle. Dennis Williams and I started playing each other, then some of our classmates joined in, and finally players from every grade got into the action. When we watched the faculty play doubles, we set up our doubles matches too. Eventually, I got so good at the game that no one wanted to play against me, including the faculty, and I considered myself the undisputed champion of table tennis in the whole high school.

One day I was sitting quietly in the study hall working on my homework, along with a number of others from my class. Without warning, Mr. Culbertson came in, walked up to Keith Jungjohann and told him in a loud voice to stand up. Then he asked him what he had been doing. When Culbertson was not satisfied with the answer that came mumbling out, he slapped Keith in the face so hard the smack resounded all over the room, and a bright red mark spread across his cheek immediately. Whoa. While Castor had the tall and lanky build of an athlete, Culbertson had the bulk of a wrestler and probably weighed over 300 pounds. Mr. Culbertson had been monitoring the study hall through the window and observed some brand of misbehavior inconsistent with diligent study. I am not sure whether his corrective action produced a change in Keith, but I do know it established an unmistakable standard of discipline throughout the school. When this scene was repeated with a few other boys, everyone was on notice, first, that misconduct would not be tolerated, and second, that Culbertson was not someone to mess with. Years later, reminiscing with one of the faculty members at a reunion, I asked him about this. "Listen," he said with a shudder, "When Culbertson walked into the teachers lounge, even *they* snapped to attention out of fear for what he was capable of doing to them."

By the time I reached the eleventh grade, the basketball team must have found itself desperate for players, because I actually made the team as a varsity player. That does not mean I actually got to play, but I considered a position on the First Twelve traveling squad, almost like one of the apostles, to be quite an honor. Around Christmas that year, my parents got a brand new station wagon and decided to take advantage of the break from school to drive out to California, where my father's sister Clara lived with her family. Before we left, my father called the Iowa Division of Motor Vehicles to be sure we would not encounter any problems driving interstate with temporary license plates. When we came to a checkpoint at the Arizona border, a highway patrol officer directed us to an office nearby, where they informed us there was a four-dollar fine for driving with paper plates. After arguing in vain with them, my father pulled out a piece of paper and started writing down names from the badges of the officers behind the counter. Then he laid four one-dollar bills on the counter and said, "I want a signed receipt, and when I get back home, I am going to take this up with the state of Iowa." With that, the officer pushed the money back over to my father and said, "You are free to go—courtesy of the state of Arizona." We had uncovered a little scam, and there is no telling how many little four-dollar beer-money "fines" they had already collected.

I had never been to California, but when we arrived, I could appreciate instantly why Aunt Clara and Uncle Wilmer had moved here. I had never seen real palm trees before, but here they were everywhere, almost like another world. It was December, yet my cousin Richard and I were playing basketball outside in our tee shirts, something quite commonplace to him, but giddily extraordinary to someone just liberated from a block of ice in Iowa. They took us across the border to Tijuana, where I ignored the caveats of all the adults and seared my palate on a real hot tamale that was a really hot tamale. I think I still have somewhere up in the attic the bongo drums I foolishly bought as a souvenir in Mexico. At Knott's Berry Farm, the mechanical man called out to my father, "Well, hello there, Elmer Pullmann, from Sutherland, Iowa" when he looked into the window of the "jail" to which Aunt Clara had directed him. Unaware that she had sneaked up to the window in advance to provide the information, I was more than curious to know how this little trick was pulled off. But when I peered through the bars, the dummy said, "Well, hello there, skin head."

When we got back to Iowa, I had a nasty surprise waiting for me. I was called into the superintendent's office, and sitting there with Mr. Castor was Mr. Erickson, the basketball coach, both of them demanding to know why I had skipped basketball practice over the Christmas break. Usually a model student, I had never done anything to warrant a trip to the office, but my parents were definitely not "my kid, right or wrong" types and would most assuredly have sided with the administration if I had. However, when I told my father about this, he immediately called the school and gave them his "you've got to be kidding" speech. In essence he told them that if this was the biggest problem they could find over at the school, he was going to come over there and point out a few they had missed. They never apologized, but I could tell from their response to his phone call that they had made a decision that the best course of action was none at all.

In the fall of that same year, Westgate was celebrating the diamond anniversary of its founding, and we were invited to it. It was shocking to see how much my classmates had changed in the three years since we left. Mannerisms were the same, but girls had been transformed into ladies, and most of the boys had dropped the pitch of their voices into a strangely unrecognizable husky range. When we drove into the driveway at Klammers, I overheard my father say under his breath to my mother, "If we are not welcome, we will just leave." Odd. Apparently, there had been a falling out between them, but we were never privy to the details. I could speculate on the problem, but the upshot was that after this visit, Arnie and Arvilla never spoke to my parents again. None of us knew it at the time, but it would be the last time I ever saw Larry Dean alive. One week after the Kennedy assassination, when the nation was still reeling from the events in Dallas, Klammers were rocked by the most devastating words any parent will ever hear. Larry Dean was driving to his job in Minnesota when a slow moving freight train collided with his car and rolled it over and over, crushing him inside. When my parents heard the news, they sent a card to the family. Arvilla returned it with a note, "We do not want your sympathy."

Everyone remembers the hula hoop fad that swept the nation during the early days of television, but there was another craze that followed at once on its heels—the trampoline. Unfortunately, that was followed almost immediately by the predictable scourge of paralysis resulting from the accidents caused by daredevil stunts. From the first moment I saw one, however, its allure was irresistible, and I not only wanted to try it, but I wanted to have one. One day when I was looking through *Popular Mechanics*, an article jumped off the page and bit me on the nose. I could *make* one—with iron pipe, steel springs and a canvas bed.

My father was a welder, so I bought the pipe, cut it with a hacksaw according to the plans, and he welded it together. The Sears catalog had canvas I could buy, and the local cobbler glued and stitched the sturdy fabric on his heavy-duty machine to fashion the rope-enclosed edging required for the bed. Now for the springs. Hmm. Ah, but the article mentioned a company that had some. The freight charges were egregious, but the company agreed to pay half when I told them who I was and what I was trying to do. Now the only problem was attaching opposing springs to connect the canvas to the frame. We were struggling with this one evening at my father's shop where we staged the assembly, when in walked Mike Johannsen. Mike was in Ralph's class, but he was as strong as a bull and already played varsity football. One by one he stretched those stiff coils with nothing more than brute strength until a trampoline stood before us. We let Mike have the first bounce.

The summer before my senior year was filled with several extraordinary events. The day before school started, two young teachers requested some help moving a davenport up the steps to their apartment. One who responded was Keith Culbertson, our principal, and while struggling with the load, he suffered a massive heart attack and died—at age thirty-nine. Replacing him was Gene Panning, who adjusted to the Castor administration so seamlessly that I would never have thought it possible—using verbal controls instead of physical ones. On the first day of school in the fall, Mr. Castor called an assembly of the entire school into the gym. He told us he had heard that some students in this room actually cheered when they heard the news about Mr. Culbertson. After holding forth with some choice words about the need for an attitude adjustment for such despicable behavior, he told us that in the course of a lifetime, we would have thousands of acquaintances, hundreds of comrades, and dozens of colleagues, but the number of those whom we could label as true friends—the kind who would give their lives for you or come to visit you on death row—could be counted on one hand. He had just lost one of his. Castor was no stranger to tragedy. He and his wife Eileen had just lost eight-year-old Rodney to leukemia, and during the birth of twins a few years earlier, an entangled umbilical cord strangled one and left the other, Dale, with permanent brain damage and physical impairments. Then Hadley, their eldest and brightest star, full of promise as he started out on his career, was killed in a plane crash. Hadley managed several successful businesses, among them an aviation venture that established a niche tackling difficult fields other crop dusters refused to service. After intrepidly swooping under some power lines one day, he experienced engine failure and was impaled on the elevator-aileron control stick, which pierced his heart, when the plane struck the ground.

The second unexpected event of the summer was something expected. Bright, promising, college-bound, attractive classmate Nancy Pingel had decided to get married. Rather, incipient motherhood was making the decision for her. Nancy had always been special to me, not only because we ended up in so many classes together, but because she was a member of our church, a fellow confirmand, fellow Walther Leaguer. Now she was also special to Gary Jungjohann, Keith's older brother. Her parents were able to work out an arrangement with the administration where she would not have to drop out of school. In fact, by working at home, she was able to receive her diploma with the rest of us at the end of the year. I have no idea how many others from my class were sexually active, but even I could suspect a number of others who might easily have found themselves in the same predicament. A teen pregnancy usually maps out a course very different from the one envisioned before the event, but Nancy and Gary persevered, turning to the farm on which they subsequently raised a large family quite successfully.

Another blockbuster event over that summer was the merger of three high schools with Sutherland. The number of students at Sutherland was in decline, and the ones attending tiny Larrabee, Gaza and Calumet had dwindled to the point where it was not cost effective to maintain them. Calumet had always been a rival, especially in basketball, so the seniors, with only one more year before graduation, were particularly disgusted with this decision and maladjusted to their new situation. They had reason to be proud, however, having just won the state basketball championship against long odds. Their players were so good that with their usual big lead in the fourth quarter, they put on a dribbling exhibition reminiscent of the Harlem Globetrotters. After the merger the only Sutherland player who made the first string was six-foot-four Harry Rahbusch. Needless to say, I did not make the team at all that year.

To this day, these émigrés from Calumet refuse to attend our class reunions, forced as they were to forsake their alma mater for the haunts of their former archrivals. I once had an instructor whose high school years were spent in White Plains, New York. When I asked him whether he goes back for class reunions, his cynical answer was that it is too painful. There were five distinct classes of students, he said: the Jewish kids, the Catholics, the lower class whites, the Puerto Ricans and the blacks. He did not feel that he belonged in any of these groups, and had no desire to go back for any reunion. He would have understood the Calumet position well. Still, when I travel 1200 miles to attend one, I am more than dismayed when a classmate I want to see lives literally around the corner from the building I am in but chooses to boycott.

Many of my classmates were dating throughout high school, but besides the fact that I did not consider myself very "dateworthy," I really did not have the time for it. For many years Sutherland staged a carnival every Labor Day, and one year I worked up the courage to ask the cute new girl in town, Ginny Ross, daughter of the vocal music teacher, to accompany me to these festivities. We had a good time, but both of us developed other interests and nothing came of that. One of the most serious students in school was shy Janet Negus. As I encountered her in many of the advanced classes we both elected, I considered her to be a kindred spirit and discovered one day she was becoming an attraction. Of all the girls in high school, she was unique—the only one that was beautiful *and* commanded my highest respect. She, on the other hand, expressed absolutely no interest in me, and since neither of us was into the dating scene anyway, that remained an ember that glowed on only one side.

In that same busy summer filled with the news of the merger, I attended a Walther League rally at Lake Okoboji. One day when I was showing off at the piano, a little blonde with a ponytail leaned over and smiled at me. She was Pauline Timm from Webster City. When she told me she was an expert on the trampoline, I told her I had one and expected her to come to Sutherland for an exhibition some time. We developed a relationship during the rest of the camp, wrote a few letters during the ensuing year at school, and then I invited her to be my date for the senior prom. When her community was throwing a luau the following summer, Pauline invited me over to Webster City to play the *Bumble Bee Boogie* that I had pounded out over and over at the rally so many times that the counselors came in to make me stop. But the kids loved it. My relationship with Pauline came to an end that same summer, but I would not know it for almost three years. I will return with the sequel later, after I lay the foundation, at which time I can explain what happened.

One of the greatest challenges for a self-conscious teenage boy is the stage. One year Mrs. Ross talked me into the lead role in an operetta she was putting together, called *Threads and Patches*, modeled upon the *Mikado* of Gilbert and Sullivan. The next year it was a turn of the century melodramatic farce called *Sunbonnet Sue*, and while I had no difficulty with the vocal parts, I was seriously miscast as the romantic suitor opposite the hapless young lady in the title role. Mrs. Skinner was the teacher of English for the underclassmen, but also the speech and drama coach, *ex officio* director of the junior and senior class plays. Incidentally, she was from Paullina, Sutherland's archrival, and the mother of twin boys who were both track stars at that school. It was bad enough when the anchor of their 440 relay could outrun a greyhound, but we always had to contend with *two* of them.

Similar to its music counterpart, a speech contest was held each spring, and the contestants were judged for a rating. Of the many categories available, I chose radio announcing because it was the only one that did not require a personal appearance before the judge. The material to be delivered was written and read by the contestant into a microphone in an adjoining room. Unfortunately, since I had no imagination, my material was a total flop, and my low rating was a serious disappointment to Mrs. Skinner. She did not give up on me, however, and cast me in both the junior and senior class plays.

One of the students who had merged into our senior class from Larrabee was Jerry Magnussen, who became one of my best friends. Jerry and I had lead roles in *Finders Creepers*, our senior class play, and in one scene my character leaps into Wilbur's arms when he sees a ghost. Later in the scene, Jerry, as Wilbur, is supposed to leap into *my* arms when *he* sees the ghost. At 120 pounds, I presented little difficulty for Jerry, but Mrs. Skinner was skeptical that I could catch Jerry, who probably tipped out at over 140. Even though I protested that I wanted to do it and argued that it ruined the scene if I did not, the risk of injury held the day, and she modified the dialogue to exclude it. The entire elementary school was traditionally invited to the dress rehearsal, and when we came to the ghost scene, these children laughed so hard that I had difficulty staying in character. For the main performance that evening, my father's sister Ellen and husband Harold Gilder happened to be visiting with us from Minnesota and came with my parents to the play. Aunt Ellen enjoyed the performance, but for years she raved about Karolyn Kastengren, who played the role of the maid. Whenever I saw her mimicking Karolyn's mannerisms, I was quite sure that if Karolyn were ever orphaned, Ellen would have been first in line to adopt her.

Superintendent extraordinaire Russell Castor reserved one class for himself—senior English. Although English was not particularly my strong suit, I look back on his course as one of the best I ever had. He was an exceptional instructor, expounding on the archaic words and phrases in the oldest English manuscripts in existence, dramatizing the exploits of Beowulf slaying Grendel, patiently explaining every obsolete word in the *Canterbury Tales*, and not so patiently exhorting that even the quaint language of *Macbeth* should not need his explanation. At the beginning of the first semester, he announced that seniors should be expected to undertake a research project and prepare a thesis that was due at the end of the year.

I was having difficulty selecting a topic, but he refused to assign one to me. When I pressed him for ideas, he finally told me that, faced with similar circumstances himself, he always chose to write about something that made him upset. "Don't you have anything that really makes you *mad*?" he asked me. With no real perspective on life at my age, I told him no. He walked away. One evening I was reading an article in an old *Reader's Digest* about a noise ordinance in Nashville, and suddenly I had my topic—the *Physiological Effects of Noise*. While many of the boys waited for the opening bell each morning boisterously telling of their hunting exploits, I was busy in the typing room working on my paper. Erasures were not allowed, so it was quite an effort to produce more than 100 pages of clean manuscript by the due date.

In my senior year, I foolishly volunteered to be the editor of the yearbook. It was a monumental undertaking, ranging from soliciting support from local boosters to formulating witty labels for pictures. The editors from preceding years had always enlisted Bob Kelly, the school photographer, to snap pictures on demand, but he had graduated the previous year. Fortunately, my brother Ralph had taken up photography as a hobby and was developing his own pictures, so I depended heavily on him for the photos of the businesses in our display ads and other informal snapshots not handled by the professional portrait photographer. Our faculty advisor was Kristin Baier, the home economics teacher, who drove the yearbook staff over to Storm Lake for a workshop one day. On the way back, Becky Struve lit up a cigarette. I was so shocked that I could not get it out of my mind for days. Beautiful, freckle-faced, redhead Becky, who could easily have been a supermodel or Hollywood starlet, was one of my idols high on a pedestal, and now I actually saw her taking up the sport of losers. Oh, I knew the faculty lounge was always so blue that any teacher who walked in would disappear in about three steps, and I respected most of *them*, but somehow this was different. There were plenty of kids my age whom I saw puffing away, but every one of them was gathering momentum on a downhill track toward Low Life. Not well-respected Becky. Why, Becky, why?

# Moving Hire

Since Iowa has a relatively short growing season, my lawn mowing business was primarily a summertime occupation, from mid-May, when the last ice-encrusted puddles disappeared, until late August when frost was already in the air. When Ivan Ploeger and Vernon Meyer became the new owners of the bowling alley in the fall, they were looking for pinsetters. They called a meeting of all the high school boys who were interested, so I asked my father whether I should attend. Of course, he said. But when I asked him what I should say if they asked me if I knew how, his exact words were, "Sure I know how, if you show me." This bowling alley had semi-automatic pinsetting machines. Pins knocked over were thrown back into a pit beyond the bowling lane. The pinsetter's job was to jump into this pit *afterwards*, send the heavy ball down a ramp back to the bowler, and then clean up any pins still lying among the ones still standing. When the second ball arrived in the pit, the pins were laid on the rack that descended to align them again all standing in place. It was hard work. By the time the pins were scooped up and racked, the bowler was ready to deliver, and the ball soon came hurtling toward me again, relentlessly until the game was over.

During open bowling the job paid ten cents a line, the term given to one complete game of ten frames on the score sheet. However, on league night there were two shifts, paying $2.50 per lane for two hours of work. With a little experience I could hustle fast enough to work two lanes simultaneously and picked up five dollars for my shift. Assignments of the evenings and shifts to work were made according to seniority. No one wanted open bowling or Thursday, the league night for the women bowlers, because they never started or ended on time, so the second shift usually ended closer to midnight than 11:00, when it was supposed to. At first I was stuck with open bowlers and cringed when I saw Doc Dahlbo come in with his friend Ed Lage every Saturday night, two old fogies who were never in a hurry to finish their game. As one of the most junior employees, my lot also fell to the late shift on Thursdays, but I got frequent calls to substitute on other nights too. Keith Jungjohann was quite often one who called, but whenever I called him, he found some excuse to beg off. When he stopped by at the last minute one evening to ask me to substitute, my father was home and demanded to know why this was always so one-sided. He told Keith I was going to refuse, just as he always did. When he turned to me, I caught a threatening gesture from Keith over my father's shoulder, so I told him I would help out. My father was angry with me, telling me later that I had embarrassed him and should never expect him to stand up for me again if I was going to treat him like that. Maybe so, but he never saw the steely glint in Keith's eye.

One night when I finished the early shift working two lanes, Irene Meyer told me the kid who was supposed to work the late shift had not shown up and entreated me to fill in. I cannot recall any time, before or since, working so hard for ten dollars. I was so exhausted that I wondered if I could make it home on my bicycle that night. I got so used to working two lanes that one evening when I got a call to substitute for someone to work just one lane, I was still in two-lane mode and had a gruesome accident. My partner in the other lane brought his ball up to the ramp at the exact same moment that I did, and the fourth finger of my right hand was smashed between the two balls. The finger split open and I knew I had to get to a doctor immediately. When I raced home on my bike, however, the car was gone and the house was dark. Although I got the bleeding stopped, the throbbing pain was so intense I did not know if I could keep from blacking out. I was cursing myself, first, for allowing this to happen, but also for not paying attention, as my parents had probably told me where they were going. We had no telephone at the time, and I did not know what to do. It was two more hours before they returned, but by then a trip to the emergency room in Cherokee would have been the only medical facility available. I really needed stitches, but since it appeared to my parents that the worst was over, I was persuaded to bandage it up and try to get some sleep. I still have a lumpy scar on the tip of that finger today.

Many of the boys had hot rods that occupied a great deal of their time. Since these were usually jalopies handed down from relatives or old wrecks resurrected from behind the corncrib, the restoration process required a considerable expenditure of effort. My father had a soft spot in his heart for their plight, so he had quite a following in and around town among these boys for advice, expertise and technical guidance. This affected me too, as in the course of staying in his good graces, some of them would go the extra mile not to cause me any offense. I became "Little Elmer," and an encounter at school with them would frequently end with, "Say hello to your old man for me."

My priorities did not include hot rods, however, and I did not identify with them. As a result, when I became old enough to start driving, I was not interested. Driver training was offered as an elective over the summer, however, and my parents thought it would be good for me to enroll. The course included both classroom and hands-on behind-the-wheel experience taught by an amazing instructor from Cherokee with unflappable calm and nerves of titanium. His favorite answer when someone would ask a question like "What do you do if you are going around a curve and a car coming in the opposite direction skids into your lane?" was a dry "Well, let's just hope that doesn't happen."

For the road portion of the training, the class was divided each day into groups of three. The car was dual controlled, so the instructor and student were up front, while two students-in-waiting were observing from the back seat. One day the student driver in my group was an elderly widow who determined she would learn how to drive the car left behind by her husband. Not only was she nervous, but senile as well. When the task was to turn the key to start the car, she turned on the radio. When the task was to select Drive, she operated the wipers. Kathy Davis and I in the back seat eyed each other and were ready to bolt for the doors, as the instructor said, "That's a very good start, Mrs. Hughes. We'll just continue our lesson tomorrow." I never saw her again. The car provided in the training had an automatic transmission, but when I finished my six weeks in that car, my father made a very important decision for me. His cars had always had a manual transmission, and he felt that learning to drive was not complete until I could manage one. I still believe that today.

The rules we see today posted in every repair facility prohibiting customers from the work area did not exist in my father's shop—or probably anywhere else in rural America, for that matter. While trying to repair one customer's car, my father found him standing in the way whenever he turned around from the car to the workbench. Eventually, it dawned on the old guy that he might be interfering, so he asked my father if he was getting in the way. "No, that's okay, I'll work around you," said my father sarcastically. One lady approached my father in the shop one time and said, "I've been watching you work on my car for an hour, and I would guess you are either Lutheran or Baptist." Is there a better testimonial to your faith than that? I am not so sure someone could watch me work on a car for an hour and come away with the same conclusion.

Every day the shop where my father worked was visited by an old retired railroad worker (at least that was what *he* told people, so maybe that meant he was a hobo) named Morgan. He enjoyed hanging around to tell jokes and kibitz, so whenever anyone asked him whether he worked there, he would say he was the second assistant to the flunkey. Morgan was no dummy. He frequently rode along when my father drove to a neighboring town for parts or out into the country to rebuild a bailer, and would call out, "What does the speedometer say, Elmer? We're doing 57.2 miles per hour." Iowa's roads are sectioned into one-mile segments, so Morgan had been timing between intersections and making the calculations in his head.

Some individuals search for a lifetime trying to find an identity. Such could probably be said for my Uncle Paul. He tried for a time to follow in his older brother Elmer's footsteps and learn the trade of a mechanic. However, repairs can be frustrating, and usually require a great deal of patience and perseverance. Paul had neither. He was fond of my father and wanted to live nearby, so he settled for a time in Peterson, a town ten miles east of Sutherland on Highway 10, working for a dealership there. When the other siblings saw that he was living by himself, they suggested that Grandma Pullmann could move in with him. It seemed like a win-win proposition—Grandma would not have to continue her itinerant existence, and Paul would have a housekeeper. However, neither one was sufficiently stable to make it work, and when Paul eventually moved on, my father found a tiny cottage for Grandma in Sutherland.

This immediately created tension in our household. Grandma and my mother never did get along very well, and now she was living only a half mile away. George Pullmann had always treated my mother well, and she reciprocated with the greatest respect and admiration for him. Hilda, on the other hand, never could accept her, and I was an adult before I really understood the reason—simple jealousy. Hilda, for most of her adult life, was plain, plump, and ponderous. Along comes Martha, well-proportioned, bright-eyed, perky, vivacious and beautiful. Whenever they were together, my grandmother found constant comparison inevitable, and it made her uncomfortable. Over the years Hilda reacted by trying to discredit my mother in the eyes of the Bender relatives and to some extent among my father's siblings, shamelessly making no secret about it.

Her attitude toward my mother, however, did not extend to me. As the first Pullmann grandson, I had always been special to my grandparents, perhaps because I became a symbol that the name would now pass to another generation. Grandma loved to have visitors and always made me feel favored when she invited us over for supper. When I mowed her tiny yard, she usually had some treat she made for me, and genuinely displayed her affection in many different ways. Although I think both she and my mother made an honest commitment to see it work out, even I could perceive the little jabs Grandma would poke at my mother. There were always the comments that she was getting older. Grandma was visiting at our house one day when Irene Shuck from next door stopped over.

In the course of the conversation, I actually overheard Grandma say, "But we don't need to worry about that at our age, do we, Martha?" My mother winced but bit her lip, barely suppressing the urge to lash back. Grandma was actually trying to bring her down with the presupposition they were the same age.

Not long after this incident, my parents announced to the family that there would soon be a baby in our house. Although they never put it in such terms, I am convinced their conscious decision to conceive a child was in direct response to these aspersions of my grandmother. Whether this was "I'll show *you*" on the part of my mother, an "oops" pregnancy that results in some families when the older kids are half grown, or, as my father put it whimsically, they needed to complete the pattern of names they had started, I will never know for sure. What I do know is that one night at a Walther League meeting at the church, one of our youth counselors showed up in maternity wear, and when some of my fellow Leaguers snickered and others slipped a peek at me, I was so embarrassed that I wished the earth would open up under me. Shortly after my sixteenth birthday, Rodney was born (August 30, 1960).

The bowling alley closed each summer, but after a couple of seasons, my father had the idea that Ralph could handle some of my lawn mowing customers, while I found other work over the summer. Sometimes farmers hired teenagers to "walk the beans." When crops are rotated, it is impossible to prevent some seed of the previous year from germinating, so corn commonly sprouts up among the soybeans. Worse, thistles, sunflowers and other weeds threaten to take over the crop or rob its nutrients. So we walked through the rows with machetes, chopping out anything that did not answer to the description of a soybean. This work was not particularly difficult, but most farmers had their own children to do it or bartered with each other, so those job offers were few and far between.

There were two auto dealers in Sutherland—Brookfield Chevrolet, where my father worked, and Farquhar Motors, the competing Chrysler shop run by Wayne and Marge Farquhar. Beryl Brookfield had two sons of his own who would one day inherit the business, so my father approached Wayne, who had no children, about a job for me in his garage. Wayne already had a crackerjack mechanic—none other than Bill Burns, our one-time next door neighbor—but he could use someone to do oil changes, grease cars and trucks, haul trash to the dump, and pump gas, all interruptions Bill could not stand. Some of the customers were allowed credit when they filled with gas, so one day when I told the driver the amount, he said with a twinkle in his eye as he drove off, "Write that in the dust and let the rain settle it."

They showed me how to work the hoist, cautioning me in the strongest terms to check the lifting bracket to be sure it was positioned under the rear axle housing before operating the hoist controls. Failure to do so could rupture the gas tank or puncture the floorboard. All went well for several months, until one day I forgot to align the brackets and started to bring the hoist up. As soon as I heard the crunch, however, I quickly backed it off, realigned the brackets correctly and lifted the car. Expecting to be doused with leaking gasoline as the car rose higher, I waited with pounding heart to see what damage I had caused. The tank was dented, but not seriously compromised, so I decided not to say anything about it. Having attended school with the children of this customer, I knew he was about as sharp as a potato, so I doubt he ever figured out why his car suddenly held about two gallons less gas than it did before.

I was watching Bill hone out a brake cylinder one day and asked him to show me how to do that. He not only let me take over, but supervised my installation of the new brake kit and explained how he could tell that the car needed that job in the first place. Each time I serviced a car on the grease rack after that, I decided to check for leaking brake fluid. In about half of the cases, I found it. Telling a customer that his car needs more work than what he brought it in for is a delicate proposition, so I always told Wayne what I found and let him consider the options for breaking the news to the owner. On the one hand he might be grateful that timely intervention prevented an accident or serious damage, but on the other he might decide to get his car serviced next time by someone who is not trying to gouge him. I did a considerable number of brake overhaul jobs while I worked there, but nothing about it was dishonest or unethical. Although this generated a good deal of additional business for Wayne, I did wonder whether or not I had done him a disservice in the long run.

A repair shop generates a mountain of trash—mufflers, tailpipes, windshield glass, filters, and cartons. My job was to hook up the trailer to the jeep once a week and drive out to the landfill to dispose of this refuse. There were two aspects of this task that would prove to be particularly beneficial to me later in life. First, was the operation of a four-wheel drive vehicle at a time when hardly anyone had any idea that such a concept existed. Sometimes the only way to climb out of the mud at the dump site was to engage it. Second, when I arrived with my load and again when I returned with the empty trailer, it was often necessary to back into a tight space. I got so good at backing that trailer that I could squeeze between parked cars to place it exactly within inches of where it belonged.

My favorite customer was Bud Peterson, a trucker who pulled his semi-trailer with a Chevrolet tractor. Most of the cars and trucks I serviced were Chrysler products, so working on a General Motors product was itself unusual. He watched me as I worked and especially liked the way I washed the windows of his cab and vacuumed it out when I finished the greasing and oiling. Bud always had a kind word to Wayne about me, and sometimes left a little extra for me when he paid his bill. He liked to crack jokes and addressed me not as the kid I really was, but on his same level, as if I were an adult. One day when Bud came into the shop with his hand bandaged, I asked him what happened, and he told me something that changed my life from that day forward. As he was jumping down from the truck, his ring caught on a hook on the rig and tore off his finger. The immediate effect of that was a vow to myself that I would never again wear a ring, and with that gruesome fate in mind I have kept that pledge to this day.

Wayne had been an aircraft mechanic in WWII, and he had stories about the radial engines he worked on, the cooling problems they had, timing issues for an engine with an odd number of cylinders, and so on. I was impressed when he could still recite the firing order of a 28-cylinder engine. One day we received the shocking news that Lyle Fogelman, the father of Dennis and Frank, two upperclassmen that I knew quite well in school, was killed in an auto accident. When his car was towed in, I told Wayne I wanted to buy the engine from it to build an airplane. Although it is dangerous to tell a teenager something is impossible, Wayne took that risk and wisely pointed out, first, that a water-cooled engine would be far too heavy for a small airplane, and, second, the shape of it was not suitable for the sleek profile that an aircraft must have. Still, the idea was planted, and I could not let go of it for many years.

In the summer after I graduated from high school, I got a postcard, addressed to me personally, from Venita Rich, a talent scout with the *Ted Mack Original Amateur Hour* television program. She had received my name as a local talent and was inviting me to an audition at the O'Brien County fair in Primghar later in the summer. The sign posted at the edge of town, incidentally, for the benefit of those entering the county seat, proudly boasts, "PRIMGHAR, the only Primghar in the world." It is. But then again, the same could probably be said for Kalamazoo and a host of other cities. The reason Primghar could be so confident of its uniqueness is that it is actually an acronym, derived from the names of its founding council. The winner of the competition at the fair would receive an all-expenses-paid trip to New York for an audition there to appear on the popular television show. One of the conditions most inimical to a piano player is cold, because fingers stiffen and make difficult passages almost impossible. Iowa can get quite cool, even in summer, especially in the evenings, so, of course, my worst fears were realized on the night of the contest. Fortunately, I was scheduled to appear near the end of the program—usually an advantage in an elimination event. However, about halfway through the program, I could not believe my ears when a young lady came on stage and played the exact same piece I would be playing, the *Rondo Capriccioso* of Mendelssohn.

When my father heard that, he came backstage to give me encouragement. He had an idea. It was an outdoor event, and he had noticed that the microphone was placed on the opposite side of the stage, so far away from the piano that the sound carried out to the audience was all but inaudible. He suggested that when my turn came, I should request the stage crew to move the piano closer to the sound system. Then when I played, I should give the flashiest performance possible. They were looking for showmanship as well as talent, he said, and the visual spectacle was as important as the music. Even though the judges had already heard my piece, I could turn that into an advantage by playing it with more flair and, well, more flare. It worked. When the winner was announced, I could scarcely believe I was actually hearing my name called. I was going to New York.

College was just ahead for me, but when career choices were arrayed before me, I found myself wishing I had several lifetimes to pursue each of the ones in which I had an interest. Career Day was no help. If anything, it made the decision worse by expanding the options, not narrowing them. One clarion message that came through all the literature was to capitalize on my strengths. With a little insightful self-examination, I wanted to do that, but I was not quite sure what those were. On the one hand, I loved the advanced algebra and trigonometry, physics and chemistry courses I had taken, but on the other, I seemed to have a talent for music and wondered if a music career might be a possibility for me as well.

My father had always wanted to be a pastor and encouraged me to consider fulfilling that dream for him, but his dream was not mine. I am far too maudlin to be leading a congregation, but how about a parochial school teacher, I wondered. I could teach math and science classes at a Lutheran high school. The SAT and other tests so crucial to college applicants today were optional for me, so I mailed off my application without any test scores for admission to Concordia Teachers College in Seward, Nebraska. Before my acceptance letter arrived, however, I got another offer. The Sherwood Music School, whose correspondence course I had worked through with Mrs. Duffield in Westgate some years earlier, was dangling a scholarship. For many years afterward I would second-guess my decision to accept it, but I knew that my parents really did not have money for college tuition and trimmed my sails for Chicago. I will never know what the course of my life would have been otherwise, but whenever I survey the landscape from where I am today, I am absolutely convinced that I was following a Plan mapped out for me from above.

Graduation day finally arrived, and the faculty had voted me Most Likely to Succeed, an honor I cherished more than almost any other they could have bestowed. The motto chosen by the graduating class was Onward and Upward. The onward part was inevitable for all of us, but I hoped the upcoming chapter in life was truly upward, not sideways or backward. Janet Negus was the valedictorian, hardly a surprise, but I was named salutatorian, which was a surprise, especially given my sagging grades in social studies and history. I did not know it at the time, but it would be the last time I saw my good friend and fellow Walther Leaguer Kenny King alive. A few short years later he was killed in a pickup accident.

# Onward and Upward

How does one gauge maturity? Can it be quantified? Can it be qualified? I am not sure I know the answer to these questions even today, but I am quite sure that in September of 1962 I did not have it. Childhood was probably over long before I moved the tassel of my mortarboard from right to left, but there is nothing that puts starch in the spine like the stark reality of leaving home. When my parents dropped me off in Chicago, I discovered that I did not really know who I was. Yes, *who*, not *where*. Was I serious or was I funny? the life of the party or the wallflower? an intellectual or a dilettante? the strong silent type or the outspoken-by-no-one type? sycophantic or bumptious? I derived cues from those around me whom I admired, but which one of them was I most like? Bob Schultz, who always had a witty comeback? or was it Russell Castor, who exuded such self-assurance? or even my father, always the paragon of integrity? Be yourself, everyone said, but *which* yourself was I?

William Hall Sherwood was one of the greatest pianists in America in the nineteenth century, a protégé of Franz Liszt, arguably the greatest pianist of all time. Sherwood was also one of the most celebrated educators of his time and founded his conservatory of classical music in 1895. Accreditation at the collegiate level, however, required courses beyond music, so the music school he founded later affiliated with the University of Chicago for the academic subjects required for a recognized degree. Although my parents were completely supportive of my decision to attend the Sherwood Music School, I was learning a little more about their program only after we arrived. The first thing I noticed was that it had no campus or dormitories. The four floors of their building at 1014 South Michigan Avenue *was* the campus, and I was about to see it from the inside for the first time.

If you remember Eve Arden as the gum-crackling, wisecracking secretary on the *Our Miss Brooks* program that had a run on radio and early television for a few years, you will have a picture of Blanche B. Bensinger, the daffy administrative assistant we first met when the elevator doors opened up on registration day. BBB, as she always signed the notes she left the students in their mail boxes, had been married about four times and, while she was now perhaps in her seventies, again unmarried, flitted all over the school like a bee in a clover patch. She escorted us in to meet Arthur Wildman, at least in his sixties, whose exaggerated aquiline nose reminded me immediately of Clarence Sutter from Sutherland. As we were discussing the terms of enrollment with him in his office, he had occasion to pull out the Chicago phone directory, and I gasped when I saw the size of it. I had never seen a book that required both hands just to lift it, and I could not wrap my mind around the concept of a city the size of all those phone numbers. At Sutherland the entire list of three-digit phone numbers occupied about two pages.

In order to help him map out my major, Wildman had me play something on the piano in his studio. When I finished, I expected some complimentary remarks, perhaps even lavish praise about my advanced abilities. Instead, he turned to my parents with a sober expression and suggested that I major in education—teaching instrumental or vocal music in the schools. I was stunned when he told us pointedly that I would probably never make the concert stage. There were three professors of piano at the school, and he was assigning me to Leon Rosenbloom, the one most patient with tearing down and rebuilding proper keyboard technique with entering students who had never learned it correctly. I was finding out for the first time that the psychomotor skills required to play a musical instrument like the piano or violin must be acquired at a very young age or they become almost impossible to master. This is particularly true for the non-dominant hand, in my case the left, for the fine-motor dexterity required to execute such devices as trills and tremolos. It was already too late for me, but Rosenbloom would spend the next four years trying to unravel the tangled mess that the likes of Rowland, Duffield, and Drefke had wrought in me, all of them music teachers but none piano teachers. It was painful, but eventually he was able to put together some building blocks to which I could relate, and although I would never be able to make my fingers fully achieve them, I felt I finally began to taste the art that might have been.

My parents probably already knew something else about the program to which I had never given much thought. The scholarship covered only a portion of the tuition and did not include room and board. Female students were required to reside in the YWCA or Three Arts Club, both on the Near North Side of Chicago, about three miles from school. For them, transportation would also need to be added to the cumulating list of expenses. The recommendation of the school for the male students was either the YMCA in the heart of the city or the 830 South Michigan Hotel just down the street, both easily walkable distances away for me. After we finished the enrollment, my parents registered me at the Y and bid me a tearful goodbye (my father told me years later that was one of the most traumatic moments of their lives, as they cried the entire drive home). Just days earlier I had been in the comfort of a real home, and now I was in a kind of dumping ground with a tight knot in the gut that would not go away. Most of all, I missed my little brother. Just two years old, he was talking and responsive, the cutest thing on earth to me, and now I felt cast away from him forever.

Feeling dreadfully alone and scared in my tiny single room, I decided to go down to the lobby to look around. When I wandered into the huge game room with a sea of ping pong tables set up, an Asian fellow walked up to me and asked if I wanted to play. Ah, this should make me feel better. Was I not the high school champion? But then I saw him unzip a leather case and extract a special paddle. The ones we used in high school were made from quarter-inch plywood with a kind of stippled rubber surface. His looked like it was made from ivory, about an inch thick with a dimpled brown surface that looked like felt. Whoa. If you ever see a guy pull out his own custom made table tennis paddle from a leather case, flee from the room or find somewhere to hide. Do not let him play you. Instead of the distinct tock sound to which I was accustomed when the ball was struck, his paddle produced almost no sound at all, which in itself unnerved me. A skunk game is 7-0, and I think that was the score when he asked me if I wanted to play again. I did not.

It was still mid-afternoon, so I decided to walk through the streets to get a flavor of the city in the direction of the school. When I stepped off the elevator at Sherwood, BBB ran up to me and said she had been trying to reach me. Another student had arrived, checked into the 830 and was looking for a roommate. When I told her I was already registered at the Y, she got on the phone immediately, asking me while she was on hold whether I had disturbed anything in the room. Assuring her I had not even opened my suitcases, I marveled how assertive she could be as she made the arrangements. I had not been in Chicago even one day and already I was moving. As I stood at the elevator to leave, the doors opened, and my prospective new roommate stepped off. BBB, who was waiting with me at the elevator, introduced me to Hubert "Lee" Whittington from Muskogee, Oklahoma.

Even with two beds, our apartment at the 830 was about five times the size of the one I had at the Y, and although it did not have a kitchen, it had a pint-size refrigerator and an electric hot plate for heating up soup. I was instantly jealous of Lee when he told me his piano professor was Dr. Podolsky, which meant his entry-level technique elevated him to the next level among the credentials at Sherwood, not in the bargain basement where I resided. Lee and I decided to walk a couple of blocks over to the heart of downtown to look around and found a store with a familiar name—Woolworth's. Or, as Lee said it, Woolsworth. I had never known anyone from Oklahoma before, but he had an Okie-from-Muskogee drawl that was infectious, as it often converted monosyllable words into two-syllable ones. His way of saying "thank you sayo muuuch" did not come out the same way in Iowese. No one that I knew before used the word *hateful* either, but he sprinkled it into his dialog quite often. I even ran to my dictionary when we got back to see if it was a real word. Chicago was home base for the Sears retail chain and had one of the largest outlets in the world a few blocks away. We discovered in its basement a huge supermarket called Hillman's, which stocked almost anything a college kid could want. Two things were on my shopping list. One was a street map of Chicago, so I could get an overview of where I was. The second was a glazed donut. No, wait, my mother was nowhere around to say no, so why not buy a whole bag of them. I felt giddily uninhibited as I gobbled down so many of those glazed donuts that to this day I glaze over just looking at one.

Back in my room I spent about two hours poring over that wonderful map, learning how the grid originating from State and Madison is so regular that every four blocks is a major thoroughfare. The Chicago Transit Authority "El" trains (because sections of them are elevated above the streets), which stretch to every corner of the city, merge in the heart of downtown and Loop like a spacecraft slingshotting around the moon back out toward the suburbs. In fact, I was to learn it was possible, using rail and bus of the CTA system in combination, to step off within two blocks of any point in the city, and transfers from one to the other were free. When I looked up from my study of this map, my eye fell on that gigantic Chicago directory sitting near the phone in our room. Curious what the last entry might be, I turned to the very last wrinkled page and found Zyzyxxy, Zyzzy. I was tempted to dial the number just to see if the name was contrived.

I had a great deal of difficulty falling asleep that night, first because of the rush of adrenaline which had washed over me all day, and I suppose the rush from a whole bag of confectionery sugar, but also because my new roommate was in the habit of falling asleep with the radio on. For me, that was an intrusion, but it would be several days before I could work up the courage to say something to Lee about it. At the freshman orientation the next day, doddering old Walter Erley, the president of Sherwood, was welcoming all of us to the school and mentioned that one of the services the school provided was assistance finding part-time jobs. I was one of those who needed a job and was first in line to put BBB in the hunt for one. Erley was largely a figure-head. It was his wife who had fallen heir to the assets of the school and gave him the title and a short list of duties that included making speeches to the student body laced with corny clichés and snoring through recitals.

77

One of my first priorities soon after I arrived in Chicago was a church affiliation. It was hard to argue with my choice—one of the oldest Lutheran churches in the country. In fact, it billed itself as the cradle of the Missouri Synod, the congregation where the first organizational overtures of "walking together" were initiated back in 1847 or so. It was located three miles away at 1301 North LaSalle on the Near North Side, about an hour's walk from my apartment. Dr. James Manz, the pastor, encouraged me to join Gamma Delta, not a fraternity as the name might imply, but a fellowship group for members in their twenties and thirties. Though I was still a teenager, I started to come to their meetings. One evening I met a member named Howard Suhr and asked him if he might be related to Henry Suhr, my one-time teacher in the Big Room in Westgate. I was not surprised when he told me he was his nephew. My fellow Deltans were all single, but well established in their careers and considerably more sophisticated than I, and some of them tolerated this new bumpkin in their midst less well than others. They all had cars, so I frequently found myself packed in with engineers, lawyers, and business operators buzzing about politics, sports or other topics I knew nothing about on our way to a progressive dinner, Black Hawks game, or some other activity I had never experienced before.

Courses at Sherwood were arranged on a traditional semester schedule, with all classes and applied music sessions in the mornings. The academic courses at the University of Chicago downtown facility on East Lake Street were two evenings each week on a more aggressive quarter schedule—twelve weeks of intensive material that a semester would have spread across about eighteen. Afternoons, weekends and evenings without academic classes were unscheduled, allowing time for study, homework and music practice. This also allowed time for a part-time job, but in a woeful miscalculation of BBB's efficiency in procuring one for me, I set off on my own my first afternoon to ply the market. It never occurred to me to pick up a newspaper to bring the market to me, so my greenhorn approach was to trot my wares around town to the market. About the only experience I felt I could offer was the exposure to auto repair I got at Farquhar Motors, but downtown Chicago has very few Chrysler dealerships. Nevertheless, I took off immediately on foot and found a Shell station up on the Near North Side. The manager needed someone who could do tune-ups and asked me how much I wanted. "You can do a tune-up for a dollar an hour?" he asked me incredulously. "You can start next Monday afternoon."

The next day when I checked my mailbox at school, there were two items in it. One was a letter from home, the first of a steady stream of news that arrived every day for about three months, dripping with unwavering parental love. The other was a note from BBB sending me for a job interview at the Chicago Tribune, at 435 N. Michigan Avenue just up the street from the school, about two miles away. I did not know it at the time, but Wallace Grigg, the office manager of the Retail Advertising Department of the Tribune, would change my life forever. Wally needed an "office boy" (a title later changed to "office clerk," a less pejorative alternative to reflect sensitivity to our, well, sensitivities) and wanted to know when I could start. The job paid $1.25 per hour for up to 20 hours per week. Perfect. I told him I could start immediately. I thought about the job at the Shell station, but, even as I pictured that manager wondering why I did not show up, I decided just to forget about it. This reminds me of the Marine recruiter who called a college student to ask whether he had thought about his offer for enlistment. "Oh sure," said the student. "I thought about it, prayed about it, laughed about it, and then forgot about it."

The job was really a shared position—I would be working every afternoon, while my counterpart, who also worked part time, covered the mornings. Bill Morton was a student at a beautician school, which had classes in the late afternoons, and did not leave until about 2:00, so Wally took me back to meet him and get me started right away. Nice looking and immaculately groomed, Bill had been in this position for a couple of years, and now had only a few months to go before graduation. I usually arrived by about 12:30, so we had a couple of hours of overlap for him to show me what the job entailed. When I got back home that evening, Lee was telling me he had also found a job, working as a clerk typist in a government office for two dollars an hour, and it was closer to school than mine. I was envious and tempted to quit my job at the Tribune immediately to seek one over there. Fortunately, I had a guiding hand from the Lord once again and decided to stay where I was. Lee was laid off before Christmas. This actually worked in his favor, however, because he found a job as a church organist, which suited his minor in organ performance.

Wally had an only daughter about a year younger than I and treated me as if I were the son he never had. In fact, he may have had ulterior motives when he invited me to his house one weekend to hear his Artie Shaw and Goose Tatum jazz collections. Wonderful as he was, Wally would never be confused with Clark Gable or Cary Grant, and his unfortunate daughter Susan would have taken top honors in a Wally Grigg look-alike contest. Nevertheless, he was justifiably very proud of her, as she graduated number one in her class and had the highest test scores in all of Cook County, I think, and may have started college at about age 16. Brilliant as she was, she may have also been some form of savant, judging from what seemed to me to be a severe social disability. Conversation was impossible, and the most I could get in response to a question was a grunt, nod or two-word reply.

This job at the Tribune worked out so well, that I had to be careful that I kept my focus on what was supposed to be my primary concern—education. In retrospect, I realize I made a serious mistake. I had not learned the difference between homework and study. Even in high school I should have made this distinction, but I was making good grades without much effort, and it never occurred to me how shallow this approach was to reach the lofty objective to cumulate knowledge. Harmony, counterpoint, and sight reading were mechanical exercises to me, when they should have been opportunities to explore the mother lode instead of the flakes that fell off. Even advanced harmony and keyboard harmony presented themselves to me as mere assignments instead of the rich opportunities for practical application to the real world of transposition, chord progression and modulation they really were. Oh, to have those days back again …. How much more diligently I would have dedicated myself to the *scholarship* of learning.

Maria Hussa, professor of voice and opera, like so many of the staff at Sherwood, had made a name for herself in her youth, but was now in her sunset years passing along her art to students like me. She had sung in the première of Richard Strauss's *Der Rosenkavalier* at the height of her career, but now in her seventies croaked and cracked when she tried to demonstrate vocal technique to me. "No, no, not strident," she would say, "cover that tone, darken it, and change to ah right here where it goes high. Support from the diaphragm. Loosen your jaw until you get that yawning feeling." At the end of the first year of voice lessons with her, she gave me a bit part in her production of *La Boheme* and talked me into studying a second year with her, when I had already decided not to continue. "You are a very musical fellow," she told me in her thick accent, when she tried to extend me for yet a third year. Saying no to Madame Hussa was not easy, but this time I held my ground and told her honestly that I could not fit it into my schedule. She seemed so wounded by this news that it suddenly occurred to me that she might have been paid according to her student load, but this time I remained resolute.

Leon Rosenbloom was a Jewish émigré from Odessa, Russia, who had studied with the great Artur Schnabel, a renowned Bach interpreter. I never found out what happened to Rosenbloom, but he walked with great difficulty. The cane he always carried helped a little, but polio or some kind of injury had left him without the ability to take a normal stride. This did not affect his fingers, however, as he glided effortlessly over the keys of his Steinway. Actually, his studio had two Steinways, side by side, and I can still hear the piercing hiss he would produce as he drew in his breath when I played a wrong note. He would then struggle to his feet, hobble over to my piano, and circle with a thick pencil mark the place on the page where the offending tones originated. Then he would settle falteringly back into his chair and play the passage with me. "No! no! that is like putting a pound of ketchup on a hamburger," he would say in his characteristic Russian roar when a section was too loud, then sing along as he played it lyrically in the proper manner.

The correct fingering of a passage is sometimes crucial to playing it as the composer intended, or even crucial to playing it at all. When I would struggle with a difficult section, Rosenbloom would stop me and play it through flawlessly himself. Then he would laboriously work his way over to my piano to write his fingering on my page with his heavy pencil marks, sometimes trying it out while standing to be sure he had it right. Himself a master of Bach, he assigned me the Prelude and Fugue in C minor from *Das Wohltempierte Klavier* as my first piece to learn, because of its demands for the left hand. When I came back the next week pounding it out with my typical heavy hand, he stopped me and said, "Your playing is like," and then looked out his window overlooking beautiful Grant Park along Michigan Avenue as he trolled through the rich catalog of similes in his mind, "swatting a fly with a hammer. You must not shake your wrist when you play Bach." Then he played ever so delicately, with astonishing speed and clarity, his fingers like precision hinges barely moving as they produced such beauty the instrument seemed to be alive. "You must achieve economy of motion," he would insist, demonstrating the manner in which each finger moved almost imperceptibly as it pressed a key. "Your fingers must be like iron. You will never play it properly with fingers like … uh … spaghetti," he scowled, daubing his hand across the keyboard like a mop to emphasize his point. "Why do you play the accompaniment so loud here? We must hear the melody," and then he would exaggerate my error by pounding the left hand so loud that it completely drowned out the right. And on it went ….

As an education major, I was preparing for any vocal, instrumental, or orchestral program that I might be asked to lead in the public school system. This meant I would need to be familiar with the instruments of each section of a band or string ensemble. My parents had never put me in band, so now the curriculum required a semester devoted to each of them in rapid succession—clarinet, trumpet, flute, percussion, violin. One semester allows just about enough time to figure out which end of the instrument to pick up first and whether the proper method for producing a sound is a scrape, blast, or pucker. Except for David Scherer on the trumpet and Dan Mensing on the French horn, I do not recall any students who majored in a brass or woodwind instrument. Because of the low numbers of such students, Sherwood had an arrangement with the Chicago Symphony Orchestra to provide instruction for them. Because of the difficulty in scheduling with these masters, I sometimes found myself at the school over the summer or in for a rare evening session. An unexpected compliment came my way one semester when the percussion instructor told one of my friends also studying with him that I was the best drummer he had ever taught. He must have had a very limited number of students on his roster or just a run of bad luck on drummers.

For the stringed instruments it was a different matter. Several students were violin majors, and at least one actually decided to go out into the world trying to earn his bread playing the double bass. One of the best in the business was Rudolph Reiners, strings professor and conductor of the school orchestra. Unlike the intense European style of Rosenbloom, Reiners had a more folksy approach. Demonstrating a passage or correcting a posture might be followed by a distorted wink, gentle sock on the arm or exaggerated facial expression. The end of the bow held by the fingers is the frog, and I can still hear his down-home accent elongating the vowel as he called it a frAWWg. Mr. Reiners died halfway through my semester on the violin with him, and he was replaced by a stuffy wad who tried to impress me by playing most of the way through the first movement of Mendelssohn's E Minor Concerto on my first session with him. Besides his bad taste in introducing himself to me that way, even I knew it was a lousy performance. I did not like him.

Reiners was replaced as orchestra conductor by Giulio Favario, truly one of the most brilliant minds and greatest musical geniuses I have ever known. As a pianist of concert caliber on the world stage, he was already on the Sherwood faculty as instructor of Sight Singing 101 in the classroom, professor of choral and orchestral conducting, professor of orchestration, professor of piano, and, ironically, vocal coach. I say ironically, because his vocal quality was terrible—and he seemed not to know it. Because of his rather large frame, Lee Whittington said he had the legs of an elephant and the voice to match. There were snickers every time he tried to demonstrate how a phrase should sound, yet he made no apology, acting as if we had just heard Caruso. A further irony is that he was an assistant conductor of the world-renowned Chicago Lyric Opera. On the piano, however, it was a different matter. These were the days before digital pianos, yet he could not only sight read an orchestral score, with multiple lines of non-C instruments, as a piano reduction, but he could transpose it into any key! Years later when the National Symphony in Washington, D.C. launched a nation-wide search for a conductor after Howard Mitchell died, I submitted Favario's credentials in nomination for the post but was disappointed when no one took me seriously. His only flaw, it seemed to me, was that he had not gone to Europe to be "discovered."

This reminds me of the story about a woman whose son played the violin. A famous conductor lived in her building, and every time she saw him on the elevator, she begged him to hear her son play. After months of rejection, she asked one day if she could at least bring a tape of his playing. In a moment of weakness, the conductor agreed. From the first moment that the recording played, the conductor was visibly captivated by what he was hearing. Such power, such control, such exquisite tone, such perfect technique, such mastery of the instrument, he thought. When the piece concluded, he turned to the woman with tears running down his cheek and asked, "Was that really your *son* playing this?" "Oh no, that was Jascha Heifetz," she replied, "but my son plays just like him."

Perhaps thirty-something, Favario was one of the few professors at the school who was not on the senior circuit. All of us received a notice in our mailboxes one day announcing the death of Blossom Sewell. I did not even know who she was, except for the Matthew Brady photo of her as a young woman featured in the Sherwood course catalog. Mr. Reiners was one of several others —Mr. Wildman, Mr. Erley and Irene Keyser—who were also becoming metaphysically challenged. According to Rosenbloom, the governing body of the school had a soft spot for its aging staff, and provided some kind of position for Irene more out of welfare than an actual need for her talents. Irene's husband Francis, on course for a rendezvous with senility himself, was the professor of freshman harmony. However, with his inch-thick glasses, he could still find covered fifths or octaves in my homework, even when I was quite sure none were there. Poor old Mr. Keyser was in front of the class one day, and when he turned to write on the blackboard, a streamer of toilet paper trailed from the back of his pants, the latest in a long list of his absent-minded foibles.

Somewhat younger than many of their colleagues were the two organ professors, Ralph Sunden and Herbert White, both about middle-aged. Although I never studied organ (and, in retrospect, might wish I had), I had the privilege to be in the classroom with both of them. Sunden was the instructor of counterpoint and advanced counterpoint, teaching us the art of the fugue. He could take a theme at random from a member of the class and improvise a fugue on the spot at the piano. Anyone who does not think that is impressive, please raise your hand.

It was Dr. White who would call me one day in 1986 to inform me that Sherwood was going out of business, closing the doors to its collegiate division and graduate programs forever. In addition to his surprisingly long roster of organ students, White was also the professor of music history, so extensive it covered two semesters. For me, this would turn out to be one of the most comprehensive and interesting courses I ever had. Before music school, I did not know the difference between a symphony and a concerto. Covering the gamut (a term of music origin, by the way) from antiquity to Stravinsky, the course required stylistic recognition, if not composer recognition, if not actual name-that-tune. I had never even seen a violin before, but now I was bathing in classics I had never heard. It was a wonderful revelation. I was discovering that the reason these works remain timeless when popular works do not (and yes, I include such "artists" as the Beatles and Rolling Stones) is the *craft* required to put them together. And the distinction between the performers of such music and those that swallow their microphones screeching themselves hoarse or gyrate around a stage like caged monkeys is the years of *practice* required to develop the technique to attain the rights of performance. Such art is so rich and so profound that no jam session in Nashville, acid trip in Liverpool or shallow gig in Hollywood could possibly put it together in fifteen minutes on a single evening, unless, of course, your name happens to be Mozart.

Composition was taught by one Florence Galijikian, who laid claim to fame with the world première of one of her compositions by the Hollywood Bowl Orchestra back in medieval times. By the time she stood before us as the professor of orchestration and composition, however, she was feeble, shaking, and tottering so close to the edge of the Great Beyond that she could doubtless peer into it just by leaning over a little. In class one day she was demonstrating a constructional technique at the piano and left the final chord unresolved. When I asked her to resolve it, she banged the tonic chord several times and, turning to me, said with a sneer that I would make a good composer, "at least you have the right temperament for it." I know one of us did. At the time I thought my student compositions were fairly good, so when Ray Byniski, the resident graduate student of composition, fulfilled his degree requirements with an orchestral piece performed by the school orchestra at Symphony Hall downtown, I decided to try my hand at writing a symphonic poem that would be performed next year. When I submitted the final draft to Mr. Wildman for approval, however, he enlisted the aid of Mr. Favario to let me down as gently as possible that it was not up to their standards. Today I know they were right.

The professors at the University of Chicago were a congenial bunch that gave the illusion that grades would come easy. Nothing could have prepared me for the extent to which the opposite was true. Unlike the stodgy atmosphere at Sherwood, where the roll was actually called before each class and the air was fastidiously clear of both smoke and foul language, erudition at UC was closer to the climate at Berkeley. "Be broad-minded!" Russell Castor had often exhorted to us in his English class. But I struggled with the culture shock that now enveloped me. Everyone smoked, including the professors, but the air was also blue from the bawdiest of concepts expressed from any direction in the room, including the chair up front. The downtown campus was established for anyone on a full degree program, as well as for those of us from Sherwood, the Fine Arts Conservatory or the Art Institute of Chicago who needed academic credits. English was required for all three quarters of the freshman year, so I signed up for the Tuesday-Thursday session with Mrs. Keranen. My roommate Lee had the Monday-Wednesday session with another professor, but from his account, that class was even worse, with pot passed freely around the room.

Our first writing assignment was simply to describe a process, but she specifically said the length should not exceed 1000 words—about a page and a half. Faced with my familiar problem finding a topic, I rummaged around in my limited bag of experience, but the best I could come up with was something from chemistry class, producing hydrogen gas from hydrochloric acid. When I got the paper back, there was a big D at the top. Surely this cannot be a grade, I thought. I had never received a D on anything in my life, especially in English. Oh, wait a minute, I know, the syllabus has a glossary and list of abbreviations. Yes, here it is, D… Diction. Diction? What does that mean? I decided to ask after class. Excuse me, but I see this D on my paper. Is that supposed to be my grade? Expecting her to say no, there had been some mistake, she confirmed my worst suspicions. "I felt as if I was reading the label on a bottle of pills," she said sarcastically. Apparently, I had taken her admonition on the length a little too literally and counted the words. In a desperate attempt to get it down under 1000 words, I thought it would not matter if I left out articles here and there. When I told her that I was not used to grades like that, she told me that her classes are usually filled with students from the Art Institute, and the only way she can get their attention is to put an F on their papers. The second assignment was a comparison and contrast exercise, so I wrote that from the point of view of a pinsetter, there are four kinds of bowlers—those who approach the line swiftly and deliver the ball with considerable speed and those with the opposites of each of these two characteristics. She liked it so much that she used it as a model for the class, but *still* gave me only a B. I worked my tail off for a C that quarter. Lee got an F and had to take the course again in the summer.

# Edwin, Not Edward

After the first few weeks of school, it became obvious that a friendship was developing between my roommate Lee and another student who attended many of the same classes with us—Ron Lakin, from Greensburg, Pennsylvania. I was increasingly excluded from their company, but I did not have time for the amount of socializing in which they seemed to be engaged anyway. A second-year student named Edwin Bodkin from Kokomo, Indiana, introduced himself to us one day and set himself up as a kind of "big brother," offering various tidbits of advice and filling us in on all sorts of gossip about the school. Ed had an efficiency apartment at the Ramada just a few blocks south of the school on Michigan Avenue and invited Lee and me over occasionally for meals, much more easily prepared in his kitchenette than we could do on the hot plate in our apartment. Steak, mashed potatoes, and steamed vegetables was certainly an improvement over tomato soup and grilled cheese.

One evening when Lee and Ron had gone out together, I was in the apartment alone and decided to go for a walk. I found myself near Ed's place and decided to knock on his door. He seemed a little embarrassed to see me and opened the door only a crack. When I peered through this crack, I saw the reason why. Here were Lee and Ron sitting at his table having supper with him. Then *they* were embarrassed. I had not intentionally tracked them down and honestly did not realize they were there, but they were convinced that I had figured out where they had gone and decided to follow them. Such was not the case.

Ed seemed to me only slightly effeminate, yet behind his back Lee and Ron started calling him Edwinna. Also, mixed into their scatological humor were occasional jabs at each other about whose turn it was to be the girl tonight. I passed this off as idle locker room jawing, but little by little I was beginning to understand something a naïve kid from Iowa knew nothing about—homosexuality. When someone explained it to me in graphic terms one day, I thought it was a joke. Surely no one in his right mind would want to touch another male's, uh, you know, or allow another male to put his, uh, you know, in your, uh, you know, or in your, uh, you know, right? Eeeewww. It made me gag when I realized it was for real. Suddenly, many things became clear. I never really understood why Sodom and Gomorrah were destroyed, and I always thought the death sentence in Leviticus was an empty and unnecessary threat, and the admonitions of Paul in Romans, Corinthians and Timothy must be referring to generic abominations, not specific behaviors. I had heard terms in high school like "cornhole" or "queer," but never understood what they meant. Yuck. Although I never had any concrete evidence about what might be going on between Lee and Ron or whether it also involved Ed, I did have suspicions. Then one day I was actually attacked—not by them but by someone else I mentioned earlier.

When Christmas break was approaching, my boss Wally at the Tribune asked me whether I was planning to get home for the holidays. I had not seen my parents for a few months but told him that without a car I was not sure how I could get to a tiny town in Iowa and back in only one week. He made some phone calls on my behalf and found that one of his neighbors was planning to drive to Charles City, Iowa for the holidays and made arrangements for me to ride with them if I wanted. Since that was nearly two-thirds of the distance home, my parents could meet me there without the need for a trip all the way to Chicago to pick me up. When my co-worker Bill Morton overheard the plan, he told Wally that his place on the Near North Side was much closer to Lincolnwood, the suburb where the travelers would be starting out, than where I lived, so I could stay the night with him before they picked me up in the morning. Perfect. I was nearly asleep in his apartment that night, when I found out his offer to stay with him had nothing to do with travel assistance. Before I really understood what was happening, Bill jumped on top of me with his hand in private territory. Confused and half asleep, I was not sure what he was going to do next. However, just as I was considering whether an attempt to fight him off might enrage him, he was realizing that his gambit was not producing the response from me that he somehow expected and with a sigh decided to slither ignominiously back under his rock.

When I got home, I was just in time to help load a moving van. My parents were moving to South St. Paul, Minnesota, later to be renamed Inver Grove Heights. Several considerations precipitated their decision to leave Sutherland. For many years my father's siblings had been telling him that he should leave Smallville in Hickstate for the big city, where incomes were more commensurate with his expertise. But he had resisted, firm in his determination to be an entrepreneur one day. Now that he had one in college, however, and faced with the simultaneous expenses of two at once when Ralph started soon, he could no longer wait for such an opportunity to develop.

The catalyst was an incident at Brookfield Chevrolet. One of his regular customers was a trucker who entreated my father one day to service some equipment in order to meet a tight deadline. This meant some long hours and even a rare Sunday workday for him, but he finished the project and enabled the customer to conduct his business on time. Several weeks later the same trucker asked again whether my father could work late to finish up a repair so that he could leave with his truck early the next morning. When my father declined, the customer asked him whether the handsome gratuity he left with Beryl for him the first time had not been enough. After my father told him he never received any such gratuity, the customer was furious. He stormed into the office for an explanation, whereupon Beryl simply explained that Elmer did not work a nine-to-five office job, and he was not entitled to a bonus unless the boss decided he should have it. Within the space of about five minutes, Beryl had just lost a good customer *and* his only mechanic. My father was applying for a job at Champion Chevrolet in St. Paul the next day.

When my parents drove me back to Chicago at the end of the Christmas break, I insisted that somehow we must load my bicycle. Uncle John was fond of telling his joke about the Native American who saw his first bicycle. "Red man walk. White man lazy. He sit down to walk." For me, it was not a question of laziness, but expediency. Because of the short distance from my apartment, I could easily walk to school each morning and was never late. But the walk to the Tribune each day was about a half hour, and I needed to allow an hour each way for church on Sunday. The bicycle extended my travel range exponentially and was a wonderful time saver, but it turned out to be a mixed blessing. A kid who just fell down from an Iowa sky in yesterday's rain does not think in terms of vandalism or theft in the city. The first day that I rode the bike to work, I did have enough sense to know I could not just lean it up against the majestic Tribune Tower along the Magnificent Mile of Chicago. But I did not have enough sense to chain it to the railing I found on the lower level below Michigan Avenue. When I came back to pick it up, I was fortunate to find the bike still there, but I noticed immediately that the canvas tool pouch I kept behind the seat with all my wrenches and pliers was stolen. I can still remember my fury. If only I had caught him in the act, I kept thinking, I would have ….

I went immediately to Sears to buy a length of chain and a padlock, but the next day, the cover off the light I had mounted on the handle bar was ripped off and the batteries stolen. Again, I was hopping mad. Come on, now, who would want to steal a kid's batteries from his bicycle, went the refrain inside my head. A few days later, when I had the bike tied to a signpost in front of the Sherwood building, I returned to find that someone had clamped another padlock on top of my padlock. Not sure what that was supposed to accomplish, I simply unlocked mine and the whole apparatus came loose. My glee over foiling this miscreant and having just acquired an extra padlock, albeit without the key, turned to fury again the next day when the perpetrator got his revenge by slashing both tires.

Another trip to Sears got me back on two wheels again, but this time I decided to park the bike in the alley behind the Sherwood building. When I returned, I found a note on it saying that the iron bars of the window to which I had chained it belonged to the furniture store next to Sherwood, and that if they found the bike there again, it would be confiscated. For several weeks I was able to chain up to the light pole on the front side along Michigan Avenue again without incident, but one day I came out to find both tires flat—not slashed this time, just the irrepressible urge of some fartblossom to hear hissing. The next day, not wishing to extend misfortune to two days in a row, I had only one class and decided to take a chance on parking it in the alley again. Surely no one would discover it in less than two hours. I was wrong. The bad news was the bike was gone. The worse news was that I knew where it was. Hat in hand, I went into the store, apologized profusely to the kindly manager, who led me to the storage room in the back where he happened to have a bike that looked remarkably like mine.

Instead of walking for an hour to church each Sunday, I was now able to ride in about fifteen minutes, although on rainy days I arrived with the legs of my pants speckled with mud. One day after the service, I discovered that God had answered my prayers with a wry sense of humor. I found the frame of the bike still chained to the signpost where I had left it, but both wheels were stolen. This time Sears could not help me, so I made the acquaintance of one Frank Sykes. "Sykes for your bikes" was the slogan he advertised in the yellow pages for his bicycle shop way out on Chicago Avenue on the northwest side. Over the next couple of years I would visit Frank quite often, and gradually so many parts were replaced that it no longer resembled that shiny red two-wheeler I had bought from George Steinbronn years before. Frank became one of my good friends, but I doubt that he ever charged me full price for any repair I needed, and he usually dispensed a good deal of advice that was already built into the cost. Oh, and I also learned to use a chain long enough to secure the frame and both *wheels* to the post.

I came to depend so much upon my bike that eventually I decided I really needed two, each serving as a backup for the other. When I heard one day about a bicycle auction conducted by the police, I rode way down near the South Side to attend. I was the successful bidder on a nearly new single-speed bicycle for fifteen dollars, but now I came foursquare against a thorny problem I had rehearsed in my mind all the way to the auction—how to ride two bicycles home at once. The answer was to ride one, using one hand on the handle bar, and guide the other, using the other hand on its handle bar. It is a technique I have used many times since, to give a helping hand to a little kid learning to ride, to escort a bike with a flat tire to the gas station for air, and so on. With a little practice you could do it too.

Problems I had with the bike were not limited to the bike. There was always the possibility of injury, especially when I tempted fate. During rush hour, when cars were backed up for blocks, I could make time almost as fast as when the streets were wide open by weaving my way through the traffic *between* the lanes. As I did this, I lived in continual fear that some day someone in the parking lane next to the curb would open a driver-side door as I came flying past. Can you see where this is going? Yes, one day as I tore pell-mell past the Conrad Hilton on Michigan Avenue, a cabby at the curb decided to help his fare with luggage and opened his door at exactly the perfect moment. I slammed into it at full speed, sailed over the top and landed on my *feet* on the other side. My shoe came off in this debut performance with the Cirque du Soleil, but aside from that, I was absolutely unhurt. Fearing the driver would have me arrested or worse, I retrieved my shoe, hobbling on one foot as I quickly slipped it on, and left him standing there agape as I picked up my bike and darted off again. A block or so away, I stopped long enough to thank God for the overtime he was paying my guardian angel.

Although my bicycle did not have a roof, windshield or heater, it was an all-weather vehicle, and I recall one day when Chicago got about a foot of snow. As I pedaled along in one of the tracks made by the traffic, a cab came up behind me. Ordinarily, I would pull over as far to the right as I could to allow vehicles to pass. In this case, however, I had no place to go and tried to keep up the pace as best I could. When we got to the Clark Street bridge, the cabby got impatient and started honking his horn because he had no place to pass. I should have dismounted, lifted the bike out of the way and stood in the deep snow to let him proceed. Instead, I stubbornly tried to reach the end of the bridge where the road widened. He could not wait. Coming up hard on my left, he struck me with his fender, intentionally knocking me off into the rough, and, for good measure, spun his wheels to splatter salty slush in my face as he roared past. This time God heard me say something different.

Racing to work one day, I took a corner too fast, slipped on a patch of ice and took a spill. Fortunately, there was no oncoming traffic at the moment, and I was again thankful I had survived unhurt. However, when I got to the office, I could not get the throbbing in my right thumb to subside. Wally noticed I was favoring it and told me to go over to the emergency room of a small hospital a few blocks away for an x-ray. Since I paid for the expenses in cash before I left, I was confused by a bill I received in the mail a few weeks later. The attending physician wanted eight dollars. Surely this was a mistake, I thought, and ignored it. Again and again the bill came, now past due, now way past due, now turned over to a collection agency, but I stubbornly refused to pay what I considered already paid. Many years later, I now realize this is common practice. Hospital charges do not necessarily include the services of doctors, but at the time I believed that if I owed anything, they should have told me when I was paying my bill. Ironically, this doctor has no idea he got his revenge. The break in the bone was set badly (or not at all), and I have an oddly crooked thumb from it to this day.

Having never seen a concert pianist perform with a splint on his thumb, Leon Rosenbloom suggested I take a few weeks off when I showed up for my lesson wearing a splint. However, at my elementary level I could still continue with the violin, since the technique which needed the most work involved the left hand anyway. When my injury healed, and I returned to the keyboard, I noticed immediately that I played better than I ever had before, and, better yet, Rosenbloom noticed it too. I had accidentally discovered a phenomenon I have seen a number of times since in my own students. I suppose the education literature has an elaborate scientific explanation and a name for it, but I call it the percolation effect. Learning seems to require a certain period of time for the mind to lie fallow, while it steeps in the material that has been presented to it. When my students ask me today what is the optimum time between lessons, I always take this observation into account and recommend no more frequently than two or three times per week.

Soon after I returned from Christmas break, my roommate Lee informed me that he was moving in with Ron Lakin. I was not surprised. They took in a stray kitten and frequently entertained the class before the professor arrived with tales of their own undomesticated life, which included the antics of this hapless feline, until it "fell" out of their sixth-floor window one day and was never seen again. When Lee left, I was now responsible for paying for the apartment by myself, but fortunately, that worked out okay. My parents were greatly pleased that the money I earned at the Tribune was enough to cover my rent and all my expenses, so they gladly paid the monthly bill for the tuition. Eventually I was even able to send a regular amount home for deposit in my passbook account. When I out found years later that as my balance mounted up, they, as joint custodians, had borrowed (yes, *borrowed*, not stole) liberally from it a number of times, I was not sure whether to be flattered or upset.

Before the school year was out, Ed Bodkin persuaded Lee and Ron to leave the 830 for the somewhat more upscale apartments of the Ramada, where he lived. When they pointed out some of the advantages they had, including a more modern facility, laundry machines in the building, kitchenette and cupboards, I applied for residency over there too. There were only a couple of months left before the end of the school year, and the difference in monthly rent was not that great, especially moving from the double room that Lee and I had to a single efficiency. As a courtesy, I decided to stop by the office of the 830 to tell old Miss Golden, the resident manager, that I had enjoyed my room and that my decision to move was not owing to any dissatisfaction with her. Expecting her to express some kind words about how nice it was that I could be there for a while or polite sentiments to this effect, I was knocked off my feet when she launched into a tirade about how "ungrateful all you boys are for everything I do to provide a good place for you to stay and then you just leave." I had not told her where I was going, yet after she extended a few more of her pleasantries, she ended with something about "well, if you think the Ramada is such a great place, just get out, *get out*." With a resounding endorsement like that, how could I refuse?

As spring approached, a letter reached me from Venita Rich, the talent scout from the Ted Mack show, giving me particulars on my upcoming audition in New York. First, they wanted a tape of my performance to be mailed within a few days. Somehow I managed to borrow a reel-to-reel recorder and tried to find a practice studio that was soundproof enough that the judges would not take my rendition of Mendelssohn for Charles Ives. When I tried to run through the piece, however, I found I could no longer play it. Rosenbloom had been reworking my technique throughout the year, and the methods I once used were of little effect. It was as though a cathedral was closed for renovation, and while it lay in disrepair with construction materials littering the landscape all over, a wedding was supposed to take place. The tape I submitted was a patchwork of starting, stopping and retaping sections of the piece countless times. The timing of this audition was coming at a most awkward moment for me.

If I ever expected to start out in show business getting chauffeured around in a limousine, I was about to find out otherwise. My instructions from Venita said I could find my own way to New York or, if I wanted to join her on a chartered tour bus, the closest they would be coming to Chicago was the Indiana Turnpike. They would pick me up at the George Ade rest area near Hammond sometime between the hours of three and midnight if I wanted to ride along. Transporting a suitcase that far on my bicycle was out of the question, but I found that the Illinois Central had a stop at Hammond. Assuming I might be able to see from there where I needed to go, but giving no real thought as to how I would get to the turnpike, I stepped off the train about midday. Across the street from the Hammond station was a truck stop, so I approached a driver to ask whether he had ever heard of the George Ade service area. By the grace of God, he not only knew what I was talking about, but was going in that direction. When we rode along for at least an hour in his rig, I began to wonder if he were in fact an angel sent from heaven to protect poor dumb creatures like me in time of need.

As I waited and watched out the window at the service area for several hours, the thought suddenly occurred to me that this might all be a big hoax, but eventually a bus bound for New York lumbered into view. I had never met Venita Rich, but when the door to the bus opened, a sixtyish lady sporting an outlandish hat and wearing lipstick and make-up about an inch thick stepped off and introduced herself. Aboard the bus was every conceivable talent from the entertainment world—singers, instrumentalists, baton twirlers, tap dancers, and prestidigitators. When I later saw them rehearse, I could scarcely believe they were only amateurs, especially one saxophone player whose jazz rendition lifted the scruffy hairs on my neck some. Typical for show tours, no overnight stays were planned. If you need sleep, you better get it on the bus or however and whenever you can. Our first stop was Washington, D.C. for a ride to the top of the Monument and a quick circuit around the A list of tourist attractions, then it was on to the Big Apple. This time we each had a hotel room on 47th Street in Midtown. It was my first time in New York, so I walked all over Downtown the first day—the short distance over to Times Square, the long distance down to the Brooklyn Bridge, along fashionable Fifth Avenue and over to the Empire State Building for a ride to the top. I had heard about the automat, a much ballyhooed innovative way to dispense food, so I dropped my coins into it for an outrageously priced sandwich. And I still have the souvenir deck of cards I bought from one of the tourist traps on Broadway. The audition itself was anticlimax. I was ushered into a large studio where Venita was sitting with the producer and several of the executives, but from the way she was glaring at me, I could only assume she had just listened to my harlequin tape. About fifteen seconds into my audition, they stopped me, said that was very nice, and promptly sent me home. No one had to convince me that show business was not for me.

The following incident is not meant to be an ethnic slur, but it does require an appreciation of a time in America when such dialect was perhaps more common. When I saw the words Empire State engraved on the building in New York, I was reminded of the story my father told about his uncle Erwin's first visit to Detroit. He was trying to find the Penobscot Building, and, without noticing he was standing next to it, asked the doorman for directions. The man said, "Penobscot Buildin'! What you see in all dem lights? What you see graben on all dem windas? What you see smeeeeahd all ova ma clothes? And you aks me whea da Penobscot Buildin'?" Ethnicity itself was the focus of another well-worn story that circulated through the Swedish communities in Minnesota. A man sitting at the bar says to the bartender, "So there were these three Swedes named Sven, Lars and Ole ...." "Wait, wait," interrupts the bartender, pointing to the sign on the wall behind him reading "No Ethnic Jokes." The patron looks around the establishment and calls out, "Are there any cave men in the room?" Hearing no answer, he continues, "Okay, so there were these three cave men named Sven, Lars and Ole ...."

Before I quite realized what happened, my first whirlwind year at Sherwood came to an end, and I was headed home to Inver Grove Heights for the summer. Wally had someone full time for the summer at the Tribune who could handle my duties in my absence, but he promised to hold my job for me when I returned in the fall. This reminds me of the college student who returned home to the farm after his first year at college. When he came down to breakfast in the morning, he saw that there was one egg left on the platter and told his father at the table that he could prove existentially there were actually *two* eggs on the plate. Having studied mathematics and philosophy both semesters, he started scribbling a formula on a napkin and continued on several more before finally declaring, "So therefore, as you see, there *are* two eggs. "Well," said his father, "I'll take this one. You can have the other one." Another story concerns a student home from school visiting his grandmother. When he told her he was studying finance at school, she asked him whether he understood the stock market. "Of course," the grandson replied, and then spent the next ten minutes explaining the law of supply and demand, local economics, macroeconomics, and business theory. "Yep," said the grandmother when he finally stopped talking, "I don't understand it either."

My father had the idea that I might find a job working for the railroad over the summer, but when I went for the mandatory physical exam, the doctor said, "You do realize I will have to fail you because of your vision, don't you?" I do not remember what the job entailed, but it must have required perfect 20/20 vision. Our house did not have a garage, so my father started construction on one that summer, a detached building, heated and big enough for two cars and enough space for additional storage. One day my brother Don, who sprang up tall and sturdy from Bender genes, started up the ladder to help with the roofing. As he stepped onto the roof, he made the mistake of putting his weight on the rung of the ladder above the roofline. Without warning, this leveraged the base of the ladder away from the building, and he came crashing to the ground on top of it. Seeing him lying there unconscious, my father jumped down immediately and called for an ambulance. While waiting, he desperately tried to bring Don around, screaming for him to "Breathe! Breathe! *Breathe*!, but when his entreaties and efforts for revival seemed futile, he feared we had lost him. Once the paramedics arrived, however, they went to work with their equipment and eventually revived him. Don was revisited by his guardian angels some time later when a car suddenly turned in front of him as he tore along on his motorcycle. After broadsiding the vehicle, he sailed over it and landed on the street, sustaining only minor injuries.

One of my father's favorite jokes about motorcycles concerns the fellow who asks his friend to hop onto the seat behind him to go for a ride. As they roared down a country road at top speed, the passenger complained about the cold air rushing down his neck and insisted that they pull over to rest. "Just turn your jacket around so the collar keeps the wind out," the driver told him, as they sped off again. A short time later the bikers lost control and slammed into a tree. When police arrived, they asked the motorist who was first on the scene to describe what he saw. "Well, I could see that the first one was killed outright," said the farmer who had stopped to render assistance, "and by the time I got this one's head turned around where it should have been, he was dead too."

This brings to mind also the sawmill employee who had an accident one day at the plant and severed his arm. His co-workers quickly wrapped the arm in a plastic bag and transported the victim to the emergency room. When they visited him the next day, they were astonished to find that the doctor had such remarkable skill that their friend was already playing his guitar. A few weeks later, the same worker was back at work standing on a log that was being processed and severed his leg as

90

he slipped into the blade. Again the other employees threw the limb into a bag and rushed him to the hospital. The next day they found that through the miracle of modern medical techniques, the doctor already had their friend in rehab, playing tennis. Back on the job again, the same worker was leaning too close to the blade one day and this time severed his head. Yet again his friends carefully placed the dismembered head into a plastic bag and raced to the doctor. When they went back the next day to check on him, they were unable to locate him anywhere in the facility. Tracking down the doctor, they demanded to know what happened. "Well, I might have been able to save him if you hadn't wrapped his head in plastic," said the surgeon, "but by the time I got to him, he had already suffocated."

At the peril of taxing your patience to the limit, I beg your indulgence to pass along one more—this time a "dumb blond" story. The witless blond this time is a mortician listening to instructions for a man who has died wearing a black suit. "He *loved* this suit," says the widow, "but I will pay any price if you can find a blue one just like it." The next day the deceased wore a blue suit as his body lay there at the private viewing for the family. "It is just perfect," said the widow, "how much do I owe you for your effort?" "Oh, there is no charge," said the mortician. "You see, I was very fortunate that we were handling the remains of another man who was brought in wearing this identical blue suit. When I asked his widow whether she minded if her husband wore a black suit instead of blue, she said it made no difference. So I just swapped their heads around."

I know, I promised that would be the last one, but I must tell you about the blind man who walked into a bar one day and asked the bartender if he would mind hearing a blond joke. "Well, I know you can't see me," said the bartender, "but I am blond and I might be offended. Standing next to you is a blond guy who stands about six two and weighs two hundred forty pounds. On the other side of you is another blond guy who stands six five and tips the scales at about two eighty. Now, do you still want to tell your blond joke?" "Well, not if I have to explain it three times," calls the blind man over his shoulder as he walks out.

One of the objectives of the move to the Twin Cities was to be near Concordia College, a seminary prep school in St. Paul, where my parents enrolled my brother Ralph to finish high school. Ralph had other ideas, however, and left Concordia for Simley, the public high school closer to home. After graduation, Ralph developed an interest in electronics and decided to enroll in MIT—not the Massachusetts one, the Minnesota one. He was also interested in the psychology of the human mind, and proved to be an excellent teacher. Little brother Rodney was reading at age two largely because of the time Ralph spent with him. Whenever I came home for a visit, I could not wait to see what new knowledge might come spouting out of this pint-size package. I can still hear a squeaky little voice telling me that August thooootieth was his birthday and that "Oooobee" (Erbe) was the governor. In those days it was still possible to order exotic pets by mail, and when I saw an ad for a Rhesus monkey, I thought Ralph would have fun teaching it all sorts of tricks. The monkey proved too smart for its captors, and, alas, for its own good. It figured out how to escape into the yard one day. When my father came home and followed the trail leading from the empty cage, he found the monkey hanging from the neighbor's picket fence, strangled by its own leash.

Two doors away from our house was a Shell station run by one Don Engel, who became good friends with my father, especially when he needed free advice diagnosing a car problem or assistance with a repair. One day Engel knocked on our door, told me his hired man had just quit and asked me if

I would like to work for him, changing oil, pumping gas and working on cars in his shop. I soon found out he was something of a skinflint, electing to use the coin-operated pay phone in the waiting room instead of the pay-per-call phone in his office. When he left for home each afternoon, I was by myself until closing time around 10:00, so if I needed to reach him, I was supposed to take a dime from the cash register, dial his number, let it ring once and then hang up. This would be a signal for him to call back from his phone at home. For several weeks I never had the need to call him, until one day when a customer pulled up and asked for two dollars' worth of gas. However, while I had my mind on checking his oil and cleaning the windshield, the pump had run to four dollars before I leapt over to shut it off. The customer was not upset but said he had only two dollars with him. No problem, he added, he lived nearby and would return with the balance. When he had not returned two hours later, I decided to call Don. In my concern for the problem, I momentarily forgot the system he had so anally rehearsed with me, and Don picked up on the second ring. He drove right over and ranted for fifteen minutes about my irresponsibility, but he seemed more upset by the dime he lost on that phone call. I fully expected him to deduct two dollars (no, wait, two dollars and ten cents) from my next check, but he told me that from my description of the car and the driver, he had an idea who it was and would talk to him about it. I was beginning to understand why his previous employee had quit.

One day when Engel's daughter Connie stopped in at the station, I could not help admiring her good looks and asked whether she was an Engel. Yes, the owner's daughter, she said. But, are you an *Engel*, I asked again. When she stared at me as if I had just escaped from St. Elizabeth's, I explained that "Engel" means "angel" in German. Then she laughed, and we exchanged a few quips before she left. When she returned to the station later in the summer again with her family to watch a solar eclipse in progress using the welding goggles in the shop, I decided to ask her out. Aware that she was already dating someone, I expected her to decline, but she agreed. The Elizabeth Taylor blockbuster movie *Cleopatra* had just been released, but as there was no chemistry in either the movie or the date, both bombed together. Her younger brother Eric had been hanging around the station quite a bit, and apparently I fed him too many of the little factoids I was fond of spouting. It did not help my relationship with Connie when he told her I was a know-it-all. Later I wondered if maybe a kid his age meant that as a compliment. Anyway, she went back to her old boy friend, and with that, the last summer I ever lived at home was over.

# The Windy City

So called not because of the breezes off Lake Michigan, but according to political pundits, because of the long-windedness of office-seekers. Nevertheless, I can attest that every winter the icy wind seemed to be against me, regardless which direction I walked, even when I turned a corner. When I returned to Chicago, I checked back into the Ramada where I had finished the year before. My parents had made the eight-hour drive loaded with my things, but were apparently as unprepared for crime in the big city as I. As we were moving in, no one was watching the car, and when I went back out for another load, I found that my new suit and most of my shirts were stolen. After my parents left for home, I started to feel sick. At first I thought it was just a touch of homesickness, and I craved a piece of the watermelon they left with me. When that did not seem to improve my condition, I concluded that I was more upset by the theft than I first thought, so I tried another piece of that melon. Soon I was retching but somehow thought another piece of melon might make me feel better and… oh, no, guess not, as I ran for the bathroom instead. Soon it all came up, and I suddenly felt much better. From that day on I can no longer tolerate watermelon.

When I checked in at Sherwood, BBB approached me to ask whether she could assign an incoming freshman to me as a roommate. Gary Bird, from Coral Gables, Florida, was the life of the party, always making wisecracks and finding humor in everything. "What's that string hanging from your sleeve?" he would say, "Oh, sorry, that's your arm." "How come you are wearing your skis in here? Oh, those are your feet, excuse me." Not sure whether he was unhappy with the school, flunked out, ran out of money, found himself too far away from palm trees or exactly what caused him to leave, but Gary only stayed one semester and returned rather abruptly to Florida to attend one of the state schools closer to home. Polaroid cameras were beginning to appear on the market about this time, and Gary had one of the original models. He needed cash one day and offered to sell the camera to me for fifteen dollars. Perhaps that says something about his sense of value and might offer a clue that his parents were summoning him home, but I still have what might be a collector's item rusting away somewhere in the basement. After Gary left, an opera major named Bill Schlichter, who strangely enough was left with only one vocal chord after throat surgery, and a piano major named Gene Montgomery, were rooming together in a two-bedroom apartment in the Ramada and asked me if I wanted to join them to save us all some rent. One of my other options had been to move in with Tim Stout from Bakersfield, who transferred in from San Jose State that year. He was actually training for the Olympics as a race walker, and when I saw him working on his technique one day along Michigan Avenue, it reminded me of a ninety-year-old pretending to jog. Everyone always thought Tim was an oddball and a bit flamboyant, but I tried not to assume it was because he was from California.

When I resumed my job at the Tribune, I was welcomed back like a long lost relative. Wally had good news. This year I would start at $1.50 an hour, and there was no limit on the number of hours I worked, although that was practically moot while I had classes. Everyone was so kind to me that I felt like a legend. Super sweet, soft-spoken Dorothy Peoplau, secretary to Mr. Nightingale, said she had noticed on my application that I had mentioned the Walther League and told me she had once been a member too. Elderly Mr. Nightingale, manager of the entire Retail Advertising Department, frequently had me pedal as quickly down the street to his pharmacy as possible for one of the many medications he needed. He knew I could get through traffic faster on my bike than he could take a taxi. Then he would have a little tip in his hand when I returned. Wally frequently, too frequently, sent me down to the cigar store to pick up a pack of Carletons for him too. But no tip. Cigar-chomping Art Levy managed the advertising account of Brooks Brothers, one of the leading haberdashers in Chicago, and when he heard that my suit had been stolen, arranged with the manager and his tailor to outfit me with a new suit at cost.

Much of my work was in the file room, where we maintained one copy of each edition of the paper in huge books for two or three years. Because these books were intended for reference only, Bill Morton would be furious to discover that some salesman had clipped an ad that had run for his client. He would put on war paint, find out what ad had been on that page, track down the salesman responsible for the infraction, and fire darts into his soul. After Bill graduated and left, I approached Wally one day with an idea. I had noticed that most of such needs of the salesmen were from the preceding ninety days or so. Suppose that in addition to the permanent files, I suggested, I made room for some shelving that would allow me to keep twenty or thirty copies of each edition going back six months as a clip file. These could be used for them to tear out whatever they wanted. Wally liked the idea and ordered the Maintenance Department to build painted wood shelving to the specifications I gave them. The salesmen loved their new trove, and it dissipated the adversarial atmosphere that had pervaded the air and gave my wary eye a rest whenever anyone looked through our file books.

I was tearing out newspaper sheets for the salesmen one day, when my eye fell on a little ad for contact lenses. A company called Vent-Air was featuring a new style lens shaped to allow air to circulate behind the inner surface. I had never heard of such an invention before, but I was drawn to their claims that I could get rid of my glasses. I would be less than forthright if I did not admit that vanity was also a factor in my decision to give them a try. When I made my first appointment, they were describing the process of touching the lens to my cornea, and I was not sure this was something I could do. Could I overcome my squeamishness and actually touch my eye like that? The technology today has progressed far beyond what it was then. There were no soft, continual wear lenses that are in common use now, and certainly none that could be worn while sleeping. These were hard lenses that required scrupulous cleaning, maximum uninterrupted wear of only six to eight hours and soaking in a special solution, changed frequently, when not in use.

Wearers today may not be able to sympathize, but for me the expense was a major consideration—not just the initial examination, but the mandatory follow-ups, and each change of prescription involved lab work for new lenses all over again. At least three times I lost one down the drain, until I learned, first, to stay away from the sink, and second, to pay for the insurance I foolishly rejected initially because I thought it was an unnecessary expense. There were also the endless bottles of solution and eyedrops, but beyond the cost was the discomfort. My eyes became ultrasensitive to any light—to the point that if I walked outside without sunglasses, I was unable even to squint without actual pain. Indoors it was impossible to turn my eyes upward in any kind of light without discomfort and tears running down my cheeks. Worst of all was the inability to switch back and forth between the lenses and ordinary glasses. After six hours my eyes were so fatigued that the lenses had to come out, and just as my eyes screamed for relief, the lenses sometimes stubbornly refused to pop out. But then for the next hour or so everything was a blur until my eyes adjusted to glasses again. After giving them a try for about ten years, I had so many problems, that I finally threw them in a drawer one day and never used them again.

The secretaries at the Tribune were such fun to tease, especially Betsy Rogers, who had recently wed one of the salesmen I worked with every day. When Hurricane Betsy came roaring into the Gulf one year, I could not resist clipping out headlines about Betsy's path of destruction, Betsy's fury, Betsy's trail of debris and leaving them on her desk. She knew full well who had done this and would just stand there with her hands on her hips and a mock glower on her face when I rushed past. One of my dearest friends was Dorothy Kelly, perhaps in her sixties, but the chain of cigarettes she lit up advanced her face well into the seventies. Dorothy and her assistant, Carol Bahret, were the two accountants in the office until Carol left for maternity at age 48, when Dorothy took over those duties by herself. The two of them approached me one day to ask whether I would take five dollars a week to clean up the ten-gallon coffee pot before I left each afternoon. Besides being freed from the drudgery of cleaning it, they both had to catch their train about 3:00 but wanted to make the coffee available to the office until 5:00 or so. Every once in a while I would push my schedule to the limit and forget to clean the pot, especially on Fridays. The next day when I arrived, Dorothy would walk up to me holding her nose and telling me about the brown fuzz she had to clean out of it herself. Then she would walk away with her characteristic giggle.

If I worked late enough, I would encounter the cleaning staff that arrived after hours, and eventually I came to know the attractive middle-aged mother named Catherine assigned to the fifth floor. I was amused by the banter in Polish between her and her co-workers, especially when one of them would call "Basta!" from the elevator down the hallway, and then they would all laugh. In Spanish it would mean "enough," but I had no idea what was so funny about it in Polish. Gentle and kind, Catherine treated me like one of her own sons and proudly introduced me in broken English to her fellow workers one time as "nice boy, work hard." One day Catherine saw me on the elevator and grimly said, "Big boss die." It was Mr. Nightingale.

Retail Advertising handled the advertising accounts of Chicago-based businesses, while the accounts of national franchises, such as Chevrolet or McDonald's, were the domain of General Advertising. My counterpart upstairs in General was an opinionated old goat named Bill Worchol. I never found out what happened to him, but he had a withered hand, and I often marveled at his ability to stand on a ladder and pull huge books of newsprint files from the shelves above. Bill functioned as a kind of resident historian and institutional memory of the Tribune as he approached retirement, so every time I had to run up there to conduct business with him, it was important to allow enough time to listen to whatever story was on his play list for that day. Most of it was trivia, but usually entertaining, if not edifying. One day he was laughing so hard telling me about an incident from his high school days that he could hardly get his story out. It seems he and several of his friends were driving down a country road in Texas or Louisiana, I forget where exactly, when they saw a guy running toward them with a watermelon under each arm. Running some distance behind him was the farmer, brandishing a shotgun, from whom he had stolen them. Bill and his friends stopped their car, rolled down the window and told the man, "Quick, throw those melons in here with us, and you'll be able to run a lot faster." When he did so, they drove off, found a quiet place to park, and reveled in their cleverness on a feast of free watermelon. This reminds me of the story Garrison Keillor of *Prairie Home Companion* fame tells about the time when he and some friends crossed the state line into Iowa and saw a fellow walking along the road with only one shoe. When they stopped, rolled down the window and asked whether he had lost a shoe, he replied, "Nope, found one."

A college kid is always alert for funds, so Wally asked me one day if I had time on the weekend to pick up a little extra money. John Haberkorn, his counterpart in the Classified Advertising Division, needed help getting the huge classified section ready for the Sunday paper. Today much of the work we did would be handled by computers, but IBM stock must have been only about two dollars a share in those days. Ad takers typed up manuscript copy throughout the week, but after the 6:00 deadline on Friday, all of this copy needed to be manually sorted into the classification categories established by the Tribune. Some classifications, such as real estate, cars for sale, and business opportunities, needed to be further sorted alphabetically within each category. When this phase of the operation was completed late in the evening, we could go home while the stacks of copy were sent to linotype operators, who worked through the night setting the ads into lead type. By early the next morning some of us were back on the job reading through the proofs, comparing point sizes set by the typesetter to the specification on the copy, then re-sorting all the copy by remitter name for billing.

If you can picture the insufferable John McLaughlin from the syndicated McLaughlin Group discussion panel program, you will have the exact image of John Haberkorn, including the orange horn-rim glasses and three-piece suit he wore. Haberkorn would allow the buzz from the sea of perhaps thirty or so middle-aged adolescents in the room that were supposed to be proofreading to reach a certain crescendo before he rapped his pencil on his desk and ordered them back to work. Arguably the worst offender was Andy Corsini, king of the one-liner, who kept everyone chuckling and buckling with the continuous patter of his monologue. King of repartee, however, was a guy named Stewart, who had just returned from a stint in the Army. The object of the game Andy and Stew played was the comeback, and they kept the office entertained with their witty badminton hour after hour. However, there was absolutely no sound in the room one time after a five hundred dollar adding machine about half the size of a Chevette somehow went crashing to the floor. John did not need to rap his pencil for at least an hour. When the phone rang one day, the caller had misdialed and assumed she was placing an order for carryout. She had the extreme misfortune of reaching Andy, who took her entire order, asking her what dressing she wanted on the salads, informing her French onion was the soup du jour, persuading her to substitute redskin potatoes for the fries, and offering a free order of hush puppies if she ordered the fried sole. Then he promptly hung up and went back to work.

Falling exhausted into bed about midnight every Friday and getting back to the Tribune by 5:00 the next morning was not easy, but it was the first of many times in my life where I learned how to function when it would be so much easier just to tell the world to proceed without me today. This schedule was not exactly compatible with two roommates either. Bill and Gene were usually still up when I got home, but certainly not running, jumping, dancing, singing or playing the piano when my alarm pierced the darkness the next morning. One night when I came home exhausted, they were throwing a party, with about twenty people in the apartment dancing, laughing, slurring their loud conversation, and singing along with whatever crooner came on the hi-fi. Not only had Bill and Gene not invited me to their soirée, but they had not even told me about it. When the festivities were still rollicking into the wee hours, I found myself getting angrier by the minute. By 4:30, when I had to get up to pedal back to the Tribune, I had not slept at all. Worst of all, they made no apology or explanation all week. By the next Friday night when I came home, I was still seething and wanted revenge. I knew even then it was wrong, but as they were going off to sleep, I turned on the TV, watched the late show, then left it blaring when I went to bed. But "vengeance is mine," saith the Lord. Not only did I get very little sleep again myself, but when I came home in the afternoon that day, Bill and Gene asked me to move out. They were too late. I had already decided to leave and had found a room at 817 N. Dearborn Street on the Near North Side.

I did not realize that the old building into which I had just moved, incidentally just a few doors away from the International Walther League headquarters on Dearborn Street, was already scheduled for demolition. That probably explains why I was able to get a spacious single room with a balcony overlooking the park across the street and a full kitchenette for about the same as my share of the rent at the Ramada. Lee and Ron stopped by unannounced one day and were jealous of what they assumed must be well beyond my means. The hotel was run by an elderly couple, Mr. and Mrs. Henry Brandenburg, who doted on me as if I were their own son, took me out for a Whopper at Burger King once in a while, and even asked me along one weekend when they headed for their luxurious second home somewhere up north. But there were some tradeoffs living where I was. While I was much closer to church and to work, I was much farther from school. This did not present much of a problem, however, as long as I kept my bike in good running order. Perhaps the worst was the neighborhood. The intersection of Dearborn and Division near me reputedly had such a high concentration of homosexuals that some wag had dubbed it Queerborn and Derision.

One Saturday I was sitting on a bench in the little park across the street when an oldish man sat on the bench next to me and struck up a conversation. He introduced himself as Everett Sanders, and I made the mistake of pointing to my building across the street when he asked where I lived. The next day my phone rang. It was Everett. He was downstairs in the lobby and wanted to show me some poems he had written. A little audacious just showing up like this, I thought, but why not humor an old geezer by taking a look at his creativity. After we looked over his writings a little bit there in the lobby, he left, and I thought that was the end of it. A few days later I got a letter from him, along with typewritten copies of a few of his poems. In the letter he was telling me that he had been insulted, because where he comes from, the proper etiquette when someone stops by is to invite him in. When he went on to say he had expected to be escorted up to my room, I had a flash of understanding. He was lonely, or, considering the neighborhood, perhaps he was "lonely" (insert wink here). Either way, I was not interested in his company and wrote him a letter back, saying that where I come from the proper etiquette is not to associate with strangers who write poetry. One of his poems, however, struck a chord with me, literally, and with some modifications I used it in one of my student compositions, which I called *Peace*. It was a tone painting my sister Deanna and I years later decided would be appropriate to sing at the funeral of a lady who had finished dozens of paintings depicting the very landscapes and scenery projected by the poem. The artist was my mother.

Although the second-year courses at the University of Chicago were still non-elective, they were considerably less draconian than the three quarters of English I had suffered through as a freshman.

As I walked into the first session of social studies one quarter, I spotted a familiar face. One of the girls from English class the year before had stood out for the way she would close her eyes and articulate what she had to say very deliberately. She seemed a cut above most of the riffraff I was accustomed to seeing in these classrooms. When I talked with her at the end of the session, I found out her name was Susan Karpin, and after a week or two of class with her, I picked up two tickets for a violin concert and asked her if she would like to attend. She lived with her parents in a fashionable condo up on Sheridan, I think, and when I stopped by to pick her up, she exclaimed, "You didn't tell me we were going to see Nathan Milstein. I *love* Nathan Milstein!" Her parents also gushed over my taste in music and were very impressed with this young man who was dating their daughter. As we rode along on the subway, she said something that made me realize she was Jewish. While I was definitely not anti-Semitic, I remembered the words of one of our youth counselors, who said, "You do not marry someone you do not meet." Beautiful as she was and attracted as I was to her, prudence seemed to be dictating to me that I should avoid a relationship that might lead to romance with someone of a religion so far afield from my own. On the ride home, I told her how much she impressed me, but candidly expressed reservations about our differences in religion. She agreed immediately, and reciprocated with kind words about me, but added that her parents would expect her to be serious with someone from their own synagogue.

Now that my parents lived in the Twin Cities, it was much easier for me to return home whenever I could get away from my increasingly hectic existence in Chicago. The Greyhound terminal was in the heart of the Loop, and the station in St. Paul was only a few blocks away from the Chevrolet dealership where my father worked. Convenient and relatively inexpensive, but a boring ride. The first time I made that trip, I dozed off, but was awakened by the announcement of the driver, "Arriving at Boston, arriving at Boston." Boston! Oh, no. How did that happen? I must have gotten on the wrong bus somehow. Now, how am I going to reach my parents who are waiting for me at St. Paul? Then I noticed the signs of the businesses that said Mauston, the halfway point along Interstate 94 in central Wisconsin. My father was amused on one occasion, when I told him what happened on my way over to meet him at his shop. Near the capitol grounds a panhandler stopped me, begging money for bus fare. "If I had money for bus fare," I replied, pointing to my suitcase, "would I be walking?"

Part of the Retail Advertising Department at the Tribune was the Amusements Division, which handled the accounts of the entertainment industry—movies, concerts, extravaganzas, art exhibits, and the like. Two dear friends who worked over there, Mary Vittorini and Nancy Kelly (no relation to Dorothy), were like mother hens to me, very protective and ready to defend against any chicken hawk that might catch me off guard. Some of their advertising clients came to the office in person, and one day one of them gave Mary two extra tickets to a live concert by Johnny Cash at Soldier Field, which she passed to me. By design, my social life had taken lower priority while classes were in session, but this came along during the summer, while my batteries were recharging. Immediately I thought of Pauline Timm, the young lady I had left behind in Webster City the summer after high school. This was her kind of music, and I had not seen her for about three years. From one of the last letters she sent, I was excited to learn that she was enrolled in nursing school in River Forest, a suburb just west of Chicago. As college started, however, I never followed up on my intentions of staying in touch with her. Now, somehow in the back of my mind I pictured her sitting on the edge of the bed with the phone next to her just waiting for me to call, so I decided to look up her number and invite her to this concert. Although she seemed less than enthusiastic when we talked, she agreed to go when I told her that it was

Johnny Cash. I took the train out to River Forest, but when she came out to the lobby of her building to meet me, she informed me she was unable to go after all. She had followed an impulse to accept my invitation, but had second thoughts after we talked and did not know how to reach me to explain she was engaged to be married. She hoped I did not mind that she had taken the liberty of arranging a blind date for me instead, as she called to one of her classmates hiding behind a pillar nearby. I would like to say that the event was a complete success and that the girl was good looking, but does "Arf, arf" convey the impression I had?

Summer was a time to settle into a little slower pace. Classes were not in session, but since electives were always available, I usually took at least one course each summer. For example, I decided speed reading might be useful some day and signed up for it one quarter. Grant Park offered free outdoor concerts by major orchestras, conductors, and performers, with names like the New Jersey Symphonic, Kenneth Schirmerhorn, and Emil Gilels. Lake Michigan was walking distance away, and sometimes it was fun to doff shoes and wade through gentle waves lapping against bare ankles. The Shedd Aquarium and the Chicago Natural History Museum lie along the lake nearby, but one visit to each of these is enough to last a while. The musical *The Sound of Music* made its debut in downtown Chicago one day, and after I saw it, I considered the experience one of the apogees of a lifetime. To this day I believe that it is certainly the greatest musical, if not the greatest movie, ever filmed. When I told Wally about it, I brashly predicted that some day I was going to create a work like this. His response changed my thinking for the rest of my life. At first, I was so incensed by it that I had to bite my lip to avoid a sharp retort for the way he was putting me down so. But the longer it stayed with me, the more I realized how profound, even spiritual, it was. "Try not to be too disappointed if the result falls short of your standards," he began softly, and then, as if looking toward some distant object in space, he added, "One of the hardest lessons we learn in life … is acceptance of mediocrity."

One day during the summer, as I was passing a recruiting office near the Chicago Public Library, I decided on a whim to check out what the Air Force might be able to offer me in aviation. One of my dreams from childhood was to fly airplanes, and I was starting to think about what I might do after graduation. When I asked about flight school, the sergeant behind the desk asked, "Do you need those glasses?" I would never pass the physical, he explained, "But let me show you some of our other programs …." Undeterred by that, I checked into civilian flight schools in the Chicago area and found one at Midway Airport that could take me through ground school and flight training for about five hundred dollars. When I talked with my father about this notion, however, he listened in silence and then his first question was something like "and what does this have to do with music school?" Flying lessons would have to wait.

# Lynneway

**W**hen classes started up again in the fall of 1965, I noticed that Amusements Division had a new employee, a perky young lady named Lynne. If you can picture Kim Raver as Audrey Raines from the white-knuckle TV series *24* or her role as Nico Reilly in *Lipstick Jungle*, you have an idea what a cute little button Lynne was—narrow face with a pointy little nose, petite, slender build, gorgeous legs and flawless complexion. When I talked with her one day, she mentioned she was taking ballet lessons, explaining the five positions the dancers learn. In response, I told her I was taking violin lessons and bet her that I would reach the fifth position before she did. When she stuck out her tongue at my little joke, my heart did little handsprings inside. I was so infatuated with her that we were together constantly, both on the job and after work. Dating without a car put me at a disadvantage with her other potential suitors, but there was an El stop very close to her apartment in Oak Park, the western suburb where she lived with her mother Caroline and younger sister Diedre (I have altered their names to protect their privacy). I made that trip countless times to escort her home or pick her up to go somewhere. As the Christmas break approached in December, I innocently invited her to Minnesota to spend the holidays with me. Matrimony was not on my mind, but ignorant of the implications, I was proud of her and simply wanted my parents to meet her. Most of all, I did not want to be away from her while I was home. After a few days with us, she made a favorable impression on my family, especially Ruth and Deanna, who idolized her as the older sister they never had. Like a Shakespeare tragedy, however, this turned out to be a fatal flaw.

That long bus ride back to Chicago with Lynne seemed like an Augenblick, and it was one of the most romantic experiences of my life. I was deliriously happy. But a portent of things to come occurred soon after we dreamily said good night at her apartment. It was about two in the morning when I transferred from the El train to the subway, and as I reached the bottom of the steps I noticed a disheveled old man sitting on the bench on the platform. It seemed apparent that he was stoned, drunk or in the final throes of hemlock poisoning from the way he was slobbering and mumbling to himself, but I paid little attention when he staggered up the stairs to street level. A few minutes later I saw a uniformed CTA detective descend the steps, followed by the same derelict I had seen on the bench earlier. Again I paid little attention until the detective seemed to be coming my way. Then he walked up to me and told me to turn around, put my hands against the wall and spread my feet. What the …? Now, with your left hand reach slowly back and pull out your wallet, I heard through the fog in my brain. So it was all a ruse—these dirty bums are robbing me, I thought. Now, verrrrry slowly open the wallet and take out all the money, he was telling me. Now I was sure of it. I wanted to shout for help, but at two a.m. there was no one else around. Besides, if CTA detectives are robbing people, whom can I trust anyway? I did as he said, and then came the next surprise. Put the money in your pocket and hand *me* the wallet, he said. When he saw my Minnesota driving license, he asked me what I was doing in Chicago assaulting people in the subway. What!? It seems the version he got from the old coot was that I had kicked him in the leg and run to the other end of the platform. Though I was absolutely certain that was ridiculous, I turned to my accuser and calmly said that I thought I had passed well clear of him when I reached the platform, but that if I inadvertently stepped on his foot or hurt him in some way, I was sorry. When this self-declared plaintiff started snarling, snapping and foaming at the mouth again, the detective suddenly saw reality. In a complete reversal, he told me it had been a mistake and wished me a good evening, just as my train was approaching. Not knowing what the old man would do to me if he got onto the train, I asked the detective if he would ride with me to my stop. With a glance at the raving lunatic a few feet away, he understood completely and was glad to oblige.

At the time I came into Lynne's life, she was attending community college, but in our conversations I gradually sensed that she was only recently beginning to get her life back together. There was something dark in her background, and although I never pressed her for details, there were some clues. The first came one day when she confided a closely guarded secret. She was living in constant fear that the administration at the college would discover that she had fibbed on her application for admission about the fact that she had not graduated from high school. Aha, never finished high school. There could be any number of explanations, but I suspected something sinister or shameful, like a teen pregnancy perhaps. Aware that her mother had been divorced for some time, I also wondered if Lynne had had an abusive father or had simply succumbed to the pressures of their broken home and become a runaway. Although someone or some circumstance along the way had persuaded her to take up cigarettes, I never had any reason to suspect any other substance abuse.

Although my Friday schedule was quite structured, Lynne and I had a standing date for a bite to eat when I finished my day in Retail and before I reported for my long evening in Classified. One Friday evening she told me she was busy and would not be able to meet me as usual. By chance I was heading down the street to grab a sandwich by myself when I spotted her a few yards ahead with another guy. I did not know his name, but I knew immediately who he was—a client I had seen earlier when he stopped by Amusements in person to place his display ad with the Tribune. He had obviously noticed something of personal interest while he was there, but I had no idea when I first saw him that he was shoplifting. This incensed me doubly. First, because of the pain of betrayal, but second, I came up against a recurring fetish. This dude was at least six four, and once again I was asking myself why tall men had to take an interest in tiny women. Someone my size had far fewer options than they, so why could they not play fair and wear their socially acceptable blinders, as I expected them to? They had the entire field to play in, so why did they need to romp around in my little corner of it? Besides the fact that this bounder was stealing something that belonged to me, they looked ridiculous as a couple. It reminded me of my father, who, in disapproval of mixed-race couples, would often say that in nature you never see a mallard running around with a teal.

Since Lynne was unaware I had seen them, I decided to feign ignorance to find out where this new development would lead. The answer was not long in coming. Usually I accompanied her all the way to the door to be sure she had her key and could get in, but the next time we returned to her house, she pushed against my chest as she let herself into the lobby, locked the door behind her and turned her back to the glass. Clearly our relationship had changed. The next Friday when I asked if we were going to our restaurant as usual, she blew up my world with a four-word grenade, "I'm seeing someone else." If this had been a movie, the double basses would be playing the music reserved for the most tragic of scenes—the theme where the hero dies in battle or the final scene of the dying heroine whispering "I love you" before going limp in the arms of her lover. I was absolutely blown into tiny fragments. I could not understand what I had done or not done to cause this to happen. Why, why, why, I kept asking. How could the sweetest hundred pounds on earth crush me so completely? Then suddenly I became materialistic. I remembered the portable typewriter I had loaned Lynne to use for class, so I raced out to Oak Park before she could get home and told her mother I was there to retrieve it. Preteen Diedre blinked in wonderment at me from the next room, unaware what was wrong as I breezed into the apartment. Wearing the same smirk as the evil stepmother in Cinderella, Caroline telegraphed, with only her unctuous manner, that she already knew this was coming. As I was leaving, I got the answer that finally made everything clear, "Well, Lynne needs to meet other people. You know she is too young to get married yet." Ohhhhhhhh, so that was the problem. Her mother was behind this. Never mind that Lynne and I were nowhere near that point in our relationship. She had assumed we were getting too serious and decided it was time to intervene—for the good of, well, all three of us, of course.

I felt as if a priceless Ming vase had been shattered, and I was so devastated by this grievous calamity that it never occurred to me that perhaps this was exactly the plan God had mapped out for me. It was on my mind constantly, completely obscuring the possibility that there might be someone out there far better for me than Lynne. How much like life itself this was. Do we not get so buried by vicissitudes that we forget the Prize waiting for us at the end? Certainly for the time being I could not concentrate on anything else; my studying suffered, and my grades took a dive. This was my first true love, and the loss inflicted such trauma on me that it took literally several years for me to recover. Even today I feel shaped and defined by what happened and can perceive the permanent change wrought by this single event in my life so long ago. Mr. Rosenbloom was one of the first to detect something was amiss and asked what it was. When I told him about Lynne, he understood. Divorced for many years himself, he tried to make me feel better with a piece of his own philosophy. "Women are like busses," he mused, gazing distantly out the window. "Another one always comes along."

My brother Don had started seminary training, and when he came through the Chicago area on a choir tour during this period, the evening I spent with him was a momentary respite from the constant emotional pain I felt in my gut. Perhaps my greatest solace during this time of crisis, however, was my dear friend Richard Murphy. Dick was a community college student from somewhere in Washington, I think, who transferred in as a third-year student and had nary a pretentious molecule in his soul. He was nominally a Mormon but apparently not very devout. Oh, he attended their testimonials on Sunday evenings, but I was under the impression that a good Mormon avoids coffee, strong language and potent potables. Not to excess, by any means, but I could connect each of these to him to some degree, including the bottle of Ripple he kept around once in a while. Dick and I were roughly on the same level pianistically, so he was also a student of Mr. Rosenbloom. Both of us were fond of him, not only professionally but personally, and Dick especially loved the cute little chuckle Rosenbloom had, which Dick would imitate in a voice reminiscent of Peter Lorre in *The Maltese Falcon*. One day as I was beginning to notice that Rosenbloom's efforts with me to rebuild my piano technique were beginning to pay dividends, Dick paid the ultimate compliment. A brilliant pianist named Robert Vander Schaaf had also transferred in from somewhere the year before, and Dick told me one day when he walked past the studio where I was practicing that he thought he was hearing Vander Schaaf.

Dick called my bicycle the Silver Bullet and always had some crack about it. Just the way he pronounced the word bullet to rhyme with mullet always elicited a snigger from me. One of his favorite pieces was the *Etude in C Minor* of Chopin, which acquired the nickname *Revolutionary Etude* when Russia invaded Warsaw, and Dick could not resist the comparison to events in Cuba at the time, which he promised to commemorate with a piece he would write called the *Turncoat Symphony*. He was one of the most selfless, and self-effacing, friends I ever had—the kind Russell Castor had described years earlier, in reference and reverence to his lifelong comrade Keith Culbertson, that I had not encountered since my boyhood friend Happy Klammer. We were both cynical enough to scoff at the pomp and stuffiness we could see around us, and I would invent the most far-flung scenarios just to hear the spontaneous, deep-throated staccato chuckle he had. Ironically, the invaluable therapy I was receiving from the laughter of this wonderful friendship with Dick was exactly what he would need himself a few years later, but I was not around to give it to him. While I was at one end of a love affair, he was at the other. He had met a young lady named Marilyn Pahnke, and suddenly the time I spent with him dropped almost to zero. Once when we went for one of our increasingly infrequent walks along the Lake, he was obviously oblivious to everything I was saying, as he stopped, turned to me pretending to be a magician and said, "Zap, you're Marilyn." In a flash I realized I was nowhere on his radar screen.

Sometimes they would invite me along when they drove somewhere in the car that Marilyn borrowed from her parents, and as I got to know her, I found out what a spoiled child she was, and I could see trouble ahead for Dick. One day, for example, when she wanted Dick to stop for ice cream as we drove through a seedy section of town, he wanted to wait until we reached a nicer neighborhood. "But I want it now, Dick, I want it *now*," Marilyn pouted. It was such a classic tantrum that I thought it was just an act. But when I realized she was not just *parodying* a whine, I could not believe Dick would tolerate such behavior, much less accede to a relationship with her. Deciding it was too risky and too presumptuous on my part to say anything, I determined to let nature take its course. That was a mistake. When they later married and settled in San Jose, Marilyn's parents sold their beautiful house in one of the northern suburbs of Chicago and moved to the Bay area to be near their only child. Meddling can wound a marriage, and when immaturity leads one partner to run to a parent with problems instead of to the other partner, the wound is often mortal. When I visited them in California about two years into their wedded life, little Miles had come along, and Dick was as happy as I had ever seen him. Several months later I got a letter from him describing a trail littered with infidelity, intrigue, duplicity and desertion that hit him like a Zamboni. How could that sweet, innocent little girl I knew in Chicago turn into such a deceitful, evil monster, he wanted to know. First, I could not provide an answer to his question, but second, I knew exactly how it felt, and third, I saw it coming and predicted in my heart it would happen.

Early one morning in my apartment on Dearborn, the landlady, Mrs. Brandenburg, knocked on my door to ask if I might be able to assist one of her chambermaids. Apparently, word of the impending evacuation of the building had affected her ability to meet their staffing needs, and she was desperate. She hoped I might have an hour each morning before I left for school to change towels and linens. Although I really did not have the time to spare, they had been so kind to me that I was moved out of compassion, if not obligation, to take this on for the short period remaining before everyone had to move out. When the owner of an apartment building at 1432 N. LaSalle, across the street from my church, showed up one day to salvage furnishings from the Dearborn place for his establishment, Mrs. Brandenburg again asked me if I could help him load his purchases and haul them a few blocks away over to his building. On the ride over in the truck with him and his merchandise, he asked me where I was planning to go when I was forced out. He had some rooms in his place, and I accepted the good rate he gave me to move in there. It was the last time I would need to move until I left Chicago.

Some time after I was settled into my new room, the phone rang one evening. The man at the front desk said I had a visitor. I was reading a book on choral conducting and would have jumped at any excuse to escape that boredom, so I slipped on my shoes to go up front to see who it was. I nearly fainted. It was Lynne! Ostensibly, she had broken up with Abraham Longshanks and wanted to talk. When she wanted to come back to my room, I reminded her of my firm rule that I do not bring girls to my room. While I am not sure that she wanted to be intimate, there had been at least one other occasion when there was little doubt. I gently stated my position that this was to be reserved for marriage, and although I was to have a few narrow escapes in the years ahead, that turned out to be a principle by which I was able to abide. I could scarcely believe that Lynne was back on my pedestal. I traveled way beyond seventh heaven, to at least number seventeen. Forget cloud nine, it was cloud twenty-nine. Alas, reconciliation was short-lived, however. One day I got the classic "It's not you, it's me" routine from her, and our relationship was over forever.

Ironically, I actually believe that it *was* she. Her mother may have taken up her mace and battle axe again, but when I reflected upon it, I remembered that Lynne herself once said to me that she believed I was destined for what she perceived to be great things and did not want to be the one holding me back. Whatever darkness it was that lurked in the shadows of her past was haunting her, and she seemed to be sure I could never accept it in the long term. I tried to tell her I was interested in who she *is*, not who she *was*, but apparently she remained unconvinced. While I cannot look into her heart to examine her true motives, I must concede the possibility that this was actually a selfless act of magnanimity and farsightedness on her part, attempting to spare my welfare at the expense of her own. It is conceivable that she could foresee what I could not—that it would never work for us—and courageously called it off before it was too late. We talked briefly again about two years later, when she told me she was engaged to be married, and that was the last time I ever saw her.

There is, however, a sequel to this sordid affair. Years later, when I would retire and return to my long-neglected music, I realized that I had not actually *practiced* the piano for some forty years. As I ran through old pieces I had once performed in my student days in Chicago, I experienced the power of a phenomenon I will term associative memory. While playing certain passages back then, I must have been thinking about Lynne, because now these many years hence those latent repressions became suddenly unlocked and flooded my consciousness. Unable to put her out of my mind completely, I found myself wondering how her life had turned out and decided I must try to locate her. After nearly a year of sleuthing, still not sure if she was dead or alive, some very resourceful friends, led by Maisie Hanrahan, who were assisting me in the search, came across an obituary for her mother Caroline and tracked Lynne to a small town in Georgia. Judging from the string of AKA names provided by my sources, I leapt to the conclusion that yes, true to form, she had left a trail of broken hearts behind. Nothing could be further from the truth.

When we eventually connected by phone, I learned that Lynne was dealing with heartbreak of her own. While she and her husband conducted a stained glass business, he had been assailed by an as-yet-unidentified intruder in an upstairs room and stabbed to death. Numb with shock and grief, which would grip her for many years, perhaps forever, the young widow attempted to rebound with a second marriage. Still reeling from the tragedy, she faced mounting tribulation as first this relationship disintegrated and then her mother Caroline lost her battle with cancer. In the end she was sustained by the memories carried on through a precious son, and I bore away the impression that she is now settled in happier circumstances with "Mickey," her current husband. Though very private and extremely guarded when we talked, she was nonetheless pleasant, and in the course of our conversation, she left me with a certain measure of justification when she refered to me as "the good one that got away." Not quite sure what sort of havoc this re-encounter might play on my emotions, I was relieved that the extremes of passion once locked in my heart had not simply taken me back to the pangs where Lynne and I left off. Traversing an upward helix in my mind, I was returning over and over to the same thoughts, but with each rotation reaching a higher plane. Now, from the lofty vantage point that comes with the passage of time, I discovered that those intense feelings of admiration and affection I once had for her have transformed into a kind of warmth and tenderness I would have for a long-lost sister who has returned to the family. We remain on good terms to this day, and at last I was finally able to put the matter to rest.

At one point in our conversations, Lynne recalled sitting in the practice room at Sherwood listening to me practice. Not only do I have no recollection of this, but also it is inconceivable that I would willfully subject anyone to such cruelty. Tolerant indeed is the person who could endure the same passage played wrong ninety-nine times before it finally comes together on the hundredth. Surely she must be mistaken. The only time I can remember that she was ever in the studio makes me wince. Bob Kahn, one of the salesmen at the Tribune, had plinked out the melody for *It Started With a Laugh*, a poem he had written for his bride, and commissioned me to write the orchestral accompaniment to it for their wedding. At one of the rehearsals, Lynne was present as he was reviewing the details with me about where his solo would fall in the ceremony, to be held at a dinner club. It never occurred to me that he was Jewish when I blurted out something like, "Wouldn't you rather be married in your church?" Kahn merely shrugged off my faux pas, but Lynne gasped and darted me such a withering laser that I thought it would sear the piano.

When our health is good, we are inclined never to think about it; when it is not good, we can think of nothing else. Because my health was generally robust, I was not prepared one day when I became violently ill, and I was quite alarmed. I looked up the name of a certain Dr. Wiedenhorn in the phone book and doggedly pedaled my bike up there to his office somewhere along North Avenue, I think it was, to find out what was wrong. After I climbed the rickety, squeaking old wooden stairs to his office, I met a tall white-haired old man with enormous ears who must have been the last surviving surgeon from the Civil War. His nurse Jane surely must have served with Clara Barton. But they were both instantly fond of this college kid who came to see them and like doting grandparents determined to help. Wiedenhorn found nothing wrong and could only conclude that I had suffered food poisoning, but he was concerned that I seemed too thin, and I can still hear him tell me in his thick Cherman ahkzent that I need to eat more "noooodles, potaaatoes and spaghetttti." He wanted me to come back each week for a while for a checkup and an injection, and each time I would hear the same speech. I am not exactly sure what that shot was, but I suspect it was nothing but a mild antibiotic mixed into a liberal dose of sucrose. His theory about food poisoning has some credibility, because I was not always the most careful about what I pulled out of the refrigerator. Although my parents had conditioned me quite well about not wasting food, even I knew better than to use an egg that had been around for so long one time that the inside was black when I cracked it open.

Much of my final year in Chicago was devoted to education courses and student teaching. My first assignment was an elementary school in Tinley Park, a suburb on the South Side of Chicago, practice teaching under the tutelage of a delightful young music teacher originally from Arkansas. It was the first time I heard anyone drawl "mash that kay" of the piano when I would probably have used the expression to press it. After three weeks there, I moved on to a middle school somewhere on the South Side that seemed more like a cellblock than educational facility. When one young man stood up to slap the back of the head of another boy two rows ahead, the teacher told him to sit. He did, but then promptly stood up to do it again. What was I was supposed to teach *them*? I felt like I had just been elected mayor of Belfast.

After three weeks of teaching junior high, I was placed into a high school in Homewood. When I arrived the first morning, they invited me to their weekly faculty meeting. Faculty meeting?! Oh yeah, I was now faculty, I realized with a lemon-sized lump in my throat. Funny, I did not feel like an adult, but everyone was suddenly demanding that I *be* one. I was not ready for this. Some time after introductions were made, I was attempting to address one of the battle-hardened old biddies at the table but apologized that I did not remember her name. She snapped back with a scathing remark I will never forget, "Yeah, just what I expected. When you are introduced to someone, the only name you hear is your own." Mr. Kincaid, the chorus teacher designated to be my mentor, took me aside later and told me not to be offended. "When I first came," he recalled, "she lambasted me as a power-hungry young upstart at this same table."

I was grateful to be exposed to the real world of teaching music, because I knew for sure this was something I never wanted to do. Each day, as I endured the long train ride to my post, I felt my blood pressure rising with increasing dread as my stop drew near, and I asked myself why I ever considered this as a career. Worst of all, not only was I not getting paid for it, but my parents were paying precious tuition money for my privilege to get beat up every day. When I was asked to evaluate my experience at the end, I was tempted to say that teaching music was somewhat like controlling a nuclear reaction. Unlike other academic subjects, in which the students are relatively passive, music courses try to incite a passion without allowing it to spill over the top out of control. Right now, my mind was swimming in mud, not sure that it was not my career path that was out of control. Little did I realize everything was proceeding exactly according to Plan.

# Army Daze

**B**efore I left for Chicago, I had never heard of a country called Vietnam, but during those four years since, the lives of young men became entwined in a plan of the nation known as the Selective Service system, which seemed to exist solely for the purpose of sending them there for an all-expenses-paid tour. All males who registered at age eighteen were assigned a classification code, depending upon circumstance. Undergraduate students could be granted a student deferment, classification 2-S, as long as they remained in good academic standing in an accredited four-year program. This deferment could be extended into graduate school only for specialties considered to be in the national interest, such as medicine, astrophysics, or certain other advanced sciences.

Since my degree in education was not exactly one of the advanced sciences, I was doubtful that I could continue the deferment, but I decided to try. Before graduation, I applied for a scholarship in graduate studies at Northwestern University in nearby Evanston. From my atrocious performance at the audition I was granted, I was not surprised when it was denied. When I graduated from Sherwood, my parents swooped down from Minnesota with the entire family and whirled us all through the eastern states where most of them had never been, retracing the same route I had made with Venita Rich three years earlier through Washington and New York. My work at the Tribune had always been scheduled for afternoons because of my morning classes, but one day Wally asked me if I could sit in on the daily sales meeting the next morning. Immediately I sensed what was afoot. It was supposed to be a surprise party to celebrate my graduation, but I had correctly sniffed out their plan. Not only was I not surprised when everyone was assembled to yell, "Surprise!" but I had already rehearsed in my mind the little obligatory speech I would make. Apparently, the salesmen were so impressed by what they thought were impromptu remarks that they wanted me to join their Toastmaster's Club meetings. Although I did not feel any shame about uncovering their plot, I did feel a little guilty about that. Then at the end of the summer, my father and a couple of his accomplices came back with a pick-up truck and a trailer, and with little fanfare my life in Chicago was over.

I started graduate work at the University of Minnesota that fall, with the intention of continuing, not with education, but testing the waters of music theory, perhaps doing some composing, teaching harmony classes, or even the unthinkable possibility of working up to an assistant professorship some day. In Chicago I had subscribed to a series at Orchestra Hall to hear world-class pianists perform, but here I was in the home of the well-renowned Minneapolis Symphony, and attended as many of their concerts as I could. I was there for one of the first performances of Ivan Penderecki's *Threnody for the Victims of Hiroshima* and again for the world première of Alan Hovhaness's *Fra Angelico*, which became one of my favorite orchestral works of the twentieth century. My professor in music theory, the University's own Dominick Argento, was an emerging composer in his own right and was attempting to write his name in the concrete of the music world. Unlike the environment at Sherwood, the demands of the curriculum here were intense, and I found myself straining to meet their high standards. But it appeared at first that despite the odds, my gamble with Uncle Sam was paying off.

One day in late October, however, I received greetings from Claryce Ransom, administrator of the Selective Service office in Iowa where I had registered. It seems they had noticed, after all, that I had graduated, and in commemoration thereof, were bestowing on me some new credentials. My classification 2-S became 1-A, the amber light before civilian life stopped at the red, and that was about the length of time I had to consider my options. First order of business was monetary. If I withdrew from all my classes immediately, I could still get a refund on the tuition I paid. From classmates on campus, I had learned that the Army had a predilection for liberal arts graduates. What outstanding ground-pounders they turned out to be, and cannon fodder for the infantry. All I had to do was to wait for the next letter, and I would be eligible to join them for the opportunity to be fitted for lead teeth.

On the other hand, perhaps I had some other options. I did not even consider Canadian citizenship, a course taken by some. Conscientious objector status was tempting, but those who followed that route were stigmatized already and would likely wear that tattoo far into the future. I decided to talk to the recruiters. Do you look like a Marine, I asked myself one day in the mirror. It was not a magic mirror, but it said no. One of the statistically safest branches of the service was the Air Force, but I had already been rejected for flight training, and I had been warned that promotions were slow in coming. My father had been in the Navy, but the four-year commitment trumped family pride and loyalty. When I talked with the Army counselor, I learned that draftees had only a two-year hitch, but enlisting as a regular army volunteer extended that only to three. As a college graduate, he was intoning, I was eligible for OCS, and a commission as a second lieutenant. Ooh, a second looie. I had heard about *them*, the prized infantrymen most likely to fill the sights of a Vietcong rifle. And where would I be assigned, I wanted to know. Oh, most likely in the infantry, he coughed into his sleeve. His words were about as straight as the guy who cleans toilets for a living but tells everyone at a party he is in the porcelain industry, as he slickly pointed out the glittering opportunities for unparalleled valor and leadership that were available. "What do you have that is least likely to get me shot and killed in Vietnam?" I asked baldly. He pored over his book for several minutes, then folded his arms and said, "How would you like a military occupational specialty where you could not be assigned to a post staffed lower than a three-star general?" I was sure I heard music when he told me it was a stenographer. He did not tell me that the Army could still do anything it wanted by simply changing my MOS to helicopter tailgunner, if that suited its purpose. But I did not tell *him* that I already knew a little shorthand, planned to finish at the top of my class and would ride out my tour in Vietnam hiding behind a flag officer. I signed the dotted line.

While the Army was grinding the paperwork to proverbial grist, I found myself hanging out to dry. My classes were canceled, I did not have a job, and the nervous wait made me, well, more nervous. The stockyards of South St. Paul were a short distance away, and I decided that if we had to endure the lofty fragrance that blew from their direction every day on the breeze anyway, I might just as well be paid for it. One of the major meat packers had set up business here and slaughtered beef, hogs, and sheep by the thousands every day. Everyone should work in a sausage factory just once, if only to witness the fascinating, if gruesome, operation producing the meat products to which we too seldom give much thought when it sits on a supermarket shelf. It was an assembly line process, except that it was disassembly. On my job, freshly killed sheep hanging by their hind legs passed me one by one on a conveyor, and I simply "racked" their front feet, positioning them for removal of their hides. When green slime occasionally dribbled from the muzzle of one of them, the fellow next to me on the line would always remark, "Ain't ya glad ya have a strong stomach?" One day a live sheep got loose and ran around all over the conveyor room before several strong arms wrestled it to the floor. I do not know whether this one was granted a final wish to see its fate before the end, but I did wonder what was going through its mind. On a lunch break one time, I had to satisfy my morbid curiosity to see how huge steers were actually taken down. I know you do not want me to tell you, but I will anyway. The beasts were driven single file into a chute, at the end of which one man applied electrodes to its head to stun it while a second man clamped a leg iron to one hind hoof. The chain attached to the leg iron jerked the animal high overhead, hanging by its hoof, and moved it over to a huge pit, where a third man wearing hip waders drained its blood from the throat until, a full five minutes later, he stood knee deep in it.

About a month later, I was notified to report to an Army bus bound for Louisiana the weekend before Thanksgiving. The foreman at the plant was upset that he just got me trained, and now I was giving him only three days' notice that I was leaving. Trained? A stupid ape could do that job, and an intelligent one would turn it down. My mother kept singing "You're in … the Ar - - my now," the theme song from the WWII movie with the same name, and annoyed me further with the claim that I was doing this just to escape Minnesota and go south for the winter. When the bus full of exuberant Minnesotans disembarked at the reception station in Fort Polk, we discovered that the nice men in Smokey Bear hats who met us there requested that we see their soil from ground level. We were told to put our hands on it and examine it closely twenty times, in fact. This soil was quite sacred to them, and they had us pay this peculiar kind of reverence to it quite often. I thought they were being especially considerate too when they spoke loud enough to hear them clearly and came within an inch or two of our faces to make sure we could understand what they were saying. We were stripped naked, and, except for the glasses on my face and the wallet in my hand, everything was to be shipped home, including my contact lenses. Those of you who are familiar with the Sixties can picture hippies, long-haired freaks, pony tails, braids, and facial hair so thick only glazed eyes were visible. All of them came down on our bus. I was next in line for my first military haircut when the barber asked young Private Longmop seated in the chair if he would like to keep his sideburns. When the recruit said, "Sure," the barber replied, "Okay, hold out your hand." This haircut was free, but the weekly ritual after this would cost us a dollar each time. One of the sergeants once said, "If you think you don't have a dollar for a haircut, here's what you do. Go out behind the barracks, squat down, think green thoughts, grunt real hard, reach back, and I will guarantee you will pull out a dollar bill."

The group of us from Minnesota who arrived together was not large enough to make up a company, so our eight weeks of training would not begin for another week, when another load of recruits was due to arrive. This was bad. It did not mean we would be issued hammocks or rental cars for a drive through the bayou. On the first day of what they termed Zero Week, a few of us were told to take the bus to the optometrist on South Post to be fitted for military eyeglasses. As we waited at the bus stop, a car drove slowly past, then stopped, backed up, and parked nearby. A man in uniform stepped out, walked up to us with a notebook in hand, and wrote down the names we had stamped on our fatigues. Hmm, strange. That evening at the company formation, the first sergeant called us to stand next to him in front of the whole company. I thought we were being awarded something. We were. "Men, take a look at these duds, these *DUDS*," he bellowed, "so stupid they don't even salute their brigade commander. While they are assigned to the mess hall cleaning out the grease trap every night this week, the rest of you are going to practice saluting. If it moves, salute it. If it doesn't move, paint it." What?! It was our first day. I did not even know *how* to salute, *who* to salute, or *what* an officer looks like. Was this fair? Wait until I write home and have to tell my parents I spent my very first week in the Army on KP, I kept thinking. So, after cleaning the blinds in the sergeant major's office, operating that runaway scooter called an electric buffing machine, and stocking supplies all day, I reported to the mess hall after chow. Thankfully, the corporal in charge of our detail was relatively laid back and really did not work us very hard at all.

When he sent me to the back of the building to throw something into the Dempsey dumpster (he had called it the dipsy dumpster), I paused for a moment to stare in amazement at the size of that container. As I stood there, a passing NCO called out, "Whatcha lookin' at there, soldier?" He called me soldier. Everyone was called by only a last name. Although I eventually knew everyone in my company by name, I knew the first names of very few. But "soldier" was a neutral reference to any of us, and just hearing that one word suddenly changed my perspective of myself. I had not really felt or thought like a soldier, but it made me realize that is what had become of me. When my week in the Army's kitchen was over, I found that it was not completely the negative experience I expected. I was eyewitness to the monstrous size of the kettles and paddle-sized spatulas, the barn-sized autoclave used to wash the dishes, the cement mixer used to mash potatoes, and the mammoth operation it was to prepare food for hundreds of hungry wolves. I was surprised to learn also that the iconic task peeling potatoes assigned to the likes of Sad Sack and Beetle Bailey on KP no longer obtained. Instead, an ingenious device resembling a clothes dryer abraded the hides off as the tubers rolled around across the rasp-like surface inside its large drum. Another discovery for *me* was that the universal joke about the bad food in the Army was not true. But then again, my mother was not known for good cooking either, so perhaps I was preconditioned. It reminds me of the oft-told story of my nephew. While the older kids went off to the water park one day, little Christopher was left with my mother at the table, gagging on one of her sloppy joe sandwiches. After staring at it for a long time, he called to my mother in the next room, "It's bad." "Now Christopher, you eat that." "But it's *bad*." "Christopher …." Then, using the dirtiest word that a three-year-old knows, he shrieked, "It's POOP - Y BAD!"

One day during Zero Week, we were called into formation, and one of the drill sergeants said he needed three volunteers. If there was any advice I ever received from anyone about the Army, it certainly was never to volunteer for anything. I need a truck driver, the sergeant was saying. From several who raised their hands, he selected one. Now I need a college graduate, he barked. All of us were. Many had degrees from the University of Minnesota or one of the other schools around the Twin Cities, and at least one had a graduate degree—Foster, a registered pharmacist, who received a commission straight from basic training. A few raised their hands timidly, and one was selected. All right, I need someone who can type, he said next. When I heard that, I had to grab my arm to make sure it did not raise itself. Of course I could type, probably better than anyone else there, but with teeth tightly clenched, I hoped I did not regret *not* raising my hand, just to get stuck working on some *despicable* project. "Okay, where's my truck driver?" the sergeant asked. To the beaming face that stood before him, he then said, "You see that wheelbarrow over there near the supply building? That's your truck today. Now which one of you is the college graduate?" One finger went up, but no beaming on his face. "Okay, you see that shovel next to the stock room? A bright guy like you should be able to figure out how to use it, right?" To the "typist" he said, "See this pile of stones here? These two are going to move it over there where those ropes are. You're good with your hands, right? I want you to spread them around in a single layer all over that area." There was the right way, the wrong way, and the Army way, they always told us. I had to admit that if the sergeant had simply asked for three volunteers to move a pile of decorative rocks, he would have deprived himself of the Army way to select the very best from his unit.

Finally, Zero Week was over, and the remainder of our company arrived—all from Louisiana. Two more dissimilar groups would be hard to imagine. It was like trying to mix lemonade and plutonium. Yanks against Rebs, and they never let us forget it. For them the War had never really ended, and the South would rise again, they were convinced. Always pugilistic, they would greet each other, and us, with fists raised, shadow punching or sham socking each other. In contrast to White college graduates were these mostly Black and Cajun street-smart high school dropouts. One we called Lightning had made it only through sixth grade. To understand how he acquired such an epithet, you will need to picture the stereotype lanky, long-armed, plodding, stoop-shouldered, shuffling, step-'n'-fetchit Negro character from Amos 'n' Andy, and you will have an exact picture of him and see why Lightning was quite appropriate as a parody. As we graduated one day from basic training, and each of us progressed to our respective advanced training courses, most could scarcely believe the Army was actually sending Lightning on to tank school.

Lights in the barracks went out at 9:00 every night (2100 hours in military talk), and came on with a harsh glare at precisely 0400 the next morning. Because these old wooden buildings from WWII era were so flammable, each fireguard on duty on a particular night would lose one hour of sleep. Woe to that guard who fell asleep on duty. I always thought of the reference to Judas when Christ said, "Good were it for that man if he had never been born." Intimidation played a factor here as everywhere else. Although it never happened to me, there were occasional rumblings about Private Terminator, who would pull the pillow over his head and refuse to get up when awakened by Private Milquetoast, who would simply elect to pull a two-hour shift rather than wake the squad leader to complain. Whining was so repugnant to the drill sergeants that it would certainly lead to some "remedial training." And if you caused your squad or the entire company to join you in this extracurricular edification, you would likely be invited to a blanket party. The invitation was not engraved, and tea and cookies were not served. Someone would switch off the lights as you entered the building, while eight or ten of your buddies would throw a blanket over you from behind so you would not be able to recognize who it was that was beating you like a rug dragged out of the basement.

If I ever thought I had come to Louisiana to escape ice and cold of Minnesota, I was in for a shock to see frost glistening in the starlight every morning, and I had to dig to the bottom of my duffle bag to retrieve those wool gloves I thought I would never need. A typical day began with a scurry through latrine duties to the first formation at 0430, followed by daily inspection, then two hours of calisthenics and aimless marching before breakfast at 0700. Those inspections remind me of the story about a trainee who received four demerits when a penny was found under his bed—the first for not having the floor clean, the second because only boots were authorized under the bed, the third for leaving money and valuables in plain sight, and the fourth because Lincoln's face was visible and needed a shave. At the noon meal one day, I was not quite finished eating when one of the drill instructors walked past and asked if I was leaving. "As soon as I finish my soup," I replied. "You're finished," he said bluntly. This was not the time or place to debate my mother's philosophy about wasting food. Each week was devoted to a block of the curriculum required for graduation by the end of Week Eight—a week for obstacle course, one for cover and concealment, one for assault and bayonet, one for target practice, one for bivouac and so on. Sometimes training was in a classroom, but if anyone dared to nod off, one of the drill sergeants would yell, "AttenHUT," and the entire class was required to stand for the rest of the session. The first such infraction might, *might*, be forgiven by your classmates, depending upon your popularity and influence, but upon the second, you would almost certainly be hustled into the shower wearing a blanket over your head. No one stood for the film showing actual battle wounds. Anyone who felt faint was allowed to bend over with his head between his knees. I was one of them.

Each company was distinguished by a letter name, which was verbalized by the phonetic alphabet, so my Company B would be voiced as Bravo. Usually we marched to our training area, and when we would encounter another company on its march, the drill sergeant calling out our march cadence would work into the sing-song who we were and what week we were in. The first time this happened, we were in Week Two and criss-crossed Company Echo in Week Six. I remember thinking I would give anything, *anything*, to transfer from Bravo to Echo and be in Week Six. Each week felt like a month, and I distinctly recall thinking of the men of my father's generation who had always laughed when they reminisced about their experiences in basic training and remember explicitly thinking I would never be able to laugh about this. No matter how much time elapsed or how old I became, I would never be able to think it was in any way funny. One day we were in Week Six when Alpha came marching from the other direction in Week Three. Oh, what a glorious feeling that was.

These deltoids in our company from "Loosiana," however, relished this brand of derring-do offered by basic training. For them it was great sport, and they were very good at it. Diminutive Pichon, even smaller than I, could slither under the meshed barbed wire faster than a scalded alligator while tracers of machine gun fire stitched the air two feet overhead. When I traversed the horizontal ladder called the monkey bars, I could reach each rung only with the last ounce of effort from the bottom of my soul. Hebert could swing through them faster than a horny gorilla, grabbing every *other* rung. Throwing absolutely as hard as my flimsy arm could fling a lump of iron, I could just barely hurl that mock grenade forty feet into the foxhole, but Lebeau had to hold back to avoid throwing it through the stockade fence ten yards beyond. To emphasize trust of our equipment and to dramatize the effectiveness of it, training was as realistic as possible. Everyone was required to sniff genuine tear gas in the chamber for a minute or so before the command came to don our gas masks, and at least one grenade toss for each of us was a live one. These and other tasks, timed with a stopwatch and scored by judges, were required by the end of Week Eight in order to complete basic training. Pride, compensation, performance ratings, and therefore promotions were all on the line as competition flared between company commanders and opposing drill instructors for the highest possible collective scores from those of us under their commands. Senior drill sergeant Vega warned repeatedly that he would personally stick a banana in each of our ears if we did not score higher than his archrivals in Company Charlie.

The closest I can say I came to raising the needle of my fun meter off the zero peg was the firing range, where electrically controlled pop-up targets resembling a human silhouette from the waist up were spaced at varying distances from 50 to 350 meters. In Vietnam the soldiers were issued M-16 fully automatic rifles (firing repeatedly when the trigger is pulled), but ours were older M-14 semi-automatic models. It was a rifle or weapon, not a gun. If anyone slipped and used the word gun, he would be forced to stand before the entire company for an hour, reciting a certain poem that cannot be quoted in polite company. "Ready on the left, ready on the right, the firing line is now ready. Commence firing," the commander in the tower would call out. Although I had never fired a rifle in my life, I found that the experience I had with my BB gun was invaluable. Already in boyhood I had learned that the correct technique for hitting a target is to squeeze the trigger as lightly as possible without allowing your finger to jerk the gun itself. This worked for the M-14 too. Each time the weapon was fired, the exhaust gas from the burned powder would automatically eject the spent shell casing, and the next round was in position to fire immediately when the trigger was pulled again (thus making it *semi*-automatic). When the commander in the tower would announce, "Cease fire, cease fire. The firing line is now closed," he would then add, "Lay down your weapons and police up that brass. No running on the firing line, but the speed limit for walking is ninety miles per hour."

My specialty was the 350 meter targets. I had discovered that a bullet traveling that far actually *falls* substantially, so I found an exact point *above* the target to set my sights, and I could actually count the delay before a round from my weapon knocked over that speck in the distance. When we qualified in Week Six, we were scored on the number of targets hit from three positions—standing, one knee, and prone. For the exam, an advanced infantryman was allowed to crouch beside each of us and coach, and I was fortunate to draw an excellent coach. A target would pop up randomly at various distances and remain standing for about three seconds, but for some reason, I was having trouble with the closest ones. My coach noticed that I was shooting too high, so he told me to fire into the dirt in front of the 50 meter targets. "The enemy is just as dead if the bullet bounces into him," he reasoned, "and if you miss, squeeze off another round right away, you've got time." It had not occurred to me that I could fire more than once at the same target, but then I started hitting targets at every range. He gave me confidence, especially when he said, "Most guys hate those 350s, but you're good at them, aren't you?" A score of at least 30 was required for a Marksman rating, 45 for Sharpshooter, and a perfect score of 60 for Expert. I was quite pleased with my 48. At the evening formation that day, the first sergeant called several to stand up front with him. "Hats off to these men who scored Expert today on the firing range," he said. Then he called a half dozen others to the front. "Men, I want you to take a look at these bolos, these *bolos*," he thundered, "who can't even hit 30 targets on my firing range." They all got that tender remedial training for which the Army is famous and had to requalify. Among them was my thickly bespectacled friend Rogers, intellectual, articulate, sensible, but about as dexterous as a spider wearing horseshoes. I had watched him wince with each pace in his struggle to run the required mile in full combat gear in less than seven minutes. From that point on until the end of basic training, this group of bolos had to march at the back, and one of them was selected for whatever onerous or odorous task, known in the Army as a sh@# detail, that came along.

One of the last days in Week Eight was a miserable, rainy day, and even the drill sergeants were tired of tromping around in the mud. We had completed most of our training and were ordered to disassemble our rifles to clean every speck of carbon from the inside before turning them in. I worked on mine for about two hours, reassembled it and took it over about 0900 hours for inspection. "I still see some carbon there, soldier," said the supply sergeant. I could not see any, but after another hour of work on it, I took it back over again. "Nope, not ready, I still see carbon," he said dryly. After several more tries with the same result throughout the day, he finally agreed it was clean and checked it back in around 1600. Meanwhile, several others in my squad had played cards most of the day, then spent about a half hour cleaning a little on their rifles, walked over to supply and turned them in without incident. Only then did I understand. Those sergeants had wanted us confined to the barracks while they goofed off, but they did not really care what we were doing. My rifle did not have any carbon on it the first time, but anyone who turned in a rifle early would have had time off to wander all over the post, and *they* might be called to task for it. But how did my buddies figure this out so early in the day? That has baffled me to this day.

Finally, came that glorious day when we were standing in formation in our class A dress uniforms receiving our orders for advanced training. When the first sergeant finished the list, there were a few dozen whose names had not been called. Then he said, "And the rest of you have orders for AIT here at Fort Polk—Tiger Land. Right over there on the other side of those trees." If I had been Catholic, those words would have induced me to make the sign of the cross over my soul, the way Eli Wallach did in *The Good, the Bad, and the Ugly* whenever he heard bad news. The war in Vietnam was approaching its zenith, and as I glanced at the faces around me, I realized in an instant that some of them would probably not be coming home. And I could not imagine how anyone could endure twelve weeks more of advanced infantry training. *Never* would be too soon for me to see another little armadillo amble across a Louisiana dirt road or a loblolly pine again, and I could scarcely wait for the first bus out of camp. It was one of the happiest days of my life. This reminds me of the story of graduation day for one class of Marines from boot camp at Fort Pendleton. Recent rains had turned the company area into a morass, and as the troops were lined up in their class A uniforms waiting for their bus to leave, one of the drill instructors walked by. Each of the troops in line gave him a smirk that seemed to signal "can't touch us any more." After passing the last man in the row, the instructor whirled around suddenly and yelled, "*Hit* it!" To a man, the recruits dived into the mud in their dress uniforms. "Now you're Marines," said the sergeant as he strode jauntily away smiling.

Graduation from basic training was not just Liberation Day from Fort Polk, but a promotion too. Woohoo, all the way up to E-2. Fort Benjamin Harrison in Indianapolis was known for two outstanding facilities—the Army Finance Center and the Adjutant General School. I could not say that in Louisiana I had experienced any of the Southern hospitality for which Dixie is so well known, and now I was back in the Midwest. I know this sounds uppity and is not meant to be a reflection upon the kind, nurturing and loving people I had met at Fort Polk, but it felt infinitely more civilized here. Instead of the tinderbox barracks with bare light bulbs and brittle linoleum floors which had housed us at Fort Polk, we lived in modern fireproof cement block structures with fluorescent lighting, tile floors and brightly colored walls. Instead of the rows of bunk beds for fifty troops in one room, we had two bunk beds in individual rooms that could be closed and locked. Our lives had become far less structured, and we could go to the library, to the church of our choice, or even (this would have been unthinkable at Fort Polk) dress in "civies" and catch a bus to go off post into the city. Suddenly life in the Army had become a little tolerable. I would soon discover also that life had females in it again. In those days women still belonged to their own branch of the military called the Women's Army Corps, and they were collectively, sometimes pejoratively, referred to as WACs. I can recall at least four of them that were enlisted in the stenography program with me.

The stenography school was run by a civilian, Mr. Goldstein, who resembled Arthur Wildman from my days at Sherwood so closely that they could have been brothers. Our sixteen weeks of training were so intensive that there were only four subjects—shorthand, English, typing, and military correspondence. The shorthand instructor, Specialist Litchfield, had neither the mindset nor style of a gung-ho career military NCO. Very approachable, affable, reasonable, yet intolerant of frivolity, he was an excellent instructor. Shorthand is uniquely adapted to the English language, capturing not spellings, but sounds, and would make little sense in German, French or other tongue. I also found out that in addition to the very different Gregg and Pittman systems of the English-speaking world, there were different editions of the Gregg system we were learning. The book I picked up in high school was a version called Simplified, but here at USAAGS we would use the Diamond Jubilee edition. The chief difference was in the way strokes are connected and the number of "brief forms" to learn—common words or phrases that could be represented with a reduced number of strokes. Because ordinary conversational speech moves along at speeds averaging about 180 words per minute, it is nearly impossible for a human to sustain that pace to record it verbatim for longer than a minute or two. But shorthand is still much more efficient than cursive, and minimum proficiency to pass the course was 80 wpm. Whenever anyone in class would struggle with a character or a concept, Litchfield would always say, "Don't fight it, write it," and this became a mantra that everyone droned throughout the course.

At the end of each week, we had time trials. Litchfield would dictate from a special book that allowed him, using a stopwatch, to read at 15, 30, 50, up to 200 wpm, whatever proficiency we were expected to reach by the end of that week. He repeatedly advised anyone who was struggling to check out the practice tapes from the office on the evenings or weekends, yet I think I was the only one who ever did. Although I was never even close to struggling, I wanted to become the very best stenographer possible and spent many hours outside of class practicing with those tapes. I was not brown-nosing, but Goldstein and Litchfield were impressed with my diligence. Little did I realize what dividends this decision would pay later. Every opportunity was there for anyone who faltered, yet every week another empty desk or two stood testimonial for someone who had washed out. One day two desks were empty for another reason. Homosexuality was not tolerated in any branch of the military, so two from our class declared that they had enough of Army life by "coming out" from the same bunk bed at the same time. This was a costly decision for them, because in addition to the branding they would wear as an undesirable for the rest of life, unfit for military service, they received a dishonorable discharge and forfeiture of all benefits—not to mention the waste of the better part of a year of their lives. I thought it was ironic that one of them was Morales, a name so close to the morals he apparently did not possess.

Although electric typewriters were starting to be introduced into the market by this time, I had never used one. Not even the first doodle for a word processor machine had been scribbled on anyone's corporate design pad at this time yet either. We were being prepared for field service, where electricity may or may not be available, so most of our training still used manual Royal typewriters, meticulously maintained and well conditioned, but manual. Because I had learned typing at an early age and had considerable experience typing papers through high school and college, I expected to be the fastest typist in the school. However, I gradually became aware that George Craighead was at least as good, if not better. The class was arranged alphabetically, and he sat ahead and to my right, so one day during a time trial, I could watch him out of the corner of my eye. Undeniably, he was reaching for his carriage return before I finished the first line. Well, maybe I can catch up with him on the second line, I thought.

No, he pulled even farther ahead on that one. I found out later that he had been a professional teletype operator as a civilian, operating his equipment at speeds approaching 100 wpm. Minimum rate to pass the course was 50 wpm, but the many hours each week I spent practicing outside of class was not only to break 80, but to beat Craighead. Despite my most determined efforts, however, I had to resign myself to the fact that in the end he was uncatchable—and he did not even have to practice.

Our "professor" of English was Specialist Stevens, cut from the same cloth as Litchfield. Because neither was a career Army type, both of these very competent instructors were sensitive to the fact that we were sitting in the same seats where they had been several months earlier, and were trying to make our ride in them seem more like the back of a convertible than a convoy truck. In terms of grammar, spelling and usage, I considered my English to be unassailable, but not everyone in the class could say the same, so we had many sessions on punctuation, possessives, tenses, sentence structure, agreement, and so on. For me, the steepest segment of the learning curve was the style rules the Army preferred, in agreement with Government Printing Office style manual or the *Chicago Manual of Style* on some points but not on others. Those principles were so pervasive and invasive in me that I follow most of them to this day, including, as you may have noticed, the manuscript you are reading. If you see any mistakes, by the way, you will need to blame them on my editors, whom I am paying a handsome salary to catch them [he's a skinflint—ed.]. Certain little factoids have also stuck themselves to my psyche, ready to pull out of the mind's toolbox whenever they need to be applied. For example, only one word in the English language, when spelled properly, ends in sede. Anyone who spells supersede any other way has it incorrect, but I bet at least half the time you will see a *c* for that *s*. Only three words in English end in ceed—exceed, proceed, and succeed. All others with that homogram end with cede (e.g., recede, intercede, etc.). See, was this not a productive excursion through a little piece of English pedagogy?

The mechanism used for bestowing credit for transcription of dictated material at the USAAGS was known as the "throw-out" system. A perfect transcription was not necessarily required, as long as the typed page did not change the essence of the message. Similarly, a typo was excused as long as the intended word was obvious *and* did not result in nonsense. A violation of either of these principles would result in a throw-out, where the entire transcription was rejected, and the student received no credit for it. Perhaps the single most common mistake resulting in a throw-out was the word *than* for *that*, or vice versa. If I intended to say "It is my hope that …" and type "It is my hope than …," the typo is obvious, but since *than* is also a real word, the rest of the sentence is nonsense and would always be considered a throw-out. I can say confidently that while I may have missed a word in transcription here or there, I never had a throw-out for anything I turned in. Transcription was inculcated in us to such a degree that even today I find it impossible to listen to someone speak without compulsively forming a mental image of the way those words would be represented in shorthand. And of course, when I take notes at a meeting or conference, my page likely contains more comprehensive information than yours. I believe it is unfortunate that when my generation dies out, this extremely utilitarian skill, no longer learned or used in a world of dictating and stenotype machines, word processors, and computers, will become a lost art.

And then there was the subject of military correspondence. In stark contrast to Litchfield and Stevens, the instructor of this course was a tired old E-6 sergeant who had been around since dinosaurs roamed the earth and had been busted down to E-5, perhaps even E-4, countless times in his meteoric career. He slurred his words and had a range in his voice of no more than about three decibels in volume and five cycles in pitch. This class was the breathlessly exciting world of cutting mimeograph stencils and learning how to type multiple copies without getting the carbon paper in backwards. We were also supposed to learn the proper method for excising sentences, paragraphs, or whole pages from superseded regulations, the proper order for maintaining memoranda in a physical folder (most recent on top), and several other topics so dry that if I mentioned them, you could give this page a little puff and they would blow away. How we managed to abide this tedium in the last hour of each day only the oracle at Delphi could answer.

Anyone who was certified at 80 wpm in shorthand, who tested at least 50 wpm in typing, and who attained at least seventy percent on the English and correspondence exams by the end of the course would score 700 points, the minimum number required for graduation. However, bonus points were awarded for performance above this minimum, up to 1000 points. No one had ever maxed the course, but as the end of our session approached, I was on a record pace. Only two of us took the shorthand exam for certification at 120, and I was the only one who was certified at 130. I had maximum scores for typing, English and correspondence, but in shorthand I still needed to reach 150. When I took the test for certification at 140, about a dozen of my classmates were gathered around to watch and encourage. One was actually an admirer—Sweeney, sitting directly behind me in class, who had watched me play ping-pong, glide my fingers over the piano keyboard, and produce sounds at the typewriter that he called making popcorn, and he always remarked about my marvelous hands. Whether this made me nervous, I had an off day or I simply bounced up against some invisible ceiling, I fell hopelessly behind on the dictation and did not even attempt to transcribe what I scribbled down. Nevertheless, I finished the course with 989 points, not a USAAGS record, but a score that remains in my own record book for all time.

Before the course was over, the entire stenography school was assembled one day for a presentation by a sergeant from the 82nd Airborne Division, recruiting volunteers for paratrooper training. When he fielded questions at the end, one student asked him whether he was scared the first time he jumped out of an airplane. "Not the first time, the *second* time," he replied. One day as graduation neared, two men came through the School, asking Goldstein and Litchfield for the names of any outstanding or especially promising students currently enrolled. I would eventually find out the two men were an Army warrant officer named Leonard Stephens and an Air Force sergeant named Steve Kerchner, from the White House Communications Agency. Without hesitation, Goldstein arranged for me to meet with them for an interview, and I was selected to begin work with them in Washington as soon as the lengthy investigation process could be completed. If I ever have any doubt that God is directing my life, I look back to this single event and come to no other conclusion. I had absolutely no control over what happened. I did not even know about such an agency or assignment. I did not apply for it or choose them—they chose me. It was the only day they were there, and I was the only one they interviewed. Others just as bright, industrious and talented were there, but I was the one who had developed to the point where my progress could be evaluated against their needs. They had not recruited candidates here for over a year and would not return for more than another. I was literally at the right place at the right time, and this could not possibly be by happenstance. As we will see, the chain of events that led from this single incident in my life would eventually be so wondrous that I could never have imagined it, and all unequivocally by the grace of God.

While I awaited my orders to Washington, I would be applying the principles I had learned in class under real-world conditions, assigned to the office of Colonel Thibeau, a congenial lieutenant colonel who had at some point in his career made his home in one of the suburbs in Maryland. He was quite familiar with the Washington area and gave me important previews of what I should expect. One day he asked me to take the minutes for a meeting of the officers' club. Freshly minted from shorthand school, I arrogantly assumed that with my superior skills I would impress them with a verbatim transcript of their discussions. It was a disaster, of course, when I discovered that I was no match for the fast-speaking Army officers and their wives in attendance. It was a valuable lesson, not only in humility, but note taking. A meeting is not a court proceeding, and no one expects a transcript. In the unknown number of minutes I have recorded since, I have learned that what I actually need to write down is a few words, names or quotes, and memory will fill in the details.

If you are not prepared for another didactic divertimento (I know, a music term) through English grammar, you should skip this paragraph. In one of the memos Thibeau dictated to me, he used the word cancellation. The rule we had learned about doubling the consonant at the end of a word when adding a suffix beginning with a vowel (wait, do not glaze over yet) depends upon which syllable of the root word is accented in pronunciation. For example, begin becomes begin*n*ing, to preserve the short / sound of the stressed second syllable (otherwise, the rules of pronunciation would make it become begīning). However, for the word cancel, the suffix can be added without doubling (hence, canceling), because the stress remains on the first syllable. So, according to the rule I had learned, I typed up his memo spelling it cance*l*ation. When I insisted I was correct, he appealed to Goldstein and Stevens. It seems I had learned only half of the rule. If the suffix was itself two syllables and changed the position of the accent of the root word, the rule I was dutifully applying should actually ... (now, you can glaze over ... aw, never mind, I have pushed you too far already). It was another lesson in humiliation (not humilliation) for me. Incidentally, I am constantly irritated by the highway departments of all those states that try to save space on their signs by telling me at the rest areas where the buses should park. Buses? You mean like fūses? Or did you mean busses?

While investigation of my background continued, I was asked by USAAGS to assist them tutoring a few students in remedial English. One of them was Dieter Quinlivan, a naturalized citizen from Germany who somehow found his way into steno school. We became friends, and when Dieter was later assigned to West Point, I made the drive through the beautiful Catskills a number of times to visit him. One day while the weeks dragged on in Indianapolis, I had a visitor from the actual Agency where I was being assigned. He was Fred Skrocki, who worked in the adjoining office to where I would be working, and he gave me a much clearer picture of what to expect when I arrived than anything that had come through official channels. While he could not disclose too many details, he painted a scenario that was difficult to believe. No one was in uniform or resided in military quarters. A clothing allowance was provided as seed money for a civilian wardrobe, and a cost of living allowance was issued to cushion the impact of local housing and expenses. In fact, one of the items of business on his agenda was to broker an arrangement with me about where I would be living. Fred was currently sharing an apartment with one Gary Voight in a place called Fort Ward Towers, a beautiful new high-rise in Alexandria with security, swimming pool and a stunning view of the city. But Fred would be getting married soon and was asking whether I would be able to take over his lease when he brought his new bride back to Washington with him in a few months. He even convinced me to join the White House credit union just to take out a loan for a hundred dollars to buy his bedroom furniture. I did not need the loan, but he reasoned that this would establish a credit history that I might need for some transaction in the future. You might get the idea Fred was quite a slick salesman in civilian life, but his family actually operated a funeral business in Perth Amboy, to which he would one day return.

Over lunch one day, Fred introduced me to a friend and former classmate at Ft. Harrison named Shirley. I had never read *Don Quixote* before, but several evenings later when I was back in my quarters cackling at the escapades of Quixote, sidekick Sancho Panza and their obsession with Dulcinea, Shirley stopped by to ask whether I felt like going for a walk. She had signed up as a WAC over a year earlier and was now discovering that life here as a specialist in the Army was a humdrum existence with a bleak future for her. Counseling is not my strong suit, but I tried to listen, increasingly unsympathetically, to her unremarkable experiences in basic training and now the "misery" of daily pressures working in her field. She had a proposition for me. As she explained it, a life-changing event could be used as a pretext for early discharge from the Corps, so she was proposing that I marry her, just long enough to effect her release, and then we could separate and annul the arrangement. *Marry* her! I barely knew her. She was a shapely blond, from somewhere in Oklahoma I think, but beyond her obvious good looks I did not really know who she was. Marry in haste, repent at leisure, Ben Franklin would say. God works in mysterious ways, but I was quite sure this was not mysterious, just crazy. I told her I would need to think about a scheme like this. By chance I bumped into her at the mess hall a day or two later and asked whether she would like to go for a walk. I had rehearsed my response to her in my mind, but as we talked for an hour or so, I kept anticipating she would raise the subject again herself. When she did not, I said finally, "Shirley, about that idea of yours …." "Oh that," she interrupted, "I already decided against it," casually moving on to another topic without further comment, explanation or expression of regret. What a fruitcake. When I related this to Fred a few months later, he told me Shirley had posed the same proposition to him.

Just inside the front door of our quarters was a desk that served as a kind of information/guard station for anyone who entered. Duty at this desk was rotated around the clock, so I found myself as charge of quarters (CQ) whenever my turn came up. Far from drudgery, this post was an opportunity for me to learn all sorts of inside information to which I would not otherwise be privy. Besides the high traffic in pizza deliveries, there was an occasional one for something called a hoagy sandwich—salami, cheese and dill pickle that arrived piping hot in a little foil bag. It always smelled so good when it came in the door that I decided to try one myself, and it is perhaps without much exaggeration to say I ordered fifty of them over the next few months. The phone rang incessantly late into the night, and eventually I came to recognize the alluring voice of a certain female who called frequently. One night when the party she was trying to reach was not in, she struck up a conversation with me. I was captivated immediately by the sweet expressiveness of everything she said, and the longer I listened to her siren song, the more my imagination carried me off toward her castle on the shore. This was not phone sex or concupiscent flirting, but I did become intrigued by what she must look like. Surely a voice so mesmerizing and vibrant must be accompanied by a gorgeous face and voluptuous figure, I fantasized. When I made some compliment about the personality she projected over the phone, she asked if I would like to meet her. "But promise you won't be disappointed when you see me," she teased. Oh, surely not, I told her confidently. But when we actually met, I realized she was not teasing. Perhaps I should just say that some fantasies are best left to the imagination.

# Gary

**N**ot the one in Indiana, not the one in *The Music Man*. One day in September 1967 my orders finally came through for Washington. Gary Voight knew it before I did and sent me a nice letter of welcome. Each class that moved through USAAGS had a number, and he mentioned that by coincidence his class a year earlier was Steno 21, the same number as mine. Although that seemed to him a good omen, I could read the thinly disguised disappointment on his face when we first met. Our two psychological profiles were quite different. While I exuded the flamboyant, too familiar, brash personality of my mother, given to faux pas and shallow ill-timed quips, Gary was reserved, circumspect, very perceptive but guarded in whatever he said. On the other hand, I was usually positive, optimistic and energetic, while he tended to be brooding, melancholy and passive. I admired his foresight, astuteness and discretion, but from my vantage point in time, I realize now I must have left him an impression of spontaneity and impulsivity in return that stirred up negative vibes for him. As he shaved in the morning, he would be thinking through the day that lay ahead, planning in detail; when I shaved, I was more likely to think about what I would throw in my lunch bag, and what lay ahead in the next ten minutes. Despite these differences, however, he tolerated my foibles, and we eventually became lifelong friends. One of my most serious missteps was the result of what was supposed to be a practical joke. When Fred got married, I sent a nice card, but as a joke I included a penny and told them to buy something nice with it. Both Fred and his new wife took it as an affront, and Fred never spoke to me again.

Although there are many details about the assignment that are classified, I found that everything Fred had told me was true. Fatigues and uniforms went into storage, except for that one day each year when we tromped into the field somewhere pretending to be soldiers. In addition to roving all over the Washington area to various agencies, including the Pentagon, Executive Office Building, even Camp David, our work took us to military installations all over the country, and many in the Agency traveled the globe. In the office in which I primarily worked, I was the lowest in both rank and seniority, but a promotion to PFC was not long in coming. Gary had been there about a year and had been promoted to SP-4. The three of us who were not expecting to be career soldiers each had our MOS changed from stenographer to administrative specialist as we arrived at the Agency, since we would never actually take dictation again. Besides Gary and myself, the third member of this group was one Tim Dempsey, an E-5 sergeant whose intellectual brilliance was marred by his cynical attitude and characteristic sardonic approach to life. He was in his last few months with the Agency, and although I did not dislike him, I felt I could never penetrate that air of superiority and cold disdain, almost contempt, he seemed to have for me and the rest of his world. The fourth desk in the room was filled by an E-6 career NCOIC named Dwight David Keith Kraschnewski. I am quite sure I have it spelled correctly because, with a name like that, he was obliged to spell it a hundred times every day over the phone, always giving out the twelve letters in groups of three. He insisted that all of his friends call him Krasch. Our boss was someone I introduced earlier, Leonard Stephens, the warrant officer who had hand-selected me at USAAGS.

Krasch was from Medford, Wisconsin and adopted a reputation as a party animal, the primogenitor of fun-seekers who could make spring break seem like a garden club. After hours he had a few favorite watering holes, but he sometimes loved to hop from one bar to another all over town. As the evening wore on, we noticed that the number of red traffic lights he observed gradually decreased until there were none at all. Once in a while Gary and I would crawl into his huge black Mercedes-Benz touring car with him and brace ourselves for a luge ride through busy streets, wondering if we would wake up dead the next morning. In the office it was often an embarrassed young lady at the other end of one of his phone calls, who might be asked for details of her honeymoon or made the object of any number of other risqué impertinences. It was this blatant sort of disregard for discretion with respect to the sensitive position he held that eventually got him booted out of the Agency one day. In the meantime we accompanied him to a number of parties to which he somehow finagled an invitation. When I was at Ft. Harrison, I actually tried to learn to drink beer but could never acquire a taste for it, and here at these bars and parties, I was sometimes handed a glass that actually repulsed me unless it had brandy or something sweet in it. My grandfather's parents and grandparents would be mortified at my flippant distaste for these distilled products, given their coveted position as Braumeister of their village in Wunstorf.

Gary and I rode to work together in his little red Triumph each day. One of the advantages of a pint-sized sports car is that it fits into parking spaces too snug for anything else but a motorcycle. On one occasion the space we found was so tight that Gary drove straight into the spot, then he and I lifted the back of the car and slid it laterally into position at the curb. Gary loved his Spitfire, but he was telling me that when he first picked it up from the dealer near his home in Pemberton, Minnesota, an unpleasant surprise awaited. As he reached highway speed on the way home, he noticed that someone's wheel had rolled up alongside his car. Then it occurred to him that it was actually *his* wheel. Instead of lug nuts, this model had a single large wing nut to fasten each wheel to the car, which was supposed to be threaded so that as the wheel turned, it tended to tighten. An error at the factory resulted in reverse threading on one of the spindles, and as it turned, it loosened the wing nut until the wheel flew off. After Gary retrieved it from where it had bounded off into the ditch, he attached it with the faulty wing nut and gingerly returned to the dealer for the car's first repair.

After a few weeks of feeling guilty riding with Gary every day, I decided it was time for me to buy my first car. My father had worked with Chevrolet for most of his professional life, so he helped me with the options and pricing of the model I ordered from Bob Peck Chevrolet in Arlington. I had been saving for this moment all through college, and until I needed rent money here in Alexandria, my expenses in the Army had been quite minimal, so it was not much of a strain to plunk down $2700 in cash for a gun-metal blue, four-speed, 1968 Bel Air. When my new car finally arrived, I was disappointed that the color was not what I had projected from the swatch in the sales brochure, but I was otherwise giddy with excitement. I had been dependent upon Gary and others to get around, but now I was able to return these favors and finally buzz around more independently, especially to join a church. The first

Sunday that Gary and I visited Immanuel Lutheran Church in Alexandria, we were invited to have lunch with Ralph Behrens, the principal of the parochial school, and his wife Lola. Gary discovered that Lola's mother, Mrs. Manthe, was his neighbor back on their farm in Minnesota, and one summer he had actually worked in her field.

Since the public transportation system in the Washington area was nowhere near as efficient as the CTA in Chicago, a car was essential for a social life as well. At the Defense Intelligence Agency, one of the offices I visited regularly, a stunningly beautiful young lady named Chandra Hammond worked at the counter. As expected, Krasch also made her acquaintance and invited her to one of his parties. Here she met and later married one of our colleagues at the Agency named Willard Hausenfluck. Krasch had also told Charlie, as Chandra preferred to be called, to bring some of her girl friends, so it was at this party where I met the two young ladies from Oxon Hill who had come with her. One was Carol O'Sullivan (not her real name), from a large Catholic family of eight children, and the other was her friend Alexis, the daughter of a military officer who had recently been buried in Arlington Cemetery. I bantered with both of them for most of the evening, and when it was time to leave, I offered Alexis a ride home. It was not until I heard Carol whisper "Congratulations" under her breath to Alexis that I realized the two of them had been vying for my affections. Carol was one of those girls who, as the familiar euphemism puts it, had a great personality. She really did have a pleasant, winsome demeanor, but, I am sorry, I must be *physically* attracted to a girl in whom I am interested.

Alexis was quite attractive, and after we were dating for a while, she pointed out that what her apartment really needed was a stereo, so I foolishly loaned her mine. We sometimes double dated with Alexis's friend Susan, but one evening those two stopped over at my apartment, where they taught me how to play canasta, a two-handed card game that can be played awkwardly with three players. As we played three-handed, Alexis delighted herself playing into Susan's hand, effectively making it two against one. Worse, she and Susan had been in French class together, and were conniving throughout the game, communicating in broken French. Occasionally Gary, who could understand a little of what they were saying, would chuckle at the tomfoolery he was overhearing. If this were good-natured teasing, it would have been quite innocent and even enjoyable for me. As our relationship developed, however, I could sense a pattern of disparagement. It is probably safe to say that any friendship depends upon a kindred spirit and a mutual feeling of support and respect. In the special friendship of a mate this expectation is even stronger, but with Alexis I was increasingly the butt of her humor, and instead of the assurance that she was really on my side, I had a growing feeling of antagonism, belittlement and mistreatment, and concluded she was not for me.

Although Alexis lived in an apartment by herself, her mother was quite fond of me, so we were invited together occasionally to her beautiful house a mile or two away. In time I found out why. Alexis had been involved in a relationship not long before we met, which had led to the termination of a pregnancy, and her mother was delighted that I had come along as a buffer between Alexis and this young amorist. I was not sure the passion had completely died out in Alexis, however, given the subtle comparisons she was wont to make between me and Mr. Wunderbar. My suspicions were about to be confirmed. Without telling her I was ending the relationship, I made up some pretext one evening to ask for my stereo back. She told me to wait for her call in about an hour. When I waited two hours and did not hear from her, I drove to her apartment and knocked on the door. She was just saying good night to Casanova. After he left, she was enraged that I had not waited for her call, as directed.

The real reason for her fury, of course, was that I had walked in on her duplicity. To leave no doubt, I called her when I returned home to tell her I was not getting a satisfactory return for my investment of time with her and would not see her again. Gary overheard what I told her and was pleased that I finally saw the light.

Although the biological clock ticks at a different rate for men than for women, I realized one day that I was approaching what I considered to be marriageable age. I was meeting a number of eligible young ladies but none with whom I would want to share a lifetime. Years later, when I finally made contact with Lynne, I learned that her relationship with Rumpelstiltlegs had ended in about six months. Even more startling was the revelation that she had broken her engagement with her fiancé and did not actually marry for *seven* more years! Had I known this, I would most certainly have tried to locate her. However, as I would eventually discover, the reason God intentionally withheld this information from me was that He had a far better plan for me. At the time, the realization that I had never really rebounded from Lynne haunted me, but since I could no longer look Lynneward, I went back with a sigh through the little black book in my mind to see if there might be someone I had missed. When Hitchcock's *The Birds* was the talk of the town, a few of us at Sherwood had gone out on a kind of group date one weekend to see it, and I recalled an attractive classmate named Arlene, who seemed to have a crush on me. In those early days I had precious little extra time for social activities, and a year or so later she had returned to her home in Rosholt, Wisconsin. I tracked her down through Gene Montgomery's wife Lois, who had been a close friend when they were students together. Arlene remembered me, and I boldly asked her how she felt about flying out for a guided tour of Washington with me for a few days. I had asked Gary whether he would mind if Arlene stayed with us for a few days and slept on the sofa, and she accepted my invitation. In those days it was still possible to meet someone as they stepped off the plane, and when I saw Arlene descend the stairs, I thought she had switched places with a starlet from Hollywood—Audrey Hepburn turned blond in the sunglasses, pillbox purse, fashionable wardrobe and shoes, and shapely figure I saw waving to me from the steps. She was gorgeous but otherwise unpretentious, unrefined, an unsophisticated farm girl throughout, and Gary liked her immediately. He took me aside after her first day with us and said, "Now this one is more *like* it." His allusion to Alexis made me wince.

By the time Arlene's visit was over, however, I found that she matched up too closely with the stereotype ditsy blond secretary of the big screen for my taste, and as I drove her to the airport, I had already made the decision that I was not all that interested in her. She, on the other hand, had had a marvelous vacation and was infatuated with me. Immediately, letters began to arrive from her, dripping with sentiment and flattery, signed and sealed with perfume, hugs and kisses. I know it sounds cruel to say that I did not answer them, but, in fact, this inaction on my part was supposed to have the opposite effect—hinting subtly rather than crushing her spirit with words. One day a gift arrived, a little jeweled turtle, which in my ignorance I considered to be no more than a knickknack, but it may have been intended by her to be worn on my lapel or something. When I returned it to her, she sent me a poem told from the point of view of the forlorn rejected turtle that had found its way back to the pond where it started. The front desk of our building repeatedly passed me phone messages from her, and then one day I even got a call from my parents in Minnesota, wondering who a certain Arlene was, desperate to reach me. I did not intend to break her heart, but her obsession did little to bring about a change of heart in me. After a while her cries from the wilderness stopped, and I never heard from her again.

One night when I attended one of Krasch's parties, I spent part of the evening talking with an attractive young lady named Leona. She had been telling me that she played the piano, so I took her over to the USO club, which had a piano in each of its rehearsal studios. We signed out one of them, and after she played a few pieces, I played the Beethoven *Sonata in F minor* for her. Then when I drove her home, I invited her to join me for church the next morning. After church she invited me to come in for lunch, and it was only then that I found out she was the wife of a soldier stationed at Fort Myer who was away on assignment. Worse yet, Leona had filled out a visitor card at the church service, and the next time I saw Dorothy Kethe, she told me that as a member of the evangelism committee, she had paid Leona a visit and asked if I knew she was married. When I said yes, Dorothy's face clouded over, and without another word she walked away, leaving to my imagination the prattle that surely must have followed.

One day when I was browsing through the library at Ft. Harrison, I had run across a book by Billie Pesin Rosen called *The Science of Handwriting Analysis*. Although I did not think I was particularly interested in the study of personality, Rosen was making some shocking claims. In the hands of an expert, she says, this discipline makes it possible to elicit an astonishing number of personal traits frozen in the strokes of a sample of writing, especially if the sample includes the signature. There are many general misconceptions. For example, many laymen might refer to a particular writing as a "woman's" handwriting. Rosen would disagree; while it might be possible to deduce that the writer is a woman from clues taken together, the clues might just as easily reveal only femininity. According to general belief, the writing of a left-handed person slants to the left, yet slant generally determines, not handedness, but the degree of acceptance of the outside world, so a rightie might slant left or a southpaw right. When I went in search of her book in the Arlington public library one day, the librarians told me that the county has a wonderful policy of ordering any book that a patron does not find in their system, so I asked them to order one.

In the meantime I leafed through another book on the shelf by A. D. Hartmark, who lived in Minnesota and was offering a correspondence course in graphology, as he called it, leading to a certificate of accomplishment. I took his course, got the certificate, and had fun comparing the handwriting of many acquaintances to what I observed in them personally, noting some amazing correlation. Once considered a black art, handwriting analysis now seems to be gaining some recognition in the field of human resources, where a sample of an applicant's writing is scrutinized for incompatibilities with a given employment opportunity. It can be used to detect personality changes or even to save the life of someone who has become despondent. I could see at a glance, for example, the despair that settled over my mother in the last years of her life in her handwriting long before it became detectable in face-to-face conversation.

Although we were not assigned to any particular base, we had full military privileges at Fort Myer near Arlington Cemetery, including the movie theater, commissary, post exchange, and other facilities. In those days the installation was divided into two posts, but several years ago South Post was razed, plowed up and landscaped into gravesites. One weekend when I walked into the USO club there, I saw a familiar face from the Agency. It was an airman named Lasch, who had somehow appointed himself the director and organizer of some of the events at the club. He asked me if I could participate in a program he was coordinating. There was a very popular show on prime time television in those days called *The Dating Game*, in which a contestant poses questions to three potential candidates hidden from view, then selects one for a date. The club was staging its own version of the show, in which local models were solicited as contestants, and Lasch wanted me to be one of his three candidates. The audience could see both the contestant and the three of us suitors, but there was a curtain dividing us from her. For some reason the audience liked my answers, and when the time came for the young lady to make her choice, they were shouting for her to choose me. She was a gorgeous brunette with long flowing hair, which probably sounds like any man's dream date, but the club sent us to a dinner-dance disco theater, which presented a serious problem for me. At gunpoint I could probably fake the two-step, but I had absolutely no interest in disco dance. This did not matter to Slinky Samantha, however, who put on such a dizzying solo performance in the center of the dance floor, arms flailing wildly, dark tresses flying in every direction and the tassels on her outfit jiggling in time to the beat, that everyone else stood back to clap and cheer. As you have probably perceived, we had little in common, and neither of us made any attempt to bridge the gap on the silent ride home.

Airman Lasch heard me practicing in one of the studios one day and asked me if I would like to participate in a contest for a USO tour. Sometimes in a vain moment I would fancy myself as someone famous, but immediately I projected in my mind what it would mean to my position in the Agency if I were to be selected to troop around the world on an entertainment billet. I should have learned my lesson about show business by now, but in a moment of weakness, I told him to put my name on his list. I do not actually remember the contest itself, but I still have the silver jewelry case I won for first place as instrumental soloist. I had played one of my own student compositions called *Theme and Variations*, and the judges were so impressed with it that they asked me to play this piece at the next show they billed at the Fort Myer auditorium. On the evening of the program, hundreds, perhaps thousands, were in attendance in the audience, including some top brass, as I warmed up back stage on *Un Sospiro,* the *Etude in D-Flat* by Franz Liszt. It sounded so good that I sent word to the announcer that I was going to play this flashy piece instead. The director of the program was furious at the last minute switch because he had planned my piece as a feature performance of a composition written by a serviceman. Worse yet, I became so stagestruck when I walked out into the spotlight that I truncated the piece after the first several bars of it. Needless to say, I was blacklisted for any further business with the USO, and Lasch never called me again.

One day Gary told me he was getting a kitten, a coal-black male that he named Andy. Although I love kittens, they unfortunately turn into cats, and my immune system does not get along well with them. In this case, however, that would not be a problem, because a second announcement followed. Gary had become engaged to his high school sweetheart, a wonderful, very attractive young lady named Carol Severson from a farm near his home, and I somehow picked up vibes that the two of them would prefer that I not stay in the apartment with them after they were married. When Gary asked me for some alternative ideas to *Lohengrin* and other traditional wedding marches, I was flattered, first, that he asked, and, second, when he accepted my suggestion to use César Franck's *Grande Pièce Symphonique in F-Sharp Minor*. Both of them loved it, and though they were not sure their church organist could learn to play such a difficult piece, it is still one of their favorites to this day. One of the greatest differences between Gary and me was our taste in music. He reveled in the pop music of our teens, Sinatra, the Beatles, but his favorite was Barbra Streisand. For me the most stirring music of all time is the rich and powerful orchestral literature of the Romantic era. I can listen to the symphonies of Beethoven and Tchaikovsky or the piano concertos of Rachmaninoff, Liszt, or Saint-Saëns for hours on end and never tire of them. When I played the *Daphnis and Chloe Suite No. 2* of Ravel, one of the most beautiful pieces ever written, for him one day he said politely, "See, now to me that piece is boring." Boring! I have to say he was more tolerant of my choices than I was of his, but instead of allowing the music he played to grate on my nerves, I tried to be intrigued by what there was about it that held out such sway for him.

Andy was such fun to tease. One day when I was sitting at the table, he saw my toe twitch and decided my sock was some quarry in the wild. When I threw a shoebox over him, I watched in fascination as the box did not move for a few seconds while kitten logic processed this new development. Then when the autokinetic shoebox started to slide all over the room, I laughed until my sides ached. Did you ever laugh so hard no sound could come out? This is what happened to me when he finally tired of this game and violently thrashed his way out from beneath that box. Most kittens will chase a little ball, so one day I wadded up a sheet of newspaper into a ball and threw it across the room. Andy leapt so acrobatically in an attempt to catch this speeding object passing just over his head, that he did a complete flip in mid-air, kicking a Kleenex box off the coffee table with one hind paw as he came around. The impact of his toe against the box and the noise it made when it landed startled him so much that the instant his feet touched the floor, he scampered under the sofa faster than I was aware a living creature could move. I thought I would split open laughing. But I would not have much time to play with Andy before I looked for a new roommate.

Meanwhile, there had been some personnel rotations at the Agency. Krasch was replaced as NCOIC by a straight-arrow E-7 sergeant named Vernon Green. Tim had mustered out, and Gary was promoted to E-5 sergeant to take his place. That meant that I could now be promoted to specialist, and a new employee named Michael Zeleny moved into the slot I vacated. In the next office, working with Fred Skrocki, was a new employee named Samuel Hubbard, from Lynchburg, Virginia, who needed a roommate. Sam and I found an apartment at Arlington Towers, near Key Bridge in Rosslyn, and, sad to leave apartment 1109 at Fort Ward, I left a good relationship with Gary to find an even better one with Sam. It would be difficult to find a better roommate. Sam was a conservative Southern Baptist, very clean in thought, word and deed. Ever neat and tidy, he was, most importantly, pleasant and agreeable. He was always willing to ride along when I wanted to answer an ad for furniture or something, and he even laughed at my stupid jokes. When I needed to go out of town for a week that summer, he agreed to lug my forty-pound tape recorder to a class in German I was taking at George Washington University to tape it for me.

When Krasch left town, his party circuit went with him, and my social calendar had an increasing number of empty dates on it. I heard about a new kind of dating service advertising a match with someone of similar interests by computer. As I filled out the questionnaire, I realized a serious flaw in the algorithm this system employed. First, it assumed that only similar interests are attractive and that these qualities are of equal weight, but second, after the questionnaire asked the usual personal questions about me, it asked none about my preferences in someone else. Nevertheless, I received the names of five eligibles in the mail and called them one by one. Two said they were already in a relationship, a third lived way up near Baltimore and did not know when her busy travel schedule would allow us to get together, and the fourth never answered the phone. The fifth one was also Lutheran, lived nearby in Falls Church and was available for a dinner date the next weekend. Hmm, promising. After an enjoyable evening, however, I was making a left turn into the parking lot of her apartment building to return her home, when we were struck by another car. It was quite late before the matter of this fender bender was resolved, and when I had the temerity to ask whether I could call her again, she said no. By the time I added the bill for body shop repairs to the fee paid to the dating service, I considered this was an expensive way to meet people anyway and concluded there must be a more productive use of my resources.

American University was just across the Potomac River and down the road a couple of miles from Rosslyn, so I decided to start graduate school there. When I tried to register, however, the administration tried to tell me that Sherwood was not an accredited institution and would not accept me as a degree candidate. All of my course work at the University of Chicago was through Sherwood also, so they could not accept that either. They would, however, accept registration as a non-degree student, so I was determined that I could take enough courses that way until I had a proven track record with the university and hoped to force them to allow the transition to degree status some day. The professor of musicology, with a doctorate from Columbia, was George Schutze, a protégé of Gustave Reese, the foremost authority on Renaissance music in the world and author of the most respected text on the subject. In case the term is unfamiliar or ambiguous to you, musicology is to music what perhaps archaeology is to anthropology. It is the scholarly approach to the history and provenance of music, not the theoretical analysis of its tones or the performance of them, and it was a discipline that appealed to me right away. It was fascinating to me, for example, to learn that solmization originated in the *Ut queant laxis* of an eleventh-century monk named Guido d'Arezzo, using the syllables ut, re, mi …, altered in due time to do, re, mi …, because *ut* was a difficult syllable for singers to express melismatically.

Unlike some of my professors at the graduate level, Schutze was outstanding, and yet he was very impressed with the papers I turned in. My parents had given me a music typewriter (actually a Smith-Corona portable converted to produce music symbols) as a gift when I graduated from Sherwood, and I used it to quote musical excerpts or transcriptions into modern notation in these term papers. I was also extremely fortunate to have the vast holdings of the Library of Congress at my disposal and spent many an evening and weekend in one of their study carrels with my portable typewriter (oh, to go back to those days with a laptop and a digital camera!). The Copyright Office of the United States is one of the departments of the Library, so the reference librarians were extremely sensitive about what could be photocopied. I had so much interaction with Jon Newsom and Wayne Shirley at the reference desk there, that I could almost consider them roommates. On one occasion the nearest library which had a source I needed was at Harvard, so armed with my Polaroid camera, I set off for Hahvahd Yahd at Cambridge for the weekend. This meant, of course, that when anyone would ask where I went to school, I would now be able to tell them that I had been to Harvard. Incidentally, when my brother Ralph spent some time in the Boston area, his wife was driven mad by the way the *r* in their English could be wrested from cah (or even caa), and yet inexplicably reappear in pizzar in the same sentence. Supported by a dozen pages of laminated source photos, my paper earned lavish praise from Schutze, who told the class that with very little more work, it could have been submitted as a thesis. Schutze raised one eyebrow when I told him in class one day that when I read Reese's book, I had noticed a few errors in it, which I pointed out to him. It was a short time after that that he made arrangements with the University to offer me a fellowship for some research he had in mind. Unfortunately, it was a full-time position with only a modest stipend, and I had to decline it.

One of the courses taught by Dr. Schutze was called Twentieth Century Music. Since about a third of the twentieth century was still in the future at that point, it was impossible to extrapolate what trends would emerge or even difficult to analyze the significance to history the music already written would have. We were still too close to it to have a historical perspective. The music of Bach, for example, arguably the greatest composer who ever lived, would not be recognized as the culmination of the Baroque era for at least a hundred years after he died, the period of time in which no one had ever heard of him. However, I asked Schutze one day whether he would like to hear what I thought the music of the twenty-*first* century would be like. He sniffed, smiled and changed the subject. Pompous graduate student, his gesture seemed to say, who does he think he is? He was not interested in my theory, but perhaps you are. The one thing that all music since the beginning of history has in common is the medium—sound, stimulation of nerves in the ears through compressed air waves. Suppose, however, that the auditory center of the *brain* could be stimulated directly, without the medium. This could be effected crudely at first, through some form of electrodes, but as our understanding of parapsychology increases, this stimulation might be possible through some form of telepathy. Whole compositions would be written by multi-disciplinary specialists who would weave their art directly upon the visual, olfactory, and tactile sensory centers of the psyche, as well as the auditory, thus making "music" a multi-media experience unlike anything possible in the twentieth century. Hey, was that a sniff from you too? Just remember, they laughed at Noah too when he tried to tell them what was coming.

One of my classmates was a skinny, almost anorexic, young lady named Carolyn. She was an excellent scholar, also one of Schutze's favorites, and I started to take an interest in her. She was quite attractive, and, with a little more spaghetti at each meal for the next year, would have been even more so. When the Agency had a formal function one evening, I asked Carolyn if she would attend with me. When she asked whether her good friend Claudia, another of our classmates, also very nice looking, could be invited also, I arranged with Mike Zeleny to be her escort. Mike was witty and quite handsome, so I was sure my effort to play Cupid would lead to a relationship between them, but there was apparently not enough flint in either of their lighters to produce a spark. The world's first heart transplant was in the news about this time, so when Claudia was having trouble starting her Range Rover, the vehicle we decided to take to the event, I suggested her car needed a new heart. I did not know the car was listening, but it started immediately. Carolyn and I dated a few times, but I could perceive she was not really interested in me, so I stopped calling her. Whenever I saw her at the library or at the Library after that, she was always pleasant, but kept it above a personal level.

Shortly after the assassination of Martin Luther King in 1968, the Black community launched a riot in Washington, which rendered some areas of the city a virtual war zone and made certain streets impassable. Any unfortunate drivers that ventured through these areas were beaten up, and their cars smashed, overturned and burned. American University was just outside the perimeter of those trouble spots, but it was on one of the evenings during this riot period that I needed to register for class, and by a circuitous route I managed to reach the campus without incident. Some of you may remember the early days of computers in which programs and input data were fed into the computer via keypunch cards. Because class registration was such a suitable implementation of this form of data processing, I was handed a pack of punch cards on which to write the information. When I handed them in to a certain black fellow at the next station in line, he turned them over one by one, then handed them back, pointing out that I had not completed the back side of any of them. "Oh, I did not notice there were two sides to the cards," I said apologetically, as he placed them in my hand. "Sir," he said, taking off his glasses and leaning over the table to within inches of my face, "There are *two* sides to *everything*." His double entendre was crystal clear.

When my high school class announced its first reunion, I was not able to attend, but it stoked the embers of my feelings for Janet Negus, who had graduated as the valedictorian. One day I got the idea to see where life was leading her, and when my letter caught up with her, she wrote back to say she was teaching in Mason City, Iowa. I asked her whether she had ever been east and had some free time at the end of the school year. When I invited her to Washington for a few days, she asked whether she could bring along one of her colleagues from school. Uh, that depends .... I was relieved to find out it was a female. The two girls booked a room at a motel in Arlington somewhere, and Sam and I gave them the grand tour of the city. We had access to a few places that ordinary tourists would not be able to see, but I was quite sure they were dazzled by everything Washington had to offer. I cannot recall the name of Janet's teaching partner, but she was attractive and very personable—just the kind of girl in whom I thought Sam might take an interest. Poor shy Sam, however, a bachelor to this day, had other ideas about that, and again my efforts playing the matchmaker failed. When they told me their flight home departed from Baltimore, I presented to them a very aggressive plan. We could drive up to New York the day before, tour the city and see a little of West Point and the Catskills, and still have enough time to see the Liberty Bell in Philadelphia on the way back. It was the kind of crazy, breakneck idea of the same ilk for which my father was famous, but they loved it, and we were able to fit them with their wings back to Iowa on time. Neither Janet nor I could get away after the school year started up again to see each other, but a flame still flickered for a while through correspondence.

When Gary one day left the Agency, I was promoted to E-5 sergeant in his place, Mike moved up into my empty slot, and a new member named George Lubert joined the team. George was married and found an apartment in the Willston area to live with his wife and young daughter. When the cost of living in the Washington area stretched their budget beyond the limit, he approached Sam and me one day with the proposition that he send his little family back home to live with kin in Patton, Pennsylvania, and split our rent three ways with us. We rearranged the apartment to accommodate him, and with a positive attitude from three directions to make it work, it did. A change came about one day, however, stemming from two developments. One was the announcement at our apartment building that the owners were initiating a monthly fee for parking our cars in our own parking lot. Those of us who were incensed by such an insult organized a protest, but the management implemented the plan anyway, installing an electronically controlled gate, security guard stations, and access cards. While I stubbornly refused to pay what in my view should already have been included in the outrageous rent we were shelling out, I was forced to wait until the end of our lease to move out. The second development was the departure of Mike's roommate, so he was wondering if he could steal Sam from us. George and I found a two-bedroom apartment near Walter Reed Drive in Arlington, but I hardly ever saw him there because I was in class nearly every evening during the week and he drove home each weekend to be with his family.

One of the degree requirements in musicology at American University was accredited coursework in French and German, although the reading exam attesting this achievement could be in either one, at my option. Most high schools did not offer foreign languages in the curriculum in my day, and although Mr. Huisman was brought in to teach French at Sutherland for the first time when I was a junior, my schedule was full, leaving me shamefully ignorant of foreign language and culture all through undergraduate school. Since AU would accept credit for this from almost any school, I enrolled in a French course at Northern Virginia Community College close to home one semester.

Since these classes were in the morning, I made arrangements with the Agency to shift my schedule so I could attend. One evening I returned home late, and finding the parking lot full, I parked along the curb on the street. The next morning when I raced out the door for class, I found the entire driver side of my car smashed, sideswiped by someone during the night. Pointing to the white streaks on my dark paint, I asked the police officer who responded whether it would be possible to take paint samples to determine what kind of car caused this. He told me frankly that because this was not a murder or some other comparable felony, that would not be feasible and instead left some forms with me to complete in order to initiate an investigation. About six the next morning, I was awakened by a knock on my door. It was a uniformed Arlington policeman asking if I was the owner of that bashed Bel Air at the curb. Why had I not reported the accident, he wanted to know. When I pointed to the envelope on the end table next to the door with the completed forms ready to mail, he electrified me with the news that they had already identified the person who had done it. An alert officer on routine patrol in the parking lot of a high-rise apartment building about a mile away spotted a white Lincoln with extensive damage to the passenger side. When he ran the license number, he learned that the vehicle was leased by O'Brien and Rohall, a large Lincoln-Mercury dealer in the area, to a woman who lived in that building. Immediately upon seeing the officers at her door, she burst into tears, confessing that she had been drunk that evening and seemed to remember striking something but since her car kept going, she was not sure whether she had only imagined it. My insurance company was very happy to be armed with this information.

By now I was a regular member at Immanuel, joining the choir and attending services and Bible study each Sunday. One evening when the choir director, Barbara Pauling, and her husband Fritz invited me over for supper, I was telling them that I grew up in Iowa. Barbara asked me if I knew where Westgate is, adding that one of her classmates had been selected for a call to a parochial school there. He was none other than Bob Rikkels, that impetuous replacement for an ailing Henry Suhr. You probably did not realize it, but Cupid is a pseudonym for Barbara Pauling, and she carried many arrows in her quiver. I felt like I was playing blind man's buff, as she gave me a push in this direction or that, hoping I would make contact with someone in the direction in which I was aimed. One was a divorcee named Karen that did not appeal to me either by circumstance or by appearance. Another was a young lady named Linda Koehlmoos, who, when Barbara introduced me as a fellow Iowan, asked if I knew where Paullina is, the town where she grew up. Paullina, you may recall, is the next town west of Sutherland that was a perennial archrival in every one of our athletic competitions. I was in school with some of her cousins, and we knew many people in common. At first Linda was very appealing to me, but it seemed to me that every time I saw her after that, she was sobbing, with one or more ladies in attendance trying to console her. In time I found out she had lost her mother to cancer, and her father had remarried. Although the stepmother, Betty, was kind and supportive, this tragedy had hit Linda hard at a crucial point in her young life. From my point of view, she seemed a little too unstable for my taste, but at the time I was not in full view of the facts.

# Sharlyn

**W**hen choir season started in the fall of 1969, a new member in the alto section caught my attention. She was very attractive, and I asked Barbara after the rehearsal if she knew what her name was. "Yes," said Barbara musically. I asked Barbara if she had her phone number. "Yes," said Barbara symphonically. Her name was Sharlyn Roehl, from Chili, Wisconsin. I did not call her right away, but she made an unexpected appearance a few days later that I took as a sign that I should. Everett Dirksen, the gravelly voiced senator from Illinois had just died, and when Sam and I went to the Capitol rotunda to view his flag-draped casket lying in state, the only face I recognized, from the crowd of thousands who were there to pay respects, was hers. Sharlyn had come with her roommate Sherry, and as Sam and I ascended the steps, they were descending. She did not yet know who I was, so I walked past them without saying a word, not even to Sam. As Sharlyn relates this incident, she will claim that she *did* know who I was, but feigned ignorance. However, I cannot attach any credence to this version, because one of Sharlyn's most endearing qualities is her total inability to feign anything. There is such a thing as being *too* honest, I often tell her. In any case, the evening I decided to give her a call, I had the familiar nervous feeling I had back in high school asking a girl out for the first time. I told her I had seen her on the Capitol steps, and when I asked whether she had ever been to Bish Thompson's, a well-known seafood restaurant in Bethesda, I did not realize that shrimp, lobster and red snapper are not what most people from Wisconsin like. Like Iowans, they love an old-fashioned Midwest fish fry, but catfish, perch and sunfish come from the river, not the ocean. From my days in Chicago, I had acquired a taste for the delicacies of the sea, especially scallops and smoked oysters, so I was forgetting my roots when I suggested this cuisine. Despite my bad choice for a first date, however, she agreed to go. I do not know how the restaurant knew she was coming, but they put rockfish and cornbread on the menu just for her. I was off to a bad start, but it got worse.

After a second date with her to see the delightful movie *Funny Girl* with Streisand and Sharif, I felt that I knew her well enough to invite her to my apartment to watch TV one evening. Sharlyn was uncomfortable on the sofa, however, and when I tried to kiss her for the first time, she closed her mouth, turned away and asked me to take her home. For the next two sleepless nights I could not get the incident out of my mind. I had obviously offended her, but the more I thought about it, the more I realized what a good sign this was. I had no nefarious intentions, but she did not know that, and she had reacted precisely the way the girl for whom I was searching would respond. Of all the choices for the soulmate I had spent literally years to locate, this one had the most promise, and I did not want to lose her before I even had the chance to find her. "Who can find a virtuous woman? for her price is far above rubies," says Proverbs 31. Already I could see she had rare qualities, nay unique, not even close to anything I had experienced before. Even her handwriting had stood up to the scrutiny of my high standards. I turned to God, asking for a sign. For Gideon, the dramatic sign came through a piece of fleece. For me, it was a binary decision, a yes or no. I simply requested that if she would forgive this one transgression and agree to see me again, that would be a specific sign from God that she was the one He had picked out for me. When I saw her on Sunday getting into her car, I ran over to apologize. Her exact words in response were, "We don't know each other that well." Uh, not exactly the answer I wanted to hear. Now came one of the most important moments in my life. When I asked her whether she had plans for Friday night, I held my breath, but then was quite relieved to hear her say supper at a restaurant in Arlington sounded good. Yes, a yes. Whenever I look back to that moment, I cannot help but see the incredible chain of events that led to it, and the clearly discernible hand of God connecting it.

One link in that chain was actually a circumstance remarkably reprehensible. Sharlyn was one of the top students in high school, yet her guidance counselor, Vera Meade, who obviously must have breathed too much fertilizer on her way to school, gave Sharlyn the incredibly unconscionable advice not to apply for college. Her high school was in Marshfield, the hometown of Melvin Laird, who represented the Tenth District of Wisconsin in Congress, and when a secretary in his home office departed on maternity leave, they approached the high school office practice instructor, Marlene Hassell, for a recommendation for a replacement. Without hesitation she gave them Sharlyn's name. Until the end of high school, her job was part time, working after school and Saturdays with a full-time veteran named Pat Trierweiler. Some months later the staff was joined by Lois "Itsy" Heide, who would become a lifelong friend to both of us. Sharlyn often tells the story of Robert Dunkel, the manager sitting in his office, who would allow the crescendo of clucking from the hens just outside his door to reach a certain level before he would rap his pipe on the ashtray. Although he perfumed the air with that pipe, and both Itsy and Pat colored it gray with their cigarettes, Sharlyn had tremendous resistance to their tobacco products and never touched them. I wish I could say the same for her lungs, forced as she was to endure the second-hand smoke that continually polluted otherwise good clean Wisconsin air.

After graduation Sharlyn worked full time for Laird for a few years and in January 1969 was offered the opportunity to move from the home office to a position in Washington. This was a major decision for her, and she would probably have declined the opportunity if not for one Rita Meshak from Stevens Point, Wisconsin, a secretary who was already in the office in the Rayburn building in Washington. She and Sharlyn were acquainted through the interactions of the two offices, and it was Rita who offered to help her make the physical move to the Washington area. But it was more than assistance she was offering. Rita shared a garden apartment with a Treasury Department employee named Sherry Spaulding at 1165 North Van Dorn in Alexandria, ironically within a mile of Fort Ward Towers, where I first lived. It was not a three-bedroom apartment, but it had a walk-in closet large enough for a bed and a dresser, so she offered that to Sharlyn. This made a cozy arrangement for all three ladies, especially for Sharlyn, but they managed it with no conflicts. Considerably older than Sharlyn, Rita guided her young neophyte everywhere around the Washington area, and even though she was Roman Catholic herself, helped Sharlyn find the Lutheran church that would alter the course of her life dramatically. "What a nice little Lutheran boy," she would say to Sharlyn in approval of our relationship after I came to know her.

Nixon was now occupying the White House, and when he named Melvin Laird as his Secretary of Defense, Sharlyn joined him at the Pentagon, working directly for William J. Baroody, Laird's legislative assistant. Rita's job moved over there too, but she never adjusted to the new climate in that building and eventually left Washington and returned to "Point," as she always called it. One of the routine pickups of my Agency was at the Pentygon, as Krasch always pronounced it, and, using my seniority, I made sure I took that assignment myself. This gave me an excuse to look in on Sharlyn occasionally, not to mention the opportunity to bask in the fawning I received, each time I stopped by, from Erma Tucker and Vera Nutt, the two older ladies who worked in the office with her. Sharlyn's own mother had scarcely the same fondness for her as all of these surrogate mothers who were taking care of her, and many of them remained friends with both of us for the rest of their lives.

The married men who are reading this will understand that it is quite easy to upset a woman over what seems like a trifle, with no malice aforethought and even with every intention of bestowing a benefit on her. Early in our relationship I made Sharlyn quite upset over a pair of opera glasses. One of my favorite performers of all time was Victor Borge, and by good fortune his tour schedule led him through Arlington one day for a live performance at the Fort Myer auditorium. We found our seats at least a half hour early, and when I saw the distance from there to the stage, it occurred to me that I have a pair of opera glasses that would be perfect for us. My apartment building was only fifteen minutes away, so I reasoned I would be back before the show was underway. It was at least an hour before I returned, the show was nearly half over, and an embarrassed Sharlyn had to stand and wave to me right during the performance because I could not find her in the huge crowd. Each time I tried to hand the glasses to her, however, she refused them, leaving me dismayed at the lengths to which I had gone for *her* in the first place. On the drive home she broke her stony silence with a demand to know why I had "abandoned" her at the concert. This was more serious than I first thought, and once again I was afraid I would lose her, but when the smoke cleared she eventually overlooked this miscalculation too. But she will never allow me to forget it.

An act of kindness as innocuous as fetching opera glasses seemed to have no perceivable adversity, yet it had resulted in the most unforeseeably acrimonious of consequences. How is it then that a benefit fraught with risk could turn out so well? One day when I asked Sharllyn when the last time her 1966 Malibu had had a tune-up, she could not remember. Since in those days a car ought to have new spark plugs and contact points every ten thousand miles or so and a new distributor cap and ignition wires perhaps every twenty thousand, I decided to surprise her by picking up these items and installing them for her. On the Saturday on which I intended to do this work, she did not answer her phone all morning, so I drove to her apartment several times with my parts and tools. When she did not answer the door in the afternoon, I saw her car in the usual spot in the parking lot but did not have a key to it. No problem, the hood opens from the outside, so I went to work on it. For the points to be gapped properly with a feeler gauge, however, the rotor must be in a certain precise position, which is usually achieved by an assistant who touches the starter motor a number of times until the lobe is in the right place. I had neither an assistant nor access to the starter without a key, but by a stroke of pure luck, the rotor was in the exact place where I needed it to be. Just in the off chance (very remote, right?) that Sharlyn might be displeased with what I had done, I left the old parts for her in a bag on her doorstep, so that her mechanic could restore her car to the way it was if she wished. She had gone with her roommates to Amish country in Lancaster for the day, and when she returned that night, I got a call.

Not only was she surprised, but *pleased*. As a bonus, the car even started up when she turned the key. Taken together, these two incidents prove that I will never be able to predict how a woman will react to anything I try to do for her.

When Donovan Wascher was processing out of the Agency one day, he told me he was entering an exploding new field called computer programming. The airwaves were saturated with commercials for training programs, the classified ads were bursting with computer jobs and increasing numbers of people with whom I came into contact every day were launching into the uncharted waters of cyberspace. So when Don told me I should consider this option when I left the Army, I dismissed it as a passing fad. However, when he insisted that I go to the Computer Learning Center for an aptitude test, I went along with him. For about six months after that, various representatives of the school called me to say I had one of the highest scores they had ever seen (probably a sales pitch), urging me to enroll. However, predicting that within five years the market would be so glutted with computer technicians that they would all regret their choice, I turned down their offers. It would be one of the biggest mistakes of my life. However, when I look back on even this unbelievably short-sighted decision, I see once again the hand of God in it, who seemed to be saying, "Patience, patience, everything in My good time." Sharlyn came to the Agency with me one day to meet Mr. Stephens, my boss, and soon after that, with reenlistment papers in his hand, he gave me the half-hearted perfunctory speech all of us who reached the end of our tours received, that the Army really is a good career. I responded with thanks to him for treating me so well and on November 20, 1969, left the Agency, never to see him again.

I planned to travel home for Thanksgiving a few days later, and since Wisconsin was more or less on the way, I offered to drop Sharlyn off at Chili if she would like to ride along. Rita saw an opportunity to get home for the holiday also, and asked if she could share expenses and go with us. As we passed the Toledo area on the Ohio turnpike, I noticed I was getting low on gas, but expecting prices to be lower away from the metropolis, I foolishly passed up a number of opportunities to fill up. Worse, it was about eleven p.m., and when the last lights of the city winked out behind us, we would see nothing but desolation for mile after heartstopping mile. Running dangerously low by now, I took the next exit at Wauseon and asked the toll attendant whether any stations nearby were open at this hour. No, he said, but he would call the owner of a station in the little village to open up for us. We found the station with little difficulty and, for all my thrift, now found myself in a desperate position willing to pay three times the price on the pump. The owner was extremely friendly, especially given what we were asking from him, yet he cheerfully refused any extra money for the trouble I was causing him. And it has been impossible for nearly forty years to pass this Wauseon exit on the freeway without a vivid recollection of the details of that fateful night.

My sister Ruth was in her second year at Valparaiso, and we would be passing so close to the university not far from the Indiana turnpike that we planned to load her things and bring her along with us too. Of all my siblings, Ruth is the closest match to my coloring, facial features and personality, so Sharlyn assumed we were all alike. When she would one day meet my brother Don, who has an entirely different frame, complexion and mannerism, she could scarcely believe we were from the same parents. After we drove through the night and dropped Rita off at Stevens Point, we finally reached Chili later that same morning, where I met Sharlyn's parents, Alvin and Evelyn, for the first time on their farm about two miles outside of the tiny village. Ruth and I continued on to Minnesota, and when we retraced our route back east a few days later, the gas gauge would not be allowed to fall below a half tank without an audible alarm from each seat in the car.

As Christmas approached, I received in the mail one day an announcement that I had won a "free" sewing machine. When I read the fine print, I learned that it was not entirely free, as everyone in the world except me would probably already have known, but if I wanted to take advantage of their offer, I would need to purchase a service contract for it for a hundred dollars (probably the exact amount of their manufacturing cost, which they would thereby recoup). Riccar, the upstart company producing it, was apparently trying to gain a foothold in the market and was willing to place as many of its portable machines in homes as possible for a price that was supposedly well below the fair market value of a Singer or Necchi. I knew that Sharlyn had already done some sewing, so I bought the machine, some fabric and a pattern for a dress and presented these items to her for Christmas. If you were to ask Sharlyn about this, she would tell you that this was all a shabby ruse, a thinly disguised examination to test her sewing skills. In her mind my only interest was to determine whether she would be able to repair my pants one day. Nevertheless, when she finished her project, it was one of the most beautiful dresses I ever saw, and she looked stunning in it. You are wondering about the machine? It lasted until the service contract expired, and then it expired soon after. I replaced it for her, not with another Riccar, but a White, the very machine she has to this day.

After the Army my intention had been to transfer to Northwestern University to complete graduate school in musicology, but a certain young lady was holding my interest here where I was at the moment. Instead, I answered an ad by a research and development company called The John D. Kettelle Corporation, and with a glowing recommendation from Wally Grigg and a kind reference from Leonard Stephens, I was hired as their personnel security officer, processing security clearances for their engineers and scientists, as well as assuming responsibility for the classified materials they used in their projects. When they noticed my typing speed, they also assigned me to produce the voluminous pages of the proposals they submitted to various government agencies, bidding for contracts. In the days before word processors, corrections in typed material were laborious. Though it was sometimes easier to begin typing a page again, the usual process was to use a special insert to type a chalk image over an incorrectly typed letter, then overtype the correct letter. For a whole word or short phrase, a white liquid known as white-out was applied to cover up the incorrect section, then after a wait of as long as two or more minutes for the liquid to dry, it was ready to be typed upon with correct data. Some typists preferred to apply a strip of white tape over the offending words to avoid the wait for fluid to dry. For a whole paragraph or large sections, the incorrect segment could be physically excised with a sharp knife known as an X-Acto, and the correct material was typed on a separate sheet, then spliced into the original using a light box. These corrected pages were then photocopied with the hope that the corrections did not create shadows that would reveal the patches. Whew, and you thought your job typing an email message was tough.

The chief operating officer for whom I worked was Daniel Carrigan, but the director of Washington operations was Michael Riess. My desk was near the door to Riess's office, and one day when I arrived for work, I found his overcoat lying across my desk. I assumed Mike had absent-mindedly left it there and would remove it with an apology momentarily, but when I saw him pass my desk a number of times on his way in and out, I could feel my resentment rising. After an hour or so, I asked his secretary Barbara Cranston, whose desk was even closer to his doorway than mine, what I should do with Mike's coat on my desk. Without a word she took it into his office to hang it up. When this happened a second time, I bristled immediately at his arrogance and disdain. I suppose I should have simply picked it up for him, but now it was a matter of principle, in addition to pride, as I was determined not to be his fool. This time I went to Carrigan to complain, and it never happened again. I did not realize it at the time, but this incident planted in my mind the first seeds of dissatisfaction with that job, which led me to despise the company itself and especially this entire approach to doing business.

Carrigan was a retired military officer, and whether he was aware of it or not, one of the principal duties of my former job was to ensure proper construction in whatever correspondence left my desk. Unlike others who simply transcribed his cursive verbatim, I actually read the meaning of his text as I typed the words and made corrections as I went along. He resented this and told me one day I was effectively overriding his authority and vetoing what he wrote by making these changes and ordered me to desist. Another of my duties was to administer the health insurance program for all of the employees, so in addition to the delicate psychiatric and physiological ailments of everyone and their families to which I was privy, I also had access to their salaries. Whenever I compared my $8200 annual salary to the $24K of these engineers, I was indignant, but it turns out that this very threefold difference would providently save me from the unemployment line one day soon. When Al Meltzer, a senior engineer on one of our projects, became impatient one day with the length of time that a security clearance was pending for a prospective team member, he called DCASR in Philadelphia himself. Not only was this a breach of protocol, but condescending and blatantly disrespectful to me in my role as the security officer. Besides, they gave him the exact information I had already passed to him each time he had asked me to follow up on it, and his officious actions served, if anything, to aggravate rather than ameliorate his predicament. It reminded me of King Saul, who grew impatient with Samuel, offered the sacrifice himself and was reproved for his impropriety. Unlike Samuel, however, I was unable to reveal to Meltzer that his kingdom or his soul was in jeopardy.

When the corporation at its zenith had nearly 500 employees and lavish offices in seven cities, John Kettelle decided to go public with his company stock. But he made a colossal blunder by failing to retain fifty-one percent of the shares, and one day his trusted executives leveraged the company away from him and forced him out. They changed the name to Kappa Systems and rolled the assets over to the new corporation. As security officer I was cast into the invidious role of debriefing John and processing him out in the wake of this fracas. To spare him the indignity of trouncing through the office like a common fired employee, I agreed to meet him on a Saturday. I was told by Guy Rucker and James Heller, two officers of the new company, to be sure he turned over all his keys and did not try to abscond with anything, but since I had never met him, I wondered what I should do if he was recalcitrant or belligerent. It was a great relief when I found this six-four red-head with an athletic build predisposed to be professional and affable in completing our less than pleasant transaction. By a strange coincidence he and I lived in the same neighborhood about fifteen years later, and I learned that he had promptly gone back out to establish a dynamic new company called Ketron, in direct competition with Kappa, and had subsequently outbid them on a number of lucrative contracts.

When Congress slashed federal funding for defense contracts one year, the research and development industry was hit hard and went into a tailspin. Massive closures following the harsh fiscal realities of early 1970 chopped the company back to about 35 employees in two offices. I knew in advance when many were going to be laid off, and I watched in sympathy as one young mother emerged from behind closed doors with a sober expression, lit a cigarette with trembling hands and started packing a box with her effects. I shed no tears when Riess, Carrigan and Meltzer all became expendable. Since someone would need to decertify security clearances and administer the separations, my position, especially at one of the lowest salaries on the payroll, would be reasonably safe as long as the corporation itself remained afloat. Leonard Greenberg, the director of Philadelphia operations in Paoli moved down to become director of the Washington office and eventually became my long-time friend. The company was so depressed financially that when it was forced to move down the street to less expensive office space, we used hand trucks to wheel furnishings and equipment, including a few half-ton safes, along the sidewalks to our new quarters ourselves. Whatever remained in the office we vacated was made available to the employees for bargain prices, so I took advantage of the sale to purchase a seven hundred dollar IBM proportional space typewriter, including the fine quality folding table upon which it sat, for about a hundred dollars.

One of my favorite employees in the company was Larry Gunn, a brilliant engineer who was also caught up in the layoffs but landed on his feet in Colorado, I think. As we left the office to attend Larry's farewell, Len Greenberg, always a quick wit, quipped to those of us boarding the elevator with him that this was to be a one-Gunn salute. It was Larry who had showed me how to sweat copper pipe, allowed me the use of his Sears Shopsmith before I had power tools of my own and once invited Sharlyn and me to his house to meet his beautiful wife Theresa and three energetic young boys. Tee, as she preferred to be called, told us as we sat at the supper table that although some people with children apologize for what the kids say, for the way the house looks, for the way the vegetables are undercooked, and so on, she makes no apologies for anything. We would have to accept them as they were, formalities aside. Of course, her home was immaculate, the boys well behaved, and the meal delicious, but with this discourse she unwittingly imprinted her stance upon us forever after. In what became a kind of private family proverb, Sharlyn and I would always say, "No apologies, Tee" whenever one of us would start to explain something gone awry.

When Sharlyn's birthday came around in March, I arranged a surprise party for her at my apartment and presented her with a new watch. When I told Sue Thompson, a newlywed at the office, about this, she told me to be careful, because when her husband had given her a watch, it was followed a short time later by an engagement ring. By April I was quite convinced that Sharlyn was the only person in the universe with whom I wanted to spend my life *and*, a serious factor many men fail to consider, the one whom I wanted to be the mother of my children. However, I was not so sure she had had enough time to make the single most important decision of her life. Contrary to the traditional approach where the young man buys a ring and gets down on one knee or any of the myriad non-traditional approaches taken by some who hire a skywriter, hide the ring in a cupcake or any of a hundred other such schemes, I decided to explore the subject with Sharlyn first. Across from her apartment was a swim club, and late one night when I returned her home, I pulled into the club parking lot, switched off the engine and asked her what she thought about getting married. I told her I did not want an answer right away, but since it was my conviction to experience this only one time, I wanted her to be very, very certain it was what she wanted too. I told her to think ahead realistically to what it would be like standing over a hot stove stirring the soup with her hair in her eyes, sweat running down her face and a squalling infant clawing her leg, wondering why she had ever agreed to put herself in such a predicament. Beyond the idyllic reverie, I was trying to tell her, comes the harsh reality of eking out an existence and raising a family. It would be hard work and would require both of us pulling together to be successful. The next day she told me she had thought about what I said and was ready to be the mother some day of that wailing infant at her feet. I choked back tears.

I had not yet bought a ring, so before we announced our engagement, I wanted Sharlyn to go with me to pick one out at a wholesaler called W. Bell & Company. As she sat on the sofa in my apartment with her new ring, the gravity of the event unexpectedly weighed heavily on her for the first time, and when I called my parents to present the good news, Sharlyn nervously said hello to them for the first time. I did not realize it at the time, but she has told me for years since that as I dialed the number, she was suddenly gripped with panic and had the strongest urge to back out at that very moment. But after everyone in the family had been notified, her feelings of remorse eased somewhat, and she began to adjust to her new status with a little confidence that maybe it could be a good decision after all. Soon all of our friends knew about it, and one day an item in the newsletter at Immanuel made a reference to the sparkle on Sharlyn's third finger, left hand. No one was happier for us than Barbara Pauling. When I told Sue Thompson a few days later at the office, she exclaimed, "See, I told you what happens when you give someone a watch."

Sentimental alert, sentimental alert. Since most men will not have a stomach strong enough to tolerate the following paragraph, only the ladies are allowed to read it. As an engagement present, I gave Sharlyn a silver charm bracelet with only one charm on it—a little silver sewing machine that actually had some moving parts. Sharlyn did not try to make a dress with it, however. Sterling silver charms were a little expensive, but I bought a number of them throughout our engagement, whenever I could afford one, and made up some excuse or other to present them. The last one to be attached to the bracelet was a pair of little silver keys on a tiny ring which I gave her on our wedding night in a jewelry box in which I had a printer inscribe "These are the keys to love. You have always had them. May they always be yours." Even *I* knew a silver bracelet with a gold ring and gold watchband was not proper fashion, but some of the tiny objects attached to it were so intricate that the bracelet was not to be worn casually anyway, if at all.

As W day approached, September 12, 1970, my roommate George found another place to live, leaving to Sharlyn and me the two-bedroom apartment in Arlington that would be our first place together. In those days a blood test was required before marriage to provide discovery to each partner of any sexually transmitted diseases, so Sharlyn and I went together to a clinic in Washington to fulfill that mandate. Today, however, legislators have apparently concluded that the widespread prevalence of premarital conjugation in a sin-cursed world, and a concomitant rise in STDs to epidemic levels, render such a requirement irrelevant. When we registered for our marriage license in Wisconsin, we received a packet of useful products as a service to all young couples provided by Clark County, including a booklet called *The Bride's First Week in the Kitchen*. Sadly, this packet of wonderful materials has long since been discontinued, perhaps an expendable budget item or perhaps another casualty of the Liberation movement in which such titles are seen as sexist in an increasingly role-confused society.

When my parents attended Bethel Lutheran Church in Sutherland for the last time, the congregation hosted a farewell for them in the fellowship room in the basement. At one point during the festivities, I noticed that my father had disappeared. I found him upstairs in the sanctuary praying, and then as I watched from the doorway in the back, I noticed he was writing something down. He had not detected my presence, and I sensed this was not a good time to intrude on his private meditation, so I slipped quietly away. He reemerged downstairs a few minutes later and handed what he had written to Earl Skaar, one of the elders, and asked him to read it to the assembly. He was so overcome by emotion, his note read, that he was unable to express himself orally without breaking down. If my father can be so suffused by a mere farewell, surely I can be granted the latitude to sob at my wedding, not so? I was grateful no videos captured this blubbering display nor seismometers monitored the trembling in my limbs, difficult as this was even from far up at the front of the church to disguise from the congregation. My father's brother Carl, one of two pastors officiating the ceremony, delivered such wonderful words of exhortation and inspiration that by the time I was forced to turn around to face the guests again, I had managed to regain my composure once again. He was a talented singer as well, so we placed him in the most unusual role of both officiant and soloist.

Sharlyn had never met my parents until the day before the wedding, but it would not be exaggerating much to say that both of them had an immediate and enduring fondness for her that exceeded their attachment to me for the rest of their lives. If true, I would not have it any other way. All the grandmothers except my mother's mother Emelia Gimbel were at the wedding, but only one grandfather was still alive to attend, Ernest Sanger, the father of Sharlyn's mother. As he passed through the receiving line, he took Sharlyn by the shoulders, radiant as she was in her wedding finery, leaned back and said, "You ought to see Pickles now." When I asked Sharlyn later what that meant, she explained that when she was a little girl he would sometimes wink at her and call her Pickles, a name derived from a record he often played on his old phonograph.

While the ceremony had been at Christ Lutheran Church in Chili, the reception was set up at Zion Lutheran Church, its sister congregation in Granton about eight miles away. It was not uncommon in many rural communities for a congregation without the means to support a pastor to partner with another and call a pastor to serve both of them. Such was the case for Roland Roehrs, the pastor who actually had the legal authority to marry us. As we emerged from the church, we could see through a hail of rice that a surprise was waiting. Over the years to come, my father would repeat the words I uttered when I saw it—"What is *that*?" Sharlyn was especially close to her brother Lavern, who added a special touch as a surprise for his sister, arranging with Willis Stichert to provide a carriage, pulled by a team of immaculately groomed chestnut Belgian horses. While I was able to clamber up onto the carriage quite easily, I had difficulty assisting Sharlyn in all her regalia to reach the seat perched high above the street. It was the kind of cold, damp day that is not unusual for Wisconsin in September, so I was grateful that our open-air ride was only a ceremonial procession through the streets of Chili for a few minutes before we reached the warm comfort of the car transporting us to the reception. My brother Rodney was barely ten, and as we embarked, my mother was compelled to yank him back by the shirt collar to prevent him from piling in on top of us in his exuberance.

Many hours of planning and hard work had been spent and many people involved to make this, the most important day of a young woman's life, possible. Sharlyn spent literally hundreds of hours sewing her own dress, and her sisters Marlene and Bernette, as well as my sister Ruth (the bridesmaids in the wedding party) made theirs also. My brothers Ralph and Don, as well as Lavern (the groomsmen) had it comparatively easy, simply trying on tuxedos, shoes and cummerbunds from the rental shop. In fact, the entire wedding was so well planned by Sharlyn and her family that I was almost a non-entity. This was both good and bad—good in that the workload on me was nil, bad in that their timetable of events was now coming into conflict with mine. We had a limited number of days for our honeymoon, and it was my hope to reach Chicago yet that same night, but as the evening wore on I was getting impatient to get started. Finally, when our smiles were tired but our guests were not, we could at last break away, change clothes and wave goodbye to our well-wishers. Of course, I had to stop our car a mile down the road to unfasten the stringers of beer cans that had somehow gotten snagged on the rear bumper.

Sharlyn had already showed me much of the Chili area where she was raised and was interested to see a little of where I grew up, so our plan was to spend our honeymoon revisiting people and places I had not seen myself for a few years. We dragged into Chicago, exhausted, about two or three a.m. and woke up the night clerk of a seedy hotel on the Near North Side, close to First Saint Paul's on LaSalle Street, from where we somehow managed to arise for church the next morning. In the afternoon I showed her the skyline of the city from the top of the Tribune Tower and, though only the weekend watchman was around, the Victorian tapestries and murals of Sherwood. From there we drove into Iowa, looking around in Maynard and Oelwein a little, then on to Westgate. The house in town where we once lived was now occupied by none other than Henry Suhr, and when we knocked on the door, I had hoped to say hello to him. Instead, his wife answered the door and told us he was at a meeting down at the fire station. To this day I regret that we did not interrupt his meeting to greet him, because it was not long after that that I heard he had died. We then had a choice to make—whether to continue west across the state to Sutherland or retrace our steps back to Chicago. We decided Sutherland could wait, because I wanted Sharlyn to meet Wally and others at the Tribune, and I wanted her to meet BBB and others at Sherwood when it was alive with music in the corridors instead of the museum we had seen earlier. It was late afternoon when we crossed back into Wisconsin, so rather than risk waking her parents by trying to tiptoe into the house after midnight, we took the exit near Poynette and spent the night at a bed and breakfast outside the village before returning to Chili the next day. The following day we loaded the car with Sharlyn's beautiful cedar chest and other belongings until the metal started to stretch, and then we pointed the car east. Parents are not supposed to have favorites, but Alvin dearly loved his "Shar," the oldest, and "the boy," his only son Lavern. As we left, I might have expected my newly forged father-in-law to say something like "Well, have a safe trip" or I might have even hoped for "We're glad to have you in the family now." Instead I was to hear an Alvinism. When I shook hands on our way out the door, he summed up his affection for me with the following words, "We sure hate to lose 'er."

# Alvin

Not the chipmunk, not the submarine. From the first moment I had met Alvin Roehl nearly a year earlier, I was captured by the color of his character. He was likeable instantly, and as he related an anecdote, I was so entertained by his country manner, his choice of words, the way his eyes danced as he turned a phrase, the way he pursed his lips to produce that unmistakably Wisconsin accent, his laugh that came from deep inside, that I would start to chuckle. Often when my face would betray my amusement, he was puzzled, unaware he was saying anything particularly funny. One of my deepest regrets is that none of us wrote down the story of his life in his own words during the thirty-five years I knew him before his death at age 90.

Like my parents, Alvin was a product of the Depression years, which might more accurately have been termed Impression years for the way that era imprinted lifetime values and forged character in those who endured them. In stark contrast to the reckless and wasteful attitudes we see around us today, their generation experienced such austere scarcity and shortage that they became unalterably frugal and ultraconservative. Sharlyn tells the story of her grandmother, Emma Sanger, who used the same laundry basket until it was in tatters, barely hanging together as a container, yet when the relatives bought her a new one, she was upset because her old one was still useable. One of ten children, Alvin lost his father Herman to cancer as a youth and left school after eighth grade to help his mother Clara run the farm. He was as much a part of the country as the rich black soil of central Wisconsin, and his horizon never extended beyond Clark County until he was well advanced in years. When he was still a bachelor at age thirty-two, no one would have predicted he would live to see his golden wedding anniversary or great-grandchildren, yet his fortunes were about to change. He had noticed two girls from the next farm over, Evelyn and Mildred Sanger, "a couple o' farm chunks," as he called them, riding their bicycles or walking along the road past his farm each day on their way to Four Corners School, and he amused himself from the field watching them play softball at recess. When Evelyn was a little older, he came a-courtin' and married her, eleven years his junior. Two years later Sharlyn was born.

Few men are as gentle and tenderhearted as he, yet it was difficult for him to be sentimental when it really counted. He had the frying pan slammed over his head, at least once literally, time and again when he could not remember their anniversary, Evelyn's birthday or even which Sunday was Mother's Day. Worse, he was actually amused at her anger, almost taking delight in the spectacle. To him, her histrionics were like a calliope at full steam. Farming is a tough, relentless business, demanding the physical stamina of Hercules and the skills of a plumber, carpenter, electrician, veterinarian, inventor and a dozen other disciplines. Alvin met all these requirements, except his farm was more like a hobby for him than a business, and he struggled to make it profitable. Under the best of circumstances, a farmer works from dawn to dusk every day for years without any time away, only to have an early frost, a late frost, too little rain, too much rain, a hailstorm, grasshoppers, or blight ruin a year's profit, and many of them felt fortunate to have two good years for every five. In Alvin's case, this was compounded by the fact that he grew up farming with horses, which limited the amount of land he could manage without expensive machinery. He was very close to his animals, so it broke his heart when his favorite horse Lady finally gave him a colt that lived for a few hours but died as he knelt helplessly by, attempting desperately to will it to survive. His bond with his horses was so strong that he could trim a hoof with hammer and chisel while the huge animal nearly ten times his weight stood patiently beside him without flinching.

Fond as he was of his horses, Alvin was also attached to one of the most valuable assets a farmer may own—his dog. When I first knew the family, a miniature collie named Penny greeted me warily. She weighed only thirty pounds, but about twenty of them were teeth. Unlike her predecessors, Penny was exclusively a housedog, expected to howl when anyone played the piano rather than pick up cockleburs chasing the cows home. After many years she and I never did make friends, not so much because I made her sing along whenever I pounded on the tinny piano in the living room, but more because I was the outsider, and she was supposed to scowl and growl at anyone who did not live there. Sharlyn belonged in the pack because Penny had known her since puppyhood, but not this renegade from some other pack. The best dog Alvin ever had was Teddy, a border collie who received an outstanding performance rating for carrying out every task in his job description with superlatives. It took Alvin a long time to recover from the shock he received one day when a horse, reflexively kicking back at a gadfly, struck Teddy in the head with its hoof and killed him. At the opposite end of the spectrum was Sandy, more like a government worker who barely manages a satisfactory rating. Perhaps no one explained to her what duties were expected, but the simple fact was that her temperament was more like that of her master—too kindhearted toward the cows and other farm animals to be effective at driving them. Sandy was too slow to react one day when a wagon loaded with stones rolled over her head, which did not kill her but caused spontaneous convulsions that plagued her periodically throughout her life. Alvin often told the story about the time a truck arrived from the "fox farm," the obtuse reference to the rendering plant near Neillsville, to pick up two horses to be sold for processing. Dull-witted Sandy tried to run along behind the truck and followed the scent all the way to the place where the gruesome transactions took place. When Alvin discovered Sandy missing , he reckoned what happened and called over to Neillsville, furnishing a description. Yes, they had seen her, but she was not around now. A few days later an exhausted, bedraggled, but not necessarily wiser, barnyard dog that answered to the name Sandy was whimpering at the door.

In the eyes of a child, one of the worst possible offenses committed against him is to misrepresent his age to make him younger than he is. For children, of course, *importance* is on the line when they are associated with their ages, to the point that many will add a fraction to whatever cardinal number they report. After all, *five and a half* is much more impressive than just *five*. Although neither time nor resources allowed much opportunity for extensive family vacation, Alvin once broke away from the farm routine long enough to take the family to a local cave. Admission was free for children under seven, so Alvin was explaining the ages of the children to the attendant at the gate. When he came to

Lavern, Alvin said, "… and this one is six." Lavern immediately bristled, "I am *not*! I'm *seven*." Alvin was more preoccupied with matters of running his farm than to keep track of such mundane trivialities as birthdays, so it is likely he honestly did not know for sure. However, whether he had a momentary lapse or had intentionally attempted to spare some pennies of his precious family grocery money, he was nevertheless now compelled to reach into his wallet for an additional fifty cents.

When the budget for a growing family outstretched the income from the farm, Alvin tried his hand for a while as a traveling salesman, selling McNess products door to door. If selling a product could be considered adversarial, Alvin found himself on the wrong side, for if a salesman were to show up in *his* driveway, Alvin was apt to run him off with a rake. His heart was not really in it, especially when he could identify so readily with the feelings of the customer. Evelyn always said he could strike up a conversation with a fence post, so establishing a rapport with the potential buyer was not the problem—in fact, he enjoyed the visits with his neighbors to the point that he forgot he was supposed to be selling them something. He told the tale of one elderly woman who was interested in the tin of salve he pulled from his case, the bottle of vitamins, the can of bathroom cleaner, the box of soap, and so on until he had the table full of products that made him think he had a sale. Then she said she really did not have a need for this product and that product until, one by one, he put them back in his case, wasting two hours of his time selling her nothing in the end. To him, however, the time was not wasted, as he had enjoyed the chance to visit with her.

When Evelyn recognized the gravity of their predicament, she decided, after four children, that she would need to supplement their income herself. When Bernette was old enough to leave with Alvin's mother Clara and youngest sister Ev in town, she acquired her teaching certificate and set off for Lone Elm and the school systems at Nasonville and Loyal to teach elementary school graders. By the time I came on the scene, she had been teaching for fifteen years, and I heard so many stories from her about the world of education I was so glad I never had to experience. She made me realize that if it were not for the students, the other teachers, the principal, the board and administration, the parents and the system itself, teaching could actually be fun and rewarding. Over the years I came to regard Evelyn as my alter ego, sharing with her similar views on politics, morals, values, and behaviors. I discovered that what irked her was often the very same as what irked me, whom she most admired was on my list too, and the same scoundrels at whom she shook her fist were the ones I wanted strung up by the thumbs also. On the flip side, Sharlyn was nothing like her mother, and in fact she often saw in me the same characteristics that most embarrassed her about her mother, particularly if Sharlyn had the misfortune to be riding with either of us stuck behind some Pokey Slow in a single lane.

When Sharlyn and I returned to the farm for a visit one summer, I noticed that the yard needed mowing, so I decided to pull the mower out of the shed and "make myself useless," as my mother might say. Alvin was coming back from the barn to the house as I was putting the mower away and said to me, "Looks pretty good once you get all them weeds clipped the same length, ent so?" "Ent so" was a true Wisconsin expression I heard quite often from Alvin, his sister Lila and others of his family. A popular brand of pipe tobacco available in those days was called Prince Albert, depicting a royal figure in Victorian regalia on the front of the flat red can shaped to fit the hind pocket of a pair of bib overalls. Alvin poked me in the ribs one day and asked, "Who is the most constipated person in the world?" Then answering his own riddle immediately, he said, "Prince Albert. He's been sittin' on the can for fifty years." Then he leaned back, squinted his eyes and revealed the gaps in his teeth toward the back of his mouth that became visible when he laughed. He always liked my story about the farmer who tried to train his mule not to eat by giving the poor animal smaller and smaller amounts of oats each day. When his neighbor asked him one day how it was going, he said, "Not good. Just when I had 'er to the point where she wasn't eatin' nothin', she up and died on me."

Yolo Cemetery was a half mile away from their farm, and if someone needed a grave dug in subzero temperatures in January, Al Roehl would never let them down. Always willing to do what was right, he was an excellent employee whenever someone would hire him to work on some project. Evelyn always said he worked better for someone else than he did for himself. Sharlyn often quoted the admonition she received from her father that if the boss told you to move a pile of rocks over to there and then had you move the whole pile back to here, that is what you did, simply because he is the boss and that is what you were paid to do. I once told Alvin about a similar task at a saw mill. The foreman directing his men to move a pile of logs asked one young man why he carried only one log at a time while the others carried one under each arm. "I guess they're just too lazy to make two trips," replied the lad with a shrug. Having worked outside sawing logs in temperatures so cold the drip from his nose would freeze solid, Alvin reflected on my story with a wry laugh. By the time he was in his eighties, he had known personally about half of those buried at Yolo, so a walk through the cemetery with Alvin produced a trove of stories. Over here was Bill Dankemeyer, so strong he could hold up a wagon while it took two men just to put the wheel back on. "All them Dankemeyers, goll' they was strong," he would say. Over there was Harvey Madler, one of the smartest guys he ever knew. "Harvey could tell you what a book was about just by looking at the cover," he would insist.

The local radio stations frequently had some contest or other involving interaction with their listeners—clues about someone's farm, for example, given over the course of several days with a prize for the first to identify it. One day the station declared a contest where someone's name would be announced over the air, and the listener had thirty minutes to call in to receive a few bags of cattle feed or something. Usually Alvin had the radio on in the barn, but on the day when the station called his name on their program, he either did not have it switched on or had duties away from the radio for whatever reason. Meanwhile, the relatives in town heard his name and were trying to reach him by telephone. Whatever it was that took his attention from the radio was also keeping him from the phone as well, and he missed his opportunity by failing to call in within the thirty-minute window. All of this had taken place shortly before one of our visits to Wisconsin, and it was the talk of the table as we sat with the relatives for supper, who were razzing him about his missing out on the prize. Alvin listened to their banter for a while, then said finally, "Well, I ain't nothin' *out*." Classic even-tempered, rational Alvin.

When Alvin and Evelyn retired from the farm in 1975, they took advantage of the resources of Gerald Nelson, husband of Alvin's sister Lila, to have a new home built for themselves in Spencer, a more progressive town some fifteen miles north of Chili. Gerald was a builder and the manager of a lumberyard in town, who could give them a substantial discount on materials, expertise on construction, and whatever hands-on assistance his brother-in-law might need. A year or so after they moved in, Alvin decided he wanted a shed in the back yard large enough that he could park a car inside, if necessary, so he called for a truck to deliver ready-mixed concrete for the slab foundation and started construction. We were in Wisconsin to help him nail on shingles and put on the finishing touches, when the local building inspector showed up. On the farm Alvin was accustomed to taking whatever action expediency demanded, without answering to any authority but common sense, so he gave no thought to such formalities as permits, setback requirements, plats and site licenses here in town either. The inspector asked Alvin whether he had a permit for the shed. "No," he replied, "but I have a shotgun inside the house, and if you don't hightail it out of here, I'll go git it." This was a little out of character for him, but like many farmers of his generation, he had little patience for government interference in matters that he considered none of its business.

Alvin was hardly ever agitated about anything, but I recall one incident where he was uncharacteristically impatient. He and Evelyn had driven out to visit us in Virginia and found that they were low on cash for the return trip home. Since they did not carry credit cards, they asked if we would accompany them to our bank to write a check for cash. It was Saturday, and as the morning wore on, Alvin began to get nervous as the clock ticked relentlessly toward noon, when the lobby doors would close. Sharlyn and her mother seemed unconcerned as they looked through one bag of clothes after another. Finally, when one asked the other whether she liked the brown dress, Alvin flared, "Forget the brown, let's go get the *green*."

In retirement Alvin was able to obtain whatever amount of well-deserved rest he wanted, so he was often content watching life through the windows. From his patio window he could watch old man Haslow, so ravaged by arthritis and osteoporosis that he was bent over ninety degrees, working in his garden. Alvin told me that one day when he saw Haslow sitting in the waiting room at the doctor's office, he did not recognize him "until he stood up, and then he fell right back into shape again." Alvin was looking out the picture window facing the front side of the house one day and noticed that the black cast iron horse heads he installed to mark the sides of the driveway were streaked with white bird droppings. Now, if I were he, I might have been inclined to rush headlong out of the house roaring and shaking my fist at every bird that landed on my precious horse heads. This was not Alvin's style. Instead, the farmer in him emerged, and immediately he had the inspiration for a solution. He went to the closet for two wire coat hangers, unwrapped the twisted section, and strapped these lengths of wire to the wooden posts at the base of the horse heads. Then he bent the wire up and over the heads and slipped three empty thread spools onto each wire, spray painted the whole apparatus black to blend in with the heads, and stepped back to watch it work. When a bird would try to land on the spools, they would rotate on the wire, and the bird would tumble off because it could not get a grip. As word spread throughout the bird community that that was not a suitable perch, the problem was solved. After a month or so, Alvin could remove his ingenious device, confident the birds had been conditioned to leave his horses alone for the rest of the season.

Alvin had a section of his basement partitioned off into a shop, and one day he answered an ad in Marshfield for a table saw. When he went to inspect it, the owner had an extra belt for it, still in its original packaging, that was to be included in the price. Two weeks or so elapsed before the sale was concluded, but when the seller delivered the saw to Spencer, Alvin expected the spare belt as well. However, the seller, a teacher at the high school, as it turns out, denied the existence of any such belt, asserting it was certainly not part of the bargain; what he was delivering was the extent of the sale. The next time Alvin was in Marshfield, he noticed that there was a hardware store not far from the high school. On a hunch he went inside, and there hanging on a hook was the very belt he had seen when he first answered the ad. When he asked the storeowner whether a certain teacher had been in to return it, he said, "Why, yes, he was in here just last week to bring it back." Alvin then knocked on the door of the teacher on Saturday, told him what he learned at the hardware store, and asked him if he would like to change his story. The teacher was livid, demanding to know what business Alvin had checking up on him like that and tracking his whereabouts. Alvin calmly told him he had come for his belt and was not going to leave without it. With a humph, this model of integrity handed over the cash for Alvin to buy the belt.

When Sharlyn took Alvin to one of his favorite hamburger restaurants one day, he had taken a bite or two of his sandwich when Sharlyn asked him how it was. He stared at it for a while, turned it over to look at the back side, then said only two words--"Kinda small." He loved to go to Perkins and always had the same breakfast there without even looking at the menu. "Guess I'll have the short stack today," he would say, as if by saying *today*, his order for pancakes was somehow different from what it was every time. Evelyn and Alvin were not fond of traveling, but one year while my parents lived in Colorado, we persuaded Sharlyn's parents that they must see the beauty of the West. Taking the long drive in easy stages, we eventually reached Fort Morgan, from where they caught their first glimpse of hazy grandeur in the distance. Before long we were in the hands of my father, who whisked them through the tight turns of Thompson Canyon and the summer snows at the fourteen-thousand-foot elevation of Rocky Mountain National Park. One day in my car, my father in the passenger seat turned around to Alvin sitting in the back seat and said, "So Alvin, now that you are retired, do you still wake up at 4:30, the same hour as on the farm, or do you sleep in?" "Oh no, I sleep in," Alvin replied. "So what time do you get up?" my father wanted to know. In all innocence Alvin said, "Well, some mornings I don't get up until 6:30."

One of the secrets of Alvin's long life was his failure to realize or acknowledge his age. When a family reunion was planned one summer at the public park in Abbotsford, the organizers had reserved the open-air picnic shelter, where the chairs were to be set up. On the day of the gathering, a cold front moved through, delivering the frigid conditions that are not unusual for Wisconsin, even in July, with temperatures down into the forties. Because of the arctic winds out of the north, Alvin asked me to help him stretch a tarp across one side of the shelter as a windbreak, because, he said, "Some of those old folks can't take that cold air." He was 76.

Advancing age brought Alvin and Evelyn to the painful decision one day to sell their beautiful home in Spencer and move into the Purdy, an assisted-living facility down in Marshfield. When the family decided to hold an estate sale to dispense with a lifetime of accumulated goods, Sharlyn and I drove out to Wisconsin to offer some help. Wisely, they engaged the services of a licensed appraiser to assess the value of articles that could be classified as antiques, but he was interested only in big-ticket items. The monumental job of tagging the remaining items with prices fell to the rest of us, primarily Evelyn and Sharlyn's sister Bernette. With little exposure to the antique market, I had no idea whether that dented up coal bucket was a piece of junk or a valuable commodity to a collector, whether enamel cookware could still grace someone's kitchen or would best be placed outside to catch rainwater. On the first day of the sale, I noticed a man who asked Bernette whether she would take less for every item he picked up. "Would you take two dollars for this?" "Could I have both of these for that price?" and so on. But then his eye fell on the horse-drawn plow out in the shed. Alvin had maintained it meticulously over the years, and now that it stood in immaculate condition with its handles polished and blades painted, it would fetch perhaps a thousand dollars on the open market. When I saw him striding for the shed, I took Bernette aside and warned her that he would be back to ask for a reduction of the tagged price, which was already better than a bargain. So as he returned, asking for a hundred dollars off, she stood firm. "Well, all right," he said, "But I will need to come back on Wednesday to pick it up."

On Wednesday I saw him drive up in a big panel truck with double doors in the back to load his plow. Before he went out to the shed, however, he and the pre-teen son he had brought along with him looked again through the items for sale on the tables. This time when he asked for a reduced price I was standing behind him shaking my head vigorously to Bernette. When he checked out, it was my turn at the cash box, and as he placed a neatly folded pile of towels on the table, I saw the tag for fifty cents on top. "Is that fifty cents for each towel, or for the whole stack?" I asked the man. "Oh, I assumed it was for the whole stack," he replied. I was suspicious. "Let me just check to be sure," I told him pleasantly. After confirming with Bernette that indeed each towel had been tagged fifty cents, I realized that this schnook, probably in full view of his own son, had removed the tags from all but the top one. With neither protest nor apology, he cast his eyes downward and quickly reached into his pocket for another five-dollar bill. Although I had caught him in his deception, I made no accusations, cheerily asking him instead if he needed help loading his heavy plow. As he swung open the rear doors of the panel truck, we slid it as far in as we could, but the handles still protruded beyond the opening. "Hold on," I said, "let me go to the side door and lift it up from the other end. I think it will slide some more." But before I could get around to the front to assist, he gave one final shove from the back and slammed the doors shut. In so doing, he smashed the windows against the protruding plow handles, shattering the safety glass in both of them into thousands of marble-size pieces. His replacement costs were far more than the pennies he had shaved off of every item he picked up from the estate sale. "Could not have happened to a nicer guy," I remember thinking. But I would learn that one of the conditions of this rare moment of universal justice to which I was being treated was that I was not to be permitted to gloat. I wanted a photo, not of his misfortune, but to capture and perpetuate the poetic ecstasy I felt at the moment. However, it was such a misty, drizzly day that the lens of the camera clouded up, and when the pictures came back, my memento looked more like I had photographed the inside of a grape.

Although Evelyn "wore the pants" in many family matters, Alvin sometimes had the old-time attitude that his women should attend to his needs. "Lady, get the clippers and shave my neck 'round," he would say to his "Ev" when he noticed he was in need of a hair trim. When he finished his chores in the evening, his long hard day was over and he expected a meal to be ready on the table. "Six o'clock, time for supper," he would say, staring at the clock as he settled into his chair. At the end of the meal, he always expected some kind of dessert. "Shar, get the cake," he would order, knowing there was usually one in what he called "the cakebox." At breakfast he liked his toast nearly coal black. When a slice of bread came out of the toaster, he would request that it be put back in a second time. To anyone who would gasp or sputter at that, he would simply say with a grin, "Good for what ails ya." Long before industry discovered the value of charcoal filters to strain foreign particles out of a system, Alvin seemed to be ahead of his time. He lived to be ninety, even though bacon lard smeared on his toast was equally as palatable to him as plum jelly.

Aside from an occasional cold that led to a nosebleed ("just changin' the oil," he would say, as he let it drip into the sink basin), Alvin scarcely had a sick day in his life until he was well into his seventies. It was about this time that he was diagnosed with prostate cancer, but the doctors advised the family to forego treatment, under the theory that at his age, the cancer would likely not metastasize before he succumbed to some other ailment anyway. For about ten years after that, his health remained so robust that the doctors were inclined to amend their advice, until Alvin contracted pneumonia one winter that persisted into the spring and summer. When he developed type II diabetes and began to experience such severe circulation problems that his extremities became discolored and would not heal, he was hospitalized and then transferred to a nursing home. For no reason except that he was Alvin, he quickly became the favorite patient of all the nurses there, but when he asked them when he could go home, they told him he must get stronger and healthier first. His desire to return home was a powerful goal for him, and with sheer determination, he rallied. The entire staff gathered for a party to send him home with balloons and party hats on one of the happiest days of his life. In the fall of 2003, he was back in the hospital when Sharlyn and I visited him with my father. Hooked up to a catheter to drain his urine into a bottle, electrodes attached to his head and chest, intravenous fluid dripping into his arm, plastic tubing protruding from his nose, he had experienced hardship before and took this indignity in stride. When a nurse came in to tell him she had to draw yet another sample of blood, he simply said, "Yeah, I think I got a little left yet." May I be half as good a patient some day when I am the one lying in that bed. This time Alvin would not be going home, but he did go Home.

# Linway

**W**hen we arrived back in Arlington after our honeymoon, I carried my bride across the threshold of our apartment and unloaded her belongings into our first home together at 4620 South 28th Road. After the biggest dream of a lifetime for both of us, it was back to reality, as we drove in separate directions to work. I was still attending classes at AU as well, and one day when Sharlyn dropped me off at the campus, she failed to realize on the drive home that during rush hour Canal Road becomes a one-way route coming from Maryland. When a police officer pulled her over, her first thought as she burst into tears was not concern for a traffic citation but the fact that she was married less than a month and already she was besmirching the family name.

One of the most energetic employees at Kappa Systems, the company for which I was still working, was a hard-working utility man named Milton Wright, the company driver, deliveryman, stockman and purchaser of our supplies. He was quite an entrepreneur, who owned an oyster farm on the Chesapeake Bay and frequently brought in a few quarts of them to sell around the office. Sharlyn somehow overcame her aversion to seafood enough to come up with the best recipe for oyster stew anyone could ever experience, still one of my favorites to this day. Milton also owned a trucking business on the side, starting with one truck and a driver, then from the profits he bought a second one, until by the time I knew him, he had three or four trucks. When Toyota first made inroads in America in the late 1960s, I scoffed at anything with a "Made in Japan" label and thought anyone was foolish to buy such a product. Leonard Stephens at the Agency had bought one, however, and had high praise for it. Now Milton had bought one too, and nearly every day he was telling me about its wonderful features, until I became convinced Sharlyn and I should trade in her Malibu, older than my Bel Air, for a Corolla Mark II. It was one of the most finely engineered, user-friendly cars we ever had. After a few months we discovered that we could actually get along with only one car, so I had my first exposure to the world of selling a used car. Although the Bel Air was well maintained and in good running order, the doors had no protective moldings, so they developed a rash from those oh-so-considerate drivers who parked beside me. After a few months without success, my father finally offered us $1200 for it, thereby depriving me of the exhilaration I was beginning to experience from *not* showing it to those who said they were coming right over to look at it.

One of my good friends at Kappa was an accountant named Tom Hoover, who with his wife Jane had just bought a house. It had never occurred to me that Sharlyn and I could afford our very own house, but Tom convinced me that we could really not afford *not* to buy one. It was the voice of an angel, as his advice turned out to be the second-most important decision of our life together. Immediately after Christmas that year, we started looking at the classified ads for houses. I could scarcely believe we were actually thinking of become homeowners. The very thought alone was awesome and terrifying at the same time. Landowners. Our names would go into history as the owners of land in Virginia, but we could also live in infamy for taking on more than we could afford.

In those days the salary of a wife could not be considered in the assets which one could use to qualify for a mortgage, ostensibly because of the probability that a pregnancy would terminate her employment, thereby increasing the risk of the lender. As a result, my meager salary put us near the bottom of the market for homes we could consider. The first few we were shown by the agents were in the next category above a cardboard box under the freeway. One shanty I recall was essentially two rooms—a tiny bathroom and a small open area of unpartitioned space. Another was a dilapidated shack hidden amongst a thicket surrounded by junk cars and machinery that made me wonder if it was a hideout for bandits. Other than that it seemed like a wonderful place to settle down and raise a family. Sharlyn called it the postage stamp place for the way it seemed to be stuck in there all by itself. To me it looked more like it had been dropped from a helicopter. Each time we answered one of these ads, the agent considered us a "client," and after a few weeks this became exponential, as each of them called us with a list of properties to check out. One was a retired colonel, who considered us his personal property, and he seemed quite possessive when he discovered we had looked at a house not on his listing. I became quite interested in a nice three-bedroom brick house with a fireplace, fenced yard, and basement near our church in the Del Rey area of Alexandria. I thought it was just what we wanted, but Sharlyn was absolutely intractable against it. I did not understand, but she could see something I could not—the neighborhood. Since Ralph Behrens from Immanuel had lived near there for many years, I told him we were contemplating a house in Del Rey, but we wanted to think twice about it. His exact words were, "I would think three times." It was not long after that we became aware of the stories in the local news nearly every evening about escalating crime in Del Rey.

One day when I closed the door of a stall in the men's room, I noticed the newspaper the previous occupant had left on the floor. As I sat there reigning supreme, I saw that the folded paper was turned to the real estate section of the classifieds, so I idly picked it up. My eye fell immediately on an ad for a three-bedroom house in McLean on the section of the page open in front of me. Tell me this was just a coincidence. Go ahead, convince me that the hand of God was not guiding my eye to the very place on that paper that led us to the most important purchase of our lives. I want to tell you more about this piece of property, but first we must go to the dentist. When I had a dental checkup a few weeks before I was discharged from the Army, the young dentist who examined my teeth noticed that one of my wisdom teeth was growing in horizontally, impacting the backmost molar. He requested my consent to remove that molar so that he could extract the errant wisdom tooth under it, and I foolishly gave it to him. Now, since neither Sharlyn nor I had a dentist, I was asking Barbara Cranston at the office one day whether she could recommend one. Sherwood Frey, one of the engineers on assignment from the Philadelphia office, overheard my question as he walked past, and asserted that the best dentist in the metro area was Dr. Livingston (no, not *that* Dr. Livingston, *Jerome S.* Livingston), his family's practitioner for many years. Sherwood warned me, however, that Livingston believed in preventative dentistry and assigned his patients rigorous home care, expecting diligent dental hygiene. When our new dentist first looked into my mouth, he asked why my molar was missing. "Well, he sure took the easy way out," he muttered under his breath when I told him what the young Army neophyte had done. Then he told me that my x-rays showed that I had three more wisdom teeth in various stages of impaction that needed to be removed also. Worse, all four of Sharlyn's wisdom teeth were impacted and would have to come out.

It was bad enough that we both scheduled the extractions of our wisdom teeth on the same Saturday in February 1971, leaving neither of us to be the caretaker of the other, but we also had an appointment with Charles Rose, the agent from Henderson Realty, to look at the house in McLean on that same afternoon. Still groggy from Novocain, with swollen cheeks, distorted expressions and slurred speech, we met Rose at 6351 Linway Terrace to walk through the house. Compared to the house in Del Rey, it was a disappointment to me, but Sharlyn liked it immediately. Again, she could see something I could not—the neighborhood. Oscar Reynolds and his wife Lucille had purchased it five years earlier, and if we could pay the equity they had accrued in that period, we could assume their thirty-year loan at five and a quarter percent. Sharlyn had more in her savings account than I, so her little nest egg was hatched to buy a new nest. Reynolds had two severely disabled children, and the pressure of five years in that house with them sent him over the edge, causing the family to split up. When I later discovered the hidden drug paraphernalia, whiskey bottles and girlie magazines he left buried in the basement, I got a different picture of what life must have been like for Lucille. Rose was supposed to be representing the sellers, but he knew we had no experience and acted as our advisor as well. When I suggested that we counter their 21K asking price with a counter offer for 20K and make it contingent upon an inspection, he told us that if we did that, we would surely lose the sale, because it was priced to sell and someone else would come along who would not ask the sellers to compromise. After we signed the contract, our "agents" still continued to call, but one by one we informed them they were too late. The old colonel had strong words for us for all the "trouble" to which we had put him in vain.

When I told Tom Hoover we had bought a house, he acted like a first-time father for having been the "parent" that brought us into the homeowner world, proudly telling everyone in the office about it. One of the engineers quipped that just having a McLean address was worth what we paid for the house. McLean was one of the most upscale communities in the entire Washington area, home to many of society's most elite—generals (Colin Powell), Supreme Court justices (William Rehnquist), sports figures (Joe Theismann), senators (Strom Thurmond), political legends (the famous, or infamous, Hickory Hill, where Robert and Ethel Kennedy raised eleven children), historical sites (the mansion to which Dolley Madison fled when the British burned the White House), and headquarters of the CIA at Langley. We were not elite, however, and our house, by contrast, was not upscale by any means. It was solidly built of cement block in 1935 by William Lockwood, by now an elderly retiree who still lived with his wife Christina (Teenie) two doors away in a tiny house about half the size of ours. Bill had actually built four houses in a row along the Old Dominion railroad line at that time. The fourth one had once stood on the tiny lot next to us to the west, but this lot now stood empty since that house burned down long before we arrived, as evidenced by a charred foundation that was still visible through the overgrowth. The largest of the remaining three was the one in the middle, between Lockwoods and us, occupied by Alan and Liz Stevens when we became their neighbors. Bill's mother had been a real estate agent, and this house was built with two stories, so that she could live in the downstairs, while her clients climbed an external stairway to her office on the second floor. This always seemed backward to me. Should the living quarters not be *upstairs* and the office *downstairs*, eliminating not only the need for clients to climb stairs but the outside staircase entirely? In fact, by the time we came along, the outside steps had been removed, and there was no evidence that they had ever been there.

That seemed to be typical of Bill's sense of design. After we came to know him, he told me once that the plan for our house was sketched on the back of an envelope one afternoon, but he did not say what he was drinking when he picked up his pencil. I would eventually learn that he had been an excellent carpenter, but the floor plan of our house left me scratching my head. It was shaped somewhat like a Stetson hat, with a center section and a wing coming off each side, which made for three separate roof lines, one for each section of the structure. Worst of all, a tiny six-by-five bathroom was carved out of one corner of the kitchen, although I suppose we should have been grateful that it had an indoor bathroom at all. Over the years we found evidence that the well that still existed in the back yard of the Stevens house may at one time have been the water supply shared by both houses. It is also possible that initially neither of these houses had indoor plumbing and shared an outhouse as well. This could explain the doll-size bathroom, which might have been converted from a pantry just off the kitchen when the houses were connected to the public water system. By the time it occurred to me to ask about that possibility, Bill had died and Teenie's dementia had progressed beyond her ability to remember such details. The basement had an entrance from outdoors and was "finished" with a rough cement floor for only about eight feet. From that point back, there were a few inches of crawl space between the bare virgin soil and the floor joists of the living space above. While the house itself was in good condition, I was compiling a mental list of all the changes I wanted to make. Little did I realize the scale to which those renovations would extend only a few years later.

On the day of settlement, we noticed that a pair of vice-grip pliers served as the handle of the cold-water faucet of the kitchen sink. This was the "repair" that Oscar, who had already separated from Lucille and the kids and moved out of the house months earlier, had made when she demanded that he come over to fix it. We demanded that he fix it too—with a new faucet and a real handle. Oscar took me outside, and as he toured the yard with me, pointed to the vacant lot to the west, where the house had burned down, and told me that it was actually the property of Fairfax County, but that he had been mowing it, picking the cherries, mulberries and walnuts that grew on it, and trimming the shrubbery for the five years they had lived there. He claimed that after seven years, he could declare ownership of it by adverse possession, and now that right would pass to me. Gullible as I was, I believed him and assumed for quite some time, without ever checking the facts, that it was essentially public land. I will explain later how I found out he was wrong. Then he took me to the back yard, where he had a lawn mower, some construction ladders and a swing set for the children. Oscar earned his living as a carpenter, and when he took me down to the basement, he showed me the hand tools, boxes of nails, screws and staples, cabinetry accessories, cans of grease and oil, paint, and various other odds and ends that he was planning to leave behind. He offered it all to me, including the items out in the yard, for a hundred dollars. It was one of the best bargains I ever made. To this day I use many of those same tools and have not yet used up some of the pop rivets and other materials he left for me.

One day I ran across a small wooden box I am quite sure he did not intend for me to see. It contained his name tag, sergeant stripes, combat medals, Army insignia, and blank rifle cartridges, as well as his stash of hypodermic needles, rubbing alcohol, and rubber bands for his drug habit, and after I pulled the last items out, I saw a message scrawled with marker at the bottom of the box, "Nosey, aren't you??" Then faintly in pencil beneath that, it read, "No Good 1st Sgt." I held this box for him for over thirty-five years, expecting him to return one day, but he never did. Apparently Oscar and his friends were not quite ready to accept the transfer of ownership. I was awakened by a commotion during the night a few days after we moved in, and from the window I watched a pickup loaded with revelers, and Oscar at the wheel loaded with alcohol, driving across the yard. When the cherries ripened about three months later, one of his gaptooth friends drove up to inform me that Oscar and Lucille had always let him come by to pick the cherries every year. I told him he would need to get them from a can this year.

The rent for our apartment had been $120 per month, so we were astounded to learn that when the PITI (principal, interest, taxes, and insurance) was computed for our mortgage payment, it came to $113—and we had a whole house and two yards! What a huge blessing this turned out to be. We were supposed to move in April 1, 1971, but a few days before that, we got a call from Charlie Rose, informing us that Lucille would not be able to vacate until April 3 and that we were technically entitled to rent for those three days. This presented a problem for us because we had already given notice to our landlord that we would vacate our apartment by the first of the month. However, when I presented our predicament to him, he was uncharacteristically sympathetic, and since he did not charge us for the extra days, we did not charge Lucille either. There was an advantage to the delay. April 3 was a Saturday, and it meant, first, that we would not need to take time off from work, and, second, that Tom and Jane Hoover, who were anxious to see what the house looked like, would be able to help us move. When we finished hauling in the last load and thanked them for all their kind assistance, the only thing our exhausted bodies wanted was some sleep. However, it was an unseasonably cold day, and when I went to turn on the furnace for the first time, we discovered that Lucille had drained the last drop of heating oil out of the 200-gallon tank in the back yard. Time to call the landlo … uh, wait a minute, *we* are the landlord. Fortunately, Lucille had not yet disconnected the phone, so I started to call around for number two fuel oil. The suppliers to whom I spoke were either unable to make deliveries on the weekend or unwilling to come out on short notice without a surcharge, so we decided to pile on blankets and wait until Monday. We had just fallen exhausted into bed, when there was a knock on the door. It was Liz and Alan Stevens, our new neighbors next door, with a plate of brownies.

Around Christmas time Sharlyn was working at her office in the Pentagon one day when she mentioned to her coworker Vera that she was not feeling well. Vera winked at Erma and said she knew why. When Sharlyn made an appointment with Dr. Briguglio in nearby Shirlington to arrange for a pregnancy test, his nurse called her in to say, "Mrs. Pullmann, you are about to become a mother." Sharlyn immediately requested the use of their phone to relay the good news to me at the office. Today it is not unusual for pregnant employees to continue working until very close to the due date, yet cases of births in the office are virtually unknown. In Sharlyn's case, however, Colonel Horne insisted that seven months into her term, she would need to resign. "We do not want you having that baby here at work," he told her bluntly. Since Briguglio had established September 5 as the target for our blessed event, it was less than four months after we moved into our new house that Sharlyn was already at home full time, preparing her nursery—and a change of careers. In the course of cleaning up one day, she noticed what seemed like ants with wings. Sure we were infested with termites, I called for an inspection. No termites were found, but we were told that in the attic there was evidence of powder post beetles, which also attack wood but at a much slower pace than termites. In exchange for seven hundred dollars, a severe blow to our savings account, a fumigation tent covering the entire house was erected for a few days to rid us of these pests while we were away in Wisconsin. Whether we actually had them or whether this was just a scam, it was probably still worth the cost for the ancillary benefit we would enjoy for several years afterward for the freedom from cockroaches, spiders and other crawlers throughout the house.

My job at Kappa involved a certain amount of interaction with various government offices. One day in October I was trying to call someone in one of the agencies and could not get an answer. When I called back the next day, the person I was trying to contact told me that the previous day had been a holiday. A holiday? Columbus Day was a holiday? When I found out I had been working while he had been paid for not working, I allowed a little resentment to creep into my consciousness. About a month later they had another one, while we worked on Veterans Day. The following February when I tried unsuccessfully to reach someone again, I was told the next day that the government had had a holiday on Presidents Day. More resentment. Shortly before I had left the Army, Leonard Stephens had suggested that I take a mid-level Civil Service exam in hopes of starting a government career, but either my qualifications did not match up to their needs or I did not score very well, because my application was never followed up with an interview or offer.

One day I learned that the Labor Department had what they termed a Job Bank, a huge room in which the postings for various government positions were displayed on the walls, so I decided to drive over there to look at them. I was in that room for less than a minute when my eye fell on a description that seemed to jump off the wall at me. The Copyright Office was looking for a music cataloger … hmm, check this out, music degree required, graduate work preferred, typing speed at least 40 wpm, call to schedule a battery of tests and an interview. It was almost as if someone had read my qualifications and invented a job to match my resume. I did not realize it at the time, but this was not a routine job change. Even more than a career change, it turned out to be a lifetime benefit, far more than I would ever know for many years. One of the top five most important events of my life was about to occur, and from my vantage point in time, I perceive the unmistakable finger of God directing me to that very place to find that posting—maybe not in your mind, but surely in mine.

Most positions with the government today are staffed through a lengthy, tortuous path governed by legal procedure and equal employment opportunity regulations. A posting may remain open for a month or two, not counting any extensions, then a rating panel is convened to evaluate the applications according to quality ranking factors, before a few candidates are selected for interview, and only then can a background investigation be initiated. It is not unusual for the entire process to extend across several months. At the time I applied, however, I reported to the human resources office of the Library of Congress for the testing they required, scheduled an interview with the selecting officer, Richard Breinig, the next day, and within three days received an offer. Although I can honestly say that I enjoyed working for Len Greenberg at Kappa, and told him that in writing when I presented my notice of resignation to him, I can also honestly say that I did not have a strong belief in the mission of the company. To me it seemed that the perpetual scramble for government contracts was one notch above begging, too much like the family dog waiting by the table for whatever scraps might fall from the master's plate. However, it meant a great deal to me when misty-eyed Len bid me farewell, and his sincere comments that I would be missed were backed up by his repeated requests for assistance with various proposals in the evenings and on weekends over the course of the next year or two afterward. This was not easy, because I was still taking classes, but I took full advantage of the fantastic IBM Selectric typewriters that Kappa possessed, to type up my term papers. These machines had replaceable type heads, which allowed me to select various fonts—large capitals for headings, italics without the need for underlining, symbols and small numbers for footnotes, pica or elite to vary quoted material, and so on. Word processors were still in the future, but this analog version of one appealed to me very much.

"God said, 'Let there be lights in the firmament of the heaven to divide the day from the night; and let them be for signs' …" (Gen. 1:14). And so it was that there was a full moon on May 10, 1971, the day I started work at the Copyright Office. Two weeks later, on Memorial Day, I was already experiencing one of those government holidays that had caused me so much consternation at Kappa. When Fourth of July followed closely behind, it prompted Mary Brewster, one of my coworkers, to quip that I was getting so many holidays in my short tenure that I would have to pay back the Office for all that time off. I wonder what she told Pat Benson, who started two days after I did and had even less time on the job. If you are puzzled what copyright has to do with the Library of Congress, you are probably in the majority. The primary mission of the Library is to provide Congress with information, which is derived in large measure from intellectual property. One of the conditions in the law for registration of a copyright is that two copies of the work must be submitted with each application, at the expense of the remitter. The Library may then retain one or both of those copies in its collections for the use of Congress. Few people understand fully what a copyright is. If I send you a letter, you become the owner of it as long as you possess it, but you may not make copies of it unless I extend the right to you to make them. In the absence of an express or implied agreement between us, you may not copy or publish it without infringing my rights. Since you have the physical object, my right may seem hollow to you, yet I can wield considerable power with it, depending upon how desperate you are to distribute the contents. Entire industries are built around this very significant principle of the law.

Many people are also unfamiliar with the scope of copyright. If the shirt or blouse you are wearing is made from a print fabric, the chances are good that the pattern is copyrighted (notice that I did not say copywritten, a common absurdity). If you send greeting cards, you are using a copyrighted commodity. If you open a can of beans, look carefully at the label; for somewhere you will find a copyright notice that makes it illegal for you to reproduce it. If you play a game of Monopoly, you might presume that it is copyrighted; it is *not*, because a concept or idea is not copyrightable—but the board and the rules will both sport a notice, and you may not duplicate *them*. A movie title is not copyrightable either, because a word or short phrase cannot be registered for copyright—trademark maybe, but not copyright. A copyright is also very different from a patent. Ironically, both derive their authority directly from the same clause in the constitution, but they are administered in two completely different branches of the government—copyright in the legislative and patent in the Commerce Department of the executive. While a patent must be a unique contribution to industry before it is granted, a copyright is not granted but exists immediately upon creation and may even pertain to identical works. If I take a picture of the Washington monument, I own the copyright of my photo and may register it; if you see me take the picture, stand in the exact same place and snap your picture a moment later, you may register yours also. Identical as the two photos may appear, I may not copy yours nor you mine. If you were to invent a pair of goggles that allows the wearer to see buried treasure, you would need to keep your invention secret until the patent process is completed; however, if you write down your recipe for chicken soup, your copyright obtains immediately, whether you register in the Office or not. No one may reproduce your recipe without your permission. So why register, you may be asking. The answer lies in the remedies available to you. If I were to steal your unregistered recipe, the burden of proof is on you to establish that you wrote it, *and* you must prove actual damages. If I steal your *registered* recipe, the ownership is a matter of record, and the statute provides damages for infringement without regard to your actual losses.

At the time I started at Copyright, only certain materials could be submitted for copyright protection if they were not published. If you wrote a poem, for example, it would need to be published before you could register your claim to it. However, if you wrote a song, the words and music together would be registrable, even if unpublished. Quality makes no difference, so why not set your poem to music to get protection even if the tune was not artful in the least, and you cared nothing about it anyway? Today the law has changed to allow registration of your unpublished poem, but in those days this was a popular workaround, and the Office received unpublished music by the thousands. If you inferred from this that you could use "la la la" as the lyrics throughout your song and, since quality is not essential, thereby prevent anyone else from using "la la la" ever again, you would have dipped below a minimum standard of creativity which is not always easy to define. "Mama's little baby" repeated forty times is probably de minimis, "Mama's little baby loves Willy" might get protection under a rule of doubt, while "Mama's little baby loves Billy, Milly and silly Willy" probably emerges substantially above the line as creative output. Judging from the volume of unpublished music sent to the Office, I would venture a guess that the songwriters of America suffer from another misconception. It would appear that these wannabes believed that by submitting their works for registration, they would stand a better chance to be "discovered" by some talent scout, agent, or producer. Sadly, registration has the exact opposite effect. They misunderstand that when their work is submitted, it becomes the property of the government, and only a court order would allow anyone from the outside to see it. In fact, since registration of an unpublished work requires submission of only *one* copy, the only one in existence may be that scribbled manuscript now stored in a warehouse somewhere.

The raison d'être of the registration system is searchability. To exploit a copyrighted work, you need to be able to find the owner of it. In the days before computers, the records were maintained in the largest card catalog in the world, known as the CCC (copyright card catalog), which provided access by title, author or claimant—but not subject. A search of it could be done in person, or the Office could perform that service for you, probably more efficiently, for an hourly fee. My job as a cataloger was to create those cards. Rather than type directly on cards, however, we composed our text on a photosensitive "mat," a strip with five frames, each representing an entry in the catalog. The mats were converted by the Government Printing Office into cards, which were shipped back to the CCC for filing. The cataloging operation of the Copyright Office is unique. Unlike a public or school library (or even the Library of Congress), which has a selection policy to determine what its holdings will be, and therefore what it must catalog, Copyright is obliged to catalog *everything* it receives. No other library operation anywhere in the world is required to describe fabric, skyscraper blueprints, computer chips and jewelry designs, yet these items are but a sampling of the scope of material we processed. As you might expect, training was extensive. The apprentice phase for a cataloger was a year, the period of time in which the massive rules for extraction of data, style and format, and copyright facts could be learned. With satisfactory performance at this level, a cataloger would be eligible for promotion to senior cataloger. Beyond that was the reviser, a competitive quasi-supervisory position responsible for training and review of all the work of the catalogers. Supervising the entire music cataloging operation were Dick Breinig, the section head who hired me, and Edward Kapusciarz, his assistant.

When I started working at the Copyright Office, the Library of Congress had outgrown its two buildings on Capitol Hill and started erecting a third one, a massive new white marble edifice that became known as the James Madison Memorial Building—not only a functional office but the only memorial in Washington to the fourth President. While the construction continued, Copyright was temporarily located in rented space in Crystal City, a rapidly developing office complex on the Virginia side of the Potomac near National Airport. This was an ideal location for me, because I could catch the bus a block away from our house in McLean and ride it directly to Crystal City, the end of the line, and Sharlyn would have the car each day. On Friday, August 13, 1971, I was working at my desk when I was summoned to the office for an emergency call. Sharlyn had taken the car to Calvert Toyota for routine service, and while in line to pay the bill, she suddenly found herself in need of the rest room. Not sure what to make of a strange-looking "plug" and tinged fluid in the toilet, she called Dr. Briguglio, who told her that her water broke. Never mind that our first child was not due for another month yet; Briguglio urged Sharlyn to come *immediately* to Alexandria Hospital, where the baby must be delivered within twelve hours, he told her, to avoid complications. Today most hospitals regard birthing as truly a family event, and husbands are not only allowed but encouraged to be present; even a grandparent or other relative is frequently on hand to witness the emergence of new life, as well. In those days, however, I was relegated to the waiting room to pace. About nine that evening, when I asked for an update, the nurse asked my name and was surprised that no one had given me the news. Our daughter Angela Marie had been born about an hour earlier, and when they escorted me back for my first peek at the precious bright pink pugilist with wisps of blond hair, determined to fight off anyone who dared to give her a bath, I had to choke back tears. This completed the quadrilogy of 1971, the most momentous year of our lives, when we experienced a new house, car, career, and future college student within less than six months. My mother had good reason to be especially pleased that the stork had scheduled the delivery of our precious package exactly on her fiftieth birthday that year.

It was by a stroke of good fortune that the reviser who first trained me was Virginia Kass. Not only was she by a wide margin the most competent mind in the whole office, but she was also the most personable—and gorgeous in the orange print dress in which I first saw her. As she disclosed a little of her background, I learned that she was my exact age, grew up in Chicago and had been a voice major at Roosevelt University, just down the street from Sherwood along Michigan Avenue. It is quite possible that she was among the bustle of Roosevelt students I passed unawares every day on my way to work at the Tribune. She had landed in the Washington area through marriage to Ralph Kass, a cellist in the United States Air Force. Under Ginny's tutelage I progressed rapidly and soon became the top producer in the office. When I became eligible for a promotion to reviser, I looked around and realized that all of the incumbents of those positions were my contemporaries, not likely to die or retire any time soon, and I silently cursed the three years I had lost to the Army plus another year and a half at Kappa, while they had been building up their seniority here. I concluded that my only option was to become an examiner, where the pay scale was higher.

# Copyright Law

**W**hereas the Cataloging Division was responsible for creating the searchable copyright record, the Examining Division dealt with copyrightability and other legal issues requisite for registration. A law degree was not required, but I had the idea it would make me a better candidate when the opportunity arose, so I decided to attend law school. But I was about to make two serious mistakes. The first concerned the graduate work I was still doing at American University. You may recall that I was forced to enroll as a non-degree student because the administration did not recognize Sherwood as an accredited school. When I completed all my course work, and only the comprehensive exams and my thesis remained, I decided it was time to confront the administration again, presenting my straight-A track record as proof that I deserved to be accepted as a degree candidate. This time, however, the officer who handled such admission matters checked his books again and found not only that Sherwood *was* accredited, but its accreditation was established long before American University existed. All this time I had been improperly enrolled, as the result of a clerical error of the admissions office years earlier. They quickly corrected their mistake, but I must tell you about my own blunder.

In the course of some research I did on a term paper, I discovered that a minor *opera buffa* composer named Baldassare Galuppi had also written a number of keyboard sonatas, but no one had published them all, much less together in a single anthology. When I contacted Edith Woodcock of the University of Washington in Seattle, the leading authority on Galuppi, for more information, she was kind enough to lend me several microfilms of manuscripts from libraries in Italy and other sources. When I paid a printing company to produce hard copy of this microfilm, it totaled over two thousand pages. Later, incidentally, when I suggested that her film, along with my paper output, would be better preserved in the climate controlled conditions of the Library of Congress than in her closet, she was persuaded to donate them. Since I did not feel that the mere assembling of these various collections rose to the level of a thesis, however, I examined each sonata and wrote an analysis. Dr. Schutze, my thesis advisor, was not impressed with my approach, and strongly urged me to modify it. Because of a number of pressures, not the least of which was that graduate work was wearing me a little thin after nearly four years of night school, I foolishly contravened his advice and submitted the thesis as it was. It was the only B I received for all the courses I took there, but it was enough to fulfill the requirements for the Master of Arts in musicology. In the process of completing the paperwork for graduation, I discovered a dirty little fraud that American University, and probably most universities, perpetrated upon unsuspecting graduating students. One of the papers I was asked to sign was an agreement signing over the copyright of my thesis to University Microfilms, a clearinghouse for master's and doctoral theses from institutions around the world. When I refused, the clerk insisted it was a *requirement* for graduation. Then when I told him that I work at the Copyright Office, and that no one may take intellectual property without compensation, he waived the "requirement." Although this would mean that my thesis would not be searchable in the University Microfilms database, perhaps that is just as well, given the low regard for it held by my well-respected mentor George Schutze.

Now that graduate school was behind me, I could turn my attention to law school. But that brings me to another serious miscalculation I made. Today admission to law school must often be accompanied by an LSAT score, which in turn realistically requires a prep course. In those days, however, while admission was less demanding, the course of study was not. There were essentially two options—full time for three years without a gasp for air or part time for five grueling years juggling a full-time job with night school, home repairs and the demands of family. I thought I had discovered an easier way. Distance learning through on-line courses is becoming quite common in academia today, but in those days, unless a university operated a campus in some remote location, coursework off campus could be completed only by correspondence, if at all. When I learned that a certain LaSalle University in Chicago offered a law degree by correspondence, I was suspicious that it was nothing but a diploma mill. But when I checked further, I found that it was accredited, led to an LL.B. degree and allowed its graduates to sit for the Illinois bar exam, and met the scrutiny of the Army as a legitimate course of study eligible for benefits under the GI Bill. After all, had Lincoln not acquired his credentials this way—simply reading for the law? In addition to several boxes of bound books on case law, the course included a series of lectures in looseleaf format kept up to date with current statute law. This approach was especially appealing to me for two reasons—first, that I could proceed at my own pace, but, more importantly, I could do most of my studying at home evenings and weekends. Each section of the course required a paper, followed by a graded exam, and after about three years I was ready for the final, an Illinois bar exam proctored by someone acceptable to the school who would agree to take an oath that I had met a list of stipulations against cheating. I chose Willner Mensing, the pastor of our church, as my proctor. After I finished the course, however, I learned the truth. It was only when I started listing my degree as a credential, that the raised eyebrows and snickers it produced made me realize it was more an embarrassment than a recognized accomplishment. If you ever find yourself in a position to need someone to get you *into* jail, for a small retainer I would be glad to represent you.

Although I had enjoyed learning some of the legal intricacies of contracts, torts, domestic relations, real property, equity, and the other subjects in the curriculum, including an elective block on patent and copyright law, I did not possess sufficient funding, motivation or interest in the field to start over in one of the local law schools. Some time after my LaSalle course was underway, however, a vacancy occurred for a copyright examiner, which may have changed my mind. I was quite sure I would get the job because I had both a graduate degree and coursework toward a law degree, but one of my rivals for the position was James Vassar, who had arrived as a music cataloger about a year after I came to the Office. Jim had a rational mind that I admired and had completed most of the coursework for his doctorate, gravitating toward a thesis on one of the sons of J.S. Bach, as I recall, and I held him in such high regard that Sharlyn and I invited him and his wife to our house once or twice. The selecting officials were Penny Keziah, head of the Music Examining Section, and Felicia Healey, her assistant, and although such matters are supposed to be confidential, information was leaked to me that they were inclined to select Jim.

While their hiring decision was pending, I was on routine business in Music Examining one day, when I noticed Jim schmoozing with Penny in her office. As this certainly seemed like a breach of ethics to me, I surreptitiously monitored his movements and found repeated visits to her and Felicia. When Jim was selected for the position, I cried foul, but I could not appeal the decision because all my evidence was subjective and did not amount to bribery, coercion or illegality—inequity without iniquity. There was nothing I could do about it, and as you might imagine, I was bitter about this turn of events for a long time. As consolation I made an appointment to discuss the matter with the assistant chief of the Examining Division, Richard Glasgow, my good friend who took an interest in my progress through law school and talked with me often about it. Dick told me confidentially that the reason the deliberations had dragged out for as long as they had was that Penny and Felicia had a very difficult time deciding between us. Over time my anger faded, and eventually I had to acknowledge they had made a very good choice, and in point of fact Jim was such a commendable examiner that one day he became chief of the Division.

Although I will never know where my career might have led if I had become an examiner, my career path, by the grace of God, took an unexpected turn. In those days sound recordings were not copyrightable, so the record producers had been lobbying Congress for years to amend the law to stem the legal piracy rampant in the industry. Finally, the copyright law was amended to protect the actual sounds embodied in any recording made after February 15, 1972. For example, the famous *I Have a Dream* speech of Martin Luther King was duly registered on paper in the Office, but this did not protect King's oration. Under the new law his actual delivery would have been protected, and we would probably not be seeing the free ubiquitous proliferation of it that prevails today. However, since the only format acceptable for the underlying work was still a printed copy, a tape or vinyl record could not be used under the new law to register the song or other work itself—only the sounds captured in the *performance* of it.

This was nevertheless historic legislation, specifying an unprecedented class of registration in the law, and because automation was rapidly invading every aspect of the business world at that time, the Copyright Office decided on a bold move. Barbara Ringer, Register of Copyrights, hired a systems analyst named Leo Cooney to design an *automated* cataloging system to generate the catalog card for any material submitted in the new class N, sound recordings. I was selected to be the first cataloger to use it. This system was built around an operating system called ATS (automated terminal system) and employed a special typewriter terminal connected by a dedicated telephone line to the computer four miles away on Capitol Hill. To me it was a revolutionary concept as a typist because no erasures were necessary. A special backspace key could be pressed to back over a typographical error or a cursor could be positioned anywhere on the printed page to overtype a correction from that point forward. If messy corrections obscured the data before me on paper to the point where it was no longer legible, I could request a clean print of the entire page. Then when I was satisfied that the entry was constructed properly in its final format, I could send it to the computer to be printed as a card. I was impressed with this new concept from the first moment I experienced it.

Since neither the chief of the Cataloging Division, Elizabeth Dunne, nor her assistant Dorothy Linder wanted anything to do with the world of automation, both decided this might be a good time to retire. Before we send them away to their rocking chairs, however, I must tell you an anecdote about each of them. Dorothy, a typical product of the Depression years, became so concerned that pencils were being discarded with two inches of lead still left in them that she persuaded the administration at the highest levels to purchase pencil extenders. Every cataloger in the Division was issued an extender, essentially an aluminum tube threaded on the inside, and ordered to use it until a pencil was worn down to a nubbin with no lead left. My mother and grandmother would have been proud of her—and Dorothy received an incentive award for her "idea."

And now a little anecdote concerning Betty Dunne. Before funds were transferred electronically by direct deposit to a bank account, our paychecks were distributed manually to us by the administrative office. One day when I got to the head of the line for my check, Eric Reid could not find it and tried to say I had already received it. When he realized the absurdity of my attempting to pick up two checks, he suggested we wait until the end of the day to see which ones remained. One of them would belong to the person who erroneously had mine. When he saw that he still had Betsy Hostetler's check at the end of the day, Eric realized his mistake. Her maiden name had been Pullen, so when she appeared, he was talking to someone and absentmindedly handed my check to her. Then came a chain of errors that defies belief. Betsy was so familiar with her usual amount that she walked a block to her bank, filled out a deposit slip, endorsed the check without looking at the front of it and deposited it. Incredibly, the teller did not notice either that the signature did not match the payee or that the check was for a different amount from the deposit slip and gave Betsy a receipt for it. The next day both Betsy and I paid a little visit to the bank manager, who informed us the check itself had already left the bank, but then, despite the numbers that had to be out of balance somewhere within his system, he would have us believe it was not the bank's problem anyway. When we went to our division chief, Betty Dunne, to find out how I was going to be paid, she called the bank manager. She became so enraged over his responses to her queries that I thought her wig would fly off, as she told him she had substantial sums in his bank and that she was not only prepared to withdraw them, but would report his actions to his corporate executives, the press and to the authorities. After she hung up the phone, she told me that the matter would not be resolved until the next day, offering to write me a personal check if I needed money right away. Fortunately, our little family was not living from check to check, and I could afford to wait several days, if necessary, but I was most impressed with her support. Her influence with the bank literally paid dividends, as they acknowledged their error and made amends.

Two developments came along about that time that proved to be career-changing for me. The first was that Mary Hull, one of the revisers in the Music Section, resigned unexpectedly, leaving a vacancy. Foremost among the senior catalogers eligible for this position was one Paul Gunzelmann, a colleague whom I considered a good friend. Paul, however, had a talent for arousing hostility, taking umbrage at corrections he was handed back, and irritated his superiors in a number of other ways. The flextime programs available to many employees today in both the private and public sectors were not in place in those days, so the arrival time for us was fixed at 7:45, with a grace period of five minutes. Day after day Paul found himself pushing the envelope, arriving at seven, eight, or twelve minutes late. He carried around a catalog of excuses in his mind, some of them quite amusing, and he might even have been believable if he had retained any credibility in reserve. One day he insisted he was late because he was crossing Wilson Bridge behind a truck loaded with Christmas trees, and as one of them fell off, the driver next to him cursed at him when he swerved to avoid it. Chronic tardiness was not his only problem, however, and as a result he was passed over for the vacancy in favor of the applicant who was second in line—which happened to be me. Paul knew that I was not responsible for his misfortune and remained friends with me after that, but as I was now sometimes reviewing his work, he kept our relationship at arm's length. Besides a skilled organist, Paul was also an organ and harpsichord builder by avocation, and one day he decided to launch out into this field full time, and I never saw him again.

A second event was eventually to alter my career in ways I could not even imagine at the time. The cataloging system for sound recordings held such promise that the Office made an even bolder decision. Leo Cooney became the new chief and persuaded the Register to automate the entire cataloging process. After I worked with him for a few months, Leo selected me to be his liaison with the software engineers, led by Dennis Chin, who had been the sole developer of that unnamed sound recordings system several months earlier. Instead of typewriter terminals, however, we would be using the most remarkable invention I had ever seen. The first time I ever saw a cathode ray tube (CRT) screen, I thought it ranked up there with the light bulb as one of best ideas that ever came from the mind of man. What a concept it was—essentially a TV screen that became an electronic slate allowing a user to compose text, erase it instantaneously with no smearing or residue, move it about, or replicate it over and over. Best of all, it was interactive with a computer, which could prompt for fields of data without the need for the user to transcribe it in a fixed order or format it into paragraphs—and the computer could even check it over for errors. I was totally captivated by it at once. Even the name COPICS that Leo and Dennis invented for this new system was ingenious; when the acronym for the Copyright Office Publication and Interactive Cataloging System represented the entire scope of what it was, I was all the more impressed by it as the perfect name for our whole operation. COPICS was one of the first automated cataloging systems in the world, so I was pleased when the *Journal of Library Automation* accepted my description of it for publication in 1978. Incidentally, a perpetual source of irritation was a perplexing mispronunciation of the word COPICS. True, it could be argued that, as a made-up word, it had no correct or incorrect pronunciation, but from the beginning it was intended to sound as though derived from the word copyright, with the short ŏ phoneme. Yet somehow it increasingly came to be expressed with the long ō, as in the word cope. Whenever Leo would hear it pronounced this way, he would say, "Cōpics? You mean the Cōpics that is used to catalog cōpies of cōpyrighted cōmics?"

Life at the office was becoming exciting enough, but events at home were about to stir up some excitement also. When Angela was an infant, we noticed evidence that items in her room seemed to be mysteriously moved about or dropped to the floor. Hmm, ghosts? A day or so later we saw teeth marks on the bar of soap on her dressing table. Aha, I bet these ghosts have fur and four little paws. Then one day, when the lamp near her changing table would not work, I followed the extension cord to the wall and discovered that it was chewed nearly clear through, exposing the bare and broken wires that protruded. It was time for a visit to the hardware store. The next morning my traps were all sprung and empty, but the bait was gone. A few nights later I was unable to sleep and heard the pitter-patter of little feet, but I knew this could not be Angela. Hearing rustling in the kitchen, I crept silently from the bedroom to investigate. I peered around the doorway just in time to see in the dim light a huge rat diving into the wastebasket in the kitchen. While my mind raced wildly trying to think what I could use as a cover to trap it in there, it must have sensed my presence, for a moment later it hopped down from the trashcan and scurried under the stove. Thinking I might be able to trap it under there, I switched on the light but could not see it. I peered carefully all around under the oven with a flashlight, and then I saw the gap around the gas pipe where it was getting in. The next day I closed that hole with a piece of sheet metal, and while in the basement, I saw how it was coming into the house. Although I had succeeded to bar the pest from our living space upstairs, it still had the freedom to roam at will throughout the cellar. Beyond the finished area of the basement was raw dirt, and my flashlight picked up the rat hole from where it was able to tunnel in from outside. No wonder my mousetraps were not working. But when I traded up to rat-sized ones, I found that this clever creature knew all about them. The traps were empty and sprung, but the peanut butter had been licked clean. There is a company called D-Con that manufactures rat poison, but this cunning rodent would not touch it. When I went back to the hardware store, I found a different product in packets that, when gnawed by a curious rat, causes internal coagulation. In a few days I was able to follow the stench to the place under the washing machine platform where my nemesis lay in repose, offering its tail as a means of transport to the back door to resume its decomposition outside.

The very first time I saw the basement of our house, I resolved to excavate that crawl space and enlarge the basement one day. The rat gave me added incentive, but we were about to receive an additional reason. I had a nightmare one night that a flood had forced us to the roof of our house, where the three of us were clinging to the chimney. Somehow Sharlyn lost her grip and slid toward the raging water around us. I thought Angela, not yet a year old, understood when I told her to hang on tightly to the TV antenna anchored to the chimney while I tried to rescue mommy. But as I inched toward Sharlyn, little Angela let go and tumbled toward us, just as I awakened in horror. A few days later, in the late spring of 1972, Hurricane Agnes roared up the east coast, and while direct damage from these seasonal storms is unknown this far inland in Virginia, the collateral damage from driving rain and tornadoes spawned from the system can be dangerous. Rain started one morning, drove hard all day and continued in heavy sheets all night long. The high water mark at Great Falls Park is still today second only to the great flood of 1936. As you stand at this pillar, it is difficult to imagine the volume of water it would take to fill the basin across to the Maryland side to a level several feet above your head. In the aftermath we drove over to the Chain Bridge across the Potomac, about ten minutes away from us. Normally, we can look far down to the water hundreds of feet below, and in fact during spells of extreme drought, it is possible to step across the mighty Potomac on the stones protruding from its bottom. But on this day we foolishly ventured onto the bridge to witness its raging roar roiling and boiling inches below the road surface. We were fortunate that the tremendous hydraulics did not wash the bridge out from under our feet.

The next morning when the furnace would not come on, I went to the basement to investigate. As soon as I opened the outside entrance, my nostrils were greeted by an overpowering odor, and when I switched on the light, I saw objects floating in eighteen inches of water covered by an inch-thick layer of fuel oil. Each time the thermostat called for heat, the sensor on the furnace opened the fuel valve, but since the burner was underwater, it could not ignite. When the fire department arrived, they peered in and assured me that number two fuel oil is not dangerously flammable. "You could probably throw a match into it from up here and the fuel would extinguish it," one of them opined. So I bought a piece of garden hose to siphon as much water as possible from the layer underneath, then spent the next few days sopping up and bagging oily goo for disposal at the hazardous waste dump. The high water mark is still visible on one old section of the original wall in the basement today. Now I had two additional resolves—one to install drainage for a dry basement when I excavated some day, but also to replace that oil furnace with gas when the time was right.

The first Christmas after Angela was born, we drove our Toyota Corolla out to Broomfield, Colorado, where my parents were living. My mother's sister Sarah was also visiting them for the holidays and persuaded us to take her along with us on our way back home, dropping her off in Sioux Falls. Never mind that Sioux Falls was well north of our route home and far out of our way. As we crossed into Nebraska, we caught up with a snow squall moving in the same direction we were traveling, so it continued dumping its load on us for several hours. By the time we turned north on Interstate 29, the snow had piled up so deep that we began to wonder if the highways would remain passable. The heavy snowfall was accompanied by such fierce winds that visibility began to drop dramatically in the blizzard conditions. As I peered intently ahead, a red light suddenly materialized in front of us. I was startled to discover that we had nearly overrun the car ahead of us in what passed for a lane of traffic. The snow had packed onto that car's taillights so thickly that they were nearly invisible. In a flash I realized that not only were ours in the same condition, but the effectiveness of our headlights to detect objects ahead was also diminished by dense accumulations of snow on them. After I pulled over to wipe a few inches of opaqueness from our lights all around, we could see much better for a time, but I worried about our heightened chances of becoming involved in a multi-car pileup. Then, of all the times to have engine trouble, the car began to sputter and cough. It never quit completely, but we stumbled and lurched along, inching our way into Sioux Falls. Another of my mother's sisters, Margaret, also lived in Sioux Falls, so we called from Sarah's place to seek refuge over there for the night. One little four month old had no idea how happy her parents were to see her Great-Aunt Margaret and Great-Uncle Gilbert. After this experience, we noticed that every time the weather was at its worst, when we most needed the car to be reliable, it performed the same way it had in this blizzard. It was not until we finally sold it that we learned that the wire harness of the ignition system on Toyotas tended to absorb moisture, shorting out the electrical charge to the spark plugs.

Some time after our little Angela was a year old, Sharlyn and I decided we wanted a second child. When Sharlyn made a visit to Dr. Amorosi in the fall of 1972, he confirmed the positive results of the pregnancy test and offered congratulations. "I hope this is good news," he added. It was. In those days ultrasound was not widely used, as it is today, so we would not know until May whether this one would be the answer to our prayers for a boy. One day in the spring, when I was preparing to construct a garage at the end of our house, I needed to move a forsythia bush growing where the building would stand. After I dug the hole in the back yard, I asked Sharlyn, now seven months along, if she could assist me to drag the bush into it. As we approached the shallow hole, Sharlyn somehow slipped into it. Whether this was the cause or not, we will never know, but during the night she went into labor. I had not told anyone at the office that we were expecting a new arrival because I did not want them to dip into the gift fund, so Ross, my supervisor, was quite surprised when I called in on the morning of March 23, 1973, to say that I was at the hospital with our new son, Thomas Richard. The name Thomas had been given to my mother's youngest brother, who died in infancy. I asked Ross not to say anything at the office, but word leaked out, and they threw a party anyway. My coworkers were teasing that we had selected the middle name to honor our supervisor, Dick Breinig, but in fact my mother's brother Richard, who had met an untimely end, possibly from foul play or even murder, was foremost on my mind at the time. Of course, the choir at our church staged a baby shower for us too, this the second at which we were so honored. Poor Sharlyn, whose birthday was the previous day, had spent a miserable evening to commemorate it.

Because he came six weeks premature, our little Thomas was put immediately into the intensive care unit. For the first few days neither of us could even see him, although with her breast pump Sharlyn was valiantly attempting to be his wet nurse remotely. Before we could enter the ICU, we needed to scrub down for a full ten minutes, then wear a gown and mask, but finally we were able to hold our little boy. He was so tiny that he fit almost entirely in the palm of my hand, and when I saw him for the first time, he looked so scrawny that I said candidly to Dr. Amorosi, "He isn't going to make it, is he?" "Oh, yes!" Amorosi replied, "His APGAR was a perfect 10. He'll be fine." The APGAR was actually developed by an anesthesiologist named Virginia Apgar in 1952, but it also became an acronym to rank a newborn on a scale of zero to ten for activity, pulse, grimace, appearance and respiration. That last one was usually the most serious for most preemies, but Thomas had strong lungs, and it was a good omen that he already had a perfect score on the first, perhaps most important, exam that life would deal out to him. After about two weeks Sharlyn wanted to bring him home, but the pediatrician, Dr. Murphy, said he needed to reach five pounds. When Sharlyn started to cry, Murphy relented and allowed him come home anyway, while still a couple of ounces shy of his goal.

# Construction 101

**O**ur house had room for a second child, but I was using the third bedroom as my study, having no other space available for a desk and typewriter. While the children were small, they could both be in the same room, but I was anticipating the day when Angela reached a certain age and would not be willing to share her closet with Thomas. From the first moment we moved in, I had my eye on the vacant back corner created by the odd shape of the house, and I decided on an ambitious project. I would fill in that vacant corner with a room to match up that end of the house with the center section, and, at the same time, straighten out that ugly roofline by building a garage at the opposite end to match it up with the center section as well. Oh, and also why not brick over that unsightly cement block from which the whole house was constructed? This plan brought about the most serious crisis we had ever faced in our young lives—and it all started with the location of our driveway.

We did not realize it at the time, but the driveway used for years at our house was actually situated on the lot adjacent to our property. Since it was at the wrong end from where I wanted to build the garage anyway, however, my plan was to install a driveway at the other end straight in from the street. The problem was that the septic tank was located exactly where I wanted the driveway. If I were willing to tolerate a sharp bend, however, I thought I had found a way to make it work. To be sure the weight of vehicles would not cause damage, I decided to ask the Fairfax County inspector how close to the tank the code would allow me to install a driveway. That is when the trouble started. When Oscar, the previous owner, had installed a washing machine in the basement, he ran a two-inch galvanized pipe across the yard to the ditch along the street as the drain for it. As the inspector was probing the ground to find the exact location of the septic tank, Sharlyn was inside the house running a load of wash. When he noticed soapy water emptying into the ditch, he asked what that was. Oh, just the washer, I assured him. No, no, no, he said, that pipe would need to be routed into the septic system. No problem, I thought, that should be a relatively small project, and since I had no experience with such things, I paid a plumber the outrageous price of ninety dollars to make the repair, and I had even dug the trench for him.

Today most parents use disposable diapers, but in those days lightweight squares of cloth were folded in such a way as to form a notoriously and distressingly imperfect seal around a cute pink bottom; however, the fact that they were reusable was both an advantage and a disadvantage. The biggest advantages were the cost savings, relief of stress on the landfill, and the stack of washrags available in later years. The most obvious disadvantage was the delight that derives from handling excrement, as well as the mountain of wash that quickly piled up. Sharlyn ran a load of wash daily, and on one occasion after we rerouted the washer to the septic tank, I was in the yard and noticed soapy water bubbling up from the ground. Worse, a few days later, when I was talking across the fence with Tom Weston, my neighbor, he spotted the suds too. As he walked away, he called back over his shoulder that if I did not address the problem right away, he would take action himself to get that fixed. Tom was not one of my favorite people, but as neighbors we had always gotten along, and since their daughter Elizabeth is almost exactly the same age as Angela, Sharlyn and Bonnie Weston are still good friends to this day. Did you ever know someone who automatically takes the opposite point of view to everything you say? This was Tom whenever we talked. If I said brown, he would say no, green. If I said chartreuse, he was sure to say no, mauve. I suppose I always expected him, as a foreign service officer with the State Department, to approach every relationship with utmost diplomacy, yet he must have kept these skills in reserve for his trips to Kinshasa. I always found conversation with him to be tedious, if not rancorous, from the contention he seemed to arouse each time.

Since that county inspector sprang to mind as the person who had caused this unpleasant development in the first place, I called him back, expecting him to take responsibility for it and offer a solution. Instead, he responded by condemning our septic system, saying the fields were saturated, and followed that up with a certified letter that we had sixty days to connect to the public sewer system or our house would be condemned as uninhabitable! In the meantime we would also be required to have the tank pumped out whenever it filled up, at a whopping fifty dollars for each service call. There was worse news. Although Westons were already on the public sewer, the main trunk of it we would need to tap into ran along their property line with Lockwoods, diametrically opposite from us, two hundred feet away. No problem, I thought, we could find the closest point in the system next door and tap in there, but the county told us this did not meet the plumbing code. We then approached the Westons to get permission to cross their property to reach the trunk line. At first they seemed agreeable, but their attorney pointed out to them that such an easement would render a significant section of their land unbuildable, thereby reducing it substantially in value. The only other solution was to run a pipe from our house straight out to the ditch, then tunnel under the ditch along the street past the Weston property, where an existing manhole could be penetrated. When we presented this plan to the county, they informed us that our street was actually a state highway, so we would need to request permission from the Commonwealth to pursue that option. Meanwhile, pressure mounted as our sixty-day clock was ticking, and after we waited more than thirty days for a response, the government in Richmond denied our request, citing maintenance concerns. As an alternative, they suggested that we extend the line from our house to the center of the street, install a manhole there, then tear up the street in front of Westons to run our pipe, install a second manhole and connect from there; we would also need to hire flagmen to direct traffic for the entire period of this construction. All of this would be at our expense, of course, but when completed, this extension would be owned and maintained by the Commonwealth.

When we realized that the twenty thousand dollars this solution would cost, almost the value of our entire house, was prohibitive for us, we decided to approach the Westons with hat in hand to ask if they would reconsider. Although I was prepared for the door to be slammed in my face, it was through the grace of Bonnie, empress of the nice people in the world, that they agreed to talk again with their attorney, who answered our prayers with an alternative solution. They would allow us to run our pipe along the *edge* of their land, just inside the highway right of way, but there was a catch. They were leaving on assignment to Germany in a few days and were giving their power of attorney to a local real estate company to handle the matter for them. With only two weeks left in the sixty days given us by the county, I tried earnestly to reach this attorney for about three days. Since the matter meant far more to us than to him, he was cavalier and would not return my repeated calls. In desperation I found out where his office was and literally sat on the steps in front of his door from dawn until he arrived, and finally he could avoid me no longer. But our trouble was far from over. Our negotiations were just beginning, and we would soon discover that his terms were stringent.

There were two pieces of good news, actually, in our favor. First, all of this happened in the spring, with increasingly favorable weather ahead, but far more importantly, the lay of the land was downhill all the way to the connection point. When I had the pipe delivered, no one told me this did not include unloading from the truck (then what does "includes delivery" mean?), so the driver was quite upset when Sharlyn told him I was at work. She said he cursed at each of the two dozen ten-foot lengths of cast iron sewer pipe he had to throw off the truck by himself, and when I got home, black pipe was scattered helter-skelter all over the lawn. I had also secured a permit from the county to lay the pipe myself, and since iron pipe requires a special tool called a puller to connect it together, I had procured one. Then I got busy with pick and shovel, dug the trench and laid the pipe from our house to the property line. In the process I discovered that the original pipe to the septic tank I was replacing was actually a kind of tarpaper tubing known as Orangeburg, which I observed to be partially crushed, so it was provident that we were replacing it anyway. Bill Lockwood noticed all the commotion in our yard, wandered over, peered down at my sweaty, grimy face in the trench and said, "Bit off a pretty big chunk, didn't ya?" Thanks, Bill, for those loving words of encouragement. Just when I thought everything was finally coming together, the lawyer pulled out his heavy artillery.

My idea had been to continue in the same manner that I had started, working my way across Weston's yard, laying the pipe, filling the trench back in and seeding grass over the wound. This was not what the lawyer had in mind. No, he said the job must be completed within three days from the time that work started, and we would pay a penalty of five hundred dollars for every day beyond the deadline. This would include backfilling the trench and laying sod, not seed, to restore the lawn. So now, with time running out, I had to find a company on short notice with a backhoe to cut the trench on the first day, then, after I worked late until nightfall laying the pipe, have them come back to backfill it the next day. Then I had to find a company to deliver a mountain of sod at a moment's notice. At the attorney's insistence, I also had to agree that in addition to the usual liability that would pass with the land to the next owners, I would become *personally* liable for life for any damages caused by any aspect of the sewer line. Then of course, just as the lawyer was about to sign the paper, he remembered that we had not paid his exorbitant fee. After I handed him the check, he was just about to sign the document again, when he paused, thought for a moment, then said, "Wait a minute, you are going to need a performance bond." What is a performance bond, I wanted to know. "Well, in case you should tear up my client's property and then walk away without completing the job," he pontificated, "they will have recourse to restore it." What!? After I raced all over the city of Fairfax unsuccessfully talking to several bail bondsmen, I finally found one that would issue one if we wrote him a check for the three thousand dollars *first*, plus his fee. With all of our expenses, we had barely that amount left in our savings account, but we "happily" drained it all out for him.

With three days left in our sixty-day window, the backhoe operator showed up at dawn to begin his work. Although he was a surly fellow who seemed like he would rather be anywhere else but here, I have to admit that he was truly an artist with his machine, deftly working that blade delicately around the buried utility lines we encountered and somehow extricating several large boulders that lay in our path, one of which was at least four feet in diameter. Before he drove away in his pickup, he made a point of telling me that after I finished laying the pipe, it was important that I backfill with a hand shovel to cover the pipe as a cushion, so that he could dump large quantities of soil back into the opening without danger of rocks rupturing the line. It was about midday when I started laying the pipe, and everything was proceeding smoothly until I reached the manhole and needed to cut the last piece of pipe. Today I would use my power hacksaw, but all I had then was the old hacksaw Oscar had left me. The teeth on the blade of it quickly ground off, while the pipe was hardly scratched. Cast iron, it seems, has a high concentration of slag, or something quite abrasive, left in the material from the manufacturing process. When I asked the man at McLean Hardware for the best blades he had, he sold me a tungsten carbide one but told me that what I really needed for cast iron pipe was a cold chisel to score it all around, then it would break cleanly at that weakened point. After an hour of scoring, the pipe still refused to break, so I went back to my hacksaw with the new blade. I was making progress with it until all the teeth were filed off, but after I went back for a second and then a third new blade, I finally had my pipe cut.

But then I still had to make a hole through the reinforced concrete casing of the manhole. Today I would use my hammer drill, and with a masonry bit I could march through those eight inches of concrete in a few minutes, but because I was not even aware that such a drill or bit existed, I got busy with my star drills Oscar had left me and tapped away. Two hours later I concluded that there must be an easier way and knocked on Bill Lockwood's door. At first he suggested I rent a jackhammer, but I was afraid that would crack the manhole. He had a masonry bit, however, and offered to run an extension cord from his house. With my electric drill so hot after an hour that I could hardly hold it, I finally penetrated that thick wall. It took another hour to enlarge the opening enough for the four-inch sewer pipe to pass through, but at last I could declare, "the baby is born," as Alvin Roehl would have said. Although there was still a little daylight left, I was exhausted and had no energy to backfill two hundred feet of pipe with a shovel. My plan was to come back early the next morning before the backhoe operator arrived, but the inspector showed up to approve my work before I could attend to that, and immediately thereafter along came Mr. Backhoe, castigating me for not following his instructions. With a sigh he climbed back onto his rig, muttering and grumbling that he had to trickle the soil back into the hole instead of bulldoze it as he had hoped. It was the last day of our sixty days, the sod was down, the job was finished, and after one ceremonial flush, we had our house back!

All of this trauma was but an overture to what was supposed to be the primary focus on the house, but we had not even started that yet. The adult education system of Fairfax County is excellent, so I was not disappointed when I signed up for a masonry course taught by two retired county building inspectors. Instead of Portland cement in the mortar mix, they used lime and sand, which has a consistency almost identical to mortar, but will not harden when dry. Like most skills, bricklaying is largely practice, so much of each class session was building up and tearing down a wall, which was critiqued by these two experts as I did it over and over until at least one of them liked what he saw. They knew the building code inside and out, so in addition to the invaluable construction tips they were imparting and advice on what tools to buy (and avoid), they could also pass along the requirements we would need to meet. One of the most important lessons I learned from these professionals is that it does not pay to buy cheap tools. "You could buy a bricklaying trowel for far less than what I would pay," one of them told us, "But even *we* couldn't lay bricks with it—and we know *how*." Len Greenberg can never resist a pun, so when I was telling him about this course, he asked me if laying bricks is hod work. In what was the only time I can ever recall outwitting him, I immediately responded that there was mortar it than you might think.

Unfortunately, I was pressured by my other schoolwork at the university and could not complete the masonry course, but I felt I had learned much of what I would need for a real-world application and had few regrets when I was compelled to drop out. When I applied for the permit to build the bedroom on the back side of the house, I was quite upset when it was denied because our addition would not meet the setback requirements from the arterial Old Dominion Drive right-of-way in our back yard, and for a moment the Alvin Roehl in me came to the surface, tempted as I was to thumb my nose at government interference and start construction anyway. However, they told us, we could apply for a waiver through an administrative process known as a variance hearing. Although I had no such experience with such matters and was extremely apprehensive at the prospect of facing off against the county this way, it turned out to be almost pro forma, as they granted our building permit without much fuss. Since I wanted to do my own wiring also, I had to study a text book they recommended and pass an exam before they would grant my electrical permit, and I would also need a separate mechanical permit for tying in the heating system and a plumbing permit to run and reroute water supply lines.

Crystal City, where the Copyright Office was renting space for a few years, was originally an industrial area, so to my great delight I found a huge building supplier and a brick factory both located literally next door to our office building. Winter set in before I could start digging my footers, but when spring arrived, I would drive over to the brick yard over my lunch period to load fifty bricks into the trunk, and in the evening I would mix up a batch of mortar and build on my wall. Sometimes the project outstripped my daylight, so Sharlyn would come out to hold the utility light for me until I could finish up. We still look back on those days occasionally, fondly remembering the time we had together discussing all sorts of matters while I worked away. Chipping away at the project like this, a little each day, I gradually transformed my block house to brick. Since I had some time on weekends to lay more bricks than I could carry in the car, I had the brickyard deliver two or three cubes of bricks and several bags of mortar mix to the driveway, and then I was able to reduce the need to drive to work just to pick up more bricks.

One day while I had those cubes of brick, a pallet of mortar mix, and other construction materials piled on the driveway, there was a knock on the door. Standing before me was an old woman who could have been mistaken for one of the hags from Macbeth. "Hi, I'm Kathleen Harrington, the owner of this little lot right here," she said. At that time McLean was still semi-rural, with a large undeveloped tract of land across the street from us that was once the estate of old Dr. Hibbing. The run-down farmhouse and weathered old barn still stood on the land, but the place was now uninhabitable after some squatters had vandalized the entire inside of the house when they were forced out. Hibbing had been a professor of botany, I think someone told me, and had planted an unknown variety of exotic plants on the expanse of his once-beautiful lawn, but now it was overrun by kudzu, poison ivy and bamboo. I assumed it was this property to which she was referring. "No, this lot right here," she insisted.

Then a terrifying thought crossed my mind—that a title search had failed to discover that she actually owned *our* house. I was quite sure it was Mr. Beall who owned two large tracts of land down the street, one of which had his large old house and barn for two cows, some chickens and ducks, and the other across the street where he grew popcorn every year. So in desperation I asked her if she were not, in fact, referring to those properties instead. "No, no, this lot right here, and I'm wondering what all this brick and other junk is that you have on it." I nearly fainted. I suppose I stammered something about our project, and how I would have the construction materials off the driveway soon, but I was stunned by this bolt from the blue.

So … we discovered that the adjoining lot was not public land after all, as Oscar had led me to believe. When we learned that Mrs. Harrington lived about a mile away from us, we went to visit her one evening, offering to buy the property. "Oh, I'm sure I would want several thousand dollars for it," she replied, but she would not give us a figure. We made small talk with her for a few minutes, but there was another woman in the house, a relative perhaps, who seemed to be her caretaker, and I gradually became aware that this attendant seemed to be getting agitated. We had our two very young children with us, usually an icebreaker with most people, but apparently the housekeeper could divine something we could not, because without warning, Mrs. Harrington suddenly erupted in anger, yelling, "Get out, get out, just get out!" We were not aware that we had said or done anything in particular to provoke this outburst, but we tucked our tails and ran. When we later acquired some land near Monticello, at face value more valuable than her lot, I wrote Mrs. Harrington with an offer to trade, but she did not respond. I sent another letter a few weeks after that, asking her to give us a price for her land, but we got no answer to that either.

Several months later her apparition came to our door. "Say, I understand you are interested in this lot next to your property," she began in a jolly mood, with no small talk first. "No," I told her, "I am no longer interested. We have tried repeatedly to buy it from you, but you have always refused." And I really was not interested. After all, we had the full use of it as though we owned it, without having to pay the taxes, and we probably could stake a claim by adverse possession, if pressed, so what would ownership give us that we did not already have? This arrangement was also beneficial to her. I mowed it for her and took care of it without compensation, so that she never needed to worry about the noxious weeds and vermin that would otherwise make it a public nuisance. "Well, why don't you make me an offer?" she bellowed. "Mrs. Harrington, the most I would ever offer you for that worthless lot is two thousand dollars," I bellowed back. I fully expected this would cause her to stomp off in anger, but to my amazement, she said, "Cash on the barrel head?" "I would give you my check tomorrow," I told her. "How about today?" was her astonishing comeback. I had never seen her anything close to friendly, but she was even approaching warm when I walked out into the yard with her and told her that in days of yore, real estate was sometimes transferred when the owner broke off a twig and handed it to the new owner. "I like you," she said, as she broke off a stem from the lilac bush and passed it to me. The lawyer who handled the exchange told me in a hushed voice that he could not remember when he had seen an individual other than Mrs. Harrington who owned so many properties scattered across so many states around. With little outside income, he speculated, she was simply "land poor" and needed to sell off some of them in order to pay her taxes. He also disclosed that he took precautions to be sure that his secretary was present as a witness and notary throughout the transaction to preclude the possibility that her heirs would declare her senile and rescind the transfer.

One of the harshest realities for us over the years was that during times of crisis, trial, trouble or heartbreak, Sharlyn and I were isolated from the support we would otherwise expect from our relatives. If we had lived a few miles away from our parents and siblings, we could call upon them to come over to help shoulder the load, but as it was, we had only each other. This had at least one advantage. Each visit was precious, and we were treated like royalty whenever we made the long journey to see them. While we listened to yammering about which one was not speaking to the other, what this one had said to that one when they had met in town, and why so-and-so had actually bought something *that* expensive, we were immune to these petty squabbles and finger-pointings. At the time of Angela's baptism, relatives who had made the long journey east were crammed into every corner of our tiny house. One was Sharlyn's brother Lavern, who has never been back to visit us since, and another was her mother's sister, Mildred Faber. Millie's husband Norman was a roofer by trade, so when we were walking around in the yard, Norman and Lavern glanced up at my roof and noticed a number of cracked, curled and missing shingles. "You need a new roof," Norman told me. Although I did not have his eye for the sorry condition of it, I knew that some day I had hoped to change that roofline anyway and would take care of it then. That day was now almost here, the old shingles, with judicious daubings of roof cement, having held up well enough to buy us the three years or so that we needed in the interim.

When the brickwork was done, I stepped back, trying to assess objectively how my masonry looked. Although I remember wishing I had started out armed with the experience I had acquired during the project, I was willing to acknowledge that, despite a few mistakes that were obvious under close scrutiny, it would pass for improvement. I was finally ready to remove the two sections of roof I so much wanted to change. Since my father had considerable experience with such undertakings, I asked him to spend a few days with us to lend his expertise and assistance. However, with my father there was no such thing as "assistance." As far as he was concerned, this became *his* project, and there was room for only one foreman. I was *his* assistant. Rodney was now a teenager, so I assumed he was old enough to operate my power saw to cut some Celotex material we used as sheeting. I am ashamed to admit that I yelled at him so vehemently for wasting one piece with a wayward cut that my father jumped off the roof and came running, thinking one of us had an accident. The cost of a hundred sheets of Celotex was not worth the tongue-lashing I laid on poor Rodney, and I feel badly about it to this day.

One day while we were in the yard working, I noticed a motorcycle slow down and stop in the street. The driver paused to watch for a moment, then made a quick turn around and pulled into our driveway. He identified himself as one of the four Ballenger boys who grew up in the house next door before Alan and Liz Stevens bought it. His father had been a Fairfax County building inspector, which probably explains why the utility room we see jutting out from the side of that house violates the setback requirement from the property line facing our house. The young man talked with me for about a half hour, telling me a number of interesting facts about their house, including one that as a lad he had once dropped his father's Indian head penny collection through a hole, and to this day that wall of the house contains a fortune in coins.

I must warn you that I am about to take you on a boring tour of a construction project. The building code does not allow more than two layers of shingles on a roof, so because ours already had two, all the old shingles on the center section had to come off. We had to replace only a few rotten boards underneath, and finally one day I could declare that Phase One of my dream for our castle was completed. The house was not only sixteen feet longer, with the addition of a garage, but it was all under one roofline. Once the project was completed, it still needed to pass inspection, however. I was about to endure my first experience with building inspectors. The first one to come out told me that an attached garage must have a three-quarter-hour fire rating, meaning that a fire that breaks out in the garage must not be able to penetrate the house for forty-five minutes. The upshot was that we were not allowed to have windows in the wall between the garage and the living space. I would have to brick them shut—or, he said, we could cover them with fire-rated drywall, which was much easier. Also, the back door, half panel and half glass, that had once opened to the outside but now led into the garage, must be solid, with a gypsum core, and it too could not have a window. "Now, wait a minute," I told him, "If someone is pounding on my back door, I want to see who it is." "Well then, I will let you install a small window of special heat-resistant wired glass," he replied. I made the changes requested and scheduled the reinspection.

This time a different inspector came out, approved my first deficiencies, but then said that the steps which had once led from the back porch to the yard needed a handrail. For two steps I would not have needed it, but we had three. So, ironically, I made use of Oscar's galvanized pipe that had once emptied the washing machine to the ditch, fashioned an elaborate handrail, cemented it to the concrete steps and scheduled the reinspection. Yet a third inspector showed up this time, approved my handrail, but then said that the entrance to the basement, which had formerly been from outside the house, had to have curbing to prevent flammable liquids from flowing toward the furnace in the basement just on the other side of that door. Also, the fiberglass door that I had installed to replace the rotting wood one we found when we bought the house would need to be replaced with fire-retardant plywood. So I fashioned a concrete curb, installed a new door and scheduled reinspection. This time a fourth inspector showed up and approved the basement entrance, but then his eyes glanced upward to the loft of my new garage. He noticed that we had intentionally placed one of the joists against the chimney to give it support. No, he said, there must be at least two inches of clearance between them. If I ever had any patience to begin with, this time I really lost it. "This is the fourth time you inspectors have been here, and each time you find something new that needs to be changed," I railed. "Give me a list right now of *everything* you see wrong, and I will take care of it, but I am getting tired of the endless hassle I am getting each time trying to finish this project." "Now, now, now, just settle down," he said. "It looks like everything else looks okay. All you need to do is move that joist over, and this should be the last time we need to come out." It was. He signed us off on just the basis of my word that I would move the joist.

The garage made a huge difference, not only to bring in the car out of the weather, but for a thousand other uses that we had not imagined. One was additional storage in the loft and a considerably more humane entrance to the attic. Up until then the only access to it was through the ceiling in the kitchen. First, the table needed to be moved out of the way, then after one of the false ceiling tiles was removed, a trapdoor about two feet square was revealed. From the top of a stepladder, we could hoist ourselves up through this tiny opening into the space above. Someone had spread a few boards across the ceiling joists to walk around up there, but none of them were nailed down, so we lived in constant fear that we might inadvertently create an alternate egress with one errant step. Later, when the old house on the Hibbing property across the street was bulldozed, I got permission to salvage some of its lumber for attic flooring and nailed everything down to provide a considerable amount of much needed storage up there. Since the garage covered what had been the end wall of the house, we could cut a doorway from the loft directly into the attic. One time when Alvin Roehl came out for a visit, he noticed that I still had to fetch my stepladder to pull down a second ladder to access the loft, and he had an idea. He helped me build a foldable stairway that could be pulled down with a rope when needed, and to this day we still use those loft stairs that he designed.

On the gable above the brickwork on the end wall of the garage, we decided to install twelve-inch siding. Since this fibrous material is only a half-inch thick but twenty feet long, it is floppy and difficult for one person to handle. When Fritz Pauling from our church asked one day whether I needed any help on the project, I knew immediately how I could use him. To save time on the Saturday when he was planning to come out, I decided to have the first piece cut before he arrived. Instead of using a hand saw, which would have been less dangerous, I decided my electric circular saw would be quicker. As the saw neared the other side of the cut, the piece was so floppy that I foolishly held the cut ends together with my fingers to keep the saw from binding. Without warning the saw suddenly kicked back into my left hand. I did not even need to look to know it was bad, so I ran into the house and told Sharlyn to drop everything and drive me to the emergency room. Fritz had not yet arrived, but when he saw the still uncut piece of siding and the trail of blood, he knew what happened and realized he would not be needed today. While my index finger still bears the scar where thirty stitches patched up the wound, my guardian angel nevertheless deflected that blade away from serious injury. A millimeter or two away in any direction was bone, nerve, tendon and connective tissue, yet the cut sliced only into flesh, and I was spared by the grace of God from permanent debilitation.

Do you cringe when you visit someone who is so proud of some construction project that you become a captive audience made to suffer through endless photos of its progress on his laptop? Although I have the feeling I am already stretching the limits of your patience beyond your endurance, I want to take you into the bedroom—yes, the new bedroom we added at the opposite end of the house from the garage. Instead of crawl space under it, such as we had under the other rooms of the house, I still regret that I took the easy way out and poured a slab of concrete inside the footers instead—at least, it was supposed to be easy. The concrete was setting up faster than I could keep up with it, so I sent Sharlyn racing down the street to rent an electric trowel. If you have ever worked with concrete, you know that it is weird, and even with power equipment, I barely managed to stay ahead of it. Now that I had the masonry walls up and a roof over it, the only way in was through the window. I had not yet cut a doorway from inside the house through what had once been the outside cement block wall. Today I would elect to use a masonry blade on my power saw to make a clean cut through the block in a couple of hours. Instead, my caveman approach was to take my stone axe and flint chisel to chip out one pebble at a time. After about two days at that pace, Sharlyn knocked on the window to say she had a birthday present for me. It was not my birthday, but the electric jackhammer she rented allowed me to thank her through an opening directly into the house in about ten minutes. Once we had the flooring in, drywall up, electricity turned on and baseboard heating installed, little preschooler Angela chose this as her room. After she told us her preference for orange walls, and even helped splash paint on them, this became her inner sanctum all the way through college and beyond.

For several years I wanted my parents to have a movie camera, so when I worked for Don Engel at the Shell station in Inver Grove Heights that last summer I was living at home, I spent most of my first pay check on an eight millimeter key-wind camera for them as a gift for their anniversary. This was apparently not high on their wish list, however, as I never saw them use it. When Thomas was a toddler, they passed it back to us, perhaps as a way of saying the pressures of their own lives did not allow them to use it, but now they could use it after all, vicariously, through the precious memories we would capture in the lives of their grandchildren. They had never completed even one roll of film, so when I finished taking practice shots with the one they already had in the camera, I was quite curious what the subject of the first part of it would be. I expected to see Rodney cavorting or making faces, footage of my embarrassed mother caught off guard in the kitchen by my father, or scenes from some family reunion. Instead, memorialized for posterity was Rodney's kitten, bounding up from the basement to face relentless teasing from everyone in the kitchen. If that was the best they could do, I was glad they decommissioned it in Minnesota and put it back into circulation in Virginia. We shot quite a few movies with it over the years, until we began to encounter difficulty locating film for it, as the industry moved toward videotape technology.

Soon after Thomas started walking, we noticed that both of his feet were turned inward, one of them quite pronounced. In our ignorance we assumed this was in the range of normal and actually thought his little toddle was cute. When Dr. Livingston saw this one day in his dental office, he was not amused and strongly urged us to see a specialist. He was right. Thomas was severely pigeon-toed and was fitted with a bar connecting both feet together throughout each night while he slept. This special brace had an adjustable shoe at each end that could be gradually rotated outward over a period of several months so that as Thomas grew, his leg bones could twist back into their normal position. While wearing his brace, Thomas could stand, but he could not walk. This did not stop him from crawling all over, but we underestimated the extent of his mobility. One morning I noticed that some of his toys were scattered on the floor of his room. He was sound asleep in his bed, so at first I thought I must be misremembering that they had been put away the night before. When this happened again, I started to wonder whether the rat was back. Although Thomas could easily slide off the bed, I was convinced it was impossible for him to climb back up wearing that brace. Early one morning I heard little noises from his room. I crept silently to his doorway to watch him sitting on the floor playing, but as soon as I switched on his light, he sensed he was being naughty and scampered over to the bed and wriggled his way up onto the mattress in about three seconds.

One day when Sharlyn went for a walk with the kids, a stray kitten followed them home. Since responsibility for two children is awesome enough, we had decided that neither of us wanted the further obligations imposed by a pet. So Sharlyn told them the kitten would need to stay outside, and if we did not offer any food, it would eventually go away. I was doing some work in the yard and noticed that toddler Thomas was standing just inside the screen door, fascinated by the kitten outside on the back porch. The kitten looked up at his face pressing against the mesh and mewed. Little Thomas was amused, smiling as he looked at me, then he looked back to the kitten and said, "Do it 'gain." Right on cue, the kitten mewed. Thomas giggled and said, "Do it 'gain." This continued for several minutes, Thomas belly-laughing harder with each mew and totally convinced he was causing this automaton to perform just by commanding it. Angela was the one who always had a soft spot for animals, so one day when we found ourselves driving through Maryland, we came across a farm of llamas. The owners encouraged visitors to feed them with the buckets of field corn they had placed at regular intervals around the enclosure. I noticed that whenever one lady proffered an ear of corn to one of the llamas, another one, the largest in the pen, trotted over to push the first llama out of the way. Thinking I could outwit this dominant alpha, I told Angela to feed it at one end while I went to the other end with an ear of corn for one of the smaller animals. The alpha saw through my ploy immediately and ran to my end.

Glaring at me eye to eye, it spit a mouthful of corn onto my shirt. Giving it the benefit of doubt that perhaps it had just coughed, I foolishly told Angela to come to my end and we would repeat the process. This time, when the alpha trotted toward me, it stopped and glared as before and then spat its entire mouthful into my *face*, covering my glasses so completely that I could not see through them. Yuck.

Although I am not sure how often little kids are true to their stereotypes, Angela was thoroughly a girl, playing mother to her dolls and dressing them up in the clothes my mother fashioned specifically for them or the ones she helped Sharlyn make. Angela herself loved to change clothes, the door of her room opening every ten minutes as she came hippy-hopping out in a different outfit. Thomas, on the other hand, was positively obsessed by anything with wheels. As a toddler, he tugged against my hand to run up to a car in the parking lot to stand admiring a wheel as big as he, patting the hubcap and lovingly stroking the tire. One of his favorite toys was a Playskool jeep that could be taken apart with a plastic wrench and screwdriver, and it was not unusual for him to spend an uninterrupted hour or so assembling and disassembling it over and over. Despite the fact that one was all girl and the other all boy, they got along very well together, Thomas idolizing his older sister and following her in every game she invented. Our home movies captured them playing their daily exercise of Round and Round, where Angela suddenly runs in a circle while little Thomas chases after. When one of them was noisy or obnoxious, Sharlyn or I might sometimes be heard to say, "Is that necessary?" Apparently the meaning of that word was not completely understood by either of them, as I overheard Angela one day say in anger to Thomas, "You're *necessary*!" Thomas thought about that for a few seconds, then retorted, "No, I'm not!"

When we attended the wedding of my sister Deanna to Peter Pavlacka in Colorado in May 1975, we decided to make a detour on the way home through Yellowstone National Park. As we passed through Cody, Wyoming, some sixty miles east of Yellowstone, late that night, I was not happy with the prices for gas I saw there and foolishly assumed we could probably do at least as well at a station in the next town. I did not know it then, but Cody was the last outpost of civilization before the park, and we drove for an hour without seeing another car, store, village or person. When we arrived at the gate on the last day of *May*, running on the last dregs of fuel in the tank, we discovered that in the wake of recent blizzards, the plows had piled snow fifteen feet high along each side of the roadway. In fact, this was the first day the park was open for the season; had we been one day earlier, this very gate would have been padlocked while snow removal crews were busy getting the roads open, and it was almost *June*. Signs as we entered announced that every campsite was full, and since it was now about midnight, we drove ten more miles or so into the park wondering what we would do, until I saw the huge parking lot of the general store. It was closed, of course, but most important of all, it had a gas pump out front, where I would happily pay three times the price we passed up at Cody. Since the back of our Corona station wagon folded flat, we pulled out our sleeping bags and bedded down for the night. These sleeping bags were actually intended for an overnight slumber party and were not rated for camping, however, so we spent one of the frostiest nights of our lives trying to keep our teeth from shattering. Just before daybreak I was finally dozing a little, when I heard tapping on the glass. A park ranger continued banging her flashlight until I cracked the window open a little. "Did you camp here last night?" she demanded to know. "No, we just pulled in here last night to park until the store opens," I replied. "So you *did* camp here," she insisted. "Officer, we arrived here late last night low on gas, exhausted from driving since early morning. Would you rather that we tried to drive on and cause an accident or would you say we did the right thing by stopping here to get some rest?" "Well, camping here is illegal and …." Her definition of camping was obviously different from mine, and I wanted to cover my ears while she railed on for several more minutes, but after the haranguing trailed off, she finally drove off without issuing the violation I suppose she could have given us.

By now we were all awake, and soon after sunrise the general store opened. Who needs coffee when the euphoria created by a full tank of gas has the same effect? Angela was not quite four, and Thomas had just turned two, so they probably had no idea the steamy ground and bubbling geysers we saw in every direction around us were anything unusual. A chain barrier had been erected along the path toward Old Faithful to keep everyone away from the hundreds of boiling hot fumaroles gurgling out of the ground a few feet away, and as we walked along the boardwalk, I suddenly became aware out of the corner of my eye that someone's child had wandered off into Nature's cauldron on the other side of those chains. My first thought was outrage at whatever parent it was who could be so careless as to allow a toddler to romp around out there in such a dangerous area, but when I actually turned to look, I saw that it was Thomas! I hoped none of the park rangers saw me leap over the chains to swoop him out of there. As we were driving through the park to leave, I noticed a short, wide gravel trail that led to a small clearing at the top of a rise, where a few buffalo were grazing. On an impulse I pulled off onto the gravel to let the kids step out to get a look at them. Angela was wearing her brand new little red tennis shoes, and as she jumped out of the car, she landed ankle deep in the middle of a huge buffalo pie. Did I ever mention that we stopped to see Yellowstone on our way home from Colorado and had a wonderful experience while we were there?

When I wanted permission to salvage lumber from the Hibbing property across the street from us, Alan Stevens suggested I talk to Carl Zimmerman, who lived about two blocks away down an isolated gravel lane. His wife Catherine answered the door and wanted to know who I was. As Carl came up behind her, I told them which house we were in. "Oh, the Jim Laurel place," he said. Laurel had been the owner of our house for many years, and apparently these old-timers had not even heard that he had sold it to Reynolds, who had owned the house for five years before us. A few days later when I noticed them walking past our house, Catherine suddenly sat down on the sidewalk. Carl was talking to her in an agitated voice, and although I could not hear what he was saying, I was alarmed and rushed across the street to offer assistance. She is just tired, Carl explained. We found out a few weeks after that that she had died. On a whim Sharlyn and I decided to take Angela and Thomas with us to visit him one day. We found him to be a kindly old gentleman who loved children, and he was delighted we stopped by. They had always wanted children, he explained, but Catherine contracted diabetes at an early age, and after many miscarriages they remained childless. Carl was an expert craftsman and turned out a number of gifts for our children from his shop. For Angela's birthday one year he made a beautiful jewelry case out of white korina, inlaid with mahogany and walnut. For Thomas he made a one-runner sled with an exquisite upholstered seat that dared anyone, even a dad, to tame it for a ride down a snowy hill.

We took Carl at his word to stop by any time unannounced, so one time when we rang the doorbell, his sister, Helen Leffler, was visiting from someplace in Ahiah. While I was trying to form a mental picture where this country was, it suddenly registered that she was saying Chillicothe, Ohio. She and her husband Alan were delightful, loved our children, and were grateful that we were spending time with Carl. Helen said his letters were always full of news about us. At Easter time, when Helen came to visit again, she and Carl dyed eggs, hid them all over the yard and invited us over just to watch Angela and Thomas scurry around the lawn, squealing at every pastel object they picked up. One evening we escorted them to see the spectacular view of the lights of the city from the observation platform at the top of the Washington Monument. Helen was so awestruck by that experience that she mentioned it in every Christmas card she sent us for the next twenty years or so until she died. When we mentioned that we pass through Ohio quite frequently on our way to visit grandparents, the Lefflers insisted that we stop by to see them on our way some time. Although Chillicothe is not situated very close to any of the interstate highways we traveled, we did include them on our itinerary one time; the children misbehaved so badly in their house that we were embarrassed and vowed we would never do this again, but softhearted Alan and Helen pretended not to notice. In the course of our conversation, Helen mentioned that their mother had intentionally selected the names Carl and Helen because she did not want them to have nicknames. So when they got to school, of course the kids always called these Zimmerman kids "Zimmie."

Following a heavy snow one winter, we mixed up a batch of homemade French vanilla ice cream and stopped by Carl's house with our electric freezer. He had been snowbound all day because his heart condition did not allow him to clear his long driveway to get the car out, so he was glad to have company. He nearly broke into tears, however, explaining that when he opened the front door that morning, his dog Margy darted outside and sank so deeply into the snow that she could not get out. He could see only a moving mound and watched helplessly as she burrowed frantically around the yard trying to find a way out. Eventually she was able to follow the sound of Carl's voice to the porch, where he dug into the snow to pull her out. He was still trembling from the experience as he related it to us while we sat eating our ice cream.

I envied the immaculate shop Carl had in his basement, so one day when I needed a band saw, he was actually flattered that I asked to use his. When I brought over the pieces I wanted to cut, Carl had a visitor—his good friend Merrill Sappington, a retired admiral and mutual acquaintance who lived up the street and around the corner from us. Merrill raised bees and was a fountain of interesting tidbits about them. He explained, for example, that bees find their way back to the hive by triangulating with the sun, and this is so accurate that one day when he moved their residence a few feet away, returning bees buzzed around the old site for a while before they discovered the new location. He explained also that when the hive needs a new queen, they need her in a hurry, so the royal jelly around the egg encasing a queen causes it to hatch in about half the time required for the ordinary worker bee.

Tragedy struck the Sappington family soon after we made their acquaintance. Their son Arthur, some ten years into his Naval career, was working in the yard one day, and after bending over to bag some leaves, had a strange sensation, almost as though blood seemed to have pooled in his head and would not drain down. The young ensign physician who examined him, apparently having neither tact nor sensitivity, told him, "I have bad news for you. You are going to die." Merrill was furious when he heard about this and worked the chain of command, as only a retired admiral can, to arrange some lessons in diplomacy for this emerging Hippocrates. The end result was the same, however, as Arthur was gone from esophageal cancer in about six months.

On one of our visits Carl started sobbing soon after we walked into the house. When we asked him what was wrong, he said he had just returned from Catherine's grave near Colonial Heights and for the first time saw his own tombstone. A few days later we got a call from Admiral Sappington. He had found Carl dead from a massive heart attack on the floor of the bedroom. As executor of the estate, Merrill brought over two quilts, willed to Sharlyn, that Catherine had made but never used because she was colorblind and was embarrassed when someone told her the patterns clashed. I took the opportunity to disclose that Carl had loaned me an iron bar made for him by a blacksmith many years ago, which I had not yet returned to him. Merrill told me to keep it, a very useful tool for prying out rocks that I still use to this day.

When the Copyright Office made the commitment to implement COPICS, I was asked to assume a new role. Eddy Kapusciarz had been promoted to head the Arts Section, and Ross Stuckey was named his replacement as assistant head of Music. Ross called me in one day to say that Leo needed an automation coordinator to provide cataloging expertise to the developers and to write the user's manual describing the system while the programmers coded the software. About a year later we were ready to begin trials, and because Arts had the lowest volume of material, Eddy's staff became our first guinea pigs. It was a dismal failure—not so much because of the software, but primarily the hardware infrastructure upon which we depended. We were among the first to use a new term being introduced into offices throughout the land—down time. Terminals, local and high speed printers, controllers, modems, land lines, backup equipment, and a mainframe computer, each manufactured by a different company and administered by a different vendor all needed to interface intricately, and when they did not, fingers were inevitably pointed at each other. Coordinating the representatives of each of these entities to resolve the issues was my job, and I was consumed almost full time by it. At first the problems were so severe that we were forced to return to the manual system for about three months, but when we decided to venture out onto the ice on shaky legs a second time, automation changed the landscape forever.

The legislation to protect sound recordings was but the first salvo in a battle that had raged for several years to overhaul copyright law. By 1976 Barbara Ringer finally had enough support in Congress to bring it about, and the Copyright Revision Bill became law. Some of the comments Leo Cooney made in confidence to me regarding his opinion of Ringer and her ideas about the cataloging operation, especially what transpired behind closed doors, are not repeatable. After considering himself her whipping boy for a few years, he finally one day took the underground railroad for Knoxville. Touting the clement weather, beautiful scenery of the Smokies, low cost of living, less frenetic pace, no state income tax, low density and benign traffic, Leo offered me a job, following up his repeated phone calls with a visit. Though I was tempted to accept it, there were a number of factors that gave me pause. What if we had a falling out? Would the job market down there allow me to move on? We were in an area with some of the best schools in the country, but with Angela starting kindergarten, could we say the same for Tennessee? Perhaps the most serious deterrent was that we were in the midst of construction on our house, and because it was not at the moment salable, I used that as my rationale to turn him down. Besides, I was more than curious to see where the massive changes to the copyright law might lead. Leo's pitch to Adelia Heller, his assistant chief, was more successful, however, as he eventually wore down her resistance enough to persuade her to resign and move south with him.

To replace them, Ringer brought in a professor of library science from Hawaii named Robert Stevens as the new chief and promoted the section head of Editing and Publishing, Melvin Peterson, to be his assistant. Stevens was appalled when he saw the cataloging and style rules, name authorities based upon the Reader's Digest, and our almost non-existent reference collection. His first order of business was to institute the *Anglo-American Cataloging Rules*, *Chicago Manual of Style*, Library of Congress name authorities and a library of reference works.

The objective of Stevens from the beginning was to put the cataloging operation on a par with the rest of the Library and to make the cataloger position seamless with the mainstream of the library world. From what I could perceive, the direction in which our operation was heading was toward professional librarianship, and since I was already a part of the largest library in the world, I decided, at the urging of Stevens, to pursue a graduate degree in library science. Although the Washington area has at least a half dozen universities, only two offer a library science program. Catholic University was a little more expensive than the University of Maryland, but it offered some of its evening classes on the Virginia side of the River, and even a few at the Library of Congress. One of my coworkers, Robert Kline, had apparently come to a similar conclusion about the direction of the Office, as he took a one-year sabbatical to complete his library degree full time. Ironically, Bob, who was Catholic and had even started a path toward priesthood at one time, chose Maryland, while I, considered a renegade among Catholics, enrolled at Catholic.

Bob is always one of those people whom you meet coming back. He is so brilliant that by the time you reason through a problem and come to some conclusion, Bob has already been to that same conclusion and is stating something that seems to make no sense when you first hear him say it—until you catch up in your logic to where he has already moved on to the next step. While he was away at library school, two developments occurred which nearly destroyed my relationship with this man, who in time would become one of the most important influences in my life. The first was that my role as an automation coordinator became a full-time position, of which I was its first incumbent. The second was that somewhere in his coursework in library school, Bob made a startling discovery—that he had a world-class automation mind. When he returned to the Office, he came back to an automated world, and his role was supposed to be that of a user—one of the catalogers using the system. However, his perceptions were brimming over, so he could neither resist stepping in to direct the troubleshooting efforts I was trying to coordinate with regard to some hardware problem nor quell his urge to advise the developers on designing the system and writing software. Not willing to accept his self-professed expertise at face value, however, most of us regarded this as mere officious intermeddling and tried to suppress it. That was a serious mistake. Bob was so farsighted that years later, we were still attempting to attain the level of sophistication that he had been advocating from the beginning, had anyone listened to him. However, he was about to be granted an opportunity to be heard.

The new copyright law brought with it vast changes in the registration process, which in turn significantly affected the cataloging content of the records to be generated. As a result, the cataloging rules and the COPICS system both would need to be completely rewritten. Because the old system, COPICS I as it became known, had to be operational while COPICS II was in development, I became almost overwhelmed with work on committees tasked with design of the new system while still maintaining the daily needs of the catalogers on the old one. When I suggested to Bob Stevens one day that I really could use a part-time assistant, he responded by making my position expandable to multiple incumbents and posted it to hire two more automation coordinators. Not only was I not consulted on this decision or on the qualifications of the position description, but after Stevens granted my request to participate in the interview process, he conducted them himself and made his selections before I was even aware the application phase had concluded. My ire was aroused, not just at the snub, but mostly because I did not need even one full-time assistant, much less two, and I had already told him I was not sure we could find enough work to keep three people busy. When I asked what my relationship was to these two "assistants" in my same grade and position, he said I was to be "first among equals," whatever that meant. I determined that I could not stay in such an environment and was about to make one of the most serious mistakes of my life.

My parents had moved to Colorado and were running a fast food restaurant that became so successful for them that they postulated there was enough income in their enterprise for all of us if we might be interested to join them in their venture. Instead, Sharlyn and I left Angela and Thomas with Deanna and Pete in Liverpool, New York in January that year and flew to Orlando for a week to relax in what were supposed to be warm temperatures. However, Florida was experiencing such a cold snap that the citrus growers feared they would lose their crop, and this proved to be an omen of events to come. While we were there, we explored ownership of a fast food restaurant down there, but by the grace of God, the sellers turned down our offer. When I returned to the Office, I noticed a posting for a position as a production coordinator in another department, headed by a protégé of the developer of machine-readable cataloging (MARC). It was a management position at a higher grade, and while I had no supervisory experience, I was half way through library school and decided to apply for it anyway. To my surprise I was selected for the job and went to work for the MARC Editorial Division. At first it seemed like perfect timing. While I considered myself a valued employee where I was, I was excited about the prospect of a whole new world that awaited me in this change of careers. But there was also a grain of revenge in this move, as I arrogantly concluded that I was indispensable to Bob Stevens, and now he was going to regret losing me. However, as someone once quipped, if you want to test the degree of oblivion after you are gone, put your hand in a bucket of water. The hole that is left when you pull out your hand is the measure of how much you are missed by your survivors. When Stevens offered his congratulations, I believe he was sincere when he told me how difficult it is to win a promotion across departmental lines, but I could not help noticing the lump in his cheek as he said goodbye. Bob Kline became my more than capable replacement, and the Office flourished as never before.

The Processing Department, in which I now found myself, was the largest at the Library, the backbone of its operations, entailing huge descriptive and subject cataloging processing, the Dewey decimal system, audiovisual and sound collections, exchanges with other libraries, "shared" cataloging with foreign nations, and so on. One day a brilliant cataloger named Henriette Avram, who had some experience with computer programming, collaborated with a colleague named Lucia Rather to develop a system for organizing the data in a catalog record. They called it machine-readable cataloging because when the information was pigeon-holed into dozens of fields, any of them could be retrieved individually or collectively in an almost infinite number of combinations by a computer. When they approached Joe Howard, director of the department, with their ideas, he was skeptical of anything that smacked of automation methods, but gave his consent to input data from material already cataloged, with the stipulation that none of their efforts would interfere with any phase of the ongoing operation in place. At first, Avram and Rather undertook this project by themselves, but after the proof of concept was successful, they were able to persuade Howard to assemble a cadre of input operators to generate a growing database of English-language materials that was increasingly being used by the Library and other libraries around the world. By the time I came on the scene, this operation had grown to over a hundred employees in an entire division headed by Barbara Roland.

The regret that I felt when I accepted this position began literally the first day I arrived. Instead of the lockable individual office I had in a modern office building in Crystal City, I was now at a desk among my employees in a converted warehouse building in the Navy Yard. This crumbling edifice had been hastily erected to construct naval vessels and to store ordnance during the War, but no amount of carpet, paint, false ceiling tile or fluorescent lighting could disguise its drab, humble origins. Its broken windows allowed the pigeons to fly sorties through our offices on a regular basis, one even expressing an opinion on the blouse of an unamused worker, and our warm minicomputers were the perfect shelter from the elements for these feathered squatters to begin parenthood. In the winter the air that rushed through these openings was so invigorating, and it was always such fun to brush away the snow that drifted through, to keep it from short-circuiting our temperature-sensitive equipment. Instead of the bus I had been able to take almost literally door to door at Crystal City, I was now forced to carpool with Mike Miller, one of my employees.

Having no familiarity with MARC data put me at a considerable disadvantage when adjudicating matters as a supervisor, as I was uncomfortable separating out administrative situations I could handle from the technical ones I could not. Besides the fact that I had no experience as a manager, I was not only a first-line supervisor as a section head myself, but was also in charge of the other section heads, who were themselves supervisors of unit heads and team leaders. Until now, all of my experience at the Library had been with professional associates, but here most of my charges were non-professional, the official euphemism ascribed to the group of employees who were less educated, lower paid and generally from minority socioeconomic classes. I know this may sound uppity to you, but I have to say the differences were quite tangible. Worst of all, I did not believe in our mission. In my view our entire operation should not even exist, and I was brash enough to express this opinion to others, including Roland, my boss, who agreed with me on one level, but who was not exactly enthusiastic about my campaign to demolish her empire. Catalogers drafted their entries on card stock and sent these manuscript cards to us for keying. But if they had to key the entry anyway, why not give *them* the four-phase terminals our data input operators used to *rekey the very same data*. Duplication of effort aside, are we not incurring the risk of inevitable keying error in this process? Besides, the cataloger has the language and subject expertise to understand the dozens of orthographic difficulties which the non-professional keyboarder must interpret or learn—matters like diacritics, abbreviations and acronyms, capitalizations and idioms. And that is not all. The sheer volume of manuscript cards overwhelmed our input operators to the point that they could handle only priority one material. This meant that the Department was forced to solicit bids from outside sources to key the remainder, so we had daily shipments of material in priorities two through eleven to and from a company called EKI in St. Louis.

I was also at odds with the organizational structure of the division. I was head of the Quality Assurance Section, with three employees. Three. File Management Section had four, Name Authority Section had about a dozen in two units, but the Input and Verification Section had about eighty spread across five or six units. This lopsided structure was an administrative quagmire that made even-handed treatment impossible. Also, because each of these entities was self-contained and relatively autonomous, there was a certain measure of understandable resentment when my nose got into their business, yet this is exactly what Roland requested me to do. I disagreed. They actually functioned better without any interference from me, so I was not exactly sure what my job was. Since I knew nothing about what they did, I certainly could offer no expertise or advice. After I was there about three months, Roland demanded a summary of my accomplishments and a projection of the direction in which I was planning to lead the office. I did not know what to tell her and suggested we meet to discuss it. When she laid out the analysis of throughput, assessment of efficiency and technical leadership she expected from me, I responded that I had no experience or training in such matters. However, with some guidance from her and Margaret Patterson, her assistant, I would try to learn. When I requested patience from her because I was a first-time supervisor, she snapped that my application for the job had stated I already had management experience. She was not pleased when I challenged her to produce my application and show me what had led her to such a conclusion.

One day when an employee requested emergency leave from his unit head, she denied it on the basis that it was the employee's third request that month. He appealed to Bernie Tyler, the section head, who came to me with it. At Copyright, leave was almost never denied for any reason, so when I found out from the unit head that the employee's wife was expecting a child any day, I told Tyler to approve it. Before he did anything I asked him to do, however, he always went directly to Roland first, so when he informed her of my decision, she called me into her office, where she and Patterson sat grim-faced to talk about this. Leave was to be requested and approved in advance, they reminded me, and since this employee had established a pattern of "abuse," he must be taught a lesson. When Barbara ordered me to draft a memo denying his leave, I put it in the terms she specified, but I told her I disagreed with the manner in which this was handled, since it did not consider the circumstances. In fact, I told her candidly that she and I were not in agreement on many points in the office and asked her to find a position for me somewhere else in the department. In response, she said that was not in her power to do and suggested that I get on board with her program. In virtually every place where I had worked before, I had always come to be regarded as a prized employee, but here for the first time I was learning the painful lesson that as long as your superiors like you, you can do no wrong, but when they do not, you can do no right. As I was sitting at my desk one day, Harold Boyd from Copyright poked his head into the doorway to say he was there to move me back to Crystal City. My heart leaped about three feet in the air, thinking that by some miracle or mistake, it mattered not which, I was being liberated from this hellhole. Then with a grin he said he had business with the Card Division downstairs and had decided only to stop by to say hello. He had no idea how crestfallen I was or how cruel his little joke was to me.

At Copyright I had hardly ever spent much time away from my work, but here at MARC Ed I took a long walk for a full hour every lunch period, regardless of the weather, and stretched every break away from the office to the limit. As the months dragged on, I wondered what I should do to break out of these bonds of despair in which I was trapped. Nothing looked better to me than the asphalt outside the door at the end of the day, and every minute of the weekend was glorious, but on Sunday night I would get diarrhea at the prospect of starting another week with Jezebel and Grizelda. Then one day my prayers were answered. Copyright was undergoing massive reorganization, as the new copyright law would take effect on the first of January 1978, and in December they posted several newly created positions for team leaders. I was determined to be one of them. However, when Gloria Ayers interviewed me for a position in the new Literary Section, she told me in clear terms right in the interview that I had never been one of her favorite people and stated she did not think we would work well together. This did not bode well. Warren McKay was the new head of the Music Section and understandably wanted to know why I was willing to move back to a lower grade and take a reduction in salary to apply for this job. I was not sure how to begin my answer to explain, because the unspoken suspicion his question implied left me wondering what chance I had. Nevertheless, I shall be eternally grateful to Warren and to Mel Peterson, the assistant chief who interceded on my behalf, to give me a second chance at life in Copyright. When I saw Bob Stevens for the first time upon my return, he chided that sometimes the grass looks greener in the next pasture. I replied that he could trust me when I told him with confidence that sometimes it is just Astroturf, where cows starve to death.

After Thomas was born, Sharlyn and I determined that with one girl and one boy, our family was complete. Contraceptives had been on the market for a short time, so it was upon the recommendation of her doctor that Sharlyn began the regimen he prescribed. In the fine print, however, we read of a tiny percentage of failure with this medication, and since someone must bear out these statistics (pun intended), we were chosen from the thousands of others vying for that honor. One day in July of 1977 Sharlyn opened a fortune cookie to read, "A change on the domestic scene is imminent." Our third child was due September 21. Unlike our first two children, who arrived before the due date, Number Three decided to wait until well past it. According to the lore of the old wives, this indicates that a girl will be born, so we prepared the children for a sister and fully expected to use the name we had picked out for her. When Sharlyn called Dr. Amorosi during the wee hours of October 11, 1977, he made light of the diarrhea she was experiencing and told her to take two tablespoons of Kaopectate and try to get some sleep. Relying on his advice, she went back to bed, and I went off to work a short time later. A few minutes after I left, she called for an ambulance, and there was a call waiting for me when I arrived at the office. When I finally got to the hospital, Sharlyn had just given birth to our second boy, Austin David, and was just being wheeled out of the delivery room when I first saw her. She was quivering, her lips were blue, and from her bedraggled appearance I was quite sure someone must have thrown her into a cement mixer as part of her therapy. This picture of her in my mind haunts me to this day, and when I witnessed so graphically the extent to which she had just risked her life to produce progeny, I vowed I was never going to put her through this again. We now knew that contraception was not the answer for us, but perhaps Dr. Schwartz was, so I had already made an appointment to see him.

Four-year-old Thomas ran in to check on "little brotty" quite frequently, and after about two weeks he was standing on tiptoe peering over the edge of the bassinet one day and wanted to know, "When will he be a kid?" Few kids say anything meaningful at six months, but, unlike his older siblings, Austin was an early talker, and one day Sharlyn and I were alert to a real word from his high chair … or was it? Nah, probably just a coincidence. But then when it was repeated with the appropriate meaning attached to it, our doubts melted. Though most of his words were crystal clear, some of them were the dainty diminutives that children express. So it is that to this day "breakins," "Thom-bus" and "pato" have permanently etched themselves into the vocabulary of the household, pressed into service as the understudies for breakfast, Thomas and potato. The words recorded in Austin's baby book as his first sentence were "Don't do that him!" Do you suppose the imprint on his mind of this sentiment had anything to do with parental admonitions to the overzealous attentions of two older siblings? One day it was a budding pint-sized scientist who was amused by his fingers seen magnified through a glass of water and observed with a grin, " 'Pider in there."

Near the end of the school year when Thomas was in first grade, his class made Father's Day cards as an art project. I wish we had saved the one he made, which he began the first line lettering "Happy Fat," then continued without a hyphen on the next line with "her's Day." His lower-case *r* looked more like a lower-case *n*, prompting us forevermore to call the holiday Fat Hen's Day.

When I became a unit head in the Music Section, Congress had just passed legislation to allow collective bargaining for federal employees. Why, I wanted to know? Government workers already had one of the best retirement packages in the world, a better leave plan than anywhere in corporate America, such reliable job security that grounds for dismissal were almost impossible to establish, a pay scale and promotion system comparable to the private sector, and health benefits unexcelled by any company in the country. Since the right to strike was withheld even under this new law, what more could a public sector employee want? Nevertheless, three unions were instituted at the Library, and they were determined to flex their muscle to address "grievances." When I was a cataloger, the Office had certain standards of quantity and quality expected for ratings and promotions. Under collective bargaining these standards were deemed onerous and were thrown out, the net result of which was that ratings and promotions became more subjective—exactly the opposite of what I should have thought the unions would have promoted. I was about to become one of their first targets.

One of the employees in the Office had been given an opportunity to cross the line from the non-professional ranks of the clerks to the professional realm of the catalogers through a special policy known as affirmative action. We might have expected this fellow to take full advantage of this program to prove to himself and to the world that he could succeed without the usual qualifications required for the duties he was now expected to perform. But he either realized early on that he was not equipped after all to handle the requirements of the job or was unwilling to make the effort to undertake tasks he found much more complex than those he had before. His supervisors tried valiantly to pull him out of the doldrums, but when he exceeded the limits of their mettle, he was transferred into my unit. Despite my experiences on the South Side of Chicago, I considered myself a very good teacher and was quite confident that if anyone could indoctrinate him in the art of cataloging, I would succeed where others failed. I noticed early on that he had the intelligence to meet the requirements of the job, but he was extremely lazy. The first sign of trouble was the attitude I sensed in him that by *becoming* a cataloger he had already achieved his objective. He saw himself in the penthouse, when, in fact, he was just turning the key to the front door. When none of my cajoling or offers of assistance produced any spark of industry or motivation, I asked in frustration one day what he was hoping to accomplish in his new position. "I'm here to git what I can git," were the exact words he uttered with arms folded. He interpreted my efforts to nudge him toward productivity as discrimination and harassment and soon engaged the support of the union. He was increasingly absent from his desk, which would seem to run counter to the problems he had with his output, and after two years of counseling, training and referrals to professionals, we had enough documentation to initiate adverse action proceedings against him. With the full support of the management above me, I suggested we transfer him back to a position as a non-professional employee. Rather than accept this recommendation, he resigned, but with a change of heart later sought unsuccessfully to have his appointment reinstated by the courts.

This incident was very expensive, not just from the direct costs of dealing with the problems of one individual, or the diversion of my time and attention away from the other worthy employees in my unit, but for my reputation as a supervisor among the other employees in the Cataloging Division. I did not realize how serious this misperception was until a reorganization came along a short time later. Stevens had noticed that certain personal relationships developing between section heads and their unit heads were not in the best interest of the division, so one day without warning, he announced a grandiose rearrangement of supervisors. While that solved the problem he was addressing, it created a host of others, resulting from mismatches of talent. Gloria Ayers, who was by her own admission the least technically minded, became head of Technical Support. Warren McKay remained as head of Music

Section, but the wonderful relationship I enjoyed with him as my supervisor came abruptly to an end. Rodney Hall became the head of Serials Section, and I, who knew very little about serial publications (magazines, journals, newspapers, and other serially issued works), was reassigned to him as a unit head. There were two considerations in this move that would prove to be disastrous for me, neither of them having to do with the fact that the timing of this reorganization coincided almost exactly with the reunification of the Copyright Office with the rest of the Library. I found myself unceremoniously uprooted from Crystal City and relocated back to Capitol Hill in the fall of 1980 as one of the first to occupy the new James Madison Memorial Building that had been in development for fifteen years.

The first of two career-changing events for me was that both Bob Stevens and Mel Peterson retired nearly simultaneously. My management style had fit well into their precepts for conducting the business of the government, and they were very supportive of my efforts to maintain the high standards they established. Diametrically opposite were their successors, Susan Aramayo, the new chief, and Raoul LeMat, her assistant. Both were extremely liberal and therefore very popular among the staff because of the concessions they made to avoid confrontation with the unions. The second factor that eventually led to upheaval for me was that Serials was the only section with a non-professional staff, a cadre of recorders who input a high volume of secondary data. This in itself was not a problem, but these ladies were a tight-knit group with a gang mentality, where an offense to one was an attack on all. As their supervisor I assumed it was my duty to break up their daily giggle klatches when they reached a half hour in length and became sufficiently riotous to attract a dozen participants from neighboring cubicles. Incredibly, the front office considered this healthy behavior for good morale and ordered me to tone down my rhetoric. When I first came to the Copyright Office, the work on hand would cause alarm if it reached 20,000. Under Aramayo's administration it soared to over 140,000 and continued to climb before the Register's office ordered her to address the backlog. Instead of examining her management techniques to improve productivity instead of "morale," however, Aramayo responded by rewriting the cataloging rules to trim out essential facts! Bob Kline and I pleaded with her not to eliminate the international standard book number because the ISBN was the only data item in the entry that could uniquely identify the work to someone searching the records, but she would not hearken to reason. Predictably, the impact of this monomania is still felt to this day.

I did not realize it for quite some time, but each morning two of the first to arrive in the office were LeMat and one of my serial recorders. In their chats over their first cup of coffee, this recorder took advantage of this circumstance to summarize the events of the previous day for him, but even if … *if* most of the facts were correct, he did me a grievous injustice by listening to them from one point of view. I cannot be sure what his perceptions might have been of the version he heard of some incidents that transpired. One day one of the catalogers asked to borrow my typewriter brush. For those who are unfamiliar with this tool, I should explain that over time the ink in the ribbon of a manual typewriter cumulates in the type heads, and when it dries, the typed character appears "filled in" or smudged as it is transferred to the paper. The brush, resembling a toothbrush, is used periodically to clean the dried black ink from these metal fonts. When I handed over the brush, I jokingly told her to be sure not to use it to brush her teeth. She took offense and complained to my supervisor that I had made a racist remark, ostensibly because of the suggestive reference to applying this black material to her teeth.

One employee I hired as a cataloger came highly recommended from her previous job in a public library, and indeed she learned her new duties quickly. Unfortunately, she was so concerned about her output that her cataloging was full of errors and always needed extensive correction. After working for several months attempting to concentrate her attention on the details, she became increasingly frustrated and came to the conclusion that the cause of her problem was my insistence on good quality. She requested to be transferred to Music Section, where the cataloging was less complex and lax supervision was more tolerant of sloppy work. Another of my catalogers had the opposite problem. Her work was immaculate, error free and well researched. Unfortunately, while most catalogers generated some six to ten entries per hour or more, her output was closer to two or three per *day*. On her time sheet I noticed that the actual productive cataloging time was disproportionate to the time she was ascribing to research, meetings and "consultation with supervisor." When I questioned this last item, I discovered that each day she made sure to ask me some questions so that she could round up her time for "consultation." Clearly she was attempting to maximize accounting in the non-productive column, so I suggested I spend a day with her to observe how she was allocating her time. Instead, she went to the union, charging me with discrimination. Since she was Caucasian, I was puzzled at first how she could arrive at such a conclusion. Since her husband was black, she was able to convince the review panel through a convoluted chain of logic that I had seen the picture of him on her desk, and extrapolated discriminatory behavior from that toward her. The panel bought her arguments and transferred her to the Audiovisual Section.

One of my recorders was the mother of eight children, and when school was out for the summer, they were home alone. She was on the phone incessantly, advising them on meals and clothing, assigning duties, and breaking up petty squabbles. Not only was this counterproductive for her at the office, but her conversations were disruptive throughout the room. The first year I tried to be sympathetic, but when the pattern emerged again the following summer, I took her aside to say that I was sorry to mention it, but from my perspective, her priorities needed to be redirected to her work at the office. I did not realize it, but she was so unhappy with this admonishment that she went to LeMat to complain. A few days later when she concluded a lengthy discourse with the oldest child at home again, I reminded her politely in a hushed voice that she would need to find a way to limit the frequency and duration of her phone calls. This time she bypassed LeMat and marched directly to Grace Ross, the executive officer, who happened to be Aramayo's sister(!), to report my "harassment" through this incestuous chain of command. In addition she staged a work slowdown among her coworkers that continued for several weeks before it became apparent to me. Upon her next phone session, I decided to approach this more formally, but when I first broached the subject, she began screaming that since I was not a mother, I could not possibly understand her children needed her and continued shrieking so vehemently for several minutes that I could not calm her down. Though we were behind closed doors, her voice carried through the walls out into the room of catalogers and penetrated several offices around.

All of this came to a head on Thursday, April 11, 1985, when Aramayo called me to her office. When I walked through the door and saw with her LeMat wearing a solemn expression, I had an immediate sense of foreboding. Without prefatory remarks or niceties, LeMat began intoning something about productivity in my unit was down and morale was at rock bottom, so I was being relieved of my duties and detailed to the Automation Group in the Admin Office. My first thought was, "They're throwing me onto the bone pile," and from there my mind was swimming so frantically I remember little else that was being decreed from this tribunal. In private industry the office hands you a box and gives you an hour to leave the building. In the government someone kicks you upstairs with a "promotion" and phony title or railroads you out of the way with a contrived position. Collectively these discarded employees are like a stack of dead bones. Aramayo predicted I would be broadsided by this news and wisely sent me home on administrative leave. I was to report to Mike Burke in the Automation Group the next morning, but since it was Friday and the stunning effects of being demolished had only intensified overnight, I took a rare day of sick leave to delay my new assignment until Monday. When the thirty days of my detail had been fulfilled, I reported back to LeMat, who slid a sheet of paper across the desk to me and asked me to sign it. He told me they had been unsuccessful to find another position as a supervisor anywhere in the agency, and since I could not remain in my current position, he was offering a transfer to Tech Support. If I refused to accept his offer, he said pointedly, they were prepared to initiate adverse action proceedings immediately. Adverse action? On what grounds, I wanted to know. Well, while you were on detail, he was insisting, performance evaluations for two of your employees were not completed, and since they are now past due, this constitutes a violation of the collective bargaining agreement, and together with the evidence we have of discrimination and harassment of your employees, we feel our case is strong.

Outrageous as his charges were, my mind raced ahead to what life would be like for me if I were successful in refuting them and achieving reinstatement. There would be other such incidents, and the next one could be worse, resulting in more than just trumped-up charges. In retrospect I stand by my actions and remain convinced that I was correct to stand on principle. By the same token I realized that my biggest "mistake" was that I did not play the game. The course chosen by most (but not all) of the other supervisors was to follow the line of least resistance, *allowing* the employees to flourish in the climate of "freedom" fostered by the front office. Discrimination? Offense can be *taken* from almost any interaction, even when none was intended, but that in itself does not constitute discrimination. Did I discriminate against substandard performance and unacceptable office decorum? Yes. Harassment? It would have been much easier to look away with a smile and a pat on the back for that employee abusing a government phone, as most others would have, but in my view I chose the *courageous* course to do what was my duty as a custodian of the public trust. Nevertheless, I signed LeMat's transfer paper and began life working for Gloria Ayers in Tech Support, yes, the very person who a few years earlier had told me in an interview that she did not think we could work well together. Like many another catastrophe in life, however, I failed to recognize that perhaps this was exactly the plan God had mapped out for me, so I could never have foreseen the extent to which I would one day rise from these ashes and be respected to a degree far beyond what I could ever have achieved in management—even, maybe *especially*, by Gloria and Raoul LeMat.

For my entire first year in Tech Support, I was detailed, along with Mary Ann McFarland, to the Documents Unit to assist with the most monumental backlog in Office history. In frustration the public had been complaining to Congress that these legal documents crucial to their intellectual property industry were being held up in our offices for many months. The improved "morale" which the Cataloging Division now enjoyed allowed them to pile up uncataloged until this unit was over a year behind. Both Mary Ann and I had been crackerjack catalogers, and we made a huge difference, reducing a fourteen-month backlog to about four. While the average output from a specialist in this unit was about two dozen per week, each of us was averaging about two hundred. When I cataloged over seven hundred one week, it caught the attention of LeMat, who came to me with raised eyebrows to express appreciation. Neither he nor I realized it at the time, but this man, who had been my greatest antagonist a few months earlier and had tried everything in his power and spared no effort in his attempt to cast me into outer darkness, was about to become one of my greatest allies and, I prefer to think, admirers a few months hence. I will tell you how that came about, but first we will go flying.

# Aviation

Our offices at Crystal City overlooked National Airport, and one day when I glanced out the window, I noticed a small plane coming in to land. It looked so graceful that I was smitten anew by a lifetime dream—to fly airplanes. As I mentioned already, I am quite sure I would have made a good fighter pilot in the Air Force, had my parents seen fit to pass me better genes for eyesight, but the idea remained in my veins, bubbling beneath the surface like an underground river for all the intervening years. Even so, my pondering kept returning to three children and a mortgage on a single income, and I was not sure this was wise stewardship. But I was already thirty-five years old, and I was afraid time would pass me by. It was just after Christmas 1979 when I found myself turning to the yellow pages to look up flight schools.

Century Aviation at Leesburg Airport was offering for $1295 a discovery flight, lessons for the license, ground school training, textbooks, a flight computer and one introductory session in an advanced aircraft after licensing. This package was about the same as the one I could have taken at Midway Airport some fifteen years earlier for $499, but after adjustment for inflation, it was still quite a bargain. I cannot say that I actually enjoyed flight lessons at first, because there was so much emphasis upon endless drills, preparation for eventualities, emergency procedures and recovery techniques. I will never forget the first time Tom Barrett, my instructor, demonstrated a power-on stall. In fact, the airplane was pitched up no more than about thirteen degrees above its flight path, but I was quite sure it was pointed straight up and about to roll over onto its back.

It was about lesson two that I first discovered that I intensely disliked the wind. Tom intentionally selected maneuvers that, as he put it, took "advantage" of the wind. What I gleaned from that experience was that it created so much turbulence that I got airsick, I could not hold a course over the ground, we approached the runway flying sideways, and I marveled that anyone could move the control wheel so rapidly to land in such adversity. After about three lessons Tom suggested I purchase the aeronautical chart I would eventually need, but since one was not available at Leesburg, he suggested we fly over to Washington Dulles about ten miles away. It was after dark, and I will never forget the sea of blue lights that greeted us when we landed. Although I have seen that deep blue sea (but never the devil) many times since, I remember asking myself how anyone could possibly trace a path through the miles of taxiways in that maze. Then came one day when Tom hopped out and told me to take off by myself. It is axiomatic in aviation that the number of landings must equal exactly the number of takeoffs, so I had this in mind as I glanced over nervously at the empty seat next to me after I took off. Tom penned

"Nice landings" in my logbook that day, and when he waved me in to tie down, I had taken this little Cessna 152 up three exhilarating times, and it had settled gently to earth the same number.

Tom authorized me to fly solo after that and encouraged me to come out to practice as often as possible. One day when I picked up the keys to the airplane, I wondered whether the wind was too strong for me, but since Tom was not around to ask, I decided I needed the practice in these conditions anyway. As I was taxiing out from the parking space, Gene Pugh, the dispatcher, came running out waving his arms and shaking his head. As he gave me the signal to return the plane to its tiedown spot, I did not realize the extent to which he had mercifully saved me from grievous harm to myself, the airplane and perhaps others in jeopardy on the ground. Hoping the wind would die down enough to try again later, I watched from the window until the sun was low on the horizon, but still it continued to make the trees show the silver side of their leaves and to reveal what was under the next layer of Virginia soil. As I drove home, I could not believe I wasted the whole day watching the wind blow. Out my car window I saw a hawk struggling to reach a treetop, and I remember feeling sorry for it. Where I had the choice to venture out or not, this poor raptor was forced to endure the liabilities of nature year round just to make a living.

If you were somehow able to take an airplane back to the Middle Ages and tell King Arthur that it was possible for him to enter a chamber with you and float over the earth for several hours, soaring over rivers, castles and hills, he would be willing to give you half his kingdom for the privilege. It was this magic I experienced whenever I was able to fly the airplane solo. One of the requirements for the license was twenty hours of solo time, including ten hours flying to other airports at least fifty miles away and back without getting lost, and in all my years of flying I have never had so much fun as these student cross country flights. As soon as I finished one, I could not wait to plan the next one. The final one had to be at least 300 nautical miles long, and Tom gave me a very challenging three-leg course—Leesburg to Newport News to Rehoboth and back to Leesburg. One of the chief disadvantages of learning to fly at an airport like Leesburg is that it has no control tower, so the opportunity to develop radio skills is limited. Tom knew that the first leg would force me to communicate with Dulles, National, Norfolk, Oceania Naval Air Station, and Newport News air traffic controllers, but I managed to run thread through each of these needles to land at Patrick Henry Airport in southeast Virginia.

The destination of my second leg at Rehoboth, Delaware, was a grass airstrip. Sometimes even a paved airfield is difficult to locate from aloft, but a turf airport often cannot be distinguished from an ordinary field of alfalfa. When I could not find the airport, I radioed the fixed base operator (FBO), who tried to provide me with landmarks, but when that failed, he sent one of his students out to practice landings, and when I saw that plane take off about two miles away, I finally saw where I was supposed to land. In those days the airspace around Baltimore International and that around Washington National were separated by a corridor only about five miles wide. The final leg back to Leesburg required me to navigate through this narrow isthmus without violating the airspace of either major airport. As I approached the corridor, I was perfectly on course, and from my commanding view of Baltimore, I saw an airliner taking off on a runway that paralleled my course. It quickly climbed to my altitude, turned perpendicular to my flight path, and then turned left again to a head-on course directly toward me. I must tell you that my first impulse was to honk the horn. This might be more amusing when you realize that an airplane does not have a horn. Because visual cues are deceptive, perception of distance is an acquired skill in the air, and it was not until much later that I realized that this passenger jet was farther away than I thought and was therefore not the threat I believed.

The grass airstrip at Rehoboth reminds me of a story about a pilot in the early days of aviation who experienced engine trouble and was forced to land in a field. When he climbed out to assess the trouble, he heard a voice behind him say, "You have a clogged fuel line." Turning around, the pilot saw no one except a cow that had walked up after he left the cockpit. Not wishing to hang around a haunted place with a talking cow, the spooked pilot ran across the field and down the lane to the farmer's house, where he pounded on the door. "Your … cow … just told me … what's wrong … with my … airplane," he blurted out breathlessly. "Was it a brown cow?" asked the farmer. "Yes, yes," came the answer. "Did it have a white patch on its forehead?" the farmer continued. "Yes, that's the one," replied the pilot. "That's Flossie," said the farmer, "Don't pay no attention to her. She don't know nuthin' about aeroplanes."

Each cross country flight must be reviewed by an instructor, who looks over the student's planning and preparation, verifies the flight conditions and authorizes dispatch with an endorsement in the logbook. One day when I came to the airport to sally forth again, Tom was not around, so I asked Bill Davis, one of my ground school instructors, to sign me off. I thought it a little strange that he refused, walking away saying he was not signing anyone off today. Then I soon learned why. One of the students in the ground school class was from Morocco, and although I could understand a little of his English, I wondered how much material he was actually comprehending from the course. We were about to find out. This particular day, Tom had signed off young Mr. Morocco to take his first solo cross country from Leesburg to Lancaster, about an hour flight in a Cessna 152. After flying for *two* hours and not finding Lancaster airport, he finally admitted to himself that he was hopelessly lost and switched to the emergency frequency for help. Since this frequency is monitored by every control tower, flight service station, ARTCC, and military base in the nation, the controller who answered his call told him to describe what he was seeing on the ground. "Oh! … I see airport," he replied. "Land!" the controller ordered. So he landed … at McGuire Air Force Base in New Jersey, one of the most secure installations in the country. On high alert, they scrambled an armored personnel carrier, an ambulance and several jeeps to surround him at gunpoint. When they saw a young man from the Middle East emerge from the plane, speaking broken English, they whisked him away in handcuffs to a padded cell for debriefing. After about two hours of interrogation, the intelligence officers started to believe his story. When they produced an aeronautical chart and pointed to where he was supposed to land, but where he was now, some eighty miles off course, he lit up and said, "Oh, I go now. I be okay." No, they told him, he was going to call the instructor who signed him off to come up to fly him out, bringing along with him another instructor to fly the second plane back. I never saw this young man again.

The regulations for a private pilot license require a minimum of forty hours of varied flight experience, and when I had forty-two, Tom decided I was ready for a check ride with the FAA. Everything was going well, when Dave Pearce, the designated examiner for Leesburg, reached behind the seat and said, "Okay, where's that hood?" Part of the exam is to recover from an unusual attitude (induced by the examiner) by the instruments alone, without benefit of outside references, using a view-limiting device known as a hood. Since it was my responsibility to provide this device, and it was to be aboard when we took off, the examiner could have reached for his tablet of pink paper immediately. I had left it in my car. However, Dave was known for his fairness, and since he did not want to disqualify me on a technicality, he suggested we return to the airport, retrieve the hood, and continue the exam from there. On final approach to land, he told me to pretend we were landing on a grass airstrip and asked me to demonstrate a "soft field" landing. Unfortunately, I mishandled the wind as we crossed the threshold and bounced as we touched down. This time he did issue a pink slip and said we could try again after I picked up some additional training on the soft field technique. So after forty-*three* hours in my logbook, I had my license.

As a student pilot, I was not allowed to carry anyone along, even another licensed pilot, but now, with freshly minted wings, I wanted to take Sharlyn and three little earthlings for a ride as my first passengers. Since the training aircraft had only two seats, however, I would need to check out in a Cessna 172 Skyhawk, big brother to the lowly 152, with a bench seat in the back for passengers. Tom made the mistake of telling me it flies just like the trainer. Maybe for him, but certainly not for me. The stall and approach speeds were higher, the controls less responsive, and the additional weight quite noticeable in the way it handled in every maneuver. After a couple of sessions to make the adjustment, I started to feel comfortable with it and proudly strapped my entire family in for a short ride. When little Austin fell asleep, I was not sure whether to be flattered by the trust he placed in me or insulted by his boredom with something about which I expected him to be as passionate as I. The very next day my parents flew into Baltimore, and I had promised to meet their flight. Not aware that my mother's last experience in a small aircraft years earlier had caused her to paint the windows in the cockpit a garish color of puce and also to produce a foul smelling puddle on the ground after they landed, I had arranged to ferry them from Baltimore back to Leesburg in a Skyhawk with me. Although they were taken aback when I led them to my plane and loaded their luggage, they gingerly climbed in and grimly set their jaws for Leesburg. My mother was able to retain her cookies this time, but the flight was not without incident. As we departed Baltimore, we set off a warning alarm and a flashing amber light on the instrument panel that I had never heard or seen before. After a few seconds it stopped, but then the alarm returned a short time later with a flashing blue light. When I reported this to Tom when we got to Leesburg, he shrugged and told me I must have crossed some marker beacons. He might have spared me the coronary I nearly had in flight by explaining to me in advance that this plane was equipped for flight in instrument conditions, and I do not think it would have been too much to ask for him also to have shown me how to turn this apparatus off.

Soon after I got my license, Sharlyn became interested in learning to fly also, primarily because of her concern that when we traveled as a family, both of us should work together to bring everyone safely back to earth. Century Aviation had increased its package to $1395, but this still seemed like an acceptable rate for us, so while she and Tom Barrett bored holes in the sky, three little bicyclists watched with me from the parking lot and country roads around the airport. One day when Sharlyn was about halfway through her training, Tom pulled into the parking lot to meet his first student of the day and found the door to the building padlocked. Literally overnight, the owners of Century had declared bankruptcy and absconded with the assets of the company, including the down payments for several new airplanes, back wages owed the instructors, and, most importantly for us, the remainder of Sharlyn's package money. Most flight schools do not own their airplanes; rather, they lease them from the owners and then make them available for lease back to the students and aircraft renters who walk in from the street. So when word of this development reached the ears of the other instructors, Dave Sullivan quickly called a meeting with the aircraft owners to see if they could continue in operation, since the student body, renters, staff, instructors and fleet of airplanes were all intact. Since these instructors regarded themselves as the squadron that took charge after their company was ravaged, they hastily put together a charter under the name Squadron Aviation. The competitor at the south end of the field, Blue Ridge

Aviation, was delighted when it learned of the demise of Century but was quite displeased to discover that its hated rival was back in business so soon. Blue Ridge was the only fuel franchise on the airport and responded to this turn of events by denying fuel to any airplane in the Squadron fleet. At first, Dave Sullivan instructed all the pilots to land at another nearby airport for refueling before returning to Leesburg, but when this became problematic enough, Squadron moved its operation to Dulles. Sharlyn was able to finish up her license requirements at Leesburg before this exodus came about, but we never did recover the balance of the money we lost on her flight training package.

When I first got my license, I was bound by visual flight rules, which did not allow me to fly near clouds or in reduced visibility. This required an instrument rating and a properly equipped airplane. It also required two hundred hours of logged flight time—and I had a mere forty-three. Given the hour and a half span of a typical flight, two hundred hours of flying was a huge block, and it seemed almost unattainable to me. To build flight time, I had the idea I could join the Civil Air Patrol, the auxiliary branch of the Air Force whose primary role is to search for downed aircraft. When I attended the first meeting, though, and saw its cadets marching to a cadence, sounding off and saluting, I decided this military diet was too reminiscent of basic training for my taste. Then when I met the wing commander and told him I had just received my license, the first words out of his mouth were, "Well, if you think we are a flying club where you will be able to acquire flight time to build up your hours, that is not what the CAP is about." How did he know exactly what I was thinking before I even asked it?

One day when I was reading through the monthly tabloid distributed by the Welfare and Recreation Association at the Library, I noticed that it had classified ads for vacation packages, tours and organized recreational activities. When I sat down to list interesting places close enough to a small airport, I discovered over thirty locales that would appeal to almost anyone who might want to avoid the time and hassle of driving—resorts like Greenbrier or Bryce, historic sites like Gettysburg or Williamsburg, seafood restaurants at places like Kentmorr Marina or Tangier Island, beaches like Kitty Hawk or Ocean City, mountain destinations like the Poconos or Hot Springs, exotic places like Cape May or Martha's Vineyard. I was not aware that I had within me the sort of entrepreneurship that would have made my father proud, but I got the idea to advertise flights to these various destinations. There was a problem, however. My license did not permit me to charge anyone, nor did it allow persons to charter a flight to a destination of their choice, so I worded my ad simply to arouse curiosity, and many called. When I assembled a suitable group to accompany me on an adventure, I found that I could fill three seats, fly to someplace where I might never have been before, and still log the full time for one-fourth the cost of the flight by myself.

Most of the time, these arrangements worked out well. One notable exception was a trip I planned to New York. Ann DeJesus, the young lady who called in response to my ad, said she had two friends who wanted to accompany us, but the day before the flight, they backed out. When Ann told me she had a friend she wanted to visit on Long Island and still wanted to go, I told her that I had scheduled the plane for four people, so she would still be paying for her two absent companions. Fine, she said, but asked whether we could return via Atlantic City, where she had another friend she wanted to visit. When I thought over these changes in her plans, I got a wild idea. I suggested to Sharlyn that since none of the family had been to New York City, I could take the boys with me in the empty back seat of the plane, and she and Angela could drive up to meet us in Manhattan. The timing would be about right, because we were landing in Farmingdale and would need to take the train in from there to Manhattan and could meet them at the Empire State Building. Problems started when Thomas and Austin got bored with the long flight, and their puerile behavior from the back caused me so many distractions that I was frazzled to wit's end. After only a short wait on the corner of 33rd and Fifth Avenue, however, Sharlyn and Angela drove up, and we had a nice, albeit brief, time together before we needed to move on to phase two of our flight plan.

The plan was that, while we flew to New Jersey, Sharlyn was to motor down the coast to meet us at the Atlantic City airport. Our flight started over an hour late because Ann had tarried too long with her friend, so I started to worry that the Sharlyn and Angela would be there well ahead of us and would begin to wonder where we were. It was late afternoon when we arrived in Atlantic City, about the time I had originally planned to *depart* for our return to Washington. Sharlyn was nowhere around. We waited an hour, which turned into two, and in these days before cell phones were in use, I was playing through every possible cause for delay in my mind, becoming more and more frantic as the minutes passed. Then, before the appointed time for Ann to return to the airport for our flight home, I realized I had failed to allow for a weather phenomenon that is quite characteristic of a coastal airport in the early evening—fog. As soon as I saw it moving in, I knew that, without an instrument rating, I would not be able to take off. When I called Ann to explain that we might not be able to leave until the next day, she cheerfully told me it was not a problem to spend the night where she was, with her friend.

Meanwhile, Sharlyn and Angela finally dragged in well after dark, explaining that traffic had been horrendous leaving Manhattan, a situation apparently so normal that young ladies selling flowers, newspapers, candy and soft drinks came through on roller skates between the lanes of snarled cars in the tunnel. This delay had created a problem for us. The original plan had been for all of us to be on our return home before dark, when the weather forecasts had all been favorable, but now I was being forced to spend the night. We did not have a credit card, and our checkbook was at home, so the only money we had was a small amount of cash between us. A motel was out of the question. My first option was to send everyone home in the car, while I remained behind to return with the airplane, but since that meant that I would have to sleep in the plane, Sharlyn chose to stay there with me, where we would all be together. Fortunately, this was May, when overnight temperatures were relatively mild, and the back of our Chevrolet Citation folded down flat to accommodate four tightly squeezed sleepers. Austin was still small enough to lie on the floor ahead of the front seat. We found a grocery store to buy a few staples, and we carried back with us several empty cardboard boxes for bedding and cover.

By mid-morning the next day, I was dismayed that the fog had not lifted, and although I could see clear sky through occasional breaks, the ceiling remained about ten feet above our heads. When I informed Ann that our return was on hold until we had a break in the weather, she decided to rent a car or drive home with her friends there. It was actually a great relief to be freed from the pressure of getting her home, because it was beginning to appear we would be stuck here for a while longer, perhaps for another night. Since Atlantic City has many amusements, we decided to make the most of our time, strolling along the beaches with the kids, who had no idea how close we were edging toward crisis. Then, surely by Providence, a man approached us as we walked along the boardwalk, offering us twenty dollars if we would spend an hour listening to a presentation by a local realty company selling condominiums. While they were quite sure they had a condo to fit our budget, we stood firm, gleefully collecting our heaven-sent twenty dollars, and on five of them fed the whole family at McDonald's. Yes, we spent a second night in the car, but at first light the following morning, I could see the sun!

Without a moment's hesitation, I hastily grabbed my flight bag, wished everyone a safe drive home and dashed for the airplane. The final outcome would have been memorable even without the uncollectible check Ann mailed me for her share of the expenses, the resolution of which is a sordid tale that evokes unpleasant memories best left undisturbed.

In addition to these flights I arranged through my tabloid ad, I was promoting aviation at the workplace, as well as at our church. Two of my coworkers were interested in the trip I suggested to Luray Caverns, and one of them was bringing her husband, who had never flown before. The day of our flight was quite windy, and when we met up at the airport, I proposed to them as a group that we reschedule. It was not dangerous to go, but the ride would be bumpy and uncomfortable, I tried to explain. Dave Culp, the husband, assured me that he had been on all sorts of carnival rides and was accustomed to this, so when he convinced the others there should be no problem, they agreed to go. The Bull Run Mountains lie only ten miles west of Dulles, and the wind flowing over them was causing some mild bumpiness on the lee side almost as soon as we took off. Before we reached the ridge, I felt a tapping on my shoulder from the back seat. It was Dave. "Do you … blrbbb … have a … blrbbb … bag … blrbbb?" his green face was asking. Fortunately, I did, and he filled it a moment later. After we landed, he continued to retch for the next hour and felt so queasy for the rest of the day that he could not enjoy the tour of the amazing caverns I had arranged for them to see. Late in the afternoon, when it was time to return, he was determined to rent a car, bicycle, or a canoe down the Shenandoah to get home rather than subject himself to another ride in the butter churn. From where we were, no such options were available, so I told him that he could ride up front, where he would be closest to the center of gravity, and that we would be flying back in the calmest period of the day, with (rather than against) any wind we would encounter. With a great deal of persuasion from Wayne and Katie, we eventually convinced him to buckle in without the use of handcuffs or any mind-numbing drugs. His ride to Dulles was smooth and uneventful, but he made a vow when his foot touched the tarmac that he would never fly again.

This reminds me of the story of a pilot earning money giving airplane rides in an open cockpit airplane at carnivals around the country. One day a farmer walked up with his wife, expressing shock at the price on his sign. "You expect us poor farmers to pay that?" he whined. After the farmer groused for a while about the cost of feed, low market prices for his produce, high taxes and adverse weather, the pilot finally said, "I'll tell you what. I will take you and your wife for a ride for free, provided neither of you makes a sound throughout the flight. But if I hear one peep, you will pay double. Do we have a deal?" After stuffing both of them into the rear seat, the pilot took off. First, he did a barrel roll and heard nothing from his passengers behind him, then he tried a loop and still heard no sound from either one of them, then he rolled inverted. Hmm, he thought, tough customers. So he started performing some serious aerobatics—a snap roll, an Immelmann, a split-S, a lomcevak—but there was still no sound from behind. After they landed, the pilot called over his shoulder, "Well, I didn't think you could do it, but you get your ride for free." "I know," replied the farmer, "But goll' darn, I thought you had me there when my wife fell out."

If you have washed and waxed your car, you have some appreciation for the intensive effort and labor involved to restore the showroom shine you want the neighbors to see sitting on your driveway. Even the *smallest* airplane has a surface area of exponential proportions when compared to your car, however, and a proper laundering requires many hours to degrease the belly of the fuselage, debug the leading edges of the airfoils and delaminate the oxidation that accumulates on paint. One day Dave Sullivan offered an hour of free flight time to anyone who would wash and wax one of the Cessna model 172 airplanes in the fleet. Foolishly I accepted his gambit and dragged home exhausted after an entire day spent returning spiffiness to this aircraft all by myself. The payoff came when I could load the entire family into it for a flight to Williamsburg, the famous colonial village in Virginia situated not far from an amusement park called Busch Gardens. After Thomas and Angela, respectively about eight and ten years old, had tried out the kiddie roller coaster with little brother Austin, they kept asking me to ride the real one with them. For about two hours I tried to convince them that it would be more scary than enjoyable, but they persisted. Finally, I thought they needed a lesson heeding parental warnings and concluded that one trip on the Grizzly, the tamest of three major thrill rides in the park, would teach it to them. To my chagrin they loved it! To my shock and amazement, they then begged to try an even wilder ride that began at a dizzying height and descended through a tight coil to the bottom. At such a response from Thomas, who would not have hesitated to jump off a hobbyhorse onto the back of a fast-moving hedgehog, I should not have been surprised. But such a reaction from docile Angela, always circumspect, never daring, caused me to reexamine the space-time continuum in which I thought I was standing. "No, no, no," I cautioned, "that one will make you sick." After they cajoled me to try that one also, they loved it with such wild-eyed enthusiasm that now they wanted to try the Loch Ness Monster, a ride with two loops, inverting each carload of passengers rocketing through them, then repeating its pathway *backward* to the starting point. Even I did not want to ride that one. However, after they had convinced me to experience its low-level aerobatics, they begged to go again as soon as our feet reached the earth!

If you sit in the cockpit of an airplane, you may see what appears for all the world to be two steering wheels. Most aircraft are fully operational from either seat, but that "wheel" before you is the control wheel, or yoke, which operates the ailerons and elevator in flight, and has almost no effect at taxi speeds. It is *not* a steering wheel, and part of lesson one in flight training is spent overcoming the powerful urge to grab this control wheel to steer the airplane on the ground. Taxiing is done with the pedals on most modern aircraft, and I am ashamed to admit I took advantage of this fact to play a little trick on one of my dear friends one day. When we received our clearance to taxi out to the runway at Dulles, I asked Tom Nichols if he would like to steer the airplane. "Well … uh … okay, I guess," he said hesitantly, curling his fingers tentatively around the control wheel. "It's really easy," I assured him, "I will help you if anything goes wrong. Now, when we get to that intersection up ahead, turn right." I already knew that the taxi instructions from the controller required us to turn left, so when I started the airplane left at the intersection, Tom turned the control wheel, slightly at first, then with increasing panic until it was fully deflected to the right. "I thought we wanted to turn right here, Tom," I said calmly, "but that's okay, we can go this way too. Just turn left at the next intersection." Yes, I turned us to the right instead, and Tom turned so red in the face, sure as he was that he was causing us trouble with a machine he could not control, that I did not have the heart to continue my cruel charade and admitted my deceit to him.

If you picked up vibes that Tom might be a little slow-witted, you would have the wrong impression. One Saturday when he was returning from the store with a small bag of groceries, he was accosted by a mugger demanding his money. Thinking quickly, Tom feigned intoxication, stumbling along and slobbering out, "Aw c'mon man, don't steal my wine." The thug ran off without wasting his time rolling a drunk who he assumed would not have much cash anyway. When Tom felt so bad to be duped about taxiing the airplane, I promised, with fingers crossed, never to do that to anyone again. That reminds me of the time one of our vicars saw the organist, Sue Westendorf, practicing late one evening and decided to slither under the pews up to the front of the dark sanctuary where she was and stand up suddenly to startle her. Years later, at a special commemoration of her length of service, this vicar could not be present, but he sent a letter to be read aloud. In it, he recalled this incident, saying that he could not remember if he ever apologized to her, but he wanted her to know he would never do such a thing again—unless, of course, the opportunity presented itself.

John Pors, one of my classmates in the ground school, wanted to buy a new Cessna Skyhawk after we acquired our licenses and had urged me to become his partner. While I was considering his offer, I made the fateful acquaintance of one Fred Tathwell, who was passionate about a sleek two-place T-tail aircraft called a Polliwagen (shaped like a polliwog, powered by a Volkswagen engine) that he could build himself. When he produced his brochures touting features like two hundred knots on less than six gallons of fuel per hour, retractable landing gear, IFR-capable and, best of all, foldable, so that it could be stored on a trailer in the backyard instead of tied down at the airport, I was intrigued. This would be the airplane in which I could train for my instrument rating and fulfill my dream of travel to all sorts of distant places in a fraction of the time to drive, for the same cost. When Joe Alvarez, its designer in California, built a prototype and started selling the blueprints, I decided to join the Experimental Aircraft Association, a support group for those afflicted with a peculiar disease characterized by delusions of building their own aircraft. Soon after I received the initial plans for the Polliwagen, I found myself cashing in the money market account we had started as a college fund for the children for an epoxy pump, yards of fiberglass cloth, polyethylene foam, and many prefabricated parts with complex curves difficult to mold without an elaborate jig. The year-long saga of my battle with Consolidated Freightways (Sharlyn took to calling them Consolidated Frightways) to settle my claim for damaged and missing pieces (which they somehow located on an "empty" trailer many months after they claimed they had been delivered) could well have been the subject of a Sophocles tragedy.

Well aware of the familiar story of the fellow who built a boat in his spare bedroom, but then had to disassemble the house to get it out, I made sure every component could fit through the basement door. When the fuselage was ready to be assembled, neighbors all around gradually became aware of the fool building an airplane in his garage. After I had the wings built, Alvarez announced that he had designed a much stronger and lighter Kevlar I-beam main spar and premolded wing skins, so I shelled out for them and started over building the wings. I was not building a dragonfly, but soon I had four wings. There is an old adage in the industry that when the project is ninety percent complete, only ninety percent remains, but when I estimated that I was approaching fifty percent, disaster struck. Alvarez abruptly declared bankruptcy and moved to Mexico, refusing to answer phone calls or correspondence. Without the complex factory produced landing gear assembly I had intended to purchase from him or at least the plans for building it, I came to a standstill. After languishing for about two years gathering cobwebs, my little Polliwagen asked one day to be given away to another builder more emboldened than I to give it some legs. Having no chance to recover any amount close to the twenty thousand dollars I had invested in the project and fearing the liability I would incur by selling it anyway, I advertised it in Sport Aviation as a freebie. I was delighted when a high school in Arizona offered to take it over as a group enterprise, but when we could not come to terms on the cost of delivery that far, a local aficionado backed his truck into my driveway one day and loaded it up. I never heard anything about it again.

The instrument rating requires forty hours of training, but up to twenty of them can be logged on an approved flight simulator. At last I was approaching the two hundred total hours I needed, so I started instrument ground school at College Park, the oldest airport in the nation, founded by Orville Wright himself. The simulators at this flight school were not motion sensing but were amazingly effective for developing the skills needed to fly the airplane without outside references in various flight conditions. By the time I finished the course, I was quite adept at flying an array of precision and non-precision instrument approaches to minimums at a virtual runway without having spent one minute of time in the air, and the hourly rate of the simulator was a fraction of the cost for rental of an aircraft. Tom Barrett, my instructor at the primary level, was qualified to conduct advanced training, but for an assortment of reasons, I selected Bill Davis for the remainder of my training for the rating. By the spring of 1983, I had the qualifications to fly into clouds. In addition to the enhanced precision and flight skills I acquired in pursuit of this rating, the expanded flight capability and options this afforded me were exponential. It is roughly the aviation equivalent of a master's degree. Though it still imposes limits on the flight conditions into which a wise pilot will venture forth seeking adventure, it is like an insurance policy against stranding a family at Atlantic City airport for three days. Some of the most awesome flights I ever experienced were those in the clouds. As you approach a cloud, it gives you the impression you will slam into a wall, but then as you penetrate the wall harmlessly and punch out the other side, you are seeing formations no one else on earth can see, forming a "landscape" as surreal as the surface of some distant planet. Those of you who remember what an E-ticket ride at Disney World was will understand that this experience could not provide a greater thrill. The first time I saw a rainbow from the air, I was surprised to see a complete circle, not the arch shape so familiar to those ground bound.

With an instrument rating I was far less likely to be grounded by bad weather, so it expanded my range considerably. When Sutherland, my home town in Iowa, announced a celebration of its centennial over Labor Day weekend in 1983, I decided it would be possible not only to attend it, but to proceed from there to Wisconsin to visit Sharlyn's family and still be back in time for the kids to start school, if we were to fly out there. A trip of this scope would not have been possible by car, and would have required a string of several days of clear weather to complete without an instrument rating—not a realistic prospect. We landed in Cherokee and had arranged to rent a car from a Ford dealer in town for the drive up to Sutherland. The football team was playing its homecoming game, so while Sharlyn and I attended the barbecue in the central park, we sent the kids over to the game. When they returned, I asked Angela, who cares nothing about football, which team Sutherland played. "Uh, I think they were the Eagles," she recalled. "The Philadelphia Eagles?" I teased. "I think so," she said, in all seriousness. We had not made reservations for a place to stay for the night, so we will always be grateful to Jerry Magnussen, my good friend and classmate, who approached us and offered to put us up for the night at his farmhouse near Peterson. At the pork chop banquet the next day, each class was served in the order of graduation, starting with the oldest. Since we needed to fly to Wisconsin yet that evening, we asked to join the oldsters and had some interesting conversations with them before we said farewell to the Iowans. We landed in Marshfield late that night, where Evelyn Roehl met us for our stay with them in Spencer. I would never have believed that she would agree to fly in an airplane with me, but the next day we did some sightseeing, viewing their house in Spencer and their farm near Chili from the air. She and Alvin enjoyed it immensely and talked about it long after. We did not know it at the time, but when Sharlyn's aunt and uncle, Millie and Norman Faber, got their rides, it would be the last time we saw Norman, who died of a brain tumor not long after.

As soon as I obtained my instrument rating, Bill Davis told me I would make an excellent flight instructor and urged me to continue with my training. This flattery had nothing to do, of course, with the fact that he wanted to continue his income from me as a student. A prerequisite of the instructor certificate is a commercial license, which requires at least 250 hours of logged flight time. Since I already had two hundred, and the training and practice itself would tally some of the remainder, I decided to pursue the commercial certificate right away. By the time I was ready to start training, Bill had taken a position as the airport manager at Warrenton, Virginia, and would be available for instruction primarily in the evenings. I had joined a flying club at Manassas Airport, about fifteen minutes away from there by air, and had purchased a large block of flight time at a reduced rate, so much of my commercial training was at night—hopping over to pick up Bill, flitting around for a lesson and dropping him off at Warrenton before returning the airplane to Manassas.

One late evening we were high over Leesburg airport practicing chandelles, when a voice came over the radio saying, "Aircraft over Leesburg airport, land and taxi to the south end of the field." Since we were under no obligation to answer this request or comply with it, or even to be tuned to their frequency, we ignored it. At that hour we were the only airplane in the vicinity and at least three thousand feet overhead, well outside of everyone's airspace and noise abatement restrictions, clearly not in violation of any rules. Again came the call, "Aircraft over Leesburg, this is the Loudoun County sheriff. Land immediately." Although this still did not require us to comply, we were more than curious and decided to land as a courtesy. There was the squad car with its lights flashing as an officer approached me, assuming I was the pilot in command when he saw me disembark from the left seat. Bill immediately stepped in front of me and said, "I'm the PIC of this aircraft. What do you want?" Someone had heard the repeated power changes overhead and called the authorities to report an aircraft in trouble trying to land. After Bill explained that the commercial maneuvers have a number of non-routine requirements, the officer told us they simply had an obligation to assure our safety, as he returned to his vehicle and sent us on our way.

The day before my flight test for the commercial ticket, heavy rains in the Washington area caused widespread local flooding. That hardly concerned me until I rounded a curve on Piper Lane, the only way in to Manassas Airport, and found several cars stopped in the roadway. Broad Run, adjacent to the field, is ordinarily a quiet brook that trickles parallel to this narrow access road, but today it had taken its name seriously, overflowing its banks to form Piper Lake. I knew that Everett Noel, my examiner, had flown in and was already waiting for me, and I could see the field a scant quarter mile beyond the flooding. I could also see the airport employees, on their way to work, standing beside their cars at the edge of the water discussing among themselves what they should do about those waves lapping against their tires. After a moment's hesitation I edged past them in my car and foolishly decided to forge into that pond, hoping my wheels hit the bottom before my engine hit the top. In seconds I reached the halfway point, leaving a wake as I dashed for the other side. When I glanced into my rearview mirror, I saw about seven cars suddenly right behind me.

The check ride went well, but when the examiner was completing his paperwork, he noticed that I still had my third-class medical. He told me that as soon as I presented second-class papers from the aviation medical examiner, he could grant the license. A few days later, Noel handed over the temporary certificate still warm from his typewriter and said, "Now you can *charge*!" By an odd coincidence, as I wrote him a check for the exam, the balance in my checkbook was exactly the same as the airplane number. When I mentioned this to the examiner, he replied, "I would run straight over to 7-Eleven and put those numbers on the lottery right now."

This ability to "charge" is quite restricted by regulation, and a commercial pilot must be very careful not to cross the border with illegality. Conducting scheduled airline operations assumes the right to charge passengers for services, of course, but this is governed by an entirely separate section of the federal aviation regulations (FARs), far outside the scope of the section for commercial pilots. Even charter operations, where you approach me to fly you somewhere specific, even if the service is for you alone, are governed by still another section of the FARs not within the rights and privileges I had just added to my credentials. However, if you would like me to tow a banner over the football stadium or skywrite a message to your girl friend, we could transact business, but by far the most common use of the commercial license is for flight instruction. Perhaps the most unusual flight I conducted under my commercial ticket was also the only one on which I intentionally dropped something from the plane—another action carefully governed by regulation. I received a call one day from the wealthy widow of the owner of an upscale Chinese restaurant in downtown Washington, asking me to fulfill his wishes to scatter his ashes over the Atlantic Ocean. She was not willing to ride along, but she pressed her brother into service holding the urn in the seat next to me until we reached the spot over the water he designated, where I opened a window for him to complete his grim assignment.

"Not in a million years would I have been able to land in these conditions," were the exact words of the aerial photographer when we returned to Dulles one day from one of his photo missions. Construction companies, real estate developers and road builders frequently needed an overview of a project for their commercial interests, and I would get a call from one of them every now and then. This particularly day was blustery and cold, and the winds were howling fiercely, so gusty and unpredictable when we approached the runway that the control wheel was a blur as I was attempting to keep the aircraft under control in the turbulent conditions in order to bring us softly back to earth. The landing itself was nothing, however, compared to the dangerous flight conditions to which we were subjected during these photo sorties. Not only were we low and slow (the two words beaten into the heads of every student pilot as the configuration *always* to be avoided), but the aircraft was cross-controlled to "clear the strut," so as to provide a clear field of view to the photographer. We were operating at the ragged edge of disaster, and the slightest miscalculation or misjudgment would put us into an unrecoverable spin in an instant. One day the photographer who called me the most charted our course for Crystal City. The site was so close to National Airport that our circling took us almost directly over the asterisk pattern of their three runways. I was wearing my headset with one earpiece *on* my ear to hear the instructions from a nervous air traffic controller a scant half mile away and the other earpiece *off* my ear to hear the requests of the photographer. Against my better judgment, I reluctantly granted the photographer's demand that I bring us lower … no, lower, *lower*, he kept saying. Now just a few feet above the office buildings, we were in clear violation of a number of minimum altitude restrictions, and I made a pact with God that if neither that controller nor anyone on the ground reported me to the FAA, I would never fly one of these photo missions again. Each of us kept his side of that covenant.

The flight instructor certificate has no minimum number of flight hours required, but it is by far the most difficult to obtain. Because of the awesome responsibility of launching heavy metal into the nation's airspace, the FAA keeps a short leash on its instructors. While most flight testing is turned over to commercial designated examiners, FAA usually retains the examinations of flight instructors for itself, and first-time pass rates are extremely low. In addition to the flight test, in which the applicant must not only perform all the maneuvers in the private and commercial curriculums but demonstrate how they should be taught, the license requires two written exams and an oral so exhaustive that it sometimes extends into a second or third day. Worse, all of the flying most pilots experience up to this point is from the left seat. The instructor must now rewire the reflexes and conditioned responses of the brain to switched hands and cross-eye parallax. My first landing from the right seat was so ugly that I was fortunate Bill Davis had selected a grass airstrip, which was a little more forgiving of the cross controls I was feeding the poor airplane. Landings had become routine for me, but now I was forced to rethink the technique in terms of what the aircraft needed from me instead of the perfunctory psychomotor inputs I had developed before. It was somewhat like looking at an exploded diagram of a landing, in which I could see it taken apart and study its components.

The day of my flight instructor check ride was a brutally cold, windy day in January, and while not every aspect of its two-hour duration was scintillating (particularly one of the commercial maneuvers called a lazy eight), I believe I clinched my certificate in the adverse gusty conditions with an absolutely perfect landing so soft that the examiner commented that he was not sure we had touched down. I had beaten the odds and passed on the first attempt. It was January 19, 1984, and I was actually a flight instructor! While the ink was drying on my brand new instructor certificate, I clearly remember the bifurcated emotion I suddenly felt. On the one hand I was quite proud of my accomplishment and basked in my newfound respect. At this writing, the number of licensed pilots in the nation is about one-half of one percent, and the number of flight instructors is about ten percent of that number. I was now an elite member of a very exclusive group. But at the same time I was staring at a daunting responsibility, and to make matters worse, I was now required, in addition to providing primary training to novice aviators, to conduct recurrent training and remedial instruction to licensed pilots. Suppose (as I feared likely) they knew more than I? Maybe you have taken a course where someone in the class, perhaps you, had more knowledge, insight and experience than the instructor. I was not prepared for the chance of such humiliation and intimidation as a flight instructor and had very little confidence.

While I was wrestling with these thoughts, I was talking with someone at Manassas Airport one day who was telling me about the aviation program sponsored by the Boy Scouts. They had purchased a Cessna 152, maintained by volunteer mechanics, and were in need of volunteer instructors to teach any youth, boy or girl, between the ages of fifteen and nineteen to fly for a nominal cost. This was the answer. Surely none of these kids was more knowledgeable than I, and it would be the perfect opportunity to gain some experience and hone my instructor skills without fear of ridicule. It was the right decision, as I learned more about flying in the first fifty hours than I had in the preceding three hundred—much of it from observing what *not* to do. One day when I was waiting for one of my students, I noticed a woman next to the runway talking on a handheld radio. As I struck up a conversation with her, I learned she was Gerda Ruhnke, the owner of Dulles Air Service, who was talking over the airwaves with one of her students on his first solo flight. I was not trying to impress her, but I had mentioned my involvement in the aviation program with the Scouts, and a few days later I talked with her again as we rode together in the shuttle to the general aviation parking lot at Dulles. She called me a short time after that, asking if I would like to work for her as one of her instructors. Dave Sullivan was still operating Squadron Aviation at Dulles, and when I encountered him one day in the GA terminal, he asked me if I would like to instruct for Squadron. Although I never flew with Dave, he had long held a favorable impression of me and I became aware that both Tom Barrett and Bill Davis lavished high praise for me as a student, so he was hiring me on the basis of this unproven reputation. Perhaps I should have mentioned that I was already instructing for Gerda, but since I did not regard this necessarily as a conflict of interest, I accepted his offer.

Flying out of Dulles was an intimidating experience at first, because I was plunged into the deep water of airline and business aviation operations, forcing me to learn the new language these controllers were using when I was told to "follow the Dash Eight" or "give way to the Gulfstream Three approaching right to left." I thought I was making some progress toward recognizing aircraft types when I heard an airline captain radio the tower to say "be advised, numerous GU-Elevens in the vicinity of one-niner right." GU-Elevens … GU-Elevens. I was racking my brain trying to picture one. Then it hit me. He was creatively warning of the seagulls circling around near runway 19R. I realized how slow I was on the uptake when I recalled that the controller who answered him had understood it at once.

Gerda was from the old country in Germany and had such a distinctive brogue that all of the air traffic controllers in the Washington area recognized her voice immediately, some even greeting her by name. She had a charming radio presence and could request almost anything from ATC and get it from them cheerfully. One day when I stepped off the shuttle to pick up my airplane, Bill Davis came hurrying over to ask whether I had heard about Gerda. It was a bright clear day, and she had departed Dulles with a student on his first flight. As they approached the Warrenton area, their Cessna 152 abruptly disappeared from radar. When I drove to the crash site in a rural area a few days later, I found, still lying on the ground, a number of pieces of the familiar aircraft I had flown several times. A hole about three feet deep in the center of a driveway and scorched trees surrounding it lent grim testimony to the place where the nearly vertical trajectory had impacted so forcefully that the wings compressed to about one third of their original size. Since Gerda was an outstanding pilot, weather was not a factor, and no conceivable mechanical failure could have caused such a catastrophic event, an investigation by several government agencies concluded that the student, whom she had never met before, must have committed suicide by overpowering her and nosing the aircraft straight into the ground. On the cover of the service folder at her memorial I read the words, "God needed another angel, so he selected the very best we had." Such a misguided pronouncement would not have had a modicum of validity even if Gerda were not a self-professed atheist.

Traumatic as it is to lose a good friend, it is also sad when that friend is an airplane. My favorite airplane is the Cessna 210, a six-place aircraft with cantilever wings, that has a reputation for being so powerful that you could pull stumps with it. I was scheduled to fly N6481N one Saturday, when Joe Bogert from the Copyright Office wanted to bring his four children along for a ride. Late Friday night I got a call from the flight school that owned this 210 that it had been due back the preceding day but had not yet returned, so they took the liberty of scheduling me in a Cessna 182RG instead. The 182 has only four seats, so I called Joe early the next morning to alert him that two of the kids would not be able to go. When N6481N had still not returned by Sunday night, search and rescue was called out. The plane had been rented by four men who met up with another planeload of pilots out of Front Royal, Virginia, and the whole group was headed for the Outer Banks of North Carolina for some fishing. The searchers plied the likely routes for about two weeks without success, until a farmer near Fredericksburg discovered the wreckage by smell. The impact was so great that the fuselage augured into the ground some *twelve feet*, and only parts of bodies were found, the largest piece of which was the midsection of one man's torso. I had been flying myself the night this plane went down and recalled the misty conditions, with a cloud deck too low for safe flight underneath it. When I read the details of the flight, there were two facts that in my mind explained it all. First, the pilot was not instrument rated, but second, at the very end of the article I read "before the flight they had gathered with friends for dinner and *drinks* [emphasis added]." This combination is lethal, and if I had to bet, I would put down money that this flight into the scud, flown by a pilot with alcohol in his bloodstream, led to disorientation and total loss of control.

Before I was a certified flight instructor for long, I wanted to add the additional certificate which would give me the capability to train students for their instrument ratings. Sometimes called a "double eye" because of the upgrade of the CFI to CFI-I, this qualification was somewhat easier to attain than the basic flight instructor credential because it required only one written exam, and the searing scrutiny of the initial FAA oral was replaced by one more humanely scaled down. It was almost the last day of 1985 when I flew over to meet the examiner at Montgomery County Airport in Maryland, but I discovered to my chagrin that I had left the official results of the written exam at home. Usually this means that the oral and flight test cannot continue, but when I promised that my wife could bring them before we finished, the examiner agreed to proceed with the test. In response to my urgent call, Sharlyn hurriedly rushed Thomas to the car and made a valiant effort to race through rush hour traffic on a holiday weekend to get this document to me on time. After I was successful in qualifying for the license, Annabelle Fera, the examiner, told me later that she was much more impressed after the exam was underway than when I first arrived. In her experience, she said, someone who forgets required paperwork is a red flag for someone unprepared, and usually the exam does not end favorably. Besides the additional qualification to my aviation career, I added a stroke of credibility to my exhortation to each of my graduating private pilot students to proceed to the instrument rating immediately. Before this, when they would ask whether I could provide this training for them, I would have to admit that I could not.

Sometimes when I wanted to fly a long trip somewhere, I would strike a bargain with a student whom I thought might be interested to accompany me. One year when my high school class was holding a reunion, I asked John McGowan, who was working on his instrument rating with me, if he and his wife would like to join Sharlyn and me, together with nine-year-old Austin, on the long flight back to Iowa. I told John that if he were willing to pay half of the costs, I would not charge him time for the instruction. For him this would be not just a training flight, but experience on an actual flight in real instrument conditions, loggable time in a high-performance retractable-gear airplane and cross country time creditable toward the fifty hours required for his rating. Awaiting them at the other end was an annual air show of model airplanes not far from Cherokee. From there they could rent a car and see the show while Sharlyn and I attended the reunion. Soon after we departed Leesburg in a Cessna 210, I noticed that the big low-voltage warning light directly in front of John was glowing red, but I assumed that since he said nothing about it, the glow was only reflection from the sun over his left shoulder. However, I had always been taught never to assume, and I kick myself all over again each time I think about this, wondering why I did not simply lean over to check it. After several minutes, I began to notice that the radios were mysteriously silent, and then I saw that the navigation radios were red-flagged. We had total electrical failure. Fortunately, we were in absolutely clear conditions, without a cloud in sight. Moments later I spotted the airport at Morgantown, West Virginia, and ordered John to descend directly toward it. Since we could not radio the tower there, we followed standard communication failure procedures, which specified that we circle near the field to attract their attention to send us light signals. As we circled, our passengers were beginning to get sick, when John suddenly said, "I see a green light!" I did not see it, but I told him, "That's our signal to land." The controller who answered the phone when I phoned from the base of the tower asked what the nature of our emergency was. After explaining we were on an IFR flight plan and lost our electrical system, I thanked him for sending us the light signal. "But we didn't send a signal," he said. The only explanation he could offer, when I insisted we had seen it, was sunlight through the green-tinted shades they had pulled to reduce the glare. Our alternator had failed, but because this was Saturday, the local FBO could not find anyone to provide repairs on the weekend. I suggested that we abort our trip and return to Leesburg immediately, while we still had daylight and those perfect visual conditions.

"There are old pilots and bold pilots, but there are no old bold pilots," goes the old adage. Aviation is not inherently dangerous, but it is far less forgiving of mistakes than motoring along on dry land. I was usually quite conservative, but I can recall at least two incidents I am able to describe firsthand only because the grace of God triumphed over undeniable stupidity. The first occurred soon after I became an instructor, when I regarded myself a superior pilot. A superior pilot, according to one definition, is one who uses his superior judgment to avoid a situation where he must use his superior skills. Good judgment comes from experience, goes another adage, but experience comes from bad judgment. Dave Sullivan had asked me to ferry a Cessna 152 to Cincinnati's Lunken Airport for an engine replacement. When I started out in the early afternoon, I knew that a line of thunderstorms stood between me and my planned fuel stop in Clarksburg, but I arrogantly assumed I could penetrate it at some point. Well before I got to the West Virginia border, air traffic controllers confirmed a solid line of convective activity ahead and suggested I divert to Shenandoah Valley Airport. The line of storms preceded me there, however, so they suggested I divert to Hot Springs. When I could not reach that either, they diverted me to Beckley, and finally I was diverted to Bluefield. Lightning was already striking the ground all around me when I touched down at Bluefield, and as I taxied to the terminal, rain and gale conditions raged outside my windows. After an hour or so waiting out the storm, crystal clear conditions prevailed behind the front, so I requested fuel while I planned my route from there to Cincinnati. The lineman who topped off my tanks approached me with a grim countenance and within inches of my face asked, "Do you know how much fuel I put into your tanks? Twenty-five gallons." Since a Cessna 152 holds only 24.5 gallons of useable fuel, I had landed within perhaps a few seconds before engine failure. According to my calculations, I should have had a half hour of fuel remaining, but no explanations that could be offered to explain my miscalculation would have made any difference if God had not spared my life that day.

Dan Morley was a successful businessman who owned two airplanes. One was a beautiful, well-maintained Cessna 172 in which he made a half-hearted attempt to earn his instrument rating. When Jerry Bullock, his primary instructor, a good friend of mine who knew everything there was to know about aircraft and instructing, gave up trying to get him to complete his training, Dan asked me to take over as his instructor. After working with him for a while, I found that we could make progress only to a point, but then I learned why he faltered. Dan had been badly injured in a near-fatal aviation accident some years earlier, while flying in low visibility with his instructor in Illinois, and he could never feel confident flying in less than perfect conditions, especially by himself. One night I got a call from him saying that he was at his beach house in Rehoboth and wanted me to ferry his plane over there early the next morning so that he could fly out for a business meeting. When I obtained a weather forecast, I learned that fog was expected in the morning, but through the night conditions were expected to be clear. It was about eleven that night when I made the decision to fly over before fog in the morning would make landing impossible. At that hour I expected to be the only customer at the general aviation terminal, but at about one o'clock in the morning, while I waited for the shuttle over to Dan's airplane at Dulles, a private jet rolled up to the terminal, and out stepped Ted Kennedy with a beautiful blonde on his arm.

Yes, I knew that Rehoboth was a grass field, difficult to find even in daylight much less at night, that the runway was unlit and that power lines at the approach end made it especially dangerous after dark, but I foolishly determined to have the plane ready for my boss when he needed it. It was a classic accident scenario, nudged along by a mortal disease to which many pilots succumb, called get-there-itis. To my own amazement, I navigated without difficulty to the field by triangulation, and after three passes to assure myself I thought I could do it, I flipped the switch in my mind labeled go-for-it. My landing light picked up the power lines, but when I touched down, I failed to reckon with the dew that rendered braking action on top of the grass almost nil. My landing light picked up the specter of the fence at the far end looming closer, but my brakes were already locked, and I could do no more. Fortunately, I was able to skid to a stop well before the propeller introduced itself to the barbed wire, and I was there at first light to greet Dan and his two sons, who rode uneventfully back to Dulles with us. Again, it was nothing short of pure grace that allowed this to end unremarkably.

Aviation has sometimes been described as long hours of boredom interrupted by brief moments of stark terror. One of my students decided one day to awaken that definition which up to this point had lain dormant within me. After Robert Hahl, a patent attorney, obtained his license, he bought an old 1953 Bonanza C35 and asked me to start him on his instrument rating in it. I told him I had no experience in this model, and I really had serious misgivings when I saw that instead of the dual controls of all training aircraft, this one had a "throwover" control wheel, a single yoke that could be passed between seats by releasing a catch at the base of the assembly. Although I would probably have declined him as a primary student in such an aircraft, Hahl was not only a secondary student but a good pilot, so I allowed myself to be persuaded. Toward the end of his training, we planned an instrument flight using the resources of the IFR system over to Atlantic City one evening. When I checked the weather forecast, I learned that a line of thunderstorms would be moving across our area, but Hahl convinced me that since they were not due until long after we departed, we could stay well ahead of that front. What about the return flight, I asked him. Well, he said, we would be in Atlantic City and could wait it out, returning in the relative safety of the conditions after frontal passage. He kept his plane in a hangar at Hyde Field near Clinton, Maryland, and told me that he had already topped off the tanks, so we should have no delays getting started. However, so many pilots were getting extensive weather briefings from the flight service station because of the approaching storms, that we waited nearly an hour to file our flight plan. Then when we rolled open the doors to the hangar, Hahl discovered that someone had broken in and siphoned off his fuel. Clinton has an auto racetrack nearby, and a certain criminal element had taken to stealing high octane aviation fuel from Hyde and other surrounding airports for their racing machines. So now we were plagued by further delays as Hahl reported this to the authorities and waited for refueling.

By the time we took off, I could already see the billowing clouds to the northwest, and to make matters worse, though our destination was northeast, our initial clearance took us northwest, directly toward those ominous conditions. When I glanced at our route, I noticed that we would be changing course to the northeast in about twenty miles and hoped we could turn the corner before we encountered any adversity. Before we reached that point, however, we entered the clouds and could no longer see the edge of the weather system. I knew immediately we were *in* it. Soon the airplane was pitching and rolling wildly. Ordinarily, I would have taken control, but Hahl had the controls and there was no time to throw them over to me. The best I could do was to *talk* him through what he needed to do to keep the airplane in one piece. As we were in what I would eventually realize was the worst of it, I remember thinking this would not be so bad if only I knew how much *worse* it was going to get. The most severe segment of our ordeal was over after about fifteen minutes, but we were clipping the edge of a thunderstorm, and our rough ride continued until finally we emerged into the clear about five miles from our destination.

The only time I actually had to declare an emergency turned out not to be one. On most airplanes with a Lycoming or Continental engine, oil is added through the dipstick tube. On the Cessna 210 I sometimes flew, however, the filler tube was on top of the engine, while the dipstick was extracted separately through a port on the side of the cowling. One day when I had several passengers waiting for a flight with me, I noticed during the preflight that the oil level of the crankcase was low and asked the lineman to add two quarts. When I returned from the restroom, I saw that he had left the cowling door to the filler tube open, so I closed it and checked to be sure the dipstick showed full. Within less than a minute after takeoff, I saw oil on the lower left corner of the windshield. At first I thought the lineman had spilled a little on the cowling, but then the amount of it began to increase and spread higher up the windshield. We had an oil leak somewhere, and I realized we needed to land immediately before we had a catastrophic engine failure. After declaring an emergency, I landed from the end of the runway at which we had just departed and taxied back to the FBO to assess the damage. By this time the windshield was almost totally covered with oil, and as I stepped out of the plane, I saw that the entire left side of the plane was streaked with a film of brown goo. With trembling fingers I pulled out the dipstick to see how closely we had come to starving the engine and was astonished to find that it still held nine quarts. We had lost only one, but I had just discovered that a little oil can cover a wide area. The lineman had not put the oil filler cap on, and I had not checked it, so oil was splashing out the filler tube and seeping to the outside. After we spent a half hour or so wiping the plane down with paper towels, we jumped back in and began our flight again.

Dave Sullivan called me one day to ask if I would like to have Tinker Bell as a student. When I first met Kim Mason, I realized what he meant. Scarcely five feet tall, weighing all of ninety-five pounds, and cute as a little fairy princess, Kim was also very bright and turned out to be one of the best students I ever had. She not only acquired her license in a very short time, but she went on to earn her instrument rating as well. Some days my schedule was so full that I played Russian roulette with the gas tank of my car (no, no, *never* with the airplane, just my car). On my way to Manassas Airport for a lesson, I was on the freeway one day and I hoped I could make it to the exit, where several choices for gas awaited. Alas, I felt the car sputter and barely managed to coast to the shoulder. Almost immediately a car pulled over and stopped just ahead of me. It was Kim! She had recognized my car and drove me to the exit with the gas can I always carried.

It was on a flight with Kim that I had a supernatural experience one day. One of the requirements for the instrument rating is a long flight in simulated or actual instrument meteorological conditions, using the full IFR system and executing specified approaches at each destination. We were returning from Pennsylvania about two o'clock in the morning, flying in the clear above an undercast, increasingly worried as each weather forecast reported lower ceilings at Manassas, our destination. When we were about twenty miles out, the weather broadcast reported the latest conditions. Kim turned to me with an alarmed look and said, "That's below minimums." While considering our options, I first said a prayer, asking God to send an angel to help us. A few moments later, ATC called to us on the radio, "Traffic eleven o'clock and five miles, *type and altitude unknown*." At night the lights of any aircraft almost directly ahead of us five miles away in a clear sky would have been impossible to miss, yet neither Kim nor I could see it. Then suddenly I understood. It was the angel I requested—and the location reported by the controller was exactly in the direction of Manassas Airport! As we began our approach, the controller, with doubts that we could complete it, intoned, "Cancel with me in the air as soon as you have the field in sight or on the ground as soon as you land. I don't want to call out the state police at this hour of the night." We broke out of the undercast, not only above minimums, but with about three hundred feet to spare.

Although Gerda's vice president, Lynne Clayburgh, attempted to continue the Dulles Air Service flight school in operation after Gerda was killed, she decided to move the enterprise to Maryland's Hagerstown Airport, and my association with her came to an end. About this same time Dave Sullivan became more interested in charter operations than his fixed base operation at Dulles, so as he started his new business at Hagerstown also, he sold his interest in Squadron Aviation to one Dan Stapleton, who was eventually to become a close, lifelong friend. At the instructor's meeting at which Dan was introduced one evening, he expressed concern that our fleet of Cessna 152 trainers had dwindled to only two, and one of them was for sale. When Dan said the owner was moving out of state and did not want to fly it to the west coast with him, I raised my hand to suggest that if all of us at the table would buy it, each share would not cost much, we could lease it back to Squadron, and we would thus not lose our airplane. At the conclusion of the meeting, Lew Miller was the only other instructor who came forward in response to my idea, so Dan, Lew and I became partners in N5448L, a wonderful little airplane we owned for nearly the next twenty years.

After instructing for a while, I began to get students by referral. However, because I was not dependent upon this avocation as the primary source of my income, I could afford to be rather selective with these prospects. One of them was an attractive coed who told me that her schedule was tight and could only fly on Saturdays. Fine. This was the day when I scheduled most of my flights anyway. On the beautiful summer day we were scheduled for her first lesson, she called to cancel because she was sick. When she arrived, appearing somewhat disheveled, for her lesson the next Saturday, she explained that she had been up most of the night and had been vomiting just before she drove to the airport. On the third Saturday she arrived late, explaining that she had just driven a couple of hours from the beach in order to keep our appointment. The beach, huh? Vomiting, huh? Suddenly a mental image appeared—a party animal who thought this kind of wild lifestyle would somehow dovetail seamlessly with aviation. "I'll tell you what," I told her calmly, "we're getting a late start today, but after getting up so early and making your long drive, you are probably not in the right frame of mind for a flight lesson anyway. The fact is, I don't think I can handle you in my schedule right now. Let me give you the name of another instructor, who can probably serve your needs much better than I …."

One day at Dulles, when I had a gap between students, I noticed a man sitting at one of the tables in the lobby staring at his aeronautical chart. When he saw my flight bag, he asked whether I was an instructor. His instructor was supposed to meet him to plan a flight but never showed up, so I offered to conduct a training session with him until my student arrived. He was very pleased with the assistance I gave him, and when I refused his offer to pay me, he told me he had just purchased a Cessna 152 so his daughter could learn to fly and asked me to be her instructor. This young lady was married to a contractor who had a very successful business installing swimming pools and who owned a Beech Bonanza A36. The husband was very interested in her progress, and when he dropped her off for a lesson, he frequently talked with me at some length about his own aviation experiences. He flew his Bonanza in all sorts of flight conditions, so I assumed he had his instrument rating. When I learned he did not, I cautioned him about the legal danger he was courting and offered to take him through the instrument training. Each time we were scheduled for a lesson, however, he found some excuse to cancel. Gradually I found out the reason. He was absolutely terrified at the prospect of the written exam because he had never learned to read. Although I had an obligation to turn him over to the authorities for his abuse of the system, I was so impressed by his flying skills each time he took me along in the Bonanza that I did not have the heart to follow through by blowing the whistle. After his wife got her license, she announced that the Cessna 152 was for sale, and Dan Stapleton jumped on the opportunity to add it to his fleet.

When I first started flying out of Dulles, it was a sleepy airport so far out from the metropolis that in those early days it was not unusual for us, while still twenty miles away, to be cleared to land. Once characterized as a white elephant, Dulles steadily increased the number of its scheduled flights and hub activity each year until Squadron was eventually compelled to shuttle over to one or another of several satellite airports for training. One day when we announced our destination as Manassas, the air traffic controller responded immediately, "Manassas is reporting level five thunderstorm activity. Say intentions." In that case, we will go to Leesburg instead, we told him. Indeed a tornado struck the airport, snapping tiedown ropes, splattering fuel and battery acid indiscriminately and intermingling aircraft aluminum with tin from hangar roofs. By the grace of God, N47105, the Cessna 152 owned by the Scouts, had been flown out earlier that day on a long cross country flight by a student who was prevented from returning to Manassas because of the adverse conditions. Unaware of this, I found local authorities standing guard when I arrived to check on our aircraft. They were there to prevent looters and to take precautions against the possibility that a careless spark would ignite flammable fluids trickling everywhere. When I picked my way through the rubble with a flashlight to our usual tiedown spot, I found another aircraft upside down in our space. Had that student been able to return before the storm struck, our plane would surely have been crushed and destroyed. Not long after that, the Scout leaders asked me to a meeting to discuss a number of administrative issues about the aviation program, not the least of which was the cost of continuing it. I immediately suggested they lease the plane to Squadron, which would take over the maintenance and provide revenue to offset their costs. Instead, they leaped at the opportunity to sell it to Dan Stapleton, and Dan gleefully added another trainer to his fleet.

I came to know most of the service personnel by name as well as the employees at the Signature service counter of the general aviation terminal at Dulles, but I was always careful to greet one of them, Jack Bolen, with "Hello, Jack," never "Hi, Jack" whenever I walked through the terminal and waved to him. One Saturday, as I was talking with Jack while waiting for my student to arrive, a man walked up to the counter to ask how he could rent an airplane. Although Signature provided fuel and many amenities to a variety of private and business aircraft, their services did not include aircraft rentals or flight instruction. Jack turned to me. The man introduced himself as Dave Abramson, claiming to be a pilot who had last flown many years ago and now needed to attend the funeral for the mother of his ex-wife in Allentown on Tuesday. His logbook had been lost for quite some time, and as I gleaned more facts of his hiatus, I told him that in my experience it seemed doubtful we would be able to turn over the keys to him by Tuesday. He explained that he was a physician with a tight agenda and could not spare the time required by the scheduled airlines to return home, and then he asked me to fly up there with him. His flying skills were so poor that I was skeptical he ever had a license, especially in setting up for landing, but by the time we returned to Dulles, he was so enamored by the flight that he wanted to start work on his instrument rating immediately with me.

While we worked toward his rating, he called me frequently to fly with him to Newark, to Providence, to Columbus and a few other cities in order for him to testify as an expert witness at trials involving neonatology, his specialty. While he was in court, I usually sat with the airplane, planning the return trip, supervising the refueling and filing our flight plans. On the flight to Newark, I took him aside when he returned from the trial to warn him that when he paid the fuel bill they would be adding a landing fee of $147. Expecting him to be nonplussed by that, I was not prepared for the disdain on his face when he responded, "So?" Once when I accepted his offer to sit in the spectators' gallery at the Providence proceeding, the opposing counsel, attempting to influence the jury, asked Abramson's annual salary. Dave explained he had several offices in Washington and New York and estimated it was about two million dollars a year. It was after we had landed at Columbus for him to give his testimony that I came out of the restroom as Abramson was coming out of the *other* one. Startled, I glanced back and saw that instead of words, only restroom symbols were painted on the doors, and I realized with mortification that I had misread them. Fortunately for me, I was the only occupant and avoided being labeled a pervert.

This reminds me of the tale Ken Medley, a DPE (designated pilot examiner), told us on himself at one of the flight instructor refresher clinics he was conducting. Medley was a raconteur with such a spellbinding delivery that we instructors could listen tirelessly to accounts drawn from the rich trove of his experiences conducting check rides and oral examinations. As he was often sought after as the featured speaker at Air Safety Foundation presentations and aviation seminars, a woman approached him on one occasion to ask whether he gets nervous before he gives a speech. "No, not really," Medley began. "After so many years I suppose I have gotten quite used to it." "Well, are you particularly nervous *tonight*?" the woman pressed further. "No, I don't think so," responded Medley. "Well then," continued the woman, "what are you doing in the ladies' room?"

On the last evening before his instrument check ride, Abramson wanted to go over to Culpeper Airport to practice some non-precision approaches with me one more time. A fast-moving cold front was on its way from the west, but it was not due to arrive until well after we would be back at Dulles. Although clouds are often invisible at night, I was quite sure I caught a glimpse of wispy clouds *below* us on the flight to Culpeper. This was not a good sign. On our return to Dulles, we requested the closest runway from our position southwest of the field, so the controller assigned us the instrument landing system (ILS) approach to runway 12, landing to the southeast. Abramson leafed through his book of approach plates and found the one for our runway. A few minutes later the controller told us the vertical guidance component known as the glideslope was inoperative to that runway and said, "Turn left heading 360 [magnetic north], expect the ILS to runway 19R instead." Abramson leafed through his book again and started to set up for 19R. Since our parking area was closest to 19L, however, I requested that runway instead, and the controller radioed, "Expect the ILS to 19L." Abramson had just flipped to this third approach plate when I noticed that all the lights at Dulles, clearly visible moments before, suddenly went out. I realized in an instant that we had penetrated a cloud. We were flying under visual flight rules, and since continuing in these instrument meteorological conditions would be illegal, I asked the controller if he could handle us IFR. His exact words were, "Oh no, you make a 180 and fly back out, and then we'll talk about IFR." Abramson turned us immediately to the south, and as soon as we were in the clear, the controller said, "You are cleared to Dulles, turn right heading 360, expect the ILS to 19L."

In a few minutes, when we were in the soup again headed north, we started to encounter significant turbulence. Moments later the controller told us, "Weather is changing rapidly at Dulles, we're switching to a north operation; turn left heading 190, maintain 3000 feet, expect the approach to 1R." As Abramson struggled mightily with the turbulence, he lost control in the turn, and in just a few seconds we lost a thousand feet of altitude. I grabbed the plane away from him, climbed back to altitude and steadied it up before I turned it back over to him. Since he had his hands full just to keep the plane sunny side up, he was too busy to look up yet another approach plate, so I found it for him and placed it on his lap. The weather system was causing diversions to Dulles, and a few minutes later, the controller told us, "Numerous inbounds into 1R, turn left heading 090, and expect the ILS/DME now to 1L." This was November, so after I leafed to this latest approach plate, I pulled out my flashlight and ran its beam along the leading edge of the wing checking for icing. "Oh God, no, not ice too," screamed Abramson, terrified. There was none. At that time Dulles had only five precision approaches, but very few pilots could say they had been cleared to all five on the same flight. After we landed Abramson, sweating profusely, turned to me and said, "I am so grateful you were here. If I had been by myself, I would have had to declare an emergency." "Why?" I asked him. "Because I … was … *scared*," he sobbed.

Had this incident occurred one day later, after Abramson had his instrument rating, he *would* have been by himself, and his flight would probably not have ended so favorably. Abramson's wife, Bonnie Nelson Schwartz, was quite glamorous and attractive, making a name for herself as a kind of impresario of local stage productions, even acquiring the rights to produce the music for the 1992 Olympics. After she had accompanied us on several flights, Abramson asked me one day to start her towards her license. We had been flying a Cessna 172 each time she came along in the rear seat, so after she flew her introductory flight in a Cessna 152, she found it too confining and preferred to learn in the larger plane, even though we flew with an empty seat behind us. One day her husband asked if he could fill it and ride along on her lesson. Still in her early stages of learning, she was all over the sky, and Dave could not believe that I calmly allowed her to put the airplane in such attitudes without grabbing it away from her. He forgot that he was watching a picture of himself at the same point in his development. Not long after that, they bought a factory-new Beech Bonanza A36, loaded with features and approaching a price tag of a half million dollars. This particular model was known as "the doctor killer" because only someone like a doctor could afford it, yet their busy schedules prevent them from retaining proficiency and currency in such a sleek complex aircraft. After we transitioned Bonnie into it, they flew together all over the country in that airplane, and although Bonnie experienced many hours in it and became quite proficient flying it, none of her time with Dave was loggable, so unfortunately by the time she received her license a year later, they had sold the plane.

That flight with Dave Abramson in which he might have ended up dead by himself was reminiscent of the flight I had with Brian Jett, a young man whose apt name gave testimony to his excellent skills as a pilot. Part of the curriculum at the primary level is to fly under the hood to simulate inadvertent cloud penetration, but if a pilot were to incur these conditions live, this minimal amount of training is intended to provide only the skill to turn around and fly out. The University of Illinois once put non-instrument-rated pilots on simulators to learn how long they might survive if they tried to continue flight after losing visual contact with the ground and concluded that their average lifespan was 178 seconds. Brian had been under the hood with me many times and was so adept at flying on instruments that on one of the last flights we scheduled before his check ride I was quite sure he would shatter any such average. On the evening we were planning to practice landings at Manassas, the ceilings were steadily coming down, so I asked Brian whether he might be interested to find out what it was like to fly into an actual cloud. We filed an instrument flight plan to Dulles, and our clearance after takeoff was to turn right directly to a navigational signal called Casanova VOR. In seconds after we punched into the overcast, the airplane was in a steep spiral to the left. By himself Brian would have been dead in about five seconds. I could not believe my eyes. For me, the first time I flew into a cloud with my instructor during instrument training, I clearly remember wondering what the mystique was all about—the technique was all the same. But I had always heard that there is a huge psychological difference between simulated conditions, where the pilot knows in his mind that he may lift the hood at any moment, and real conditions, in which this safety net does not exist, and here before me was graphic proof that such was the case.

One of my best students was actually my son Thomas. As a little kid already he was what I would call an expert on his tricycle. Those skinny little legs were a blur as he pedaled toward a curve in the sidewalk one day, and as I watched from a distance I knew he was going to be skinned up from the inevitable spill I could see coming. To my amazement, however, I witnessed the inside wheel of the tricycle lifting slightly as he rounded the turn and roared on past the curve. He knew the exact limits of his vehicle, and I always thought he had the dexterity, reflexes and natural aptitude to be a credit to the armed forces one day as one of their best pilots. After he had his license, my sister Ruth came to town with her three young boys, and after we spent one morning canoeing with them on the canal parallel to the Potomac, I suggested we drive out to the airport for some rides in our plane. When I overheard David and Christopher arguing about who was going to ride first, I told them the one who would ride first is the one who proved to be the *nicest*. Immediately little conniving Christopher said, "David, wouldn't it be really nice if you let *me* go first?"

After we finished our rides with a few circuits over the field, I asked Thomas, who had ridden out with us, whether he would like to take it once around the traffic pattern just for the practice. While he was preparing to go, I noticed that the sky was darkening to the southwest, and before I realized this was a bad idea, Thomas had begun his long taxi to the runway. I had taught him never to be in a hurry to take off, so I watched nervously as he methodically ran through the runup procedures endlessly. I could see heavy rain falling from the clouds in the distance, but when I started to run out to the runway to stop him, I saw him start his takeoff roll. Before he finished his climbout, the rain was already reaching the far end of the runway, where he would be coming back to land. Foolishly having left my handheld radio at home, I frantically went from airplane to airplane tied down, trying to find one unlocked to radio him not to land from that direction. Too late, I saw him turn the base leg at the south end to land and moments later he *disappeared*! "I just killed my son," I kept thinking over and over. As I feverishly searched my mind trying to remember if I taught him what he should do in such conditions, we all dashed for cover under the wing of a nearby plane as the system now began dumping rain on our location. Never had I prayed so desperately, and then by some miracle I saw him emerge from the soup and land. When he taxied up to shut down moments later, I ran through the downpour to see if he was all right. A typical teenager, he responded to my wild-eyed questions with, "What?" Perhaps he had no idea how miraculously God had just spared his life.

This was not the only instance in which I nearly sent Thomas to destruction in that airplane. Worse, the next time it happened, Austin was along with him, when I put both of their lives at risk. Across the highway from Orange County Airport was a little tavern widely known for its great hamburgers, so one Sunday afternoon I proposed that Thomas and Austin fly over to sample them while Sharlyn and I drove over to meet the boys there. The ceilings at Manassas were about three thousand feet, and the weather at Orange was not much better, but it was a very short flight with low terrain, so I determined that should give them enough room below the overcast in which to maneuver. I was wrong. About halfway there I gradually became aware that the ceilings were much lower than first reported. When I heard a small plane flying very low overhead, I was terrified that Thomas was trapped in it. This time I had my handheld radio along, so I stopped the car and called to him. No answer. When we got to Orange a short while later, I found that the ceilings were so low it would have been impossible for them to land, so we started back, stopping with heavy heart every few minutes to radio them. Thinking perhaps my radio was too weak when we got no response, I drove to the office of the FBO at Culpeper Airport to use their powerful signal, but still there was no response. Frantic with worry, we raced back to Manassas. The relief we felt when we saw our plane sitting there on the ground with the doors open and two Mountain Dew soda cans resting on the instrument panel cannot be described in words. In a few minutes two young aviators came strolling back to the plane, where Thomas related that they had actually tried to fly over, but when he saw the poor conditions, he got cold wings and decided to return. We commended him profusely for one of the wisest decisions he ever made.

My sister Ruth was Thomas's godparent, so we saw them as often as possible, despite the fact that they never lived very close—unless you consider Papua New Guinea close. Her husband Bob Riedel was a pastor and accepted a call as a missionary for eight long years to the island, where two little boys eventually joined them. Most of their travel around the island was by small airplane, so David, their oldest, knew all about "a'plane" and "popeller" from a tender age. Tiny as he was, he could distinguish between Mission Aviation's single-engine Cessna circling the airstrip for landing and an arriving twin-engine commercial aircraft just from the pitch of the engine sound. One day when a shipment of Western items arrived at the little trade store on the other side of the seminary campus where they lived at the time, Ruth wanted to buy some onions before they sold out. As she walked the path with little David in tow, she told him to remind her to buy onions when they reached the store. Every few minutes Ruth asked him, "Now what do we need to buy at the store?" "Onions." As they walked among the produce and goods, Ruth asked, "David, what did we need to remember to buy?" "Onions." When they laid their groceries on the counter at checkout, Ruth said to David, "Tell the man what we want." "Cookies," said David.

Once when they came to visit us, I asked Bob how it was going. "Well, I can't seem to stop gaining weight," he replied, rubbing his stretched shirt. Indeed his middle resembled a beach ball, to the point that our boys disrespectfully invented the saying, "We need a Bob in every pot, but not a pot on every Bob." "Oh, really?" I said in response, "Well, here's how you do it. Set yourself a goal to lose one pound a week and step on the scale every Saturday morning. At that rate you will lose the weight safely, and it gives your body the time to adjust so that it will not go into 'starvation mode.' In a year you will lose *fifty* pounds. Now, when you find that you are hungry between meals, you tell yourself this is exactly what should happen. It means your plan is working. You will need the willpower to resist a snack right then, because your body will adjust to that too and soon those pangs will go away. The key to the whole plan is to *eat less*." I wish I could tell you it worked for Bob.

When several of the college kids in our church were accepted into Virginia Tech one year, they found few options for worship in and around town, so the congregation decided to institute a campus ministry for them. The success of this venture was due at least in part to the flights I donated, fortunate as we were to have a wonderful airport adjacent to the campus. By car, Blacksburg is at least four hours away, depending upon success avoiding police radar, but by plane it was less than two. The pastor and vicar could leave at midday on a Sunday, conduct a communion service for the students, take some time for supper with them and still return by evening the same day, thus avoiding the overnight stay which would realistically have been necessary at the hands of all but the riskiest of drivers. On one trip the only plane available was a Piper 140, known as a Cruiser, which I had not flown before. Our pastor was six feet six, nearly three hundred pounds, and the vicar was not small, so we had a full load with just the three of us. According to my calculations we were not overweight, but I could not explain why the plane seemed so sluggish on the flight down. When we were loading for our return flight home, I topped off the tanks as usual, but our daughter Angela, who had her car down there, had two spare tires for it and asked me to bring one of them back with us, so I loaded it aboard. On the takeoff roll the plane seemed so sluggish that I wondered whether it was going to lift off. Just as I was ready to abort the takeoff, it lifted feebly and climbed slowly but steadily between two peaks near the departure end of the runway. It was only when we got back that I realized what the problem was. Unbeknownst to me, this plane was equipped with long-range fuel tanks, and when they were full, we were carrying far more weight than I had calculated when I computed our weight and balance. Shame on me for not knowing that before we left. Had we not had smooth air in both directions, the excessive load on the airframe could well have been disastrous, especially with a spare tire the plane could not even use.

One day a student named G. Richard Little came to me saying he had his license but had not flown for nearly twenty years. I did not realize it at the time, but this man was to become one of my best friends—albeit indirectly leading me to my only aviation accident. Before we started any air work, I wanted to see whether he could remember how to land. He not only could not, but he could barely control the airplane in a straight line or a level attitude. After about three circuits of the traffic pattern, however, it seemed as if someone turned on a switch in his brain, and we both discovered that a real pilot lay underneath that thick layer of rust and tarnish on his gray matter. Rich went on to get his instrument rating with me and subsequently answered an ad to partner with two owners of a Piper Dakota. After the Dakota was sold and the partnership dissolved, Rich made the acquaintance of my friend Elwyn "Bit" Fretwell, an instructor at Manassas airport, who convinced Rich to pursue advanced training there, so he eventually went on to be an instructor.

While Rich was working on his instrument rating with me, one of our training flights took us to Chesterfield Airport near Richmond. Soon after we landed, a young man stepped out of the airplane next to us and walked over to me with his open sectional chart trailing behind him, to ask me if I could show him on it where he was. At first I thought this was some kind of joke, but when I took a second look at his ashen face, I realized in a flash he was a student pilot who had become lost. After I showed him on the chart where he had landed, I asked him what his destination was. Accomack County, he told me—a small airfield near the tip of the Delmarva peninsula. "Did you file a flight plan?" I asked him. When he nodded, I said, "Run! Don't walk! *Run* to the phone. Close out your flight plan and tell flight service you have landed safely. If they haven't already initiated search and rescue for you, you are a very fortunate young man." He had departed from Cape May on a beautiful clear day attempting a cross country flight that could not have been easier to complete. As soon as he saw ocean to his left and land to his right, all he had to do was keep it that way until he reached Accomack. Instead, he had somehow turned inland, flew for over an hour beyond his ETA, violated the airspace of busy class C Richmond Airport and landed some *eighty-five miles* off course.

One of Rich Little's co-owners of the Dakota with him was Richard Sugarman, a mortgage foreclosure lawyer, who, in response to Rich's lavish praise of me as an instructor, frequently asked me to conduct recurrent training or accompany him on a flight somewhere. Sugarman's skills as a pilot were passable, but I observed several bad habits I was trying to break with him. Ultimately it was greed that kept us in contact, for if it were not for the handsome stipend he paid me for my services, I should have refused to maintain a professional relationship at all. My biggest problem with him was getting his attention. While I was reviewing the details of an approach plate with him, he would be glancing over a brief from his office; while I was rehearsing a list of emergency procedures, he was organizing a stack of papers. "Yeah, yeah, I'm listening," he would say, but he was not. On April 27, 1994, when all government offices were closed for a national day of mourning at the funeral of Richard Nixon, Sugarman called to ask whether I wanted to take advantage of my day off to fly with him. He was not legally current and needed a flight review. It was a fateful decision when I met him at Dulles, where he and his two partners kept their Arrow.

Although I had many hours in an Arrow, I had not flown this one. I noticed as we started the takeoff roll for our flight to Leesburg that my seat suddenly slipped to the full aft position. After this problem caused a number of accidents in various Cessna models, FAA issued an airworthiness directive to inspect the seat tracks of them at least every year, but I was not aware that any problems had been reported in Pipers. Since Sugarman was at the controls for the takeoff, this slippage was uneventful, so I readjusted my seat, thinking it was probably my fault for not locking it into place properly. However, it happened again without warning when we were practicing stalls, and I realized there was clearly a malfunction. For the remainder of the flight this was in the back of my mind, wary as I was that it could recur at any moment. On every flight review various emergency procedures are reviewed, so we were practicing simulated engine failure from the traffic pattern. When Sugarman was having difficulty reaching the runway after several attempts, I handed him the checklist and offered to demonstrate the proper procedure for him. Throughout the approach I mentally rehearsed my reaction in case that seat slipped out of place again, but I was able to maintain my concentration and guided the airplane perfectly to the runway. "You did it!" Sugarman exclaimed, as if I had just reached the summit of the Matterhorn. Moments later, I heard a scraping sound, the propeller stopped turning and we skidded a short distance before the plane came to a grinding halt in the center of the runway. In a breach of self-discipline, I had allowed that faulty seat to become a distraction and had forgotten to lower the landing gear!

Gear-up landings rarely cause any injury, unless, of course, wallet, career, reputation, and credibility are taken into account. Immediately I recalled the old saw which divides retractable-gear pilots into two camps: "Those who have and those who will," and my vow to myself that this would never happen to *me* also came ruefully to mind instantly as I realized I became another grim statistic. The first words out of Sugarman's mouth were, "Well, I'm sure glad it was *your* fault." Did I mention he was a lawyer? There is also a whimsical question that circulates around the hangar asking what the first thing a pilot does when he lands gear up? Answer: put the gear handle down [in an attempt to avert any suspicion of pilot error in the ensuing investigation]. Like many accidents, this one was life-altering in a moment, and I was soon to discover how far-reaching the consequences were. For one thing, we had departed from Dulles, so I had to call Angela to drive out to Leesburg to pick us up and return us to our cars. Although at least two airplanes landed over the top of us on the remaining runway, the airport was officially closed until the wreckage could be removed. Two tow trucks had to be summoned to lift the fuselage from each end enough for someone to manually extend the landing gear, and then it could be rolled, not dragged, to the shop. Besides the obvious damage to the lights, antennas, skin of the belly and to the propeller blades that struck the asphalt, the sudden stoppage of the engine can cause a broken crankshaft and other internal damage which must be carefully inspected by disassembling the engine. The accident was such a severe psychological blow that I could think of nothing else day after day, as I played out the sequence of events over and over in my mind, agonizing anew over each *if, whatif* and *ifonly*. When Sugarman called the day after the accident to say he had found another plane and wanted to schedule again, I told him my credibility as an instructor was in shambles and I was seriously thinking of quitting. "Oh, no," he replied, "You're the best there is." If only such a remark were coming from someone I could trust. After the insurance company paid for the repairs, they tried to subrogate the claim for nearly fifteen thousand dollars to me, as the pilot in command at fault in the accident. In response, I argued that at most I was only twenty-five percent liable. For one thing, if Sugarman had been paying attention when we discussed the procedure, I would not have been the one performing the maneuver. Also, part of the protocol was to follow the checklist, which he had in his hand. And what about the partnership, which must have known that anyone who flew from the right seat was at risk for an accident? Barring improper maintenance or damage to the seat by the owners, the manufacturer itself had some measure of liability for its seat design. When I summed up these offsetting factors, gulped really hard and mailed a check for one-fourth of the bill, I never heard from them again.

My problems from the accident were not over just because I had paid the bill, however. When the FAA heard about it, I got a call from the Flight Standards District Office one day, informing me that a certified letter was coming my way. If you ever receive a stern official reprimand with such phrases as "it has come to our attention that …" or "you are hereby directed to …" or "if you fail to show cause …," it probably means the government is rather displeased with something you did. I was being ordered to surrender my license or submit to a flight test with one of their examiners under section 609 of the aviation regulations. Usually I was the third party in these "609 rides," as they were known in the industry, the instructor who prepared some unfortunate miscreant for his moment in the sun with the FAA. One that comes to mind was a pompous senatorial aide (who shall remain nameless) who mishandled the winds at Tangier Island and landed in the bulrushes. Now the spotlight was aimed toward me, so I decided to engage the services of Tom Oneta, a former FAA examiner, as my mentor to prepare for my trial by ordeal. Under section 609 the FAA may require any pilot to demonstrate his right to hold his certificate, usually for cause, but it could be for any reason or no reason, somewhat the aviation equivalent of an IRS tax audit. When I asked Oneta whether FAA was persuaded by mitigating circumstances, he told me their primary concern was contrition. If they sniff any arrogance or recalcitrance, he warned, they will respond with a high hand, so when John Brown met me for our showdown, I was apologetic, submissive and receptive to his suggestions. When he asked me how it happened, I told him it was my fault for not following the checklist. "You don't even need a checklist," he insisted and forced me to fly the entire flight without one. I retained my license. Ironically, Brown had a dirty little secret, and he was not aware that I knew he was not lily white himself. In his official capacity with the FAA, he had rented a plane from Squadron Aviation a short time before this, flew around for several hours in it and landed at Manassas Airport to use the restroom. While he was taxiing out to the runway to take off, he ran out of fuel (a clear violation of more than one regulation), thus preserved by the grace of God from certain disaster.

With some misgivings about my own competence, I eventually went back into instructing again, and as enough time passed, the gnawing regrets I harbored for several years eventually faded from consciousness. One day Jose Andrade, a student from Spain who had flown his first solo, came to me to ask if I would take over his instruction. His primary instructor, he told me, yelled at him whenever he made a mistake, and he wanted to change. Some words in Spanish soften hard consonants, so when Jose radioed to clearance delivery that we were flying to Frederick Airport, he pronounced it Frerick. The controller said, "What is your destination?" "Frerick," said Jose again. "Still didn't catch it, what is the identifier?" came the voice at the other end. "F ... D ... K, Frerick," repeated Jose. "Oh, Frederick," said the controller. Jose turned to me and said, "Isn't that what I said?" "Sounded like it to me," I replied.

On our flights from Dulles, I usually scheduled the airplane for a three-hour block to allow plenty of time for delays at an increasingly busy airport. No one, especially I, embraces someone who brings the plane back late, eating into the precious minutes allocated for a flight, whether to beat approaching weather or to cram into a lesson all of the material required for an upcoming check ride. The usual excuse I would hear was, "Well, we got the plane late ourselves." Not an excuse, I would always say. It was the responsibility of my students to call in to schedule the plane, and each of them knew to call me if the time slot agreed upon between us was not available. As a lesson progressed one day, I asked my student to confirm that we had the plane scheduled until two o'clock—an allocation of three hours, but the point at which I asked the question would have allowed us to return in two hours, if necessary. When we got back, Jack Bolen called to me from the service counter to say someone had been looking for me but had just left. When I asked what he wanted, Jack said he was hopping mad because we were an hour late returning the airplane. I checked the schedule and learned that indeed my student had reserved only two hours, not three, so I called this pilot to apologize. He was a Navy commander whom I had never met, but within three seconds after I identified myself, he launched into a tirade that lasted for ten minutes. After his rant trailed off, I said, "I know exactly how you feel. Although I rarely do this to anyone myself, it happens to me all the time, and I don't like it either. Again, I apologize, and if there is any way I can make it up to you, I will." This set him off again, and I could not stop him for several minutes. This time I said, "Let me ask you something. Do you normally get this upset over something so insignificant?" This produced such a rage from him that each time I walk into the general aviation terminal I still hear it reverberating. Perhaps you can hear it where you are.

As Dulles became busier, we noticed that the air traffic controllers started to suffer hearing loss. Whenever we wanted to transition back in for landing after a flight lesson, no one could hear our radio calls, and this malady seemed to affect all controllers on all frequencies. From their perspective it was equipment failure, as the radios on all of our planes in the fleet were becoming weak. Sometimes when they answered, it was "Calling Dulles, stand by" or "Expect a thirty-minute delay." One day I was number one for takeoff with my student when the controller asked us to give way to the 747 behind us. After we taxied over to the runup block as requested, I politely asked why. The exact words of the female voice came back, "Because he is carrying more passengers than you, he is burning more fuel than you, and he is on a time schedule." This is clearly illegal. Dulles is a federally funded airport, which makes preferential treatment except for emergencies prohibited by law. The next day we were on the phone to the tower chief, who said he would review the tapes and get back to us. When he had not called back for several days, we rang his number again. "I listened to the recordings from an hour before you said this happened until an hour after, and I not only did not hear the conversation you allege, but I did not hear the voice of any female controller," he stated. Clearly, he was lying—or someone got to the tapes before he did. In any case it offered an insight into the mindset of the controllers. They were supposed to be operationally neutral, yet they were clearly biased against us. We were worse than a nuisance to them.

One day I was with a student on his first cross-country flight, where the dead reckoning we practice requires a direct climb to cruise altitude and an immediate turn to course. Instead of turning us on course and granting our request to climb over the Bull Run Mountains west of Dulles, however, the controller took us five miles south to clear Dulles airspace and turned us loose. Because we were too low to clear the ridge safely from there and because we were far off course, I radioed back requesting clearance to transition through the terminal control area. The controller denied it, saying simply, "I said 'Frequency change approved.' Good day." He left us in an awkward position at a hazardous altitude and forced us to remain below Dulles airspace and improvise our way out of danger. This was even worse than the fact that the whole point of our lesson was ruined, as ATC was teaching us its own lesson from a different podium. The entire air traffic control system exists as a service to pilots to promote safety to the public. I recognized the voice on the radio, an experienced controller who clearly did not understand his job. If that student pilot had been at the controls by himself, an accident might well have been traceable not to the system but to the warped understanding of it by that one individual in the tower. Finally, Dan Stapleton had enough of these shenanigans and threw in the towel. We moved our operation to Leesburg.

Dan called me one day to ask whether I had any experience with handicapped students. Handicapped? How? He gave me the phone number of one of the most remarkable students I ever had—Jeff Parker, whom I would soon discover to be not only one of the brightest, but one of the most level-headed and competent as well. Though he and his wife Gail have since moved to Illinois, Sharlyn and I remain good friends with them to this day. Jeff had been in an automobile accident twenty years earlier and had lost the use of his legs. This did not deter him from pursuing his dream to become a licensed pilot, however, and after researching the requirements, he came to us at Squadron because we had the Piper Arrow II he needed to accommodate the hand control device he purchased. He carried a socket wrench in his flight bag, and while he conducted the preflight before each lesson, I affixed the hand controls.

Jeff then eased himself onto the wing and pulled himself into the left seat while I folded and stowed his wheelchair. After he acquired his license, he asked me if I thought he could obtain his instrument rating. In my experience, I told Jeff, about eighty percent of flying an airplane on instruments is a mind game, and because his mental capacity was not found in his legs, I saw no reason he should not pursue the rating. Annabelle Fera, the examiner who administered the check ride later called me to say he had impressed her very much and extended her congratulations to both of us. Jeff turned out to be such a competent pilot that he subsequently purchased his own beautiful Arrow—which no longer would require him to install and uninstall the hand controls with each flight.

Long after he was burned out from the struggle to run a flight school for many years, Dan had been trying to sell his interest in Squadron Aviation and finally found a buyer. By the time Congressional Air swooped in to absorb Squadron into its existing enterprise at Gaithersburg, Dan had expanded his operations to Manassas and Winchester. Because Av-Ed Aviation was firmly established as the reigning fixed base operator at Leesburg and occupied the tin-roof terminal where Century Aviation had been years earlier, Squadron, and now Congressional, was relegated to an office trailer in the weeds behind the building. Although that tall grass may have been a contributing factor, the demise of Congressional after the transition was due in no small measure to the mismanagement of its operations. Instructors left for Av-Ed next door in droves. I was almost one of them, as I had already interviewed with Don Robb, the owner, and sat through his orientation class for new instructors. But I took compassion on Monty, the owner of Congressional, when I realized the effect this drain of his instructors would have on his business and decided to remain loyal to him on principle. The new office manager, one Lee Revell, called me one day to say that one of the students in the instrument ground school I was conducting was falling behind and wanted to know what I was doing about it. I asked him what he *expected* me to do. When he replied that it goes without saying that I should work with him outside of class, I asked who was going to pay me. Since Congressional was paying me less than ten dollars an hour and I was driving almost two hours through rush hour traffic to get to class as it was, I was not receptive to his notion that I was expected to do this as part of what I was paid for the course. But if the student were willing to pay my private rate for ground time, I would be willing to tutor him, I said. When he replied that that was not consistent with company policy, I reiterated that at the outset of the course I warn the class that the course is very intensive, that they must devote hours of time outside of class for reading and study, and that they will certainly fall quickly behind if they expect to keep up with the enormous amount of material if they come to class unprepared. Then I promptly resigned—with three weeks remaining in the course. Six months later Congressional was out of business.

Since our Cessna 152, N5448L, was now being leased to Aviation Adventures in Manassas, I followed it down there and started instructing for their flight school. When the town of Leesburg announced one day that it was erecting a palatial new terminal building, Av-Ed was forced to move into the office trailer once occupied by Congressional Air, and Aviation Adventures decided to expand its operation to Leesburg to compete head to head with them in a second trailer, insisting on a share of the office space in the new terminal when it was completed. Aviation Adventures fancied itself the premier flight school of the area, establishing a covenant with the manufacturer to become a Cessna Pilot Center and aggressively soliciting owners of expensive new aircraft fitted with the latest avionics, virtual instrumentation and satellite navigation systems. In addition, Cessna 152 models such as ours with old analog "steam gauge" instruments were increasingly being passed over as training aircraft in favor of much more expensive Cessna 172 models and sleek new composite aircraft manufactured by Diamond, so we began to notice that revenues from N5448L were falling off sharply. When my partners, Dan and Lew, wanted to sell it while a market still existed, I tried to persuade them that the answer was to convince the flight school that it should point to our plane as the least expensive in the fleet and therefore the cheapest route to a license. My argument was to acquire the basic flying skills inexpensively first, then upgrade to sophisticated equipment at the end, in one additional lesson. AvAd ignored my pitch, and eventually I and my students were the only ones still flying our plane.

One day in spring, when I arrived to fly it, I discovered idleness had allowed a pair of starlings to take up residence on top of the battery. After I removed all of their nesting materials and tore up their lease, I tied down in a different parking space, but they were back by the next weekend with two eggs in the nest on their battery mattress. I removed the nest carefully and laid it over on the grass, but when I tied down after our flight, both of the parents came strutting boldly toward us, each with a straw in its beak. When I found *three* eggs the following weekend, I stuffed rags into every orifice and laid a rubber snake on top of the battery box for good measure. This time I found droppings around every one of my rags as they tried to claw their way in, but they were finally able to read my "occupied" sign and decided to give up.

Dan and Lew were becoming insistent that we sell N5448L before it was time to shell out the ten to twelve thousand for engine replacement again. Reluctantly, I agreed, bidding a tearful farewell to a faithful companion that had served us well, including at least three trips Sharlyn and I had made to Iowa. No longer with a fiduciary connection to Aviation Adventures, I nevertheless continued my association with them as an instructor, but I began to weary of the obsession of its management with revenue. At the instructor meetings we were being berated for not charging enough ground time with each flight, and the collusion in schemes to beat the competition that was expected of us pushed me too close to the business aspects of aviation, where I was not comfortable. Schemes against competitors were one thing, but against our own customers, clients and students, they were another matter. When a student completed his curriculum and was ready for the flight test, the chief pilots insisted on a costly series of review flights to assure the student would pass on the first attempt—not for the welfare of the student but for the advertising value the company could claim.

One day I was asked to take over the student of another instructor who was moving up to the airlines. When I looked over his logbook, I noted that he had over sixteen hours logged. When any of my students has that much time, they have usually already flown solo or are very close, but this fellow had no solo time logged. On our first flight together, I was shocked to learn that although he had been flying from the outset at a tower-controlled airport, he had never used the radio and did not know how. He could not hold an altitude within 300 feet or a heading within thirty degrees. When I asked him to perform maneuvers from the Practical Test Standards that I saw listed in his logbook, he had no idea what the specifications were. Then I realized what was happening. His instructor had been bilking him with "fun" flights in place of legitimate instruction and stretching out the hours to increase revenue. The poor student did not know the difference. When we landed after our first lesson, the student said, "I want to thank you." For what, I wanted to know. "You are a *fantastic* instructor," he began. "I learned more in this one hour than I ever learned before, and also I want to thank you for not cursing throughout the lesson." I was not so fantastic; he was simply getting from me the standard fare that every scrupulous instructor ought to be providing. I sent word to Bob Hepp, the owner, that

I would need to take a leave of absence for a while because someone needed my help with a disabled child. It was the truth, but it was not the real reason I never spoke to him again.

I might be inclined to join those critics who point to the hours of time I spent instructing, over the years. There were several months when Samantha "Sam" Picard, the office manager at Squadron told me I had logged more hours than some of the full-time instructors. Many Saturdays it was approaching midnight when I dragged home after as many as five lessons, yet when I realized that Austin had mowed five lawns that same day and made more money than I, it made me wonder if what I was doing made any sense. It is fair to say I put myself at considerably more risk than he each time I strapped into an airplane, but the percentages were in my favor, and teaching people to fly was immensely gratifying. I once compared the statistics for an accident with a flight instructor aboard to fatalities on the nation's highways and calculated that statistically it would be safer for a student to fly with me from Washington to Chicago than for him to commute from Dale City. As for the money, I was determined to earn back all I had lost on my failed Polliwagen project, and as it turns out, I was not only able to do that, but also to pay for all of Angela's orthodontics, a work-study project in Europe and Asia for each of my children, a college car for each of them at Virginia Tech, and a number of other essentials we would not have been able to afford otherwise. In one sense the time away from family was reinvested and returned to the family in other ways.

Nowhere in the world, including Canada, Mexico, Australia or Europe can someone fly with the freedoms that we have in America. In fact, many pilots from other countries come here to learn to fly because of the extreme hardships in their own homelands. Yet, new rules and internal strife are threatening to destroy the fabric of which the magic world of flying, as I have known it, is woven. After the attacks of 9/11, the face of all aviation, including general aviation, changed drastically, especially the fifty-mile radius around Washington in which my students and I fly. Although by the grace of God I still have health good enough to maintain my medical status, I continue to read the literature to stay current, and I am occasionally persuaded by Don Robb from Av-Ed to teach the ground schools, most of my aviation career is now largely symbolic. One thing never seems to change—the image of aviation by the general public, and I often find myself in a position to correct some concept or other that persists in the mind of someone who has no experience. Small airports of the nation are closing at the rate of twenty-five per day, largely due to ignorance of local communities unaware of their value or to the greed of developers who do not care. Highway accidents are so commonplace that those which earn a place in newsprint appear on the back page, but it is actually a testimonial to the tiny percentage of aviation accidents that they are the lead story on the six o'clock news. I discover each time an aviation accident makes the news, however, what a sock in the eye we endure as I suffer through the inaccuracies and misconceptions that get reported, not as news but as sensationalism.

# ADP

Not Austin David Pullmann. When I told Martha Arnott, one of my colleagues at the Office, that was the name of our youngest son, she laughed, immediately leveling the accusation that only someone in automation would select a name with the initials ADP. At the time I branched into a technical support position at the Copyright Office, automation was exploding into every facet of our lives. Positions for automated data processing (ADP) began filling the pages of the Sunday classifieds, and ADP was on the mind and lips of every executive in the business world. A few years earlier I had intentionally steered away from this field, as I mentioned, but now it seemed there was no way to avoid it. In all the years I worked with software developers, I had the impression that computer programming was an obscure specialty, an arcane science of black arts best left to the alchemists who I always saw hunched over their flowcharts. Then one day I started a course in library school that allowed me to push aside the curtains to peer inside, and I was not only astonished at the revelation I saw, but it changed my life forever.

I found most of the courses in the library science curriculum to be little more than tedium to be endured for the sake of the credential that came dropping out of the slot at the end. One that was particularly memorable was a mandatory core course called Technical Services, taught by an old-school professor named Mathilda Rovelstadt, who subscribed to the medieval German tradition of scholarship, where only a tiny percentage of the best were allowed to advance. "I am a tough grrraderrr" were the very first words out of her mouth. "You get a B frrrom me, zat is a gud grrrade," she warned, raising her finger. True to her word, the class of nearly a hundred students yielded two A's. I was not one of them. The midterm and final exams were perhaps more fitting for entrance into Heidelberg, and I felt fortunate to pull down a B for the course. One of the electives in the course catalog was called library automation, and by the grace of God I signed up for this course that was to alter my career. We were taught the rudiments of a computer language called Beginner's All-purpose Symbolic Instruction Code (BASIC) and asked to write simple programs using this incredible language that could talk to a machine, telling it what to do. Each week of the semester a new project was assigned, and I could scarcely wait for the next one. The final project was to take a list of titles as input and print the list again, sorted alphabetically. I had so much fun with this that I even built into my routine an algorithm to handle the nettlesome problem of a title beginning with "The" to assure it would not sort under T. One of my classmates, Francine Liem, struggled throughout the course and could not believe I actually enjoyed these assignments that represented such torture to her. I helped her with some of her projects and spent hours on the final one to enable her to meet the deadline, but she never really understood what was going on. Francine was a cataloger at the Library and for years after that, whenever I saw her in the corridor, she would roll her eyes and give me a disgusted look that testified wordlessly to the repressed pain she felt anew each time she saw me.

As soon as I finished my comprehensive exams and collected a sheepskin that read M.S. in Library Science, I remembered the masonry course I took through the Fairfax County Adult Education program and looked through the course catalog for computer courses. The name of one language I saw everywhere was COBOL, an acronym for Common Business-Oriented Language, so I signed up to take it. This course did not measure up to the excellent standard I had come to expect from the experts who had taught me to lay bricks, so I decided to explore an educational program run by the U.S. Department of Agriculture for its computer courses. While it did not offer degrees, this informal university issued certificates of accomplishment in a wide range of disciplines, including computer programming, so I decided to sign up for COBOL again. This one was much better, so I decided to try a language called P/L I next, taught by Charles Tobin, one of the best instructors I have ever had in any school anywhere. I loved his course so much that when I saw his name in the catalog for JCL, the job control language used on large mainframe computers, I signed up for that too. Many programmers in those days were versed in Assembler, a complex low-level language tailored to large IBM computers. Various high-level language compilers were also being developed at computer science labs and universities, one of the most powerful of which was C, with its capability to exploit addresses in memory. In fact, C was invented at Bell Labs in 1978 for use by an operating system called Unix to run telephone equipment and was later adopted by Jet Propulsion Laboratory to control rockets. Here I really found a challenge, exploring its rich trove of functions and commands to make the computer perform an endless variety of tasks. It was so much fun that I could hardly wait for each new assignment.

These computer courses were offered in downtown Washington, so I walked over from the office to school two nights each week for a couple of years until I fulfilled the requirements for my certificate. Since our children were old enough by then to be left alone briefly, the plan was usually for Sharlyn to pick me up at the exit to the university building after class. This was intended to be an opportunity for her to relate the domestic events of her day on the ride home and an opportunity for me to vent about something that may have occurred at the office that day. It was this arrangement, however, that often brought to the fore our polarized concept of timetables. No, to be brutally frank, I would have to say it exposed our diametric natures. One of Sharlyn's most admirable qualities is her unflappable calm in a crisis, yet it is paradoxically this same trait that arouses my hostility to the point where I am not only flappable but flapping. The down side of someone who is never excitable is that, well, they are never excitable. *Hurry* and *punctuality* are not words that register with such a person. "The world operates on a *schedule*", I find myself fuming over and over into ether that has no listeners. Stewing every Sunday as we depart late for church yet again, I find myself asking Sharlyn the same facetious question whether she intends to ride with me or run along behind. So how is it that *I* am the one criticized—for wild driving in my desperate attempt to make up for our late start? I have often told her I hope I never get bit by a snake if she is the only person to run for help. This does remind me of a story about two soldiers on patrol in Vietnam. One of them gets an urgent call from Mother Nature, so the other tells him to squat behind a nearby tree. As he does, a snake lurking in the weeds strikes him directly in the anus. His buddy waiting over on the trail hears the shriek and tells him to lie down right there while he runs to the nearest ranger station to fetch the medic. Too busy to leave the infirmary, the medic tells the soldier he can treat the wound himself. "Just cut an X across each fang mark with your Army knife," he instructs, "then put your mouth directly over the site and suck out the poison." When the soldier returns, he finds his buddy writhing in agony, screaming, "What did he say? What did he say!" "Doc says you're going to die," answered the soldier.

"The Lord God said unto the serpent, '… and I will put enmity between thee and the woman ….'" God is really addressing Satan in this Scriptural reference, but Sharlyn and Angela seemed to overcome the innate ancient aversion to these reptiles one day when a large black snake became entangled in the mesh covering our blueberry bush. After watching it struggle for several minutes, they decided to contravene their primordial instincts to avoid it and to render assistance instead. One ran for the scissors, while the other stood ready to pull the mesh away from the reptile as each piece was snipped. Now oozing a milky white musk, apparently produced either by its distress or by a nick of the scissors, the snake seemed to understand they were trying to help and stopped wriggling while they hacked away at the cords of the mesh. At last it was free and lay totally exhausted for several minutes without moving. Moved by pity for their eternal enemy, Sharlyn and Angela walked away to leave it in peace. When they returned to check on their patient several minutes later, it had slithered away.

Both of my parents were dynamos from a long line of type A personalities, whose energy, ambition and work ethic would rival Alexander the Great or Genghis Khan. I have watched John Gimbel literally *run* from task to task all day long on the farm. My mother's prodigious productivity was legendary, leaving many of her associates in wonderment at the mountain-sized gross domestic product she was able to generate routinely. I am not sure whether this is a genetic trait among the Germanic people or whether it came about from the necessities of Depression and hardship, but such is the character of many people in the Midwest. If Hurricane Katrina that devastated New Orleans had struck South Dakota, Iowa or Nebraska instead, say some in my family, everyone would get busy cleaning up the mess, and by now everything would be rebuilt. There would be none of this standing around months and years later whining and waiting for "the government" to come in to help. Many in my father's generation never trusted the government anyway, and besides, they would say, did we not learn in school that we *are* the government? If there is one mantra from the lips of both parents I can still hear ringing in my ears from childhood, it would be "Get busy!" But the down side of all that drive and productivity is the juggernaut syndrome. My father's brother Carl ascribes to the Pullmanns the term "eighteen wheelers." "Lead, follow, or get out of the way," reads a bumper sticker I saw once, and that could well be the maxim on the Pullmann coat of arms. My father was once naming off which of his sisters had inherited this trait he was calling the "Pullmann spirit." "But Dad," I interjected, "I am not so sure that is something you should be proud of. They are domineering, create strife by bossing everyone around, including their husbands, and have no patience with anyone moving at a slower pace than they." After spending a few days with us one year, my sister Ruth observed Sharlyn's modus operandi around the house and remarked to me, "She's not a Pullmann, is she?" This is by no means an inference of laziness. Sharlyn works tirelessly all day to compile a list of accomplishments at least as long as my own, but while I lie exhausted, collapsed into a heap of lifeless bones, she still plods along pulling her dray for several more hours.

So when I came dragging out of that USDA classroom at ten o'clock dog-tired from a full day at the office followed by three hours of schoolwork, the only thing left in my head was a desperate longing to get home. As soon as I saw that Sharlyn was not at the curb waiting, though, my mind would begin to race. Sometimes I would finish down the street at the building where the computer lab was located, so I would then suspect that she was waiting there for me instead. After waiting for five minutes, then ten, I would trudge over to the lab, watching every car that came past, in case she *had* been waiting and concluded I was at the classroom instead and was in transit *there*. Not seeing the car here either, I would begin to fume as I picked up the pace back over to the classroom, again watching every car for her. Still no sign of a car that resembled ours. Then I would start to speculate and worry. Was she confused about whether I would be taking the bus? Did she forget which night this is? Surely she could not be this late unless she had an accident. What if one of the children is in the hospital, and she has no way to reach me? Finally, a half hour late, Sharlyn would drive up. Because there is not a mean, spiteful or hurtful fiber in her being, she was not intentionally arousing my ire. Just the opposite, she was late ironically because she was so *selfless* and was not even conscious she was causing any distress! After putting the kids down, she took the time to fix a sandwich and heat up a pan of soup for me, but then she was hurt when I was so furious I could not even enjoy it. If this were an isolated incident, it would be easily forgivable and forgettable. But the following week we would conduct the same drill all over again. In all the years since, I have never been successful to get her to look at time through the same pair of glasses with me. This reminds me of the businessman who, while driving through Arkansas, sees a farmer carrying a pig into the orchard. After the pig is allowed to eat the fallen apples for a few minutes, the farmer carries it back to the pen and brings another one to scavenge for apples on the ground. Observing him carry one pig after another into the orchard in this manner for a while, the businessman approaches the farmer and says, "Wouldn't it save a lot of time to let all the pigs into the orchard at once?" Musing over that for a few minutes, the farmer drawls, "But what's time to a pig?"

Some time after the Cataloging Division had an automated cataloging system to handle materials received under the new copyright law, the Office requested the Automated Systems Office to expand this system to include an accounting routine to replace the manual process in use. When claims were received for cataloging, they were sorted by registration class and logged into a paper register. Clerks in each section bundled the work into packets for an individual cataloger, administered the distribution for processing, logged it out of the register when completed and dispatched the materials for storage. When ASO received the request to automate this manual operation, they informed the Office it would be several months before any of their systems analysts would be available to work on it. In the meantime the Technical Support Section, where I was working, had acquired a personal computer, one of the most revolutionary innovations of any age, putting into the hands of ordinary office workers greater power than a mainframe but with much more versatility. It was the beginning of the end for unwieldy central processors and opened the market for an explosion of software products, including a database management package called dBase III.

I was playing around with dBase one day, and as I looked through its documentation, I discovered that it had its own programming language. This meant that it was not only a static repository for data, but it could be made interactive, so that a user could be prompted to interface with the data without having to know anything about dBase itself. This was intriguing, and I wanted to exploit it. The software itself was written in C, and I could identify certain C functions underlying the dBase language shining through here and there, so I soon found myself building a little system which did most of the tasks we had requested ASO to do for us. It was not my intention to steal this role away from them; I was merely applying techniques from the dBase manual to a practical application, and this little system came out. For some reason that reminds me of what Aaron said to Moses, "I cast it [the gold] into the fire, and there came out this calf." I do not know what ASO's might have been called or what tasks it would have performed, but mine simply logged material in and out, so I dubbed it the Log-in/Log-out System (LILOS). At first the Division ran it in parallel with the manual system to be sure it had the capabilities everyone wanted, but to my great surprise, the day came when they were not only using it, but *depending* upon it. When I noticed that the clerks spent many hours writing up a cover card for each bundle by hand, I got the idea that since all of the data was already in the computer, we could hook up an impact printer to the PC and let the computer print each card. Better yet, if the card stock could be printed on continuous form tractor feed stock, the clerks could print them in batches instead of dropping them into the platen one by one. About a year later ASO came back to us, offering to start on that project to automate the logging operation we had requested. Raoul LeMat, assistant chief of the Division, told them thanks, but we already had what we needed. I felt like a prince.

Whenever I needed advice or assistance with some difficulty, I found that my friend Bob Kline was not only light years ahead of me in his comprehension of everything in the field of automation, but he was always incredibly willing to help. Best of all, he was a superb mentor and a great teacher who could explain a thorny concept in clear terms—except when I was too dense to comprehend it. One day when a certain operation in LILOS had been chugging away for three hours, Bob suggested that we install a clone product called FoxBase using the same structure, commands and functions as dBase. I doubted his claim that it was ten times as fast as dBase, but when we purchased and loaded a copy of it, we ran that same algorithm that had dragged me down earlier and found that it finished in about fifteen minutes—*more* than ten times as fast. Ever curious, Bob looked at my program code and told me he thought he could rewrite the functionality directly in C and reduce that time even more. When we plugged in his patch the next day, the same task finished in about twenty seconds!

When I noticed the clerks in the Documents Unit typing up certificates one day, I got the idea this could be much more efficient if it were automated. When they finished processing a transfer, affidavit, mortgage or security agreement related to a copyright that was submitted to the Office, the legal document was returned to the remitter along with a cover letter and an official certificate attesting the facts of recordation. No erasures were permitted on these certificates, so even when the clerk had a good day, a considerable amount of certificate stock was torn up and wasted. LILOS was working so well in FoxBase that this time I did set out intentionally to develop a parallel database to track all the documents received in the Office, and once this data was captured, it was not only searchable but could be manipulated in various ways. I called my new system DocLog, which the clerks used to print certificates error-free in large batches. Names and addresses of recurrent remitters could also be retained on file, so that the cover letters could be generated error-free as well, without the need to retype the entire name and address of the same parties over and over.

For nearly a hundred years the Copyright Office maintained a card catalog of items submitted for registration and recordation. If a user discovered an error in the CCC, however slight, the Office was mandated to correct it. Those of us in Tech Support fielded these requests for correction, physically typed up correction cards and sent them down for refiling. Since these replacement cards themselves had to be error-free, correction chalk was used liberally, or time-consuming erasures were made to produce them. One day I decided to apply what I learned in my C programming class to develop a little routine for entering the data at a PC, so errors could be corrected electronically, and the data could be thrown into fields on the screen without the need for manual formatting. In the process I was enlightened anew by what every scholar since Socrates discovers sooner or later—that a huge gulf exists between classroom theory and practical application. It is one thing to take a class in laying bricks, quite another to build a fireplace. The only real way to learn a discipline is to apply and exercise it. My little cataloging system was crude, employing the escape sequences (command codes) of a device driver known as ansi.sys in the DOS operating system to control the PC keyboard and display, but it worked quite well. We could thread pin-feed card stock through an impact printer and print out corrected cards at a considerably faster rate than before.

This prototype led to a more ambitious project a short time later. Bear with me while I explain the background for you. The Copyright Act of 1976 (the new copyright law I told you about before) allowed, for the first time, a novel concept in the registration process. Large foreign publishers, especially, were interested in registering their works in the United States market, but they were reluctant to pay the fees for such a large volume of materials, so section 407 of the law struck a compromise for them. Since the Library was interested in their scholarly publications and wanted to encourage their submissions, this provision allowed a remitter to deposit a copy without a fee. Although the copyright owner was not entitled to statutory remedies under the law, the Office would maintain a file of these deposits as evidence that a copyright existed. In exchange for this service for which the Office incurred an expense but was not compensated, the law also contained a clause by which the Library could *demand* that a work be deposited, even from a publisher who was otherwise unwilling to register *or* deposit a copy. Also because it was not a fee service, the cataloging of the deposits was intentionally excluded from the cataloging system already operating on the mainframe. At first the volume under this new legislation was light, so a small cadre of catalogers was able to type up entries on library cards and file them. To minimize workload, these records had only two access points—the title of the work and the depositor (no authors, publishers or subjects), so the catalogers typed on a multicolor carbon pack. Each error had to be erased, chalked or blotted with fluid not only on the top card where the error was struck, but also on the carbon copy underneath.

Esther Cashion had been the prodigious spearhead of this project for the first few years, so when she retired, the glue that held the operation together dissolved, and the remaining technicians were unable to keep up, either with the cataloging or the filing of the cards. When a huge backlog resulted, the Office enlisted those of us in Tech Support to address it and solicited additional volunteers from among the catalogers to assist. As I overheard the cursing at those unwieldy carbon packs, I got the idea to develop a little interface with the PC that would allow the user to create the record at the computer, making all corrections on screen until the catalog entry was complete, then push a function key to type the card at the printer. This was very well received by the catalogers, who could set aside their typewriters, bottles of colored correction fluid, erasers and chalk. However, now a backlog of unfiled cards began to develop until a table was stacked with piles of them eighteen inches high. That gave me an idea for a more ambitious project. Instead of throwing away the data after it was printed, why not save it into a database, eliminating the need for cards altogether? And why not enhance the cataloger interface, breaking the data into fields, employing format recognition and error checking? There were several obstacles to this approach, however, the most obvious of which was the collection of the data. Although local area networks were beginning to appear in the business world, none were yet in existence anywhere in the Library. I did not realize that the solution I found for that problem was already widespread in the industry and had even acquired the pejorative name Sneakernet—where the administrator puts on his sneakers to run around collecting the data captured on floppy disks and to transport it manually to the central repository for loading to the database.

That was the easy part. Setting up a searchable database in C was far beyond anything I had attempted before, so I found a book on database administration. When I read of an ingenious indexing algorithm called a B-tree, I asked Bob Kline whether he had ever heard of it. Not only was he well aware of it, but he had built one himself, and he pointed me to some third party shareware that I could purchase, which would handle the indexing for me. In a few weeks I had a self-contained system for input, storage, retrieval, maintenance and statistics for all of the Copyright Office deposits that was ready for beta testing. I called it DEPOSICS, and when Laila Mulgaokar, the chief of the Acquisitions Division for whom the system was designed, saw what it would do for her operation, she thought I was some kind of wizard.

Because some of the maintenance operations of my systems were easier when all the users were off their computers, I requested an office key from Raoul LeMat, assistant chief of the Cataloging Division, so that I could come in on Saturdays. I was not asking for overtime, just permission to come in on my own time to work for an hour or two. When he forwarded my petition to the Admin Office downstairs, however, Mike Pew, the operations officer not only denied the request but ordered Raoul to "soft pedal" these maverick projects I was doing. Such software efforts belonged within the purview of CAG, the Copyright Automation Group, he said, and no one from that organization had authorized such activity. Instead, Raoul gave me his own key and invited me to attend the next meeting of the section heads, where he reviewed what Pew had said and asked them what would happen if we pulled the plug on LILOS, DocLog, OldCards and DEPOSICS. When they testified that returning to the manual methods used earlier was unthinkable, Raoul said, "We're going to 'soft pedal' this to the metal." The irony! Only a few years earlier, he had tried to get rid of me when I stood on principle as a supervisor, and now *he* was the one standing firm on his convictions. I had to admire his courage for defying his supervisors, risking disciplinary action *himself* by his insubordination to support me. Of course, I believed he made the right decision, but then again I still believed *I* had as a supervisor too.

Before long, the Library purchased a local area network called Banyan, named for a tree in the East Indies that propagates by sending shoots from its branches to the ground to form new trunks. When FoxBase issued a new version that supported networks, I purchased a copy and gained some experience with multi-user technology. Although LILOS ran considerably slower on the server than it did on a single host, the clerks were willing to accept that as a tradeoff for having the software on their individual machines instead of the single, centrally located workstation they all shared before. This little network was a novel idea in the industry, and I wanted to exploit it further. When dBase had first appeared, an examiner named Phil Gill purchased a copy and set up a database with it in each of his sections to help track referrals, the polite term for registrations returned to the Examining Division for correction. When Phil unexpectedly died, I was asked to take over the administration of his databases. I soon discovered that Phil knew nothing of programming and was requiring his clerks to perform complex operations with commands to manipulate the raw tables of dBase directly. Since most of these referrals came from Cataloging, where they had been accounted for by LILOS, I needed to reconcile the two sets of data anyway, so I built an interactive system for the Examining Division clerks in FoxBase and networked the operation to benefit both divisions.

For some time I had been musing over another idea that I considered a timesaver for the Office. Suppose that instead of, or perhaps in addition to, a paper application, which had been a requirement of registration for at least fifty years, the remitter could send the information to us already in digital format. The cataloging time would be reduced by a significant margin because the information would not need to be transcribed from the paper copy by a cataloger; instead, the remitter would have already done that work for us, so that we could import it into a catalog entry without any keying. Although errors in transcription would be eliminated, the cataloging operation would still serve a useful function to apply style rules and correct the inevitable orthographic errors that would occur. According to my plan, a remitter requesting a paper application would also be mailed a diskette, which would already be loaded with my program soliciting the particulars of registration. When received in the Office, the diskette would be checked for viruses and uploaded to the cataloging system—yes, a new system which would somehow need to interface with the massive COPICS database of twelve million records on the mainframe. Because I could envision a number of detractors to such a scheme, from the general counsel to the Admin Office to systems office administrators, I decided to develop a prototype in secret, so that I could produce a proof of concept when it was time to sell my idea. Several weeks later I had a workable model that I hoped to demonstrate to Mike Burke, the chief of CAG. When I invited him to my office to discuss my idea with him, however, he dropped a bombshell I had not anticipated. The Office already had plans for electronic registration, not only for the application, but for the work itself, using digital signatures. I lost my nerve even to mention to Mike the software I had been developing and quietly put it aside. Undoubtedly my concept for interacting with the public would never take wing, but perhaps the module for populating the cataloger screen, with the power of word processing techniques and error checking, would one day serve a useful purpose, so I continued to refine it.

Instead of developing its electronic registration system in-house, the Copyright Office contracted this effort to CNRI, a software house that dispatched a team of some of the most competent developers I had ever encountered. Public/private key technology was emerging as an industry standard for validating digital signatures, and Dave Ely, the project leader, spent several months applying it to the emerging new system the Office called CORDS. As the Cataloging Division representative to the CORDS task force, I marveled at the complexity of the requirements set by the general counsel to satisfy the copyright law and secure the data, and I was glad I never had to address that. As the model grew into a megastructure, the cataloging module always appeared on it as a circle labeled Cataloging. When discussion actually reached that circle one day, Ely listened to the requirements and, looking intently at Mike Burke, told us that would add several more months to the project. "Suppose," I began softly, surprised to hear my own voice actually venturing to speak, "I could tell you it already exists. I have developed a prototype that has all of the features we discussed and more, and if you can plug it into your code and pass control to it, you could check that task off your list." Mike whirled his head around to me and with an astonished expression asked for a demonstration. "However," I continued, "my module only *collects* the data. It must still be exported to the database on the mainframe. I would need to work with ITS [Information Technology Services] to convert it to EBCDIC and map it to emulate a COPICS record." Mike could scarcely believe his eyes when he saw my demonstration later, and asked me what I had named it. Since I did not want to mention any connection to its original purpose, I said it had no name. He suggested we call it CORCATS and eagerly handed over my source code to Ely for incorporation into CORDS.

One day I was looking at the job postings and noticed one for a systems analyst in CAG, but I was not sure I should apply for it because I was not by any means unhappy where I was. On the contrary, I was enjoying the respect and appreciation of my division chief, his assistant and my wonderful supervisor, Gloria Ayers, who rewarded me with an outstanding performance rating year after year, and her words of acknowledgment of my accomplishments were genuine. Best of all, I had found the end of the rainbow. I liked my work so much that I could actually make the rare comment that I could hardly wait to get back to work each Monday, while feeling a certain disappointment that the week was ending when Friday approached. Yet, I realized much of the technical work I was performing belonged with the automation group, so when Raoul LeMat gave me a veiled order to submit my application, I complied. When Mike Burke, the selecting officer, told me in the interview that his systems analysts do not write software, I realized I did not want the job. For me, that was the source of all the fun, so afterward I told Raoul I was inclined to withdraw my application. Before I could act on this position, however, Raoul went straight to Mike's office. I did not know it at the time, but I was at the top of the applicant list, and when Raoul told Mike I that was withdrawing, Mike made the historic decision to modify his long-held position. Raoul then told me he had talked with Mike and asked me to reconsider my decision. A few weeks later, on my first day with CAG, Mike told me the full story, adding that he was broadening his policy to include whatever programming might be of benefit to his office. Little did he realize the extent to which that fateful decision would affect the Office one day in the future. More on that later.

I suppose it was the old German builder locked deep inside my genetic code that made system development so appealing to me, but whatever it was, it was immensely gratifying. When I worked with Lafayette Johnson in ITS, the Library's systems office, to merge those CORDS records into COPICS, I got the idea that the principles in its cataloging module could be applied across the board to a stand-alone version benefiting the whole cataloging operation. By now, all of the dumb terminals in the Cataloging Division had been replaced with IBM PS2 computers, which used token ring technology instead of dedicated wiring to connect to the mainframe. But it also meant these same users could now connect to the Banyan network, so I developed CORCATS as a data input system for them as an alternative to COPICS. It was during beta testing of this system by a select group of volunteer catalogers, however, that I made a mistake of such magnitude that I feared the plug would be pulled on all of my work and I would be issued walking papers. Each Friday my maintenance routines reviewed the records input for the week and divided them into two groups—those more than a week old that were ready for upload to COPICS and those less than a week old that needed to form the nucleus of the new week. Did you detect a flaw in this logic? What about those records that were *exactly* a week old? Although I had asked each of my testers to keep all of their materials at their desks until we were sure a record for it appeared in COPICS, the *implication* was that they would check their records each Monday morning before dispatching the materials. They, on the other hand, assumed *I* was checking this and after several weeks elapsed, someone noticed that all records that had been done on a Friday were missing. Since no one remembers every piece of work done yesterday, much less several weeks back, it was a horrible mess that was eventually resolved only after several weeks of backtracking. Although the users of CORCATS never wanted to go back to the relatively featureless world of COPICS, my credibility was subzero in the minds of one or two of the section heads, who forbade their staff to use this piece of junk. One had such fierce opposition to me and my work that she launched into a fiery exchange with upper management in a concerted effort to stamp all of it out. None of us knew at the time the crucial role that CORCATS and some of the counterpart systems yet to come would play, nor that one day this same supervisor would actually come to embrace them.

When Congress passed the North American Free Trade Agreement (NAFTA) in 1994, one of its provisions permitted member countries of the Berne Convention to restore certain copyrights in the United States that had lapsed into the public domain. Mike Burke, true to his word about writing software, actually asked me if I thought I could develop a client-server system, using newly acquired IBM AIX servers, to handle the flood of documents anticipated under this latest round of the General Agreement on Tariffs and Trade (GATT) talks. When he emphasized that it must be up and running by January 1, I candidly told him I had no experience with Unix, especially in a multi-user environment where the server is on a different operating system from the client. In response he simply said softly, "That's okay, you will learn it." The only person in the world who could help me now was once again my dear friend Bob Kline. Bob was such a genius in the world of automation that he had by this time actually forsaken his relatively comfortable career in the Copyright Office, with its outstanding benefits and retirement package, to work for Phoenix Systems, a software house in Arlington. After a short time there, he assessed his remarkable talents and one day, without a second look back, made a bold leap into self-employment, relying upon only his wits to sustain his family—his amazing wife Elaine and their two small children.

When Bob heard the requirements I laid out, he told me that my best course had a rather steep learning curve, but, without disparaging my ability to explore that option, he offered a safer alternative in the relatively short time frame available to us. Today we would undoubtedly have built a web-based system, but in 1994 Java, C++ and other object-oriented languages were still unsettled or did not yet exist. To orient me to the Unix world, he handed me a list of excellent texts, especially one by Dennis Ritchie, the co-inventor of C, and walked me through the built-in library of functions known as the "man" pages. To handle the screen displays, Bob suggested we use a Unix subset called Curses and pointed me to a few books on the subject, especially one outstanding text by an Australian named Berny Goodheart. To manage the key controls and data exchange, he recommended that we consider licensing a telecommunications package called Kermit from Columbia University to take advantage of its superior telnet protocols. At first, I feared that the name Curses would be consonant with my skill level, provoking me instead to exercise the blasphemous kind, but mercifully Goodheart's straightforward approach made sense to me and remained within my ken. By September I had a system called PcDocs ready for alpha testing, and by November, more than a month before the deadline, it was ready for prime time. Once again, Lafayette Johnson from ITS huddled with me to work out the import of data into the Documents subsystem of COPICS, and on January 2, 1995, when the employees returned from the holidays, the first "notices of intention" filed in the Office were processed in PcDocs, my first automated system actually commissioned officially.

Owing to my inexperience, the short development time allotted, and the paucity of users I could liberate from their regular duties to exercise the test system during development, PcDocs tended to be buggy. However, this turned out to be a benefit to me. The NAFTA legislation provided for a two-year window for filing the NOI, so it was fortunate that PcDocs was a throwaway system that I could consider a dress rehearsal for a production more ambitious. I patched it together for the two years it was needed and used the experience I gained from building it to design a whole new system for cataloging all of the documents of the Office that I called CORDOCS. In its utility as an alternative front end to COPICS, it was parallel to CORCATS, but operating on a much more powerful server and in the Unix operating system instead of Microsoft. As I was finishing CORDOCS, Banyan was already a fading star, and the Library announced it would be phased out. I immediately took advantage of that opportunity to add a number of enhancements and new features in rewriting CORCATS in Unix also. One of my most ardent supporters was a supervisor named Tom Felt, one of the most talented supercatalogers I ever met, who advocated a number of useful ideas during testing that would not have occurred to me otherwise and who tried his utmost, citing significantly superior efficiencies, to inaugurate CORCATS as the official data input system of the Division.

With no malice aforethought or intention to denigrate my work, Mike Burke could not help but refer to my software as the "little systems." In his mind they did not have the stature of the "legacy systems" which had been his focus for many years. As the project leader for both COPICS II and the stodgy COINS system which handled the accounting operations of the Office, and as the contract officer's technical representative for an ill-fated contract to develop an imaging system known as CIS, Mike was at ground level for the backbone of technology in the Office from the beginning and could not let go of his starring role in it. All of that changed as the year 2000 approached, however, when much of the world became increasingly alarmed that programmers had taken the easy route with dates, allowing for only two digits of the year and letting the software *assume* it was in the 1900s. Many developers recognized the relatively short lifecycle of their software and planned to upgrade or allowed that it would be replaced anyway before the century was out—a dangerous presumption for the many agencies who continued to maintain old systems long beyond the sunset originally projected for them. For example, 01/01/00 entered in dBase would by default populate the field as January 1, 1900, not the January 1, 2000 the user intended, thus creating havoc with date arithmetic throughout an entire system. When the Library ordered each service unit in the agency to develop a contingency plan in case any or all of its mission-critical systems should fail, Mike asked me if all of my systems were "Y2K [year 2000] compliant," the buzz word coined by the industry. When I assured him I had already anticipated this and had built that capability in, he promptly listed all of them officially as fallback to any date-intensive programs of the Office and proudly proclaimed to the administration that we were in compliance.

Operations officer Bob Dizard observed one day that the total number of items processed in the Examining Division was consistently higher than the number coming in the door from the accounting office. When he learned that the statistics he was getting from Examining were based on tallies made by individual examiners, he asked himself whether these examiners might be padding their self-reporting productivity figures turned in each week. Duh, ya think? In fact, since he had himself been an examiner for a time, he had some strong suspicions that perhaps human nature was a factor, especially when productivity played a role in performance evaluations. To find out, he asked me to develop an Examining Productivity System for him that would require each examiner to scan the barcode associated with a claim in order to count the items they handled. Immediately I saw a flaw in his plan. When I pointed out that an unscrupulous examiner could simply read the in-process number more than once, he asked me to build in duplicate checking. Since this meant I would need to maintain a database of in-process numbers, I suggested that to prevent this list from cumulating to gigantic proportions, I would retain the numbers for one or two weeks before discarding them. I winced when he suggested I save them for a month. As I met with the supervisors in Examining to work out the details of the specifications, however, they wanted to ensure that no examiner would try to replicate an entry for a *year*. These supervisors were delighted with Dizard's plan, because they had few doubts about the prevarication that had prevailed for years, but until now had little choice but to accept it.

Because I could retire from the Library at age 55, I promised myself that when I turned age 50, I would begin to inaugurate whatever enterprise I would undertake in retirement and transition into that while still relatively young. Since aviation does not match up well to advancing age and is not very lucrative as a source of income anyway, I was quite confident that I could leverage my experience in automation for a secondary career outside of public service. Accordingly, I submitted my resume to an employment agency specializing in cyber projects and soon found myself writing a program for a company in Arlington to convert data on their magnetic tapes. When I tried to run it on my client's machine, however, it produced a "stack overflow" error message. I had always used the small memory model in C, and for the first time discovered that I would need to dig out my documentation to upgrade to the medium model. It worked, but besides the embarrassment I felt in presenting the initial finished product to the customer, that shook my confidence and cast long shadows of doubt whether I really knew what I was doing.

My next assignment from the agency was to take over a project begun by a programmer who was soon leaving on maternity. In my experience I found that if I looked at an old program I had not seen for months or years, it was difficult without meticulous documentation to reconstruct in my mind exactly how it worked—this for a program I had written *myself*. Now I was being asked to evaluate half-completed, untested programs of someone *else*. Not only was I unable to follow what the program was doing, but the programmer was using conventions I had never used, such as four-dimensional arrays. In addition, these programs were to interface with a third-party package called C-Tree, with which I was unfamiliar, and the whole system needed to be operational by the start of the school year in the fall. It was already May. As usual, I turned to my trusted friend Bob for help. Not only was he able to look at the code and figure out how it functioned, but he had used C-Tree himself and tried to give me a crash course in it. After thrashing around for three or four weeks, I got a call one day from my client, who politely told me they were handing over the project to others in their office to finish up. Although the employment agency told me the company had praised my efforts to assist them, I never got any more calls for an assignment. This was just as well, because I would probably have declined another one anyway. Without realizing it at first, I had become one-dimensional, and in addition to the experience and intellect I lacked to be competent, I discovered painfully how important it was to be constantly at the cutting edge of the technology in order to be competitive. Before the ink was dry on my automation certificate, it was already obsolete, a situation that is perhaps true in many disciplines but especially in this field. Powerful new C-derivative languages were proliferating throughout the industry—C++, Java, XML—and although I took a few courses in them, I found that without application in the environment of the real world, they were pointless exercises.

If the dictum of academia is "publish or perish," the equivalent in automania might be "diversify or die." Although this could certainly be applied to me as an individual, it could also be directed institutionally. While the business world was forsaking its lumbering old mainframe systems from the Bronze Age with a frenzy, the Library was merrily content with tools of flint until we were perhaps the last agency in town still using them. IBM had long ago declared that it would no longer support our equipment, so for quite some time ITS had been cannibalizing parts from the carcasses of Amdahl and System 2 machines in whatever graveyards they could be found. Finally, when reality could be ignored no longer, the Library announced the mainframe would be shut down in one year. Twenty million copyright records would need to be moved to some other repository. Most of the library industry throughout the world had adopted the MARC standard for its records, and the Library of Congress was not only trying to lead the way but had instituted a MARC-based product called Voyager to create, store and disseminate the data for its holdings. So it seemed natural for the Copyright Office to join forces and march in that direction also. In fact, said the Office, this is such a fundamental change to our operation that this would be a good time to reevaluate our entire methodology of conducting business. Yes, we need to undergo a thorough business process reengineering (BPR) effort, and we are proclaiming BPR the watchword in the ears of everyone in the agency.

After careful and exhaustive research with other government agencies, the Office selected a company called SRA with a good track record of success to guide us through the BPR effort. After an initial review of our requirements, SRA was confident that a commercial, off-the-shelf (COTS) software package called Siebel would provide the shortest route for us to be operational again after the big red switch of the mainframe was flipped to the OFF position. It is quite customizable, will interface well with Oracle databases like Voyager when it becomes the primary repository for the data, and is quite compatible with the kind of business operations we see here at the Copyright Office, they told us in their pitch. Business operations? Although Copyright has an accounting operation and provides services, many other similarities to commercial interests are found wanting. Some of us were immediately skeptical that a turnkey suite providing tracking of prospective clients, suppliers, contacts, and profit margins would be suitable to a government operation, but the mood was upbeat and everyone seemed confident that Siebel was the answer. At last, all of the "little systems" and independent self-absorbed software that did not talk to other software would be unified into one interdependent whole.

When the one-year ultimatum was issued for shutdown of COPICS, I made a pitch for switching to CORCATS and CORDOCS, both capable of handling the full cataloging load in the Division except for serial publications (magazines and journals), for which I had never created an alternative to COPICS. And I even offered to develop a system for that, which I pledged to have ready in a few months, well before shutdown. In the face of vehement opposition to the very idea of such a plan by one supervisor and her cronies, however, the Office recognized two other options instead. The first was a half-hearted plan by ITS to create a client-server replacement for COPICS. Unfortunately, its recent track record to move COINS from old Data General equipment to Oracle and to develop a lackluster imaging system left the Office with a less than warm feeling of confidence, so the Admin Office gave ITS a polite refusal. The second option was put forward by SRA, who promised that they could support the full load of the Office, including serials, with Siebel before the year was out. What? I tried to protest that refusal to acknowledge my systems as proven technology was a risky proposition, not unlike refusing to step into a lifeboat already at the side of a sinking ship, in the hope that another one might come along …. When tech support specialist Linda Ricco asked what the fallback plan was in case this failed, the answer from SRA was, "We have the resources of so many people that we can throw at this project that it *will not fail*." Why did that remind me of the Titanic?

Almost forgotten in the delirium resulting from impending shutdown of the mainframe was one of its subsystems to control the physical storage of certain deposits. Operating at the periphery, it was known as COBN, the box number system, because the physical deposits were packed tightly into containers, each assigned a control number. Yet this low profile resource was a crucial access point for retrieval of items that might be required by a court in a legal challenge. To allow SRA to concentrate on the mainstream issues, Mike asked me to develop a stopgap system for the Deposit Copies Storage

Unit to use until Siebel was ready to address those tasks. Although I knew little about box numbers, I did some analysis with Angela Brewer, one of the supervisors at the DCSU offsite facility, and started collecting data in an interactive system I called the Box-number Control System (BCS). Meanwhile, the data from CORCATS and CORDOCS, which I had for a few years been loading to the mainframe, now had to be mapped to MARC as well. Though the structure of a copyright record divided the data into fields, the granularity of MARC was much finer, so a task group was assigned to work feverishly on the mapping. The actual conversion effort to migrate the staggering number of records in Logic Library on the mainframe was left to the one or two specialists in ITS who could still remember their Assembler language, and I did not envy them their monumental task. As the committee fleshed out specifications and chiseled the data into MARC fields, I converted CORCATS and CORDOCS records which could sing in the clarion key of Voyager, as well as in the swan song of COPICS.

You can probably predict, from the way I have been arranging the stage, that the drama playing out in the Office had a predictable ending, right? Yes, but there was a slight twist in the plot. For many years I had been warning my managers that it was not prudent for the Office to be running so much of my software without anyone as backup to understand it, in the event I should be incapacitated or suddenly removed from the picture. Also for many years my colleagues in the automation group had been advocating for an upgrade of our positions as analysts, which were a grade lower than our counterparts in ITS, and in many cases we were, with all due modesty, more knowledgeable and expert than they. Accordingly, one day at a staff meeting, Mike announced that certain of our positions would be elevated to the next grade. Then the other shoe dropped. There were only three positions—as working managers that would be staffed competitively, requiring an application, the scrutiny of a rating panel, an interview, and a selection process. As I glanced around the table, my heart sank, noting the protégé Mike made no secret of favoring, the attractive and gifted young black woman being groomed for advancement, and the most senior analyst who had been a project leader working for Mike since the formation of the Group. Yup, there were the three selectees tied up with a ribbon, so why did they bother to pretend this was open to all? But when I read the qualifications on the posting, I was quite sure I was at least equal to the most obvious candidates on all the ranking factors and superior on some of them. No one already had management experience, none had attended graduate school, none had designed and developed entire systems, and certainly my master's thesis satisfied the writing qualification better than the sloppy memos at third grade level I always read from some of these candidates.

When I got to my interview, I pointedly told Mike and the panel that, while I was not issuing an ultimatum or threat, it was decidedly my intention not to become the employee of one of my colleagues if I were not selected. I explained further, for the benefit of the selection panel members who did not know me, that I could have retired five years earlier, but chose to continue with the Library for two reasons—first, that I loved my work, but second, I enjoyed working for Mike and even considered him to be a model supervisor. This was not casual flattery; I honestly admired his style, especially marveling at the way he never talked down to anyone, but most valuable to me was that he was not a micromanager. I prized my independence, and Mike sensed that he could expect the greatest creativity from me by granting me wide latitude. Best of all, he had first-hand experience with development and understood that mistakes come with the territory, always trusting me with the confidence I would not disappoint him. And I never did. But at my age, I told them, I was unwilling to subject myself to the scrutiny of an intervening layer of management.

On Friday, August 6, 2004, as I was heading out the door to start the weekend, Mike asked me to step into his office, closed the door and knocked me to the floor with the news that I had not been selected for the position. I suppose it was preoccupation with this stunning realization that in a flash my world had been turned on its head that while driving the carpool home that evening, I crashed the new Honda we had just bought. No one was hurt, but the car was extensively damaged, and the devastation of this one-two punch made me feel like bawling. Although I entertained the notion of retiring immediately, without returning on Monday, in order to make good on the warning I had issued in the interview, the following week I was scheduled to begin an offsite class in Siebel for two weeks, and the concern that the Office might hold me responsible for reimbursement of this expensive training actually weighed on my mind. After listlessly going through the motions of participation in the course for the first week, I stopped by the office on that Friday to perform routine upload jobs for the weekend. Mike spotted me as I passed his door and called me into his office. While I was away at the class, he had met with the staff to discuss reorganization into teams and asked me to think about which new supervisor I preferred. He was going away to Europe for two weeks, but when he returned, we could discuss it further. "Well," I responded, "by the time you return, I will have retired, so I will take this opportunity to say goodbye." Visibly pained, as if hit in the stomach, he said with an ashen face, "Goodbye!?" "Why yes, I thought I mentioned this in my interview." "Yes, I remember what you said, but …," he blubbered. "But what? Did you think I was bluffing, or that I might change my mind?" I interrupted. "You can't retire now," he pleaded, "We need you right now." Well aware that he already knew it, I replied, "Actually, I *can* retire, since I am eligible, but I will finish out the pay period next week, and then clean out my desk next Friday." "But didn't you tell me how much you appreciate the way I don't micromanage you? You owe it to me to stay on until we can work out a smooth transition," he tried to say. "No, I'm sorry, I don't owe you that," I told him, "Out of respect for you, though, I will make it as easy as I can for someone else to step in and take over. It is not my style to leave you with a mess. When I leave, everything will be cleaned up, files uncorrupted, systems in good working order, all backups in place, and documentation up to date." And with that I went on to my desk to start my tasks.

This could not have come at a worse time for Mike. High turnover rate in SRA had slowed their progress to a crawl, and with only a few weeks left before shutdown of the mainframe, they were still not very far along with *specifications* for a new system, much less even *close* to the implementation they had promised by now. Furthermore, the migration of the data from COPICS to Voyager was bogged down with complexity, and it was very likely the Office would need to beg for an extension. Although I was not taking advantage of his predicament to spite him, I was nevertheless unwilling to subject myself to the new environment he was creating for me. A few minutes later he was at my desk. "I know what we can do," he said excitedly, "We can structure it so that you can continue to report directly to me in a staff position." I thought about that for a moment and had to admit that it had some appeal, but almost immediately I realized it was problematic. "No, I would still need to work with my colleagues," I replied, "and this will create resentment among them when they perceive this as preferential treatment." "Well, here's another way," he continued undeterred, "I have discussed with Julia the need for a technical security officer, and we can place you in that position." "Would there be a grade increase in it for me?" I wanted to know. "Well, there might be," came his answer. Security matters were, if anything, a hindrance to me, but even with that aside, it was not within my field of interest. "I'm sorry, Mike," I replied, "At my age I cannot afford to wait around for a 'might be.' And besides, the responsibilities of a security officer would occupy most of my time and detract from the work that I enjoy as a developer."

About a half hour later, Mike came hurrying back into my office. I thought the matter was closed, but he had sounded the alarm with Julia Huff, the operations officer. "I was just talking with Julia," he began confidently, "And she agrees that we can bring you back in retirement as a contractor." "But I don't want to come back at all," I told him bluntly, "I am making plans for retirement. For one thing, I have not spent enough time with my dad and have already made arrangements to spend a week or two in New York with him." "Well then, at least promise me this," he pleaded, "that you will wait until I return from Paris in two weeks, and we can talk about it further. Our flight does not leave until Monday afternoon, and my cell phone will be on all weekend. Please think about it and call me any time to let me know you will stay." "I will make no such promise," I said, as I turned back to my work. When Sharlyn and I discussed this whole exchange that evening, she looked at it from Mike's point of view and convinced me that my plans for retirement could wait. "If they allow you to continue your same work as a contractor, you are still doing what you enjoy, you would report directly to Mike as you did before and you allow Mike to save face," she pointed out. "At the least, you can afford to wait until he returns to discuss it some more." Despite Mike's assurance that his phone was "on all weekend," I dialed into his voicemail and lifted the cloud of angst which hung over his vacation with my message that I would still be in the office when he returned—this by contrast to the anguish he had stirred up for *me* for the whole weekend with his Black Friday pronouncement of my non-selection a week earlier.

When Mike returned, I told him I would be retiring at the end of the next pay period, but that I would take a look at a contract, if one were offered by the Office. My father had given up his car by this time, so he was delighted to be on wheels again for the few days I stayed with him in his assisted living facility near Oswego. As we ran errands and visited shops, I smiled at the "kid" in the passenger seat next to me excited to be going to the mall again. In my official capacity I had never done any website design or development, so when I got home, I enrolled in a USDA course in Dreamweaver, a wonderful package that suddenly illuminated what I remembered from XML and Java, while I waited day after day for word of a contract that never came. Although I should have known by now that nothing in the government ever happens quickly, I did extrapolate from the urgency in Mike's voice when I left that I would hear from someone at the Library within a few days after I left. Soon I would need to be making more long-term decisions, so I was becoming increasingly impatient with the uncertainty over whether they would need me or not. Finally, one day, an official envelope from the contracts office arrived in the mail, but when I looked at the terms, I thought it must be a joke. Their offer was for less than I was earning as an employee, so I promptly mailed it back with an explanation why I could not accept the offer. Almost immediately I received a call from Contracts asking what rate I expected, and to my surprise Copyright accepted it, offering me a one-year agreement.

Nearly two months had elapsed when I returned to the Office, and I spent the first week cleaning up the messes my surrogates had inflicted upon everything they touched. The mainframe was scheduled to be shut down by now, but the quality of the conversion effort by ITS had been substandard, so the Office insisted it be kept on life support for another quarter, then another and another until it was extended for an additional year. When they told me that Siebel was nowhere close to completion either, I repeated the exhortation I had made well over a year earlier that CORCATS and CORDOCS could be used to support every piece of material in the Cataloging Division except serials. This time they listened, pulling the plug on data entry into COPICS in preparation for total shutdown. My contract was for one year, but as the end of it neared, Siebel was still far from useable, so Mike asked me if I could extend for a second year. Since everything was going well so far, I agreed. As the end of the second year approached, SRA was still bogged down by personnel and staffing issues, but it was becoming increasingly clear that the fly in the ointment was Siebel itself, in which progress was still a struggle. Although the Library encountered legal issues extending my sole-source contract for a third year, Mike persuaded his top brass that the Office had no choice but to continue with my "gap load" systems, as they came to be called, for at least another year.

Over lunch with Bob Kline one day, as I was encapsulating some of the issues the Office was facing, he remarked that it reminded him of many a situation in which he had been called in to salvage a project spiraling down the drain. When I asked Bob whether he might be interested to step in if asked, he looked off into the distance as he replied, "No, the Copyright Office rejected all of my offers to help when I worked there, and since a prophet is without honor in his own country, I doubt they will listen to me now either. But my friend Meyer is a specialist in this kind of work. I will ask him if he might want such a project." A short time later a frustrated Mike flopped into the chair next to my desk, lamenting what a serious mistake it had been to select a COTS package in the first place, but Siebel in particular. Without hesitation I ventured the comment that I had a friend who specializes in rescuing failed systems. "I am not calling Siebel a failed system," I added quickly, "But if you reach the point where you decide to apply that label to it, let me know." "Oh, God no," Mike replied emphatically, "We have spent millions on Siebel already. We can't turn back now." "Think of it this way, Mike," I ventured. "If you travel down a road and find the bridge out, you can probably still get across the river with enough expenditure of time and wasted effort, but wouldn't it be easier in the long term to come back to the first fork in the road and take an alternate path?" I wanted to ask if he thought spending *billions* was going to make a difference, but because that might sound sarcastic, I bit my tongue. Instead, I asked whether he could put his finger on a specific problem. He said the most recent snag was the difficulty loading the MARC data to Voyager. Since I was already doing that routinely, I suggested that SRA give their MARC file to me, and I would load it for them, but then Mike said plainly, "They are having difficulty mapping their data *into* MARC."

The next day that remark gave me an idea. I asked Dinesh, the project leader for SRA, whether his team was having difficulty converting the XML file from Siebel into MARC. When he described the difficulty this was causing them, I offered a solution. "Suppose," I began, "we let Siebel do what Siebel does best—present an attractive GUI interface to the user, with its well-structured applets, checkboxes, pulldown menus, and displays. Then when you capture all the data you want, scrape the screen and drop it into a file that you pass to me. I will then convert it to MARC21 format, ready to load to Voyager." "That would be fantastic," he exclaimed, "But Mike won't buy it." "I think I can sell it," I told him. When Mike was in, Dinesh and I pitched the idea to him. "Here's what it buys you," I explained. "Think of my conversion as a black box that is independent of Siebel. That way it doesn't matter what front end you use to collect the data; just feed the conversion box a file that it can read, and out the back comes a Voyager file. Each time Siebel upgrades to a new version, all of the custom code that you are building into it now will need to be rebuilt over and over, but with my solution, each of those transitions will be much smoother because complex custom-designed conversion routines are not involved. Besides all of that, SRA is relieved from the logjam that is holding up progress right now." At first Mike was skeptical because he was concerned that after I was out of the picture, he would have no one to maintain the conversion software. "Look down the road ten years," I continued, "And tell me how many people you see who have even heard of Siebel, much less have the ability to maintain it. Now tell me how many thousands you see who know and use C. Besides, once it is written and tested, it should be relatively static and never need maintenance." Mike warmed up to our ideas, but when he presented them to the administration, they rejected such a suggestion on the basis that conversion was a deliverable in SRA's contract, and shifting it to my contract raised concerns that it could cause legal challenges down the line. Perhaps their rejection was based upon something else that they could not yet divulge to Mike—that my contract was not going to be renewed for a fourth year. The funding had run out, and my contract, along with a few others for vital Copyright services, became expendable. This time Mike had no choice, when he received word that he had been entered into a six-week marathon to transfer all of my responsibilities to someone else before the end of the year. And with that, my career came to an end. I was retired for a second time and was finally put out to pasture.

But wait …. As this goes to press, I am being asked by the Office to return under another contract. Although they are making progress with Siebel, it is *still*, years overdue, under development. Meanwhile, long after its intended useful life, my software still has a heartbeat and has continued to be pressed into service. However, whenever a cron job fails, an index is accidentally erased or a file becomes corrupted, the techs at the Office have been calling me. After I appeared at my own expense several times to fix problems, their collective consciences apparently brought them to the realization that this might be a bit unfair, as they dug up some funding for me to "consult" with them three days a week about a number of ongoing projects, eventually including a graceful shutdown of some of my systems.

# Twin Cedars

Whenever we visited Carl Zimmerman, our elderly neighbor down the road, we passed the hand-painted sign posted above his garage door reading "Homecroft." This always seemed to me to have a touch of self-indulgent snobbishness, especially when his sister Helen would mention in a letter of their visit to Carl at Homecroft, as if it were some expansive English country estate, replete with stables for foxhunting. One Sunday when Sharlyn asked me whether we were taking the kids to a restaurant after church, I put on my best stuffy aristocratic British air, looked down my nose haughtily and replied, "Why yes, madam, would you prefuh Humecrawft or Twinn Cedahs?" Sharlyn thought a moment before she latched onto my reference to our own house, with its two beautiful cedar trees in the front yard. There are actually three, but when we first purchased the house, the third was considerably smaller. This epithet appealed to Sharlyn, and she often uses it whimsically to this day.

The Zimmermans were not nobility, but another of our neighbors actually was. When the Library of Congress offered free parking to carpools, I made the acquaintance of one Wlada Koziebrodzki, a supervisor in Shared Cataloging down the hall from my office, a lady in her seventies. Wlada lived a short distance away from us with her husband Leopold, a feisty curmudgeon at least five years older than she. Leo was descended from Polish royalty, growing up in a grand palace in luxury and wealth. When Germans marched through his country, they forced Leo's family to flee for their lives, as Nazis occupied the land and usurped the villa, making it their headquarters. Now in the fading twilight of his life, Leo had never recovered from the deeply embedded trauma of this tragedy, and the resulting bitterness was reflected in a perpetual scowl frozen on his countenance and a most crotchety, snarling personality. Despite our diverse ages, Wlada and I were kindred spirits as supervisors, trading many anecdotes about the problems with which we dealt in the office every day, and I suppose it is fair to say that each of us grew to admire the style of the other in handling them.

Cantankerous as Leo was, he was always deferential to me, undoubtedly because Wlada spoke so favorably, so he frequently called for advice or assistance on some project or repair. Because of his frail health, I was the one to whom he turned after a storm tore off a tree limb or dumped twenty inches of snow on his long driveway. Since they were already well past middle age when they met and married in Paris, Leo and Wlada were childless, which was just as well because Leo could not stand children. Once when I came over to mow his yard, I brought along five-year-old Austin, who idly picked the buds from one of his rhododendrons. Leo, who had been spying suspiciously from inside the house, came raging outside cursing so loudly that I heard the commotion from the back side of the house above the roar of the mower. When I came running to see what happened, I rounded the corner of the building in time to witness Leo snag Austin by the collar, his other hand raised to strike him.

When it was Wlada's turn to drive the carpool, she became so rattled that we were constantly on the verge of disaster, as she swerved unexpectedly, braked far too belatedly or drifted unconcernedly toward other drivers. One morning, after yet another incident where she absentmindedly bumped the car ahead, not realizing in her nervous fog that her car was creeping forward, one of the other carpoolers took me aside after we mercifully reached our destination and said, "Someone needs to address this problem. If she ever drives again, I am leaving the carpool." Later that morning I walked over to Wlada's office to speak to her. "Wlada," I began, not knowing for sure what words to choose, "would you be terribly offended if, on the days you are scheduled to drive, I were to drive your car for you?" She closed her eyes, tilted her head back and sighed as if a piano had been lifted from her back. "Ohhh, *wuud* you?" she gushed, in her thick accent, "dat wuud be wuundahfuul!" On some occasions, when Leo had an appointment at the office of their HMO downtown, he would be the driver. One day as he was backing out of our driveway, I could see from my position in the right rear passenger seat that a car was barreling down the street toward us. As Leo continued to roll backward, I called out, "Hold it!" Leo ignored me and kept backing to the end of the driveway. As the car in the street continued to hurtle toward us, I called again, "Hold it, *hold it*!" Oblivious and unfazed, Leo proceeded into the street, now directly in the path of the other vehicle, which was forced to lock its brakes and skid noisily to a stop to avoid a collision. Only when Leo heard the screech of tires did he exhibit any awareness of impending disaster, but instead of thanking me for alerting him to it, he turned slowly to me and said with a scolding rasp, "Dun't meck unnessessaddy noiss."

Our street, Linway Terrace, is used as a cut-through, and traffic always roars past well above the speed limit. Once when we sat with guests at our picnic table, one of them remarked, "*Lin*way Terrace? It should be called *Race*way Terrace." Incidentally, this table was so inviting, as it sat in the shade of a majestic old cottonwood tree, that once in a while a family would mistake our beautiful yard for a park and set out paper plates, potato chips and watermelon for a picnic. Their impression was no doubt enhanced by the tire swing I installed when the boys were young, a long pendulum of nylon rope suspended from a huge branch thirty feet above the ground. I can recall that moment vividly. When I reached the top of my twenty-foot ladder and started shinnying up to the next limb, I felt I could view at least five counties from there and had such acrophobia that I was imbued with a bad case of "sewing-machine leg" and had to climb back down for a few minutes to think about this. After a time I recomposed myself and climbed back up halfway to the stratosphere to put up the swing. Thomas and Austin spent so much time on this swing that there was a perpetual patch of bare ground beneath it, but when I chided them one day for wearing out the grass, Sharlyn took me aside and reminded me that "we're raising boys, not grass."

Whenever someone stands up at a civic association meeting to whine about the speeding cars on a quiet street where they are trying to raise little kids, I am tempted to stand up and rebuff them with our experience successfully raising three babies on a much busier street. If your children are so young that they cannot recognize the danger, I am wont to say, it is your responsibility to keep them away, not a driver's to swerve around them. But just as quickly I recall how many times it was only through the grace of God that no car happened along when one of our boys darted out on a bicycle or skateboard. Though nearly five years separate the boys, Thomas always related down and Austin related up, and they grew up very close. This was helped by the fact that Austin grew faster, and after a time they could even wear each other's clothes. When we visited Thomas at college years later, he would take Austin around the campus and pass him off as one of his college friends. When they went riding together on the sidewalk or a side street, I noticed that Thomas was so much faster on his bike than Austin, furiously pedaling his tricycle attempting to keep up, that I wondered if he could actually learn to ride a bike. We bought a little sixteen-inch two-wheeler, and, not yet three years old, Austin learned to ride it. Although he could physically tear around and could now keep up with big brother, he had absolutely no *sense* and gave no thought to how easily he could end up as road kill under the wheels of a car. The gravel path along the C&O Canal parallel to the Potomac River was one of our favorite places where the whole family would often bike together. Incidentally, this towpath was built during the time of Washington, who did the surveying, for the mules that provided the locomotion for the barges which plied the Potomac. Although we had a standing rule for the boys that they must remain in sight at all times, Thomas and Austin loved to ride ahead as fast as their legs could pedal those bicycles. Angela was much more restrained, remaining behind with Mom and Dad, so when the rest of us lagged behind, we would hear a little voice calling, "Hewwwy hop!" One day Austin discovered that if he dragged his toes through the gravel, he could raise a cloud of dust behind him. When I caught up with him, I asked him not to do that because he was ruining the toes of his shoes. Five minutes later he was far up ahead, creating his cloud again. I raced up to him and said, "Austin, what did I just tell you?" He looked down sheepishly at his feet and said softly, "Not to make smoke with my feet." To me, it was wearing out his shoes; to him, it was making smoke.

When Thomas was five, the local McDonald's restaurant sponsored a bicycle rodeo for kids between five and ten, with a contest to traverse an obstacle course. Thomas was such an expert on his bike that I was sure he would do well, but when we got to the parking lot where the event was held, he was intimidated by all the cones, barriers and apparatus set up and cried to go home. I was convinced, however, that if he understood what he was expected to do, it was well within his ability, so I asked one of the judges whether we could walk through the course. Assuring him that we were not asking for a practice run with the bicycle, we got his permission to step through it. After I showed Thomas where he had to weave among cones without hitting any, squeeze through a narrow place without touching the chalk and ride with one hand while throwing a beanbag through the clown's mouth, he felt a little more confident. He passed through the course flawlessly and was one of only three that I saw throw the beanbag through that clown's yawn. We got the call that evening to come down to McDonald's for his trophy, since he had won first place, scoring even more points than the older riders. The restaurant had already calculated that we would celebrate with a hamburger, fries and a drink, and of course we would not disappoint them.

Growing up in Iowa, I would read in *Boys' Life* magazine about an event called the All-American Soap Box Derby and dream of building my own racer. While this had been out of the question for me, perhaps it was not for Thomas. The summer after Thomas turned ten, we made inquiries about the program and learned that his age group was in the Junior Division, which required us to purchase an official kit from the racing organization in Akron. The rules specified that a parent could supervise and could perform any task that required power tools, but that the child entering the race must assemble this kit. After I cut out the base from a sheet of plywood for him, Thomas mounted the shell pieces on it, rigged up the steering and brakes according to the plans and painted the exterior glossy blue from a little spray can. On the evening before the regional race, all the cars were to be brought to a certain warehouse for inspection and weighing before they were impounded there for the night. As soon as I got my first glimpse of the other racers, I realized these cars were not built by kids—racing stripes and flames that were not decals but actually painted on by a professional, bodies polished to a mirror finish as shiny as a showroom Corvette and expertly molded fairings custom-fit over cable connections. The judges told us our car was one-sixteenth inch (!) too long and insisted we return home to file it off. When I noticed a fair amount of jocularity between the officials and a certain group of the parents, I gradually became aware that three or four families formed a group of insiders that had been involved in these races for several years, going back multiple generations. I also began to suspect this local chapter of the organization was a bit footloose with the rules.

On the official race day, a section of Eastern Avenue (the street that forms the boundary between D.C. and Maryland), which has a long steep hill with a shallow upslope at the bottom for deceleration, was cordoned off and set up with starting gates and safety bales for the contest. It was a double elimination event, and Thomas was doing well through the first two or three heats before he had his first loss. By chance, one of my aviation colleagues was there with his son Justin, who was eliminated after only two heats, but neither of his losses was head to head with Thomas. As the day wore on, I noticed that most of the winners seemed to be in Lane 1, and then I recalled that both of Justin's losses and both of Thomas's were in Lane 2. More significantly, the winners always seemed to be members of the Family of insiders. Curious how lane selection was determined, I walked to the top of the hill, where I observed that each driver reached into a cloth bag to pull out a wooden ball marked with the number 1 or 2. So how did the Family draw Lane 1 so frequently? I could not determine for sure what there was about Lane 2 that made it slower—whether it was less shaded and therefore absorbed more sun to make it softer, whether it had a rougher surface, whether nefarious individuals had seeded it with sand or gravel, or a dozen other possibilities. But it seemed to be more than a coincidence, and the Family knew about it.

The next year I kept a tally of the winners on my program and found that about eighty percent came from Lane 1. Thomas's fortunes were about the same as the year before, using the same car, but again both losses came from Lane 2. He was a very good driver and had not made the mistakes of some, who swerved on the descent or traveled an oblique path, but he had fun and took his losses well. Although I suspected that foul play had somehow been subtly pulled off, I concluded we would bow out gracefully without whimpering about it. That all changed when the final race in the Senior Division between a member of the Family and a black teenager was declared a dead heat. I was at the finish line, and from where I stood, it seemed that the black boy in Lane 1 was the unquestionable winner. Race officials ordered a rematch, and this time the Family car was in Lane 1. From a photo taken at the finish line, I could not determine which car crossed over it first, but the judges somehow declared that the Family car was slightly ahead, so the other driver was issued his first loss. Was it a coincidence that in the subsequent heat the Family car drew Lane 1? This time the photo showed the car in Lane 1 about two inches ahead at the finish line, and he was awarded the trophy. Although I asked the investigative reporters of each of the local TV stations to look into this and also reported the incident to the CBS program *60 Minutes*, nothing ever came out of it. But I still cry foul whenever anyone mentions Soap Box Derby to me.

Although each of our kids received an allowance from us, they encountered affluent classmates at school every day who could afford amusements and expensive electronic games and gadgets of every variety. When the conversation of Thomas became increasingly peppered with cravings for such toys, I was well aware what was in his mind when he began to express interest in earning additional income. I had the idea he could deliver newspapers from his bicycle. The *Washington Post* put us in touch with the distributor for our area, one Gene McClellan, who had a route in our neighborhood that was being mishandled by the young man currently making the deliveries, but he was reluctant to turn it over to Thomas at the tender age of ten. When I volunteered to assist, McClellan promptly liberated the incumbent working for him from his duties and passed his map and paperwork to us. When we asked Angela and little five-year-old Austin whether they wanted to share in this responsibility, neither of them really had any idea what was in store when they agreed. It was supposed to be a positive experience, preparing young minds for some of the lessons of life, especially that actually *earning* money is hard work, but when I reflect on the extent to which my involvement in this enterprise was essential to keeping it running, I wonder whether they learned anything except how loud Dad can yell.

My idea about throwing the papers onto the porch from a bike was incompatible with McClellan's rule that the paper must be placed at each door quietly, inside the storm or screen door if possible, so a bike would actually be a hindrance. The coaster wagon the boys were still using for fun was pressed into service for the route, and on most days it carried the load from which we ran left and right through the neighborhood. At first we did not know the names of our customers, so we whimsically invented our own references—those three together high up on the hill were the Mountains, the one with the long driveway was the Drive-Up White One, the bungalow with the double garage and wide driveway to the door was the Motel, and so on. One of them earned the name Dog Lady, for the woman who would hide behind the door as she let the dog out or who would appear in her nightgown to let it in again. One neighbor was an early morning jogger who ran through the streets while his two dogs nipped at the kids as they ran from house to house. When I tired of this after the dozenth time, I approached him one morning to remind him that he was in violation of the county leash laws. I do not recall his words, but I can still see his teeth gnashing about three inches from my face as he grabbed the front of my shirt to express his diplomatic response. The owner of another dog that terrorized us as we tried to run through the route was simply too lazy to take the dog out in the morning. We tolerated that for a while, but when the nuisance, and especially the danger, persisted, I called to ask them whether they might use the back yard instead of the front. When the dog's owner called Bob Dant, who by this time had taken over for McClellan as our boss, to complain that their paper carrier's father had called him about his dog, Dant was sympathetic to us and told the customer he had no control over his carrier's father. The next morning, when the dog was deliberately released from the front door again, I rang the doorbell to have the owner witness his dog chasing my children through the yards across the street. This time the customer called Dant to complain that I had awakened his whole household at 5:45 in the morning. Dant simply told him that was out of his hands. Nevertheless, we never again had a problem with the dog.

Bundles of newspapers were dropped off to us by 4:00 a.m., regardless of the conditions outside, and the Post promised delivery to its customers by 6:30, so I was the taskmaster who sounded reveille every morning at five. Although all three little carriers liked the money they were earning, it was not long before novelty turned to drudgery, so we instituted a system where each of them could choose one day off, except Sunday, when we needed all hands and feet to distribute the massive load. In addition, I volunteered to let everyone sleep in on Saturdays while I trudged around the route alone. Before anyone

243

could claim a sick day, they were sent to Doctor Sharlyn for evaluation, and she could probably write a number of medical journal articles about some of the shortest illnesses on record, speedy recoveries and the miracle cures she worked. At first Austin seemed to have misunderstood his day off. He awoke and ran out to help, but when we told him he could stay home and sleep, he said, "But I want to get *paid*." Sharlyn and I took none of the profits, but we exercised authority over how the money was allocated. The first ten percent was taken off the top as a tithe for Sunday school. Fifty percent was set aside for what we termed long-term savings, money that could not be touched, while twenty-five percent went into "short-term savings" to be held for big-ticket items that required parental approval for purchase. That left fifteen percent that they could use as spending money for almost anything else. This spending money revealed some interesting personality traits in each of the kids. Austie Little, as I called our youngest sometimes, wanted to spend his as soon as his fist grabbed it. Thomas was the best saver, allowing his spending money to cumulate for some item with a more expensive tag or simply adding it to his long-term savings. Angela liked to buy things too, but when she went shopping, she so often saw items she thought someone else would like that more than half of her purchases were usually gifts.

We prided ourselves on our good service, and most of our customers were very appreciative. One of our deliveries was to the convent, and the good sisters there would say ironically, "You're so faithful" to describe our dependability. When McClellan was our distributor, we were plagued by his deficient counting skills, often ending up one or two papers short for some reason—never long, always short. In this event the SOP was to call him, so that he could drop a paper at the customer's door later. But since this might not be until mid-morning, I usually had enough time before my carpool arrived to pedal up to Chesterbrook Shopping Center to buy one from the newsstand. After Dant took over, he always added one extra to our count, and we literally never had this problem again.

All of us hated the collecting each month. With a little experience, however, we were able to predict the most likely time to find our patrons home, especially during football season. Most of them were very kind, but I must confess that because human nature has a tendency to be more generous with tips to children than to adults, our insistence that the kids be involved in this operation was a part of the strategy. Individual customers gave little thought to the major effort involved in collecting from a hundred homes, so they perhaps did not realize the impact when we finally found them home, but were then requested to stop by another time simply because they were in the middle of dinner. Since they got up to answer the door anyway, could they not reach into their wallet right then? One of our patrons subscribed only when the *Post* announced a special offer to sign up for the Sunday edition and receive the rest of the week free. When the eight weeks of this offer elapsed, it was the responsibility of the customer to cancel. We could always count on her to take advantage of this each year, but one year she forgot to cancel and was furious with us for charging her for one additional week at the regular price, insisting that we should have known that she did not wish to extend her subscription. Sharlyn and I never allowed the children to do this collecting alone, but Austin sometimes ran ahead to the next house to ring the bell before I could catch up. One day I came around the corner as the customer was closing the door after handing him two rolls of nickels. As soon as she saw me, she quickly reopened the door to say with mock cheeriness, "Wait a minute, I didn't give you enough there, did I?" Young Austin's unquestioned acceptance was based upon the fact that the heft of those nickels seemed the right amount to him, but if I had been ten seconds later, she might have been successful in her attempt to short him.

Declining numbers of postulants eventually closed that convent along our route, but it was soon revived as a center for "youth apostles," young men in the service of the church who seemed to cloister there without the austerity or formality of an institutional monastery. This reminds me of Sharlyn's favorite story about a fellow who decided to join a monastery. As he enters, the abbot warns him about the strict code of silence that allows only two words every ten years. After ten years go by, the abbot calls the monk into his office to commend him for his service and asks if he has anything to say. "Food cold," mutters the monk, before returning to his cell. After the second ten years, the monk is in the office again, where the abbot again permits him to express up to two words. "Bed hard," grumbles the man this time. At the end of the third ten years, the man is summoned to the office of the abbot, now grizzled with age, who says, "Well, you have been here thirty years now, and your record shows that you have been doing nothing but complain ever since you got here. Can you explain such impious behavior with only two words?" As the monk stands up and walks slowly to the door leading to the street, he answers, "I quit."

Carpools are at the same time a wonderful blessing and a fountain of frustration. In my case it was a constant shifting of personnel, as individuals would change work schedules, move away or drop out for one reason or another. One evening Tom Ripy was the driver on the ride home on Interstate 66, as Paul Morgan sat up front with him, turned partially round to face me in the rear seat as we talked. Tom had apparently had a tiring day, for I thought I saw him drift toward the next lane, then swerve suddenly back into his own. When it seemed we were headed for the shoulder a few moments later, I interrupted Paul to verify it, and he yelled, "Tom!" in time for him to snap out of his nap. "Tom, if Paul and I are boring you," I offered, "we would be glad to change the subject."

For a time I was riding with a cataloger named Kamel Gaballah who worked in Regional Cooperative Cataloging around the corner from my office. Since there just two of us, we could not secure a parking space inside the building, forcing us to scrounge for a spot on the street into which we could shoehorn our car. Kamel had learned to drive in Egypt, from whence he had come to America as a young man. It was at the same time refreshing and terrifying to ride with someone who regarded signs and signals on the streets not as instructions to be obeyed, but as suggestions to exercise discretion. To Kamel a red traffic light meant slow down a little, stop if you must, but if there is no cross traffic coming, why stand there idly wasting time? In one sense this approach to motoring was appealing to me, because while I was of the same mindset, I would never have the guts to try it. To Paul Morgan, who joined our carpool some time later, Kamel was known as Kamel-Kazi. One morning, as we crested a hill, the Arlington police were waiting for us with a speed trap as Kamel roared along at his customary pace about thirty miles per hour above the speed limit. Driving licenses in those days were paper, and when Kamel produced his, the officer observed that it had been left in his shirt pocket so many times when his wife did the laundry that most of the writing, insignia and picture were washed out. In my experience the Arabic people are born to argue, so Kamel accordingly launched into a vehement protest when the officer insisted he did not have a valid license. After the histrionics continued for a time, the officer said, "Look, if you have someone with you," glancing at me, "who has a valid license, that person may drive your car. If not, we will impound it." After they handed Kamel his ticket for speeding, I got behind the wheel, drove until we turned the corner out of sight, stopped the car to trade places with Kamel again, and we continued on to work.

The parking places near the Library along the streets of Washington were not always in the most desirable neighborhoods. I foolishly kept a few quarters visible on the console between the front seats for tolls and parking meters and one day found my window broken out by the poor homeless beggar who desperately needed them, of course, to stave off starvation with the bowl of soup on which, I am sure, he spent them. One day when I had driven in alone, I came back to my car and noticed that it seemed to be a little low on one corner. When I investigated, I noticed that someone had stolen my right front wheel, lug nuts and all. Now what would someone do with one wheel, I wanted to know. I was in a hurry to get to the airport to meet a student, but I spent my time filing a police report at a substation— ironically quite nearby—instead. Fortunately, there was a salvage yard just around the corner from where I parked, which even more fortunately had a Chevrolet Citation just like mine sitting there with four good wheels. Most *un*fortunately, however, the owner was reluctant to part with one of those wheels, which he claimed made the car undrivable. Undrivable? This is a junk yard. Did he think someone would mistake it for a used car lot and come by to ask for a test drive? It took me a half hour to persuade him to sell it to me, and another half hour to persuade him to accept my check—the only way I could pay him, since I rarely carried that much cash around.

About two weeks later I left the office early and was walking to my car in this same neighborhood. As I came along on the sidewalk, I passed a car along the curb where a woman was standing with the passenger side door open. Lying prone on the front seat was a man working at something underneath the instrument panel. As I walked past them wrapped in my thoughts, I paid little attention … until it struck me they were breaking into that car. Snapping my fingers, I turned around, pretending I forgot something. I wanted to reach that police substation in the hope this pair could be caught in the act. As soon as I turned back toward them, however, I heard the woman whisper hoarsely, "He's coming back!" In an instant the man who had been lying across the seat popped his head up, and both of them ran to the car parked immediately ahead of the one they were invading, jumped into it and roared off. Though they were getting away, I would not only be able to identify them, but now I would also be able to describe their car and its license. As the car pulled away, I noticed that they had covered the license plate with a towel, but as they whipped out of the parking place, the towel fluttered up enough that I could read the whole number. Armed with all this information, I proceeded to the substation to file a report, and when I finished I added, "And if these are the two who stole my wheel, I still want it back." I never heard from the authorities again.

In America you are in serious trouble, of course, if you strike a person with your car. In Egypt, Kamel told me, you might stop to see if the victim was still alive, but if not, you would simply say, "Oh, poor fellow," and drive off. One morning as we streaked down the piece of the Potomac Parkway that parallels the river and passes under Memorial Bridge, I could see a brown spot in the road ahead. I could not make out what it was, but it seemed to be a cardboard box. As we came closer, the spot seemed to be moving slowly, so I assumed the box was empty, the wind sliding it into our lane. Meanwhile, Kamel did not yet see it or perhaps came to the conclusion that it was harmless, as he roared along without slowing. Soon we were close enough that I could see that it was a female duck ambling across the highway. Incredibly, Kamel made no attempt to change lanes or slow the car. Did he still not see it or did he simply not care? Either way, I glanced at him in wonder and disbelief. Was he consciously choosing to hit the duck? No, any moment he will surely do something to avoid damage to the car, even if he has no feelings for the duck. I could not believe he would intentionally do nothing, but in a few seconds there was a loud thump, and I whirled around to gape through the rear window at a cloud of feathers and a red clump where the duck had been. As I stared at Kamel with my mouth wide open, unable to express a word, he looked at me and said, "What?" He never offered an explanation, but as I reflected on this many times, I came to the conclusion that drivers in some countries must take the position that an animal, or even a person, so stupid as to put itself in the path of a speeding car actually deserves whatever consequences result.

Kamel was always most generous to me. One afternoon after Sharlyn began working for the Library, she became ill and needed to go home. Since Kamel had been the driver of the carpool that day, I considered taking her home on the bus, but this would have involved transfers and consumed over two hours of time she needed to be in bed. Without hesitation Kamel gave me the keys to his car and insisted I use it to drive her home. I was the one who became sick on another occasion when Kamel was the driver. I had a hot dog for lunch, and after about an hour I noticed that it was not sitting well in my stomach and began to suspect food poisoning. As the afternoon dragged on I became increasingly nauseous, but I reached the point where it would take more time to get home on the bus than to wait for the carpool, so I tried to remain at work and tough through it. On the trip home, I became violently ill and had to request that Kamel pull over a few times to allow me to decorate the weeds along the side of the road. It was a Friday, and that evening was the graduation ceremony for the eighth graders of our parochial school. As chairman of the board of education, I was expected to be in attendance for the presentation of diplomas. Vainly conscious that if I called in sick, it might be perceived as an insult or a ruse to evade my responsibilities, so I decided to force myself to go. It was a mistake. While Sharlyn was driving us to the church, I reclined the passenger seat to rest and started to see huge spots in front of my eyes, an indication that already my brain was oxygen-starved. As one of the "dignitaries," I was seated in the front pew and staggered to my feet for the presentations. I felt faint immediately and knew I had to return to my seat. I did not make it. That graduation ceremony will be remembered for many years as the one where the board chairman collapsed to the floor and had to be carried out feet first by four strong men while the ambulance was summoned to revive him with some oxygen.

As a faithful Muslim Kamel spent considerable time reading the Koran, attending the mosque in Washington each Friday and conducting a prison ministry at the penitentiary in Lorton. He was deeply religious and fervently preached his message in the car on our ride to work, engaging me in many a spirited discussion about repentance and faith. His only understanding of Christianity, unfortunately, was based upon Roman Catholicism, and he steadfastly rejected any such notion that forgiveness could be effected by the deeds of others or purchased from the church. He was surprised that I agreed. But Islam has no room for Christ, and when he repeatedly thundered that "God *has no son*," I tried to warn him that the Savior he was denying was the very one who was going to be his judge when he died. I made no inroads on his beliefs, of course, but Kamel did not realize how soon he would find out that I was right. He developed a severe headache one evening when he went home and was admitted to the hospital when none of his wife's remedies at home gave him any relief. When I visited him there a day or two later, he complained of constant pain. Three days later he was dead. I think of him often, recalling our discussions and wonder how many times he berates himself from his place in the afterlife for rejecting my counsel, especially as he realizes that the impossibility of escape from his predicament is *forever*.

By coincidence, Kamel's son Balal was one of our son Thomas's best friends in high school. This was fortuitous for both of us as parents, because we could compare notes with each other on what caper or other our two teenagers were planning next. Kamel would tell me what Balal said they were doing, and

I could inform him what Thomas had told us, and together we would sometimes discover that the truth was far afield, at variance with both. Ironically, Kamel would often complain about the "headic" Balal was always causing him. One day when Kamel pulled into my driveway, I noticed a big crack across his windshield that had not been there the day before. He seemed quite agitated as I stepped into the car, so I assumed he had some kind of accident. No, in his impatience to remove the frost that morning, he came to the car with a pan of hot water, which instantly cracked the glass when he splashed it on the ice. But that was not the source of his anger. No, he and his wife had discovered that Balal had, without their consent and against their express objections, purchased a motorcycle. The parents had responded by slashing both tires with a kitchen knife, but Kamel spent most of the ride to the office telling me about the extent to which the deception and disobedience had disappointed them. As I reflected on this, I was thankful that Thomas would never treat us like that—or could he? Unlike Kamel and his wife, who had engaged in many heated arguments in their household with Balal in forbidding him to own a motorcycle, we had never discussed such a thing with Thomas.

When Thomas found out I was recording some of these memoirs, he told me he plans to write his own rebuttal some day, yet it is with apologies to Thomas that I must relate the following incident. Curious whether both boys might have made a pact to buy their motorcycles together, I asked Sharlyn, who was custodian of his savings account, to look through his passbook to determine if any large withdrawals had been made recently. When she spotted one for several thousand dollars about six months earlier, our hearts sank, realizing the truth. Every Sunday afternoon Thomas and I headed for Manassas for his flight lesson, and with his learner permit in hand he also acquired some freeway experience driving us to the airport. That next Sunday as we rode along, I casually asked him whether there might be something going on in his life that he ought to be sharing with us. "No," he said without hesitation, but I thought I caught a glint of suspicion as soon as he said it. I let that percolate for about five minutes, then asked, "Have you made any large purchases recently?" "No!" he said defensively. Now I knew he was lying, but we rode in silence for about seven more miles before I said, "Maybe we already know about it." Then it all came bubbling out. "Well, I knew that if I asked you, the answer would be NO," he said emotionally. "That's right," I agreed, "and do you know why? Because we don't want to lose you. When you are in your car, what do you have all around you? Steel. When you are on your motorcycle, what do you have around you? *Skin.*" "Well, if I ever had an accident," he retorted, "it wouldn't matter because I would be dead anyway." "It would sure matter to *me*," I replied, "and just suppose it didn't work out so nice and neat for you that you were killed. Suppose you were only a quadriplegic or on life support for the rest of your days. Who is going to take care of you then? *Me*?! How considerate of you."

A few days later the doorbell rang about two o'clock in the morning. Aroused from a sound sleep, I was instantly furious at the pranksters who would do this and sprang to the window to see who it was. When I opened the door, someone was shining a flashlight through the storm door into my face. It was a police officer. "Is this where Thomas Pullmann lives?" he asked, without any preface. "Are you his father?" he asked next. "Well, I regret to tell you he is in the hospital," came his stunning revelation. "I'm sorry, there must be some mistake, officer, Thomas is in bed sleeping," I said with relief, absolutely sure that I had seen Thomas go to his room earlier that evening. "We have positive identification," he insisted. "Give me a moment," I said, determined to assure him he was wrong. When I opened the door to Thomas's room I found the bed empty and the window standing wide open, cold November air pouring into the house. He and Balal had decided to go for a midnight ride on their motorcycles, and fearing we would hear the window closing and wake up, he simply left it open. It seems that the lights on Thomas's bike were not working, and this caught the attention of an alert police officer, who pulled up behind with lights flashing. When the officer stepped out of his cruiser, Thomas took off through the residential neighborhoods of McLean, with the police in hot pursuit. By cutting across yards and through narrow passages where the squad car could not follow, Thomas managed to get away. However, as he raced along in the dark, he could not see a T intersection in the road ahead and realized too late that a sturdy wooden fence stretched in front of him a few feet away. Instead of slamming into it head on, Thomas thought he could lay his motorcycle on one side in an attempt to slide under the fence. The commotion woke up the inhabitants of the house, who came running out to render aid to a dazed, scared and badly skinned-up teenager. His misfortune deepened, for it was the home of a retired police officer, and soon he was not only in the hospital, but in the custody of law enforcement.

If you have a fifteen-year-old in your house, I will wager you have told this sophomoric genius fifty times that actions have consequences. "Life does not require you to experience everything firsthand. There are some things you can learn from others, especially their mistakes. What you do does not happen in a vacuum, but impacts other people—like parents, for instance." Does that speech sound familiar? It reminds me of the message I read on a T-shirt recently, "I'm not totally useless. I can always be used as a bad example." For us the consequences were far-reaching. While we were grateful that God had spared his life, we now had to deal with the aftermath. First, I needed to redeem the hulk of a wrecked motorcycle from the impound lot and haul it home on my trailer, but a few days later we received a letter from our auto insurance company canceling our policy, not for the accident but for the unlawful acts of fleeing the scene and eluding police. What!? This was *my* insurance company, not Thomas's, *his* accident, not mine; it had nothing to do with me and I did not even have *coverage* for a motorcycle. We had been with the same company for nearly twenty years and never once filed a claim, much less for this incident. When I called them in a rage, first demanding to know how they skirted the law to pry open sealed records of a juvenile, but also why I was being punished for his offense, they put me in touch with one John Pew, an agent with a soft spoken North Carolina drawl who could sympathize immediately. He had a nineteen-year-old who had had several wrecks, and the very company for whom he worked canceled his insurance twice. Yes, John was the man for us. When I requested that we be reinstated, but excluding Thomas from the policy, he enlightened me that under Virginia law everyone in the household with a license must be insured or must pay a prince's ransom in uninsured motorist fees. So are you telling me that if a husband is a reckless driver, the wife cannot exclude *him* either, I wanted to know. "That's correct," he replied, "But don't you worry, I think we can get you insured again." We were, but for the next two years, the amount of money we normally put into our savings account went for insurance, and for that entire period, we could not afford to put anything extra aside.

When Thomas came home from the hospital, I asked him what I should do with that pile of junk still on my trailer. He offered to help me unload it to the back yard until he could sell it for parts. But when we got to the trailer, still hitched to my car, the motorcycle carcass was gone! I am not sure whether Thomas ever figured out which of his friends pulled off their prank, but we found it a block away in the parking lot of St. John's Catholic Church. Thomas placed an ad for a motorcycle "slightly damaged" in an accident, hoping to salvage five hundred dollars for it, and one day two lads showed up to look at it. One of them, a fifteen-year-old named Zach saw that the damage was confined to one side and was quite sure he could fix it up, gleefully rubbing his hands for his good fortune discovering what he perceived to be a steal—a four-thousand-dollar motorcycle for only five hundred. When he told us he had no means to transport it, I quickly offered to deliver it to his house in northwest D.C. Because he did not want his parents to know he was buying it, he gave us the address of a friend and asked us to meet him at the door of a garage in an alley behind the house.

It was rush hour when Thomas and I reached the traffic light where Canal Road meets Foxhall, and as I foolishly whipped around the sharp left to clear the intersection before the light turned red, our load broke free of its ropes, slid completely off the trailer and crashed to the pavement. A few more pieces lay beside the wreckage now, and Thomas was so angry that he grabbed the electronic control console that had broken loose and flung it far into the weeds along the side of the road. "Wait, it's not so bad," I told him optimistically, "it landed on the same side that was already damaged, and Zach needs to repair that anyway." As we struggled to reload the wreckage while traffic snarled behind us, a police car pulled up. Oh boy, I thought, here we go—a ticket for obstructing traffic, another for littering the streets, and another for operating an illegal trailer (which had a license plate but no lights). But when one of them approached and assessed our situation with hands on his hips, I asked him whether he had teenagers at his house. When he said no, I said, "Some day you will, and when you do, this is what will happen to *you*." That coaxed a wan smile from him, and to my amazement, he and his partner directed traffic around us while we cinched our ropes as tightly as they should have been in the first place and took off. They followed us for several blocks until I nervously pulled over and stopped, encouraging them to drive on by. When we met up with Zach, he put his hands on his head and said immediately, "Oh, I didn't remember that it was damaged this *bad*. And without that control panel, it will be a lot harder to get it working." "Oh, I think I know where that missing control panel is," I interjected quickly, fearing he would renege, "I'll go get it and leave it here with the motorcycle, in case you are not here when I get back." With that, he handed Thomas five one hundred dollar bills, and we drove back to where Thomas had vented his frustration. After a few minutes thrashing through the weeds, I found the piece and returned it to the floor of Zach's garage. To this day, whenever we have something for sale, especially if few calls are coming in from prospective buyers, we have a standing joke that perhaps Zach will show up to buy it.

The boys climbed in and out through that window of Thomas's room so many times that the aluminum frame of the storm window was in a constant state of disrepair. When the lower storm panel refused to slide in its track to allow the screen panel to be slid into place behind it during mild weather, it was necessary for me to remove the entire window, realign the panels, reassemble the frame, mount the window again and recaulk around the edges. Does this sound like a fun project to add to your job list every few weeks? One day when the storm panel was stuck in its raised position yet again, I was investigating why it was jammed, when suddenly, without any warning, the glass frame suddenly dropped with a bang. Unfortunately, the index fingers of both hands were in its path as it slammed like a guillotine to the bottom of the frame. The fleshy tip of my right finger was sliced off slightly, but the left did not fare so well. As I instinctively jerked it away from the "blade," I saw instantly that a half inch of my finger was nearly severed. A tiny piece of the nail was still intact, but the other piece was hanging by a flap of skin. I was feeling faint, not sure I could avoid losing consciousness, but I desperately held it together until the ambulance arrived and was reluctant to let go when the EMT on board insisted I allow him to look at the injury. A wonderful surgeon removed the nail, stitched the tissue underneath together and assured me the nail would grow back normally. He was right. Today only a slight scar gives silent testimony to how narrowly I was saved, by the grace of God, from adopting the name Stubby.

Since it would not be fair to reveal the teenage exploits of Thomas alone, I think I might as well provoke the ire of Austin also to reveal one of his secrets. Bear in mind as you read this that it comes from the point of view of a parent and, in accordance with the Universal Teenager Code, is therefore based only upon partial facts, others of which will never be known for sure—unless, of course, you happen to hear Austin's version of it some day. While he never surprised us with the purchase of a motorcycle, we were totally unaware that he had bought a car until one day when we got a call from the mother of one of his friends, asking if we could come over to her house to pick him up. Her daughter had called her from Maryland to report that she and Austin had been "stranded" in Austin's car and needed a ride from there. Wait, wait, wait, Austin's car? I could hardly wait to hear the prequel to this one from Austin, as soon as I got my hands on him. What were you doing in Maryland with a girl? Research for a class project. How did you get there? In the car I bought. You bought a car? Where? From some guy in Springfield. Where is the car now? The police have it. Why? Well, when I tried to get license plates from DMV, they would not give them to me without a title, so I took the front plate from your car and put it on mine. Grrr, I could already see this was only going to take a turn for the worse.

When I pressed him for details, the following sordid tale emerged. As I listened in disbelief that the 1978 Mustang he bought for three hundred dollars came with no title, I asked what information was on the bill of sale. There was no bill of sale—only a slip of paper with the seller's name and phone number. A good start, I thought, but when I asked for it, Austin said that when DMV would not accept it as a bill of sale, he tried to call the number on the slip but got a message that it was not in service, so he *threw it away*—our only evidence in the event the car was stolen and we needed to prove Austin was not the thief, and he threw it away! The current dilemma began when Austin was on the Clara Barton Parkway, where a Park Police officer noticed that he was missing his front license plate, and after Austin could not produce registration for the car, impounded it for stolen plates. First, I wondered why I he was not calling from jail, but I have a feeling the officer took pity on the young lady who convinced him it was a legitimate class project. Not sure where to begin, I went over to the impound lot to reclaim my license plate. "Hmm, federal boys," murmured the burly attendant as he pulled out an index card from the file in his trailer office next to a heavily fenced yard full of cars, "Nope, can't give it to you until the car is released." "Well, how do I get that back?" I wanted to know. "Show me a title and registration and I will release it," he said with steel in his eyes. "But it is *my* license plate," I protested, "and I have title and registration to prove it." "Sorry, but those are my orders," he said, leaning on one elbow.

The next day I loaned our car to Austin and told him to hightail it back to the place where he bought his jitney and demand the title and a bill of sale. When he got there, the parking lot which had been full of cars on the day of his purchase was empty, the building was vacated and everyone had vanished. This was December, and I had almost three weeks of time off because I had accumulated excess leave at the office, but I did not know at the time that I would be forced to use up nearly all of it sleuthing. The first thing we needed to do, I believed, was to pray that the car had been registered in Virginia and to find out from DMV who the owner was. Our first break came when they found the car listed in their records as an abandoned vehicle and provided us the name and address of the last known owner.

251

When Austin and I drove to that address in Prince William County, however, the young mother who answered the door informed us no one by that name had lived there for at least two years, the period of time they had been in their townhouse. Our next move in such a case, according to DMV, was to send a registered letter to that last owner, and if we received no response within the specified period of time, we could establish registration of the vehicle ourselves. It was a happy day when an official envelope from DMV arrived in the mail a few days later. Meanwhile, the car was still in impound, racking up twenty-five dollars per day in storage fees, which at that rate would soon amount to more than the car was worth. Nevertheless, I doggedly refused to give in to them, not only for the principle of getting the car back, but I still needed my license plate.

Hoping to catch them off guard, I went to the impound lot, triumphantly waving our registration, still in its envelope from Richmond, and asked for the car. Not without a notarized bill of sale, growled the toothless Harvard MBA grad in disguise behind the counter. A *notarized* bill of sale, he said. From whence cometh that new requirement? This one put me at wit's end, not quite sure how to get around it. I know I should not tell you this, but I resorted to chicanery. Crumpling a sheet of paper, I unfolded it and penned a bill of sale on it by hand, scribbled the "signature" of the last owner with my left hand, dated it and drew a blank line for my own counter signature. Then I went to our bank to ask if someone could notarize my signature on a document. Although he cheerily said yes, I bated my breath, hoping the young man would not ask me any questions as he read through the note. Was this dishonest? unethical? Sharlyn and Angela will surely say yes without any hesitation. While you and your high school forensics class are debating the question, I will race over to the impound lot again and try to free my imprisoned vehicle. When I got there, the owner of the lot himself was behind the counter, and my heart pounded as he scrutinized my papers at some length before ordering that the car be handed over to us. When Austin and I reached the front gate, however, he flagged us down and told us we were not allowed to leave. What now?! I wanted to know. "Well, your vehicle is illegal with only one plate, and I cannot allow you to drive off my lot with it that way," he said, beckoning us to step out. But he had a solution. It was not illegal to *tow* such a vehicle, so for a mere fifty dollars extra, he would be happy to deliver it to our house. How could we refuse such a generous offer?

Austin was still facing charges in traffic court for driving without insurance, registration and proper license plates. John Pew at our insurance company agreed to backdate the insurance coverage on the car, and after we had procured a title, registration and plates for it, I tried to contact the arresting officer to have the charges dropped. He would not return my phone calls, and because of his shifting schedule, it was several days before I finally reached him in person. He agreed that if, on the day of our hearing, we could show him an insurance card dated before the incident, he would drop that charge, but unless we could demonstrate proper paperwork from before the arrest, the other offenses were still on the table. "But we are talking about a sixteen-year-old," I wheedled, "Does this have to be a matter of record?" "Yes sir, it does," he said, unmoved. "So are you saying you *want* him to be punished?" I asked, taken a little aback at his insensitivity. "Of course," he shot back immediately, "Don't you?" Now that we had paid dearly for it, Sharlyn determined this additional vehicle was fair game to use for errands. It did not exactly provide the same driving experience as a BMW, however, and when she described the play in the steering that required a half turn of the wheel before the tires responded, I told Austin to put it up for sale immediately. Such a death trap should really have been relegated to the scrap heap, but a lady from Fairfax was desperate for a cheap car, and when by coincidence we saw her streak through the intersection in it as we sat at a traffic light one day about six months later, we felt some relief that she had figured it out and seemed to be adjusting to it just fine.

To be sure, the singular brand of genius reserved for teenagers was not limited to Thomas and Austin. In predawn darkness one Saturday morning recently, I was awakened by a disturbance on the street outside our bedroom window. My first recollection was a rumbling noise, which I took for the rolling of my neighbor's trash bin to the curb, and fitfully drifted back to sleep. Soon, however, the sound of tire screeching penetrated my unconsciousness, and with annoyance now amplifying my grog, I made my way haltingly to the window. In the dim light I could make out the figures of two high-schoolers darting about their SUV, which I could now observe perpendicular to the roadway in our ditch. The vehicle pivoted on the edge of the road surface with the rear wheels suspended in the air, and the screeching sound that had awakened me had come from repeated attempts to extricate the four-wheel-drive vehicle without sufficient weight upon the front wheels to provide traction. Having nothing else to use for leverage, one of them desperately attempted to pry the vehicle free with the head rests he had snapped out of the seats. My first thought was to phone for the police, but in the recesses of my mind I could picture teens of my own in this scene and decided to exercise compassion for what had all the earmarks of an all-nighter involving alcohol. Besides, I was intrigued by the entertainment this was now affording me, and I caught myself chuckling at their antics as they puzzled over their predicament.

When I saw one of them talking on his cell phone, I initially found myself silently congratulating them that they had reached their senses and were phoning a parent. Just as quickly, however, based upon my own experience with teenage boys, I dismissed that thought with the wager to myself that another teen would soon be upon the scene. True to form, a lad their same age showed up moments later, stepping out of a white pickup. I wondered what their plan was now. With amusement I watched the pickup back up to the front bumper of the beleaguered SUV, where one of them connected the two vehicles with a couple of bungee cords. Through the thick pane of my window upstairs I could hear three unanimous muffled moans when the cords snapped in an instant. These genius-IQ mechanical engineers actually seemed surprised when their plan failed. While they stood there literally scratching their heads, another from their group of friends drove up. After several minutes of animated brainstorming, one of them pulled out his phone again. All activity now stopped, and while they seemed to be idly waiting for something to develop, I noticed that they were all looking intently toward our house as they talked. Anticipating that it was only a matter of time before my show would be interrupted by the sound of the doorbell, I made my way to the basement to retrieve the ten-foot log chain I keep in reserve for such occasions. As soon as another member of their fraternity drove up in a dual-tandem-wheeled extended-cab truck, one of their party came to our door. Without a word I handed the chain over to him. Minutes later, a *very* grateful and polite young man was standing on the porch again to hand me back my chain, ecstatic to be back on four wheels. He made it quite clear that he knew full well that I could have called the authorities, and he seemed more gratified that his secret was safe than that he had been liberated from his imprisonment. "The first thing I would do, if I were you," I called after him as he bounded down the steps to dash off, "would be to get that car up on a hoist to inspect for damage. For example, after you drag the bottom across the asphalt, you will want to know right away whether the oil pan plug has been sheared off." "Oh, yeah, I never thought of that," he said wistfully, and then he tossed me a quick salute and disappeared with a leap across the ditch.

When Chevrolet introduced its Citation model in 1980, we were in the market for a new car and bought one of the first ones off the assembly line. We came to love that car and eventually believed that it deserved the Car of the Year award it earned from the industry that year. But when we first brought it home, it was a different story. We noticed almost immediately that, because of a factory defect, the manual transmission was difficult to shift into first gear. When we returned to the dealer under the warranty, the service department determined that a part was needed, but the factories were still in full production mode and did not anticipate that parts would need to be manufactured so soon. As a result, no parts shop in the entire nation had what we needed. Soon it was possible to shift only into third gear, and we really should have immediately insisted upon a loaner on the basis that the car was unsafe in that condition. Instead, we believed the continuous lie of the dealer that parts would be arriving "any day." We did demand that the requisite piece be removed from another car still on the assembly line, but since that would delay delivery for some other buyer, General Motors refused that solution. In addition to this transmission problem, the emergency brake had a bent cable and could be only partially engaged, so it too could not be fully used. Because our driveway was on an incline, we usually parked with the car in gear and the parking brake on. But since I could not trust the feeble brake, I placed a block behind one rear wheel. One day when Sharlyn went out to the car to run an errand, I heard a scream and ran to the window in time to see our car gathering momentum backward as it sailed into the street and crashed into the bushes on the other side with a resounding thump. For whatever reason, the car had not been fully in gear, so when Sharlyn removed my block, the gear handle popped out of position, and the brake could not hold it. By the grace of God she was not run over as she bent to remove the block, and, almost as importantly, no traffic was driving past at the moment that the car bolted for freedom. Needless to say, Sharlyn was as angry as she can get and drove straight to the dealer to report what happened and to declare she was not driving such a dangerous contraption one more mile. They gave her one of their demonstrators to use until repairs could be made.

Despite the unfavorable impression the Citation made on us initially, we discovered after it was repaired that we came around to love its hatchback loading, carrying capacity, pep, economy and other features. Four years later we had worn that car out with annual trips to Colorado and Wisconsin to visit grandparents, in addition to our local commuting all over. We had been so pleased with our Citation that we bought another one. For the first time, however, we owned a car controlled by a computer, and it left us underwhelmed from the first moment we drove it. Perhaps General Motors was still trying to get it right, perhaps the software had design flaws or perhaps we simply had a lemon, but we were sorely disappointed. If I tromped on the accelerator of our previous four-cylinder Citation, it responded with plenty of zip; however, the computer of this new car with *six* cylinders seemed to be saying, "I know what you asked for, but according to my calculations, you actually need about forty-three percent of that, so I will be generous and give you half." One problem that we had when the car reached about 70,000 miles was not its fault. On a trip to Wisconsin that Christmas, we left Virginia in relative warmth, but when I stepped out of the car in Ohio to pump gas, I was sure we must have been detoured through the Yukon, from the blast of cold that nearly sucked the air out of my lungs. We continued from there into the teeth of gale-force headwinds from the west fed by Arctic air pouring out of Canada. Steady snow and sleet lashed our windshield, and with the heater and defroster at maximum output, frost was coating all of our windows on the *inside* so thickly that we were wiping and scraping almost constantly to clear a small hole. Suddenly, for no apparent reason the car stopped running. As we coasted to the shoulder, I turned to Sharlyn and said grimly that unless we could restart it, there was a good chance we would all freeze to death before anyone would realize we needed help. After about a minute of silence, I decided to turn the key, and to my great delight, the engine started right up. However, after about an hour the problem returned. Again we waited a short time, and the car started right up. At irregular intervals the stoppages continued, but, thankfully, each time the engine would restart.

Trying to assess the cause, I concluded that the fierce winds were forcing so much ice into the air intake that the moisture was affecting combustion. Surely once we rounded Lake Michigan and turned northward, the headwinds would diminish and reduce the induction of ice. Indeed, when we had no further problems from Chicago onward through Wisconsin to Spencer, I was sure my diagnosis had been correct. The next morning the mercury was reading twenty-seven below zero when we dashed through crunchy snow to the car for church. Everyone in Wisconsin has an engine block heater to preheat the car through the night, so anyone who heard about a certain tinhorn from Virginia who tried to start a car in this weather without one would snort in ridicule. Yes, when I turned the ignition, the poor car responded with "rr (pause) rr (pause) rr …" as if to ask, à la Balaam's donkey, "You want me to do *what*??" The day we left Wisconsin the temperature had warmed to twelve degrees above zero, and the contrast was so palpable that to me it seemed like shirt-sleeve weather. We were continuing on to Broomfield, a suburb of Denver where my parents were now living, and had no problems with the car, so I was sure our troubles were over. I was wrong. On the trip east, while caravanning with my sister Deanna and her family on their way back to New York, the failures were becoming increasingly frequent, but with two vehicles, the camaraderie of family and less frigid air, we felt far less vulnerable. By the time we reached Hazelwood, near St. Louis, we were all exhausted and decided to check into a Howard Johnson's to regroup. The next morning, as we were planning to drive to a local church for Sunday services, the car refused to start at all. It was around New Year, and since our prospects of finding a shop open on a holiday weekend were slim, we all crammed into Pete and Deanna's van and headed for the church, hoping someone there could advise us where to find help. More than one member responded to our plea, and when one of them asked, "When was the last time you changed your fuel filter?" I could not remember that it had ever been changed. He came around to the motel parking lot with his tools and removed the old filter, and the engine roared to life. He directed us to a station not far away that could install a new one, and the rest of our trip home was far less exciting.

There is more to tell you about this 1984 Citation. After Angela had a little fender-bender with it when she was driving home from school one day, I told Sharlyn that besides the repairs and body work, there were enough nicks and scratches to justify repainting the whole car, as long as such a large section of it would need to be sprayed anyway. The original color was a metallic brown that almost seemed deep purple under fluorescent lighting, so I assumed MAACO would check the factory color code and match it. When two ladies select a color, however, whether it be for a birdhouse, wall, rug or vehicle, I will never understand how they arrive at their choice. Sharlyn and Angela decided they liked "antelope beige" instead of the factory original color, and when I first saw it, the hideous hue looked for all the world like *pink* to me. We had acquired a nearly new Corsica as a second car by this time, but from that moment on, this one was the "pink car." By the time Austin's experience with his Mustang wore off, the pink car was already well worn and advanced in years, and when he began openly hinting about buying a motorcycle, we offered to allow him to take the pink one to school. But I was quite sure he would be too embarrassed to accept. On the contrary, it was such a distinctive vehicle that he became "legendary," to use his term, when his friends instantly recognized him zipping around town in it. One Sunday when we returned from church, we discovered that Austin's trademark vehicle had succumbed to a huge limb that had fallen from the cottonwood tree. In addition to crinkling the roof, it had poked out the rear passenger-side window. Undeterred, Austin taped a sheet of plastic over the window and drove off with Brian Hevelone to a youth gathering in Elizabethtown, Pennsylvania. When the insurance company declared the car a total loss, I asked whether I could buy it back from them. For a hundred dollars as salvage value, they retitled it back to me. With the check they handed me for the coverage, I took it to K&G, my favorite body shop, run by a wonderful Jamaican family I have come to know quite well, and soon Austin had his beautifully restored pink bomb back in commission again. However, its final demise came about tragically a few months later, when Austin T-boned a van that was running through a stop sign. This was well before airbags were in wide use, but we are forever grateful he was listening when we insisted that he always wear a seat belt, and because of it, God spared the life of our son.

Our Corsica came along just in time to relieve our boys from embarrassment. Its classy lines, stallion black color and red interior were at least an improvement over the fogeymobile family cars out of which their parents usually made them slink for baseball practice. Angela and I were both reading quietly in the living room one cold winter evening when we heard a muffled whump sound from outside. It sounded as if a car had run over a cardboard box, but we could not see anything unusual from the window, so we shrugged and ignored it. An hour or so later Thomas returned home and asked what the Corsica was doing in the ditch in front of the house. What?! I shrieked in horror when I saw my precious chariot nearly on its side in our deep ditch out front. I depended upon this car for so much and could not afford to be without it. So *that* is what had made the sound we heard earlier. From our window Angela and I had not seen it because it was hidden by the twin cedars. A little reflection allowed me to piece together what happened. When I pulled into the driveway, I had not straightened the front wheels completely, and I seldom set the parking brake because I always left the transmission in gear. However, I remembered that this time as I stepped out of it, I had had a twinge of doubt whether it was fully in gear, but instead of double checking that, I stood for a moment to be sure the car did not roll backward and foolishly decided it must be okay. It was not. Whether it was the wind, constant pressure of the downward slope or whatever else, the gearshift lever popped into neutral, allowing the car to back partially into the street in a curved path, then roll forward downhill and into the ditch. Several times in recent weeks I had seen a tow truck parked in the driveway of one of the homes up the street, but when I walked to that house, no truck was there. The woman who answered the bell said it was her boyfriend who operated it, and a short time later he graciously agreed to come by to extricate my beautiful car so skillfully from its predicament that my mechanic who checked it over could not detect so much as a scratch underneath.

A few months later I would gladly have driven that car right back into that same ditch, however—permanently. I had finished a class and found that after I buckled up to leave the parking lot, the car would not start. There was plenty of cranking power, so the battery and starter motor seemed to be fine, and the gas tank was nearly full. Yet after a few seconds' wait, it started up without any hesitation. I was reminded at once of our earlier problem with the fuel filter, but that was now an item of regular maintenance, so I doubted it could be a factor. Several weeks later, when the problem returned, I took it to the dealer for service. They investigated the possible causes, ran diagnostics on all the computerized components, and found no anomalies. The problem was infrequent and intermittent, but then for the first time, the failure to start graduated to engine stoppage. After a short wait, the car started immediately and continued running for many miles. When we got an invitation to the fiftieth wedding anniversary celebration of my mother's brother Sam, living with his wife Hilda in Fort Collins, Colorado, Sharlyn and I planned to attend. The plan was to travel first to the home of my parents in Rolla, Missouri, and then caravan with them from there the rest of the way to Colorado. We got almost to Morgantown, West Virginia, when the car suddenly stopped running. When it failed to restart after several tries, we held up a sign asking for help and got towed several miles into town. When we reached the repair shop, the car started immediately, and after they spent two hours trying to ascertain the problem, they found nothing. As we resumed our travel, we had a few more stoppages, but each time the car eventually restarted and continued for two or three hours before failing again.

By the time we reached Columbus, I decided to pull into a Chevrolet dealership to have them give it a thorough checkover. They could not get it to fail in the shop, and when their state of the art diagnostic equipment again revealed nothing, they tried to persuade us to replace the main computer. This was not covered by warranty and would set us back a whopping eighteen hundred dollars. We thanked them and continued to Missouri to meet up with my parents. As we left Rolla, I told my father in the lead car to watch for my signal in case the car failed, as we would need to stop for a few minutes before it would restart. By the time we reached Abilene, Kansas, the frequency had increased to the point where we were stopping every hour, so I asked my parents to continue on to the celebration, but Sharlyn and I would need to turn back for home while the car would still run at all. On the return we got near East St. Louis before the car stopped again. We waited our usual five minutes, but it would not restart, so we waited ten, then thirty. Surely after an hour of cooling down, it ought to start up, we thought, but this time it was totally dead. It was Labor Day. What were our chances of finding a shop open today? We had managed to coast close to an overpass, so I told Sharlyn to lock herself in while I climbed up to the highway overhead to see what services might be available. A mile or so down the road was a small town, and as I crossed into the city limits, I saw an old VW van for sale sitting on a driveway. For a fleeting moment I entertained the notion of abandoning our car and buying this one, but it was in tough shape. The odometer read 85,000, but from the look of it, I wondered how many times the dial had spun around to that number. Returning to the car, I told Sharlyn that we had little choice but to walk to a callbox and ask for a tow, hoping someone was open on the holiday for repair. We were in luck. Not only was there a shop about seven miles away, but for the first time, the diagnostic equipment they had could be used for an actual failure. They found a faulty electronic fuel sensor, and in less than an hour, we were singing with Willie Nelson.

On another occasion when we had car trouble, it is quite possible that we were the beneficiaries of divine intervention. I will let you decide for yourself. As we were traveling on Interstate 70 across Indiana, we came to a construction zone, where the highway narrowed to a single lane adjacent to the median for several miles. We found ourselves in rain so torrential that the windshield wipers at top speed were unable to keep it clear; in addition to the deluge, we were following closely in the wake of a truck that sprayed us mercilessly. Visibility was so poor that we could barely discern the boundaries of the lane, much less the road surface. Suddenly, without warning, we heard a tremendous bang, as the car shuddered violently, followed immediately by the rapid sound of whup, whup, whup, whup …. We had struck something in the roadway, and I knew right away that we had blown a tire, but I had no idea whether the object was animal, mineral or metaphysical. By the grace of God we were a few yards from the shelter of an overpass, so we limped a short distance farther and pulled to a stop on the median, a mere three feet or so away from the whoosh of traffic in the lane next to us. Within seconds a pickup materialized in front of us, rolling to a stop. A heavily tattooed young man sporting a ponytail and smoking a cigarette stepped out and shouted over the roar of traffic for us to stay in the car while he undertook the dangerous task of changing the horribly damaged right rear wheel inches from the roadway. Whatever it was that had delivered such a blow to us probably remained a hazard to other motorists, so while he was putting on the spare tire, I pulled out the umbrella I kept under the car seat and walked back to investigate. Finding a chunk of concrete about the size of a football still in the roadway, I moved it off to the side, out of reach of anyone else's wheel. When I returned to the car, our Good Samaritan told us the hard rubber "donut" he had installed was low on air and pointed to an exit sign about a quarter mile away. "Follow me to that exit," he ordered. "You will find an air hose at the top of the ramp." We pulled up beside him at the station, where he had directed me to the hose, but as I stepped out of the car to pay him, or at least thank him for his efforts, he and his pickup had *disappeared*. When I related this incident to my father, he said, "You know who that was, don't you? It was actually an angel sent to help you." Was it also just a coincidence that a tire repair shop was directly across the road? A man there took a big hammer, pounded out our badly dented rim enough that it would hold air, charged us nothing and pointed us to a salvage yard about thirty miles ahead for a new wheel.

When Thomas was in high school, his friend Brian Sansone introduced him to the world of skiing. Thomas was by then already an expert on his skateboard and took to this exciting new sport instantly. One year the boys asked if I would drive all of them, as well as Austin, up to Ski Liberty, near Gettysburg, Pennsylvania. The ski lodge had a huge window overlooking the slopes, but as I sat there watching the skiers for about two hours, I could never spot any of the boys I had brought along. Then Austin came in, angry, wet, cold, covered with snow, his face all skinned up, crying that he was quitting. "What happened to you?" I asked with alarm. As Thomas later told it, the way he himself had learned to ski was when Brian took him over to the expert slopes the first time, gave him a few pointers and wished him luck. So they tried this same method with Austin. "No, no, no," I protested, "As a beginner you go over there to the bunny slope and learn how to stand up first, then how to stop and turn. I'll tell you what, why don't you sit here by the fireplace and warm up and dry out. I think I can fit into your boots. Let me try this out." When I grew up in Iowa, I remember getting a pair of skis one Christmas, but they had no bindings, so I drilled through each ski to insert a roller skate strap. With my first attempt on a short hill, I found them hopelessly uncontrollable and was never on them again. After about an hour struggling with the rope tow and learning how to ride Austin's slippery boards to the bottom, I started to get the hang of it and went back inside to find Austin. "You have to try this," I told him excitedly, "it is really fun." He was feeling better, so I sent him back outside to the beginner slope. In a short time I saw he had gotten so good that the slope was no longer steep enough for him, as he stroked violently against the snow with his poles to gain as much speed as possible. Before long Thomas and Brian found him again, and off they went to some more intermediate slopes. By the time the sun was setting, the boys were having so much fun that they wanted to stay for night skiing, and I had difficulty convincing them it was time to go home. Today Austin has become such an expert that he describes one slope he tried in France so steep that when he stopped to rest, he could reach over and touch the mountain. That awes me—especially when I realize I will never be that good.

The next Christmas I was given a lift ticket as a stocking stuffer, and soon I became hooked myself on this wonderful sport. Although I am still not any good, I have reached the point where I will attempt every slope at least once, wherever I go. Angela absolutely refuses to give it a try, citing this one and that one at her office who came back from a skiing holiday on crutches and wearing a cast. Then one day, just to fulfill her prophesy, I became a casualty myself. The story really starts at the trash dump, where a woman was depositing a long ski bag, a pair of boots clamped in a carrier and a set of poles into the truck. When I asked her whether she was really throwing this equipment out, she said they had belonged to her son, who was never going to use them, and offered them to me. At the time I did not understand the importance of the proper length in the skis one uses, but at my next opportunity I joined the boys for a day on the slopes at Snowshoe, and for the first time had my own equipment. I soon discovered the skis were too long for me, and I was having difficulty turning, which is crucial to controlling speed. As I approached a point where the trails merge, my skis were getting farther and farther apart, as I frantically tried to avoid the splits and bring them back together. I could see the steep slope ahead where I would need to slow down, but I could not turn. In desperation I tried to sit down to stop, but in so doing I twisted in my boots and snapped the fibula in my left leg. By the time I stopped, I was in the middle of the steep slope, from where I could see the lift at the bottom, maybe fifty yards away. At first I thought I could scooch along without putting pressure on my bad leg, but the pain was excruciating, so I crossed my skis in the snow and waited for the ski patrol to haul me down. When I finally made it to the first aid station, I thought the pain was going to blow the top of my head off when the attendant removed my boot. He told me he did not think anything was broken, so I drove five hours home, using that leg to operate the clutch. It was still quite painful the next day, so I decided to visit our local orthopedic, who took an x-ray to confirm the bone was broken. When I asked him whether he thought it would heal in time to do more skiing that season, he said probably not, but that if I were a football player, the coaches would probably have taped it up, injected a little painkiller and sent me back into the game. From the discomfort I felt, I could not imagine doing anything more stressful than sitting in a Jacuzzi. It was my first, so far only, experience on crutches.

My brothers Rodney and Don, who now live in Colorado, are the real experts, and it is always an unforgettable treat to join them every few years at Vail, Copper Mountain, Winter Park or Keystone for a couple of days living a dream. My sister's husband Pete is at about my same level, so he and I have an annual tradition shussing down various hills of New York, as well. Near tragedy and real tragedy followed me to the slopes recently. Don and Rodney invited me to spend a day skiing at Mary Jane resort, near Winter Park, not far from where Rodney lives. As we traveled home along U.S. Highway 40, it was snowing so heavily that low visibility forced traffic to a crawl as we approached Berthoud Pass over the continental divide. When we reached Don's house, we turned on the news to learn that an avalanche had closed U.S. 40 at Berthoud Pass about two hours after we had passed through. Several motorists had narrowly escaped being buried or swept to their deaths in the valley below. We might have been one of them. When Sharlyn and I returned to Virginia, we learned that, by a strange coincidence, my good friend and colleague Dennis Chin had been skiing at Steamboat Springs, just down U.S. 40 a few miles, on the same day we were at Mary Jane. When he stopped for a rest room break, he suddenly collapsed, and although medics were on the scene within about a minute, he succumbed to an embolism.

Another recent skiing adventure to Whitetail with Austin and Retta could have had tragic consequences for me, but I was spared serious injury only by the grace of God. We were taking advantage of a promotional event called "demo day," where manufacturers of skis, poles, bindings and boots not only offer a sharp discount for lift tickets but are also willing to outfit skiers and boarders with loaner equipment for trial. Though I had been to several demo days before, I was never dissatisfied enough with my own skis to exchange them for a pair of theirs. This occasion, however, was my first run of the year, and after an hour or so on the slopes, I had the feeling my own skis were exceptionally sluggish on certain patches created by snowmaking equipment. After strapping on some demo skis and giving them an initial try on a relatively gentle slope, I decided to slip over to one of the black diamond slopes for a real stress test. Soon after exiting the lift, however, when I made my first cut to the right near the top of the trail, I was cast suddenly, without warning, tumbling headlong down the slope. One ski was left ten feet behind me, and I noticed a curious black object come to rest about ten feet ahead of me. It was the toe of my right ski boot. Whether the borrowed binding had been cramped too tightly, whether the boots were inherently defective, or whether the twelve-year-old plastic had simply outlived its usefulness, the result was the same. I was extremely fortunate to be so near the beginning of my run when the boot separated and released the ski from my foot. This provided my first experience riding the lift *down*, whereupon I hobbled into the retail shop for a new pair of boots and a wax treatment, which made a dramatic difference in performance when I happily ventured back out strapped to my own skis.

One year when my leave balance at the office exceeded the maximum that I was allowed to carry over to the new calendar year, I took a few days off around Christmas to catch up on some projects at home. Sixteen-year-old Thomas came rushing in, as I was busy with a drywall taping knife in my hand, to say that one of his friends was selling a car, offering him a good deal on a Ford Boss Mustang. Although I hated to squelch his enthusiasm, I tried to point up the huge liability of a car—not just the obvious costs of the selling price and fuel, but the hidden ones of taxes, licensing, insurance, inspections and repair. "But Dad, it's a great *deal*," I can still hear him say. I know he was angry, but I persuaded him to wait—or so I thought. About six months later he was wheedling for a Pontiac Firebird another of his friends was selling. This classmate had a fondness for tinkering with cars, and one day when his father tired of seeing so many vehicles cluttering the yard, he gave the son an ultimatum to get rid of them. By happenstance my parents were visiting at that time, so I told Thomas to ask his grandfather for his opinion, adding that if Grandpa thought it was a good idea, I would not stand in the way. I was up on a ladder picking cherries in the yard while Thomas and Elmer sat at the picnic table talking, and I overheard some of my father's sage advice. Although Thomas's glazed eyes probably started rolling, expecting the old man to launch into some tale beginning with the classic "I remember when I was a kid …," what I heard instead was the following from him. "I had to learn a lesson when I was a lot older than you are about the difference between the things we want and the things we need," he began. "For many years I dreamed of buying an RV, because it has such appeal to someone who loves to travel as much as I do—you carry everything you would have at home around with you. But the price tag was always far out of reach for us. Then one day I realized that for the cost of such a vehicle, the operating expenses and its low resale value, we could stay in the finest hotels with superior service and still be money ahead without the headaches of ownership that go along with an RV. Now, my advice to you is to ask yourself, not just for this car, but for anything in life you find yourself desiring, is this something I want or something I need?" Thomas did not buy the car.

However, by the time Thomas was graduating from high school, the lure of a cherry red 1977 Pontiac Firebird with a four-barrel carburetor and nearly four hundred horsepower under the hood was too hard for him to resist. It roared like a P-51 Mustang and nearly flew like one. Although I warned him it was a police magnet, he decided he wanted it with him when he went off to college in Blacksburg, and for a time he was the envy of every hot-rodder on campus. One day when he was driving home for the weekend, he got as far as The Plains, about an hour away from our house, when the car made a loud bang and stopped running. He called me from the shop to where he had been towed and said he needed a ride home. The shop owner was not sure, but the engine had seized, indicating possibly major damage. We made arrangements to have it towed from there home, and for over a year it sat on our driveway while Thomas applied himself to more important matters at school. When Angela graduated from college, we had transferred to her, as a gift, the title of the little blue 1982 Honda she had come to love, so when Thomas went off to Russia on a work-study program over the summer, I decided to surprise him by having his Firebird repaired as an early graduation gift. When I found a shop near us in Arlandria specializing in engine repairs that estimated two thousand dollars to get the wheels turning again, I arranged for the car to be towed there. The next day I got a call from the owner of the shop saying he had never seen an engine so badly damaged. Sometimes a connecting rod will penetrate the block when it seizes, but this one had two, one of which showed most of the piston protruding through as well. The estimate he had given me assumed that the block could be rebuilt, but this one had to be scrapped, and we would need a whole new engine.

Over the next month I had a call from the shop almost every day. It was obvious that amateurs had been tinkering around, they told me, as many of the modifications were not according to specification, some even dangerous. The owner's first question was about what engine I wanted in it. The one it had now was a replacement from a more powerful Chevrolet Impala, but we agreed that it would be best to downgrade to the Pontiac engine that was originally intended for the car. The next day he called to say that when they pulled the old engine out, they noticed that the throw-out bearing had been installed backwards, asking whether I wanted them to fix it. After that, he called again to say that in making that repair, they noticed that the clutch was worn out and suggested that while everything was apart anyway, it would be advisable to replace it. In the next call he told me that the original fuel lines had been rerouted to accommodate the bigger engine, but the new tubing had kinks, and where it contacted the firewall, vibration had abraded a hole in the line, pumping raw gasoline directly onto the top of the engine, some of it spilling into the cabin. On it went like this until I thought the project was finally nearing completion. But then he found the radiator hoses dry-rotted and suggested they all be replaced. When the new engine finally got its first test run, the mechanics found the radiator leaking so badly that it needed to be replaced also. Ah, so maybe this was a clue why the engine failed in the first place. Thomas had said that when he heard a knocking sound, he pulled over to check the oil, but found it at a normal level. Perhaps he did not notice the temperature gauge pegged in the red. At last, after a month without seeing the sunshine, the car was ready to squeal its tires on the pavement again. Although the bottom line was nearly twice their original estimate, stretching the limit of the flight instructor funds I had budgeted, I was probably more proud of the accomplishment than I anticipated Thomas would be.

When Thomas returned from his long swim in the Volga near Ulyanovsk, he was so excited to tell us about his venture that he failed to notice the bow on top of his shiny new red car in the driveway. After we saw his videos of the Hermitage and photos of his new friends in Russia, I invited him back outside to see if he noticed anything that might have changed while he was gone. "No way!" he exclaimed. "Are you telling me it runs again?" I threw him the keys, and he did not return for twenty minutes, falling in love with his baby all over again. Although I gave it little regard at the time, we still had a problem with the car. The Commonwealth had legislated tough new emissions standards, and without a catalytic converter this Firebird could not meet them. Any car at least twenty years old qualified for an exemption as an antique or classic car, but this one fell short by a year or two. Both of our boys had an elaborate network of friends, and soon Thomas was working his for a solution. It was not long before he found that John at the Amoco station would apply the sticker and file the approval paperwork. Why was I not surprised that the next time I took my car in for inspection, John was no longer working there?

After Thomas had the car at school for a time, he decided it was a distraction, so a short time later it was back on my driveway with a sign on it. One prospective buyer with thick facial hair and a ponytail rode up on his motorcycle with a girlfriend on the seat behind, and I was quite sure I was finally rid of it until he crawled underneath and let out a string of expletives. It was the first time I was aware that it was so rusted out, so he claimed, that he could see through the floorboard into the inside. Even though I offered to lower the price, he was no longer interested. Then one day a man showed up with his teenage son. When they returned from a test drive, the father exclaimed, "That car's got *balls*. What do you think, son?" Virginia requires an annual inspection of vehicles, but when these buyers from Maryland expressed concern that it would not pass their tough one-time inspection, I played my trump card. Although I was careful not to guarantee it, I said, "If it will put your mind at ease, I can show you the paperwork from the Virginia inspection that we just completed. That should carry some weight with the Maryland DMV." With that, they handed over my asking price. That evening, however, I got a call from the dad again, saying his son did not have enough money in his account to cover the check. This is usually a ruse, but it sounded sincere, so I quickly offered to lower the price for him rather than risk that the car would wait "For Sally" on my driveway again for several more months. Thomas was never aware of it, but because I had made that decision without consulting him, I made up the difference myself, so that he got his full asking price.

Thomas and Austin may someday write a book of their shenanigans, but I suspect many of them are not repeatable, especially as long as I am alive to hear them. I was mowing the lawn one day behind the garage, when I noticed a blotch of discoloration on the cinder block wall. Hmm, I wondered how that got there. I had laid the block myself some years earlier, finishing the surface with a special masonry paint that contains a gypsum sealer. But something happened in this one patch that made me worry I had some kind of leakage that was causing the paint to break down or, worse, the wall to disintegrate. After sorting through a list of possible causes, I was baffled. Then one day I heard the story about two boys with time on their hands while parents were away. When I installed our sewer line across the property next door, it was necessary to pass over the stream that flows through their yard. My solution was to run my pipe over some culvert, but I had bought too much culvert and had three leftover pieces stashed behind the garage. Hooligan boys found them and somehow came to the conclusion it would be fun to fill them with leaves and light a fire, but they failed to reckon with the chimney effect on the other end against the garage wall. With parents due home at any time, they desperately searched through cans of paint in the basement, praying for some shade of white that would cover up soot. It worked about as well as work-righteousness covering up sin.

# Construction 102

From the first moment I saw the partially completed basement of our house, I dreamed of all the extra storage I could get by excavating out the vast area in the back that was just crawl space. When my father had undertaken a similar project in Westgate, Iowa, he suspended half of the house at a time on jackposts while he built the foundation right up to the floor. But his house was wood frame construction, which would be somewhat forgiving of a slight shift when the building would come back to rest on the new foundation; mine was masonry, and I was worried that I would end up with cracked and weakened walls. So I concluded it was vitally important that the original foundation not be disturbed at all, hoping I could excavate close enough to build a retaining wall to hold it in place. The problem for me was the center, where the floor joists rested on the fireplace foundation. I would also need to leave that foundation alone as an island in the center of the new basement surrounded by its own retaining wall. I would run a steel I-beam lengthwise from one end of house to the fireplace foundation and then a second beam from the fireplace to the other end of the house.

When I located a foundry near Baltimore that sold I-beams, I should have borrowed or rented a truck, but I confidently drove into the factory with my little Corolla, put a blanket on the roof and motioned the crane operator, shaking his head incredulously, to carefully lower two chunks of steel on top. Although I got home without incident, this was not very smart, as I probably risked a serious accident or at least a citation from a state trooper who would not have listened sympathetically to my story. Starting with narrow channels to support the center of the house on jackposts, I put my pick and shovel into action on this exciting new project. Nothing is ever as easy in implementation as it is in concept, however, so where I was shoveling dirt in that picture in my mind, I had not foreseen striking rock. In my ignorance I had no idea how fortunate we were that our house lay where it was. Two doors away, Bill Lockwood some time later took me to his partial basement to show me the vein of solid bluestone upon which his house rested. A few years later when new houses were built across the street, developers spent most of a week dynamiting rock in order to construct their foundations. My vision was to use the soil for landscaping all over the yard, but when Carl Zimmerman heard that, he scoffed that nothing will grow in that "mineral soil you are spreading around like it was topsoil." He was wrong about that, as I would discover in time, but it served to remind me what a tenderfoot I was in taking this on. Needless to say, I had not anticipated that at least half of the volume I was unearthing was rock. Fortunately, most of them averaged about football size, but soon Stone Mountain was building up in the back yard. When the pile reached about twenty feet long and four feet high, Bill Lockwood asked me one day what I was going to do with it. It was not an idle question. A branch of Pimmit Run that flowed through his property was gradually eroding his back yard, and he asked if he could load up his trailer with these stones to shore up its banks. What a godsend that was to solve a problem for both of us, and he even did most of the work hauling that pile away.

When I found that my wheelbarrow was useless for hauling such a heavy load of earth up the ramp out of the basement, I rigged up a boat winch on the far wall of the garage and pressed the little blue coaster wagon we had bought for the kids into service to carry out rocks and soil. Although it worked perfectly, this wagon was intended as a toy, never for the heavy duty to which I was subjecting it, and as pieces began to snap off and bracing eventually broke through the metal, I patched, bolted and wired it together as I willed the poor thing to continue its life just a little longer, and a little longer …. Everything was going well until I hit the big one. It was a rock about three feet in diameter and nearly two feet thick. While I was contemplating my options, whether to dig a hole deep enough to bury it or to attempt breaking it up with a ten-pound sledge hammer, my parents came for a visit, accompanied by my mother's sister Lorene and her husband George. Both my father and George convinced me that the three of us could roll it out of there and haul it away somewhere. George and Lorene had never been to Washington, so we took a few days off to show them "all dem cement buildin's" in town, and even flew them off in my airplane over to an island for some seafood one afternoon. All of the Gimbel sisters on my mother's side were very attractive, and Lorene was quite a lovely woman even into old age, yet George always pretended to be a ladies' man, even into old age. "I always told Lorene that when she got to be forty, I was gonna trade 'er in for two twenties," he would say boisterously. Sometimes he would add, "I would rather smell perfume than liniment."

There was a story I often told about George in his later years that, at the time, I considered to be amusing. When I later found out that he had been showing signs of dementia, perhaps full-blown Alzheimer's syndrome, it turns out to be a little tragicomic. At the family gathering for the fiftieth wedding anniversary of my parents, each family was asked to bring a nine-by-thirteen baking dish of frozen lasagna. As I approached the main cabin one day, where everyone assembled for meals, devotions and announcements, I met George carrying two of these foil wrapped glass dishes stacked up and asked if I could help him carry one. When I asked where we were going with them, he said he was taking them back to his cabin to heat them up in the oven. As he led me into the cabin, two young children who had been watching TV asked us what we were doing there. As soon as George realized this was not his cabin, we pulled the lasagna back out and entered another one he was quite sure was his. When an adult came out of the bathroom and asked us what we thought we were doing, I asked George to look at his key, which would have the cabin number on it. Lorene had the key, he said, so we headed back to the main cabin to find her. When we finally located her in the crowded cacophony of people, George asked her for the key. "Why, *you* gawt it," she drawled in her distinctive, slow South Dakota-German accent. George fished around in his pocket for a few seconds, then grinned saying, "By goll', I do," as we left again, bound for the right cabin this time.

My objective was to have a dry basement, and I was willing to go to great lengths to achieve it. Although it involved breaking up the partial floor already there and digging over a foot deeper, soon leaving me slopping in mud as I hit the water table, yet I considered this an essential step in order to do the job correctly. The strategy I adopted was actually to allow moisture reaching the walls to drain *into* the basement. With several pieces of cast iron sewer pipe I had left over from our septic tank conversion a few years earlier, I built weep holes into the footers of the retaining walls. As the walls went up, I pargeted the outside of the cement block with mortar and, when that dried, covered it liberally with foundation tar and filled the void between the wall and the original soil with gravel. Then I laid piping all through the basement area leading to an underground drainage trunk to the outside. I covered this network of piping with a layer of gravel and then spread plastic sheeting over that before pouring my cement floor on top. Once again I underestimated the magnitude of a project involving concrete. I rigged up a curved chute from the driveway for the ready-mix truck, and our wonderful neighbors Pierre and Bakhtavar Sales next door helped me haul load after wheelbarrow load, sloshing through wet cement to spread it evenly throughout the basement area. Seriously miscalculating that in such a cool, enclosed environment away from direct sunlight concrete would not set up quickly, I must say that I discovered a newfound respect for what weird stuff cement is. When I saw that we were not keeping up with it, I had Sharlyn place a frantic call to Lorena Stiles, a nearby member of our church, who had two teenage boys willing to rush over to lend a hand. Nevertheless, to this day we have an uneven floor with a few rough untroweled sections, but it has provided excellent storage space for over thirty years without a drop of moisture.

By the time I finished this project, I envisioned another which would involve major renovation, but Sharlyn had already endured so many reconstruction efforts on the house that she would not bear even to imagine yet another one. So it would not be until we had an empty nest that Freud had predicted that my dreams would finally come true, but that was several years away. Meanwhile, three members of the family were rocketing through childhood, and by the time Sharlyn and I turned around twice, one of them was knocking on the door to college. Was this not the same little girl who only yesterday was boarding the school bus for her first day of kindergarten? And the one who stormed into the house a few days later to say she was never going back because, "Dara said … my … picture … was YUCKY," as she sputtered between sobs. Never was a parent prouder than we were of Angela, who graduated near the top of her class of almost four hundred, and with SAT scores of 1400, her choices of schools were wide open. When I once made the mistake of pointing to Angela's achievements trying to motivate Thomas, he replied, "But I don't want to be a megatron like Angela." After visiting the University of Virginia, Duke and one or two others with her mother, Angela selected Virginia Polytechnic Institute and State University, better known as Virginia Tech. Although we greeted her choice with relief because the instate tuition was considerably lower, it was still necessary for us to play the ace we had been holding in reserve for quite some time. Until now we were able to exist on one income, so Sharlyn was able to care for children at home. Now, however, to avoid drawing down our savings completely or incurring debt for college expenses, Sharlyn took a job, first for a temporary agency and later part time for the property management office of Laughlin Realty in downtown McLean. Then one day Ginny Kass, one of my colleagues at the Office, told me that APPWP, the company for whom her husband Ralph worked, needed someone with Sharlyn's qualifications. After a short stint with this small human resources company, Sharlyn resumed her government career by landing a position at the Motion Picture, Broadcasting and Recorded Sound Division at the Library of Congress. Yes, we both worked for the same agency, and it was very satisfying for me to have her there with me.

After Thomas whirled through high school, he chose to follow in the footsteps of big sis, as he still calls her, and was accepted at Virginia Tech also. Because of the school's excellent reputation for turning out military officers, I had the idea that Thomas could be an ROTC cadet, with a career in aviation. However, Thomas was not cut from military cloth and had different objectives, opting out of the program before it even began. We noticed quite a change when he came home for the first time at Thanksgiving, when the impetuous high school youth that went out the door at the end of summer was replaced by a polite, circumspect, reflective young man. This quality deepened in him dramatically in the wake of a tragedy the same weekend he was home that hit him like a thunderbolt. He and some friends were traveling down the George Washington Parkway headed for Georgetown in two cars, when the driver of the car following behind Thomas lost control, crossed the median and was broadsided by an oncoming car. The impact crushed the door of the rear seat of the Volvo where Tom Peterson was sitting, causing grave injuries. He survived about a week before he died. For a parent there is no greater pain on earth, and for all the empathy we felt for Ron and Elsa, it was really impossible for any of us to share the excruciating anguish they endured. We had known Tom since elementary school, where one insensitive teacher, upon discovering she had two boys named Tommy P., ignored both the snickering of the class and the self-esteem of our Thomas by actually suggesting the one be addressed as Tommy P.E. and the other as Tommy P.U. Young Tom Peterson had been in our house a number of times and had flown with me in my airplane, and now in a blinding flash he was gone. I can still feel the shock to this day.

Angela retained her lofty principles all through school and graduated at the top of her class with a degree in mathematics. In the spring before graduation, she received job offers from a number of companies, one of which flew her to Washington for an interview. As we sat in the airport for her return flight to Roanoke, the airline announced the flight was overbooked and offered a voucher for a free flight to anyone willing to give up a seat. When we learned that she could catch a later flight to Roanoke that same evening, we traded in her ticket. With the voucher she was able to fly to Denver, where she basked in the summer air for a few days on the hammock of my brother Rodney and his wife Barb at their beautiful chalet high in the mountains near Boulder. Think about that—she had traded a mere three hours of her time for a round-trip flight to *Denver*. Someone else was even paying for the initial flight, and the delay only meant that she could spend additional time with her family and arrive at her destination with her next-day schedule intact. Whenever I reflect upon what a good bargain this was for Angela, my thoughts arrive at a magnificent event Sharlyn and I experienced some time later, which I shall describe in more detail shortly. While it is a common theme among fresh graduates to set up housekeeping in an apartment when they start out, I recalled my father's principle never to rent the house in which you live if you can own it. So we suggested to Angela that she move back into her old room in our house until she could save up enough money to buy her own place, whether that be a townhouse or condo, or even a single family dwelling within her means. She perceived the soundness of this advice immediately and settled in with us again as she started her new job at American Management Systems, Inc., a research and development company in Fairfax.

As Angela watched her nest egg grow, we learned one day that the young girl who loved to spend her newspaper carrier money on other people was back. In gratitude to her mother for returning to the job market in order to put her through school, Angela was sending us to southern England to retrace some of her steps a few years earlier when she had gone to England and France. Sharlyn and I had not only never been to Europe, but we had no *desire* to go. After all, I had seen Westminster Abbey, Big Ben, double decker busses, bobbies and beefeaters, and all the rest of Britain any number of times in the movies and on TV. Why would I want to travel all the way over there just to see what I had already seen? I was wrong. It was awesome. When you are looking down at the floor of the Abbey where Chaucer is buried (yes Chaucer, *Chaucer*, right there!) or standing at the exact spot where Anne Boleyn was beheaded, your experience is not just with your eyes as from a photograph or electronic screen but from an emotion that wells up from deeper inside. You will need to read Sharlyn's journal for all the details, but the itinerary through the Cotswolds, Shakespeare's home at Stratford-upon-Avon, Roman pools and ancient coins at Bath, Oxford, Tintern Abbey in Wales, Stonehenge and the plains of Salisbury, Rye, Brighton, Canterbury, Kent Castle and the theaters and sights of London was the thrill of a lifetime.

It was my impression that English is spoken in England, but we sometimes had difficulty understanding what the people of London were saying to us. A little shop we visited near the British Museum was offering a variety of sandwiches arrayed in a glass display case. When I pointed to the one I wanted, the clerk asked, "TGUAY?" "Excuse me, what are you asking?" I replied. "TGUAY?" he repeated. As I turned to Sharlyn to see whether she had understood it, he pointed behind his head to the sign that announced two different prices—one for carrying the food out and the other for dining at a table inside the shop. What we heard was the Cockney version of "Take Away?" We were continually amused by the accent and delightful expressions of our tour guide Patricia, who instructed us where the bus would "set you down" and "take you up" for a tour "whilst I am engaged in my nuvel." "Now, you Americans commonly shorten Patricia to Pat," she admonished, "But here in England, Pat is what we call someone named Patrick, and since I am neither Patrick nor Irish, please do not call me Pat." "How many of you on the bus are from either America or Texas?" queried another local tour operator with a smirk as he stepped aboard. When the tour took us past the "flat" of actor Benny Hill, the guide took the opportunity to explain that "what you Americans call an apahtment we call a flat, and what you call a flat we call a punct-chuh." As the coach moved slowly through the streets, he pointed out the former home of the Earl of Montague, who was beheaded after falling out of favor with the crown. When the king realized that no official portrait had ever been made, he ordered the head sewn back on and the corpse propped up for the painting. "But the ahtist had the veddy devil of a time getting the Euhl to smile," quipped our tour guide dryly.

Around Thanksgiving of 1995, we received a strange letter in the mail. It was from one Elfriede Pullmann in Germany, explaining in German that she had recently seen a book listing Pullmanns who had emigrated to America, and from the twenty-odd names on this roster, she had selected me at random as the one to whom she would write. She was asking whether my ancestors had, by chance, come from Germany. At first I was excited, thinking she might be a link to valuable genealogical information, but then I remembered that we were descended from Püllmanns, not Pullmanns. Our name was the same as hers now, but only artificially, through anglicization. Though my German is not good, I provided her with family tree information, stressing that in addition to the spelling differences, my relatives were from Lutheran territory around Hanover in the north, not the Catholic Bavaria and Hessen areas in the south from where hers originated. Over the next few months we gradually became friends through an exchange of letters, until I suddenly got an idea. We have a family reunion of all the Pullmanns in America every five years, and the next one was approaching the following year, July 1997. Even though I was quite sure she was not a relative, I decided to explore the possibility that she might want to attend it with us, not as a genealogical trophy to present to the family but more as a symbolic representation of the Old Country. Not expecting her to take me seriously, I was at the same time surprised and pleased when she accepted my invitation. It had always been her dream to come to America some day, she said, but she had never thought the opportunity would arise.

We told Elfriede that her only expenses would be her airfare and whatever souvenirs of America she wanted to buy. Otherwise, she would be our guest, and we would cover the costs of food and lodging, wherever we traveled. Here was a lady seventy years old, willing to come alone to a country in which she did not speak the language, trusting that strangers would not leave her stranded at an airport in a foreign city. Not willing to rely on recognizing her from a photo, we mailed her one of the T-shirts everyone would be wearing at the reunion and asked her to be wearing it when she arrived—to help us identify her. We stared intently at every passenger deplaning at the international terminal, and finally there was one smiling broadly, not wearing the T-shirt as we had requested, but waving it instead. Unmistakably, it was Elfriede. When I rolled down all the windows of the car to let overheated July air escape, she motioned for me to roll them up—not only because the draft bothered her, but she was actually basking in the wonderful heat. Back at our house, she asked for "ein Glas Wasser." But when I poured a glass of water for her, she said, "Haben Sie Wasser mit Gas?" Wasser mit Gas, Wasser mit Gas, ah, I bet she means soda pop. But when I opened a can of Pepsi for her, she wrinkled her face and said, "zu süß, zu süß." Too sweet, huh. Now stymied, I was unsure what to offer next, not realizing that in Germany everyone prefers carbonated sparkling water, not the water straight from the tap, even though it is perfectly safe to drink. After her nine-hour flight I considered that stretching her legs a bit might be good for her, so I asked if she was up for a stroll through our neighborhood. Again she soaked up the sunshine, and as she looked left and right at spacious yards and homes, we heard the words "viel Platz, viel Platz," so much space, over and over.

Though Sharlyn spoke nary a word of German, the two ladies bonded instantly, and when we got home from our walk, the first thing Elfriede wanted to do was to fix supper for us—Haferflockensuppe. Haferflocken, Haferflocken, oh, I should know what Hafer means, I told myself as I disassembled the compounding the German language is so fond of doing. Oats, that was it. You want to fix oatmeal soup? Oh, that should be yummy. Never bashful, Elfriede was a whirr as she whipped open cupboard doors, looking for her ingredients. "Haben Sie Sahne?" She wanted cream, but when we showed her the jug of milk in the refrigerator, she raised her nose, but then said, reluctantly, "Ach, ja." Eventually her creation was finished and ready to serve. Not expecting much, I sampled a half spoonful from the edge of the bowl Elfriede had liberally ladled out for me. It was delicious. My mother sometimes made what she called milk soup, with noodles or maybe flour-egg dumplings stuffed with a little cottage cheese, and it was one of my favorites. Elfriede's soup was much like it, and I wondered if they had learned from the same kitchen. The next day after church, Elfriede wanted to buy lunch for all of us, but I tried to remind her we had an agreement that she would not pay for anything. We thought the Three Pigs Barbecue would have the slaw, pork ribs and sausages on the menu that we perceived Germans would enjoy, but while everyone was finding seats, I placed our order and paid at the counter. Elfriede wanted a beer with her lunch, but she was astounded that there could be such a thing as a restaurant that did not serve it. When we finished eating, she wondered where the check was. "Ich habe bezahlt," I told her, attempting to explain I had already paid it. She was upset when I refused the fifty-dollar bill she extended. Crossing her arms across her chest, she stubbornly proclaimed, "Dann ich bleibe hier," informing us in no uncertain terms she would not move from this spot until we allowed her to treat us. Reluctantly, I accepted the fifty she proffered.

We had warned Elfriede that the journey to Kansas City by car would be a long, perhaps boring, one, farther than a drive across the entire length of Germany, but we felt this was the best way for her to see the land and soak up the flavor of America. Since we would not begin our trip until midweek, however, we had a day or two to show her a little of Washington. After we strolled past the White House, she saw a kiosk on the Ellipse selling postcards for ninety-nine cents. When Elfriede handed over a dollar for one she selected, the clerk asked for three cents more. Elfriede set her jaw, turned to me and said in English, "Why?" In Germany the price is the price, so she expected a penny *back*, not to reach into her purse for three *more*. "Steuer," I told her, explaining our crazy system of sales tax. "Ach," she humpfed, as she pulled out her three pennies. We remembered from her letters that she grew flowers in her yard in Groß-Zimmern, so Sharlyn suggested we take her to the Botanic Gardens at the foot of Capitol Hill. A place like that requires no translation, and she enjoyed it for at least two hours. When we emerged, she stopped to gaze at the huge Capitol building a short distance away. Sharlyn and I assumed she would be content with a photo of herself against the Capitol in the background. No, she motioned toward it, indicating we should get closer. While Sharlyn waited on a bench, Elfriede and I crossed over the street to the grounds of the Capitol. Thinking that would satisfy her, I was surprised when she started up the long stairway on the west side of the building. When we finally reached the top, she waved to Sharlyn far below and motioned to me that we should go around to the front side. In those days it was still possible to walk in unescorted, so we ascended the long set of steps and passed through the main entrance leading to the rotunda. As she gazed in awe, slowly letting her eyes reach the top of the dome high overhead, a tear rolled down her cheek, and I finally figured out what she was saying to me in German, "I never thought I would see the day that I am *standing* in the Capitol of the United States."

Every time we stopped to eat on the way to Kansas City, Elfriede reached for her purse to pay, but each time we reiterated our promise that her stay in America was going to be at our expense. When we reached the Mississippi River, Elfriede became excited to reach another item on her list of symbolic places in her mind that represented America to her. Part of the plan I did not mention to you before was that Elfriede's twenty-year-old grandson, Torben, was flying directly from Frankfurt to Kansas City, where we would meet him at the airport. The Midwest would host a double reunion that day, as Elfriede was overjoyed to welcome Torben to join us. Communication suddenly took a quantum leap forward, as Torben's excellent command of English made understanding Elfriede so much easier. As we were returning to the car after collecting Torben's luggage, he spotted a water fountain and wondered what it was. "We do not have such things in Germany," he informed us. Following three fun-filled days introducing the Germans to the Americans, we bade our farewells to many we would not see for at least five more years and a few we would not see until we reach the Church Triumphant one day.

Our plan with Torben was to drive across farm country to Wisconsin, where we would spend a day or two with Sharlyn's family. Angela had traveled with us from McLean to Kansas, so now we were packed five together, sweltering in temperatures that soared into the triple digits. Only then did I discover that the air conditioning in the car must have been low on Freon and was barely putting out any cool air. From my rear view mirror I could see Angela's anguished expression as she sat squeezed in the middle of the rear seat, barely suppressing the urge to throttle me. Halfway across Iowa I could see a tremendous thunderhead building up, and I knew that in a short time we would have some relief. As we passed through those welcome showers, the temperatures outside went down twenty degrees, but more importantly, Angela's thermometer inside the car also dropped back into the normal range. Fortunately, she was planning to spend a few days with Grandma and Grandpa in Wisconsin, so she would not be continuing with us from there. From Spencer the plan was to travel south again, pass

269

through Chicago, swing around Lake Michigan and cross into Canada. Elfriede was excited again when we came to Chicago, as she ticked off another of her most memorable sites, but both she and Torben were blown off their feet by the spectacular Niagara Falls, where we reentered the United States. My sister Deanna graciously hosted us for an evening of games and camaraderie when we passed through Syracuse on our return through New York City and Philadelphia on the way home. We allowed just enough time for Torben to tour Washington with us for a day before they caught their flight together back to Germany. As we bid them farewell, Torben told us that next year they would play the host to us in Germany. We did not yet know that we would have a wedding to plan the following year, but we left room in our schedule for a return to our roots in Europe, and as the photo journal of our tour all over Germany with Torben and Elfriede will attest, they gave us by far the better part of the bargain.

As Thomas approached graduation, we extended to him the same offer we had given to Angela to live with us until he could stand firmly upon both feet. When he seemed cool to the notion of moving back in with parents, we promised to give him as much privacy as possible, but it was not until Sharlyn heard the beeping of a truck backing into our driveway to drop off his belongings that we knew for sure that he intended to occupy his old room again. When I came home and saw the sofa, lamps, chairs and boxes filling half of the garage, I asked Thomas what he intended to do with it. "Well, I was thinking it could go in the basement," he suggested. "What about the things we already have in the basement?" I asked, wide-eyed. "Well, I was hoping we could get rid of that stuff," he ventured. "But what if your mother and I need it?" I wanted to know. "Well, maybe we could build a shed then," he offered. "I'll tell you what, Thomas," I answered, "go down to the land office of the county and take a look at our plat, and if they can show you any place on our land where we can legally have a shed, I will build it." Bless his heart, he came back later that week from the office of records and informed me that we could erect a shed at one end of our property next to the garage I had built. "Are you sure?" I asked suspiciously. "That's what they told me," he replied, producing the business card of the clerk with whom he had discussed it. Relying on that information, Thomas and I started digging the footers for our shed. As we encountered pesky rock again, we hit one that was too large to move, so I decided to break it up. To this day I thank God that Thomas's guardian angel was on duty to deflect a piece of shrapnel that zinged an inch past his eye when I gave the stone a whack with my sledge hammer. The local lumber yard dropped off the kit we purchased, and before long we had a beautiful shed spacious enough for not only all of Thomas's wares but my lawn mower, bicycles and garden tools as well.

Austin had just graduated from high school, and against the odds that Sharlyn and I had laid that he would not choose to attend Virginia Tech, he forsook his wanderlust that might have taken him to join friends already accepted at the University of Arizona and his desire to be near the ski slopes in Utah in order to follow the now established tradition to enroll at Tech that fall. About a year later Angela met a young man named Paul Keiser, whom we remembered as a little toddler crawling around under the chairs as we sat in the Bible class of our former congregation in Alexandria. Until that moment Angela's credo was close to the message I saw on a lapel pin at the airport one day, "I don't like your approach, but I would like your departure." Several months after they met, Paul approached me formally to ask for her hand, and we were pleased to welcome a new son into our family. When Angela and Paul moved the last of her things into their first home together not far away from us, I started to make plans for major changes to our house. The most urgent need was for an additional bathroom. If the one bathroom we had was occupied just as I got up in the morning, you would be greeted by a spectacle remarkably resembling a Hopi rain dance. Years earlier I had hoped to install a toilet in the basement, but the floor was lower than the sewer line, and the very thought of pump failure was reason enough to defer that idea. But there were other considerations. We had the attic and loft full, junk stashed under every bed, and a card table or game board behind every door. And it was not just storage. Not only were there no guest rooms, but all the rooms were on one floor, most of them bedrooms. No, we needed to get the bedrooms upstairs on a second floor, where they belonged. What is more, for the first fifteen years or so we were in our house, we had no air conditioning, but when too many summer evenings produced insomnia, we eventually invested in window units. But every spring they were hauled from the basement, and every fall they were uninstalled and returned. With a developing hernia I finally had enough of that. Our baseboard heating system was useless for radiating cold. No, we needed a central air system. It was time for major renovations.

To submit such a project to a commercial developer would have cost a fortune, but since most of that cost is labor, I had the idea I could save thousands by doing most of it myself. Although I had never discussed my plans with my father, he had over the years assisted various relatives with renovations and sometimes referred to ours as "next." Not sure what he meant by that, but with his advancing age I noticed these prophecies from him had ceased. As I approached retirement age, I kept my ear to the ground for rumors of a buyout, a program of the government to purge its rolls by offering a bonus to those willing to retire early. Such a bonus would give me seed money, and the retirement itself would provide the time to devote my full energies to the project, but, alas, the rumors floated by without substance each passing year. A growing sense of urgency pervaded the air if I was ever to consider asking my father for assistance. Once I had convinced myself to proceed, however, I now had to present my plans to Sharlyn, who greeted them with a less than enthusiastic response, recalling the trauma we always had with those infernal building inspections. Angela and Thomas too tried to dissuade me from such a major undertaking. But when one of our carpoolers referred me to Bill Williams, a retired architect who was willing to take on a small assignment inexpensively, I had him convert my sketches into pretty blueprints. Although this did little to stir up much more passion in my detractors for the plan, I decided to explore the formal process of securing the necessary permits from the county. It was then that I got my first shock. One of the hurdles along this idyllic golden road is plan review, and when they pulled up the plat for our land, I realized in horror that this was the same one Thomas had seen a few months earlier when he explored building a shed. It showed our property *before* the garage was built, and when they advised him to build a shed at that end of the house, he did not realize they were actually referring to the exact location *where the garage was now*. I was about to take off my hat and ask for a permit, and here I was coming in with an illegal shed!

In case my neighbors had taken notice of this too, I immediately informed them of our mistake and assured them I was planning to remove it. To my surprise they begged me to leave the shed there; not only did they not object to it, but they were comforted by the additional layer of privacy it provided between us. Nevertheless, when I noticed that the property that our church provided for the principal of the parochial school had two dilapidated sheds in the back yard, I convinced the trustees we could tear at least one of them down and replace it. Furthermore, I told them I knew a source willing to donate a brand new one. So with heavy hearts we emptied our shed of its contents, sliced off with a chainsaw the pilings upon which it rested, winched it onto the bed of a Jerr-Dan tow truck, and transported it to the teacherage, where I had already spent several weeks chopping tree roots and digging a foundation for its new resting place. Now we could proceed with a new land survey required in the permit process, and this time it would not reveal any illegal structures on it. Because my first concern with the magnitude of a second story on the house was the uncertainty whether a sixty-five year-old foundation was sufficiently sound to bear the weight, but worse, whether my retaining walls had compromised it, I engaged the services of a structural engineer to take a look. He advised me to fill the hollows of the cement block with concrete and half-inch reinforcement bars every sixteen inches. Instead, I interspersed half-inch with *five-eighths* rebar, alternating every *eight* inches. This was a step I probably should have taken anyway when I dug out the basement, and even if our plans went no further, this could not be anything but a benefit.

Sharlyn had endured renovation for years and contended with the disruption, noise and mess dragging endlessly on, but what engendered the most resistance to yet another project in her mind was that we would now be required to deal with the county government again. She hated confrontation, but worse, she would be forced anew to listen to my rants about it. We had already experienced the trauma of zoning code proceedings, inspectors and bureaucratic red tape at every step of our other projects, and now we were asking for more of it. Her reluctance to proceed, however, took a turn in January 1999, when an ice storm brought a tree branch down onto our house, puncturing the roof. Yes, the roof we would now be replacing anyway if we proceeded, but which would need extensive repair if we did not. In the spring, after I had removed the limb and installed a temporary patch, we used this as an argument in our petition for a variance with the board of zoning appeals, and together with my report that carpenter ants had found their way in, they granted our request. A short while later, on the very day I was planning to take some time from work to apply for the permits we needed, something strange occurred. About midmorning our building was evacuated, and everyone was sent home for the rest of the day. The timing of this hiatus was eerie, giving me a sense of foreboding, almost as if something was wrong. I remember asking God for a sign—that if my request from the county proceeded without a hitch, it would be an indication we should go forward with the project. On the other hand, if I encountered snags, it would not be too late to reverse course. I knew I had my answer when I secured all four of the permits in about a half hour, including the electrical permit, for which I had expected an exam to be required again.

For nearly thirty years I had been longing to demolish that ugly fireplace in the center of the house, which we never used and which occupied so much precious space. So as my very first official act in the project, I fulfilled that long awaited dream before the summer was out, dismantling it brick by brick from the top. Even if we never got our second story, at least I would finally be rid of that eyesore. Poor Thomas could not bear the tap-tap-tap of my chisel every evening, and when he realized for sure that any day he was literally going to lose the roof over his head, he decided to cash in his savings on a down payment for a townhouse. This was a mixed blessing. On the one hand, Sharlyn was beginning to worry that he was becoming too comfortable living at home with few domestic responsibilities, but on the other hand, I regarded him as a good companion and liked having him around, especially if I needed a second opinion or assistance. As my pile of reusable brick in the back yard continued to grow, I eventually reached the area around the flue, where we made a shocking discovery. Stove pipe buried in the walls provided evidence that at some point in the past the house had been heated by this fireplace. But at whatever point a furnace was installed, these branches of piping, instead of being sealed off with non-flammable material, had been stuffed with newspaper. So it was a good thing we had never tried to use the fireplace. The walls would have caught fire from the inside, and by the time the problem was detectable, it would have been too late. From the dates on the newspapers, I could determine that Oscar had never used the fireplace either—in fact, no one since at least 1954 ever had. I sealed up the chimney hole in the roof with a temporary patch, and after many weeks of reverse brickwork, we finally had a gaping hole in the floor all the way to the basement. Now I could remove the retaining wall I had built around the fireplace foundation years earlier, replace it with a section of I-beam supported on steel pillars and reclaim not only all that additional floor space in the basement but all the floor space on the main floor we had given up for a hearth we had never needed or wanted.

So far nothing we had done on our project would prevent us from terminating at any point. Reinforcing the basement walls was only a benefit, as was the removal of the fireplace, and I could still convert the temporary patches on the roof to permanent repairs. But I was about to reach the point of no return. The top course of the brick work I had done some years earlier terminated when I reached the eaves, but if the roof were to be removed, that overhang would also be removed, requiring that several more courses of brick be laid to reach the top of the exposed wall. The company from whom I obtained my bricks twenty-five years earlier was no longer in business at their original location in Arlington, but I was happy that I had saved a few from that lot, when I found a distributor in Manassas who could match them. Winter was approaching, so I would need to hurry if I wanted to finish this phase before mortar would freeze. Now came decision time. I took a deep breath, paused for a moment, then started my saw. The overhang along the entire north side of the house was coming off, irreversibly. The last few courses of brick went on before the first little snowsels of the season arrived, and we were ready to tear off the rest of the roof. But that would have to wait for spring.

Winters in Virginia are usually relatively short and relatively mild, but there was plenty of work inside that I could begin. The new stairway to the second story would occupy most of the tiny room that had once been Austin's bedroom, and, before that, my study. Small as it was, this room had two windows, one of which would be almost completely covered by the staircase and would need to be plastered over. Thankfully, this turned out so well that today it would be nearly impossible for you to detect that a window had ever been there. One of the most difficult challenges of the entire project for me was to calculate the stair risers. The stairway was to be in a U shape with two landings, each with three steps leading away symmetrically so that the bottom and top steps were in the same vertical plane. I would need to know in advance what type of floor joists we would be installing upstairs in order to find out the exact dimensions. The architect had suggested composite I-beam stringers rather than solid wood two by tens, but we had not even talked with building suppliers yet to determine what was available or what specifications were involved. We would also need to know the exact thickness of the subfloor material and what kind of flooring would be installed over it. You have probably seen projects where the builder miscalculated, resulting in a staircase with one short step at the top carved out of the upstairs floor. Not sure I really knew what I was doing, I made my calculations and started building what Thomas called my "staircase to nowhere," because it led to a ceiling that was yet to be removed. If you look at the finished product today, you will see that somehow, miraculously, it turned out perfectly.

As soon as the first warm currents of spring started fooling me into thinking winter was over, I decided to start removing the roof. My strategy was to remove small sections of the roof at a time, leaving as much of the old roof as possible for protection, while we stretched a huge sheet of plastic over the section exposed to blue sky—or should I say, what we *hoped* would be blue. I was optimistic that we had chosen a good year for such a project. The previous two summers had been exceptionally dry, and the long-range weather prognosticators had forecast that the La Niña pattern of the planet would continue for another year. They were wrong. The two months in which we were the most vulnerable to the weather turned out to be two of the wettest on record. My father had just finished building a home in Rolla, Missouri from the ground up, so I was of the opinion that at the age of seventy-eight, he could still give me some assistance rebuilding mine. Only a parent would agree to the deplorable conditions I was holding out for both of mine, which included sleeping together for two months on a twin bed practically under the open air. When I had about a third of the roof torn away, he and my mother drove up with their car, nearly dragging on the street loaded with equipment, including his table saw and power miter. They got to work immediately, and within a few days we had not only the roof and ceilings removed, but the floor joists installed. In order to conserve my leave as much as possible, I started work at the office at 6:30 each day, which allowed me to finish at 3:00 for a full day, or to leave around noon or so to minimize official time off.

A construction site is always ripe for accidents at any moment, so I had to intervene when I noticed my parents inviting trouble one day. The switch on my father's reciprocating saw was not working, so each time he was positioned to operate it, he was having my mother plug it into the extension cord. My mother's seventy-eight year-old ears, however, did not always detect his voice over the perpetual din of traffic past our house. At first it was comical to see their little vaudeville routine. "Okay, turn it on." No response. "Martha, turn it *on*." No response. "Martha! I said TURN IT ON." Without a word from her, the saw suddenly jerked to life. "Okay, turn it off …," and the same sequence would continue again. This was bad enough, but the reverse was more dangerous. While my father was still repositioning his ladder or not yet ready to cut, my mother's tired old ears would imagine he was hollering again and connect the plug. "No, no, no, not yet!" No response. "Martha, turn it OFF." The saw stops. "Can't you *wait*?!" I insisted we put down the saw immediately and make a little trip to Home Depot for a new one.

No one lost a finger that day, but a few days later disaster struck—and not the kind in the ribald old aviation joke about what happened to the woman who backed into a propeller. I was working up on top when I suddenly heard a blood-curdling scream from across the street where we had parked the huge dumpster to collect construction scraps. It was my father. "Daaaa … viiiid! DAAAA … VIIID! Help! Help!" shrieked his voice. Not sure what to expect, I leaped down and ran over to investigate. The latch to the massive front door of the dumpster was faulty and had closed prematurely on my father's finger, nearly severing it. I was quite sure my selfish request for his assistance had not only been far too costly but had put him out of commission for at least the duration of his visit, if not for the rest of his life, but after a trip to the emergency room for stitches, my indomitable father was up on the ladder working away with a heavily bandaged hand when I came home from work the next day. His surgeon had done excellent work, and within a few days he had the full use of it again without even the need for a bandage. I called the waste management company to insist that the dangerous container be replaced with one with a working latch, and as we were explaining what happened to the driver who delivered the new one, he showed us *his* hand, which had one of his toes sewed on in place of the thumb that had been jerked off in a shredder accident.

It seems we were asking my father's guardian angel to work overtime, as he was spared yet again from catastrophe one day. As he knelt on the floor framing a window, a huge section of an outside wall, assembled and ready to be moved into position, was resting lightly against an interior wall behind him. When I passed between him and this wall section, I must have brushed against it slightly, for a moment later I watched in horror as a half ton of assembled lumber came hurtling down on him. Helpless to stop it, I could only witness what seemed like slow motion, cursing myself before it even struck him that I just caused his back to be broken, paralyzing him for life. Instead, he sensed the motion and braced himself in time to absorb the blow, and when we lifted the wall off him, no one was more relieved than I not only that he could stand unassisted but that he could stand at all.

After we had a section of the old ceiling removed, my father was at the top of a ladder on the outside one day looking over the wall to the inside, while my mother sat on the unfinished stairway to the second floor. Sharlyn was ready with the camera and captured this scene on film. I had an eerie premonition at once when I saw the two prints of this. Taken together, they were a picture of my mother, silhouetted at the top of the stairway to heaven, waiting for my father, who was peering over the edge and could see where she was. I became convinced in that instant that my mother's death was not far off, and that she would precede my father, while he was still climbing his ladder resting on earth. I will have more to say about their last days in a subsequent chapter, but this picture turned out to be uncannily accurate, as almost exactly three years later she was gone. Nevertheless, it was also one of the few pictures of my parents working on the project, so I suggested to Sharlyn that we have these photos enlarged and framed for them as a reminder of the last project of their lives and a token of our remembrance of their unselfish sacrifice for us.

We had rain nearly every day, sometimes pounding, sometimes drizzling, and with our constant struggle to provide cover, my father remarked that he hoped he never saw a sheet of plastic again. To hold the plastic down, we sealed it as best we could by tacking strips of lath directly into the old roof, and where the roof had already come off we held it down with cement blocks on sheets of plywood. On Easter Sunday, as we were hastily pulling our plastic cover into place in anticipation of a rapidly approaching storm, a microburst associated with the gust front picked up one of our cement blocks from its resting place and slid it crashing into one of Sharlyn's beautiful end tables below, smashing it to pieces. Once we got a few of the floor joists installed, we quickly pulled plastic over them for the night when the showers came. Shortly after midnight Sharlyn woke me, calling my attention to the bathtub of water between joists. As the water accumulated, it pooled in the void between each span, bulging downward with hundreds of gallons and threatening to stretch the plastic to the bursting point. As I pushed upward with a broomstick on a piece of board I placed against the plastic, attempting to clear the massive pool to the outside, the stick slipped off, puncturing the plastic. Sharlyn let out a shriek that woke anyone in the neighborhood who was not already awake from all the commotion, but by an odd coincidence we had covered this section with a double layer of plastic, thus sparing us, by the grace of God, from commemorating that room Lake McLean. I have never known anyone as optimistic as my father, never allowing himself to be downcast, so he was quite confident that once we had sheets of flooring installed above us and waterproofed with sealant, we could lay our plastic on it and be fully protected. When the rain still leaked in everywhere, we deployed both mortar pans and every plastic washtub, pot, pan, dishpan, cereal bowl and tin can in the house catching the drips. Not admitting defeat when I pointed out that the water was seeping through the cracks between the sheets of flooring, he said we could fix that too. After I spent most of the morning in sunshine meticulously caulking every crack and nail with roofing tar, I was sure we were ready for the afternoon downpour. When it came, water leaked in everywhere. No matter what we tried, we could not stop it.

After we got most of the walls and framing erected upstairs, my wonderful brother Don flew out from Denver for two weeks to lend a hand. What a godsend he was, as his fresh viewpoint, light humor and positive attitude buoyed our sagging spirits after several weeks of exhausting labor and frayed nerves. I had rescued a fifty-pound box of sixteen penny common nails that a building supply company was throwing out because they had a thin coating of slightly brown oxidation. I was determined to use them up before we started into the box of shiny new silver spikes I also had ready to use. In addition to those, my father had selected a box of special gold-colored coated sinker nails designed to grip into wood and resist pulling out. When Don first arrived, I told him that all new recruits must start out on brown nails, then when they have served their apprenticeship and become worthy enough, they may graduate to the silver nails, but only the most elite master builders among us are allowed to touch the gold nails. To this day we joke about someone on the bottom rung of any endeavor as someone who is still using brown nails.

Don came onto the project as we were puzzling how to get twenty-odd enormous trusses up to the top of our building. Contractors and almost anyone else with any sense would use a crane to hoist them up rather effortlessly, but at the tune of nearly a thousand dollars for us to rent one, we concluded that perhaps we could build a ramp and somehow winch them up instead. When I came home from work one day, Don and my father had a marvelous surprise for me. They had pooled their money to rent a forklift, which Don already had the expertise and license to operate, thus saving several hours of manual labor building a ramp and dragging hundred-pound trusses halfway to heaven. But it nearly turned into tragedy. When we loaded the first truss onto the forklift, we found that it slid off because the vertical member of the fork was too short. So we contrived an extension, lashing a stud to the fork as a support for the truss to lean against. This worked well, and we should have been content to raise the truss, unload it and repeat the process twenty-some times. No, we got lazy and concluded that if this held one, we might as well load on two, no wait, I think it will hold three .... Only after we had seven stacked on the lift, bowing that stud slightly, did we decide to raise our first load to the top. Halfway up, the stud snapped like a popsicle stick and the load shuddered precariously. If it fell, those trusses would break apart, crushing Don beneath a ton of useless Lincoln logs. Only the grace of God prevented them from crashing to earth, and to this day I do not quite understand mechanically why they did not slip off. Don was so expert with the controls that he was able to ease the lift up the rest of the way so gently we could barely see it move. Finally, it was at the top, where we could gingerly remove the trusses one by one and pile them up safely on the floor above.

Critical as the time was to get our building sealed to the elements as soon as possible, we were pleased to be interrupted. Austin was graduating from Virginia Tech that spring, and his grandparents and one of his godparents, his uncle Don, just happened to be in town to attend with us. When we heard the forecast for severe weather in McLean that evening, Austin's grandparents stayed one more night with the house, opting to make the long journey to Blacksburg early the next morning for the ceremony. The hard work on the project and sleep taken in snatches, however, took its toll on them, as Deanna's video shows a whole row of celebrants seated in the balcony dozing. Having already missed the scrumptious breakfast the rest of us had that morning, my wonderful parents now missed lunch, volunteering to race five hours back home immediately following the ceremony to babysit the house for the late afternoon thunderstorm predicted. Austin had met a young lady named Loretta Jones, known to some of her friends as LoJo, but she introduced herself to us as Retta. Direct and outgoing, she impressed us from the first handshake, and we liked her instantly. Austin had inherited that hard-charging "Pullmann spirit," as my father had termed this family characteristic, but when we watched Retta stride so purposefully to the stage to receive her diploma that she nearly overran the graduate ahead of her, we realized she had as much of it as he. If you ever have a chance to see the video we have capturing this event, you will see what I mean. We were not surprised when these identical dynamos announced their engagement a few months later.

We had another pleasant interruption to our project again eighteen months later, when our wonderful son Thomas sent us on a tour of Israel, presenting his gift out of gratitude for the years he had lived with us while he built up his equity for the down payment on a townhouse. As with our journey to England three years earlier, however, we had no particular desire to go. Some time after all his children were established in their careers, my father had attempted back then to put together the funding to take the entire extended family to the Holy Land. But when he disclosed this idea to me, I told him candidly, "Dad, I have no desire to see a gas station or tobacco shop that today stands on the exact spot where Jesus once performed some miracle." I was wrong. As the photojournal of our trip will attest, it was the dream of a lifetime. Motivated by similar sentiments to those of Thomas, Austin, out of gratitude for his mother's unselfish exchange of leisure at home for the workplace in order to keep him funded throughout college, gave generous sums for the furniture and accessories he knew we would need to decorate our new home when the project was finished.

I shall be eternally grateful not only to Don, but also to Rodney, who really did not have the time to spare but came out from Boulder anyway one long weekend to help us erect trusses and nail on sheets of roofing. Although he looked quizzically at me at first, he quickly adjusted to the jargon we had adopted, handing me the four-pound hammer when I called for the Quarter Pounder and passing me the ten-pound sledge for the Big Mac. The rains pounded us so hard, as we set up trusses and formed a catwalk on them, that Don and I were drenched in a few seconds. Yet when my conscience forced me to suggest we climb down to seek shelter, Don shrugged and said, "I'm not going to get any wetter now, we might as well keep working." Meanwhile, my parents were below us pushing gallons of water off the new second floor with push brooms, and Rodney counted over sixty times that he emptied the wet-dry vacuum tank, which holds *five gallons*. Fortunately, the carpet on the first floor was going to be replaced with entirely new flooring anyway, because brown leakage from above soaked and stained it thoroughly, despite our valiant efforts to catch the drips that fell in everywhere. The next day we caught a break and took advantage of fair skies to cover those trusses with sheets of plywood. As Don and Rodney gathered up their tired bones for the airport to return home, I scrambled up onto my new roof to tack on tarpaper, thinking that would finally stop the indoor waterfall we had endured for nearly three months. However, when the rains returned in the afternoon, so did the drips—no longer torrents, but still drips.

The roof was now so high above the ground and pitched so steeply that I was scared to be up there and wondered if I should not have it shingled by the professionals. That next Sunday, when we pulled into the parking lot for church, I parked beside a panel truck advertising roofing, siding and windows. I took that as a sign that I should call the number emblazoned on its side, having no idea whose business it was. Expecting to reach an answering machine that afternoon, I was surprised when John Adams, a long-time member of the congregation, answered the phone. He did not mind talking business, so we invited him and his wife Kathy, who was already suffering from terminal liver cancer, over for some pie that same day.

Later, as John sat at the picnic table outside looking over at our project, he said, "I think you can do that roof yourself, but what are you doing about your windows?" Sharlyn and my mother had already been shopping for the high-grade Anderson windows we thought we wanted and had all of the specifications and pricing ready at hand. After glancing over the list, John said, "How would you like to have them *installed* for that price—and with a better window than Anderson?" He was representing Bryn Mawr windows, which had nearly one-inch separation between panes for superior insulating quality and the noise absorption properties we needed for the side of the house facing busy Old Dominion Drive behind us. "In fact," he added, "we can replace the old windows you have on the first floor too with matching custom-made ones for relatively very little more." How could we refuse an offer like that? When he saw the bare walls of the second story, he asked, "Do you have any experience installing vinyl siding?" Although I had nailed a few pieces onto my father's house in Rolla with him, I really had none. "You are going to need some serious scaffolding to do a project that high up, but I can give you a price for that too, if you want," he offered. Shuddering at the yearlong project I would face doing it myself, especially the risk of an accident or a shoddy result, we allowed ourselves to be persuaded by his salesmanship.

By the time Don and Rodney left, Memorial Day was approaching and my parents had been with us for nearly two months. I had hoped I could persuade them to stay longer, but they had obligations back home, which included their medical appointments and all of the surprises of the mail not forwarded to them in Virginia. After my father tacked on the first course of shingles, I watched from the window with a heavy heart as he packed his car for the long drive to Missouri. By the time I came home from work, they were gone. A tremendous amount of work remained, but I was now on my own and cannot recall ever feeling so alone, scared and abandoned. Despondent for several days afterward, I could barely force myself to climb up that ladder every day to nail shingles on such a huge roof. I can remember looking at the vast sea of black roofing paper before me and thinking the task ahead was so monumental that I would give almost anything to be looking back on it as a completed job. At long last I finished the south side, and when I was halfway up the north side, Thomas showed up one weekend with a carload of his friends, and I will never forget the way they danced around on that roof and helped me finish it in one day. Finally, finally, only now, finally, we had no more leakages from the rain—until, that is, the subcontractor who put on the vinyl siding had the audacity to anchor his scaffolding with a spike directly through my brand new shingles!

One day when Angela's husband Paul was out of town, she invited us over for supper, so I wrapped up the task I had started inside the house, threw on a shirt and drove to her house about three miles away. While we sat at her dining room table, I started to experience that feeling I get when I am allergic to someone's dog—a tightening in my chest, followed by sneezing and wheezing. Angela and Paul did not have a dog, but I asked her whether some visitor had stopped by with a dog earlier in the day. She said no, but I continued to feel worse as the evening progressed. Finally, I told her I was just not feeling well and would need to go home. By the time Sharlyn and I got to the car, I noticed that my arms, legs and neck were aflame with red welts, and I began to itch so severely that it felt as if I was on fire. I raced through the streets, trying to get home for some relief as rapidly as possible. My standard joke with visitors from out of town is that Virginia is a very green state, though half of it is poison ivy. Whenever I have come into contact with its urushiol yet again, I have discovered that the best treatment for the itch is hot water, not scalding, but as hot as I can tolerate. This not only provides instant relief, but the sudden heat seems to create confusion for the nerve endings, causing the immune system not to release the histamines that cause the itch, for a period of several hours. When we arrived home, I dashed through the door, tore off all my clothes and jumped into the tub for a hot shower. I asked Sharlyn to get a pitcher to pour a concentration of hot water on my back, which was bothering me the most. As she went for the pitcher, she suddenly had an inspiration, "*I know what the problem is. You had on one of Duane's shirts, didn't you.*" Her sister Marlene had passed some of her husband's outgrown work shirts to Sharlyn on her last visit to Wisconsin, and their house on the farm was always full of cats. Both Marlene and Sharlyn had washed them before I put one on, but there was apparently enough residual dander remaining in the fabric to bring on the anaphylaxis I was experiencing. Because of my sensitivity, we have never been able to have pets in the house, but little Austin wanted a dog so badly when he was growing up that one day he cut out a picture of one, taped a piece of string to it and took it for a "walk" by dragging it around the living room.

To someone who looked at the house from the outside, it would appear that our project was done, but we were literally years away from completion. While the exterior was beautiful, the work on the inside had scarcely begun. Our long-awaited central air system was installed in July, but we could not use it because none of the upper floor was yet insulated. As the summer simmered away, I installed all of the electrical work upstairs and called for the inspector in the fall. When he saw that I had grounded some of the outlets to the clamp screw, he told me that did not meet the code and disapproved my wiring. But I was beginning to worry that the snows of winter would be arriving before I could cover up the wiring with insulation, so I secured his permission to proceed with insulation. Already before the outside walls were erected, we had had the foresight to have several stacks of drywall hoisted by crane to the floor of the second story, but I was becoming concerned about its tremendous weight concentrated for any length of time on these single points in the structure. So I asked the inspector whether he saw any problem with my nailing up some drywall too. As long as I did not cover up anything that needed inspection, such as plumbing, he affirmed I could proceed with it. That is when trouble started. After I checked more than sixty outlets to be sure they had the proper grounding screws or clips, I called for reinspection of the wiring. But a different suspector showed up this time. He saw that I had installed insulation and some drywall and issued a formal stop work order, effective immediately, on the basis that I had covered up electrical work before it was authorized. His brain and ears stopped functioning when I pleaded that his colleague had approved what I did. His exact words were, "I have more experience in the field than he does, so I am revoking his approval. You have a good day now, okay?" With that, he turned on his heel and swaggered back to his pickup.

Not sure whether I was dealing with a turf war or a real violation, I called around to obtain the email address of their supervisor and wrote a plaintive message laying out the conflicting information we were getting from the field inspectors and asking for clarification of the confusion. I was careful to point out that we were not trying to cover anything up and would be cooperative in every way, including the tearing out of any work already done, if necessary. We received a "they were both right and both wrong" response from her, but with approval to proceed as before, with the proviso that nothing except insulation would be covered over. This was good news, not only because I could relieve those floor joists holding up the load with all their might, but because cold weather was on the way, and I had no reasonable way to close off the stairway between floors to contain the heat loss through the attic.

For me the most formidable challenge of the entire project was yet to come. The one bathroom we had was to be removed and replaced with three others. While I had no problem running the supply pipes to these three new locations, I simply could not wrap my mind around the concept of drainage from three distant points to the far corner of the basement where the soil pipe exited the house. The first rule of plumbing, so I had been told, was that sh@# does not run uphill. I decided to ask for help. Approaching one of the oldest and most respected plumbing companies in the area, I inquired about their rate for consulting. When I met with the master plumber they sent out to talk with me, I was most impressed with him and made arrangements to have him advise me how to proceed. He would direct the operation, he agreed, but I would do the work. Whew, his expertise and experience were exactly what I needed. But a few days later I was shocked to receive a letter from the company, citing liability concerns, rescinding our agreement. I was to be on my own. In the process of formulating a strategy in my mind, it suddenly occurred to me that I could exploit the T joint. If I started with the most distant fixture, I could splice in the next one downstream of it, essentially proceeding from there with a single pipe again, splicing in the next in turn, and so on, always making sure I was working my way downhill toward the corner of the house. Although this plan eventually worked out perfectly, it took a great deal of courage to make that first cut through my beautiful brand new floor to install a bathtub. When the job was finished, I had installed three toilets, two bathtubs, three vanities, six sinks and two garbage disposal units. Retta was working for Ferguson, a plumbing wholesaler, at the time, so we were very grateful when she offered to secure over ten thousand dollars worth of materials and fixtures for us at a forty percent discount. I was dreading the inspection and could not bring myself to make the call for several days, morbidly fearful Dracula would return with vengeance in his eye. However, not aware such a thing as benevolence existed out of the county inspection office, I opened the door to a kindly old gentleman from the country, who looked around for about ten minutes, made a few non-mandatory suggestions and told me to hook it up.

When it was time to apply sheets of drywall to the ceilings, I decided that the project would extend for such a long period of time that I could not justify the cost of renting a lift to raise it into place. That was a big mistake. Instead, I followed the methodology of my frugal father, who pressed my mother into service as an assistant to position a "cripple" to prop up strategic points of a sheet after he had maneuvered it into position. My assistant was to be Sharlyn. As I carried a sheet on my back to the top of a stepladder and held it into position, her job was to quickly pin it in place with two props. Already near the limit of my strength and endurance just getting it into position, I had little reserve for delay. With both hands and my head occupied supporting the weight, I could not gesture, so I tried to direct her where to position the cripple by shouting directions. Each time I would yell, "Move it more to the east," Sharlyn would have to run through in her mind how the front door faced north, so east must be … uh … let's see … this way. While I frantically wait for some response from her, I somehow think it helps to yell louder, "East! Move it EAST! There is a longstanding axiom admonishing that if you value your marriage, you should never try to hang wallpaper together. The same is true for drywall.

One of the most difficult areas to paint was the stairwell. How does one position a ladder upon steps to reach the corners high overhead? Oh, I know there are special ladders for this purpose, but my solution was to rig up some scaffolding, using stepladders and planks. It was crude but effective. One of my planks, however, was somewhat longer than the other, so I needed to be careful not to step on the end of that one whenever I dismounted, to avoid raising the other end off its support. As I was painting merrily along one day, a neighbor up the street called to request my help moving some furniture up her steps. In order to minimize the interruption to my painting project, I accelerated, attempting to reach a stopping point before I left. Can you see where this is going? Yes, in my haste I forgot about the long plank and sent a nearly full, five-gallon bucket of paint crashing to the landing below. Paint splattered twenty feet in every direction, as I quickly scampered through a two-inch deep puddle of Swiss Coffee to find something to scoop up as much of my hundred-dollar bucket of paint that I could salvage. Horrific as it sounds, however, there was good news on every front: dried paint can easily be scraped from window glass, the steps and the landing were as yet unfinished, the walls would need to be repainted anyway, carpeting was being replaced, bare wood floors would be eventually taken up to be replaced with subflooring, and, most important of all, no expensive furnishings or furniture were within range—even in the basement, to where some of the goo oozed its way through heat register cutouts.

When the months of taping drywall, painting walls and laying flooring upstairs were finally finished, we moved our bedrooms ceremoniously up a level, in preparation for phase two—renovating the downstairs. Before we proceeded very far with this somewhat smaller scale project, however, we were interrupted by an unexpected call one day. Torben Pullmann was in America on a six-month project, some kind of cooperative agreement between George Mason University in Fairfax and the Technische Hochschule, his employer in Darmstadt. Since Torben has the Alps in his back yard, I was not sure how he would greet my invitation to ski the slopes of Pennsylvania, but he strapped on a snowboard and found the gravity at Whitetail works much the same as in Austria. His beautiful partner Beate, whom we had met when we were in Germany, later joined him for a few weeks, and the two of them took advantage of their opportunity to visit America by jetting off to the west, bound for Las Vegas and the Grand Canyon. Because Torben was unable to accommodate Beate in his tiny room near the campus, to where he could bike to his lab, he asked if they could stay with us. Although we warned them they would be living in a construction zone, they dodged shrapnel, ducked under dangling wires and stepped around piles of debris downstairs to become the first inhabitants of our freshly inaugurated guest room upstairs.

Now that we had three new bathrooms, I could finally demolish the one we had as part of the kitchen for all this time. Sharlyn had been worried for several years that the floor under the toilet was rotting away at an alarming rate and had been saying for quite a while that some day when she was "busy," I would be able to tell by the yelp that she had gone down to the basement. Indeed, when I tore everything out, I found that I needed to replace the full joist. This was okay because the entire kitchen floor had to be stripped to the joists anyway to lay new subflooring for the ceramic tile Sharlyn and Retta had picked out. Then all the old cabinetry was also stripped out to make way for new cupboards and counter tops. After about four years, we could finally stand back and take notice that we had made a few worthwhile changes. The best moment of all was when my father walked through the door for his first visit since making his monumental contribution to the shell, gazed at the banister and balusters of the staircase and said, "This is a beautiful house." My father does not toss out idle compliments.

# Ain't Life Grand (Great-Grand)?

**A**n elderly couple in their nineties was sitting in their lawyer's office asking him to arrange a divorce for them. "Aw, come on now you two, you have been married for, what, over seventy years? Why *now*, why after all this time?" "Well," answered the husband slowly, "we promised ourselves we would wait until the kids were dead." My parents nearly reached their sixtieth anniversary, but while the family was planning a celebration, my mother reminded us that life on earth is only temporary. She was very close to her mother Emelia and decided the time for a reunion was at hand. Sharlyn's grandmother Emma was the only other person in the world like Emelia—two of the kindest and most gentle ladies who ever walked the earth, so much alike they could easily have been sisters. Sadly, I saw very little of my grandmother after I left home because of the great distance between us, but near the end of her life, when she was placed in a nursing home in Colorado, we stopped in for a visit with two of her great-grandchildren. Somewhere we have a photo of a squalling infant and a toddler, eyes still red from bawling, pictured with their great-grandmother, the last and only time Angela and Thomas ever saw her. On December 6, 1974 this beautiful jewel passed quietly into the Light. Sharlyn's grandparents, Ernest and Emma Sanger were alive when their great-grandaughter Angela was born, but on our first return to Wisconsin with her at Christmas time, the hospital in which Ernest was confined would not allow tiny visitors, so we carried a little package wrapped in a furry pink snowsuit around to the outside of his room on the first floor and waved to him through the window. He died the following February. Emma lived alone for a while, but morbidly expressed her desire to be with him almost every day. When her depression affected her ability to live independently, the family moved her to Memorial Home, a nursing home in Neillsville, where she lingered semicomatose, unresponsive for many interminable years before she finally slipped away from us.

My parents were visiting us just after Christmas one year, when we received a call from my father's brother Martin. Their mother, Hilda, had just died. In her later years she was in a nursing home in Winfield, Kansas, where Martin lived and could look in on her daily. In the last few months she declined rapidly, suffering from diabetes, macular degeneration, dementia and lethargy to such a degree that she had no desire to arise for meals. After long periods of sleep, she still preferred to remain bedfast, resisting all efforts of the nurses and family to keep her "active," a relative term for this woman who had the ability to move her walker ahead only a few inches and shuffle six steps to catch up with it. When Martin stopped by on a certain Friday to say he was traveling to Hoxie, where he had once been the pastor, for a ninetieth anniversary celebration of the congregation there, she wished him a good trip.

On the following Sunday morning, January 7, 1979, when the nurse came in to give her an injection of insulin, Hilda remarked, "I'm sure hungry—I just can't wait to go to breakfast." Those were probably her last words. As she sat in her wheelchair in the dining area, she seemed to be turning blue, so the nurses wheeled her back to her room. As soon as they laid her on the bed, she gave out three sighs and stopped breathing. One nurse administered oxygen while the other ran for the doctor, but she was already gone.

My mother became a grandmother exactly on her fiftieth birthday, when Angela was born, but still the mother of a preteen herself, she had mixed emotions about it. She had always loved children, ours in particular, but her vanity stood in the way of complete acceptance of her new role. Perhaps it was not so much the role, but the title Grandma that came along with it that bothered her so much—especially that she would now be called "Grandma Pullmann," the reference to her mother-in-law which had been so abhorrent to her for so many years. Still quite attractive even into old age, my mother did not picture herself as her own mother, who, after all, in her mind was the one we should all properly call Grandma. Incredibly, she would try to pass Angela off as her niece when Sharlyn took the new grandma along shopping with them. Sharlyn and I were ever amazed also, when my parents came to visit, that someone who had so much experience with children could be so naïve about how to approach them. Although Angela and Thomas were their only grandchildren for several years, the great distance between Virginia and Colorado made my parents practically strangers to two small children who saw them only twice a year. Yet instead of starting off from a respectful distance when they arrived, allowing tiny little personalities to become accustomed to them gradually, my mother would burst into the room with a boisterous greeting, scoop them off their feet, toss them around in the air and dance around the room swinging them by the arms. Both kids were terrified and ran away shrieking, slamming the doors to their rooms behind them. If my parents were seated on the sofa when either Angela or Thomas was compelled to emerge for the bathroom, a fearstruck child would press flat against the opposite wall, inching past until it was safe to make a run for it into the safety of the next room.

Sharlyn's parents, on the other hand, were models of grandparenthood. Though they saw their only grandchildren no more frequently than did my parents, their approach was to stand watching them play when they first came through the door, waiting for that moment when one of them brought something over to show them. Then they would bend down to child level to softly admire it and give a gentle hug. They were masters at this. Alvin and Evelyn were not travelers, however, so when their long drive was replaced by airline travel, they soon tired of racing through the confusion of connections at huge airports and eventually made it known that an exchange of visits was no longer possible. Some of George Pullmann's travel genes were running around through my veins, however, so when the onus of biannual visits shifted to us, I did not mind the journey at all. I was probably the only one. Air conditioning in a car was an expensive option we felt we could not afford in those days, so the only relief from hot summer travel was known, tongue in cheek, as four-sixty AC—where you open all four windows and drive sixty. Our boys in adulthood still ridicule the one-inch rule I imposed on them as they sweltered in the steam of the rear seat on these trips. Because I believed gas mileage was substantially reduced by open windows, I allowed them to be lowered only an inch. Besides that, however, I was traumatized by my father's account of a man he witnessed lose an arm because he had hung it out the window. A repetition of such a gruesome scene would not be made on my watch. Further relief came from our discovery of driving through the night, when the air was much cooler and traffic was considerably reduced. Although I no longer have the stamina for such a marathon, we would sometimes drive nonstop to Broomfield, Colorado, thirty-five hours away. Through the marvels of the interstate system, the likes of which George Pullmann could only have dreamed, we could actually complete this *seventeen hundred* mile trip to Denver without encountering one traffic light!

When my parents lived in Rolla, Missouri a few years later, Sharlyn and I offered to fix breakfast one morning so they could put their feet up to relax a little. While Sharlyn cooked up the eggs, fried the bacon and heated up the tomato soup, I ran a few potatoes through the shredder for hash browns to round out the trademark menu we had often enjoyed at home on Saturdays. When I asked my mother what she thought of the hash browns I had so proudly fried up for them, she had no idea how deflated I felt when she said, "Why, they're nothing but potato pancakes." By the time my parents came out to help us with the massive renovations on our house in 2000, the ravages of Parkinson's disease were already advancing upon my mother, as her physiological age was catching up to her chronological one. By 2002 she was in nursing home care, but she could never accept the fact that she needed it. More than once she tried to walk out, and when the staff locked her into her room, she climbed out the window and was in the process of scaling the fence separating her from the highway when they pulled her back to safety. When my father was experiencing difficulty adjusting to his medications, the family decided it was time to move him from independent living in Rolla to a facility near my sister Deanna in New York which could provide some assistance. After they sold off most of their belongings and put on the market the beautiful house my father had just built for themselves, I flew out to accompany them on the emotional journey half way across the country in their car.

When we were growing up, we were forced to endure the constant word-fracturing of my mother. As she read a billboard or business name, her logological mind would twist the letters or sounds into another form. Thus Mobilgas became Bubblegas, spaghetti became *spag*-hetti, Gulf became Gluf, wristwatch became witchwatch and so on. Whether by genetics or by simple exposure to such an environment, some of these annoying characteristics have rubbed off on me. Each time we passed 32nd Street on our way to church, Sharlyn and the kids groaned when I asked yet again, "What is the shortest street in the world?" So it was that as we started out from Rolla, my mother wanted to know where Interstate 44, the highway we traveled toward St. Louis, went. Well, right now we are in Misery, I told her, and straight ahead was Little Noise, but the opposite direction would take us into Homely-oka. Unimpressed, she decided not to pursue such a ridiculous comment. "What state are we in?" she wanted to know several hours later when we stopped at a rest area in Ohio. "A state of disrepair," I said first, out of frustration from driving through construction zones, but when I told her it was Hiohi, she lashed back disgustedly, "I sure wish you'd talk right." Excuuuse me, look at the pot calling the kettle black, I thought. How ironic, after all the years of this sort of abuse we had tolerated, and now that she was getting a taste of it herself, she was assuming such airs of self-righteousness. But then it occurred to me that perhaps the Parkinson's had turned off that center of her brain where such frivolity was amusing to her. In any case, it was good that we would not be going as far as Massachewednuts.

When we saw my parents at Deanna's house that Thanksgiving, my father announced at the end of the meal in the evening that he and my mother would be starting back in their car to Springside at Seneca Hill, their facility near Oswego. Alarmed at that, I insisted that while *I* drove him in his car, Sharlyn and my mother could follow us up there in ours. As we started out from Liverpool, there were a few snowflakes falling, but as we reached the freeway in inky darkness about five miles away, the snow suddenly seemed to be pouring from confetti buckets in the sky. Before we advanced a half mile, we were in whiteout conditions so severe that were it not for special reflectors on posts placed along the edge of the roadway, we would not have been able to determine where the roadbed was. Accumulations were rapidly increasing as we proceeded northward, and before long we were tracking through a foot of snow. Sharlyn was barely able to keep us in sight, struggling to follow in our tracks as we crawled along a few feet ahead. I will never know how they would have fared on their own, but when we arrived an hour later, my father was grateful I had contravened his bravado and the assurances they would not need assistance. My mother seemed alert, active and engaging, accompanying us outside through the snow and frigid conditions back to her nursing home facility. I was remembering that this was the last time Sharlyn and I saw her alive, but Deanna reminded me that we were all together one last time the following January for the birthday celebration of Becca, her first grandchild. In any case, a scant two months after that my mother would be gone.

Although it was not easy for Deanna to make the thirty-mile drive to see her, she visited my mother often, reading to her, spoon feeding from her tray and attempting to make conversation, some times more successfully than others. My father's facility was about a half mile away, so he walked, drove or rode the shuttle up the hill to spend much of each day with the diamond of his life. He loved a game called Zilch and carried his little box of dice around with him everywhere, but my mother was less than enthusiastic when he insisted they play it yet again. No matter, he would make all the decisions for her anyway, add up the points, sometimes even roll the dice for her. "You want to keep that one and roll these two again, don't you, Martha?" he would coach, and of course she would nod agreement. Or "Uh oh, that's the wicked split, you'll have to try to beat it," as she dutifully followed his direction, not really caring what that meant.

Whenever my father was able to be with her, my mother seemed to be holding her own. However, when he was hospitalized around Christmas from a chronic problem with aneurysms in his legs, my mother decided to undertake the daily walks, which they usually made together, by herself. She would never admit that she needed a walker—that was for *old* people. However, she seriously underestimated the effect of the Parkinson's disease on her balance and was prone to falling, which nearly landed her in the hospital when she struck her head and probably cracked a rib on one of her stumbles. Her general health seemed sufficiently robust that her doctors decided to proceed with cataract surgery on both eyes within a week. When that was successful, they elected to undertake knee replacement surgery two weeks later. The next day, however, the stress levels of the preceding weeks caught up with her and her cardiac enzyme levels became erratic, causing a mild infarction.

When Deanna visited her at the hospital in Oswego, my mother was unable to communicate verbally but kept pointing downward. The nurses assumed she was experiencing pain in the knee and discontinued the machine therapy they were conducting. Doctors administered additional doses of morphine, but my mother only became more agitated, trying to express her extreme discomfort with desperate gestures. In the mean time my father had a pancreatitis attack and was hospitalized in Syracuse. When he was strong enough to visit my mother, he was able to determine that the cause of her distress was simply the need for a bowel movement. One of the side effects of opiates like morphine is constipation, and the doctors had aggravated the pain resulting from locked bowels with more morphine. Following that episode, my mother rapidly lost her grip on life. Her coordination and vigor had deteriorated to the point where she could not hold a spoon, and she refused to cooperate if it meant she was no longer able to do this simple task by herself. Soon she was in and out of the hospital with complications, infections, dehydration, and alternation of intravenous fluids and diuretics, but when she was finally sufficiently stable to be discharged, a CT scan revealed an aortic aneurysm ready to burst at any moment. Deanna and my father could not interest her in conversation, games, singing of hymns, prayer or even just opening her eyes. Her only solace was to curl up into a fetal position so stiffly that her legs could not be straightened. My father said that she could feebly squeeze his hand when he asked her to pray with him near the end, but when he finally realized she would not survive the night, he was torn between staying at her side until her last moment came or returning to his room for rest, to keep up the strength he knew he would need for the inevitable days ahead. At four o'clock the next morning, March 21, 2003, we were awakened by a phone call from my father, giving us the news that she had slipped away. For the rest of his life he remained convinced that the doctors had killed her with overdoses of morphine.

It was at her funeral that Deanna and I sang that composition called *Peace* I mentioned earlier. It is not written as a duet, but I asked her to be singing at my side for several reasons. First of all, she has a beautiful voice, but the accompaniment is quite pianistic, and she would need to arrange for someone local who could play it. Moreover, it has a high A-flat, which I was not sure my voice could still reach, but even if I made it past that, I was not sure I could get through the whole piece alone without breaking up emotionally. For over two years after my mother's death, my father resumed his life at his apartment so energetically that we were sure he would live forever. As part of his exercise routine, he pushed his "Cadillac," the three-wheel walker he probably did not really need but used for an extra measure of confidence, down every corridor at Springside, volunteering to deliver the stack of newspapers that arrived in the office each day.

I would never have expected him to use email, but Rodney and Don got him set up on a computer, and he not only maintained regular correspondence with an extensive list of addressees, but whenever I saw him, he would rail against Fergie, one of the imaginary players in the Hearts game he played every day on his machine. He held himself to a rigid exercise regimen in the equipment room on a strict schedule, taught a catechism class to members of his church, assisted with bingo and other games up the hill at the nursing home, and argued vociferously with Catherine Salisbury about theology. Catherine was a retired Methodist pastor who conducted a Bible class every Wednesday morning for any and all who would attend, and my father challenged her doctrine constantly. She maintained, for instance, that the days of creation could actually represent longer periods of time—years even. When he asked her what *yom* means in the original Hebrew, she did not know. Then she would have him believe that when the ages of such figures as Adam, Methuselah and Noah are given in hundreds of years, their lifespans could actually be similar to our own, since we do not know for sure what period of time a year was in ancient times. But then my father asked her what it means when it says in the same book of Genesis written by the same author that Joseph was thirty *years* old when he became ruler in Egypt. Did that mean he was really only three?

My father had a more powerful urge to travel than Gulliver, so after Sharlyn and I had made a successful and fulfilling trip with him through memory lane in northeast Iowa on our way to the Gimbel reunion in South Dakota in 2003, we tried a similar venture the next year, with an aim to reach Colorado. However, the popliteal aneurysm behind his right knee brought this to an unmitigated disaster. An aneurysm is a widening in the vessel that allows blood to pool, rather than flow through it smoothly, causing coagulation and clotting in the stagnation. When normal flow sweeps one of these clots along with it, smaller diameter vessels downstream can become clogged. The lower leg has three primary arteries supplying blood flow, and in my father all three had frozen shut, causing him sudden and excruciating pain as we drove along Interstate 90 across Wisconsin. We rushed him to Gunderson Lutheran Hospital in La Crosse, where they performed emergency bypass surgery with only minutes to spare before amputation would have been the only other option. His recovery extended across several weeks and seemed to mark a turning point in his health that sloped gradually downward.

Medication in the hands of even the most skilled practitioner is a double-edged tool. On the one hand it is a miracle drug that saves lives, but on the other it is a silent killer, wantonly striking down the unwary through unknown, undetected, ignored or underplayed side effects. One of them killed my father. Sometimes a miscalculation in dosage can even lead to fatality, as it nearly did for him. A slight overdose of his blood pressure meds caused dizziness and fainting, so one day he blacked out while driving, resulting in a chance encounter of his Chrysler New Yorker with a stump in the ditch. It was a total loss of the car and the end of my father's driving days forever. Though the aneurysm was repaired, poor circulation in his lower extremities led to problems with edema. But when his right leg failed to respond to diuretics, the doctor ordered compression stockings to reduce the swelling. Then he discovered he was allergic to the latex in them. This caused a severe rash everywhere on his skin that taxed the skills of a dermatologist to the limit and required months of aggressive treatment attempting to control it.

When I saw him in the fall of 2005, he told me that, by comparison to the preceding year, he felt "weak," yet he had just come from his checkup, where his doctor made the pronouncement that he had the heart and lungs of a fifty-year-old. Soon after this, I noticed that he coughed continually all through the night. Originally attributed to allergies, this cough was, in fact, a rare side effect of his blood pressure medicine. When his doctor switched him to another, however, the cough was not only unrelieved, but the new medication caused diarrhea. Attempts to control that, in turn, caused him constipation. The specialist called in to deal with the coughing discovered a hiatal hernia. The nasal tubes inserted for the treatment of that caused nosebleeds, but my father was convinced the blood in his stools was caused by the Nexium used to control his reflux, so his doctors switched over to Prilosec instead. Finally, one day my father concluded the doctors were not really helping him and made the decision to take over the management of his health, self-medicating on a concoction of home remedies, diet and tablets obtainable over the counter. Still, the cough persisted.

Although Sharlyn and I considered hernia surgery ill-advised, given his increasingly fragile condition, my father felt it was important to have it repaired in October that year. By November he began to have breathing problems so serious that the doctors began an oxygen regimen, but the apparatus he was required to drag around with him was such an awkward nuisance that he refused to use it. When he found the meals served at his residence difficult to eat, he switched to a liquid diet, primarily of Ensure. This, in turn, caused a rapid weight loss, which affected his facial structure, but he refused to consult a specialist to address this new problem with loose-fitting dentures he was now experiencing. His tribulations were mounting, and they began to affect his outlook on life. He was always happy to see us when we came for a visit, yet when we drove up to see him after his hernia surgery, we first saw him coming down the corridor toward us when we arrived, strangely waving his hand with a gesture for us not to say anything as he brushed past us on his way somewhere else. One of his fellow residents came up to us later and asked, "What is happening with Elmer?" Ralph had provided him with a cell phone and ordered him to use up the minutes every month, and at first he loved his new toy and called everyone. Now, however, he seldom called out, and when I tried to call him, he would invent some excuse for not talking, telling me I should not call back later either. When one of his friends at his facility asked him one day how he was, I heard him make the shocking statement that it was time for him to join his wife. When Ruth asked him the same question around Christmas, he responded that "changes will be coming in the new year." As I reflect on these symptoms, I am convinced that while his failing condition was partially responsible for his mindset, he was also heavily influenced by a mélange of medications. Yet, he was losing perhaps his most prized asset—control. He had always been in charge of his life, sometimes to the chagrin of those around him who were unwillingly swept along, and now for the first time in his life he felt that slipping away irretrievably.

As he gradually grew weaker, a battery of tests revealed pneumonia, congestive heart failure and bronchiectasis resulting from the cough. Bronchiectasis is a lung condition in which the bronchi and bronchioles have lost their elasticity, have expanded and filled with fluid. The constant coughing had destroyed the bronchial walls of his lungs, and he was dying from it. When Sharlyn and I visited him in rehab at Seneca Hill Manor in January, we met up with Ruth, who gave us as a gift the first orange from the tree in her yard in Florida. When we walked into his room, my father was sitting up in bed with his arms folded in disgust. I showed him the orange and asked him if he knew what it was. His unamused expression told me he was not in the mood for show and tell. "No, no, it's a special orange," I tried to say cheerfully. Ordinarily, he would have shared in the joy of such a moment, but he would not be cajoled. When I asked him how he was, he snapped, "Miserable!" We soon found out why. He was on megadoses of diuretics, severely restricted on fluid intake, and just when he saved up his water from breakfast and lunch to take with his food, the nurse had just come in to snatch it away. He was furious. Our attempts to steer his thinking toward the positives were futile. After all, I tried to point out, others around him were much worse off. He was not racked with constant pain of cancer or heart attack, was not on dialysis, was not facing amputation from diabetes, and so on. He refused to be comforted. It was to be the last time we saw him alive.

When Don and Ralph visited on April 1, he had been moved to West Side manor, an assisted living facility closer to Deanna, and they estimated he had less than two weeks left. Don assured my father that it was okay to release his grip on life whenever he was ready, with the promise he would meet him on the other side. Preparations were made to move him to hospice care. On April 3 Deanna got a call from the facility to say my father was too weak to go to the bathroom and was requesting to be moved to the hospital again, where lift assistance was available. Instead, Deanna stayed through the night with him to avoid transporting him back to the hospital. After Deanna left for home to get some sleep, Ruth's husband Bob and Deanna's blind daughter Kate came to visit about noon in order to help feed him lunch. My father was always a light sleeper, and when Kate greeted him, he opened one eye to acknowledge their presence, then closed his eyes forever. Before they left, Kate placed her hands over his, then felt along up to his face and held his head in her hands. Before she left, she paused to hold his feet in her hands, and it was then that her blind eyes *saw* a bright glow that faded slowly to black. It was April 4, 2006, and my prince was gone. Yet, it was almost as though he was still in control after all. What better time for a funeral than Easter, he seemed to be saying. The service was on Holy Saturday, and the promise of resurrection on Easter Sunday the next day was the most meaningful and memorable I can ever recall. In accordance with the arrangements my parents had made years earlier, the family gathered in Delta, Colorado, on September 2 that year for the burial of their ashes, and my father's own brother Carl conducted the service committing their remains back to the earth. One of the most considerate gestures parents can make for their children is to prepare for their own burial, so even in their deaths my parents were still providing for us.

The western slope of the Rocky Mountains in Colorado is one of the most beautiful places on earth, so when the families gathered to say goodbye to the mortal remains of Elmer and Martha, it was also a time to celebrate the joys of life. Rodney and Austin had arranged lodging at Beaver Lake Resort in the tiny village of Marble, where everyone could choose between activity and leisure, hiking or sunbathing, biking or watching the hummingbirds hovering at their feeders, playing horseshoes or striking up a card game, strolling to the edge of the lake with grandchildren to throw in pebbles or simply leaning back to "marble" at the grandeur and serenity of the mountain. It was a time for reflection, realizing that on the conveyor belt of life, we were now the oldest generation alive, poised for our turn to tumble off the end into eternity one day soon. The following year those who could not come for this occasion would be meeting us at another—the reunion of all the Pullmanns in America, descendants of George and August, held every five years since 1947. It would be the first that Elmer and Martha would not be joining them. However, Sharlyn and I had arranged for some special visitors to attend in their place.

Much to the admiration and gratitude of everyone in the family, Angela had become the keeper of the genealogical record, and she discovered a source in Missouri providing the names of over fifty Püllmanns all over Germany. Several years ago I drafted a letter in my halting German requesting genealogical information and mailed it to every one of the addresses on the list. About half came back as undeliverable for various reasons, and most of the remainder went unanswered. Among the small number of those who responded, however, was one Heike Püllmann, writing in fairly good English on behalf of her father Gunther, to whom my letter was addressed. Only gradually did it become apparent to me that most Germans are not much interested in maintaining, much less tracing, the record of their lineage, so Heike was unable to provide any information, but her family lived close to the area in the country from where my ancestors originated. It was intriguing to speculate that we were possibly somehow related, so over the next years we maintained a sporadic correspondence. She wrote of her father's death, her marriage and subsequent birth of a daughter, but just when I had not heard from her in quite a while and was about to write her off as preoccupied with her own life, the attacks of September 11, 2001, prompted an email from her, anxious to learn how we were affected by them. In 2007, when Sharlyn expressed the desire to return to Germany to visit an aging Elfriede while she was still alive, I asked Heike whether she wanted to be included on our itinerary. We borrowed Elfriede's car and made our way to Gelsen-Kirchen, where Heike lived with her husband Chris and two little girls Julia and Luisa. She had taken the opportunity to assemble her entire clan to welcome us warmly—her widowed mother Kathe, sister Helga and son Dominik, brother Hans-Gunther and his wife Petra, even Chris's father Willi, a widower who seemed so affectionate with Kathe that we suspected they were an item together. Heike told us her father Gunther, in the typical German penchant for long names, was actually Louis Gunther Albert Karl, and when I shook hands with Hans, I became quite emotional to be actually meeting someone with the original family name Püllmann for the first time. Before we left, Hans told us that Angela had mailed them information about the upcoming reunion in Minnesota and told us they hoped to attend.

From the first moment Hans, Petra and their son Christoph arrived in America on July 22 for the reunion, we were quite sure they had come hexed. When they changed planes in Amsterdam, their luggage had not made it aboard their connecting flight and would not be arriving until the same flight returned the next day. Unfortunately, we had planned to whisk them up to New York early the next morning and would not be here when the flight with their bags came into Dulles. Hmm, this presented a dilemma. I gave them two options. We could borrow clothing from members of our church until we returned in a few days, or we could quickly dash to Wal-Mart, which would be closing in less than an hour, for a shopping spree. Although they had not yet eaten anything, they wanted new clothes, so we bolted for the door and dashed down the highway to the store. I had promised their visit would not cost them anything, but I was not prepared to buy them each a wardrobe, so I offered to provide whatever toiletries they would need, and they filled their carts with the rest.

Our misfortunes were only beginning. We had an aggressive plan for them to see Niagara Falls and then drive diagonally across New York yet the same day. My father would have loved such a plan. We arranged to overnight with Deanna's daughter Teresa in Cheektowaga, about a half hour away from Niagara, and as we approached Grand Island the next morning on Interstate 190, I suddenly heard tick, tick, tick, tick …. When I pulled over to investigate, I found that some construction vehicle had an open box of nailgun cartridges, which were scattered all over the highway for at least two miles. Several nails were embedded in my left rear tire, and one of them was protruding enough to strike the wheel well, causing the ticking we heard. The interstate was much too busy to change a tire so close to the roadway, but fortunately the last exit before the big toll bridge to the island was just a few yards ahead. We found a parking lot at the bottom of the ramp, unloaded everything out of the trunk, changed to the spare tire, loaded our bags back into the trunk and headed for the ramp back to the bridge. We had no sooner driven fifty feet, however, when I heard whump, whump, whump, whump …. The hard rubber donut was flat. The pincushion we had just removed, though, was not yet leaking air, so I reasoned that if we hurried quickly enough, we could put it back on and make it to a repair shop for a new tire. So we unloaded everything out of the trunk again …. About three hours behind schedule now, we were back on our way, showed off the spectacular Falls to our visitors and dragged exhausted into a motel in Newark, New Jersey, late that night. Despite our misfortune, we tallied up the blessings for which we could be thankful—the ticking had alerted us to a problem in time to fix it, only one tire was affected, the weather was clement, it occurred during daylight hours, it was a weekday when a repair shop was open and the bad wheel held up until we could reach a safe haven.

Still, the worst was yet to come. Hans had told me their flight to Minneapolis for the reunion departed from Reagan Airport, so I tried to match our flight as closely as possible to the times he gave me. When we planned our departure, however, I found out they were leaving from Dulles, requiring me to drive them first to their airport before Sharlyn and I raced to Reagan. As we reached the exit for Reagan, Sharlyn pulled out our tickets and let loose such a woeful shriek that I was sure she was suffering a heart attack. Then *I* nearly got one as she proclaimed that our flight was leaving at that moment. We had a connecting flight in Detroit, and she had read on our itinerary the departure time from *there* as our departure from *Reagan*. Although I had visions of starting over with reservations at premium prices, the kindly agent at the counter assured us she could convert our tickets to standby status. Within a few minutes we were rushing down the corridor and soon boarded a flight to Chicago. This was going to be easy, I thought, because I assumed it would be much more difficult to fly from D.C. to Chicago than to catch the relatively short hop from Chicago to Minneapolis. When we checked the standby board at O'Hare, however, I noticed that there were thirty-four names ahead of us, then a little later thirty-seven, then forty-three. But when only twenty-six were boarded, the airline moved the rest of us to the end of the list for the next flight. This time we were number twenty-two, but only one was boarded, so we were bumped again. Meanwhile, Hans had a direct flight, but we had told them to wait for us at their baggage claim area. They had no idea we had missed our flight. Fortunately, we had their cell phone number. Unfortunately, it was a European number, which gave us an error message when we tried to call it. Fortunately, Hans had Sharlyn's cell number and eventually called us, puzzled what happened. Unfortunately, we had no way of knowing if or when we would ever see Minneapolis and told him they would need to wait for us. On our sixth try we were twelve on the standby list, and Sharlyn and I were the last two to make it on that flight. Although we finally arrived at Minneapolis, our bags did not, but we finally made contact with some very relieved Germans about ten o'clock. Again, we tried to think positively, realizing that if we had missed that flight, we would not have arrived until the early hours of the morning. And our bags were delivered to our Holiday Inn by mid-morning the next day.

After three wonderful days with Hans, Petra and Christoph at the reunion, we found that we had enough time to take them to visit the Mall of America in Minneapolis, which bills itself as the largest in the world. Hans and Petra had asked us whether we owned a game, unfamiliar to us, called Phase 10, currently all the rage in Germany, so when Sharlyn and I strolled into a toy store at the Mall, I idly asked the clerk whether he had ever heard of it. He had the deluxe version, the travel version, the dice version … every possible variety of the game imaginable, so we picked one up. We had no way of knowing, as we crossed the bridge over the Mississippi on Interstate 35W the next day for at least the fourth time, that two days later it would collapse, killing a dozen people and injuring over a hundred more as cars were crushed under the debris.

Our airline travel troubles were not over either. This time we traveled with reserved seats, but we learned an important lesson every seasoned traveler already knows—always book a direct flight whenever possible. At the time our plane pulled into the gate at Detroit, we had twenty minutes to board our connecting flight on a different concourse. Since Sharlyn would not be able to hurdle over luggage with me like O.J. Simpson in that old Hertz commercial, I told her to hurry as fast as she could over to the new terminal, while I raced ahead to try to stall the boarding process until she got there. At first the agent told me we had plenty of time, but soon she said she would need to close the door in five minutes. Surely Sharlyn would be here by then, I assured her. In five minutes she asked whether I could see her coming down the corridor. Straining for any glimpse of a turquoise blouse, praying for her to appear at any second, I had to tell the agent she was not in sight. Standby passengers were lining up at the counter, eagerly anticipating that two more seats were coming their way. After five more minutes the agent told me she could not wait any longer and started keying into her computer. Just as I saw her hand poised to strike the Enter key of her terminal, however, Sharlyn rushed breathlessly to my side. For some reason security agents had compelled her to pass through inspection again, and we had come within a microsecond of missing our flight.

The reunion itself had a startling surprise. Angela and Paul had spent a few months in Germany when Paul was stationed near Würzburg and had trekked throughout the area around Hanover, leafing through records. Their genealogical sleuthing, together with Paul's phenomenal linguistic facility reading old German script, paid off handsomely when they confirmed a branch of the family previously unknown—some of them right here in America. One Joan Schmid from Missouri provided a link to a few names that matched up with church archives in Germany, so Angela and Paul proudly laid out their data in a PowerPoint presentation to some very grateful family members at the reunion. Although we have yet to establish a link to Hans and Heike, we are quite confident that somewhere in the ancestry are two brothers—one from whom Hans is descended and the other that leads to me. Paul has already been able to link our family to the *area* from which Hans's ancestors originated.

All of my father's family grew up with the assumption that it was my grandfather George and his brother August who were the first of the Püllmann family to come to America. Since both of them had anglicized the ancestral name to Pullmann, the new spelling was so unusual in America that they had always assumed that anyone with this spelling was definitely a relative and that we had accounted for all of them. Recent efforts by Paul and Angela, however, have made some rather startling discoveries, which my grandfather probably never disclosed to the family. At least four of his grandfather August's siblings settled in Missouri long before George ever arrived. One, named Friedrich, who was known in his local community as "Uncle Fred" until he died at age 99, retained the original Puellmann spelling. But should the family have known about this after all? Upon George's death, a nephew and foster child of Friedrich named Conrad Meese, nine years older than George, penned an open letter in 1956 describing life in the Friedrich Püllmann household in which he was raised. In this letter he refers to a brother and uncle of Friedrich and a brother and sister of Friedrich's wife Sophie (née Tornei) Püllmann living in America before George's brother August emigrated. Paul and Angela have identified three of these four people and confirmed his statement to be true for them.

Even more recent research by Paul indicates that August's father Ludwig seems to have originated from Seesen. Some churches in Germany have records dating back into the fifteenth century, but this varies by location and size of the church. Unfortunately, the community in the Wolfenbüttel region of Niedersachsen in which Ludwig was born in 1771 did not start keeping church records until 1810, yet dauntless Paul was able to unearth not only a birth record for him from an alternate source but references to some of his siblings. In addition, Paul has sifted through the records of Eime and Northeim to uncover the names Johann Zacharias and Johann Phillip, most likely the father and grandfather of Ludwig. Tantalizing as it is to speculate that the Johann Heinrich mentioned with the same birth date as Zacharias in the records of the same town is his twin brother and indeed the long-sought ancestor to Hans, that conclusion is still in abeyance pending further research. A curious clue as to the possible *Ursprung* of the family name itself comes from a court case in which two brothers are squabbling over the estate of their father with the ancestral name Püllm. In the record of this litigation, the name of the brothers is rendered as "Püllm(an)," and one of them is apparently from Klein Rüthen, a suburb of Seesen. Hmm.

There was also an update at the reunion on the custody of some family artifacts. According to the account of my father's older brother Martin, their grandfather Friedrich walked into a shop one day in Wunstorf to find his local butcher tearing a page from a large book to wrap his meats. Taking a closer look, Friedrich was shocked to see it was an old Bible and rescued it at once from such irreverent hands. The last of Friedrich's children remaining in Germany at the time of his death was Johannes (Hans), the youngest, who inherited this possession. Before he died, Hans had stipulated that this Bible be passed to the oldest Pullmann in each generation, accordingly presenting it to Martin. As the oldest member of the next generation bearing the Pullmann name, I became the next owner of the Bible after Martin died. As it was ceremoniously passed to me at the reunion, I humbly expressed my gratitude for the honor; however, I was careful to point out that I perceive a clear distinction between possession and ownership. While I pledged to afford it the best care possible, the Bible belongs to the family, not to me, I stated, and I see myself merely as its temporary curator.

There was initially a mystery about the whereabouts of another family heirloom. When my grandfather George was a pastor, he maintained a diary of his work, which extended to some thirty volumes. Although the chain of custody of these little red diary books after the death of my grandmother Hilda is somewhat nebulous (I have never seen them), they somehow found their way into the hands of my father near the end of his life. Unable to read them, my father intended to pass them to my cousin James Gimbel, a Lutheran pastor with a doctorate in divinity, with the request that he or some graduate student at the seminary take on the translation of them as a research project or thesis. Instead, Jim advised my father to hand them over to the Concordia Historical Institute in St. Louis to include them in its archives. The volume for the year 1941 was missing, however, when Angela and Paul subsequently traveled to the Institute to create a digital record of the diary. That mystery was eventually solved when we learned that my cousin Judy (Kumm) Wendt (eldest of the forty cousins of my generation) had borrowed the diaries for awhile when conducting her own family tree research, but because of the value of that one volume to her as a memento of the year she was born, she kept it as a sentimental treasure. After she is finished with her research, it will likely join its fellows in the collection.

After all the years Sharlyn and I had tried to provide a healthy relationship for our children with their grandparents, we received the news one day from Angela and Paul that we were ourselves going to be grandparents. There was an additional surprise in the news. For over thirty years my military records had followed me, listing my blood type as O-positive—on my dogtags, DD214, discharge papers, everywhere. Angela's doctors at National Naval Medical Center had typed her blood as B-positive. When Paul found out that Sharlyn's blood type is A-positive, he deadpanned that Angela is not our daughter—as it would be impossible for us to produce a child with her blood type. Some mix-up at the lab, I told Angela. Just have them check it again. When the result came back the same, I told Sharlyn to have the technician retest hers the next time she gave blood. Then when *her* result was the same, they all glared at *me*. Oh no, I told them, the Army would not make a mistake like that—it could prove fatal on the battlefield to the poor soldier who fell victim to it. All right, all right, I will donate blood and have the lab recheck it. It came back B-positive. Paul may one day tell you about the medical circumstances surrounding the birth, in which an undiagnosed separated placenta nearly caused a stillbirth, but on December 23, 2000, little Rachel Marie Keiser was born. By coincidence Angela's best friend from high school, Kris Shue, delivered her second child a few days later on January 1, 2001. When Angela ribbed her friend that they missed out on a tax deduction by a few hours, Kris responded, "Yeah, but how cool is it to say you were born on 01-01-01." As I was commenting to Angela that their two infants were born in different millennia, I heard on the news the report of twins born as 2001 approached, one just before midnight and the other just after. These twins who entered the world minutes apart would not only have different birthdays, but were separated by a different weekday, month, year, decade, century *and millennium*! I realized too that it was not out of the question that Rachel, with good health care and modern medical techniques, could actually live in *three* different centuries. Unless you have been where we were, as newly minted grandparents, it may be difficult for you to imagine the emotion of that precious moment. We could not descend from our high for days and simply could not get enough of Tiny Little. If more than two days passed since we had seen her, I told Sharlyn we *must* drive over to their house to get our "Rachel fix."

Of course, it was my responsibility to spoil her rotten, and I had every intention to measure up to it. Paul loved to give Rachel an "airplane ride" before bath time, flying her all through the house while she held her arms open to the breeze. As she got older, she came to realize that bathtime meant bedtime, which marked the end of playtime. One evening when we were visiting, Paul was upstairs running the bathwater and called for her to come. "No," cried Rachel from the living room. Without saying a word, Paul merely appeared at the top of the steps, when Rachel said "No" again. This time she had her back to him, so how did this smart little kid know he was there? "Come, little miss," said Paul, as he scooped her up and threw her over his shoulder. All the way up the steps, Rachel shrieked, "No, no, NO … Grandpa! Grandpa!" as if I had the power to swoop in to rescue her from the Evil One.

Some kids seem to take a verbal track at an early age, while others develop physical skills first. Rachel was most definitely verbal, speaking at a very early age and very clearly. By the time she was a year old, Paul had taught her to sing the first verse of *Von Himmel hoch* in German. She noticed early on that adding "ed" to a weak verb made it past tense, but when a tiny voice said "I just waked up," I realized she was still in the formative stages with some individual strong verbs. Some concepts presented a little more difficulty, so when I would say, "Should Grandpa carry you?" she would request, "Grandpa, carry you." I understood, but when Paul would ask "Should I carry you?" and she responded "Carry you," he always insisted, "Rachel, can you use the correct pronoun?" Some of her words melted my heart. One day on a walk with her, I noticed a lawn sprinkler in one of the yards ahead. As I was formulating in my mind how I would describe to Rachel its purpose and what it was called, she called it a "prinker" and explained to *me* what it was for. When we read a Ranger Rick story with pictures for some of the words, it was delightful to hear "munket" each time I pointed to the chipmunk. My bicycle was a "bicio" whenever I rode over, but the one that sent me into convulsions was "bwewbwewwies." That extra *w* added to the "bwewbewwies" I expected charmed me to such an extent that I gladly paid any price for blueberries just to hear her say it as often as possible.

When Rachel was barely walking and talking, Sharlyn and I bought her a Radio Flyer coaster wagon. On her first ride in it through the residential streets near her house, we stopped to talk with some neighbors. After a while Rachel became impatient that the wagon was no longer moving and climbed out. As soon as a little girl much older than Rachel saw that the wagon was empty, she came running over to sit in it. I was not sure how Rachel would react to this, but I did not have long to wait. The instant she noticed this interloper sitting in *her* wagon, she was jealous and bristled immediately. As fast as little toddler legs could carry her, she hustled over to the big five-year-old and glared at her indignantly, saying, "No. *Wagon*." She did not yet know how to say "*My* wagon," but that was clearly what she meant. When the big girl sat there staring back at Rachel with a puzzled expression, Rachel repeated, "Wagon, Wagon" and became quite agitated, crying and pushing against her nemesis trying to force her to dismount. At this point the parents were compelled to intervene and ordered the older child out. Rachel quickly picked up the handle and trudged along with her wagon, darting a quick look behind occasionally to see if her competition was gaining on us.

At her first party Rachel was indignant that the other children her age were allowed to play freely with *her* toys. Worse yet, she could not comprehend why her parents not only did not rally to her defense when she insisted that they intervene, but they insisted instead she must do something they called *share* with these intruders. With a sullen glare at each offender, Rachel soon realized this social gathering was not the well of merriment promised by its billing, and before the first hour was up she was righteously demanding to know when they would be going home. Now that I think about it, I can recall an occasion or two retreating to similar such sentiments myself. If Rachel's parents were ever to wonder whether their rules were getting through into her consciousness, they would need only to listen as Rachel laid them out for her little visitors. "No jumping on the sofa!" she would admonish the first to stand on it. "No sitting on the coffee table!" one hapless little girl was to learn. "No toys in the kitchen!" she scolded the boy who pushed the little school bus across the threshold.

One day when I was riding along with Angela and Rachel, a car suddenly cut into our lane in front of us without warning. "Oh, you dirty weenie," I muttered without thinking. "Weenie," repeated little Big Ears from her booster seat behind me. "Da-ad!" exclaimed Angela immediately, accentuating her displeasure by making it a two-syllable word. I failed to remember that Uncle Wiggly was present on another occasion when I made a deprecating comment about Paul's Buick. After a number of trips to the shop, it began to suffer a particular malaise that results from inferior factory craftsmanship combined with repair at the hands of incompetent mechanics. We were sometimes involved in dropping off or picking up the vehicle, so one day on the way home from the shop, the car began to lurch and belch smoke, forcing Sharlyn to jerk it to a stop at the curb. As she explained this latest in a long litany of its maladies to me at the table that night, Rachel heard me mumble under my breath that the best thing we could do for that car was to drive it into the river. "Why would we want to drive Daddy's car into the river?" piped up a small voice whose receiver had been tuned in to my frequency.

Sharlyn and I were astonished at Rachel's phenomenal memory, which experts profess can be greatly enhanced by association. We saw this phenomenon again and again with Rachel. Once on a walk when we took her in her stroller, Paul was driving home from work and saw us about two blocks from their home. Not even a year old, Rachel lit up when her daddy stopped, rolled down the window and greeted us. About a week later, as we came to that same place along the street, Rachel softly repeated, "Daddy? … Daddy?" On our way to the playground with her one day, I picked up an elastic band lying on the bridge over a little stream, and as I showed it to Rachel, I stretched it with my thumbs and said, "Boing, boing, boing …." About a month later we were crossing that bridge again, when Rachel suddenly said, "Boing, boing, boing." The stream under that bridge is bounded by a strip of flood plain on both sides for a few yards before it gives way to woods. One day Rachel saw some deer near those woods, later explaining to me excitedly what an ideal location this was for them, providing the water to drink, the trees for hiding and the "meadow," as she put it, "for the fawns to play." When we saw a sign reading "Turtle Crossing" along the road one winter day, it was soon obvious that Rachel had seen it before and had already received a full explanation. "The turtles are sleeping," she told me, "in their *beds*," she added, causing me to wonder whether this was also part of Angela's explanation, or whether the imagination of a not-quite-two-year-old allowed for some embellishment. But when she continued, "with their *blankies* on," I still was not sure where the explanation left off and the fantasizing began.

Rachel became familiar with eating at restaurants at an early age, and once when we were seated at our table for Thai cuisine, a waitress hurried past. Rachel raised her finger to stop her and said authoritatively, "Rice!" She *loved* eating out, especially if she got a chance to have rice, her favorite. Shopping with her mother and grandmother was such an adventure for Rachel that she was almost fanatical about it. One evening as we were returning from a restaurant, Angela and Sharlyn decided to dash into the mall for a few items while I waited with Rachel asleep in her car seat. As soon as they returned to the car, Rachel awoke, and when she saw the Target sign, she cried so pathetically realizing she missed out on the shopping that I interceded for her to go back into the store with them for a few more minutes. Before she had her own little pink purse, she discovered a certain clock on Paul's dresser that had a brass handle for carrying it. Rachel brought this into the living room one day as her "purse" and announced, "Shopping. J.C. Penney." One day when she was showing me her new shoes, I asked her where she got them. "Actually, we bought them from Pay-Less, because Stride-Rite was too expensive." She was not even two, and already she was learning the names of the stores and how to shop the market. That word "actually" was peppered into her speech liberally, and she could be quite smug when she used it. I introduced her to Sandy Jones at my office one day, who asked the usual questions about her name and age. Sandy expressed surprise when Rachel carried on a conversation with her and said, "You're just two? You seem so much bigger." To which Rachel replied, "Actually, I'm just two." One day when I took Rachel to McDonald's, I noticed a group of high school girls seated at the table next to us admiring the cute little curly-haired blond with me. Eventually one of them asked her name. As soon as Rachel told them, they chorused in unison, "Ohhhhhh, she's so cute." When one of them said, "I like your hair," Rachel said, "Yes, it has curls." All the girls again said, "Ohhhhhhh." Then one of them asked how old she was. When Rachel said, "Two," they all gushed, "Ohhhhhh" again. A few minutes later I asked Rachel what she thought of the big girls. Where are the big girls, she wanted to know. When I gestured toward the highschoolers, Rachel said, "Those are *wadies*." To her, I suppose, big girls were about age five.

At a restaurant one day, Rachel wanted to know what the red flakes were in the shaker bottle on the table in our booth. When I told her it was pepper, she was confused. "But isn't this pepper?" she asked, picking up the shaker next to the salt. After explaining to her that some restaurants give us both red and black pepper, I pointed to the sugar shaker and asked her if she knew what it was. She knew. "What do we use it for?" I quizzed. "*Recipes,*" replied the tiny little smartie next to me. "What do we use recipes for?" I asked next. "For making cookies, silly," she said with a tinge of disgust at my ignorance. "Do you make cookies?" I asked innocently. "Of course," she replied. "What kind of cookies do you make?" I asked with mock surprise. "Scarecrow cookies," she explained, without any reference to Halloween, when she had apparently "helped" her mother make a batch. "What do you put in them besides sugar?" "Spices," she said hesitantly, not really sure if it was the right answer. "What kind of spice do you use?" I wanted to know. "Uh, *scarecrow* spice," she said with a straight face, hoping I would buy her improvised answer. I did.

As precocious as Rachel was verbally as a toddler, she was ungainly in coordination. It was comical watching her try to step on an ant, moving faster than Rachel's little foot could find its target. One day when Austin and Retta were visiting, we took one-year-old Rachel to the playground. Someone had left a basketball lying on the ground, so Austin told Rachel to go kick it. Although she knew what "kick" meant and what she was supposed to do, she could not make her foot strike the ball. First her foot landed beside the ball, then too far in front of it, and with the next attempt, her foot came down on top of the ball, causing her to fall down. Finally, in frustration she bent over and swatted it with her hand. As it rolled a few inches from her, Rachel started to walk away, but then stopped, turned around and yelled at the ball, "Go … *away!*"

One of the darkest moments of my life occurred a few days before Rachel turned two years old, when I nearly caused her to be killed. I could not relate this incident to you in person without breaking down, and it is even difficult for me to write it, but for the sake of catharsis, I must tell you about it. As a military officer, Paul could get special permission to go deer hunting on federal property at Ft. A.P. Hill, an Army post some sixty-five miles south of Washington. Angela invited Sharlyn and me to stay with her and Rachel in the cabin they rented, idyllically set alongside a pond among the thick woods of the base, while Paul was off hunting. It was late in the evening, Monday, December 16, 2002 when we arrived. The next morning, after Paul had left to find some additional hunting supplies, I wandered down to the pond, where four new fiberglass canoes were lined up along the edge of the water. This pond was roughly the size of two football fields end to end, and our cabin was situated at the west end of that rectangle. Although I noticed there was a thin coating of ice on the surface, the air was unusually warm and calm for a day in December, so I decided to take one of the canoes lengthwise across to the east end. While Sharlyn, Angela and Rachel ate breakfast, I grabbed a paddle and life jacket I found in one of the closets inside the cabin, dumped out the rainwater from the canoe and dragged it to the water's edge. The canoe and paddle broke through the thin ice easily as I glided through it, cutting a trail of clear water to the other end.

By the time I got back, the sunshine was much warmer and the day so tantalizingly beautiful that I suggested Rachel take a ride with me in the boat. As I strapped on a life jacket, Angela remembered seeing a child's life jacket in another room and put this one on her instead. It would turn out to be a lifesaving decision. Sharlyn insisted that she herself ride along to help keep Rachel still, and after last minute instructions from Angela for Rachel to remain seated in the canoe, the three of us started across. As we reached the midpoint of the pond, the unthinkable happened. In an instant the boat capsized and we were all pitched into the freezing water. If the canoe had been aluminum, this might not have happened, but this fiberglass craft was extremely buoyant, riding high in the water and raising the center of gravity by several inches. No one had stood up, none of us had made any sudden moves, but although I cannot recall for sure, I may have shifted slightly on my seat while planting my feet for rowing. In any case the only refrain racing through my head was that *this cannot be happening*. Disbelief and shock numbed my senses, so the gravity of our predicament settled over me only gradually. If there was any good news, it was that all of us were floating. So was the boat, albeit upside down beside us. How does one right an overturned canoe, I wondered. But then I remembered that everything I had read about canoe accidents in *Boys' Life* magazine was that from the water it was impossible. As long as the inverted canoe remains afloat, the water safety experts had said, stay with it and hold on. Poor little Rachel was beside me in the water, not considering this much fun, and kept repeating, "All done, all done."

I was hanging onto Rachel with one hand and to the submerged end of the canoe with the other. Sharlyn had been thrown out of reach altogether and was drifting gradually away in the slow current. My first priority was to get Rachel out of the water, if possible, onto the canoe bottom protruding into the warm air. After I succeeded with that somehow, I was not sure what to do and started calling for help. What happened next was nothing less than a miracle. We were in the midst of several cabins surrounding the pond, but none of them were occupied in winter. Yet in the *nearest* one was a cleaning lady, who immediately phoned the military police and called to assure us from the water's edge that help was on the way. Meanwhile, Angela at the far end of the pond heard our cries of distress and ran inside to call 911. When she found the phone did not work, she tried Sharlyn's cell phone, but the area was too remote to pick up a signal. In desperation she threw on a life jacket and ran to one of the three remaining canoes. Not realizing the paddles were inside the cabin, she grabbed a stick and started paddling frantically with it toward us. I am not sure why I did not try sooner, but I discovered that by kicking my legs I could propel the floating canoe. Sharlyn was by now about ten yards away praying fervently aloud, so I pointed the canoe toward her and set my course for her position, scissoring my legs until we reached her. My submerged hand was rapidly becoming so numb that I asked Sharlyn to work her way to my end so that she could hold onto Rachel if I lost my ability to hang on any longer. Our highest priority, I felt, was to reach the shore as soon as possible, so I tried to tow the weight of all of us toward the nearest point of land as best I could by continuing to kick.

We were making progress toward the edge, when I noticed that a pickup truck had stopped along the road at the east end of the pond. In a few moments he found a boat and was paddling furiously toward us with a snow shovel from his truck, the only paddle he could find. I do not recall his name, but he had been working on a water tower nearby and overheard the distress call on his radio. Before he could reach us, however, we could hear the sirens of our rescuers in the distance, and moments later a swarm of them were churning the water to a froth as they paddled out to us. After hauling each of us out of the water into a separate boat, they thrashed furiously back to the shore and hustled us into the warmth of the cabin. There they whisked us into separate rooms, stripped off our wet clothing and wrapped us in blankets, but when they tore open their emergency heat packs, the medics found they did not work, so they wrapped me with towels soaked in hot water from the bathtub. We had been in the icy water only about thirty minutes, but hypothermia was well advanced in all of us. Fortunately, little Rachel fared the best, perhaps because of her youth and the fact that she had spent much of the ordeal in the relatively warmer air. On the other hand, I was the worst off, feeling no pain but such discomfort that I was not sure I was going to survive. Although I was not gasping, the feeling I had was similar to the time the wind was knocked out of me. By the time they loaded me into the ambulance, I began to shiver—convulsed violently for about two hours, shaking so hard continuously and uncontrollably that my abdomen ached when it was finally over as if I had been forced to perform sit-ups for some cruel drill sergeant. I do not know what my core temperature was initially, but after they started a hot IV in each arm it had warmed up to 94.2.

Meanwhile, Angela found her way to the cabin and asked the EMTs to reach Paul. She was four months pregnant and was feeling some abdominal pain from the stress of launching a canoe and rowing with a stick. She described Paul's car and the military police tracked him down. He was returning from picking up supplies when one of their cruisers came toward him at high speed with lights and sirens, then made a power turn behind him and pulled him over. They led him to the ambulance and told him to follow it—all the way to the hospital at Fredericksburg an hour away. When the doors to the ambulance in which I was riding were thrown open, I was surprised to see Paul standing there waiting. He had been told Angela was in this vehicle, and his expectant look withered quickly to disappointment, as he said simply, "Oh" when he saw me instead and dashed off to check the next one. After two hours in the warmth and comfort of the emergency room bed, I was beginning to return to normal. Then a little visitor wrapped in a blue gown appeared in the arms of Paul. It broke my heart when she took one look at me and stiffened, sensing that I had been the cause of her suffering, not understanding that this was not supposed to happen. When Paul laid her next to me, Rachel became hysterical, shrieking uncontrollably for fear I would harm her again. At first I was shocked by her reaction, but when I realized that she was continuing to associate me with the horror, I could not have been more devastated. She had terror in her eyes even when Sharlyn tried to touch her. Then Paul was pushed away as this poor delicate child would cling only to Angela. I feared she might be traumatized for life.

Since we had arrived with no clothes, Paul was elected to make the two-hour drive back to the cabin to pick out a wardrobe for each of us. Before he could return, the hospital issued us paper "suits" and discharged us. If we had known this, we could all have piled into the car with Paul, but instead we repaired idly to the cafeteria to wait for him to return. It was a tense time with Rachel, but when she became bored, she allowed me to set her on the seat of a wheelchair, and as long as I was pushing from behind, where she could not actually see me face to face, she granted me the supreme honor of allowing me to push her in it. Gradually the familiar curly haired girl emerged from her shell, and I wanted to shout for joy when she eventually said, "Grandpa, carry you" again. We walked all over the hospital together, trying out the buttons on the elevator that could always take us back to the floor where Mommy and Grandma were. When some nurses found us on the eighth floor, where they were startled to see us, I explained that one of their little patients was just a bit bored. They melted when Rachel, fascinated with some miniature potted Christmas trees, described the red and white "fwowers" with "pwaid" bows. How did she know what plaid is, they wanted to know. It was about 7:00 that evening when we all finally returned to the cabin, but I suffered a sneezing fit that rendered me sleepless most of the night.

The next morning I was up early, musing about walking over to that vacant cabin to retrieve our clothing. Since I had only the one pair of shoes, which had been stripped off yesterday, I was borrowing Paul's, while he wore his hunting boots. Just as I was puzzling about what I would do if I found the cabin locked, I heard a car drive up outside. Oh, it must be Paul, I thought. He had gone out before dawn to try hunting once again, and I assumed he was bringing the good news that he bagged a deer. Instead, I opened the door to find a woman and two uniformed officers standing there. "Are you the lady who saved our lives yesterday?" I asked. As soon as she nodded, I broke down, giving her a hug. That angel of mercy who had phoned for help now had organized the cleaning brigade and was accompanied by two of the men who had been in the rescue boats, each carrying hangers of drycleaning and bags of apparel, cleaned and pressed, ready to wear. It was a tearful reunion as we invited them in for some Christmas bread Sharlyn had still had the energy to bake the evening before. When Rachel woke up later, they presented her with a huge teddy bear from all the personnel of the A.P. Hill Fire and Rescue Department. A few minutes later the chief came by, someone I recognized as the calm commander who directed the operation to bring order to the madness and frenzy in that cabin the day before. We had no way to express our profound thanks adequately to these wonderful strangers who quite literally had our lives in their hands. One of them, who became a first-time grandfather the night before our ordeal, had called every hour to inquire about our progress until we were discharged. The other, a grandfather of his own precious seven-year-old, took me aside and told me he could identify with the pain I felt gnawing inside me for having caused the accident. He related a similar experience of his own that had ended tragically, but he had to learn to stop beating himself up for it over and over, and so must I. We tried to find out the names and addresses of as many of our rescuers as we could, including the one who attempted to paddle out to us with a snow shovel, in order to send a note of thanks and a generous gift certificate. Yet whatever we spent for that was far too little. We thanked God for sending them all to us and especially for sending Rachel's guardian angel to spare us. If you still believe all of this happened by random chance, come and talk to me.

It was a scant three months later that my mother died, and although I know it does not work this way, I remember thinking that perhaps in some mystical way she had worked out an exchange, offering up her life so that I could live. Another month after that, her death was exchanged for a birth. Our second grandchild, Kathryn Elizabeth Keiser, was born April 28, 2003. When Sharlyn called me to pass along the news, however, I nearly dropped the phone when she also shocked me with the revelation that little Kathryn was born with Down syndrome. How could this happen? Paul and Angela had none of the risk factors that should have made such a result possible, I was sure. There was no family history, they had not been exposed to radiation, their first child was in the upper echelons of normality, Angela was of normal child-bearing age, the spacing between births was not abnormal, they were both of normal weight, both of brilliant intellect, and so on through a long list of superlatives. I was not sure I could accept it. To Paul and Angela, however, this was simply their new daughter, and they were determined to provide as normal a life for her as possible. It was almost as if God were telling them, "I am sending a certain number of these children into the world, and what better parents could I find than you to take care of one of them for me?" I had difficulty getting past the life of cruelty, abuse, and ridicule that society would foist upon poor Kathryn, however, and must admit I was less than enthusiastic in my welcome of this tiny little newcomer into the family.

The news was even worse. Birth defects among babies with Down syndrome occur at a rate of incidence higher than average, many of them quite serious. Kathryn was born with a defective valve in her heart and a leak between chambers, causing pulmonary hypertension. Ordinarily the blood pressure from the right ventricle into the lungs averages around 15 mm of mercury. Normal systolic pressure of the rest of the circulatory system is around 120 mm, which means that if the left ventricle is allowed to pump blood directly into the lungs, this abnormally high pressure causes the delicate vessels of the lungs to become fibrous and thicken as a defense, resulting in constrictions which in turn create back pressure into the heart. Uncorrected, this condition produces heart failure that is likely to be fatal before age twenty. Kathryn would need open heart surgery without delay. I hope none of you is ever compelled to witness such a stark picture of wires, tubes and instruments that was seared into my memory following one of her procedures. I could hardly find a recognizable human being spread eagled among the tangle of hardware that resembled the inside of a mainframe. Although the doctors were able to close the hole in the wall between the heart chambers, they were only partially successful repairing the flawed valve, so it is possible that one day Kathryn will need to undergo the scalpel again for the implant of an artificial one.

While the parents were involved with Kathryn's doctors and attending to her needs before and after her surgeries, Sharlyn and I were put in charge of Big Sister. Rachel was only two and really did not understand what any of this was about. One day when we were trying to keep her entertained in the private waiting room for families of patients with serious illness, Rachel found the phone sitting on an end table. At home she was not allowed to play with the phone, so it was a source of constant irritation with Angela that when Rachel came to Grandpa's house, the rules were different. I did not care how much she played with my phone. The chances that she would push the 911 keys in the proper order were relatively remote, and even more remote that she would punch in a real area code and a working number. Even if she poked around and actually dialed someone in India or Machu Picchu, I would gladly pay the bill for the call. Just as she was learning the concept of a telephone, I startled her one day when I called her on our intercom. After playing with it most of the evening, Rachel told Grandma as they were leaving that she liked her "inside-the-house telephone." So when she was pushing on the keys of this phone in the hospital, I asked her whom she was calling. "Aunt Sandy," she said demurely, referring to Paul's sister. "Do you know Aunt Sandy's number?" I asked her. She shook her head no. Because she was so precocious, I fully expected that she might know their number at home. "Do you know *your* number?" I asked Rachel. "Yesss," she said confidently. "What's your number?" I asked. Without hesitation she said, "Two!"

For several months after surgery, Kathryn was required to wear a nasal cannula that delivered supplemental oxygen. At home Angela could plug in a bulky machine which had a length of tubing that could reach anywhere in the house, but whenever she went out, she had to load oxygen tanks into the car and transport them on a little cart wherever she carried Kathryn. As if this were not onerous enough, Kathryn developed such a serious case of acid reflux that she was experiencing difficulty retaining food. It meant more surgery, this time to install a feeding tube directly into her stomach, forcing Angela to use a breast pump and to puree everything for well over a year so that it could flow through yet another machine. Even though the plastic line of the feeding tube was securely taped into place on Kathryn's abdomen, it would occasionally pull out, prompting an immediate trip to the emergency room. Through all of this Angela handled her role as guardian of her precious package with such aplomb that Sharlyn and I marveled at her seemingly boundless sources of inner strength. It required a superhuman effort I would never have been able to pull from the depths of my soul. Although Kathryn's development lagged behind her peers on a traditional learning curve, she seemed to be at the high end of those with Down syndrome and would probably be even closer to the mainstream were it not for her medical problems which gave rise to a slow start and many interruptions to learning at those critical early years. Before she learned to crawl, she discovered that if she wanted something out of reach, she could roll to it, so she became quite an accomplished roller. Kathryn learned sign language while still a toddler, so she could communicate some of her wishes even before she could voice them. Rachel also picked it up quickly and reinforced all of Angela's lessons with Kathryn exponentially.

On one of the many occasions on which Kathryn was brought into the hospital as an infant, Sharlyn and I were present as one of the technicians spent a half hour attempting to find a vein in her arm to draw blood. To this day we are haunted by the unending screams from our grandchild we heard down the hall. Soon after Kathryn was born, Daisy Barrett, one of the nurses in the health room at the Library, was moved with compassion when I mentioned Kathryn's condition in conversation one day, so when I brought Kathryn into the office a few months later, I decided that Daisy might want to meet her. Poor little Kathryn, however, was so traumatized by her first glimpse of all the white coats in the health room that she began to shriek uncontrollably and would not be consoled until I whisked her away. She was unalterably convinced someone would be mutilating her yet again.

Kathryn seemed to make up for the slow start which life handed her, as she quickly caught up with those her age. She learned to walk within the range of normality, especially for children with Down syndrome, and today she can *run* so fast that Grandpa can scarcely keep up. Her motor skills are exceptional for those with a chromosomal disorder, who ordinarily are unable to jump with both feet. Kathryn astonishes her therapists by not only leaping from the sofa but jumping *up* stairs with both feet. It is impossible to drive past a playground without a fuss from Kathryn. She loves everything a park offers—the slides, swings and every conceivable climbing apparatus. But her favorite activity is swimming, to the point that she will lie on the carpet at home and demonstrate her strokes and breathing techniques. Angela enrolled her in a ballet class composed mostly of those with typical development, and Kathryn practiced diligently at home to be equal to them for her first recital. She knows many songs from Sunday school, but by far her favorite is *Happy Birthday*, appropriate almost any time in her mind, which manifested itself early in her singsong version of "happy day you." More recently she surprised me with her rendition of *Do Re Mi* from *Sound of Music*, which she sings *on key*, and she knows most of the words to *Edelweiss*, certainly better than I. Her speech is improving steadily, to the point where she can hold a conversation until she gets frustrated with her inability to express in words all of the thoughts she has inside. Still, it is cute to hear her refer to Uncle Thomas as Unkie Nomas. Kathryn is exceptionally compassionate, whispering softly to her dolls as she lays them down tenderly for their naps. When she noticed a spot of paint on my knee one day when I was wearing shorts, she was sure I had injured myself and bent down to kiss it. When I took her for a ride on her bicycle with the training wheels attached, her foot slipped off the pedal, and she was afraid she had hurt it. "Are you okay, little bike?" she asked, "Sorry." Although her fine motor skills are underdeveloped, she writes her name and draws recognizable objects, but her *appreciation* of art is so advanced that she is fascinated for long periods of time when someone draws pictures for her, squealing with delight as she recognizes what has appeared on the paper or slate. Most astonishing to me is her ability to put together jigsaw puzzles. Starting with the simplest, she has now progressed to those with one or two hundred pieces, which she finishes in less than an hour of steady work. Each time she finds a fit, she is her own best cheering section, exclaiming, "Oh, you did it! Good job, Kathryn!"

One of the chief reasons for whatever advances Kathryn has made is that Rachel is a natural therapist, tirelessly reading to her and drilling her from books. When Rachel was still a tot, I was sitting on her bed one day with a coat hanger in my hand, using it as a pointer to touch the pictures and shapes on the page as I quizzed her about each object. When I finished, Rachel took the hanger and, imitating my exact mannerism, took over as the tutor. "Now, Grandpa, what is this called?" she would ask, "And what shape is this? What color is it?" She learned to read at a very early age and had such an astonishing range of expression, comprehending the meaning perfectly, that when she was four, Sharlyn dialed up her mother Evelyn, who once taught third graders, to have Rachel read to her over the phone. One day I saw her reading to Kathryn, facing toward her, looking down at the book from the top, reading with expression at full speed *upside down* as she turned the pages for her to see them. The girls have a book of children's Bible stories, mostly pictures, from which Rachel was teaching Sunday school one day. "See, Kathryn, here's Noah, and he says to his wife, 'Get … in … the … boat!'" When Rachel turned to the picture of David and Goliath, depicting the Philistine army arrayed behind the giant, she explained to Kathryn, "Look, Kathryn, this is Goliath, and these are … uh … the *other* Goliaths." In the nativity scene she pointed out to Kathryn, "Here's Joseph giving baby Jesus a toy giraffe." Rachel had been hearing in Sunday school about the Virgin Mary and the parable of the ten virgins and one day asked me, "What do virgins do?" When I related this to Retta later, she quipped, "It's not what they *do*, it's what they *don't* do." But I think Retta was satisfied with the answer I gave Rachel, probably adequate for an inquisitive five-year-old, "Well, it's talking about a young girl who isn't married yet."

One fall day Thomas met a young lady named Olivia Majesky, and after a whirlwind courtship, they announced their engagement the following spring. Almost a year after they were married in 2002, Sharlyn and I were in the waiting room with Olivia's mother and two grandmothers when little Anna Isabella was presented to us, born June 29, 2003, about two months after Kathryn. Olivia's father, Gregory, was from the Harley school, complete with a full eight-inch gray beard, bandanna, and American flag waving from the back of his motorcycle—not the sort of person I sought out growing up. On the other hand I was probably not the type with whom he would associate as his best buddy in school either. Yet he was a genuine article, so we found common ground in the middle and became good friends. Rachel was not yet two at their wedding, but never was there a cuter junior flower girl. Paul was one of the groomsmen, and when Rachel ran over to him for security during the ceremony from the crowd, he picked her up and stood up front holding his little angel in her lacy white bridal regalia. This brought back a painful memory for me. When Angela was two years old, Sharlyn's sister Marlene asked little Angela to be the flower girl and wanted me to be one of the ushers. During the ceremony Angela was supposed to stand near the front of the church with the wedding party, but when she saw me standing at the side, she started toward me. As I play this scene over and over in my mind, I wonder why I did not just allow her to come over to where I was. She was very shy, feeling alone and intimidated by all the people and just needed a reassuring hug. Instead, I gave her a stern look and motioned for her to remain where she was. Poor little Angela responded with the most otherworldly, unladylike wail anyone in Abbotsford had ever heard, disrupting the ceremony as she fled to her mother for refuge. No one knew that I had caused it, and the very thought of my cruelty in denying her to come when she needed me haunts me to this day.

In the lives of many young couples, it is not unusual that more time is spent with one set of in-laws than the other. For example, Angela feels much more comfortable with us than with Paul's parents, resulting in a decidedly one-sided relationship in our favor. Perhaps this is not a fair example, because Paul's position in the military sometimes takes him off to faraway places, leaving Angela in real need of our assistance. One day the phone rang soon after we came home from work. Angela was screaming, "Get over here fast! I've got a big problem! Get over here *right now!*" before she abruptly hung up. It was left to our imagination to guess what horror awaited us as we tore up the streets of McLean to race over there. Was one of the girls struck by a car? Was someone lying there bleeding? What? When she met us at the door, she was dripping wet from head to toe. They had just moved into their new house, a pipe had burst in the basement and she could not find the main cutoff. When I ran to the basement, I found storage boxes, cans and other objects littering the scene, floating in six inches of water, the source of which gushed from overhead. In seconds I was drenched as thoroughly as if I had jumped into a swimming pool, while I waded underneath Great Falls attempting to trace back from the break to the wall. Eventually I found the cutoff valve hidden behind some cans and stopped the torrent. When Angela had dialed 911, the operator told her this was not an emergency, urged her to calm down, directed her to solve the problem herself and promptly hung up.

The bond Olivia has with her parents is also very powerful, resulting in this same one-sided relationship, but this time decidedly not in our favor. When Sharlyn and I are invited over to their house, we find that she is most comfortable surrounded by her extended family—grandmothers, uncles, cousins and close friends. Despite our most earnest attempts to adopt her into the family, she has felt uncomfortable with us from the beginning and remains a challenge for us to gain her favor. However, she is an excellent mother to Anna, and while we continue in our attempt to melt some of the frost, we understand the syndrome. From the glimpses we get of Anna, we see quite a contrast with Angela's girls. Where Rachel and Kathryn are into reading and the arts, Anna is cut from the same cloth as her father—physically coordinated and driven by speed. She is a blur on the playground, unintimidated by the most challenging equipment. When I push her as fast as I can run on her little bike, she relishes it, always ready for more until I am exhausted, almost as if to say, "Is that all you got?" Truly a child of the twenty-first century, Anna plays for hours with her gadgets—especially the toy computer she got for Christmas one year, operating it instinctively like some office worker in miniature. When poor Psalms, the family poodle, repairs to his bed to curl up for a nap, he often finds Goldilocks already stretched out in it, talking to someone on her little toy cell phone like a teenager.

My father occasionally noted that all of his great-grandchildren were girls, wondering whether the Pullmann name would die out in his line of descendants. Sadly, he died before he could learn that not only would a great-grandson be born, but there would be two of them. Austin and Retta announced one day that they were expecting fraternal twins. Soon the sonograms showed the boys so distinctly that they had their individual names already in the womb. Retta had the printout made into a plaque reading "We Love You Dad," with each name lettered under its corresponding embryo, and presented it to Austin as his first gift from them. Then on May 1, 2007, Jackson David and Matthew Barrett were born, the middle names honoring the two grandfathers. Retta lost her mother as a child, but Nancy, Barry's second wife, is as close to Retta and her sister Virginia as if they were her own daughters. Sharlyn and I have also come to know Barry's parents, Everett and Gene Jones (derived from the name Eugenia her mother loved), as two of our most favorite classics, holding them in such high regard that we wish we could adopt them as our own parents. Although the twins are still toddlers, they leave us little doubt they are boys. Instead of tracing the shape of the magnetic letters on the refrigerator with his finger or carefully arranging them in a row as Rachel did at that age, Jackson is not satisfied until they are all knocked to the floor with a few swipes of his paw. Forget the stuffed toys and give us the ones with *wheels*, they seem to be saying. And these drumsticks work just as well on the walls, right? Hey Matthew, look how high I can reach if I climb up on top of the gas station. What is this mirror for, anyway? Let me see if it comes apart. Hey Jackson, look, someone left the gate open, we can climb up the steps and check out the upstairs ….

As cute as the twins are, they probably do not mind comparison to their newest cousin, little Christie Michelle Keiser, born May 2, 2008. Angela and Paul suffered the heartbreak of losing their attempt for a third child a year earlier, so this one was especially precious to them. Unlike her older sisters, Christie has a dimple, and if her smile is so broad that it squeezes her eyes closed, a second one appears in the other cheek. Christie reminds Sharlyn and me so much of Angela as a baby. In the days before car seats, we transported little Angela in a car bed on the rear seat. When she was supposed to be sleeping, she was more interested to know what was going on outside the walls of her confinement, so we would see a little head peer over the top as we drove along. As an infant Christie too was such a light sleeper because she was interested to know everything that was happening in the world, straining to lift her head to look around in every direction. Perhaps I have forgotten how strong an infant can be, but she seemed exceptionally strong. Is it normal for a baby to support her own weight at one week? Christie preferred a standing position to such an extent that I often had to buckle her knees to get her to sit on my lap. She was so active that Angela could not utilize the special Bumbo chair that is supposed to provide back support while an infant learns to sit up. Christie would arch her back and roll right out of it. Is it normal to be rocking on all fours in crawling position at four months? That was Christie. When Christie was about six months old, still only on breast milk, Kathryn tugged Angela's sleeve one Sunday during snacks after the service to say how much Christie had liked her tuna salad sandwich. One of Christie's chief duties when I held her was to inspect the contents of Grandpa's shirt pocket. The pens were, of course, for chewing and my pocket calendar was not only for chewing but also for tearing. What a fun toy box this is, she thought. But I was not paying attention closely as she pulled out my sunglasses on one occasion and was soon handing them back to me in two pieces. One day when I was sitting in the children's corner at our local library holding Christie while Rachel and Kathryn were reading through every book on the shelves, Christie got my attention with three sharp blasts from the diaper end. At first I thought it was gas until I noticed that my shorts, the chair on which I was sitting and the carpet underfoot were all being painted a peculiar shade of yellow. Sorry, I hope that did not catch you sitting down to an expensive steak.

This is the same Dolley Madison Library in McLean that served all three of our children when they were growing up. Every Saturday morning we brought them to the conference room to watch cartoons, followed by a visit to the shelves to browse through those same books that now captivate their children. One day while Angela and Thomas were reading in the children's corner, I was idly looking at the bulletin board in the lobby, when my foot brushed against an object on the floor. When I glanced down I saw that it was a license plate, frame and all. Hmm, DFR-544. That number seemed familiar. With a shock I quickly recognized it as my own! Because of a poor design, the license frame on the car I was driving hung below the plastic molding of the bumper, anchored on with two plastic screws. From such a low position, it was frequently susceptible to getting snagged on something or other, so this was not the first time it had come loose, but it was the first time I had driven around for who-knows-how-long without it, unaware a curb in this parking lot had yanked it off. Some well-meaning patron must have found it, propped it up against the wall in the lobby and hoped I would come back for it.

One day I set Christie down on the piano bench for a discovery lesson, allowing her to learn that sounds can be produced by pushing keys. As she was playing her rhapsody on their Roland digital piano, Rachel ran up to turn on the record feature, thus preserving for posterity Christie's very first improvisations at the keyboard. We listen in awe to it quite often. Her position as third child in the family forced Christie to hold her own at a very young age against pushy big sisters. The next time I positioned her at the piano again, Kathryn noticed the attention from me that this was eliciting and rushed up to squeeze onto the bench beside her. Christie would have none of this, as she immediately cried "na na na na" and attempted to elbow this unwelcome newcomer out of the way. When she realized that this was ineffective in moving a stubborn block of sisterhood out of the way, Christie defiantly reached over in front of Kathryn to block her access to the keys down there. Whenever Sharlyn and I rang the doorbell, we heard squeals of delight from all three girls on the other side of the door. To them, grandparents represented a diversion from whatever drudgery that had been assigned or perhaps even represented some sort of present they sometimes brought along. To Christie, this meant only that if she toddled up to Grandpa, he would always pick her up and carry her about—sometimes even for a walk in the yard to experience all sorts of exciting adventures outside. This was one of her favorite activities. She would start to chuckle as soon as I asked her where her shoes are and giggled through the entire operation of putting them on. As we put on her jacket, she could not contain her glee as she ran to the door. She melted the heart of everyone we met on the sidewalk as she imitated my hello with a "wewwo" of her own—not hewwo, but wewwo. Can you guess what was coming into view as a little curly-haired blondie excitedly scanned skyward for the "ha-hopter" we heard approaching? At first I did not understand what was meant by the "pompone" to which a tiny finger was pointing over on someone's porch, but eventually even thick-headed Grandpa finally figured out what a pumpkin was. On the other hand I had no difficulty comprehending that the last pieces of detestable broccoli could be tolerated with a squirt of "sup-sup" from the Heinz bottle. When she finished her plate of strawberry shortcake recently, she had berry stains all around her mouth and whipped cream covered her face from her nose to her chin. As soon as I showed her her image in a hand-held mirror, she noticed immediately that her face was covered with food, but she attempted to clean it by rubbing her finger on the glass. One day when I was talking with Angela on the phone, she put Christie on to hear my voice. As soon as she heard it, she assumed it meant I was at the door. She squirmed out of Angela's grasp, then ran to the door saying "Paw-paw, Paw-paw…." There are some who would give their souls to hear such precious words.

# Lost and Found

**W**hat is the most valuable thing you own? Did you say your house? your business? your car? your art collection? your stamps, coins or gems? Some might answer that it is their children—not a bad response, considering they represent the only tangible you can take with you into afterlife. I say it is your soul. Yet I am continually amazed at the number of people I encounter who have utter disregard for it. The purpose of this life is to prepare for the next one, my father often said, and what happens to you after you die outweighs all other worldly considerations by an infinite margin. This reminds me of one of our evangelism calls several years ago, when Sharlyn and I had a conversation with a man who scoffed when we invited him to our church. When I asked if he ever thought about what will happen to him after he dies, his exact words were, "The same thing that happened to that cockroach I killed this morning." Poor fellow did not even know he *had* a soul.

Eternity is *forever*. You cannot undo *then* a mistake you make *now*. Sherman is supposed to have uttered once that war is hell. I disagree. As horrific as war may be, I submit that it is not even close. Hell is a place so horrible that no one living can possibly imagine it, yet how often have you not heard someone say frivolously, "See ya in hell." How often have I talked with someone who simply shrugs and says, "I'll take my chances." No one in hell will ever be happy they played those odds. Just think about it—try to imagine third degree burns over your whole body while you writhe in agony continuously, with no chance *ever* to escape. But in the real hell that would seem like a spa by comparison. Believe me when I tell you that you do not want to go there. I implore you to square up with your Savior now, while you have time. It does not work to show up at church once a year at Christmastime to get a white stripe painted on you that will last until the next year. The manual you need is *Basic Instructions Before Leaving Earth*, an anthology so shallow a child can play in it, yet so deep an elephant can drown in it. Hurry, death stops the clock.

In the carpool one morning, the subject of evolution arose in the conversation. Jim Allgeyer and Ron Gephart, my antagonists, were arguing aggressively against my foolish notion of Creationism. What proof did I have, they demanded to know. As we passed the Rayburn building on our way up Capitol Hill, I said, "You see this building here? Well, I have it on good authority that it once started out as a grain of sand. Over time that single grain spontaneously joined an adjacent grain to form a pebble. The same phenomenon occurred along a city block until there were thousands of pebbles. Soon contiguous pebbles joined together to form a brick, and when this action was repeated over thousands of years a wall started to rise from the earth. Eventually perpendicular walls were formed in the same way until they reached a height of sixty feet, when a covering began to grow over the empty enclosure. After several thousand more years, inner walls took shape, as wires and pipes began to thread themselves through them. After only a million years we can finally enjoy this magnificent edifice that we see today. Your body is the most complex machine ever built, far more complex than this building, yet my explanation is no more preposterous than what you would have me believe about how you and I came into being." Even the simplest creature is part of a grand design. We think nothing of swatting an annoying gnat pestering us as we work in the yard. Yet could the pooled resources of the most brilliant engineers and scientists in the world build something that tiny that can *fly*, much less recognize and avoid objects, lock onto a moving target, comprehend a larger creature's eyes and attack them, navigate without external controls, find and tank its own fuel, fly in formation with its own kind, take evasive action when attacked *and* replace itself with an identical copy before it is worn out? And you are asking me to believe that this little guy acquired all these characteristics by *chance*? I saw a cartoon recently depicting two donuts talking. Says the first, "I believe that I was created in one day by a master baker." Its fellow replies, "Well, I believe that I evolved from the lower pastries over the past several weeks."

According to reports I read, a growing number of scientists today subscribe to a theory called the Big Bang. Recently I saw a bumper sticker that read, "I believe in the Big Bang Theory—God spoke and BANG, it happened." I would like to introduce you to the Big Bag theory. Think of the entire universe as a big bag. Inside the bag also are all the laws of mathematics and science. It is a place where time ticks, colors light up, gravity works and one plus one equal two only because God says so. Some say the universe is infinite, but that too is a relative term that has a meaning only inside the bag. Vast as the universe, and even infinity, may be, God exists not only everywhere within it, but far outside of it as well. The understanding of man is confined to observations made within the bag. Everything that makes sense to us is based upon experience within a tiny portion of this universe. Yet even if we could explore all of it, our understanding would still be confined to what we learned inside the bag. It is no more possible to comprehend existence outside the bag than for a fish to understand what it is like to ride a bicycle. Yet all of us will one day *go* outside, where both heaven and hell are. We must, because the bag itself and all of its contents will be melted away. How do I know all of this? Because I read it in a Book. Not long ago I had a discussion with someone who was telling me he had recently read a book which pointed up numerous errors in the Bible and carefully analyzed the writings of Genesis and other parts of Scripture, questioning the provenance of the manuscripts, consistency of the authorship and its literary style. This writer (and his reader) came to the conclusion that such a flimsy platform was ridiculously unstable as a foundation for faith and could never support the claims of organized religion that are built upon it. Yet is this reader not doing even worse, gambling his *eternity* on the writings of a single author? If it comes down to my Book against his book, which would you choose? For me, doubts about divine inspiration in Scripture quickly dissolve away when I read such passages as the one in Jude, where he quotes Enoch. No words of Enoch are mentioned anywhere else, so how did Jude, born thousands of years later, know the exact words of Enoch's prophecy? Did he just *make that up*?

Perhaps we should come back to Earth for a moment to look at some things in my temporal Lost and Found box. One of my most traumatic memories goes back to when I was about eight years old. We were walking across the parking lot of the airport at Waterloo, Iowa when I spotted an object. I could not believe my eyes, but there before me on the asphalt was a real jackknife, which I eagerly ran to pick up. On the way home my parents made a rare stop for ice cream. While my younger siblings gobbled down their cones quickly, I licked the soft-serve treat slowly, keeping just ahead of the melt. Then with fiendish delight I observed the desire in their eyes as they watched me continuing to eat mine while they realized theirs were already gone. I paid dearly for my sadistic pleasure, however. When we got up to leave, I forgot that I had laid my precious new jackknife on the table where we sat outdoors, so we drove off without it. A few miles down the road, my father was compelled to turn around in response to the incessant wailing of my grief, but we were too late. By the time we reached that table, some other boy had experienced the joy of disbelief that someone would leave a real jackknife for him there. The pain of that experience lingered for a long time, as I replayed it over and over in my mind.

When we lived in that old farmhouse just outside of Westgate, Ralph and I were walking to school one day, and as we reached the intersection where the road turns west into town, I spied an object lying on the gravel road. At first I could not determine what it was, but then I recognized it as a box wrench that was bent into a U shape, the two box ends nearly touching. My father straightened it out and told me I could keep it as my own. Do you remember that when I first had my bicycle in Chicago, all my tools were stolen? I think I now know who committed that offense. It must have been the original owner of that wrench who hunted me down to get it back. Although this wrench was another item found, then lost, it did not leave the same searing emotional scar as the jackknife. In a similar easy come, easy go category was a bicycle my parents brought out on one of their visits. When they had taken a troubled youth named John Czarnecki (not his real name) into their home for a while, he repaid them with hostility, abuse and disrespect, so they sent him packing in such haste that he left behind some belongings, including his bike. As they were unloading their bags from the car, this Czarnecki Zephyr was leaned against the cherry tree in our yard, and moments later it was gone—whether due to poltergeist, hobo, serendipitous hitchhiker, the spirit of Czarnecki himself or just some kid happening by who asked himself, "Why am I walking?" At first glance I had seen it as just a rusty mass of pipe and rubber twisted into the shape of a bicycle anyway, so I was secretly glad someone else besides me could actually use it.

In all the years I have known Sharlyn, I have never met anyone who has more good luck than she, whether it be playing gin rummy or finding lost items. If I have turned over every article in the house looking for my keys, Sharlyn can find them within fifteen minutes, always, of course, in a place where I had already looked. I can recall only one occasion when I outperformed her. Austin had lost his car key in about a foot of snow somewhere between the driveway and the back door, where he had come in. After both he and Sharlyn had searched for it, I decided to try, even though it was already getting dark. If the key had been attached to a red tag, a leather key chain or something distinct against a sea of white, it would have been simple to find, but his key was on a thin ring with a clear plastic tab. Whereas they were looking for a mark in the snow where it might have fallen, I suspected it was actually lurking under one of Austin's footprints and found it by pawing through each one. Sharlyn outdid even herself once, when she found a fifty-dollar bill lying on the sidewalk. Quickly checking her pocket, she realized that it was the very bill that had fallen *out* of her pocket about a half hour earlier when she had walked by that way.

By contrast, Thomas had bad luck multiplied by two. He is fond of nature and decided to go for a jog through a forested area of Prince William County one time. The only place he could find to leave his car was the parking lot of the marina at the Lake Jackson boat launch. As he started out running, he found that carrying his keys was an unnecessary burden, so he hid them under some rocks near the trail and covered them with leaves. When he returned, the keys were gone. Farther back he had met a park employee picking up trash, and after making small talk with him, Thomas had offered to help him carry some of his bags to the truck. Meanwhile, it was approaching sundown, when the gate to the marina was padlocked shut, so when Thomas got back to his car, he found it trapped inside. In such a remote area, his only hope was to find that caretaker who had been loading trash. After Thomas poured out his tale, the man told him that he lives in the direction of McLean and would drive him home after he dropped off the trash truck and picked up his personal vehicle.

It was approaching eleven o'clock when Thomas came in and related his story to me. His theory was that a raccoon or squirrel had found the keys, but I had a feeling the animal who had seen where he hid them had only two legs. My concern was that whoever it was would be back early the next morning when the marina gate opened and drive off with his car. I told Thomas it was imperative that we take his spare key and go back out there immediately to see if we could find a way around the gate or enlist help from the police to unlock it. At worst case, he could sleep in the car until morning, which, if my theory was correct, might allow him to catch a thief with some keys in his hand. Since it was daylight when Thomas had driven to the marina and had stumbled upon it while driving aimlessly through the area, we had difficulty finding it again in the dead of night. When we finally got onto the road Thomas recognized and found the marina about one in the morning, we were in for a shock. There waiting at the gate was a pickup with the Prince William Park Authority insignia on the side. It reminded me of the Resurrection, when the women approaching the grave wondered how they would roll away the stone. "Sweet!" exclaimed Thomas as a seventy-ish man stepped out when we drove up. But this was too extraordinary to be explained by ordinary coincidence. "Do you know who that is?" I asked Thomas, "None other than an angel sent by God to help us." I was tempted to call the administrative offices of the County the next day to ask about this employee and would not have been surprised if they asked me what I was talking about. The man unlocked the gate after Thomas explained his car was inside, and moments later, as we left for home, the gate was locked again and the pickup had disappeared. Thomas had duplicates for all of his keys, so nothing was really lost except the time subtracted from the end of my life from the worry.

Some time after this Thomas took his mountain bike to a challenging trail over near the Shenandoah. As he approached the summit, the trail became so steep, rugged and strewn with boulders that he could go no farther. Not wishing to get this close without pressing for the mountaintop, he noted his location on his map and walked several yards off the trail to stash his bicycle, lying down, hidden in the brush and covered with branches. I am sure you have already surmised that when he returned to retrieve the bike, it was gone. After checking his bearings, he tromped all over the area to be sure he was not mistaken about his hiding place, but there was no trace of a two-wheeled vehicle. The next day he hiked up to the same place and searched for hours, but still came away empty. While he was considering a third search the following day, he came to the conclusion that his time, fuel and effort were not worth wasting on a twenty-year-old bike that needed replacing anyway, so he simply sent away for a new one. After losing his keys from a foolproof hiding place, he certainly did not expect lightning to strike him twice when he hid his bike the same way. This reminds me of the two men sitting in a bar watching the TV. When the ten o'clock news reported the story of a man threatening to jump from a bridge while the police try to dissuade him, one of the men, already sloshed from too much beer, said, "I bet you twenty dollars he doesn't jump." "Okay, it's a bet," answered the other. After the deranged man leaped, the second man said, "I can't take your money. I already saw the story on the six o'clock news and *knew* he was going to jump." "Well, I saw the six o'clock news too," said the first, "But I didn't shink he would actually do it *twice*."

One night after I and a few of my Army friends had seen a movie at the theater on South Post at Fort Myer, I was running my mouth as we walked across the parking lot to our cars. Those who know me well are quite aware that I am notoriously bad at multitasking, so even though I was looking straight at a twenty dollar bill lying on the asphalt, it did not penetrate my rambling psyche until Gary Voight bent over to pick it up. I had actually seen it before he did, but the thought I was expressing somehow rejected the interruption. I was the beneficiary of this same phenomenon at work once again several years later. This time it was Angela wrapped in conversation as we walked along, and I spotted, yes, a twenty-dollar bill lying in a puddle. Although I suspect she actually *saw* it before I did, her concentration on the point she was making to me prevented her from reaching down to pick it up. A generous father should have given it to her anyway, but I suppose I was still stinging from the one that got away some thirty years earlier, so the twenty got stuck in my pocket. Not everyone picks up pennies, but I delight in each one I find, as if it were some priceless artifact. Although pennies are the most common coins dropped on the sidewalk, I find higher denominations occasionally, even a presidential dollar once.

When Austin and I were at a used car lot one day, I spotted an object half buried in the gravel. Upon closer inspection I saw it was a silver dollar made into a tie clip. No one else was close by, and when I saw that none of the men on the lot was wearing a tie, I claimed it as my own. And, of course, it is not only currency that has value. Though I find subway fare cards occasionally, some valued at amounts that are not insignificant, it was another medium altogether that piqued my interest one day. When I walked to the airplane on a particular Saturday to meet my student, I kicked at a small circular piece of cardboard lying on the tarmac. As it rolled away, I was curious and picked it up. I saw that it was a casino chip from Bally's, stamped with a "25" on both sides. Not sure whether it was really worth anything, I had it on my dresser for several months until one day Parham Haghighi wanted to fly to Atlantic City. Ours was one of the last flights into Bader Field, a relatively short walk from the famed boardwalk, before the airport closed forever. With some trepidation I approached the window at Bally's where chips are cashed in. Fully expecting the cashier to tell me regretfully it was no longer a valid token, she handed me twenty-five dollars instead. "Lunch is on me today," I told Parham.

The kids and I were out riding our bikes one Saturday, when we happened upon a sweater along the sidewalk. A short distance farther was a blouse, then a few more single articles, then a small pile of clothing. Curious, I stopped to investigate and noticed that a few feet away from the pile was a storm drain bunker, which had several of its vertical bars broken out. When I looked into the storm sewer, now dry from lack of rain for several days, I saw a suitcase lying open, with many of its items still intact. After crawling partially inside the bunker, I carefully extracted it so that nothing would spill out. From the apparel and jewelry among the contents I could determine that it had obviously belonged to a woman, but then on a small plastic prescription bottle I found the name and address of the owner in Baltimore. Picking up the clothing loosely strewn along the path and packing it back into the bag, I brought everything home and called her. Fortunately, the long distance operator had a listing for the name printed on the capsule of pills, so I explained to the woman who answered the phone that I was not someone she knew but that I had found a suitcase that seemed to belong to her. After I described some of the items and asked her whether it was hers, I expected her first words to be some expression of relief, surprise or gratitude. Instead, after a long silence I heard the startling words, "This is a joke, right?"

Confused, I found myself in the ridiculous position of trying to convince her, almost defensively, that I was trying to reunite her with property that was actually hers. Then she explained that several *months* earlier this suitcase was missing when she went to retrieve it from the baggage claim area after a flight, and the airlines had already reimbursed her with a cash settlement for lost luggage. Nevertheless, I gave her our address and said she could pick it up from us whenever it was convenient. The next day, Sunday afternoon, a man in a Delta Airlines uniform rang our doorbell and asked for the suitcase. Some day when I get to heaven, one of the questions I will have for God is whether he could play the video of the prequel to this story for me. I am still curious how that suitcase got to the place where I found it.

Another incident without prequel occurred not far from this same spot. On my way to the post office one day, I was wrapped in my thoughts and scarcely paid any attention to a scrap of paper lying next to the sidewalk. After walking a few paces past it, however, I was suddenly gripped by the pervading thought that the logo on it looked familiar, so I retraced my steps to investigate. It was a vehicle registration card for the Chevrolet of none other than four-star General and Secretary of State Colin Powell. This presented me with a dilemma. How could I return it to him without arousing his suspicion that I had somehow acquired it illicitly and was trying to gain his favor? I decided to mail it anonymously with a note telling him briefly where I had found it. Nevertheless, hoping he might offer some explanation about the apparent careless disposition of such a valuable document, I left our return address on the envelope. A few days later I received an envelope in the mail from "CP" addressed simply to "Friends" at our address. Inside was a note that began "Dear Neighbor," thanking us for returning it. I was disappointed that he offered no further details.

Over the years we have found at least four wallets, but the first two have some facts that you might find interesting. En route to Denver one time, we were descending the ramp onto the Pennsylvania Turnpike, when I spotted a black object, in the center of the lane, that looked like a wallet. Nah, not likely, I said to myself at first, but still …. About a quarter mile farther, my curiosity overcame my doubt, so I pulled over and ran back to pick it up. It had seventy dollars in it and the driving license of an eighteen-year-old in Hazelwood, Missouri. As we drove along, I asked Sharlyn to help me watch for a state trooper or a sign for one of their patrol headquarters occasionally found along the interstate highways. But then I recalled my father's experience with those corrupt police in Arizona and concluded that perhaps this was not the best course for getting the wallet back to its owner. We usually carried a few empty grocery bags along on our trips as an expedient for any number of purposes, so Sharlyn suggested we cut one of them up as a brown paper wrapping to mail it. Before we acted upon that decision, however, I noticed that the house number in the address was five digits, which sometimes indicates a place in the suburbs of some city. When I asked Sharlyn to pull out our atlas, she found that Hazelwood was indeed a suburb of St. Louis, and we would be driving right through St. Louis. Maybe we could hand the wallet to him in person!

About nine o'clock that evening we had just turned onto the I-270 bypass north of St. Louis, when I suddenly saw a sign reading, "Hazelwood City Limits." At the top of the next exit ramp was a gas station, but as I drove up, its lights went dark. Moments later the owner emerged in a hurry to say he was closing and suggested I ask for directions at the bowling alley next door. When I asked the attendant over there whether he could direct me to the street we were trying to find, a lady sitting at the other end of the counter said, "What was that? Oh, I live on that street," and scribbled a map to the address we were seeking a short distance away. When I asked the woman who answered our knock whether this was where Jeffery Unger lives, she said, "Well, I'm his mother, but he's not here right now. Jeff's had a bad day. He was supposed to be home by now, but he ended up losing his wallet and had to call me at the office to wire money to him, so with those delays he probably won't be getting in here for several more hours yet." When she invited us in, I said, "Well, actually I already know he lost his wallet, because I have it here." Her jaw dropped, as she nearly fainted. His wallet had arrived before he did. When I said I was curious how the wallet got to the place where I found it, she explained that Jeff and a buddy were driving back from Pennsylvania in a car that had just been overhauled, so they stopped every hundred miles or so to check the oil and inspect for leaks. On one of their stops, Jeff had his wallet in his hand and set it down on the radiator cap, not giving it another thought as they slammed down the hood and drove off. As we left, I said, "Well, I really have only one regret—that I didn't get a chance to see the expression on Jeff's face when he got his wallet back." "Well, you got to see *mine*," she replied.

On the ride home in my carpool one day, we were about two blocks away from our house, when I glanced out the window and saw a wallet along the side of the street. What made it especially noticeable was that instead of lying flat on the pavement, it stood up on edge, as if someone had placed it there for target practice. Sitting in the right rear seat, I asked the driver to stop immediately. Everyone in the car was curious what I had found, and then eager to see the contents. Inside were two one-hundred-dollar bills, two silver-certificate one-dollar bills, a silver dollar, a wad of French francs worth over a hundred dollars and two business cards—one for a beauty shop in Washington, DC, and the other for a restaurant in Baltimore. But no identification. I posted a notice reading WALLET FOUND on the telephone pole closest to the spot where I picked it up and waited for the owner to call. Each day in the carpool, everyone was quite interested to know whether anyone had called yet, and after several days passed, they urged me just to keep the money. Instead, I called the beauty shop to ask whether anyone had inquired about a lost wallet. Since that was a local call, I had hoped I might get some clue from it, but it was a dead end. I phoned the restaurant in Baltimore, even though it was a toll call, and asked the same question, with the same result, but I left my phone number in case someone should come in later.

The next evening the owner of the restaurant called to ask whether we had found a wallet. When he claimed that his grandson had lost his wallet, I asked whether he could describe it. "Well, I don't know," he replied, "But I know it had two hundred-dollar bills, a silver dollar, two dollar bills ...." There was no doubt that I had located its owner. The caller asked me to hold it for a day or two longer until his grandson could arrange to pick it up. After two or three more days the phone rang again, and this time the caller was claiming to be the brother of the owner of the wallet. I was suspicious and asked him to identify it. "Well, it's black cowhide and has two one-hundred-dollar bills ...." Seemed legitimate. When he found out where we live, he said, "Oh, I'm about two blocks away from there. I'll be right over." Two blocks away, coming right over, he should be here in about five minutes, I thought. Ten minutes went by, then twenty, then a half hour. Nearly an hour later the doorbell rang. There standing on the porch was a man holding a huge bottle of Moët champagne with a bow on it, which he presented to me. I invited him in, with a mild scolding for bringing his gift. "So is this your wallet?" I asked, showing it to him. "Well, it actually belongs to my brother," he said with a slightly embarrassed look. "Where is your brother?" I asked, "And why isn't he taking care of this himself? First his grandfather called and now you." "Because he just arrived from France," said Frère Jacques, "And he doesn't speak English." "Well, tell your brother two things for us," I said, now less suspicious, "First, 'Welcome to America.'

This is the way people are in America. And second, tell him to put some identification in his wallet, so I won't have to work so hard to get it back to him next time." As he started to leave, I added, "By the way, I'm curious to know how the wallet ended up on the street." "The whole family was going out for pizza," he explained, "And my brother set his wallet on the roof of the car as we were deciding who should sit where. I guess it fell off a short time later." The place where I found it was about a half block from where they lived. Why they never saw my notice on the pole right at the intersection of their street I will never know.

I was the beneficiary of human integrity myself one day when I lost my wallet in the men's room at the office. I was not even yet aware I had lost it, when Jerry Tuben came to my desk to ask if it was mine. One of the contractors with whom he was working had found it and brought it to Jerry to ask whether the name inside it was anyone he knew. I shudder to think of the pain I would have experienced if it had not been returned, and I was very grateful to find that by the grace of God it had fallen into the hands of an honest man.

# Is It Just Me?

The most delightful piece of creative writing I have ever found is a book called *Eats Shoots and Leaves*, by Lynne Truss, devoted entirely to the power of punctuation. Her title without a comma simply describes a cuddly panda bear, but a comma after the first word changes it to a diner gone berserk. Obviously, there is a great difference between "I am God" and "I am, God." Here the comma changes one statement into its opposite—one blasphemous, the other submissive to divine authority. It would never have occurred to me to attempt to hold anyone's attention with a discussion of correct punctuation, of all subjects, for an entire book, but Truss manages quite brilliantly. Nevertheless, while her tour de force will make you cheer "Bravo!" my ranting in this chapter may make you sick. I really must warn you in advance that you will need to have a broad tolerance for whining and strong opinion to wade through the muck that follows. On the other hand, perhaps some of these observations are consistent with your view of the world also.

I suppose I can excuse my mother for saying, "I was so aggravated," since her education came in fits and starts. She was attempting to mollify the word *angry* with a euphemism, but, though she was using a popular colloquialism, the word *aggravate* properly means to make *worse*. When I was in elementary school, we were taught proper English. Is this not taught even in the high schools today? Or is it just cool for young people everywhere, it seems, to say, "so me and him went to the concert"? In casual conversation perhaps such idiosyncrasies can be tolerated, but it is far worse when professional speakers we are compelled to endure know no better. How is it that the personalities we watch on the news can choose the field of broadcast journalism, where grammar, pronunciation and diction are their very stock in trade, and then sit in front of a camera projected at me polluting the airwaves with *Wimbleton, Febuary, jewelry,* and *very unique*? Did they not notice that *Wimbledon* is spelled with a *d, February* has two *r*'s and *jewelry* has the *l* at the <u>end</u> of the second syllable? And how can something be very unique? It is either unique or not—there can be no comparative degree of being the only one in existence. Did they mean to say very *rare*? At best they might have said, "He is unique—like everyone else." When the weather lady tells me about "the tempature of the water over which Hurricane Babara is moving," is she being pressured by her producer to economize on the letter *r* to speed things along? If a pastor wants me to stay focused on his sermon, he should not divert my thinking off the main road into a cul-de-sac with such expressions as *would have went, irregardless, drownded, Holloween, nuculus, athalete* and *keep tract of*.

Meetings at the office are the worst—well, second worst, if you count the illiterate rubbish that passes for memos sent by email. Is not "ability to write" one of the qualifications in your job description,

I am wont to ask. Were syntax, possessives, spelling, usage and grammar omitted from the English courses you had in school? Did no one ever tell you there is a difference between *it's* and *its*? that there is no such thing as *her's, their's* or *theirselves*? Perhaps the apostrophe should be renamed the *approxtrophe*, a mark that can be thrown onto the page somewhere close to the word with which it is intended to be associated, so that the reader can supply the correct meaning. When I see *sugar 'n spice*, I can only come up with a handful of possible omissions—is it *sugar* <u>in</u> *spice, sugar* <u>on</u> *spice, sugar* <u>then</u> *spice*, what? Or did you mean *sugar 'n' spice*?

I feel wounded when I hear "we're still waiting on Gail," "we can flush out this idea," "like I said," "then we can try and see," "we need to hone in on," "we called a realator," "it just doesn't jive" and so on. We are waiting on Gail? How very kind of you to stand there with that towel over your arm and a tray to serve her some tea. But did you not mean we are waiting *for* Gail? We can flush out your idea, but perhaps you would rather that we *flesh* it out. When the Winston cigarettes commercial jingle some years ago was, "Tastes good … (clap, clap) … like a cigarette should," the Reynolds tobacco company was flooded with protests for their use of *like* for *as*. Today, few would even know it was wrong. Did you not learn in *your* school that *like* is a preposition, not a correlative conjunction?—unless, of course, you are a teenager and overwork it as an interjection. Austin's friend Ashley in high school used "like" nearly every other word, so every time she called saying, "Could you tell him that, like, Ashley called?" I left a message for him that Like Ashley had called. If we are already going to "see" what happens, what is it that we are going to "try"? Do you not mean try *to* see? Remind me to bring my little grinder and electric drill to the next meeting, so we can hone in on your idea—or did you mean we want to *home* in on it? One is a tool for a mechanic, the other a navigational principle to aim for a target. And what is a realator? I suppose a relator might be a storyteller, but should we consult one to sell us property? Or should we be talking with a real estate agent instead? Or did you really mean to say Realtor, a trademark for a member of a proprietary association, *not* a generic word for an agent? I think "jive" is something I saw once on a New York subway—or, excuse me, did you mean to say that something just does not jibe? Is there a difference between "in" and "into" or "on" and "onto"? Some seem not to notice or care, yet one could put you in more danger than the other. If I run *in* the street, I am continuously out there with vehicular traffic, but if I run *into* the street, I am in control of my own safety before I step off the curb. The difference between jumping *in* the water and jumping *into* the water is the difference between already having wet feet or about to get them. If I hop on the bus, will the other passengers think I am nuts if I am the only one hopping? But if I hop *onto* the bus, I will merely be joining what many others are also doing.

* * *

One of the most serious plagues of our area is the voracious, unsatiable appetite of developers for land. Any stand of more than ten trees must be cut down so that eight more houses can be plunked down. It is bad enough that the courts slap down our injunctions and moratoriums against these rapacious practices, but it is even worse when our politicians actually participate in them. Mr. Developer goes to Mr. County with a proposition, "If you let me change the zoning of these thirteen acres from R-1 to R-3, you will get three times the tax revenue from the same land." Mr. County falls for it every time, pulls out his rubber stamp and says, in the manner of Mickey Mouse's friend Goofy, "Gawrsh,

Mr. Developer, yer purdy smart." Then with incredible chutzpah, Mr. Developer goes in the next time with his request to change from R-3 to R-100, so that we may now introduce ourselves to the four hundred new neighbors moving into their condominiums down the street. How can we be so stupid as a society to allow ourselves to be hoodwinked time and again by these deceptions? By the way, I love the definition of chutzpah in Leo Rosten's *Joys of Yiddish* as the quality of a man who shouts "Help! help!" while beating you up—or the one who, after killing his parents, begs for the mercy of the court because he is an orphan. It is only after the developer is long gone that the local government realizes that it has not the infrastructure to support such a rapid exponential influx of citizens clamoring for schools, hospitals, roads, fire departments, trash collection, police and other services which will ultimately cost far more than those "tax revenues" the charlatans no longer on the scene had promised. Worse, have we learned nothing about the impact of population density upon social conditions—increased traffic, crime, pollution, trash, noise, juvenile delinquency, and classroom size, to name a few? Zoning laws exist for the very purpose of avoiding this malaise, yet we willingly, intentionally and casually discard the immunity they offer. Two rats in a cage will find a way to get along, but a hundred rats in the same cage will fight and bite every time. In high school I remember the football cheerleaders chanting "Push 'em back, push 'em back, farther, farther. Hit 'em again, hit 'em again, harder, harder." The marketing cheerleaders for the developers have come up with their own mantra, "Pack 'em in, pack 'em in, tighter, tighter. Hit 'em again, hit 'em again, harder, harder."

* * *

Few things in life boil my blood faster than traffic. Why do manufacturers even bother to put turn signals on cars any more? Equally useless are laws requiring the use of them, since they are never enforced anyway. I notice the car ahead of me is slowing down, then the brake lights come on, but why is he stopping here in the middle of the block, I ask myself as I use up my margin of safety concluding he is probably braking for a squirrel and will resume his speed any moment. No, he slows to a crawl, without signaling, before turning into his driveway. Similar is the car in the left lane at a red light. I pull up behind, ready to proceed when he does. When the light turns green, he pulls into the intersection and stops, waiting to make his left turn. At that point it does not matter whether he engages the turn signal or not, because either way I am now stuck behind him. A courteous driver would have signaled the turn two hundred feet *before* the intersection, as the law requires, to afford me the option to choose the right lane and go around. Some drivers intentionally refuse to signal for a lane change in order to prevent the sadistic motorist in the next lane from gleefully closing up the gap. Yes, I have experienced this too, but I take the opposite position—that by announcing my change I can allow the traffic in the next lane to adjust to my coming over, and I find that these motorists, whether motivated by pity, courtesy or guilt, it matters not which, award me a high percentage of success.

How can you not love the adorable weenie who diddles, fiddles, twiddles and piddles along in the left lane at five below the speed limit? Does he fancy himself the self-appointed Enforcer, a vigilante trying to control the scofflaws who are trying to stay with the pace of traffic? Is his left turn coming up twenty miles ahead? Is he ignorant of the danger and the laws forbidding such tactics or just so shabbily base that he does not care? The left lane should be sacrosanct. The law in some states now requires that you must continue moving right if you are not passing a car to your right. It is not your responsibility to block speeders. And why is it that on a busy two-lane road, *one* car should be allowed to hold up fifty while stopped waiting to make a left turn? I declare that no one should be allowed to stop in such a roadway unless no traffic is coming up behind. No, I am sorry, you will need to make your left at the next intersection, if it is clear, or turn off to the right and cross back over. Oh, to be emperor for one day ....

In my experience the worst are the truckers. The long stretch of Interstate 81 from the Tennessee border through Virginia is heavily packed with trucks, as it brushes the Blue Ridge Mountains for the length of the state. Time and again I have been behind a convoy of fifteen or twenty of these behemoths through the mountains. On the long, downhill side of a slope, this moving wall roars along at speeds approaching a hundred miles per hour, but on the next three-mile upslope, twelve crawl along at thirty miles per hour until one of them suddenly swings out to pass the others at the dizzying speed of thirty-*three*, blocking the left lane for many minutes until the crest, when the pattern repeats. If I were in the legislature, I would introduce a bill to make it illegal for a truck to be in the left lane except for an emergency. My father was fond of saying that the truckers used to be the knights of the road but are today the nightmares of the road. Their bullying tactics anger me the most. If construction ahead will block one lane, traffic tends to queue up in the lane that will not be blocked, sometimes for several miles. Some motorists consider it "cheating" to continue to use the lane that will be closing. Among them are many truckers, who play God to prevent this by setting up a rolling blockade with another truck, sometimes as far away as five or six miles from the merge point. If a car tries to pass such an illegal barrier on the shoulder, I have seen the truck ride the shoulder to prevent that too, sometimes forcing the car into the median. Surely even the most adamant adherent to the belief that the lane should not be used must admit this goes too far, with its potential for accident, road rage, fisticuffs, or even gunplay. Apparently state legislatures agree, stipulating that *both* lanes are to be used all the way to the merge point. When I see these cowboys behaving in this manner, I copy down their numbers and report them to their companies. In every case the owner has agreed with me that this projects an unacceptable corporate image.

\* \* \*

Some people are of the opinion that the perpetual state of construction on our roadways is due to our system of awarding contracts to the lowest bidder in the road building industry. These critics say those companies maintain their copetitive edge by cutting corners and using inferior products that hasten deterioration of the surface and in turn proliferate new contracts. As evidence, they point to the superior quality of materials used in the highways of Europe and other places in the world. Whether this is true or not, I am angered by the arrogance of these contractors. Have you ever been squeezed into a single lane for twelve miles and observe not only that the lane which is closed is perfectly serviceable, but also that *no workers* are anywhere around? First of all, the work should be so carefully planned that the extent of a closure is minimized. It should not be necessary to block a lane for eight miles if two hundred feet of it are under repair. Second, a maximum period for closure based upon working around the clock should be established, and the company should be heavily fined for every hour beyond it. We were tormented by a ten-mile stretch of Interstate 81 north of Harrisburg that was a heavily trafficked one-lane bottleneck for five *years* (!), yet whenever we tried to pass through this segment, we *never* saw any work being done. Worst of all are toll roads which not only force me to crawl along at twenty miles per hour, but then hold out their hand for the full amount at the gate. When I reached the tollbooth in Ohio one time after suffering inch by inch through construction for thirty miles, I asked how much the discount was. "Discount?" questioned the puzzled attendant. "What do you mean, *discount?*" For what was I paying, if not for the privilege of driving unimpeded at high speed over their stretch of roadway, I wanted to know.

* * *

I seem to remember, when I was a teenager, encountering pay toilets for a brief period of time, but even if they were not legislated out of existence, they were surely sabotaged out of existence. Americans historically have never tolerated any form of taxation or exploitation well, so I am surprised we tolerate toll roads, especially those that double as interstate highways. Any private enterprise should be free to build a toll bridge or roadway anywhere it chooses to purchase the rights, but the instant federal funds are used, the freeway should be free of fees. How is it that in my state you can freely use the interstate highway that belongs to all of us, but that in your state I can use the interstate highway that belongs to all of us only if I pay a user fee? And how is it that on the segment of Interstate 90 through New York, the so-called Thruway, the highway commission not only assesses me a toll, but haughtily sends me away with a flea in the ear by refusing to conform to the rules of the interstate system? Exit numbers are supposed to be assigned according to the mileage post, rather than sequentially, and mileage posts are supposed to be numbered from west to east, not the reverse.

In the same vein, I am always irritated when I enter one of our national parks and find someone from the Department of the Interior standing at the gate with his hand out. Is this not a federal park? Does it not already belong to me as a tax-paying citizen of the country? So then why am I paying to see what I already own? I thought I was going to be arrested one time for failing to pay one of these fees. No, I was not *intentionally* a gatecrasher, but that is not how the park officials saw it. Sharlyn had never been to western South Dakota, so in 1996 when we were invited to the centennial celebration of Golgotha Lutheran Church in Nebraska, where my grandfather had been pastor for many years, we decided to extend our trip to visit the majesty of Mount Rushmore and the stark beauty of the Badlands. The Badlands Loop Road has two lanes winding some thirty miles from one end of the park to the other, allowing entry from either direction. If I were designing the system, I would establish toll collection at the entrance at both ends, not the entry *and* exit points at both ends—and I would install a gate arm to stop each car until it had paid the admission, if there must be one.

As we approached the entrance to the park near Wall, at exit 110 off Interstate 90, we encountered a glass-enclosed toll collection building. As we approached the window, the young lady inside motioned us forward, and then as we came abreast I saw her stride purposefully to other side of the building where cars were exiting. I was confused. Was I supposed to wait until she came back eventually, or was she waving us through? Was it because certain days are free, out of town license plates are admitted without charge, every hundredth car is exempt, what? When I saw her interacting with the car exiting, I assumed we would pay on the way out, so I shrugged and drove on through. As we reached the midpoint of the Loop, I saw a police car with lights flashing coming toward us at a high rate of speed. As soon as it passed us, it skidded to a stop and made a U-turn in a cloud of dust before pulling up behind us. A uniformed officer asked to see my gate receipt. When I told him I did not have one, he said sarcastically, "You don't *have* one? Why *not*?" "Because the lady at the window where we entered the park waved us through," I explained. "That's not what she says," he retorted. When I insisted I would testify under oath that she gestured for us to pass on through, he talked at some length on the radio back in his car before approaching us again to tell us to pay the fee as we exited. Now, here's my question. Why, exactly, are we collecting admission to see the Badlands? Is it so that we can pay salaries of the people collecting fees? Is it so we can construct and air-condition the building in which they work? Or is it to buy police cruisers and pay salaries of park officials to descend upon those who slip through? Could we not save all of the overhead required to maintain such machinery and simply allow those of us who already own the Badlands to drive through and see it? And do we really need to send out the militia with guns a-blazin' for such a minor offense?

* * *

Blue smoke can often be seen coming out of my ears when I see traffic lights. Surely they were invented by the devil himself. Surely local governments must seed the streets with fertility powder to make them proliferate overnight. It is becoming impossible for me to drive through any familiar area without seething over yet another new one hanging there glaring at me. Every church must have one to let its parking lot empty, every condo forms a civic association demanding one for its garage, every strip mall with three stores must enable soccer moms to get in and out to pick up dry cleaning, every …. At this rate we will not be content until we have a red light every ten feet coast to coast. Such short-sighted and self-serving policy actually sets out with the proactive intention, not to *facilitate* traffic flow, but to *disrupt* it! I have a theory that ninety percent of our traffic lights are simply unnecessary and that if we cut them down, traffic would not only *not* be adversely affected but would actually improve. As evidence I offer the conditions we see following a storm, when widespread power failures knock out the traffic lights over a broad area. At certain major intersections, where even I am compelled to admit some kind of control is necessary, police are out to direct the flow, but at the myriad secondary intersections, traffic is managing quite well without any controls, humming along without incident, thank you. At an intersection like that I contend that a red light is unnecessary, but if you insist, it should function exactly as a yield sign. Stop if you must and give way to a vehicle in conflict with your own, but proceed with caution if the coast is clear. If this is too much to ask, because of the confusion between the secondary and primary intersections, we could make these a different shape or color—say a triangle, a swirling spiral, or the color purple.

Poor Sharlyn is so tired of hearing me rail against the stupidity of the traffic engineers in our area that she has taken to adopting *their* point of view whenever I start up again. But why should I sit at a red light for forty seconds at eleven o'clock at night when I am the only one there? My first question is why that light is even needed at this hour, but also what is the purpose of those sensors we expended such great effort and funding to embed in the roadway? Is this not the very reason they exist, so that I am not compelled to wait some arbitrary cycle of time before it is my turn? And when one vehicle has tripped the sensor from a little side street, why is it that the light remains green for several more seconds as twenty cars queue up on the primary road, waiting while *no one* is allowed to use the precious intersection? Why are forty cars piling up at the red light while the next light ahead, which none of us can reach and no one is using, is green, but then by the time ours turns green, that one has turned red? Think of the time and fuel wasted when this idleness is multiplied a dozen times in a row. What was the engineer thinking when he set up an intersection at a boulevard where I sit at the red light while the second half of the boulevard twenty feet farther is green? As mine finally turns green, that one turns red. Was he forcing me to linger again at the second half just to admire the beauty of his boulevard or enraging the bull with red at the bullevard? My favorite is the four-minute light, especially during rush hour, when it short cycles three or four times before I finally get across. How can we be so stupid as a society as to transform all of our arterial highways into a string of Christmas lights with all red bulbs? Do we not have developers and shortsighted local government to blame for this too? After all, it is much easier and far less expensive in the short term to link housing tracts and shopping malls directly to the highway than to build frontage roads, overpasses and on-ramps. But those of us who live afar must pass through these densified areas and do not get to vote on the impact this has upon *us*. This is a very self-serving point of view taken by a few at the expense of the many, and eventually all the main corridors to get from here to there are choked by an endless string of traffic lights, and nobody moves anywhere, especially the ones they were meant to serve in the first place.

I must admit that traffic lights collectively are a great equalizer. Have you ever seen the giraffe in the next lane who sees only orange as the light turns red, leaning his neck through the intersection? Is this not the same dude to whom you pull up alongside a half mile later at the next red light? You may have noticed that it really does not matter what speed you drive over a given distance. You will arrive at nearly the same time whether you are a snail or a cricket. This was a lesson I was taught by Loyle Stiles several years ago. As we drove a half hour across town every Sunday morning for church, it was our custom to start from home late so that I could be sure to build up my blood pressure enough to arrive in a reverent mood. Loyle, Lorena and their boys lived only a couple of blocks away from us and left for church on time. If I drove like a madman, I would catch up to their car at a traffic light. When the light changed, I was off like a jackrabbit, while Loyle eased through the intersection like a frozen daiquiri. Three lights later, as I sat fuming at the red, Loyle's car coasted slowly up in the lane beside me. Then I screeched away again at the green, only to have Loyle drift up again farther down at the next light. He arrived like a country gentleman, while I arrived like Yosemite Sam.

* * *

The very next item on my list after traffic lights is speed limits. Oh, I know all about the traffic surveys, population density, volume and vehicle counts that supposedly determine them, but I still contend the number is arbitrary. It seems to me that when we ask how fast someone is driving, we are asking the wrong question. The speed limit posted on Linway Terrace where we live is twenty-five, but *everyone* passes my house at speeds up to seventy or so. But what is that to me, really? As long as they are driving *past* my house, not *into* it or *through* it, why should I care? Instead of how *fast*, should we not be asking how *safe*? One day when Hoda was driving the carpool, we were pulled over for driving forty-seven in a zone for thirty. First of all, this was rush hour, when anyone who can *attain* the speed limit ought to receive a plaque. Facetious as that might be, I am quite serious when I adhere to the notion that during rush hour, traffic will regulate itself. Not only do we not need squad cars out there contributing to the congestion, but also I question whether they are not actually *jeopardizing* safety by snarling traffic flow with flashing lights blocking a precious lane. People are simply trying to get to work, and in the evening rush, they are tired, simply trying to get home. Why not just leave them alone? Was Hoda doing anything *dangerous*? If the answer is no, then why should she be hassled? I realize I am skating on thin ice here, but while acknowledging that speed is a factor in safety, I contend that most drivers do not need a sign to remind them what speed is safe. I am especially irked by those neighborhoods whose civic associations proclaim to the world that they shall not only determine what speed I must drive but shall install speed humps to *force* me to comply. They anger me, first because I usually play by the rules and drive through their precious residential areas close to the posted speed anyway, but if the sign says twenty-five, why must I bottom out on each of a half dozen lumps in the roadway slowing me to *ten*? If these civic associations were to conduct an honest self-appraisal, they would discover that most of the infractions stem from their own members right there in the same neighborhood. And does a wide four-lane roadway with a boulevard separating opposing traffic really need a speed limit of twenty-five in the first place—and heavy patrol to snag me for going thirty-one?

Part of the problem, as I see it, is that police are given too much power for acts that are *malum prohibitum*, those offenses which are merely *declared* wrong. We want our police to have full power to provide protection for the citizenry against acts that are *malum in se*, those violations of moral or natural law, such as robbery, murder and rape. But we allow our police to confuse the two. When Ralph was traveling from Georgia to Texas several years ago, a local law enforcement officer stopped him for speeding. When the officer claimed he was going seventy-five in a zone where the limit was fifty-five, Ralph knew that was false. "I have you on radar," lied the officer. "Show me," said Ralph, striding back to the squad car to see for himself. Having considerable experience with radar units in the Air Force and at Raytheon, he noticed immediately that the officer had it turned off. Confronted with his deception, the officer said, "Well, if you insist, I can cuff you right now and take you to jail until the judge hears your case." If I were Ralph, I might have been tempted to call his bluff, except for two considerations. First, the judge was likely as crooked as the officer, and second, there was the matter of his car, which would certainly have been impounded while the wheels of "justice" ground slowly toward their conclusion several *days* later. On top of the indignity of being falsely convicted, he would still have paid extravagantly to redeem his vehicle, probably damaged, from Bruno bunkered behind barbed wire.

Clearly, this was unjustified and inappropriate. No one is denying that this officer had the *power* and was within his *right* to threaten handcuffs and jail, or even to draw his service weapon, but that is precisely the point. *Should* he have such a right and *was* this really an appropriate response against an otherwise law-abiding citizen? Armed with power and weaponry bestowed upon them by the government, hammer-handed police forget their role as protectors of the public and zealously revel in their ability to harass the public. Why did the police need to stop poor little Hoda *during rush hour* on her way to work? It is true that she technically disobeyed the literal words on that sign, but did she violate the terms of her contract with society to drive safely? I was there, and I say no. Ultimately the respect upon which law enforcement depends in order to provide service to society quickly disintegrates into a *dis*service which fosters *dis*respect and mistrust.

\* \* \*

I had just gotten home from work one day when a police car pulled into our driveway. The officer demanded to talk to Thomas Pullmann, who, according to reports, had been seen throwing apples at a school bus. It turned out to be a case of mistaken identity, but the officer was impressing upon me that, if apprehended, Thomas would be charged with a felony. "A felony?!" I thundered. "Officer, let me tell you something. School boys have been chucking snowballs at gentlemen in top hats for centuries and will continue to do so for centuries more. You are never going to stop such behavior by declaring it *felonious* to throw snowballs—or apples—at school busses either. The only thing that accomplishes is disrespect for the law and for *you* when you try to enforce it." It reminds me of a call I got one day at the office from the principal of the middle school, telling me that Austin was in his office for running in the hallway. I was confused. "Why, exactly, is he in your office then?" I wanted to know. "Well, it's against the rules to run in the corridors," he enlightened me. "You have a rule against *that*?" I asked in disbelief. "*I* run in the corridor here at the office every day. Mr. Lynch, let me tell you something. If you have rules which even I think are questionable, you should not be surprised when your students begin to disrespect them."

* * *

If it is a felony to throw an apple at a school bus, then surely it ought to be quite serious to throw a rock at a house. Moments after Sharlyn had gone into the back yard one evening after dark to hang up a towel on the clothesline, we heard a sharp bang from some object that struck the roof. Busy Old Dominion Drive runs along behind our house, so my first thought was that a truck had flung some debris from the roadway high into the air and onto the house. But when I rushed outside, I saw immediately in the dim light from the street that a rock about the size of a baseball was lying underneath the clothesline, about four feet over from the towel. On the roof I could make out another, somewhat larger, still resting on the shingles. As I dashed up the bank to the street, I witnessed a young man heaving a cardboard box of debris onto the roadbed. As soon as he caught sight of me, he ran toward one of the houses in the neighborhood across Old Dominion. As I chased after him calling for him to stop, I approached a half dozen more youths milling around on the driveway. The sight of a homeowner with fire in his eyes barreling toward them made them run for the house, locking the door behind. When they refused to answer my pounding, I called through the screen, "Boys, would you prefer that I talk to you or to your dad?" A sheepish face appeared at the door and mumbled an apology. I had not made any accusations, but the apology seemed to be an affirmation of guilt nonetheless. After my tutoring session on the hazards of blindly hurling stones in the direction of humanity, which included a stern lecture on their close encounter with manslaughter, we had no more problems with them—and without the necessity to involve the authorities.

* * *

Speed traps, especially of the sort that Ralph encountered, are a bane of society that should be outlawed. First, they all too often discriminate by targeting any driver with a license plate from out of state. A local judicial system takes advantage of the fact that a motorist is unlikely to expend more to contest the charges than what he stands to lose by simply paying a fine which he knows, or strongly suspects, is fraudulent. Second, the objective of law enforcement should be to promote public safety, not to solicit taxes, yet these communities thrust their police into the machinery of an elaborate revenue mill. This is not only an overextension of authority, but also a conflict of interest that amounts to extortion. Third, they encourage law enforcement officers to be overzealous and dishonest. Under pressure of superiors to wring fines out of the citizenry, officers who have been issued broad authority will posture with intimidation and deception to exercise it. We know from the testimony of Mark Fuhrman in the infamous trial of O.J. Simpson and myriad other cases that police lie, but dishonesty aside, such officers have a misplaced sense of purpose of their role in society. But it is not their fault. Rather, it is ultimately our own, for putting them in this position. Finally, if the intent is really to curb speeding, these traps simply do not work. Oh, yes, they work for *me*. I remember even twenty years later where every one of them in our area has been set up and watch my dials assiduously when passing through. But the very next day after the police dismantle their apparatus, traffic is back to the pace it was before. To me this suggests that not only are police wasting their time with such tactics, but more importantly, society is sending a message to government which is being ignored—that the numbers on their signs are wrong.

\* \* \*

All too often it seems to me that police are simply following the line of least resistance. It is much easier to wave over someone who willingly stops to cooperate than to take on a drug cartel, den of bank robbers, or car theft ring. But as Leon Rosenbloom often told me, "If it takes an effort, you must make the effort." If resources marshaled for issuing tickets for minor infractions and moving violations were reallocated to solving real crime, the interests of the community would be much further advanced in the long run. When I witnessed a man and woman breaking into that car in D.C. and filed a report furnishing their license number, I fully expected to be contacted by the prosecutor's office, or at least the Metropolitan Police, to testify. Yet I never heard from them. Did they even investigate whether there was a connection to my stolen wheel—or was it simpler to deploy their army of officers to write parking tickets and arrest tourists for littering?

Late one spring evening, when Sharlyn and I had the windows open as we watched the Miss Universe pageant, we heard a noise across the street. I sprang to the screen door in time to witness a young man swinging a piece of two-by-four down upon our mailbox, bashing it to the ground. Foolishly, I darted out the door after him, chasing him down the sidewalk. He crossed the street to a waiting car a half block away, and as he opened the door, the courtesy light revealed the raucous gaiety of a carful of young people. As they sped away, I made a mental note of the license number. This was not the first incident of "mailbox polo" in our neighborhood, and I expected this evidence might be just what the police needed to put a stop to it. Instead, the detective to whom my case was assigned called me about two days later to ask whether I was sure of that plate number. Assuring him I was absolutely positive, I was not prepared for what he said next. The owner of the car was from Lorton, some twenty miles away, who said he had never been to McLean. The case was simply dropped after the officer asked me whether I thought I might be able to identify this miscreant whom I saw at midnight running away in the dark with his back to me. What more could I have done to help them solve the crime? To the police I say, "If it takes an effort, you must make the effort."

When Angela and Paul returned from Germany one year, they were arriving by military transport into Dover. Because their family needed their car from there and because we could not all ride together, Sharlyn and I drove over to meet them in two cars. As I approached an overpass in their station wagon, I heard a sharp snap and noticed immediately that an object impacting the windshield left a mark about the size of a silver dollar. More than once, my windshield has been struck by a pebble thrown from some truck I am following, but when I saw no vehicle ahead, I realized that someone had just taken a potshot at me. Fortunately, the pellet did not penetrate the glass completely, for the mark was directly in my line of vision, and a more high-powered projectile would have struck me between the eyes. Whoever fired the shot knew what he was doing and had very good aim. When we arrived at Dover, I told Sharlyn that I had been shot, and she immediately exclaimed that she had too. Indeed, there was the mark of the silver dollar on her windshield in the exact position where a bullet would have struck her in the forehead. By coincidence there was a Maryland Police barracks near the place in Prince George's County where the incident occurred, and late that night on the way home, we stopped in to report it. The officer behind the desk not only doubted our story, but also refused to look at our car, belittling us and threatening to charge us for making a false police report. As we left in disgust, we flagged down another officer about two blocks away, who told us to follow him back to the barracks and to wait for him at the front of the building, while he drove around to the back. After waiting in vain for over fifteen minutes for him to appear, we assumed he had talked with the Ostrogoth behind the desk and was not likely to come out. We decided to forget about our civic duty to report crime and drove back in the wee hours of the morning to civilized Virginia, where we replaced two windshields at our own expense.

Why was I not surprised when Angela and Paul some time later had that same station wagon stolen and learned that it was recovered in Prince George's County? And why was I not surprised that such crimes are so common and so voluminous there that the police incredibly did not even dust it for fingerprints? It is precisely the long string of such unsolved cases that plagues many police departments throughout the nation that mandates the need for a national, perhaps international, DNA database. Part of the process of issuing a birth certificate ought to be a registry of an infant's fingerprints and distinguishing DNA markers. Squeal all you want about infringement of fundamental rights or Orwellian totalitarianism, but I contend that the overarching benefits to society far outweigh whatever negatives such a policy might bear. I see it simply as the price to pay for tranquility. Not only would it serve to some degree as a deterrent to crime, but it also offers swifter justice and even protection for suspects. Several death-row inmates have recently been exonerated by such genetic detection techniques.

But advances in scientific technology do not excuse laziness or unconcern on the part of uncaring police. One Saturday as I walked across the pedestrian bridge over Pimmit Run near us, I glanced down and saw that someone had thrown a shopping cart, an office chair, a traffic cone and other small items of debris into the water. When I called the non-emergency number of our local precinct to report this, the officer told me to hold for a moment. A few seconds later I found myself connected to the answering machine of the county park authority, to which she had transferred me, ostensibly because Stream Valley, as the flood plain is called, is actually a county park. Of course, their offices were closed on a Saturday, so I called back to the police station to explain what happened and to present again the details of what I saw. This time a different officer said, "Well, sir, there is really nothing *we* can do." Nothing we can do! Is not a crime involved here? Was the shopping cart not stolen from some local store? Did that office chair not belong to someone? What about the offense of polluting the rivers with debris? Surely the person who committed that ought to be the one seining it back out. As a minimum I expected a shift of the responsibility I had fulfilled as a citizen to an agency of the government that should have taken it on instead of unconcernedly pushing the switchboard button marked Dumpem. "If it takes an effort, you must make the effort."

In my experience police often carry a certain swagger that telegraphs the message that they are above the law. The opposite ought to be true, where, with the eyes of the world on them, they hold themselves up as model citizens, the paradigm of behavior in society. Nowhere is this more evident than their behavior behind the wheel of their cruisers. We see them streaking along the streets well above the posted speed, charging through stop signs, engaging the infrared feature of their turn signals and sending pedestrians in the crosswalk scurrying out of their way. Yet, as a community we provide an avenue for them to carry on in exactly this manner in order to execute their duties, if *necessary*. When legitimate police business demands, they may switch on flashing lights and a siren, and *then* cloak themselves with whatever expediency that desperate measures may require. This is not a toybox to be opened during routine patrol, however, nor are the maneuvers required for a car chase to be practiced while cruising. What I see instead is arrogant abuse of power and haughty disdain for those of us who have little recourse to stand up to it.

* * *

Although you probably already have the idea that I have a real fondness for the police, I will relate an incident in which they eventually responded somewhat favorably to us. When Austin was a senior, he preferred to drive to school rather than to take the bus, because of the flexibility it provided for him after classes. A neighbor boy we will call Trampus frequently appeared on our doorstep with his sister in the mornings to ride along with him. One day when Austin returned to his car to drive home, he discovered he had locked his key inside and foolishly allowed Trampus to witness where he kept the spare in a magnetic Hide-A-Key hidden underneath the car. Next time Austin went to the bank to withdraw some money, the teller told him there were only a few dollars in the account. "Someone" had appeared with the passbook and nearly cleaned it out. Since Trampus was the only one who knew where Austin had the passbook hidden in his car, he did not need Sherlock to solve the mystery about who "someone" was. Because this was a teller mistake for not requiring proper identification, the bank made restitution.

A few weeks later, when we came home from work one day, I noticed a piece of dried brown leaf on top of Sharlyn's sewing cabinet directly beneath the window of our bedroom. When I saw another little piece of leaf lying nearby on the carpet, I suspected that "someone" had crawled through that window. Fearing a break-in, I immediately checked the top drawer of my dresser, where I foolishly kept three hundred dollars in cash for emergency use. It was gone. In response to the incident report we filed with the police, our local McLean district office called us in to talk with their detectives. Asking Austin to wait outside the conference room into which Sharlyn and I had been ushered, the spokesman soberly told us they knew who took the money—Austin. This was a classic scenario, he explained, where a teenager steals money from parents and arranges an elaborate hoax to make it appear like a robbery. I did not buy their story. Convinced as they might have been, I was not. But they considered the case closed.

Although we kept that old sash window locked, and the storm window could supposedly be opened only from the inside, it was nevertheless not difficult to break into our house, and a few days later we found evidence that "someone" had been in the house again. When Austin got home from school, he came running out of his room to say some four hundred dollars he had collected from his newspaper customers was missing from the pouch in which he kept it. Our report to the police fell upon deaf ears, as they remained confident this too fit the pattern they laid out for us, contending their theory was still valid. They told us that if we watched Austin's spending habits over the next few days, we would discover where all the money went. However, a few days later we returned home to discover still another break-in. This time the thief walked off with Angela's beautiful jewelry case Carl Zimmerman had made for her when she was a little girl. Although it perhaps had little intrinsic value and held nothing of much mercenary value, it was priceless to Angela, containing as it did all of her medals, awards and ribbons for her accomplishments through school, the souvenir French and British coins she brought back from her European trip, and irreplaceable memorabilia that held sentimental value to her. It broke her heart when she found out it was gone forever. Ironically, had she not kept a tiny padlock on its clasp, the thief might have rifled through it without the compulsion to carry off the whole chest.

When we notified the police again, they called Austin in for questioning. After they finished with him this time, they had a new suspect—Trampus. Austin was quite sure by the way their relationship had changed in recent weeks, and especially by the association of Trampus with an older boy with whom he had recently taken up company. Hoping to catch him, or them, in the act, two detectives arranged to hide in our house while we were away at work. Although they lay in wait day after day for about ten days, the break-ins mysteriously stopped, whether because the suspects were somehow tipped off or spooked, acquired a conscience, feared a growing risk or simply felt we had little else worth stealing. Acting upon Austin's suspicions, however, the police decided to have a little talk with Trampus. He not only confessed to the thefts, but also named his accomplice, who by then had fled to another state to avoid prosecution. We never did recover our losses. However, we were pleased this time with the efforts of the McLean district police on our behalf.

* * *

Although I do enjoy some professional sports, I really do not understand how fans tolerate them. I have never attended a live game of the NFL or the NBA and have seen major league baseball only two or three times. The cost is frightful—and shameful. Do fans not realize that billion-dollar contracts with players come from their pockets? The value of anything is only what someone is willing to pay for it, and no one on earth is that valuable. I have a theory that if we paid our pastors, teachers and medical researchers in this country what we pay entertainers and sports figures, we would have a stronger moral fiber, a more creative and inventive populace, and a united front to eradicate disease. After all, what is really accomplished when your team wins the championship? When our local team won the Super Bowl one year, I must admit it was exhilarating—for about two days. By the end of the week it was already stale news, and by the following week most of the world could not remember who had won and were busily preparing for next year. If a bench-emptying brawl breaks out on the baseball field, players are heavily fined. If two players slug it out on the gridiron, they are ejected. If two basketball players swing their elbows and knock each other to the floor, officials assess technical fouls and toss them out of the game. The rules do not tolerate fighting because it is outside the rules of the sport. So why is it that every night on the sports segment of the news I must watch highlights—yes, the *highlights*—of some hockey game showing two players slugging it out while the referee stands by with hands on hips? Some tell me the fans like it this way, but how is this any more sportsmanlike in hockey than in basketball? If I were a hockey referee, I would warn both benches before play begins that this is a team sport, not an exhibition of pugilism, and at the first outbreak, both players will be sent to the showers.

If I played the game, one of the most difficult challenges for me would be to resist the urge to argue with the officials. When I watch the World Series, I can never understand how the home plate umpire calls pitches. One pitch is called a strike, while two pitches later in the same position it is called a ball. Pitchers, catchers, batters and managers contest pitches in every game, sometimes so vehemently that the umpire issues the heave-ho. Why do we tolerate this? At the major league level we have the technology to determine the strike zone electronically. For each batter the machinery could be adjusted for the player's size, and multi-positional cameras could easily determine balls and strikes. In fact they *do*, as the replay of the pitch clearly portrays. No, the home plate umpire does not lose his job, because he is still needed for plays at the plate and other functions. How is it that instant replay can be used to settle disputed calls in football but not in baseball? Could the camera not settle the argument over whether the catcher missed the tag at the plate or the throw to first base was in time? Similarly, a sensor could be implanted in every football used at the professional level that could track precisely where a punt passed out of bounds without the need for an official to say subjectively that it went out … oh, about … here. After a fumble, the ball passes around at the bottom of the pile of scrum through the hands of multiple players, but with the electronic sensor, possession could be determined by the first player to have it. The sensor could be the arbiter for spotting the ball, determining first downs, settling questions of goal line crossing, and so on.

\* \* \*

I am especially fond of the dipstick who rolls down the windows of his car and turns up the volume to share his beautiful music with the rest of the world. Even better is the one who puts the top of his convertible down at two in the morning during the summer so that I can get the full effect of the boom-*boom* … boom-*boom* … boom-*boom* of the bass beginning a mile away. How did he know that was my favorite song—and the best time of the day for me to enjoy it? What a pity it is that these free concerts are illegal. Just as enjoyable is the scruffy youth in dreadlocks who sits ten rows behind me on the bus, yet I hear the heavy metal coming through his earpiece as loud as if *I* am wearing it. I have been in quieter machine shops.

Human nature is selfish, but does it seem to you that as a society we are becoming increasingly inconsiderate of each other? There is a story about the guy who enters a stall in the restroom. As he sits down, a voice from the adjacent stall says, "Hi!" Not sure whether he should answer or just ignore it, the man decides that it is probably harmless enough to reply, so he responds, "Hello." Then the voice says, "How ya doin'?" Not willing to get involved in a conversation with someone under these circumstances, the man is not sure he should answer again, yet, not wishing to be totally impolite, he says, "Fine, how are you?" This time the voice says, "Do you mind? I'm on the phone here!" The proliferation of cell phones has turned public places into chat rooms. It is such a delight to ride all the way home on the bus after a long day at work listening to the woman on the seat behind me chattering away loudly in Spanish or the one way in the back who turns on the speaker phone to rage at a client until the whole bus begins to take sides in the argument. I am always interested to know what the woman across from me on the subway wants her husband to pull out from the freezer, how long to let it thaw, when to put it in the oven, and what time they need to leave for the meeting. Is there anything in this that he could not figure out for himself? This brings to mind the story of a fellow in the locker room at the gym. Among the personal items on a towel on the bench is a cell phone ringing incessantly. In annoyance the fellow answers it. The voice at the other end is saying, "Hi, honey. That house we liked is back on the market for only 900K." "Well, make them an offer for 1.3 to make sure we get it. Gotta go," replies the stranger as he hangs up.

I have deluded myself into thinking that I keep pace with technology reasonably well, but a recent experience in Seattle confirms that I am quite outstripped by the next generation. Since our flight home departed at 6:10 a.m., I asked the front desk of our hotel for a wake-up call at 3:00. However, quite well aware from painful experience that the reliability of such service is far from foolproof, I suggested to Sharlyn that perhaps I should buy an alarm clock. Because we had already turned in our rental car, I hoofed about three miles down the road to find an all-night drugstore that had one. As I suspected, no wake-up call came, and I felt quite smug that my belt-and-suspenders failsafe method worked when the alarm got us up on time. When I asked the desk clerk at checkout why we did not get the call, he referred to his log and said it indicated we had gotten it. Curious why the phone had not rung, I asked him if he would mind conducting a test of the phone with me. When he dialed the room but was unable to connect to me, I found that the previous occupant had disconnected the phone, apparently to plug in his laptop. Both the hotel and I had assumed that the phone was in working order. When I related this incident to Austin and Retta, gloating about my astuteness to obtain the alarm clock, they hooted in derision. Almost in unison they both chortled, "Why didn't you just set the alarm on your cell phone?" I had to confess I did not even know it had one.

Have we not yet reached the end of our tolerance for those who try to drive while on the phone or engaged in some other activity—applying makeup, squeezing a pimple, reading the stock quotes, text messaging or changing shoes? Paul Morgan once remarked that he did not mind seeing such behavior result in an accident because it tended to keep imbeciles out of the gene pool. True enough if the accident involved only such a fool by himself, but all too frequently he takes an innocent life along with him. This brings to mind comedian George Carlin's solution for this. We should all be allowed to fire suction-cup darts, he says, each bearing a flag with the word Idiot, at any car doing something dangerous. Then the police can readily identify those drivers loaded up with darts that need to be removed from the roads. Carlin also pointed out that by nature we use ourselves as a reference, calling any driver moving slower an idiot and any moving faster a maniac. Time and again, when I see a car doing something in traffic resulting from inattention, I find that when I am able to pull abeam, I see that he is on the phone. Incredibly to me, many states are still reluctant to outlaw cell phone use while driving. Some that do still allow a hands-free device. Although it is a step in the right direction, I still disagree. It is not merely the engagement of hands that causes errant behavior and accidents—it is engagement of *attention*. No one, and I literally mean *no one* can have his mind occupied by a phone conversation and at the same time give full time and attention to driving the car. Indeed, I submit that some drivers should not even attempt to talk to me sitting next to them in the car because the brain is diverted from analyzing roadway conditions into the emotions of the conversation. I can tune out the radio completely when traffic demands my full attention, but if you are one of those with a terpsichorean bent as you play karaoke, I really must request that you turn it off.

* * *

Have you ever performed a little dance with someone coming toward you in the office corridor? As you zig to the right, she zigs to the left, then as you zag to the left, she zags to the right. Finally both of you stop, each waiting for the other to make a move. All of this could be avoided if everyone simply remembers what we were taught all the way through school about staying to the right. Did you never have Mr. Lynch yell at you in middle school about this, or Mr. Culbertson in the hallway in high school hollering, "Keep to the right, people. Keep to the right!" Why do I constantly need to face pedestrians on a busy downtown sidewalk who force me off the curb because they insist upon hugging the left side? I have come to the point where I refuse to give way, stopping dead in my tracks with a glare, daring them to run over me. Is it hard to figure out that when you approach double doors, the one on the left, even though it is not labeled, is *not* for you to use? Do I deserve that dirty look I get when I open the right door and smack into you trying to open it from the other side? Or do *you* deserve the bonk on the nose that results from not following custom? When you step into the elevator car, are you the one who stands in front of the panel after pushing the button for your floor? Might it not be better etiquette to step to the back afterward, to provide access for others to reach the selection panel? Before the door opens at a stop, some at the back do not seem to realize that "last on, first off" works better than pushing to the front to be the first one off. Have you never learned that etiquette, if not common sense, dictates that you give way to those coming *off* before you crowd your way *on*? When I approach the checkout counter with the sign reading "Limit 15 items," I am never sure whether to count my seven boxes of Jello, five cans of tomato soup and ten candy bars as three items or twenty-two. But I have to gnash my teeth at the hubris of those who march right up to unload more than forty, no matter how they are counted. I once read about a checkout clerk who challenged one of these illiterates with, "Uh, excuse me, *which* fifteen items did you want me to ring up?"

I realize I am probably beginning to sound like Andy Rooney, but he might ask sardonically why we persist in our unsanitary tradition to blow out the candles on a cake. Do we really like the flavor of chocolate icing enhanced by the saliva of an eight-year-old? If the idea is to extinguish the flames, why not just hand the kid one of the paper plates to fan them out? Rooney might also observe with me that when I was a kid, we raked our leaves. Are we getting so lazy in this country that we are willing to burn a hole in the ozone layer, destroy our hearing and annoy our neighbors for two hours by strapping on a roaring leaf blower? Judging from the news I hear every night, we have apparently forgotten what the eighth commandment says about responsibility and consideration toward our neighbor. How is it being a good neighbor to me when you buy a house next to my airport, which was intentionally built far away from housing developments forty years ago, then *complain about noisy, dangerous airplanes.* You knew the airport was there before you ever saw the house, but what is even worse, you launch a campaign to petition the government to shut it down!

When I must suffer through the daily crime report in Prince George's County night after night on the TV news, I begin to ask myself how this can be "news." If the same crime happens every day, do I care that only the *names* are different? How is that *new*? If this is supposed to be a factual report, why is it packaged as entertainment or sensationalism? It is difficult not to associate these reports of crime with race, but in the final analysis I find myself prejudiced anyway—not against skin color or socioeconomic status, but against *behavior*. To be sure, we do not need to go to Maryland to find people who do not understand how to get along with each other. When Austin was about a year old, we took the whole family to the public swimming pool at Lake Fairfax Park near us in Virginia. After witnessing the behavior of the denizens of that neighborhood, we understood why private swim clubs are formed in our area to keep such riffraff out. Granted, the pool was crowded with too many swimmers, but that did not justify rowdy hooligans deliberately leaping from the edge onto small kids unable to move out of the way. This was far too dangerous for me to be in the water with Austin, but when we realized that Angela and Thomas were also at risk of serious injury, we pulled them out of the water too. When Sharlyn and Angela returned to their changing room, they discovered little Angela's clothes had been stolen. Outside was a train that gives rides in a circuitous route through the park, and we eventually found the clothes strewn along the tracks of this little railroad.

\* \* \*

I am discovering that as I get older, I am becoming increasingly intolerant of negativity. I have reached the point where I find it difficult to watch television news because of its bias toward the dark side of everything. Perhaps doom and gloom sells newspapers, but when I pick up a magazine, I now gravitate toward those articles that put a positive spin on a topic and avoid those that tell me what I already know about a sin-cursed world. Fortunate indeed are those spouses who have discovered the positive energy that comes from supporting each other's position. My parents did not agree upon every color in the spectrum of life, but they *always* worked together toward a positive result without Hardy blaming Laurel for getting them into another fine mess. As I have stated before, my father was the most optimistic and positive person I have ever known. If my mother had an idea that he saw would not work, he set about immediately to find a way to make it workable instead of scoffing and simply vetoing it outright. The idea itself was important to him, and he derived energy from her wish to fulfill it. If my father came up with some hair-brained scheme, my mother did not snarl "No!" at him, but trusted so deeply in him that they stood shoulder to shoulder, both of them wading deep in kimchi, if necessary, never once complaining about whose stupid idea *this* one was. This relationship they had was a wonderful thing rarely seen today, but I see it as the very essence of the word *love*, putting the welfare of the relationship ahead of self-serving individualism.

One of the reasons their relationship was successful was that both of them subscribed to the Scriptural model of marriage. They believed that when God himself instituted marriage, He provided a woman for Adam and made him responsible for her. Even when the woman Eve led them into sin, God held *Adam* accountable for it. Ever since, this corruption of sin they brought upon the world passes through the Adam of each generation from one to the next. This is why, incidentally, the Messiah would not be born corrupt to sinful woman, but could not be sired by sinful man, because sin passes through the *male*. My parents also believed Paul's explanation to the Ephesians that the husband is to *love* the wife totally, as if she were himself. The very word husband, in fact, connotes someone who devotes his life to his vineyard, tending to it lovingly as his beautiful garden. In the same way that the wife risks her life to bear children into the world, the husband is to risk his life for her and these children. He has been placed in this role by God, as Ephesians goes on to say that the husband is the head of the wife in the same way that the heavenly husband Christ is the head of His bride, the Church. The woman was provided for the man, not the other way around. In families where the woman "wears the pants," whether by choice or of necessity, turmoil almost always abounds as the distraught wife is exasperated fulfilling both roles and the cowering husband is frustrated fulfilling neither.

With few exceptions this acceptance of the respective *roles* of man and woman has gone unquestioned for centuries, whether in the home, the church or in government. This is seen by some, with a shrug, as domination, where men subjugate women simply because they are bigger, rather than the expression of love for the woman it was intended to convey. In recent times women have led a rebellion, which men sometimes join, against this "oppression" and declare that they now refuse to be "secondary." We are already seeing the effects. The institution of marriage itself is under attack as indiscriminate cohabitation and divorce soar to levels unimagined only a generation or two ago. Some men have so little regard for their responsibility toward woman that they seem to maintain the proposition that the world is just a big barnyard, where the rooster attempts to jump upon as many hens as possible. Some women think their newfound "liberty" allows them to experience all pleasures of life that their voluptuousness will allow. When man marries woman, God says in Genesis, they become "one flesh," a concept affirmed by Christ himself in Matthew when he quotes this passage in response to a pharisaical trap. Does this mean the man and woman wear the same pair of jeans? That they both use the same public restroom? That the righteousness of either one guarantees entry into heaven for both? Certainly not. Whatever else it assumes, it means a new social construct instituted by God himself has been created, a family unit with a name and with the husband as the head of it. Refusal to accept this arrangement is nothing short of rebellion against God. Today many women balk at this notion, refusing to submit and insisting they are selfishly going to keep their *own* family name. Some try to solve the problem by combining the names. So when Dingleberry marries Turnip, they defiantly determine that the new family name shall be bifurcated. One of them will remain Turnip while the other is now going to be Dingleberry-Turnip. But what is to happen when their daughter marries the son of Taxcabbage-Slushpump and they arrive at the same solution as their parents? Are the teachers now keeping report cards for the Taxcabbage-Slushpump-Dingleberry-Turnip kids? Where does the ludicrousness end, as once again the genius of God is corrupted by the folly of man?

As expected, the courts have stepped in to clarify things for us. So now we have "equality" in entitlements to everything, including sports programs, employment, public office and profession. For much of my working life, the classified ads read "Help Wanted—Men" and "Help Wanted—Women." This is no longer acceptable. Do we really want this as a society? Do we want our little boys aspiring to be nannies, nurses and chambermaids or our little girls to grow up as lumberjacks, bulldozer operators and ditch diggers? Do you really want your little daughter to be *required* by law to be conscripted for war as though she is no different from the rough-and-tumble boy next door? If you have the idea that men and women perform equally in warfare training or in actual battle conditions, you should read the candid comments of soldiers who have been there. Should we be surprised, when men and women are thrown together in the same military academy or aboard the same submarine, to find that conjugation and rape take place? Many women, I suspect, are unaware how powerful the urge to mate is within men. Many others, I wager, *do* know, and derive pleasure from their ability to turn it on. When Paul says in Ephesians that women are to keep silent in the church, many women today take this as a put-down, rejecting it out of hand as an archaism. But once again God has some reasons for this. If the woman is allowed to stand up and argue in meetings, she usurps the responsibility of the husband or another elder to do it for her. There is no room for the kind of "chivalry" where the cause of a woman who engages in a caustic verbal exchange is taken up by some "protector," probably a husband, who socks the "offender" for his "insults" to her. This is not conducive to the requirement for the church to conduct its affairs "decently and in order." Worse, if the husband and wife disagree, they air their views publicly, shaming both of them and the institution of the family when their heated exchanges reveal personal and private matters. Do you suppose these scenarios ever actually played out in a congregation meeting attended by St. Paul? However, when men shirk a responsibility, someone needs to step in to shoulder it, and the woman often takes it on out of exigency rather than obstinacy. When not enough men pursue the ministry of the Gospel, for example, should we wonder that women come forward to become pastors? If this is an act of open defiance of God's ordinance against it on the part of the woman, she brings shame upon her own head, but if she reluctantly takes accountability because no male wants it, this is to the shame of the *men*, not the women, for allowing it to happen. Fortunately, all of this is a temporal convention, where the earthly natures of men and women are different, but their divine ones are identical, so that both have equal footing in the kingdom of heaven.

# Acceptance of Mediocrity

To be sure, mediocrity is a relative term. Before Roger Bannister came along, the ability to run a mile in less than four minutes was considered an unattainable threshold. Today anyone who can *not* exceed such a pace is deemed mediocre. When I was in high school, fifteen feet in the pole vault was considered a nearly impenetrable ceiling. Today anyone who cannot rocket over the bar as a member of the six-meter club is mediocre. No one is immune from mediocrity—even those who are unexcelled by their peers. Michael Jordan, arguably the greatest basketball player of all time and one of the best all-round athletes in the world, discovered that his talent for baseball merited a pat on the back for effort but a kick in the pants from the League. Even Bo Jackson, who successfully managed a professional career in both baseball and football, could not sustain superiority for more than a very short time. While we could argue that no one would ascribe the term mediocre to Babe Ruth, Roger Maris, Hank Aaron, Jack Nicklaus or Mark Spitz, along come the likes of Mark Maguire, Sammy Sosa, Barry Bonds, Tiger Woods and Michael Phelps to eclipse their records.

In fact, excellence itself is defined by mediocrity. Would Arnold Palmer be anything special if he were not standing upon the shoulders of the hundreds and thousands of weekend duffers and wannabes that also played their hearts out, only to finish far back in the standings? But the fact that a competitor puts forth his best efforts and still falls short is exactly what Wally Grigg so long ago was trying to tell me when he said it is one of the most difficult concepts in life to accept. This has not been easy for me. If I were to compile a list of my accomplishments, capabilities and proudest moments, I would be found wanting in each of them by an objective observer, who would be compelled to tick them off one by one as falling short. When I realize my maximum efforts can so easily be exceeded by hundreds of others, the experience is at the same time awesome and demoralizing. It is simply disheartening to hear Philippe Entremont play a difficult passage from Mendelssohn or Liszt flawlessly at a tempo about twice the speed at which I can stumble through it.

For most of her life, my mother had a strong desire to be admired. Whether this is a normal human aspiration, whether it might be a trait passed down from her, or simply because both of us were born under the sign of Leo, I too must admit to a certain measure of this vanity. In my case, however, it is less a need to be liked by everyone than a need to be respected. With increasing age seems to come an increasing requirement to be taken seriously. After all this time I suppose it is natural to feel I have earned it. Blessed with a wide variety of talents and abilities, I assumed one of them would one day make me widely acknowledged as important, perhaps even famous. Thankfully, it never happened. Fame is quite often accompanied by misfortune for those who actually achieve it. All of us could cite dozens of examples of superstars who are seen under the brightest lights so suddenly that egotism quickly swallows them up before spitting them out. It is as though they were transformed into Faust, very soon wishing everything could be reversed, as they discover no dark glasses, wig or disguise can dissuade the paparazzi from suffocating them. The happiness purchased by increased wealth is fleeting also, as it so often leads to drugs, debauchery and, ultimately, to that inevitable dizzying fall from grace.

Fortunately for all of us, mediocrity, when put into a spiritual context, is an absolute requirement to avoid a fall from the grace of God. Jesus says to us in Matthew that "except ye be converted and become as little children, ye shall not enter into the kingdom of heaven." All true Lutherans believe, in fact, that in the eyes of God, everyone is less than mediocre, and when we stand before him on the Last Day clothed in our own righteousness, He will say we cannot come in here in those worthless rags. To those of you who have not accepted Christianity, this must seem to be the height of foolishness, for what kind of judge would say, "I sentence you to death. But I'll tell you what, I will have my son serve your sentence for you"? Yet, if that really happened to you in an earthly context, would you be so foolish as to reject it with a casual, "Uh, no thanks, I'll just accept the death sentence"? But that is exactly what your unbelief earns you. Paul explains it to the Corinthians this way: "For the preaching of the cross is to them that perish foolishness, but unto us which are saved it is the power of God." If you are the kind of person for whom everything must make sense, this is a difficult concept for you, because you are so good at approaching your world from the standpoint of reason. But there is another viewpoint that is most important for you. When you listen to a comedy routine of Abbott and Costello, you understand that it makes no sense. It is not meant to. When you listen to *Claire de Lune*, you hear it with that part of your brain that understands beauty and art, not with the synapses that handle logic. In a similar way your spiritual life is a matter of the heart, not of syllogism. God takes on the form of a human and dwells among men? Is this not straight out of Mythology 101? Why then do I believe such nonsense? Is it because my parents believed it? Because *their* parents believed it? Yes, and I thank God every day that I was born into this saving grace. But, you say, what about the little boy who was born into a Muslim, Hindu, Mormon or Jewish family? Does he not believe just as fervently what *his* parents believed?

To them I say the documentation and the evidence before us cannot be ignored. If *one man* with a known propensity toward prevarication weaves a fantastic chronicle based upon some golden plates he claims he found, I am suspicious, especially when he cannot produce the plates for examination. When *one man* with a gift for leadership relates an elaborate account of visitation by an angel who transports him into the seventh heaven, I find it too easy to suspect fabrication, especially when he has no way to verify it and much of his material smacks of corrupted plagiarism from preexisting sources. But when dozens of writers, most of whom never knew each other, all testify seamlessly to the same event, their witness is difficult to discount. When we read in the tabloids the predictions of modern psychics, we are apt to be awed when a certain event occurs as forecast, but even the most credible among them is wrong more than right. But suppose *every* prophesy of even one Old Testament prophet was fulfilled in the New Testament. Should we not attach credibility to him? What should we conclude when *every* prophesy of *all* of the prophets come true? Does this not become a body of testimony that is impossible to refute? It reminds me of the young man I saw board the bus recently wearing a T-shirt that read "I make stuff up." As I read the Bible, I find it impossible that someone, anyone, much less all of them collectively, could make this stuff up, and I am increasingly amazed at the consistency of its message taken in context throughout its pages. For one thing, Judeo-Christian theism is the oldest, traceable back to the beginning of time, so I must ask what those who died before any other cult or religion was invented were supposed to believe. It is unfortunate that the writings of the Scriptures were not translated into Arabic until some three hundred years after Mohammed began to formulate Islam and foist it upon his powerless subjects. He wove whatever oral traditions he had acquired about the law of Moses, the virgin Mary and the Messiah into his "revelation," but the information came down to him corrupt, so although he ironically concludes that Jesus was the greatest of the prophets, he received the Jewish version that He was just a man and could not possibly be a Son of God. The Jews who could not accept the Messiah who stood before them in the flesh are still today refusing to match up what their own prophets said about Him to the events of history. To me they are a little bit like someone waiting for the bus into town. Along comes the bus, with all of the transit authority markings on its exterior, clearly marked Downtown on its marquee. When you are surprised that he does not board with you, he says, "No, this is not my bus. Mine will be painted pink and purple, with flowers and balloons on it. I will recognize it when I see it."

Some have said that it really does not matter which religion you follow, since all paths lead to heaven, and ninety-eight percent of what they all teach is identical anyway. To me that is like saying that there is no difference between a human and a chimpanzee, since ninety-eight percent of the DNA between the two species is identical. Does that remaining two percent make a difference? I can picture all of the chimpanzees reading this who are hopping around in gratitude screeching that it *does* to them. Of all the religions of the world, Christianity is the only one that teaches we cannot *earn* our way to heaven. Because it is so natural to feel that, after a life *free* of seemingly unacceptable behavior, we deserve recognition for it, even some within Christianity find this a difficult concept to swallow. After all, they might say, I never committed murder, car theft, bank robbery, rape or fornication; on the contrary, I helped my neighbors, gave generously to charity and became a respected leader in my community, so I deserve recognition for my good behavior. Harsh as it may sound, God says no. "I demand *perfection* from you," He says. "Did you achieve it? Was that not *you* who left that can of peas on the shelf with the rice because it would be some trouble to return it two aisles back? Did you not realize that amounted to *stealing* from the merchant? Was that not *you* whose desire was aroused when someone attractive entered the room? Did you not realize that your very lascivious *thought* was covetous and adulterous? Uh, oh, tsk, tsk. That's not perfection. Nope, can't let you in here." Strange as it may seem, Jesus lived perfection to such a degree that he never once in his time on earth had to say "I'm sorry" or "Excuse me" to anyone—for accidentally stepping back onto anyone's toe, entertaining a sexual thought or misreading the "No Admittance" sign. When I stand before God after my time here is finished, I will be able to say, "I want that robe He is wearing—to cover up the filth, scabs and stench I was covered with when I left earth."

By the time you read this I may be wearing that robe, but today I am still that small-town boy from Iowa, who like an ear of corn from one of its fields, is getting mellow and more mature on the inside, while the husk turns deeper shades of brown. As I get older, I am reminded by the stiffness I feel putting on my socks or the nettlesome visits from Arthur and Itis that occasionally afflict my knuckles for no apparent reason that one day both the kernels and the husk will dry up and blow away. When you reach a certain age, the rules change. You discover, for example, that those second helpings with which you always indulged yourself without another thought are now inducing you to buy Fruit of the Lump underwear. As the readings from my blood tests reveal PSA numbers that are climbing into double digits, I realize that these are reminders from God that time is at hand. After forty-two biopsies no malignancy has been found, but I am aware that before long I will be sitting in a chair discussing a decision concerning which of several unpleasant options I must choose. Incidentally, for those of you men who have not yet experienced this thrilling procedure, I can describe it to you as one where the doctor rams a flagpole, with the eagle still intact, up your rectum, twists it around for about twenty minutes, and makes it fire burning darts into your private parts while he tries to convince you the ultrasound screen upon which you are watching all of this in real time is your favorite sports event.

Health will fail quickly enough without any assistance, so I ask myself why I had to hasten the deterioration one day with a bike accident. Sharlyn and I were out for a leisurely ride, and as I was streaking down a steep hill, I judged that I could turn the corner at the bottom of it without applying any brakes. As I careened around the bend, I thought I could simply push off against a pickup parked along the opposite curb. Instead, I slammed into the truck with such force that I do not remember striking the pavement. Besides the concussion, I dislocated my jaw, fractured my cheekbone, destroyed my sense of smell for several months before it gradually returned to partial keenness, chipped a front tooth, and cracked two molars that eventually required root canal surgery. While bystanders rushed to render aid, Sharlyn pedaled to fetch the car to transport my twisted frame and that of the bicycle back home. What had started out as an afternoon of idyllic pleasure had quickly turned my mood into a morass of misery and grogginess. In the post-mortem analysis of the accident, Sharlyn and Thomas, assuming my brakes had failed, sent the bike into the shop for a thorough overhaul. However, while it emerged good as new, I would not be able to say the same for myself for quite some time. Oh, and for my next birthday they also bought me a bike helmet.

These days I try not to dwell upon the regrets and unpleasantness from the past but to focus my thoughts upon the comforts that come from relationships to family, friends and church activities. After fifty years I thought it was time to look up my boyhood friend Hap Klammer, my respected mentor from high school Russell Castor still alert at age eighty-nine and cousin Nathan Bender who emerged one day from the murk of the past. Private detectives have so far been unsuccessful at locating my college friend Richard Murphy, but after a long hiatus Sharlyn and I have reconnected our friendship with Gary and Carol Voight, which had cooled to a pile of ash. Soon after we were married, they invited us to have Thanksgiving dinner with them in their new townhouse in Dale City. The next year we invited them for Thanksgiving at our house, and a tradition began. Soon, however, there were three of us coming for pumpkin pie, then four. Some time after Austin was born, our custom of trading recipes for the holiday came to an end. One year when we invited them for some of Sharlyn's oyster stuffing and cranberry-Jello salad, they coolly announced their plans to visit Minnesota instead. When we did get together, our conversation, laced with tales of domestic life chasing three children, was not compatible with their refined cultural tastes and relatively carefree existence that drew xanthic stares from us as they related their exploits in Paris and Hawaii.

Although we were rapidly drifting apart, Sharlyn and I were fond of them both and made an attempt to stay in touch every few years, even visiting them once with our teenagers at the gift shop they owned in Sterling. We gradually sensed that they, for reasons not altogether clear to us, preferred to keep us at arm's length, so we reluctantly allowed our contact with them to dwindle to zero out of respect for their feelings. Then one day I received word that Carl Franke, our mutual colleague at the Agency, had died, and since

Gary had always been one of his favorites, I decided to clamber over the stone wall that had sprung up between us to leave a message for him. Both Gary and Carol came on the line, and the short conversation we had for a few minutes was quite pleasant. They had recently retired and were making preparations to return to their roots in Minnesota. An entire chapter could be devoted to the obstacles they encountered selling the classic century-old Victorian house in Leesburg they owned for thirty-five years, but at long last they were able to settle unencumbered into their beautifully furnished home back in the heartland.

After the broad space of nearly forty years, I have finally returned to the pleasures of playing the piano. However, it was not only my technique that had fallen into disuse, but also the old rusting hulk upon which I was to play that sat forlorn and neglected, buried under rubble waiting for someone to push its keys again. When I tried to call the piano tuner who had last serviced this old upright in the basement some ten years earlier, I found that his number was no longer in service. The next one I called from the Yellow Pages seemed like a good bet, judging from his ad touting thirty-five years of experience. When he arrived, he insisted that he pull out the action and "recondition" it in his shop before he returned to do the tuning. I was surprised that he was finished reinstalling the action and tuning it up in about twenty minutes. When I went down to try it out, however, I noticed immediately that it was still woefully out of tune. "Oh, well let me work on it some more," he said cheerfully, as he pulled out an oscilloscope from his bag. Hmm, an oscilloscope. In a flash I understood why his tuning had not succeeded. Even *I* know that a piano cannot be tuned with an oscilloscope. I quickly realized that this old duffer, at least seventy-five years old, could no longer hear the wow-wow-wows essential to a proper tuning technique and was attempting to extend his art artificially. After he banged away for another fifteen minutes or so, the instrument was still nowhere close to pitch. When I told him to stop trying and asked his price, he wanted a whopping $450. I should have sent him packing with nothing, but I took pity on him, and mostly to compensate him for the work he had supposedly done in his shop, I cut a check for $200 and told him to hit the road.

Next I called John Bowen, who was referred to me as the technician who serviced all the pianos in the Fairfax County public school system. This seemed like a good prospect too—especially when he told me his fee was only ninety-five dollars. When he finished, I picked away at the keys a little without actually playing through the full range of the keyboard, assuming that with his experience and credentials, a good tuning was assured. However, when I sat down to play it after he left, I found that the treble quadrant at the upper end of the keyboard was not in tune. A short time later I found myself explaining all of this to Ron Boyd, a piano dealer in Fairfax, who had several questions about the age and condition of the piano, especially whether anyone had ever told me the pins could not be set to hold a pitch. I honestly told him no. When I handed him my aviation business card with my address and phone, he mentioned that he had once owned a Cessna 182, so we talked for almost an hour, not about pianos, but airplanes. Although I expected Boyd himself to come to the house, he sent one of his subcontractors. As I listened from upstairs, I soon heard the distinct snap of a string breaking. Several minutes passed before I heard tuning resume. Seconds later I heard another snap. This time tuning did not resume. Minutes later a sober-faced technician was upstairs explaining to me that to bring the piano up to pitch, he was going to be breaking some strings, perhaps as many as twenty of them. When he laid out a surcharge of ten dollars for each string that would need to be replaced, I wanted to know why the previous tuners had not encountered the problem. "Well, they did you a disservice," he said quickly. "When they saw that the upper register was likely to break strings, they simply left it alone."

Before I could decide whether this latest escalation was worth the cost, the tuner suggested I call the office. By the time I reached Boyd, he had already talked with his technician and told me that he stands by his price quotes, that he would be out himself to raise the piano up to pitch and that he would replace any strings he broke along the way. "Mr. Boyd," I began, "I do not necessarily expect the piano to be brought up to A-440, but only to be in tune to *itself*, so I don't want you to ...." "You didn't hear me," he interrupted. "I said I would bring it up to pitch *and* replace any broken strings." After working on the piano for two hours, this dear man finally came upstairs exhausted to report he had finished his task. Not having heard any strings break while he worked, I asked him how he accomplished such an incredible feat. He revealed a secret—WD-40 sprayed ever so sparingly at the point where the string crosses over the bridge of the sounding board. "But," he warned, "In the wrong hands this stuff can ruin a piano. Any overspray or runoff that reaches the pin renders it useless." When I asked him how soon I would need to call him again for re-tuning, he rocked me off my feet when he said, "I don't ever want to see this piano again." The piano was tuned beautifully, and for about two days I experienced once again the exhilaration of its rich tone. Then suddenly one of the keys went dead. When I removed the panels of the instrument to reveal the action, I found that the glue holding a tiny wooden fork to its key apparatus had come loose. By splitting a popsicle stick lengthwise, I could reach far back into the action to apply a dollop of Elmer's carpenter glue, and by the following day the piano was back in commission. But after a day or two another key went dead, and then another, and another .... After repairing perhaps twenty or twenty-five of these little forks one by one, I finally decided enough was enough. A simple fact was gradually settling over me—that the piano was trying to tell us it was tired. Boyd had checked the serial number of this Newby & Evans we had bought second-hand years earlier and learned that it was manufactured in 1927, so I arrived at the conclusion that it was time to enter the digital age. When I answered an ad for a Roland, I found that now I not only had an electronic piano that theoretically never needs tuning, but also I could slip on headphones to practice without disturbing anyone else in the house who might be trying to carry on a conversation or watch a movie. In addition, I could convert the instrument to a harpsichord or organ, if the spirit so moved me, and the capability to record a performance or interface with a computer was built into it. Such marvelous machinery could never have been *dreamed* by Bach, Mozart or Beethoven.

As I observed the ever-widening circle of pills spread out on the dinner plates of my parents, I started to realize that the ages beginning "sept" become even worse when they begin "oct." Well aware of the health issues they faced during that period of their lives, I know that it was not fun for them. Now that my own pile of pills is beginning to mount, I sense that the bittersweet twilight years will be increasingly more bitter than sweet. However, whether that dark tunnel looming ahead is to be long or short, golden or leaden, smooth or turbulent for me, I am confident that the visibility will remain clear as I emerge into eternal Sunshine. Bob Long was one of those who could not share such a vision with me. Bob was the lead programmer on the serials subsystem of COPICS, and when the Copyright Office one day wanted extensive modifications to it, he was heard to exclaim to all in attendance at the meeting, "Oh God, why couldn't I have been born five years earlier, so I would be retired by now?" This complex project had so vexed him during development that he could not bear the thought of reopening it, so it was handed off to someone else. His blasphemous appeal to the Almighty, however, was ironic, because he was a vehement self-declared atheist. An amateur photographer, Bob kept on his desk one of his framed creations depicting an old country church, the charm of which must have appealed to his artistic sense of rustic beauty. Attached to the clapboard siding above the doorway was a large professionally lettered sign reading, "Believe on the Lord Jesus Christ, and thou shalt be saved. Acts 16:31." When I first saw this picture on his desk, I assumed he was a Christian and one day asked him where he attended church. This sparked the first of a number of animated conversations with him about his beliefs, and I encountered over and over his vociferous opposition to Christianity and adamant refusal to acknowledge God—any god.

Perhaps you identify with Bob. If so, picture a foundry pouring molten iron. If you were to tumble into this cauldron accidentally, you would probably have enough time for one muffled squeal before your life would be mercifully extinguished. Now visualize a molten lake thousands of degrees hotter than the iron. "And whosoever was not found written in the book of life was cast into the lake of fire," reads Revelation. That is you. Do you think you will blithely splash around doing the backstroke, as you eternally scream for the chance to die or escape, with no hope for either? The fact is that this was not *intended* for *you*. Hell was created for Satan and the evil angels who co-conspired against God and fell from grace. But in the end you leave God no choice when you refuse to accept what He offers you. It reminds me of the time Don and I were in Florida helping Ruth clean out her garage. As Don swept the floor, a little tree frog came hopping in from outside. When Don flicked it back outside with the broom, the frog immediately dusted itself off and returned toward the doorway. Again Don nudged it outside. Again the frog licked its wounds and insistently came limping back. "If you do that one more time," said Don, bending low toward the tiny green lump on the concrete, "you are not going to like where you end up." When the little creature still refused to listen, Don carried it into the house, where Ruth had an enormous glass tank containing a bearded dragon lizard. When Don lifted the lid and dropped the frog onto the sand, it looked slowly over its new surroundings and then, frozen with fear when its eyes met those of the lizard, seemed to say, "Uh … oh, I think I just made a big mistake."

If you are one of those clinging to your atheistic or agnostic views, I issue you the following challenge. If you are correct in your thinking, you and I end up in the same place after we die, right? But if you are *wrong*, you will be herded through a gate leading to an existence so horrible that it would be better that you had never been born. If you are willing to scoff at this, as my cousin Terri once did with a disdainful "I'll take my chances," you will certainly one day experience grim, gruesome regret. Therefore, what have you got to lose by coming around to my point of view? You would at least afford yourself the opportunity to be ushered through a different gate leading to unimaginable bliss. Otherwise, I must leave you with a quotation of Paul to the Galatians two thousand years ago, "O foolish Galatians, who hath bewitched you, that ye should not obey the truth, before whose eyes Jesus Christ hath been evidently set forth, crucified among you?"

# Appendix A. Selected Photos

Elmer with the ski buggy he describes in his book, *Putting Out the Fleece*

Ralph and David in front of the Little House

Hilda (holding Lorene Shore and Ruth) and George Pullmann (holding Marjorie Gilder) with all of their grandchildren in December 1949: Ralph, Sharon Kumm, David, Richard Shore, Judy Kumm, Donald, Allen Kumm

Elmer and Martha Pullmann at David's baptism, Bethlehem Lutheran Church, Detroit

Richard Gimbel, Emelia Gimbel, Elmer

Steven Kaune

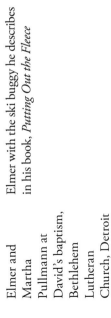

Donald, David, Ralph (baby Ruth in front) at the basement home in Maynard

A - 1

Hubert Firnhaber with his third grade class: David, Thomas Bender, Rollin Stedman, Dianne Hoehne, Theresa Bartels, Carol Bartz

Newlyweds Mabel and John Gimbel share their first Christmas with the Pullmanns (Ruth, Deanna and Martha sitting, David, Donald, Ralph on the floor in front)

Mabel Timm with her Little Room class (David is the fourth student in front of her)

Suhr with his eighth grade class: Patricia Fitz, Eunice Buhr, Verla Potratz, Pauline Steinbronn, Burton Hoehne, Joan Nus, Larry Sabin

Henry Suhr with his fifth grade class: Janet Nus, Jerry Meyer, George Steinbronn, Virginia Potratz, Jodene Fitz

Christmas 1955 in the southeast corner of the remodeled house (David, Donald, Ralph, Ruth, Deanna)

David gives Ruth a ride on his new bicycle (along the sidewalk where many hours were spent roller skating)

House in Westgate before remodeling

David's tenth birthday, in front of the picture window of the remodeled house (back row: Dianne Hoehne, Carolyn Ohl, Lavonne Klammer, Marianne Ohl, Jackie Ohl, Happy Klammer, center: Russell Klammer, Rollin Stedman, Larry Dean Klammer, David, Ralph, front: Donald, Ruth)

Robert Rikkels with his Big Room class: David seated closest to window right of center (Nathan Bender in foreground, older brother Reuben seated behind him)

Southeast corner of the remodeled house, with the Kumm cousins (back row: Ruth, Sharon, David, center: Deanna, Allen, front: Donald, Ralph, Judy)

A - 3

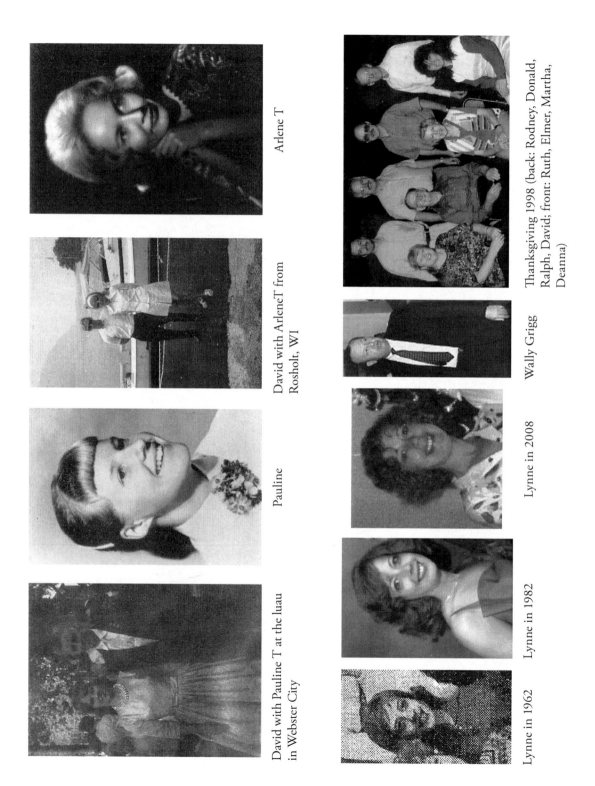

Arlene T

David with ArleneT from Rosholt, WI

Pauline

David with Pauline T at the luau in Webster City

Thanksgiving 1998 (back: Rodney, Donald, Ralph, David; front: Ruth, Elmer, Martha, Deanna)

Wally Grigg

Lynne in 2008

Lynne in 1982

Lynne in 1962

House on Linway Terrace in McLean, VA in 1971

Angela poses, Thomas runs off as remodeling begins in 1974

"Suitcase" bunker

Sharlyn on her engagement in 1970

Remodeled house on Linway Terrace in 2008

… while Elmer still climbs the ladder resting on earth

Mishap at Whitetail

On the road to Whitetail

Martha waits in "heaven" …

Peter Pavlacka with David at Whitetail

# Appendix B. Pullmann Rules of Croquet

## Section I. Equipment.

The design and type of croquet balls, mallets, arches and stakes are standard manufacture for up to six players and are left to the agreement of the players before play begins.

## Section II. The Court.

A. The croquet court is laid out with two stakes and nine arches in the following pattern, the two stakes forming a center line from which measurements are made:

B. The two stakes are set in place 16 yards apart (or 16 even paces). The center arch (arch 4) is in the exact center of the court—eight yards from each stake and set in place on the center line between the two stakes. Optionally, a second "interference" arch is set in place over the center arch, perpendicular to it and in exact line with the center line. The court may be reduced in size to accommodate a smaller lawn, if necessary, but the configuration of arches and stakes relative to each other must be maintained.

C. There are two end lines, each passing through the stake, perpendicular to the center line.] Four arches are positioned at the sides of the court (arches 3, 5, 8, 9). Each is four yards in from the stake (i.e., in from its respective end line) and four yards to the side of the center line. Two arches are placed near the stake at each end (1-2 and 6-7), all four on the center line; these arches are one mallet-handle length apart and begin one mallet-handle length from the stake at each end of the court.

D. The boundary of the court is a rectangle which is one mallet-handle length beyond the end lines and one mallet-handle length beyond the line formed by the outside edges of the arches (3-5 and 8-9) at the sides.

E. All obstacles which are permanently in place within the boundary of the court are considered part of the court, and play must proceed around them. Examples include tree roots, buildings, utility meters, bird feeders, plants (including lawn grass), and embedded stones. If such an obstacle interferes with a particular stroke a player wishes to make, the player's ball and/or a croqueted ball may be moved up to one mallet-head length away from the object in the direction of the nearest court boundary to provide a clear shot. However, the new placement of the ball(s) must not reduce the difficulty of the original stroke and may not otherwise provide an advantage (for example, a stroke which would be impossible from the original position if the obstacle were not present may not be turned into a possible one from the new position). In cases of doubt, play around obstacles within the court should be resolved on a case by case basis by mutual agreement among the players in each instance. Objects which are easily moved and not considered a permanent part of the lawn may be removed. Examples include twigs, leaves, pebbles, mulch chips, paper, bicycles, toys, and vehicles.

F. Any ball which rolls outside the court is immediately (i.e., before another stroke is taken) moved to the outside boundary of the court in a line directly perpendicular to the boundary line from where it comes to rest. If there is already a ball at that point, it is placed adjacent to that ball on whichever side of it the player whose ball is being moved chooses. If the new position brings the moved ball into contact with another ball, the contact does not satisfy other rules where contact must be made before privileges or penalties ensue (for example, rules for croquet or Snake.)

G. The course is traversed when a player's ball passes through 14 arches and against the two stakes as follows: Play on the front course begins at arch 1 and continues in order through arch 7. The ball must pass completely through each of these arches from the side of stake A. After passing through arch 7 from the side of stake A, the player completes the front course when the ball strikes against stake B. The back course is traversed in similar fashion to the front course and begins from wherever the ball lies after the ball strikes the stake. Arches must be passed through in the following order from the side of stake B on the back course: 7, 6, 8, 4, 9, 2, 1. After passing arch 1, the ball ordinarily must strike the stake to complete the game. However, certain post-game options may apply, depending on the agreement of the players (see the rules for Snake and Rover below).

H. Completion of an arch is determined from where the ball comes to rest; the arch is not completed if the ball passes through the arch but subsequently rolls reversely back into it. In determining whether the ball is completely through an arch, the mallet handle may be laid carefully across the front face of the arch without moving the arch; if the ball touches the handle, it is not completely through. In cases of doubt as to whether it touches or not, the ball is through. If the ball passes through the arch in the wrong direction, the player is not penalized, but the ball must rest completely outside the arch before it can begin to pass through in the correct direction. Ordinarily, the ball passes through the arch as the result of a direct stroke from the player's mallet; however, the arch is also completed when the ball is struck through by another ball.

I. If the optional interference arch is used over the center arch, some special rules apply: Seen from above, the pattern of the two arches forms a kind of plus sign as follows:

The dual arch can be completed only on the diagonal. On the front course, this is 3-8 or 9-5; on the back course it is 8-3 or 5-9. As for all arches, passage can be completed in more than one stroke; however, the arch can not be completed if the ball comes to rest entirely outside the wrong exit (for example, entry at 3 and exit at 5). In such cases entry must be begun again. When using the mallet handle to determine whether the ball has passed this arch, it is laid across the front face of the two wires which form the exit.

J. An alternative layout for the center arch is to convert arch 4 into two separate arches. They are positioned on the center line one mallet handle-length apart and each a half handle-length from the exact center of the court. The resulting pattern is as follows:

This allows for the possibility that a player could be awarded three additional strokes for completing either arches 3, 4 and 4a or arches 8, 4a and 4 in one stroke (see Strokes section III.D. below).

## III. Strokes

A. Each player begins by placing the ball between stake A and arch 1 at a distance from the arch of the diameter of the ball. Each player is given three chances to send the ball through the first two arches with one stroke.

B. The mallet must strike the ball directly, even when the ball is against the stake or an arch wire, and the mallet must not be touching the ball when the forward swing of the stroke begins. Normal follow-through may be used after the stroke to push the ball along, but the ball may not be steered in this manner in a curved path. Only the flat surface of the mallet head may be used to strike the ball, and it must make contact only once. If a player inadvertently taps against the ball before delivering the stroke, the ball may be repositioned and the stroke taken again without penalty—provided the ball moves less than the diameter of the ball and does not strike another ball. On the other hand, there is no minimum distance that a ball must travel (but see Appendix for stalemate rules).

C. The player is not penalized if an arch is inadvertently bent or pulled out of the ground in the course of a stroke, but the alignment of the arches must be immediately restored. However, if realignment would provide an advantage to the player who made the stroke, the realignment is deferred until no advantage exists to that player. In any case, realignment must be made before the next player's turn. If the other players decide that disturbing the arches was done recklessly or intentionally, the balls must be repositioned and played again.

D. A player is awarded an additional stroke for each arch completed. This means that if two arches are passed with one stroke, the player receives two additional strokes. Additional strokes do not accrue to a player whose ball is driven through an arch by another ball. The center arch is considered one arch even when the optional interference arch is used. When the ball strikes stake B to complete the front course, an additional stroke is awarded. However, this additional stroke cannot be cumulated with strokes awarded for passing arches. In the case where the ball both passes arch 7 and strikes stake B on the same stroke (or arch 1 and stake A), the player has the option of accepting the additional stroke from the arch or from the stake, but not both. Upon accepting the additional stroke from the stake, any others are canceled. Upon accepting the additional stroke from the arch, however, the front course remains uncompleted until the ball strikes the stake again.

E. Order of turns is decided by mutual agreement of the players or by the order of the colors painted on the stake, but once determined remains the same throughout the game. If a player is eliminated or drops out, that player's turn is simply skipped over. If a player plays out of turn, all balls must be returned to their original positions if the out-of-turn position affects the play of any player whose turn was skipped. Otherwise, play continues until order is restored in the following rotation of turns. If a player strikes another player's ball directly with the mallet, neither player is penalized, but the balls must be returned to their original positions and the stroke is replayed.

F. It is the responsibility of each player before beginning a stroke to assure that the court is clear of spectators and other players in the direction that balls will move. If a ball strikes a person on the court, the balls must be returned to their original positions and the stroke is replayed.

G. It is not necessary that each player remember the next arch of each other player. Any player must reveal this information when asked.

H. Events which occur during a stroke are significant in chronological order. Whenever a stroke provides an option, the player may exercise the option; however, when options are not available, the consequences of a stroke are evaluated in the order of occurrence. If the order of elimination from the game is significant for any reason, it is determined from the moment of the event which causes the elimination, even when the player's ball may be kept in play for the purpose of croqueting it (see Croqueting below).

## IV. Croqueting

A. When a player strikes the ball against another ball, the ball which is struck may be croqueted. It is not necessary that the target ball actually be seen to move in order to be struck. If the balls are in contact or the sound of contact is clearly heard, the target ball is considered struck. On the other hand if the target ball moves, it is considered struck, even if grass or other object on the court prevented actual physical contact. However, an arch wire or stake are explicit exceptions to this rule: the ball is not considered struck if it moves by intervening contact only with an arch or stake.

B. Croqueting always awards two strokes; all other strokes previously awarded are forfeited. The second of these strokes is at the discretion of the player, but the first must be taken in one of three ways: (1) the croqueting ball is placed against the croqueted one and both are driven together with the stroke, or (2) the croqueting ball is placed against the croqueted one and the former is held in place with the player's foot as the croqueted ball is driven away with the stroke (called a roquet), or (3) the croqueting ball is placed away from the croqueted one at a space of one mallet head before the first stroke is taken. The mallet-head distance is an absolute; it cannot be shortened or lengthened to benefit or handicap any player. If, in the execution of the second of these options (the roquet), the foot of the player is struck instead of the ball, the player is not penalized and may strike again. However, if either or both balls move out of position, the stroke will count.

C. An arch may not be partially or completely passed merely by the placement of the croqueting ball. To complete the arch, the ball cannot be placed into the arch before the first stroke; it must first be placed entirely in front of the arch before striking the ball through. If the ball is placed against another ball or a stake, the ball or stake is not considered struck unless the player subsequently strikes the ball against it again.

D. The croqueted ball must be played from where it comes to rest after being struck. It is never moved first unless it lies out of bounds. If the ball which is struck subsequently strikes stake A to put that player out of the game, it must be removed and can not be croqueted. If the croqueting ball tends to roll away from the spot where the player wants to position it, the player may tap on it lightly to hold it in place. If the croqueted ball is struck with the mallet during croqueting, the balls must be repositioned and croqueted again.

E. After croqueting, the croqueted ball is "dead" to the croqueting ball. The croqueting ball may strike the croqueted one again but may not croquet it; however, the former may strike and croquet other balls which are not dead to it and the latter, of course, may strike and croquet any ball, including the croqueting ball, which are not dead to it. For all balls to become "live" again, the player must complete the next arch in the course or strike the ball against stake B to complete the front course. Whenever the game involves more than two players, it is advisable to designate a gamekeeper to maintain a list of the balls which are dead to each player. It is not necessary that each player remember balls to which other players are dead; any player must reveal this information when asked.

F. The two strokes awarded for croqueting are not cumulative. If an arch is completed or contact with the stake is made with the first stroke, the player has one additional stroke, not two (i.e., the player has the option of taking the next stroke as a result of the arch/stake or the croquet).

G. Croquet is a privilege, not an obligation. If the privilege is not exercised, the ball which was struck remains live to the player. If an arch is completed on the same stroke during which a ball is struck, the player has the option of accepting the arch or croqueting the ball. Accepting the one forfeits the other. If two or more balls are struck on the same stroke, the player may croquet only one (the player may choose which); the others remain where they lie (except for laying them in bounds).

## V. Snake

A. When a player completes the course, the game continues as normal for the remaining players. If the players have so agreed before the game begins, the completing player, however, may continue in a post-game role as a Snake. After striking the stake, the Snake player's ball is played either from where it lies or is placed one mallet-handle length in any direction from the stake—at the Snake's option.

B. The Snake has one stroke per turn, taking the first stroke immediately after striking the stake. If the Snake strikes its ball against another player's ball, that player is eliminated from the game immediately, and the Snake is given an additional stroke. If a player's ball strikes the Snake's ball, the player is eliminated and the ball is immediately removed. However, if the ball which is removed was intended to be croqueted by another player, it is no longer considered to be in the game and can not be croqueted.

C. The Snake itself is eliminated from the game if its ball passes completely through any arch in any direction or strikes against a stake for any reason. This means the Snake is eliminated even when a ball which strikes the Snake's ball sends it through an arch or against a stake. If the optional interference arch is in place over the center arch, the Snake's ball is eliminated if it passes through in any direction, including laterally or longitudinally. If the ball comes to rest within an arch, it must exit in reverse of the way it entered; otherwise the Snake is eliminated. If the Snake's ball passes through an arch and subsequently strikes a ball, both are eliminated, but the player whose ball is struck is not eliminated (the ball remains where it comes to rest); however, both are eliminated if the target ball is within the arch when it is struck and the Snake's ball subsequently passes through the arch. More than one player may become a Snake, and whenever one Snake's ball strikes another Snake's ball, the player whose ball was struck is eliminated.

D. If a player's ball is driven into stake A to complete the course, that player immediately becomes a Snake. If this new Snake's ball subsequently passes through an arch on the same stroke, the player is eliminated from the game. If the new Snake's ball subsequently strikes another ball (even the one which drove it into the stake), that player is eliminated.

## VI. Rover

A. In partnership play, a player who has completed the course except for the final stake (stake A) may become a Rover, if the players have so agreed before the game begins. Turns continue as normal, with the Rover in the same place in the rotation of play. The Rover must croquet balls in a fixed order—i.e. once croqueted, the same ball may not be croqueted again until all other balls have been croqueted in order. The order is determined in one of two ways, as agreed among the players in advance: (1) It can be of the Rover's choosing; in this case, it is advisable to write down the order, since there can be more than one Rover and play can become complicated (in any case, the Rover must reveal the rotation order when asked). (2) The colors painted on the stake can be used to predetermine the order, either from the top or beginning with the next color after the Rover's color, as agreed.

B. With either option, the Rover must maintain the same order throughout the game and may continue a turn indefinitely, as long as balls are croqueted in order. The Rover's ball is available for croquet by any other player to whose ball the Rover's ball is not dead. Any ball which is not next on the Rover's rotation is dead to the Rover's.

C. At any time that the Rover's ball strikes stake A (even if unintentionally or by another player), the Rover is eliminated from the game; the rotation of turns minus the Rover remains the same. However, if the Rover's ball strikes another ball for the purpose of croqueting it and the Rover's ball then ricochets against the stake on the same stroke, the Rover is not eliminated. The game is over only when all members of the partnership complete the course.

# Appendix. Play and strategy.

A. The game is intended for one to six players. In solitaire, the player either plays two balls alternately or traverses the course with one ball in the fewest number of strokes, as in golf; a very skilled player could theoretically finish in as few as 12 strokes.

B. When there is more than one player, each plays in turn in the same rotation. Since the player who starts is at a disadvantage, the order may be determined by rolling a die or some other method as agreed among the players, such as following the order in which the colors appear on the stake. A player may choose to better another player's position or not; typically, each plays to his own advantage and tends to leave an opponent in a less advantageous position.

C. When the number of players is four or six, partnerships may be formed (with six players, it may be either two teams or three). In partnership play, the rotation of turns must be set up so that no players on the same team play in succession; when there are three teams, the first player on each team must have a turn before the second player begins, and the second players must play in the same order as the first. In multi-game sets, the team which wins each game must play first on the succeeding game. If the players agree, teams must be broken up after each game in such a way that players who finish first must be teamed with players who finish last.

D. A skilled player can make considerable progress through the course by croqueting a ball beyond the arch to be croqueted again after the arch is completed. Part of the success of this is in the mastery of the croquet stroke. When croqueting with considerable follow-through in the stroke, the croqueting ball will tend to travel along with the croqueted ball. On the other hand, if a sharp quick stroke is used, the croqueted ball will travel a much greater distance than the croqueting ball.

E. Another part of the success is in the angle of the stroke in relation to the alignment of the two balls: If the stroke is delivered in the same direction the balls are aligned, both balls will move in the same general direction; however, the greater the variation in the striking angle, the greater is the divergence in the paths of the two balls. Accurate croqueting is a skill which often depends on both the character of the stroke and the proper striking angle together.

F. When assisting a partner during croqueting, a player attempts to place both balls in a more favorable position; the player tries to leave an opponent's ball in a less favorable one. It is usually advantageous for a player to eliminate a rival from the game when the opportunity arises. This can be done, for example, by driving the other player's ball against the Snake or driving the Rover's ball against stake A.

G. The arch wires and stakes can be used to advantage in a number of ways, as the following examples show: (1) A ball may be bounced against them in order to change its direction to strike a ball or pass through an arch when doing either would be difficult or impossible to do directly. (2) They may be used as interference to prevent being struck by another player's ball. (3) They may provide a haven from the Snake, who must avoid them.

H. If a stalemate develops, where each player taps the ball without changing its position, the first player to begin the stalemate must on the next turn stroke the ball at least the distance of the diameter of the ball; otherwise that player is eliminated from the game.

# Appendix C. Trip to Germany, May 18-June 4, 1998

As we were boarding the plane at Dulles, the ticket agent hurried up to us and asked if we were traveling together and left with our tickets. When he came back a few minutes later, he said that coach class was overbooked and, since we were "so nice," we were being upgraded to business class. The seats were spaced farther apart, reclined farther, and had footrests for a more comfortable ride. Each passenger received a little pouch with travel socks, ear plugs, eye coverings, mouth wash, hand lotion, and extra tissues inside.

We departed Dulles about 6:00. At daybreak I looked out the window and noticed that we were over land. Then we were over water again for quite a while before we reached land again. The first landfall was probably Scotland, followed by a crossing of the North Sea, then the mainland of Europe. We could not recognize specific countries we flew over, but we probably entered the coast of Holland first. After about an hour we seemed to be descending, and soon I recognized the place where the Rhein makes a bend to the east and realized we were over Germany on our approach into Frankfurt airport.

I expected to see the cities close together in Germany, but what I first noticed was wide areas of green space between relatively small areas of civilization. Later in our stay we learned that Germany has a very strict building code. Development is tightly controlled, which results in relatively little new housing. This tends to help control the population also, since those who cannot find an apartment are inclined to leave. Building new is expensive and restricted. More common is to strip an old building down to its frame or foundation and rebuild new. Except for massive old timbers used in the original frame, wood is used very little in construction. Instead, walls and floors are made of concrete or "backstein" (brick). Where Americans build homes to last several decades, the Germans build to last centuries. Roofs are made of clay tiles which are not attached, but hook over horizontal furring strips and are held down by their own weight. Repair is easy after a major storm or other disaster because broken tiles can be lifted off and new ones laid into place.

We landed at Frankfurt about 8:00 in the morning local time. The time difference in Germany is six hours, and they have daylight saving time. In America this is set by Federal law and can be predicted years ahead, but in Germany the week in which the time changes is fluid and is announced by the government only a few weeks ahead. Since Germany is at approximately the same latitude as Canada, we had daylight until about 10:00 p.m. while we were there. The 24-hour time system most familiar only to military Americans is in use throughout Germany, so this would be called 22.00 Uhr. However, since the clock is only numbered to 12, they are a little ambivalent and might sometimes refer to it as 10.00 abends. Since all Germany is in the same time zone, a powerful transmitter which reaches all parts of the country provides a continuous electronic broadcast of the current time. Thus the train system, computer networks, news agencies, TV and radio stations, even personal watches can be constantly set to the same time automatically throughout the country.

Elfriede Pullmann and her grandson Torben met us after we passed customs, loaded our two bags and headed for the freeway south out of Frankfurt. I noticed that most, but not all, of the car licenses began with F and asked Torben if there was some system. All license plates on the cars begin with the Kreis in which they are registered. We had fun throughout our travels trying to figure out what Kreis various cars were from (there were some even Torben did not know offhand, particularly the ones from the former East Germany). After the German emblem which follows the Kreis, the owner can take the sequential number supplied by the system or can pay for a "vanity" designation as in America. At the highest level of their government is Germany itself--the Bundestaat. Then come some 16 or so relatively independent cities or areas each called a Bundesland. The Kreis is within the Bundesland and usually named for the largest city within the Kreis. Elfriede, for example, lives in the village of Gross-Zimmern. Her Kreis is Darmstadt, which is in the Hessen Bundesland (some neighboring ones are Baden-Württemberg, Bayern, Thuringen, Nordrhein Westphalia, etc.). Thus her license plate starts with DA (for Darmstadt), then following the emblem is her personalized number EP 89 (Elfriede Pullmann 89).

On our way through Darmstadt, Torben gave us a quick tour. One of its most prominent landmarks is "Tall Louie," a statue of Ludwig IV atop a tall pillar. We saw a few of the buildings of his Technische Hochschule in Darmstadt. He drove through the area called the THD Lichtwiese, and when we saw the sign pointing to it several days later, he had to remind me what it meant. Literally, Lichtwiese means "light meadow," and he explained that where the building now stands was originally a clearing in the woods.

Soon we reached Dieburg and checked into the Mainzer Hof, which was to be our home and headquarters for the next two weeks. It is a two-star rated hotel which provided us with a wonderful room overlooking the Marktplatz in the center of the village. The office building next door, however, was undergoing renovation, and we never had to worry that we would miss the next day's events by oversleeping. Construction began promptly at 7:00 with demolition debris hammered off and sent crashing through chutes to the street below. The plaza seemed to be a haven for the young people late into the evening, so if we tried to sleep with the windows open, our last thoughts of the day were usually accompanied by the laughter of teenagers and the sound of broken bottles. Our room was otherwise quite comfortable, but we noticed some differences that we were to find in every hotel in which we stayed. A washcloth is not furnished. Towels and bathmat are exactly what you would find in an American hotel, but if you want a face cloth, you bring your own. The fixed shower we are familiar with in America apparently does not exist in Germany, even in the homes. Showers and bathtubs are equipped with a shower head to be held in the hand, connected to the plumbing by a piece of flexible tubing. It can be hung up and used like a shower or lifted off and moved around the body to rinse wherever it is needed. The third oddity to us was the way the top sheet of the bed is actually a large sack which encloses the blanket. Instead of the blanket on top, as in America, the sheet is on the outside and ends up on top.

We wanted to adjust to the time change as quickly as possible, so we forced ourselves to stay awake after little sleep on the plane. Already noon in Germany, our bodies were still functioning on 6:00 a.m. American time. We went first to Elfriede's house on Ritterseestrasse 22 and met Berthold Bannat and her little 8-year old dog Bella. While they are not actually married, Berthold is, practically speaking, her husband. Her son Jörg explained that Berthold wanted to marry her 19 years ago when they got together, but under German law she would lose the the pension she gets from her husband's death if she remarries. Berthold speaks no English, but we understood a little of his German, and he has a great sense of humor. At one point we were talking about vitamins A, E and so on. He said his favorite was the vitamin W in his whiskey. He also joked that Elfriede, who likes to freeze everything from her garden, would even freeze her cup of coffee if she could. When we were eating cherries one day, he got his bottle of cherry schnaps and said he preferred his cherries that way. He is feeling much better after surgery to remove a tumor near his lung a year ago, but we watched sadly as he lit one cigarette after another. I was bothered by the smoke, but I did not get a rash from it, as I sometimes do.

Smoking seemed to us to be far more prevalent in Germany than it is even in America. Many, many people of all ages smoke everywhere. Free-standing cigarette machines line the shopping areas. Non-smoking areas in restaurants are rare or non-existent, and the smokers are unabashed about blowing their smoke or letting it drift into your face.

We had lunch with Elfriede, if you can call it "lunch." She brings out bowl after bowl of food and does not take no for an answer when she offers more. She will literally dish food onto your plate for you if you refuse more. We were already familiar with the German way of eating from their visit to us last year. Most Americans eat with one utensil most of the time, keeping the other hand on the lap. The Germans almost always eat with two, the right hand operates the knife, the left the fork. Even salad is cut with the knife, then loaded to the fork and eaten left-handed. We adopted their custom and learned to eat that way too.

Elfriede's dog Bella is the cutest mixed breed little spaniel you ever saw. She absolutely adores Elfriede, and constantly strives for her attention. Berthold is a close second, however, and he, in turn, has a lot of fun teasing and playing with her. Throw or kick an old tennis ball, and she tears off after it. If she doesn't bring it back close enough, Berthold says "nein" and "hier" until she nudges the ball to his feet or "throws" it back to him by dropping it from her teeth in his direction.

While we ate lunch, Torben's mother Anita and sister Svenja dropped in with their little dog Donna--our first meeting with them. It is no accident that both dogs have Italian names, nor that spoken together "bella donna" means "beautiful woman." (Jörg and Anita, as we found out, love Italy. By car it is only six or seven hours away over the Alps, and they spend as much time there as possible.) I was surprised that I was not allergic to either dog. Bella was short-haired, but Donna was a frumpy, long-haired mutt that left her aroma in the room after she had gone. Also surprising was Anita's command of English. We expected both Jörg and Anita to speak only German, like Elfriede and Berthold, but she told us she had taken some Berlitz courses, and we communicated in English quite well.

After lunch Elfriede took us for a walk into her village of Groß-Zimmern. In English the name means "large rooms," but I never learned how it acquired that name. The adjoining town is Klein-Zimmern ("small rooms"), and Torben tells us that the dialect of the people in both towns amongst themselves is so local that even most Germans outside the area cannot understand much of it. They speak regular German outside of their community, but they still have an accent that is recognized immediately by the towns around. Elfriede is quite proud of all the shops in town and, oddly enough, her local "kirche." Like most Germans, she hardly ever attends church, but seems to have the idea that by belonging to the parish and admiring the beautiful churches and cathedrals all over the country she can acquire salvation. One street is entirely tore up, and she refers to it as "Pullmann Canyon" because most of the construction on the street is the work of her son Jörg, a developer by profession.

We wandered the streets for an hour or longer and found ourselves at a Renault dealership at the edge of town. To our surprise, Berthold and Bella were there waiting for us. It turns out that the dealership is owned by Berthold's daughter Ingrid, whose English is quite good. We also met her pre-teen daughter Mira and her husband so briefly I didn't catch his name. Behind the building were two or three goats (I don't know what role they played). As Berthold was playfully making bleating noises to them, I meant to make some reference to the Ziegen ("goats") and must have used the word "zeigen" instead. He didn't understand what I was saying, so he said something in German to Ingrid and the next thing we know she says "of course we'll show you around" ("zeigen" means "to show"). We got the grand tour. It turns out that Berthold was the parts manager there for several years and still enjoys coming in to razz the people there.

Berthold drove us all home, including Bella, who loves to run back and forth between Berthold and Elfriede, licking first one face, then the other. By now it was getting late in the afternoon, and though our bodies were noticeably starved for sleep we were invited to Jörg and Anita's for supper. We arrived at Ahornweg 7 about 7:00 that evening and brought each of them an American proof set, as well as a salami from Wisconsin made to look like a beer bottle. Never saw it again or heard about it after that, so I don't know if such a thing was a good idea for them or not. Torben's fiance Beate Garfon? was there, and the two of them gave us a tour of the beautiful house. Large bedrooms with balconies upstairs, huge family room downstairs, patio and pool, and even the basement were all nicely furnished. Jörg runs a pretty mean grill, and our plates were heaped with at least three different waves of meats (including his own special concoction of meats blended into a kind of sausage), then piles of onions grilled over the fire, and this was on top of the bowl after bowl already on the table of Anita's salads, potatos, and, of course, Spargel.

Spargel is a kind of white asparagus which is in season for only about six weeks in the spring--right at the time we were there. And it is everywhere. Every market has it, stands are set up along the roadsides to sell it, and every restaurant has its big sign out front advertising it--even a special Spargel Speisekarte ("spargel menu") inserted into the regular menu with every soup, salad and spargel dish there is. It is planted in sandy soil which is formed into long hills. It grows very fast when the ground warms up, but if it is allowed to reach the air above ground, it changes to green within a few minutes. So the harvesters watch the hills closely. When it is about to penetrate the surface, they can actually see the ground move. This is the time to dig down quickly and cut off the long spargel root (about 8 or 9 inches long) below ground and put it into the basket. I still can't accept the taste of green asparagus, but I found I could tolerate a little of the spargel. But only a little, and I had my fill about ten minutes after I first tried it. Torben says that when the season is almost over, they all start praying the weather will turn crummy so the farmers can't pick any more of it.

We had the impression that the Germans like their sauerkraut, sausage, and beer. But we found that these Germans, at least, don't like sauerkraut much--or eat it only occasionally in the winter time. Sausage (or "wurst") is available, but isn't nearly as prevalent as I had imagined. It is only one item on the menu, if you can even find it at all. They like their beer, but it seemed to us what they really like is their wine. They are connoisseurs and know what they like. The very same grape grown in the same soil produces a different wine in one place than in another, and they taste the difference. Jörg's favorite is a very dry Franken Weißwein ("white wine") from the area around Bayreuth and is always sold in a specially shaped wide-based bottle. He served some to us, but the magic it worked on his palette was lost on our untrained one and we did not enjoy it. We talked late into the night and finally fell into bed close to midnight.

The next morning, Wednesday May 20, it was our intention to sleep late to catch up with our jet lag. The developers in the building next door had other plans. Torben met us for breakfast at the Mainzer Hof. In America one would usually find "bed 'n' breakfast" only at certain places which advertise it specifically. Every German hotel, whether it has only one room (more on that later) or 1000, must provide breakfast for its guests. So the Mainzer Hof also had its breakfast room with a variety of breads you can toast yourself, muffins, fruit bowl, dry cereals, pots of marmalade, and a little padded basket shaped like a hen which, as we discovered, held boiled eggs kept warm inside. All this, together with coffee and tea, one would expect at any American breakfast too. But the German breakfasts always had a display of cold cuts and cheese as well: ham, several varieties of bologna, little packaged braunschweigers, slices of several varieties of cheese in addition to little wrapped cheeses. In the center of each table was a big plastic cup labeled "für den sauberen Tisch" ("for the clean table") used to hold all the refuse generated by the breakfast--egg shells, muffin papers, cheese wrappers, even your napkin at the end.

After breakfast Torben gave us a tour around Dieburg (in English it means "the castle," and I was teasing him that everyone in town lives in the castle). We saw the schools he and Svenja attended, the business places Jörg owns, the buildings around town they have built, the parks and recreation areas, shops, churches, hospital, the local prison in town (not for murders or other serious crimes, he told us), and even an old tower which was used in days of old for imprisoning and executing unfortunate women considered witches. Soon it was time for lunch, so we met Anita and Svenja at the Bistro Mainzer Hof, a "Biergarten" behind the hotel. Jörg bought the Mainzer Hof about 13 years ago as a run-down eyesore and spent two years completely renovating it. He added the Biergarten to attract more business and at first ran it himself along with the hotel, but now leases it as a separate business. After lunch Torben drove us to Elfriede's while he and Jörg went off to celebrate "Father's Day."

In Germany Mother's Day is observed in much the same way as in America. In fact, it is set up there for the second Sunday in May also. But no such thing as Father's Day was ever declared as a special day, as it is here. So the fathers claim the right to have their day too and go off together in a kind of annual bachelor's party away from the family. Older sons also get to go along, so Torben and Jörg were planning to take their boat up the Rhein to meet some other men at Scheinheimsee and make whoopee that night.

Meanwhile, we had tea with Elfriede and Berthold in the afternoon and later drove to Otzberg, an old fortress atop a hill about an hour from Groß-Zimmern which can be seen for many miles around. Otzberg is a quiet place out in the country, and it was quite a steep climb up the cobblestone pathway to the fortress. Although we had some concern for our companions in their seventies, all of us reached the inner Hof ("yard") of the old fortress. Here was an old Brunnen ("well") some 90 meters deep, a chapel, long buildings probably originally used for housing but now converted to a museum, and a Turm ("tower") looming high (probably some 10 or 12 meters) above us--all with huge thick walls of stone built hundreds of years ago. Sharlyn and I climbed up the steep steps inside the tower yet, and the view from the top was spectacular. Here Germany was exactly as I had pictured it. The villages of Oberklingen, Niederklingen, and Langenfeld lay in the beautiful valley below. In the distance lay Groß-Zimmern and Dieburg and towns beyond. But most charming of all was the bells. Like a scene from the Sound of Music, the pealing of the bells from all over the valley was like stepping back in time. Too bad the picture we took from the tower couldn't begin to capture the visual and aural magic of that moment. We waved to Elfriede, Berthold and Bella below and descended the narrow stairwell back down to the Hof.

Elfriede wanted to see the museum yet, but the woman attending the desk at the doorway announced they were closing. We started to leave when another woman, probably the manager who wanted to add as much admission money to her meager daily intake as she could, suddenly appeared and eagerly waved us in. The museum had an extensive Topferei ("pottery") collection, many old farm implements and tools, clothing used by the local people in bygone days and an entire spice shop preserved as it might have looked a hundred years ago. On the first floor was an elaborate exhibit devoted to bats, with taxidermically preserved displays, models of caves in which they are found, even a sales counter selling bat kites, fans, and umbrellas.

After leaving the museum, we descended by a different cobblestone route to the tiny village of Otzberg. In a Friedhof ("cemetery") nearby Elfriede and I visited the grave of her brother Hans Henrich. On the drive home, Bella paid me the compliment of trusting me enough to sit on my lap rather than her usual place on the middle of the back seat during our travels. Actually, she was used to sitting on the lap of whoever was in the right front seat so she could see out the front window. In about an hour we were back at their house for supper, after which we were entertained for a few minutes by Berthold on his concertina.

On Thursday, May 21, after our breakfast in the Mainzer Hof breakfast room, Elfriede and Berthold met us for a tour of the Odenwald several kilometers to the south. First though, we paid our respects to the graves of Elfriede's husband Georg Pullmann and Berthold's wife Margarethe, both buried in the local Groß-Zimmern Friedhof.

Our first stop on the tour was Michelstadt, known widely around Germany for its shops selling Elfenbein and Bernstein ("ivory" and "amber"). They had many beautiful items of amber, including lamps and other pieces of such size that I was surprised amber could even exist in that quantity. Ivory is illegal in many civilized countries, including Germany, but supposedly the items offered here for sale were made before the ban or re-crafted from other pieces already in existence. Elfriede was pressuring us to buy something for Angela here, and against my better judgment let Sharlyn pick out some earrings of Elfenbein.

Up to this point we had not spent any money in Germany because Elfriede and Torben had been paying for everything. The American Express office at home had advised us to take at least 100 DM in German cash and travelers checks in DM, which "all the shops accept." To pay for the earrings I first offered a credit card. The 24 DM price was apparently too low for credit card, and the clerk refused it. Then I offered one of the travelers checks which "all the shops accept." To this the young clerk was not sure and in a moment another woman, who seemed to be her mother, took one look at the check in my hand and said "Nay" as she hurried past us and out the door. Not "nein," as my German textbooks told me means "no," but most of the people in Germany use "nay" instead. Also, most of them say "nit" instead of "nicht" for "not." I should have followed my instinct not to buy them at this point, but we had taken 100 DM in cash with us from home and just like that 24 of them were gone. The exchange rate, incidentally, is about 60 cents for one Deutschemark. So to determine the value of something in dollars we would take about 2/3 of the DM price.

We went on to Erbach, where we had our first meal at a German restaurant. My image of lots of beer in Germany was fairly accurate here, as everyone orders beer with lunch. Torben had explained that Germany has over 1000 name brands, not including many local brews which may or may not have names as they are served in the homes and restaurants. Here the local brand was Erbacher, which Jörg told me had a campaign going to make it an international favorite in 10 years. The sponsors of the campaign were expecting and prepared to lose a million DM each year during this period before starting to see the payoff in the eleventh year. Quite a gamble, considering its competition in the area. Sharlyn spied the bratwurst and sauerkraut on the menu and had her first taste of what we considered was true German food. I tasted a little of hers too and it was superb to my taste. For myself I ordered a fish plate, which was wonderfully prepared. But on several plates in the room I noticed large white dumplings, nearly the size of a tennis ball, with beef covered with gravy. Elfriede told us this was Kloß, called Knödel in some places, made from whipped potatoes. Several days later I tried it and liked it so much that Elfriede made some for us on our last day in Germany and agreed to send us the recipe.

After lunch we toured the hunting lodge of a well-known Graf ("Count") nearby, with room after room of the thousands of horns of his trophies mounted on the walls. The tour was conducted entirely in German, and even though the guide enunciated her words slowly and extraordinarily clearly, I was disappointed in the small amount of it I could comprehend. We went on to Amorbach and toured the Abbey cathedral, which boasted a powerful organ built by the Stumm brothers. We stopped for hot chocolate, walked around the streets a bit and then went to Miltenberg beautifully set on the Main River. Both little towns are preserved much as they were four or five centuries ago, with narrow cobblestone streets, houses with walls of the familiar V- and X-shaped timbers seen all over Germany, and the charm of little shops and homes intermixed to the point where sometimes we weren't sure which was which. Some of them had the date they were built engraved by the builder into the stone.

That evening, back at Elfriede's house, Berthold's daughter Ingrid dropped in, accompanied by a man who I first assumed was her husband, but though we had met her husband only briefly, I didn't remember that he looked like that. She introduced him as Peter, and it was only later in the conversation that we learned that he was her cousin--from Köln, I think. I was most amused at the antics of Bella, who was well aware that there was "company" in the house. She twirled about, barking, rolling over, and jumping on everyone, as if to say to all of us, "look what I can do," much like kids do when they are "showing off." She was quite insistent that someone play ball with her, and went from one person to another repeatedly dropping her slobbery ball on the floor at their feet and barking until she had their attention. Peter spoke English quite well and we had a nice conversation with both of them despite Bella's histrionics.

Friday, May 22, Torben and Beate picked us up from the Mainzer Hof after breakfast for a day of boating on the Rhein. We drove about an hour to the ferry crossing the Rhein at Gernsheim, where Elfriede, Berthold and Bella were waiting for us. From there we traveled together about twenty minutes to the Pullmann country house on the Eichersee, a small cove off the Rhein near the village of Eich. When we arrived, Jörg and Svenja waved to us from their boat moving very fast not far away out on the Rhein. They were having fun whipping the little craft around like a jetski, then made their way through the narrow entrance to the cove and around to the floating Steg ("pier"), where they tied up for lunch. They gave us a tour of the beautifully furnished house. Torben explained that when they bought the house it was little more than a shack, but the strict building code would not let them tear it down. Instead, they rebuilt little sections of it at a time until the whole place was effectively rebuilt. At first, they were so remote that it had no electricity, so they installed a solar power unit which they proudly showed us. Now that they are connected to the commercial power source, they use the solar system to reduce the demand and could switch back over completely to it if necessary.

Lunch prepared by Anita was bread, salad, and "wurst" accompanied by two different kinds of mustard--regular "Senf" and "Löwensenf" ("lions mustard"), the hot version. Despite Jörg's warnings, I tried the Löwensenf and it wasn't bad at all. Svenja gulped her lunch and ran down to the pier to her little rubber craft with a small outboard motor. Her little dog Donna, who loves the water and often goes boating and swimming with the family, jumped in after her, and in moments they were putting all over the cove. Jörg explained that at 12 she is too young to legally drive even such a small vessel, but in the privacy of their cove and within sight of the pier he lets her do it anyway.

Soon it was time to board their huge boat with two 900 hp engines and four propellers. Anita and Berthold stayed behind with the two dogs while seven of us climbed aboard. Bella barked furiously at being separated from Elfriede, but Berthold held fast and off we went. The weather was a little cool even in still air, and whipping along at the 40 or 50 knots that the High-Lighter was capable of got chilly. Sharlyn was not sorry she brought her wool cap and gloves, and I was soon wishing I had remembered the jacket I brought to Germany but left at the Mainzer Hof. The Rhein has huge kilometer markers along the shore, much like we would see mile markers on our interstate highways, and the first one I noticed said 466. The Rhein flows into the North Sea and the numbers were increasing, so we were starting out already 466 km from its source, or maybe from its first navigable point.

This is wine country, and hundreds of vineyards could be seen up the steep slopes high above the water. Many old fortresses can be seen at the tops of the highest hills above the water in various kinds of condition. Some are completely intact and appear straight out of a fairy tale book. Others are partially or completely in ruin, some in use for museums or restaurants, some in restoration, some totally abandoned. In days of old these were the domain of the tolltakers. As ships came up or down the river, the tolltaker was little more than a pirate who could swoop down and demand a "toll" from you. One can only imagine the disagreements that must have resulted and the competition among the tolltakers themselves--hence the need for a fortress to retreat to. Even today the Rhein is far more than a pleasure waterway, though the tour cruises are aplenty all along the river. We saw many huge barges loaded with machinery, automobiles and barrels of goods. Where the current is strong, they need tugboats to assist on their way to the interior of the country. At one point Torben pointed out a tanker with a triangle flag flying from it. He explained that after a tanker unloads its fuel, the fumes remaining in the hold can be extremely dangerous. One flag means the danger is low, two that it probably unloaded diesel fuel and only moderately hazardous, while three indicates the cargo was gasoline and all vessels are warned to give wide berth.

We passed the cities of Mainz on the left, Wiesbaden and Biebrich on the right. Along the river at Mainz was our namesake hotel, the Mainzer Hof in big letters atop it. Jörg explained that in days long ago noblemen from Mainz liked to spend time away from there in the country near the present Dieburg, where they once had a villa called the Mainzer Hof. They decided to keep the name when they took over the hotel. Near Rüdesheim we passed the statue of Germania, the German equivalent of the Statue of Liberty. Facing France, Germania holds up her hand in warning to all challengers that this is Germany--respect us. In places the pilons of what was once a bridge across the Rhein remain. Bombed during the war, the bridge was now too expensive to rebuild or could not be justified for the little amount of traffic it would bear.

As we approached Assmannshausen (I have no idea what such a name represents) near km marker 550 the river becomes quite rocky. Little sailor Svenja had been sitting on Jörg's lap wearing her cap with "BOSS" in big letters emblazoned across the front and doing some of the steering up to this point, but here Jörg took over and slowed the boat, explaining that many inexperienced boatmen lose their boats on these rocks. Torben added that though the Rhein is not a tidal river, for some reason the river was low today. Many of the rocks we saw were often underwater, and he said he had never seen the stone foundations of several structures we could see today. The current was quite swift here, as evidenced by the white water around the buoys, and we saw many barges now assisted by tugs. It was near this point that we saw the word LORELEY (I had to look twice to believe that it was spelled this way) painted in huge letters near the water line at the bottom of a cliff high above. This is where the legendary Lorelei sat combing her hair and lured sailors to crash on the rocks trying to reach her. In another version she loses her lover in the war and jumps to her death from the cliff above.

At km marker 555 we swung the boat around and started back upriver. The red and green buoys marking the channel were now reversed. This is based on an international navigation system where red means left (based on having your back to the sea), so the red buoys were now to our left. By now some members of the group had gone below to get in from the cold up top, but against the current now the temperatures were noticeably warmer in the slower airspeed. Before long we approached Wiesbaden again and pulled into a cove which had a floating restaurant along the shore called "Noahs Ark." We stopped in for restrooms, some hot tea and a snack before heading back upriver.

Shortly before reaching home we encountered a large tourboat generating a huge wake behind. At the speed we were going our boat was jolted hard and actually seemed even to leave the water momentarily. From our position on top, it was exciting and even fun. But below the passengers were more directly against the hull of the boat and felt the shock quite severely. Elfriede banged her knee against the table at which she was sitting and was bothered with it for several days afterward. A little while later we were back in the Eichersee, and Bella was so overjoyed to see her beloved Elfriede again that she jumped all over her and covered her with kisses as soon as she set foot ashore.

Some of us walked to the other side of the cove, others drove, and we met at a little restaurant there for supper. We were surprised that the dogs were allowed to come into the restaurant with us, but our hosts told us that any restaurant or shop who would dare to exclude them wouldn't stay in business long. We did notice later in our touring that some of the cathedrals had signs with a dog picture and the words "Wir warten draußen" ("We will wait outside.") We were amazed how quietly both dogs lay underneath the tables, and everything was fine until a poodle entered the restaurant with its owners. For several minutes there were three languages going--German, English and dog greetings. At one point Jörg said something to Torben, who suddenly realized that the last ferry was an hour sooner than he thought, only 20 minutes from now! So we said our hasty goodbyes and dashed off to catch it with a few minutes to spare.

By now, we felt we had already seen so much of Germany, but our biggest tour of the country had not even started yet. The next day, Saturday May 23 we started what Torben called our South Tour. We took off to the south, retracing some of our Odenwald steps and then turned off onto some backroads which took us into the Schwartzwald (the Black Forest).

Germany has basically three kinds of roads through the countryside. The A highways (sometimes called the Autobahn) are always marked with blue signs. In theory they have unlimited speed limits and are the pride of the German highway system. From what we saw, however, this has little practical application. We traveled at speeds up to 240 km/hr, the top speed the car we were in could go. And cars which are capable go up to 300 km/hr or more. If you could sustain this speed for any distance, travel would be quite rapid. For reasons not always clear to me, though, speed limit signs of 130 or 120, even 100 or 80 suddenly appear, and we must brake to decelerate to those speeds from whatever we were before. Cameras are set up all over the place to catch speeders, and the penalties are not insignificant. This happens so frequently that the net effect forfeits the advantage of the high speed, and a more moderate speed at which your cruise control could be set would get you to your destination in the same amount of time. As it was, we rarely traveled above 130 for more than a few minutes. Add to these signs the construction sites (there were many) slowing us to 60 or so or the many thoughtless motorists who pull into the fast lane without much warning doing 100 into the path of a car doing 200, and the appeal of the unlimited speed limit seemed to me a rather hollow dream.

I noticed two things about the Autobahn system that would be serious deficiencies to me as a driver in Germany (although I could not get Torben to agree with me about either one). First, exits have only recently been numbered, and the number does not exist at the exit, but rather at the first place the exit coming up is announced. This could be a km or two and many minutes, depending on the traffic, before the exit itself, and this number must be both noticed in time and remembered if needed. Secondly, the direction the highway runs is never given. In America, whenever we come to the interstate, the access ramp is marked so we know which one to take--east or west, say. In Germany, the ramp is marked only with the name of the city in that direction. This works for the people familiar with all the cities, but the newcomer would need to know which direction that city is from here.

The B highways are marked in yellow and automatically have a speed limit of 130, even when not marked. Still a very good highway the B road sometimes lets you cover as much territory as the A road, but, like our U.S. highways (not the interstates), they often pass through towns instead of around them, and all in all let you see more of the real character of the country. Then there are the backroads which are not marked by number. Worse yet, they are not found on most maps we saw. These would compare to the county roads in America and really take you through the rural areas.

It was on some of these backroads that we passed through the Schwarzwald. My idea of the Black Forest was that we would pass through a relatively small area of trees so densely packed together that it was relatively dark, but that in a few miles we would leave them behind. Instead, the Schwarzwald is a huge section of southwest Germany that has both areas of dense forest and scenic valleys, lakes, even farms between them. Sharlyn was never sure if what we were seeing was still Black Forest, and Torben was getting upset whenever she would ask if this was still the Schwarzwald. Near the village of Freudenstadt is an area known for its cuckoo clocks. The shops are full of them and, uncharacteristically for Germany, signs announcing the big "Uhrhaus" ("clock house") Wall-Drug style appear miles ahead of it.

We stopped near here, not for cuckoo clocks, but to see Triberg Wasserfall, the highest waterfall in Germany. While it might be true that it is the highest, it really wasn't much to see--little more than a small stream with several drops of 5 or 6 meters. We took advantage of the souvenir shop there to pick up a few items, but they would accept only cash, so we realized we would need a trip to the bank before too long--and this was late Saturday afternoon.

We continued southward through the beautiful Schwarzwald country and by evening we reached Schaffhausen across the border in Switzerland. Here the Bodensee drains into the Rhein, and not far away is the beautiful Rheinfals, the German equivalent of our Niagara Falls. Not nearly as big as Niagara, the Rheinfals is still impressive and worth seeing. Across the stream at the base of the falls is a glass-enclosed restaurant overlooking the falls and the place where the river continues northward. Still in our casual traveling attire, we felt a little out of place as we dined in one of the fanciest restaurants in the area. We stayed that night in an elegant Victorian-style hotel called the Park Villa. Fancy as it was, Sharlyn was uncomfortable there and would have preferred our more modest quarters at the Mainzer Hof.

Sunday morning, May 24 found us not in church, as we would have preferred, but in the breakfast room of the hotel, which even though Swiss, had exactly the same format as the German breakfast. We crossed back into Germany again and soon traveled along the north edge of the Bodensee (the Swiss call it Konstanz, Americans Lake Constance). From the many resorts along here, we chose the village of Meersburg to stop, walked around a bit, and took some pictures of the Bodensee from our vantage point high above.

When it was time for lunch, we found ourselves on one of the backroads near Isny. On an impulse Torben turned down a gravel road which led to a small country restaurant with two or three tables outside. As we sat there in the pleasant breeze eating our lunch, a farmer nearby let his cows out to pasture. They filed past us a few inches away on their way up the same gravel road to the pasture--a rather unusual experience at a restaurant.

We continued east again and crossed into Bayern (Bavaria). Soon we got our first glimpse of the Alps in the distance. The transition was so gradual, we weren't even aware it was occurring, but they lived up to their reputation for beauty. Our first stop in Bayern was one of its most famous places--Neuschwanstein, the castle of the unfortunate Ludwig II. Although there is transportation, including cable car up to the castle from the parking areas, we chose to walk--perhaps a questionable decision for Elfriede, who still suffered the effects of the boat trip on her knee. But she didn't complain much and, with a number of rest stops along the way, we huffed our way to the top. Of course, we didn't come all this way just to see it up close, so we took the tour of the inside. Tours were offered in several languages, so Sharlyn and I took the English tour, while Torben, for Elfriede's sake, took her on a simultaneous German one. Although I might question the justification of the cost of some of the things on our trip, this one was worth it. We learned many things and enjoyed the tour immensely.

The castle is set on the side of a mountain high above the valley below, but it is also surrounded by other peaks, one of which had a scenic waterfall cascading from it. Across another valley hang-gliders and paragliders were flying out over the land. We were brought back to reality quickly, however, when we discovered the bane of tourism in Germany--pay toilets. Largely regulated out of existence in America, they are everywhere in Germany, and this was our first real encounter with them. They occur in several variations. Sometimes you voluntarily throw a coin into a bowl, dish or box near the door, sometimes the urinal is free but the stalls are coin-operated (with varying operational success), sometimes an attendant stands barring the door with his hand out. In whatever form I avoided them whenever possible, waiting instead until we reached our restaurant or hotel. Separate restrooms are provided for the handicapped, and only they have a key to enter (all have the same lock throughout Germany).

We walked back down from the castle and pressed deeper into Bayern eastward. The view looking up at Neuschwanstein from the west side of the lake in the valley below as we drove away was spectacular and I am still regretting that I did not ask Torben to stop for that picture. It was this same vantage point that inspired Disney to copy Neuschwanstein for his Castle of Sleeping Beauty in Disneyland, incidentally. I found out later that it had been Elfriede's plan to go from here to Schloß Linderhof, a lavish castle nearby, but that would have meant we would not have been able to see Innsbruck, and Torben overruled her. How fortunate for us that was, because I wanted to get into Austria very much, and we saw a video of Linderhof at Elfriede's house the next week anyway. It was ornate, but not worth giving up Innsbruck for.

After this enchanting stop we proceeded on our way again to Oberammergau (there is indeed an Unterammergau nearby, as I found out). Though the famous passion play is still two years away, we had hoped at least to see the huge theater in which it is performed and the layout of the area. Instead, we found the theater under construction, entirely surrounded in scaffolding, plastic, and canvas. The area was all fenced off, and we couldn't even find a way to peek inside. The place is beautiful, though, and even though it was starting to rain, we walked around a bit and saw the cross hundreds of feet up on the top of the mountain overlooking the Oberammergau valley. The town is famous also for its wood carvings. Many shops, already closed for the day by the time we got there, had thousands of statues, clocks, and beautifully decorated figures for sale. We saw shops in Frankfurt later offering wood carvings from Oberammergau.

The day was moving toward evening now and we headed south to Garmisch-Partenkirchen. Actually two cities, they are usually referred to as a single place (like Minneapolis-St. Paul perhaps). After calling several places, Torben found a room at a pension called the Hotel Shell. I had seen the sign Pension over and over as we traveled and finally asked Torben what it meant. He explained that when people have raised their families and now have an extra room or two in their home, they often choose to rent them out to travelers and tourists. It must be profitable, because the owner must meet rather stringent specifications and regulations in setting it up, including bathroom and "Duschraum" (shower room), heating, cooling, TV in each room and the mandatory breakfast room. This one must originally have been a good-sized house, because it had at least seven or eight rooms on three floors, each with a balcony. There must be an American military installation nearby, because we saw two or three USA license plates in the parking lot of the Italian restaurant where we had supper that night.

We were now almost 800 km into our South Tour, and Torben needed to "tanken" (fill with diesel) for the first time. This seemed extraordinary to both of us, and we were curious about our fuel efficiency. In America we want to know how many miles per gallon our cars get. In Germany it is liters per 100 km. We computed it to be 5.9, which Torben said was fantastic--3 or 4 is considered good. I was curious how good this would be in America. It worked out to be about 48 miles per gallon.

Monday, May 25, after breakfast we had our first opportunity in several days to find a bank open to cash in some travelers checks. We found our bank and when my turn came to step up to the teller, a woman from the next line over quickly stepped in front of me, and without apology transacted her business and left. I thought this was a bit rude, but I found out later that the same rules of politeness which we had seen in England and which, for the most part, we would find in America do not always apply in Germany. Women tend to use their elbows in lines, and in this case, the woman in the next line over had been waiting longer than I had and therefore felt entitled to move in front of me when my teller opened up. In America this maxim would almost certainly provoke a fight, but seemed to be taken for granted in Germany. Later, on a tour, where the group passes through the narrow doorway between two rooms of a castle, we were literally elbowed out of the way by one "me first" woman.

Garmisch-Partenkirchen lies at the base of Germany's highest mountain, the Zugspitze, on the border with Austria in the Alps. Our plan was to take the cable car to the top. Torben and Elfriede were buying the tickets when I heard Elfriede exclaim, "300 Mark!!" Yes, each ticket to the top was 75 DM. We thought that the 40 DM in the literature we brought along was outrageous, but we had no idea it had gone up to 75. I still feel a little ashamed that we let them pay that much, but we did not interfere at the time. Later, I told Torben that we needed to have a little talk about how much this was costing, and that there would be many things we would be content to see without the cost of going inside. He told us not to worry about it, that it was their miscalculation, not ours, so up we went, first by bus to the base of the cable car station.

Part of the ascent was supposed to be by cogwheel train, but since this was off-season, they were all out for maintenance and repair. At the cable car platform the conditions at the top were displayed--as of 8:00 the top was obscured by clouds and the temperature was -6 C (about 21 F). We had on our warmest clothes and started for the top. Just before we penetrated the clouds was one of the most breathtaking views from the cable car we had seen. The top itself was somewhat of an anti-climax by comparison: fog so thick we could hardly see 10 meters and snowing a kind of ice pellets. The height is variously given as both 2964 and 2966 meters. The difference seems to be whether the cross standing at the highest point is counted or not. In better weather we would have been allowed to leave the climate-controlled building at the top, cross a small chasm and climb a ladder to that cross. Today the entire way over was covered with snow and the door to it was barred.

A large platform on the opposite side of the building was open to the air, though, and we went out into the snow to see what was out there. Large ravens were sitting on the railings, eating whatever the tourists fed them. Some distance away was a crowded souvenir stand and beyond that a checkpoint for entering into Austria. It is possible to ride the cable car from there back down on the Austrian side of the mountain. We went back into the building and had lunch at the restaurant there at the top of the highest point in Germany.

Over lunch Torben and Elfriede seemed to be arguing about something in German, and I couldn't quite catch what it was. Later, Torben explained that as we left the hotel that morning, Elfriede didn't quite have her door closed as he was moving the car. While the car was moving, she opened the door and bumped the car next to them slightly. In Germany, if you cause damage to somebody's car, however slight, you must contact the owner directly, if possible, and offer to repair it. If you cannot contact the owner, you must file a report with the police. If you do neither, and someone sees it happen and reports you, you are subject to a fine of 2000 DM and suspension of your license for one year. (Imagine how many times our cars in America are bumped carelessly in the parking lot by the guy next to us getting into his car!) Since Torben had done neither, he was concerned that someone might have seen it happen. We went back to the hotel and found the car gone, so he filed a report with the police.

It was time to continue southward. We crossed the border into Austria. Though there was a checkpoint at the border, I was surprised that the guards simply waved us through without checking our passports or anything. Innsbruck lies in a valley, and we first saw it from the mountain highway while still about 10 km away. What an awesome setting. We descended into the valley and into the city. Spotting a post office, I asked Torben to let us check for some Austrian stamps for Angela, and we picked up a commemorative set for her. We weren't planning to spend much time in Austria--after all, we came to see Germany. We hoped to visit München yet today, so we continued northward.

On the way Torben wanted to know why Americans say Munich, Switzerland, Dutch, and so on instead of the names used by the people who live there. He even insisted that the way Americans pronounce Berlin is wrong. I argued that German is very consistent in its pronunciation, and that to pronounce it Ber-leen, as he said, would be an exception without merit. In some cases, since the teletypes and typewriters of English-speaking countries have no umlaut, the name may have been altered in some bygone time to accommodate an easier form. Besides, I pointed out, France doesn't refer to itself as Frankreich nor Poland as Polen, etc. But I had to agree that if Roma has a name, who are we to change it to Rome? If Deutschland has a name, why should we insist on Germany?

When we got to München, Torben made sure we got to arguably the most famous place in town--the Hofbräuhaus. Here we found the picture of Germany many Americans fancy in their minds. The oom-pah-pah band playing in a room full of tables of beer-drinking patrons. We saw the Biersteins of the regulars locked up in long rows along the wall, and their tables with "Reserviert" signs waiting for them to appear at any moment. We found a place at a table, where Elfriede had told us we must try their famous Weißwurst ("white sausage"), sweet mustard, and pretzels--and, of course, a beer. Torben claimed that the beer here had one of the lowest alcohol contents anywhere in Germany, and it was possible to drink great quantities of it without getting drunk. It was probably the worst eating we had in our entire visit to Germany. First of all, we don't like beer and certainly didn't find this any better. I was hoping the occasion would at least be saved by the sausage, which ordinarily I love. It was awful. That, in turn, I hoped could at least be saved by the mustard, which ordinarily I love. It almost made me gag. At least I thought the pretzel was good, but Sharlyn said she could hardly even eat that. At one point Sharlyn asked if I thought they took requests. I teasingly asked her if she wanted to hear the Beer Barrel Polka, when suddenly they started playing it! Right there in Munich. There, I said it, Munich, Munich, Munich.

Torben told us that München was his favorite city in Germany and was anxious to show us more of it. As we approached the Marienplatz (the "plaza"), we saw the twin spires of a magnificent old cathedral called the

Frauenkirche (literally it means "Lady's Church", which is probably some reference to Mary). Instead of the turrets we had seen atop other towers, these were capped with turbans, somehow acquiring a decidedly Russian influence. Entering the huge Marienplatz, we saw that München had not one Rathaus, but two--the Altes and the Neues. High up on the face of the Neues Rathaus was a large clock with the mechanical figures of its Glockenspiel. Since it was still about 15 minutes before the top of the hour, we strolled around the shops a bit and returned to see the glockenspiel in action. But apparently it only runs at certain times of the day, because we stared for several minutes in disappointment as no knights, horses, or woodcutters did their little dances.

We returned to the car for a tour through a large park in the city called the Englischgarten. In the center is a small tower called the Chinesische Turm ("Chinese Tower") with a large open-air Biergarten nearby that today stood empty, but in warmer weather in summer is thronged with customers. Torben told us the tower and the area surrounding it are often used as a setting for movies and German TV shows. Nearby was a restaurant where we had supper. I assumed that it was a Chinese restaurant, since it seemed to be associated with the Chinese Tower, but it was not, and we found much better fare than we found at the Hofbräuhaus. It restored my confidence in German food again. Since we had a big agenda for ourselves tomorrow, and since München is one of the most expensive cities in Germany, we wanted to put some kilometers between it and us before the night became late. So we traveled as far as Ingolstadt, where we stayed the night at the Gästhaus Bauer, a Pension owned by the Bauer family.

Tuesday, May 28, after breakfast, we left for Nürnberg. This is the place famous for its trials of Nazi war criminals after the war, but since I felt this might be a sensitive area for our German hosts, I did not ask to see where this took place. I thought it was also famous for its long bratwursts sold hot off the open air grill on bread to the tourists, but we saw none of that either. Instead, we were starting to see a familiar pattern in the way most German cities seemed to be laid out. At the Zentrum ("center) was the Altstadt ("old city") or Mittestadt ("middle of the city"), where there was the Rathaus (the closest American equivalent would be the city hall), the city Dom ("cathedral") and/or large Kirche, and its Marktplatz. This was all off limits to cars, and available to pedestrians only. If there were two churches, one was Romankatholische, the other Evangelische (in Bayern) or Lutheranische (in the more northern areas). The Marktplatz was a large plaza where open-air stands of produce, flowers, and other transportables are sold. About 6:00 they all start putting their things in carts and in a short time the whole market disappears. Around the perimeter of the Marktplatz and coming away from it like the spokes of a wheel are the shops, also for the Fußgänger ("pedestrians") only, the quality of which depends upon the city--in some cities quite exclusive fashion items can be purchased, while in others, the mode is more scaled back. German law regulates quite strictly the hours that a business may be open, which varies somewhat according to the type of business.

There is very little American influence in evidence, and whatever imported businesses (we saw McDonald's, of course, Pizza Hut, Woolworth, Foot Locker, etc.) must conform to the character of the rest of the shops--no golden arches or big signs standing out anywhere. Usually the Hauptbahnhof ("main train station") was close to the Zentrum and outside this zone was the traffic and the rest of the city. We didn't spend much time in Nürnberg, but as we reached the Marktplatz, the first shop I saw was a large Buchhandlung ("bookshop"). Since I wanted to buy a German Bible while I was in Germany, I went in. I ended up buying two--one for me, the other I fancied Paul might like.

We left Nürnberg and went on to Bayreuth. This is Richard Wagner's city, but before we saw much of it, it was time for lunch. As we entered the plaza, however, we passed the Markgräfliches Opernhaus and went inside. The doors to the theater itself were locked, and we were at the wrong time for a tour, so that was all we saw. The opera house is named for Margravina Wilhelmina, sister of Friedrich der Große, who was the opera patron who first brought Wagner to Bayreuth to begin with.

It was here in Bayreuth that I first remember developing a slight irritation at the eating habits of our German friends. In America when we are traveling and seeing things, eating is secondary to the travel events--getting to the places we want to see and grabbing food along the way. In Germany, the eating is very much a part of the activities. To my way of thinking, we were wasting a lot of time sitting there eating while the weather outside was great and the world was out there waiting to be discovered by us. It was not unusual for us to spend two hours or more finding a place to eat, ordering, talking and talking, and still order cappuccino or dessert yet before finally getting back to the first order of business--seeing Germany. Still in the heart of Bayern, Torben and Elfriede tended to be particular about their choice of restaurant. We found one to their liking, and had our first taste of Knödel. It was as wonderful as they had looked when we first saw them.

While eating we were sketching out what we wanted to see here, and Torben couldn't believe that I wanted to waste my time visiting the grave of Richard Wagner. In a sense he was right. He argued that the legacy the person leaves behind is the only thing of importance, not the mortal remains. But I said if that were completely true, why should the grave be marked at all. Just plow it up and use the space for somebody else. In any case we must see the famous Festspielhaus where some of his operas were first performed. While he fetched the car, Elfriede, Sharlyn and I wandered over to Wahnfried (it might loosely be translated as "Freedom from Illusion"), the house he built for his family in his later years, which had a statue of Ludwig II, the patron who became fanatical about Wagner and his operas, and, yes, the grave (though unmarked) where he and his wife Cosima are buried. I have in my notes that we saw the Schloßkirche here also, but I must confess it must not have made an impression, because I cannot remember seeing it.

We went on to Bamberg, where we saw a majestic cathedral called the Kaiserdomkirche, inside which is a rather famous sculpture of the Bamberger Reiter, an equestrian statue supposedly ahead of its time stylistically. From there we drove to Würzburg, but reached it too late to tour the Residenz palace--a mild disappointment, since the description we had read of it in our tourbook made it sound magnificent. We had supper at the Residenz restaurant on the grounds of the palace, and on the night walk back to our car, lighted high on a hill was the famous Marienberg Schloß. It was quite spectacular. We arrived back at the Mainzer Hof that night exhausted, our minds swimming with all the things we had seen on our South Tour.

Wednesday, May 27, Torben had to take care of some business at the Hochschule, so we would not see him today. Elfriede planned to pick us up at 2:00 to tour Darmstadt about 15 km away. This gave us a much needed morning free, and we planned to take advantage of it. After over a week in Germany, I was running out of clean underwear and socks. I had asked Torben where the nearest coin operated laundry was and I was pleased to learn it was only about 20 meters from the Mainzer Hof front door. But when I went in, I asked the lady if she speaks English. "Nay." Do you have a coin operated wash machine? "Nay." It was a dry cleaners, but from the counter I could see a couple of wash machines. I was not about to try to ask what it might cost for them to wash my underwear. So back at the desk of the Mainzer Hof I asked the lady there, who speaks quite good English. Without hesitation she offered the use of the machines in the basement of the hotel. Though all the dials and instructions were in German, we managed to get that task out of the way and were very grateful for the use of those machines.

Next I wanted to buy a bottle of the best Franken Weißwein I could find as a gift for our German hosts. Torben had told me where I could find the wine shop in Dieburg which would have it, but to my dismay, its hours were 3:30 to 6:30 only. Short hours for a shop, wouldn't you say? But when I mentioned this to Torben later, he said, "Of course, who would want to buy wine in the morning?" Don't drop in unannounced on someone in Germany and expect them to pull something out of the refrigerator for you. Their refrigerators are very small, and intended to store something for only a short time. They go to the market every day to buy only what they need for the day, use that, and throw the rest away.

Temporarily I gave up on finding the wine, but another thing on my list was to find a good German map. Dieburg had a little bookshop, and there I found a wonderful set of maps of the country divided up into 12 sections, each showing every highway, backroad, village and point of interest in Germany. Immediately I thought of Torben and bought it for him. But the more I thought about it, the more I wanted one for myself too. Later, I found the same set in Heidelberg and bought it.

I had passed a little bakery advertising Rhabarber Kuchen ("rhubarb cake"). I knew Sharlyn would love it, and when I got back to the Mainzer Hof, she said yes, but she really wanted to try a McDonald's hamburger in Germany. We got out our map of Dieburg and found one about a 25-minute walk away. On the way we shared a piece of that Kuchen. Torben and Elfriede wouldn't be caught dead in a McDonald's, scoffed at them as something only the kids do, so Sharlyn was afraid someone would recognize us and report to them what we were doing. We were using up our time more quickly than we wanted though, and after picking up that familiar American fare we only had twenty minutes to get back to meet Elfriede, and she is very punctual. To make matters worse, as we hurried back (as best Sharlyn can hurry), the train came along, stopping all traffic, including the pedestrians. This ate up another 10 minutes of our precious time, and we started to worry that Elfriede would not know what happened to us. But by some miracle, she was running late and was never the wiser that, one, we had gone to McDonald's and, two, that we were late too. And we never told her.

Darmstadt is possibly most famous for its being the home of Alexandra, wife of Nicholas II of Russia. They visited there often, but Nicholas felt uncomfortable not having a Russian Orthodox church to attend, so he built a beautiful chapel. No picture does justice to this exquisite Russische Kappelle with its Eastern architecture and gold turrets. I bought a postcard photo of Nicholas and Alexandra leaving the chapel taken in 1908. Elfriede was most proud of the rose gardens of Mathildehöhe ("Mathilda's Hill"), so she took us there first. Unfortunately, the roses are still in bud in May, so she was quite disappointed for Sharlyn's sake. But the park itself had many magnificent old trees, including one or two sequoias, which I was surprised could thrive in Germany.

Near the Kappelle is a tall commemorative building called the Hochzeitsturm ("wedding tower"). At the top the architecture has five tall arches, representing the fingers of the hand, and beneath that is an observation deck. We took the elevator up and had quite a view of the entire city. We went into the city and walked around a bit. Sharlyn took Elfriede to look at purses and found one to her liking and bought it. On the way to the car a vendor was hawking his produce, so we bought some strawberries and bing cherries. After one of Elfriede's wonderful suppers, we had cherries and chocolate while watching a video on Germany (narrated in German) she had bought.

Thursday, May 28, Torben was back with us, and the four of us drove to Heidelberg on the Neckar River. We spent quite some time at the famous Schloß ("fortress") there. It stands, partly in ruin, high up on the bluffs above the river and has quite a spectacular view of the city below. Inside the Schloß is the world's largest Weinfaß ("wine cask"). Of course, we took the stairway up to the platform on top of it and another down the other side. Big enough to contain a small restaurant, it has the capacity for some 225,000 liters of wine. In days of old it was used to hold the tribute brought by the wine-producing peasants of the valley (one can imagine how watered down that tribute must have been), but stands empty today as little more than a curiosity for the tourists.

Heidelberg is a university town, and as we walked near the university, the student presence was unmistakable. On one street we saw a line of parked bicycles so long we just had to take a picture of it. In Germany it is not only the students who ride their bicycles, however. In America most bikes used by adults are for exercise. But in Germany we commonly saw many people we would judge to be in their seventies and eighties biking--not for exercise, but as transportation. They all have baskets on the front or back or both, and the women, young and old, use them to go to market. Here it is common to see two women standing in conversation, each holding a bike, everywhere in the market. We never saw anyone lock up the bicycle when they went into the stores either. I suppose theft happens, but people seemed to be very trusting in the places where we went.

The day we were there a demonstration was being organized--something about the treatment of children in Third World nations I think, so while we had our lunch outdoors at a restaurant along the river, the marchers came along with their bullhorns chanting and shouting. In the center of town is a huge Lutheran cathedral--the Peterskirche. We went inside and found, as usual, no one inside--except for one student sitting at a table near the pews who had discovered a quiet place to do homework.

We wandered around the Marktplatz and the shops a little, still trying to agree on some gifts we wanted to buy yet. Earlier, near the little souvenir stand at the Triberg Wasserfall on our South Tour I had seen a shop selling every description of Swiss Army knives. I thought Thomas and Austin would like a real genuine Swiss Army knife, so I wanted to buy them. But Sharlyn didn't want them to have knives, and hoped to buy some CD for them instead. I argued that this wouldn't be very representative of Germany, since we could buy the same thing at home. Suddenly we found ourselves at a little shop selling beer steins. Here we picked out a glass one for each of them, and later picked up a bottle of premium Warsteiner beer to go with it. We worried a little about how we were going to get these breakables home, but even that worked out.

On the way back from Heidelberg we passed through the Odenwald again, and Elfriede insisted that Torben, who was anxious to get back to spend some time with his Beate, take a little detour up a winding mountain road to the little village of Lindenfels. Here was a marvelous view from the top of a lookout in the mountains of the valley below. Lindenfels is one of several places in Germany known as a Kurort ("cure place"). Anyone needing a quiet haven in the country to rest and recover from a lingering illness or malady can come here away from the noise, excitement and hustle of the city. Back in Groß-Zimmern Elfriede fixed supper for us and showed us another video (also narrated in German) of several big nature parks in Germany.

Friday, May 29, after breakfast at the Mainzer Hof, Torben picked us up for a tour of Frankfurt. Since Elfriede had to attend to some personal matters today (and probably needed a break from us anyway), Anita would be accompanying us instead. Frankfurt is one of the largest cities in Germany and breaks the pattern I described earlier of most of the other cities. It has its Marktplatz, Rathaus and cathedral, but it has a much more extensive "downtown" area like an American city. The many modern-looking office buildings, large department stores, and skyscrapers are curiously juxtaposed with the older buildings unlike any other city we had seen. We parked near the downtown area and rode the subway from Eschenheimer Tor one or two stops and strolled along the wide avenue.

We first went into a kind of vertical mall--an eight- or ten-story complex where the floors were connected by ramps arranged in a square all the way up, much like we would have escalators. In the center of the square was a glass-enclosed elevator. Torben told us that the developer who had built this and several other buildings was currently in jail for misrepresenting the floor areas of his buildings to acquire his loans to build them. Years ago Anita had worked in the big Peek & Cobblestone department store here, but it had moved down the block and she was anxious to have us see it. Sharlyn was interested in buying a scarf for Elfriede anyway, and Torben wanted to check on Lee jeans, so while they shopped, I went across the street to explore a big Woolworth I spotted. Anita pointed out a six- or seven-story shoe store where her friend Mary was a manager (remember this point for something which happened to us later).

Torben was always on the lookout for a good place to eat, and soon we were sitting in an all-fish restaurant. Sharlyn is not much for fish and was hesitating to go in, but the perch she had was very nicely done. The salads were accompanied by a little pitcher of the "green sauce" for which the restaurants in Frankfurt were known. Anita is learning English quite well, and we had fun over lunch discovering the English equivalents for the various spices in the green sauce.

After lunch we walked a short distance to an older part of the city. On one side of the plaza, with its fountain in the middle, was located the Römer (town hall) and on the other the huge Dom (cathedral) of the city. The Dom has a high Turm ("tower") and I could see people way up there looking out over a stone wall near the top. In Germany there is a charge for everything, but I was still a little surprised that we had to pay for this too. There wasn't even an elevator to take us up. Inside the tower was a circular stone stairway to the top which was so narrow that you needed to flatten yourself against the wall to let someone pass coming the other direction. I don't know how Anita made it up and down in her 3-inch heels, but she seemed to have little difficulty.

Coming up behind us was a group of seven or eight young men bearing "Buena Vista" on their sweatshirts. At the top I learned that they were in Germany to play football and were from Storm Lake, Iowa (in Buena Vista County) not far from where I grew up. One of them even had the name Pullman, which he says was once Pullmann before his grandfather dropped the ending n when he came from Germany. It is more likely he is related to Torben than to us. This part of Germany is noted for its Apfelwein ("apple wine"), so, of course, we had to try some from a little cafe near the Römer. Sharlyn liked it, but even though we had requested it cut about 50/50 with "wasser," I still preferred the Apfelsaft ("apple juice") I usually ordered.

Jörg had told Torben we must check out a famous bistro called Adolph Wagner's in a section of Frankfurt called Sachsenhausen. We had some difficulty finding it, but we went in and sat down at one of the old tables in the dimly lit room. Sharlyn considered it nothing but a glorified tavern. Torben was particularly unimpressed and said out loud he would never come back--too far from home and offered nothing for him and Beate. Several of the locals were already there and two more couples from the neighborhood came in and sat next to us. Anita started chatting in German to the lady across from her, who explained that Wagner's was founded three generations back and was still a family business. After Anita explained what she had just learned to me in English, I pointed to a large old photograph of a man on the wall behind her and asked her if that was Adolph. She turned around and then looked back at me with a shocked look and asked what I said. Again I asked if that was Adolph. She turned pale as she said no. Then she wanted to know why I thought that might be Hitler. When I told her I had meant Adolph Wagner I thought she would split open laughing so hard.

Later that evening we had supper with Jörg and Anita at the Biergarten behind the Mainzer Hof and we had a good laugh about it again. Torben stopped in near the end of our meal, and when we finished, Jörg offered us an after-hours tour of his office, the headquarters of his "empire" in Dieburg. First though, he wanted to show us another building he owned across the plaza from the Mainzer Hof. Official records have documented it as the third oldest building in Germany. It is in use today as a pub, but the upper floors have been restored following a recent fire. Of most interest to me was the Keller ("cellar"), which made me think of descending into a catacomb. This part of the building was built by the Romans and had walls of stone, an uneven floor of cobblestone, an arched ceiling also of stone and in one corner of the room a stone well perhaps two or three meters deep. The tour of his modern office a couple blocks away was an anticlimax compared to that. It was after midnight before we returned to our room that night with the souvenir umbrella he gave us--bearing the name PullMann (with its trademark M shaped like one of his buildings) which appears when it is opened.

Saturday, May 30, we began what Torben called our North Tour. As Lutherans, we had requested to see some of the places where Luther had lived. This took us into what had formerly been East Germany, where Torben had never been. Our first stop was Eisenach, where we stopped for lunch first at a little restaurant along the highway. Except for that awful Weißwurst in München and a little taste of Sharlyn's lunch in Erbach, I still had not had any bratwurst in Germany, so I ordered bratwurst and sauerkraut. It was delicious to my taste. I had not noticed slot machines elsewhere in our travels, but this restaurant had one. Torben and I each threw in a Mark or two hoping to get lucky, but after all the dazzling lights were out, the machine still read zero in the end. Elfriede had as much fun watching us as we did playing.

We checked out the Bachhaus in this town where Bach once lived, but it was only a memorial to Bach where his music was sometimes played. The Lutherhaus nearby was the building where Luther had gone to school until about age 15, I think, but nothing of any real interest. Far more significant was the Wartburg visible from our restaurant window already and looming high above us at the top of the mountain. We drove up as far as we could, but had to either walk or take a carriage pulled by horses up the steep climb from there. Torben wanted Elfriede to ride, but she took it in easy stages and before long this magnificent fortress stood before us. Elfriede had been here not long ago, so she elected to wait for us at the outdoor cafe while the three of us took the tour. The lines were long, and as we stood waiting to enter the massive Schloß, a cold mountain rain started, and our umbrellas were in the car.

Lutherans remember the Wartburg most as the place where Luther took refuge for ten months and translated the New Testament into German. The room in which he lived and worked is preserved much as it was, except for the desk itself, which burned and was replaced long ago with a similar one. But as significant as this event is to Lutherans and as important as it is to the Germans for the stabilization of the written German language, it is a tiny part of the history of the Wartburg itself. The tour was primarily devoted to those other events in its history which were in themselves interesting to me. After the long wait to get in and the lengthy tour itself, Elfriede thought she must have missed us and walked back down the mountain. Meanwhile, we were searching all over for her up on top. Concluding that she must have gone down, we finally caught up with her down near the car. She was so relieved to see us, and Sharlyn and I were both relieved and delighted that she was not upset.

We had spent far more time already than Torben had expected, and he asked us now to reconsider what we really wanted to see in north Germany. He had underestimated times and distances and this seemed to put him in a bad mood. He muttered something about most Germans not even wanting to see most of the places we had requested (Eisenach, Erfurt, Weimar, Wittenberg, Leipzig, Dresden, Wunstorf, Bielefeld) but he had tried to include anyway for us. In any case, Dresden was too far and would not be possible. Elfriede agreed. So we chose to go next to Weimar, a city rich in art, music and literary history. This is the city of Lucas Cranach, Schiller and Goethe, Bach and Weber, but we spent a frustrating hour driving all around the Altstadt looking for the Schillerhaus and Goethehaus. We did eventually catch a glimpse of both of them, but this was somewhat of a disaster and did little to humor Torben. Just outside of town to the northwest is Buchenwald, which I might have wanted to see, but didn't have the nerve to bring up--in deference not only to Torben's disposition but to their possible sensitivity to the issue of concentration camps. We had hoped at least to get a picture of the famous statue of Goethe and Schiller in front of the National Theater, but we never saw it. It appeared we were not destined to see much in Weimar, so it was on to Wittenberg.

This was eastern Germany now, and the rebuilding effort was evident everywhere. We became aware of a distinct American influence here. The Autobahn looked more like an interstate. I couldn't recall seeing rest areas in the west, but here they looked just like the American ones. We had not seen billboards along the highways, but here they were popping up everywhere. In the west the McDonald's was not usually a stand-alone building with a big sign seen from the highway, but here they were exact replicas of their American counterparts. All of this seemed to irritate Torben and Elfriede. We started to see the sullen, gray apartment buildings formerly occupied by the East Germans, now abandoned and looking quite shabby. Amongst the blight stood the bright new building of a business, sometimes with an American name. Occasionally we saw one of the tiny Trabant cars still running, originally built for an East German family who perhaps saved up for ten years to buy it. Torben told us many social issues are still in transition as the former East Germans learn that they now must do real honest work to get what they want. The people here are still quite poor, so it is difficult for the smaller businesses like restaurants and shops to take hold. Their best hope seems to be for big business and industry to move in and offer employment, and that seems to be slowly happening. Toward evening we reached Lutherstadt-Wittenberg and found rooms in the Sorat Hotel.

Sunday, May 31, we were in the city where Luther nailed his 95 theses to the door of the castle church--one of the most explosive religious events in history. How ironic it was to see signs advertising an "Erotik-Messe" (an exhibit for sex freaks) on every lamp post between the parking lot and the Schloßkirche, each one showing a woman's bare behind. It was around 9:00 and the next church service was scheduled to begin at 10:00. If I were convinced I would be worshipping in a real Lutheran service with Lutherans who believe as I do, I might have insisted we wait for it. Instead, we took some pictures, including the famous door. The original wooden door to which Luther nailed his paper burned long ago and has been replaced by the present bronze one given as a gift. Luther is buried inside the Schloßkirche, but we did not realize we were looking at the tomb until it was too close to service time to get a picture. We stopped by Lutherhaus, where he and Katherine had lived with their family, but our Catholic companions were anxious to get to Berlin yet today, so we did not spend any more time here.

As we approached Berlin from the southwest we passed Potsdam, where Friedrich der Große (Frederick II) established his famous Schloß Sanssouci. Regretfully, we did not take the time to see it. Torben had never been to Berlin and told us the Siegesäule monument standing prominently in the Kaiserdamm Bismarckstrasse was more significant to most Germans than such things as Checkpoint Charlie or the Wall. We passed through the Tiergarten ("animal park") and soon saw the famous Brandenburg Tor ("gate"). I asked Torben if he could pull off near here for us to get a picture. While pulling into a little construction area (construction was everywhere in this part of Berlin), he drove over a section of concrete curbing with a loud scraping sound, and a few minutes later we noticed a puddle forming underneath the car. Torben became quite alarmed and upset, and I feared that my request for a picture had turned out to be a costly one. But we soon concluded that it was condensation from the air conditioner.

We had taken our pictures when we noticed a man nearby who had pieces of the Berlin Wall for sale. We did not expect to be able to buy such a thing so easily, so we suspected they were fake. But we had seen whole sections of the wall still standing nearby that were being demolished in the construction projects. The graffiti on his pieces seemed to match the ones on one section of the wall we had seen, so we gave him 20 DM (about $14) for a small piece. The wall originally proceeded southward from Brandenburg Tor and curved around to the east. We followed this path along Niederkirchnerstrasse and came to a section of the wall intended to be left standing permanently as a monument. This section stretches for a block or two with vignettes along the entire east side illustrating the conditions and stories of those who lived through the worst days. Another block or two beyond that we came to the former Checkpoint Charlie, the passage between East and West in the American sector of old West Berlin. Nearby was a restaurant where we had lunch. Since the government buildings were still under construction, we could not see or tour them, so we proceeded to Hannover.

Torben had only been to Hannover for the big computer exhibition they hold every year, so he didn't know much of what the city had to offer us. Elfriede estimated it to be about 400 km from home, so she too hardly ever came here. In my role as navigator, I had one of Elfriede's brochures to use in getting us around in Hannover as we entered the city. When we passed the Hauptbahnhof, I found it on my map, but I couldn't orient any of the streets whizzing past to the map. Frustrated, Torben grabbed the map at a red light and noticed immediately that I was looking at a map of Göttingen. The brochure Elfriede had handed me, which I assumed was for Hannover, actually described several cities, and had a map for each.

As we did with the other cities, we parked near the Mittestadt and walked into the Marktplatz. We spotted an interesting building on the other side of the plaza marked Staatoper ("state opera"). We planned to check it out, but as we came closer we became more aware of loud rock music in that direction. Then we encountered more and more young people in spiked hairdos, fluorescent green or yellow hair, six earrings in each ear, one guy with a big safety pin pushed through his eyebrow. When we saw girls holding hands and kissing each other, we decided the state opera building was not that interesting after all. Torben assured us it was harmless, so we had supper at a restaurant on the plaza.

We were now in the area I had most wanted to see, and my first impression was a disappointment. My grandfather had left the Hannover area almost 100 years ago, where his family had lived for at least 100 years before that. I could only hope that Wunstorf, the little village some 30 km to the west where the family actually lived, would be more interesting. After supper, we walked around a little and looked at the big Lutheran church along one edge of the plaza from the outside, and Torben suggested we find a hotel. But since I had hoped to spend some time in Wunstorf the next day, I asked if we could try to find a place there for the night, so I could get an early start. This proved to be a bad decision.

We arrived about 10:00 p.m. and found a small Hotel Garni with one double and one single room. I told Torben to take it. Sharlyn and I would be happy to stay in the single. No, they told him of another hotel across town, he said. When we found it, the name was on the building, but the place was dark. We found out later that they had gone out of business. Torben wanted to check out a third name they had given him, but I was afraid we would lose the one sure thing we had. By now it was almost 11:00, and we persuaded him to return to the Garni. As Torben went into the building to reserve the rooms, a car pulled in beside us. They wanted a room and were turned away. We had just taken the last two rooms in town.

Monday, June 1, was the most important day of the entire trip to Germany for me. I was in Wunstorf, the village of my great-grandfather and his father before him--Fritz and August Püllmann--community brew masters of their day. As much information as was possible had already been squeezed out of the local records in town by my more genealogy-minded cousins, but I wanted to see things for myself--the way the little Aue flowed through the village, the old houses, the character of the shops, the layout of the streets, even the smell of the air. I wanted to walk where they had walked. Though I was warned in advance it would be a waste of time, I walked through the big cemetery looking at names. I gave up only when it started to rain.

Torben, Elfriede, and Sharlyn had been talking with the caretakers of the cemetery. Plots in Germany are not bought as they are in America. They are rented for a period of 30 years. If no one renews the plot, the site is plowed up and reused again. Only wooden caskets are allowed, to minimize recycle time, and the bones are considered part of the soil. The markers are ground down and sold as second-hand, if useable, or simply made into walkways or used as ordinary stone. The Aue flowed through town in two branches--Nord and Süd. I didn't know it at the time, but in 1975 the north branch was rechanneled about 100 meters farther north and, for some reason, was now called the West Aue. This meant that the house in which they had lived along the river is today some distance from it. No wonder I couldn't find the right house on the Aue, and the picture I did take of the West Aue shows nothing of consequence. I had fulfilled my dream, though, so we left the past behind and headed for Bielefeld.

My cousin Terri Ebner had invited us to spend a few days with them, and I was getting an idea. I wanted to see more of north Germany than Torben was planning for us, towns which I figured I could see using Germany's wonderful train system. This was fine with everyone, so after lunch with Terri, Alois (they call him "Lewis"), and son Johannes (daughter Leah, a highly ranked chess player, was away at a chess camp), the other three of our group left for Köln and Bonn and I remained with Terri to spend the night. I remember wondering if I was making a serious mistake.

Terri gave me the grand tour of Bielefeld that afternoon, including Lewis's "Bethel"--the health care facility he runs as part of his specialty advising surgeons precisely where to operate on epileptic patients. I was surprised to hear her say that Bielefeld too, like most cities in Germany, was heavily bombed during the war. From what little was ever mentioned of it, to me it seemed to be of no strategic importance. But she said it had enough light industry (making such items as cutlery), and its topography had a few natural passes through the northern-most range of mountains in Germany, to make that necessary.

My plan was to see Hamburg, then travel to Flensburg on the border with Denmark, cross into Denmark just to see what it looks like, perhaps even get a glimpse of the North Sea, then down to Bonn and back to Dieburg. When I told Lewis of this notion, he raised his eyebrows as if I were crazy. To do it in one day, as I hoped, he told me, would be impossible. I was considering doing it anyway, by staying overnight in Flensburg somewhere and coming back the next day. Lewis suggested that I just see Hamburg, then Bonn as I wanted. I followed his advice and, as I was to find out, probably saved my life. The train I would have taken on the second day from Hamburg to Hannover crashed, killing 100 people.

Tuesday, June 2, Lewis dropped me off at the train station a little before 8:00. I discovered that the time your train is due is all important. In the airlines you need to know the flight number to find out information--what gate, whether it is on time, passengers on the flight, and so on. City bus systems usually have a number also, while cross country busses have a destination city. But I had never used a system governed by the departure time. Your train may or may not have a number, such as ICE 879, but that is largely ignored. Look up which Gleis ("track") your train is leaving from according to that time.

From what I saw, the trains fall into three categories: the intercity express (ICE), the intercity (IC), and the Stadt (SE). I think Torben may have pointed out the elevated track of a super 300 km/hr train that runs into Berlin, but that would be something quite special and not really part of the system. You try to get the ICE if possible, because it is the fastest--it travels up to 250 km/hr and makes the fewest stops. I was amazed how punctual every train was--every time right on the minute. This is done by controlling the speed between stations. Running behind, speed up; running ahead, slow down. All is regulated by the computer and that central clock signal beamed all over the country. Connecting trains are easy to catch, even if you have only a few minutes between, because each one is so precisely on time. Often too, the connecting train is conveniently controlled by the computer to be on the same platform, so all you do is walk across to the other side.

By 10:30 I was in Hamburg, having changed trains in Hannover. Conveniently, the tour busses were all lined up in front of the Hauptbahnhof, so I took a 2 1/2 hour tour of the beautiful city of Hamburg, the largest port city of Germany at the mouth of the Elbe. The tour circled both parts of the Alster, passed the U.S. embassy (and the embassies of many other countries, as well), St. Michaelskirche (the church with the tallest spire in the country), the Köhlbrandbrücke (a majestic suspension bridge across the Elbe), the famous Fischmarkt (where every Sunday nearly everything can be bought or traded), and the Reeperbahnstraße (a red-light district well-known all over Germany). The schedule worked out perfectly, since my train back to Bonn was 13:53. I was feeling a little cocky about using the system, so I wasn't prepared for what happened next.

I couldn't find a train going to Bonn anywhere in the huge station. My train was due in about 20 minutes, and I started to panic. I started running from one person to another asking if they could speak English, since I didn't feel I had time to explain in my fractured German. "Wo is der Zug nach Bonn?" would have produced a volley of explanation I wasn't ready for. Most people simply gave me a cold "nay" and hurried off. But finally one kind lady with her husband said "a little." These were sweet words. She pointed me to the track to Köln and Koblenz. It had my departure time, but Bonn was not on the list of destinations. I decided I would take it and hope for the best. At least I knew Köln was close and I could probably get another train from there if necessary. After I boarded the train and saw the Reiseplan ("itinerary") for this route, suddenly I understood. Bonn was the 10th stop and there were several more after that. The sign board couldn't possibly list them all, so it selected a few and left it up to the passengers to figure out the others. Again, it was that departure time that held the key. Most important, I was on the right train, but it shook my confidence.

I was traveling second class, which meant each car had eight or ten compartments, each with six seats. There is no such thing as non-smoking, and three of the passengers in my compartment kept the air blue constantly. A fourth was a black young man who had his earphone pulled out too far, so we heard coosh-cooh, coosh-cooh for many miles before he finally got off in Düsseldorf. We saw very few black people in Germany, but Terri had told me that in Germany the Turks are in roughly the same socio-economic status as the blacks in America. They were welcome soon after the war to assist in rebuilding the country, but now into their third generation, they are somewhat non grata. In the remaining seat was a sweet older woman who pulled out of her bag a bunch of Weintrauben ("grapes") that she shared with me. I was able to talk a little German with her and learned that she happened to be getting off with me at Bonn. She pointed me in the right direction, and I ran off quickly to see a bit of Beethoven's town and snap a picture of Robert and Clara Schumann's tomb before the next train exactly one hour later. I was back in Dieburg by 10:00. In contrast to my hectic but exciting day, Sharlyn had spent a day of marketing and leisure with Elfriede, even squeezing in a nap. I found out they had also spent a lot of time sitting in her "Garten" drinking wine and eating Erdbeeren ("strawberries"). But I was not envious.

******

This is Sharlyn's account of her day:

It is 9:30 a.m. and some shops are not yet open in Dieburg, Germany, near the Mainzer Hof, the hotel in which David and I have been staying during our 16-day stay in Germany, so before shopping for a scarf for Elfriede Pullmann (she and her grandson, Torben Pullmann, are hosting our stay), I may as well write a bit. She and Torben came to America last year and even attended our Pullmann Family reunion in July. We doubt that there is any real family connection, but they are certainly nice people to be related to. Once we met up with David's first cousin Terri Ebner, of Bielefeld, and her family and had lunch yesterday, David decided to stay on with them and either take the train yet last night or certainly first thing this morning to see Hamburg and then get over the border into Denmark. In short, he planned a biggie trip for just the day with the plan that he'd get back late tonight and when given the choice of hurrying along with him without food or rest and lots of walking (the Pullmann method) or coming back with Torben and Elfriede via Köln (Cologne) and possibly Bonn yet yesterday and doing today whatever Elfriede chose to do quietly, I chose the latter.

Back to my story, we left America Monday evening, May 18, from Dulles International Airport (Washington, D.C. area) about 6:00 p.m. and landed in Frankfurt, Germany Tuesday, the 19th, about 8:00 a.m. (their time) after an eight-hour flight. German time is six hours ahead of America's Eastern Daylight Time. Germany too has daylight saving time but sometimes begins it as early as February. Each year's period is different.

You wouldn't believe the construction noise outside our window as I write. Workmen are renovating a building, I believe, and start always at 7:00 a.m. too. We're used to city noises, luckily. Clocks and bells are continuously announcing the time in Germany also but that is rather nice. Although we saw cuckoo clocks for sale in the Schwarzwald (Black Forest area), people here do not seem to use them.

I think I'll check out the shops. I know a few words of German--ja bitte for yes please, and danke for thank you. I need to mail my last postcard too. I have some over 70 DM plus some American Express travelers checks which shops here are not too ready to accept. There have been a number of scams with money here which accounts for some of this.

******

Wednesday, June 3, was our last full day in Germany. Elfriede had promised us some of her home-made Kloß balls and invited us over for lunch. They were wonderful. After lunch Torben was elected to take us (just us three this time) to Mainz and Wiesbaden. In Mainz we toured the Gutenberg museum, where printing from moveable type was born. Three rare paper copies of the Gutenberg Bible dating from 1452 are found here. The museum was filled with old presses and printing memorabilia. Mainz was organized along the same plan as the other German cities we had seen, so we did not plan to spend much time here. Close by the museum, however, was St. Martin Dom, which warranted a quick peek.

We had already seen a bit of Wiesbaden from the Rhein, but Torben planned to drive through to give us some more of its flavor. He explained that everything here was more upscale than the other cities nearby. As soon as he said that I noticed that the price of diesel fuel, for example, was 1.27--10 pence more than in Mainz. The best price I ever noticed for diesel in our travels was 1.07 DM per liter. More typically, it was somewhere between 1.15 and 1.20. We saw a few high mode shops and expensive apartments before heading down the road toward Rüdesheim. We wanted to see the huge statue of Germania near here yet before Torben needed to get back by 6:00. The statue was quite impressive up close, but the view from the bluffs high above the Rhein was equally spectacular. Visibility was unlimited this day, and we had no difficulty seeing what I would judge to be 70 or 80 km away.

We still had one more surprise waiting for us. On the way home, Torben needed to pick up some shampoo. We thought Germany had only small shops. From what we had seen, even their "Supermarkt" was quite tame by American standards. But near Groß-Zimmern he took us to their Interspar store, which looked to our eyes as if we had just stepped into Wal-Mart. Torben was almost apologetic for bringing us here. Looked too much like America for his taste.

Since it was our last evening with our German friends, we planned to get the whole group together for a farewell dinner and toasts. We met at 8:00 at the Limoncello restaurant in Groß-Zimmern, which Jörg had been instrumental in getting started only about three weeks ago. In the same restaurant were some friends of Anita, including Mary, the manager of the shoe store in Frankfurt she had told us about. They were invited to join us. Mary speaks fairly good English and mentioned that her brother is in America for a year. When we asked where, she replied Virginia. When I asked where in Virginia, she didn't know but had his business card in her wallet. I looked at the card and read McLean, Virginia. Her brother, Wolfgang Kaufeld, lives less than two miles away from us. Little Svenja had bid us a sweet farewell earlier in the evening, when Anita drove her home, and now Berthold bid us farewell as he and Elfriede left for home. Jörg and Anita drove us back to Dieburg, where we bid them a rather emotional farewell also.

Thursday, June 4, Elfriede and Torben drove us to Frankfurt for our flight home. After breakfast with them at the airport, we bid them Auf Wiedersehen and headed for our plane. The umbrella Jörg had given us would not fit into our luggage, and Sharlyn accidentally left it at the metal detector conveyor. We only discovered that after passing customs, and we quickly found out that going backwards against the flow of a system designed to flow passengers in one direction is difficult. I was beginning to wonder if she would be successful in retrieving it in time to catch our flight, but a half hour later she returned with umbrella in hand. One official had ridden his bicycle some distance over to the gate through which we had passed to pick it up for her. We departed runway 25R, which has its elevation posted at 364 feet, at 12:55 local time. We first saw North America over Newfoundland, near Goose Bay, where even in June we saw it covered with snow. We landed at Dulles right on schedule at 3:00.

******

Sharlyn's account of June 4, 1998, 4:20 p.m.:

We are back on U.S. soil. We have come through customs and baggage claim, so David is now walking to satellite parking to pick up the car Angela, Paul, and Thomas left us, and I can write once again. I vowed when David and I flew to England and I spent most evenings writing a journal plus postcards that I would not do that again. Therefore, this will be short. In fact, let me just say that Elfriede and oftentimes "her Berthold" plus dog Bella or Elfriede and Torben took us in their cars to many, many town/cities in southern Germany to see their Deutschland. Torben's family--father Jörg, mother Anita, and sister Svenja had us to their home for a super cookout and took us out to eat to get the full flavor of German dining several times. They also took us for what proved to be a rather cold boat ride in their boat down the Rhein River! Torben's girlfriend, Beate, joined us for this. And if this were not enough, Elfriede and Torben took us for an abbreviated northern tour also. In this way, we got to see some Martin Luther-related sights such as Wartburg Castle and the church at Wittenberg on which Luther posted his 95 theses.

In an effort to see more of the north, David, as written earlier, took the train. As it turned out, his original plan to get into Denmark was too ambitious. He had all he could do to take the train from Bielefeld to Hamburg, tour Hamburg on a 2 1/2 hour sight-seeing tour, take the train from Hamburg to Bonn, see Beethovenhaus as well as a gravesite (took photo of the Haus from outside only), take the train from Bonn to Dieburg, and walk to the Mainzer Hof, where I was waiting wondering just when he would be back. He had spent 10 hours that day riding the train as he says, "with chimneys"--people who smoke nonstop. It had been rush, rush, rush so I'm glad I did not go along. He was back by 10 p.m. which was especially good since the hotel locks its doors by 11 p.m. (make that 2300 hours). The next day there was a horrendous accident of this same train system in the northern area where David had just been. Over 100 people were killed as they thought a car from an earlier accident dropped down from an overpass to the train tracks below and the train (except for the engine?) hit it. There is/was quite a chance that had the Ebners not convinced David to forego a Denmark visit, he would have spent the night somewhere after his day's touring, made it to Denmark and the North Sea the next morning, and been on that very train midday coming back. We will never know, thanks to God.

As it is, we are enjoying sweet memories of Germany and the people we came to know who live there. I, personally, would like to go back again someday. David feels all the towns are the same with their Rathaus, cathedrals, platzes with markets set up primarily selling fresh fruits and vegetables, etc. that he does not need to see another one. He is basically right. I myself will enjoy drinking milk again, something served only at breakfast in Germany. And I certainly will not miss being asked to drink Wasser ("water with gas"), wine, or beer. Even so, we had a lovely time in another part of the world.

# Appendix D. Trip to Israel, November 5-14, 2001

Despite State Department warnings against travel to the Middle East and pleas from family and friends not to go, we were finally on our way to the Holy Land. Made possible as a gift from our son Thomas three years ago, the trip had been scheduled and rescheduled as trouble erupted in this volatile land again and again. When the phone rang after the terrorist attacks in New York, I was sure our tour organizer was calling to postpone it indefinitely. In fact, I had been liberally dipping into the vacation time I had allocated for the trip, because I was sure it wasn't going to happen. To my complete surprise, however, we were not only still on schedule, but we were told of other TTI Travel groups that had been coming and going all along for several months, even throughout the tumultuous events surrounding September 11. Nevertheless, we still were not sure we were making the right decision.

Most of Pastor Paul Schroeder's tours bring Christians within range of his radio program *The Word Today* together from his home base near Milwaukee, so we were meeting this group of ten fellow sojourners in Newark to begin the long flight to Israel. We had never met any of them, yet before the week was out, we would be forming life-long bonds.

Things did not go well as we began the short connecting flight from Dulles. The Continental Airlines computer "randomly" selects passengers to be pulled out of line and searched from top to bottom. I don't know what our odds were, but soon we were emptying our pockets and dumping our suitcases upside down. After hurriedly stuffing our things back into the same bags we had already spent hours carefully packing, we boarded the Boeing 737 for departure. The arm rest of Sharlyn's seat came completely apart as she settled in, and my overhead light didn't work, so we began to wonder if maintenance was this good on other components of the airplane or if this was a sign of something more ominous to come. At last flight 618 was off at 6:14 p.m. and pulled into terminal C in Newark a half hour late at 7:35.

Our companions would be arriving at terminal A from Chicago in about a half hour, so we decided to take the monorail over to meet them at the gate. We did not know what our host Pastor Paul Schroeder looked like, so when I noticed limousine drivers holding up signs to make connections with their arriving passengers, I got the idea we could do the same. I found a candy vendor nearby who graciously gave me the largest-size bag she had. On it I scratched his name, and after a seemingly interminable wait, a hand was waving to us from the other end of the long corridor among the last passengers to disembark.

We were introduced to the other members of the group and heard "Avanti" for the first time as we joined forces with them back to the monorail and over to terminal B for international processing. Our tour of Israel was Pastor Paul's 19th, and Avanti (Italian for "forward!") was the word he used frequently to pick up the pace or call the laggards (often Sharlyn and me) to catch up to the rest of the group. It was 11:07 before flight 90 on our Boeing 777 finally lifted off. Sharlyn does better than I at sleeping in a sitting position, but both of us attempted fitfully to get some rest on the ten-hour flight. It didn't help that our seats were against the bulkhead that houses the rest room. This meant that not only did the seat backs not recline, but we could count each whoosh of the toilet behind us--and it reached a very high number.

Israel is seven time zones ahead of us, so dawn arrived long before our biorhythms were willing to accept it. All the shades were drawn on the windows, but since I couldn't really sleep, I decided to sneak a peek outside. Even though I raised the shade only a slit, bright sunshine immediately flooded the cabin, and I'm sure that aroused the ire of my fellow passengers still trying to sleep. It wasn't worth it either, because the cloud layer beneath us prevented eye contact with the ground anyway.

One of the most fascinating features of the 777 is the moving map display of the flight. I amused myself monitoring our position, altitude, ground speed, time remaining, local time, time at destination, all being continuously updated as the flight progressed. The display zooms in to show detail to include the cities we were crossing over. We were following the great circle route, which took us over Dublin, London, Paris, a corner of Switzerland, along the entire eastern coast of Italy, and out over the Ionian Sea.

When we reached southern Greece, I decided enough people were awake that I could lift that shade again for another peek outside. This time I was rewarded with a clear view all the way to the surface, and I watched us fly over snow-capped mountains of Greece, then pass north of Crete, south of Cyprus, and soon we were making our descent into Tel Aviv. It was 3:55 in the afternoon when we landed at Ben Gurion International Airport--not even 9:00 in the morning yet back home!

An armed Israeli soldier stood guard as we descended the high stairway that had been wheeled up to the door of our aircraft and crossed the tarmac to a modern mobile lounge that transported us to the terminal. There was some confusion about whether we were supposed to be in the Foreign Passports or Israeli Passports line, some telling us it didn't matter, so we stood in at least five different queues (some with the Open light on but with no one at the desk by the time we got up to it) before we were finally processed through. On the other side we were met by a man who asked to see our return tickets. We were a little reluctant to hand over such a valuable thing to a stranger, but Pastor Paul assured us he was the local representative of TTI Travel, Inc., who needed them to prepare the paperwork for our return trip next week.

Avanti again! We retrieved our luggage, including Big Rover, and, ever conscious to stay together with our group, made our way out of the terminal to our tour bus. Big Rover was named by Sharlyn. I had been urging her to upgrade our old hand-carry Samsonite to a wheeled suitcase for a trip she and Angela were making to Wisconsin a few years ago. She kept putting it off until the night before departure, so I went out that very night and bought a huge one. The first thing she said when she returned home from the trip was how much she hated that thing. It was way too big and made her feel like she was walking around with a big dog on a leash, so she called it Rover. She went out immediately and bought Little Rover, a smaller version much more to her liking. But here we were with both Rovers and grateful for the immense volume they could contain.

As we waited for the others to rejoin us from the rest rooms, I remarked sarcastically to Pastor Paul standing next to me that our group was in at least second place among famous groups of twelve in Israel. He thought a minute and then said "third." I was referring to the Apostles, but then it was my turn to think a minute before I remembered the tribes of Jacob. At the bus we met our tour guide, a wonderful young Palestinian woman named Rula Shubeita, who was to be quite a beacon of hospitality and Christian faith for the next week. We were also introduced to our Palestinian bus driver, a Muslim named Ahmad. While Ahmad understood very little English (and spoke even less), Rula impressed us with her fluency in at least three languages--English, Arabic and Hebrew. It was our first exposure to the exigencies of existence in the clash of cultures and ideologies in this troubled land.

Most of the population are Israeli Jews, about half that number are Palestinian Muslims, and a relatively tiny minority are Christians (some 1.5%), Ba'hai, Druze and some others. For the most part they remain segregated, each group not welcome in a particular pocket of territory belonging to another. While animosity runs deep among these diverse groups, stemming from ancient hostilities, embers of political intrigue are constantly fanned into flame by the Hassadim. Instantly recognizable by their broad-rimmed hats, beards and distinctive long curled sideburns, these Hassidic Jews are fanatically dogmatical, tyrannically territorial and politically intractable.

The Hassadim cluster into their own sector of the city, which is blocked off to cars and made off limits on the Shabbat (Sabbath). Darren Duke (who lives in Jerusalem and whom I will identify later) told us of a family returning from the beach still in their swim wear who mistakenly turned into a Hassidic neighborhood and barely escaped with their lives as their car was stoned for their indecent affront. With families of ten or twelve children, they are subsidized by the government so they can devote full time to Scripture study and prayer. Exempt from taxes and military service, they are seen as a privileged class and incur the resentment of most other sectors of society.

We boarded our bus for the first time, and I noticed that the jumbo size LED digits of its clock were still set to daylight saving time--an annoyance throughout the week as we had to make the mental adjustment with each glance at the time. We were now passing through the streets of Tel Aviv during rush hour, and Ahmad was doing his best to find the shortest route through traffic out of the city. Tel Aviv was once a suburb of Jaffa (the city of ancient Joppa mentioned in the account in Acts 9 from where Peter was summoned by Cornelius after raising Dorcas from the dead). Before the founding of the state of Israel in 1948, so many Jews settled in this suburb that today Tel Aviv is the city and Jaffa is the suburb. Today it ranks second largest in size behind Jerusalem, with Haifa in third place.

The behavior of the drivers was consistent with a general rudeness we were to observe elsewhere during our stay. Darren explained that an Israeli is extremely sensitive to a perception of subservience. Allowing someone else to go first or some other simple politeness might be mistaken for being someone's fool. We noticed, for example, that when elevator doors open, the ones behind us brashly push their way forward past us and force their way on without regard to others trying to get on or off. Here Ahmad was trying to merge right and was being forced out by a city bus, whose driver simply closed his window and looked away when Ahmad opened the door to our bus and expressed his admiration with a few choice words in blue French.

Tourists and members of the public who cannot afford a car travel on these city busses. Trains are non-existent except for two trunk lines stemming from Jerusalem, one connecting north to Haifa and the other southwest to Ashdod in the Gaza strip. Most of the cars are European or Japanese, compact models not only to conserve precious fuel but also to accommodate the narrow streets in the cities, especially Jerusalem. Prices for gasoline were identical at every station we saw, starting at 95.9 cents per liter for regular. Billboards are rare along the roadways, but here in Tel Aviv I saw an advertisement for a Chevrolet for 124,900 shekels (more on that later). In the heavy traffic I couldn't believe that I saw a car merge directly in front of a police car with its lights flashing. Rula explained that police cars always have their lights flashing and use their sirens to pull cars over.

Soon we were in the posh suburb of Herzliyya (Herzlia). It was after dark now, so we probably couldn't fully appreciate the expensive real estate and new home construction our guide was describing. This is an entirely Israeli Jewish neighborhood. Official policy of the government is to encourage Jews from other countries, particularly Russia, to emigrate to Israel, offering them a place to live, exemption from taxes and military duty for three years, five months of intensive language training, and job placement as incentives. This brazen plan intentionally uses settlement as a weapon to force Palestinians out of territory where the Israelis believe they shouldn't exist and is probably the single most provocative issue igniting turbulence in the country today.

After a two-hour ride we reached our hotel in Netanya, a city on the Mediterranean Sea about 30 kilometers north of Tel Aviv. Somehow in the review of the plan for tomorrow I erroneously got the notion that one of the sites we would visit would require a lady's head to be covered. Sharlyn didn't have a scarf along but thought she might be able to get by tying on a handkerchief. While she unpacked our bags in the hotel room, I decided to try the gift shop down in the lobby. Indeed I found a modest assortment there and selected one priced 25 shekels (sometimes written sheqels). The exchange rate is four NIS (new Israeli shekels) to the dollar, so I handed the young lady at the counter a ten dollar bill. As she handed me a fistful of coins in change, I realized I didn't know how to count it. Too embarrassed to ask her, I left to do the homework I should already have done to understand and recognize the local currency. I later determined it was the correct change, but in a less hospitable environment I could easily have been cheated.

Two members of our group, Tom and Mickey (originally a native of Berlin, her real name is Mechthild) Weathers, invited us to go with them for a moonlight stroll along the shore of the Mediterranean after supper. But a brisk wind greeted us as we stepped out onto the beautiful deck outside, and we discovered we were situated on a cliff overlooking the shore some 150 feet below. When a cold rain started, we decided to abandon the idea and regroup to get ourselves organized for the long day of touring which would begin early tomorrow.

All of us would be receiving a wake-up call at 6:00, but I found myself awake at about 2:15. I wasn't sure whether the constant rushing sound I was now conscious of was the wind howling or the waves on the shore, but it was intrusive and, in combination with jet lag, kept me from sleeping. Do I just lie here or should I get up, early as it is, and start my morning routine? The first faint streaks of dawn were the last thing I remember when I heard a knock at the door. This must be the way they make their wake-up call, I thought. Through the door I called "thank you" and the voice came back "We've been worried about you." It was Mickey. Sunlight was streaming into the room. We had 20 minutes to be on the bus!

Our wake-up call never came, and I must have dozed off after my bout with insomnia. At home my circadian rhythms ordinarily have me awake within a few minutes of the same time each morning, without an alarm clock. We had a travel alarm along with us, but Sharlyn couldn't find the batteries for it right off, so we decided we probably wouldn't need it anyway. Now we were frantically throwing toothpaste and brushes, shave cream, soap and dirty underwear back into suitcases as we scrambled in all directions to make it downstairs on time. Our luggage was supposed to have been set outside the door before breakfast to be picked up by the porters and loaded onto the bus, so we would lose even more time as we now became responsible for this ourselves. This was Wednesday morning, November 7, we missed breakfast, and it was not a good start to our tour.

Rula was teaching us a few words of Hebrew as we traveled down highway 2 out of Netanya. Boker tov ("good morning") we all repeated in unison, and toda raba ("thank you"). For its size Israel is extremely diverse topographically, and we were now passing through the lush coastal Plain of Sharon. Produce is the number one industry of the land, and we were seeing many greenhouses growing an assortment of vegetables year round. Vineyards and banana plantations were in abundance, as well as groves of mangoes, oranges and other citrus. Each cluster of bananas was covered with a plastic bag, some blue, some gray. Rula claimed that this produced blue bananas, which some of us accepted quizzically until she cracked a smile and explained that no, this protected them from pests and allowed the growers to control the ripening rate. The banana tree dies after producing its fruit, and a new shoot emerges in a few months from the root.

Our highway followed one of two ancient routes which once connected the two great civilizations of Egypt to the south and Mesopotamia to the north. This one was the Via Maris ("way of the sea") along the Mediterranean, the other the famed Kings Highway of Solomon roughly parallel to it some 40 or 50 kilometers to the east. Both met at Damascus, from where a single route continued northward and eastward through the remainder of the Fertile Crescent. Soon we reached the first stop on our tour, the site of Herod's once luxurious palace at Caesarea. Tom, now retired as a director of parks and recreation near St. Louis, was also interested to learn the only golf course in Israel is located here.

While excavation and reconstruction are still underway, much of the structure which now lies in ruins has been exposed. Columns, arches, capital stones, and huge building blocks have slowly emerged from the sand, as workmen reconstruct this magnificent resort on the seashore. The Romans had to have their horse races, so the hippodrome stands there today completely unearthed, as if ready for the trumpets and pageantry to begin. We sat on the stone seats of the theater high above the stage below. Rula explained that because it is semicircular this is a theater, not an amphitheater, which is circular. When she called for a volunteer for a demonstration of its acoustics, I descended to the stage below. Everyone said they could hear me clearly, but my performance as a Roman ham did not get good reviews.

When I saw black numbers painted on each stone seat, I was impressed with how close their theater ticket system must have been to ours today and how well preserved those numbers were. But wait a minute, these were Arabic numerals--in a Roman theater. We soon found out that the theater is in modern use again for live concerts.

Today the audience overlooks the Mediterranean directly, but originally a high stone wall behind the stage served as both an acoustical backdrop and a screen from the distractions of the waves and activities along the shore.

Artifacts lie everywhere, and to my great surprise we were allowed to pick up whatever we found. Shards of pottery were in abundance, so I pocketed a small piece which Rula assured me had an ancient origin. Pastor Paul, a recognized scholar of antiquities and author of *Pathways to Palestine*, found a green piece of genuine Roman glass from the first century. As I wandered over the rough stone pathways where ancient buildings once stood, I came across a large stone slab with the following chiseled inscription:

S TIBERIEVM

PONTIVS PILATVS

PRAEFECTVS IVDAEAE

Rula had almost forgotten to show us, but this is an exact replica of the only extant primary source which mentions Pontius Pilate as Prefect of Judea. The original stone is housed in the Museum of Caesarea Antiquities.

A short bus ride away we came to one of the most famous and photographed sites in Israel--a half-mile section of the ancient Roman aqueduct system. Originally 16 miles long, it brought fresh water from the springs of Mt. Carmel to Caesarea. Its proximity to the shore also gave us our first opportunity to dip our toes into the Mediterranean. It occurred to me as I doffed my shoes and rolled up my pants that some 2000 years later another Gentile was about to step into the same waters as many Romans did on this very spot. Back on the bus, Pastor Paul was having fun asking each person coming aboard whether they had climbed up the steps to see the dual channels on top of the aqueduct. Of course nearly everyone had, and with a straight face he maintained that they were for hot and cold running water.

We said farewell to the beautiful Mediterranean and turned to the east. Our next stop along the Via Maris took us to the top of Mt. Carmel. Actually, Carm-El ("vineyard of God") is not a single mountain, but a range of mountains extending from the point of land near present-day Haifa southeastward along the Jezreel Valley. From the Carmelite monastery which stands on top today we had a spectacular view across the valley to the town of Nazareth and Mt. Tabor (believed by some to be the mount of the Transfiguration described in Matthew 17), with Mt. Hermon dimly visible in the distance. A statue of Elijah wielding a well-worn sword over a slain false prophet has been erected in the courtyard to commemorate his standoff with the prophets of Ba-al near here, as described in I Kings 18.

Near the base of this statue was a small plaque with a Bible verse in English and German. Pastor Paul rubbed the mud from the lower corner of it to reveal the initials M.B., and asked those of us who saw him do that how he knew they were there. He told us we would be seeing these plaques quoting an appropriate verse or meditation (sometimes including Latin) at sites all over Israel. After seeing them himself on earlier visits, he was curious about the initials and launched his own private quest to determine their meaning. After some research, he learned they stand for Mother Bernice, an early 20th century nun who originated the project.

We were in the area which would have been known as Samaria during the time of the kings of Israel and into New Testament times. When the highway we traveled near En-Ha-Shofet was built a few years ago, the road crew cutting through the rock discovered the ancient tombs of a family who once lived here. The bones have been removed for study and respectful preservation, but the open tombs, complete with the large rolling stones to close them, stand at the side of the road inviting anyone passing by to stop and look inside. As I ducked through the narrow opening, I expected to see a single tomb, but discovered instead a chain of shafts with several cells in each for the members of an extended family.

As we passed into the region of Galilee now, Rula pointed out a kibbutz. Before 1948, when Israel became a nation, the Jews had no cities of their own, so they congregated into quasi-cities called kibbutzim. A kibbutz is a kind of commune or settlement of families who raise livestock and farm the land with collective home rule;

anyone is free to leave at any time, but while there, is subject to a kind of socialism where work and reward are shared. The architecture of the buildings in a particular community sometimes betrays the ethnicity of its inhabitants, and Rula could tell the next village was Druze. The Druze are an offshoot of the Muslims who have rejected some of the traditional teachings and adopted others, such as reincarnation. Because the Jews, Muslims, and Christians each have a different day of worship, schooling in Israel is segregated. Israelis follow a Sunday-Thursday schedule, while a separate system for Muslims and Christians together meets Monday-Thursday and Saturday.

After a time we arrived at the site of Megiddo, or Tel-Megiddo. A tel is a mound where multiple civilizations have been built one on top of another, and some of them reach astonishing heights. Structures in the ancient world were built of stone, and when a city was destroyed, there were no bulldozers to clear the rubble, so it was easier to build up from whatever lay there already. Here at Megiddo archaeologists have identified a stack of 25 distinct civilizations--a city built, destroyed, and rebuilt 25 times! The reason for this is the strategic location of this site on the Via Maris. Whoever controlled Megiddo could exact a toll from the steady stream of merchants passing through this valley between Egypt and the kingdoms of the East.

We walked a gravel path to the top. A palace built by Solomon once stood here, and excavations have produced a little evidence of his fabulous wealth. We saw the foundations of a large stable, which may have been constructed for the 1000 horses he kept here or may have been the work of Ahab several generations later. Nearby also was a stone manger of the type in which the baby Jesus was laid. Yes, the manger was stone, not wooden--the kind we see so often in our American crèches. As we know from I Kings 9, heavy levies were placed on the citizenry to build this and many such palaces, but much revenue could also be generated from the military control over Megiddo Solomon enjoyed throughout his reign. We also saw the cavernous grain silo which has been unearthed, with its two staircases to provide a different route into and out of the grain store. We descended the 183 steps into the tunnel Ahab carved to bring the water supply inside the city walls in readiness for siege.

Because of the frequent convergence of kings and armies at Megiddo, it is also known as Armageddon, the final great battle of annihilation described in Revelation 16. Rula was telling us that many Christians believe this to be the actual location where Armageddon would be fought at the end of time. The Armageddon of Revelation, however, is on a spiritual plane and is never fought. We read in verse 17 that just as Satan has amassed all his forces of evil to destroy the last remnant of the Church on earth to achieve victory, God booms out from heaven that it is all over and doesn't allow the battle to take place. I decided not to embarrass Rula or myself by introducing what I perceived to be controversy.

It was lunch time, so we stopped at the village of Mizra, the only place in Israel where it is possible to buy pork. The entrance to the restaurant routed us through a small grocery store stocked with cheese, salami and ham from the deli, fresh produce, bread, drinks and packaged snack foods. One rule Pastor Paul urged us to follow was not to drink the tap water--not that it was bad, but just that our systems were not used to it. Most people would probably not react adversely, but until we had enough of the local product in our systems through tea and coffee, we should stave off dysentery with bottled water. Even fresh produce that might have been washed in their water was to be avoided. So Sharlyn picked up a package of figs, and everyone paid the outlandish price of two dollars a bottle for water or soft drinks from this little store.

After lunch we drove a short distance to Nazareth (nazaret meaning "lily" or "offspring"), situated high on the slopes of the mountain above the restaurant. With a population of 100,000, the Nazareth of today is really two cities, lower Nazareth for the Palestinian Muslims and upper Nazareth for Israeli Jews. As our tour bus labored up the steep incline snaking its way up the rugged terrain, Rula pointed out the high cliff thought to be the "brow of the hill" where the synagogue rulers described in Luke 4 intended to cast Jesus down.

There is also an apocryphal tradition that there were two Annunciations in this city. The first took place when the angel appeared to Mary as she came to the spring for water. She was so startled by this encounter that she ran home, where the second Annunciation took place. While the Roman Catholics have built a church over the house of Mary, the largest church in Israel, we visited the beautiful Greek Orthodox church erected over the place where the spring is today. From this 100-year-old church we could peer through glass down to the excavations of an earlier church dating back to the Byzantine era. Appropriately enough, a local shopkeeper was hawking bottled spring water for "one dolla" as we exited the church, and, as encouraged by the admonishment of Pastor Paul, many bottles of it were sold to the members of our group. In other shops here were tiny ornate tear bottles for sale, from the ancient custom of collecting the tears of the mourners to be buried with the dead mentioned in Psalm 56.

As if following the route of Jesus as he left his home town to begin his ministry, we too now departed Nazareth for the place of his first miracle, the changing of water into wine at the marriage described in John 2. Here at Cana the home of a wealthy person has been excavated which would have been large enough to accommodate these festivities. Some of the gold, silver and jewels that a rich man would store were found in one of the ancient rooms, but more convincing was the recent discovery of one of the six "water pots of stone."

In the picture in my mind of this account, the water pots were carried to the "governor of the feast" to sample, but when we saw the huge size of the stone block in which the "jar" was carved, that picture was shattered as I recognized the impossibility of carrying it anywhere by ordinary means. A more careful reading simply says they were told to "draw out now" from the jars. A small shop outside the chapel erected over the site of the home was selling bottles of wine from Cana, so how could we resist that opportunity? We bought two--even though they were not claiming it was the same wine Jesus made.

It was at the rest break at Cana that I first encountered the spartan accommodations a tourist might discover at a public rest room. I could probably do without a seat on the cold porcelain, but this one was also open to a small courtyard with no door! Worse yet, it had no toilet paper, and I needed some. What was I to do? The urgency of my predicament, the price of regularity, prompted me to take the chance that someone might happen along before I could finish, and I had in my pockets two paper napkins from lunch. So I hurried as fast as I could, but as I pushed the handle to flush, I thought of the poor Canan plumber who was probably now going to wonder who it was that could be so inconsiderate as to flush table napkins down the toilet.

Back on the bus, we continued our journey eastward through Galilee. As we crested a hill just west of the city of Tiberias, there it was--the sight I most wanted to see in Israel. We caught our first glimpse of the Sea of Galilee lying before us in the valley below. Familiar as I was with its size, I was still surprised I could view the entire body of water all at once. The hour was approaching sunset, and the beauty of those purple and orange shadows along the famous shoreline made a permanent imprint on my memory. On our descent into the city we passed the sign along the roadside marking sea level. Yes, the Sea of Galilee is some 600 feet below sea level.

We would be staying overnight in Tiberias, but first we were going to see one of the country's primary industries. While it has no diamonds of its own, Israel represents some 65% of the world's diamond cutting business. When our bus arrived at the chain-link and barbed-wire gate of a fortified facility, I thought we were entering a military base. It was the Caprice Diamond Center. After a short video and a tour of the sorting, cutting, polishing, and mounting operations, we found out why we really were welcomed there, as they ushered us into their showroom.

The suave sales team who greeted us were very happy to remind us how fortunate we were to have this opportunity to try on Israeli jewelry (or "jewlery," as Rula called it). My ignorance about gems gleamed brightly, as I was surprised to learn that there are some 5000 grades of diamonds. Most come from the Kimberly mines of South Africa, but the fact that Australia furnishes one-third of the world's supply raised my eyebrows. Sharlyn and I felt fairly secure in our resistance to the lure of their diamonds, but we melted when they showed us the gemstone which is found only in Israel. Called Eilat Stone for the location of the King Solomon mines near the city of Eilat on the Red Sea, the gem is unique in the world for the veins of turquoise, lapis lazuli, and malachite that converge to form it. Sharlyn had Retta in mind for a gift, but she did an admirable job of resisting the high pressure of the young lady showing us earrings, brooches, rings, and bracelets until just the right necklace she wanted came along.

I wasn't sure we would ever get one member of our group, Jane Irving, out of that place (to the chagrin of her husband Dick too), so it was dark when we left the diamond factory to board the bus for our first night at the Carmel Jordan River Hotel here in Tiberias. Jesus never set foot in this ancient city on the western shore of the Sea of Galilee because in the first century it was Roman and unclean to the Jews. The lights of new Tiberias were arrayed high above us on the steep slopes of the shore here as we stepped off the bus into old Tiberias, so weary from our first incredibly memorable day, we could scarcely recall how it began.

Pastor Paul remembered a shop near the water's edge that specialized in almonds, hazel nuts and other specialties. As if we still had any energy left, he asked us if we felt like taking an evening stroll along the shops of Tiberias and then stop for a beverage and some nuts to munch on over conversation. Most of us were game for adventure, so he pooled a dollar from each of us and off we went. At first he thought we were on the wrong street, but then realized the shop had gone out of business. A beauty salon now stood at that location. We were to see this scene over and over on our tour, as one business after another indicated signs of suffering the effects of the poor economy.

Tourism is the number two industry in Israel, and the Palestinian intifadah ("uprising") a year ago has taken its toll on every sector of society--brand new hotels closed for lack of occupants, shops standing chained and dark, and a plethora of goods standing unsold. Israeli and Palestinian alike recognize the significance of its effects, and everywhere we went, merchants pleaded with us not only to buy but to spread the word back home that it was safe to travel to Israel.

What was bad for them, however, was wonderful for us. Foremost was the paradox of safety amid the daily potential for outbreaks of violence around us. The word was out--don't touch the tourists. Secondly, there were some good bargains to be had. If an item laid on your arm didn't impress you, the merchant would offer two for the same price--or three. Unfortunately, most of the time we didn't need one. Another huge advantage of the downturn was the absence of throngs and long lines at the sites we visited, especially the most popular ones. Pastor Paul's wife Sylvia gasped as we entered this or that place to find *no one* inside. This place was packed with people last time, she would recall.

The next morning, Thursday, November 8, I looked out our seventh floor window just before the sun broke over the horizon. Silhouetted on the water of the Sea of Galilee below was a boat which exactly fit the picture I always had of the craft Peter and Andrew must have used in their fishing business on this very lake. I didn't know it at the time, but it was an exact replica of a first century relic found nearly intact at the bottom of the Sea and was the very boat (the "Jesus boat") we would be aboard right after breakfast. We were still adjusting to the time difference, but our wake-up call came through on schedule this time.

Unlike the boat used by Zebedee and his sons, this one was motorized. In minutes we reached the center of the Sea, shut the engines down and drifted in solitude. Rula was filling in details as we soaked up the experience. While in the New Testament we find it called the Sea of Tiberias, the Old Testament refers to this body of water as Chinnereth ("harp"), derived from its harp-like shape. Only seven miles from east to west and thirteen north to south, it is not really a sea at all--or even a very big lake.

In its third year of serious drought, it is still 120 feet deep but according to one source 2.14 meters below "normal" levels, and we saw pathetic evidence of this along the shore where many huge craft lay on their sides, stranded by the receding waterline. Drinking water for much of the land comes from the Sea of Galilee, which in turn depends on runoff from Mt. Hermon 40 kilometers to the north. Average rainfall there is 70 inches per year, 45 in upper Galilee, 30 in lower Galilee, 20 south toward Jerusalem and down to only 4 in the Negev in the southern extremes.

From our position in the center of the lake we could see the high slopes of the Golan to the east, the city of Magdala ("watch tower") on the northwest shore (where its most famous resident Mary the Magdalene was from), and just west and south of that the Valley of the Winds. This is the narrow funnel-shaped canyon that functions like a natural bellows to turn a breeze into a gale in minutes (exactly what happened in the account of Matthew 8). After our devotions, prayer and song, we started the engines and headed for shore to explore by bus the places we could see from the water.

Travel in almost any direction from the Sea of Galilee is a steep climb, and our tour bus was soon chugging its way slowly up the hills to the north. Even today these hills are much the way they must have been when our Lord walked through them. Big black basalt boulders are strewn everywhere, evidence of volcanic activity centuries ago oriented near the peaks to the west of the Valley of the Winds. The terrain is so rocky in this region that Mark Twain once reported that the sheep here eat gravel. "They must," he quipped, "because that's all there is to eat."

When we reached the top of the sharp incline we had been climbing, we came to the place where Jesus is said to have addressed the crowd with his Sermon on the Mount (Rula said from Mark 5, but she meant Matthew 5). It is known as the Mount of Beatitudes, from the Latin for "blessed," for the famous verses that begin his lengthy discourse ("Blessed are the poor in spirit..., Blessed are they that mourn..."). The question often arises how Jesus could be heard by the large crowd that sat on this hillside. Rula explained this is a natural amphitheater, with superb acoustics to amplify the human voice. An octagonal Roman Catholic church (for the eight beatitudes) has been erected here, with a lush garden overlooking the shore of the Sea of Galilee far below. The garden was not only extraordinarily beautiful but remarkably peaceful, and we planned to spend some time here in devotion and meditation.

Communion was offered to those who chose to participate, using olive wood cups and wine from Cana, and Pastor Paul took the opportunity to tell us a bit of his radio ministry. He pointed out that per capita wealth in the United States is nine times greater than Israel or any other country of the world and had been pondering for some time why this is. Because Americans are somehow better? Because God loves Americans more? Certainly not. One day he was in the midst of a broadcast when the answer struck him, and he interrupted himself in mid-sentence to explain to his radio audience. Luke 12 spells it out: "To whomsoever much is given, of him shall much be required." We are expected to use that wealth to share the Gospel. Even if we tithe (and many do not), is that enough? Do we need $100,000 to live on? Do we need a Mercedes or BMW, much less one of each? What is 10% in view of this abundance? If Americans were to give 50%, their standard of living would still be far above the rest of the world, and the perennial cry by our missions for funding would go a long way toward an answer. If we do not, we can expect the terrorisms to continue, as God's patience runs out, waiting for repentance from our poor stewardship.

As we were boarding the bus for our next stop we passed a citrus stand selling either a cup of freshly squeezed orange juice or four oranges for a dollar. Of course, we chose oranges freshly picked from the groves nearby. Near the base of the Mount of Beatitudes is Tabgha, the probable site where Jesus fed the multitude of 5000 (the only miracle except for the resurrection recounted in all four Gospels). Tabgha is an Arabic corruption of the Hebrew word Heptapegon ("seven springs"). The present-day Church of the Fish and the Loaves was built 100 years ago on this site by the Benedictines, on top of the fourth century structure built by the Christians, destroyed by the Byzantines, rebuilt by the Crusaders in the 11th century and destroyed by the Muslims in the 13th. Inside at the altar is the famous mosaic of two fishes and four loaves (in one version the fifth loaf is Christ himself, in another a real loaf is placed on the altar next to it) replicated on pottery, tee shirts, plates, mugs and glassware all over.

In the courtyard here at Tabgha was a fifth century baptismal font which argues against immersion as a doctrinal necessity. This stone basin would simply not be large enough. While the early Christians were not opposed to immersion, the notion that it is required came along only as recently as the 19th century. Also in the courtyard was a well-preserved old olive press. Later in Capernaum we would be seeing accessory stone equipment used in the entire olive process.

The olive tree is ubiquitous in the land and has been a symbol of peace since the dove returned to Noah's ark with the olive leaf (Genesis 8). Some of the trees we were seeing were in a sense actually hundreds of years old, as the root never dies. Occasionally we would see an old tree which appeared dead with a new shoot emerging from the base. No part of the tree is wasted. We saw olive-wood carvings in shops everywhere, but the wood is so oily that it must dry for six years before it can be used. Although the olive fruit is often picked green, it is bitter and hard and must be cooked or soaked for several months before it becomes edible.

The olive harvest was occurring right about the time we were there, but we were surprised how infrequently we could see any black on the trees we saw. When ripe, the olive is processed in four grades: After pressing for 20 minutes, the first oil produced is for use in the temple and ritual blessings (the first fruit). After four hours the oil produced is used for cooking, after six hours for olive oil soap, and the residue after eight hours as fuel for lamps. Even the pits are not wasted, as they are strung into necklaces or rosaries, or are ground up by the indigent and burned for heating.

As we were leaving, we passed a souvenir stand selling postcards, trinkets and knickknacks. Hanging on a rack outside we spied baseball caps each with a little solar-powered fan to cool your face built into the visor. We had already heard "Avanti" from the bus, yet the novelty of such a thing captured our fancy as we thought of Austin and Retta sitting in the hot sun at Virginia Tech football games. Even though it wasn't very representative of Israel, we quickly bought two.

A very short distance away the bus stopped again at the place where seven springs feed into the Sea of Galilee. The relatively warm waters from these springs attract fish, and this spot was a favorite haunt for John, Peter and the other disciples who depended on them for their livelihood. Sylvia was shocked to see the shoreline receded some 100 yards away from where it was the last time she visited here. It was a chance for us to dip our feet into the Sea of Galilee and to pick up stones, shells, and water itself as mementos.

It was here that Jesus appeared to the disciples for the third time after his resurrection (John 21). The place is known as the Primacy of St. Peter, because it was Peter who had denied Jesus three times during His arraignment, and here Jesus was giving Simon Peter the charge to "feed my sheep" with reassurances of His grace in restoring his apostleship. On the grounds of a small chapel on the shore is a statue of Peter on his knees with Jesus. Outside the chapel wall and continuing under the wall and into the chapel is the Mensa Christi ("table of Christ"), a large flat rock which some believe held the coals on which Jesus was cooking fish as the disciples dragged their catch of 153 large fish to shore.

Not all fish caught by the disciples from these waters could be eaten. Unless it had scales, it was considered unclean. One of their favorites was the tilapia (the so-called "St. Peter's fish"), characterized by a large black spot on each side of its head. Legend says these marks originated when Peter's hand opened the fish's mouth to extract the coin for his taxes (Matthew 17). We were now going to taste some. We drove over to the Tanureen Restaurant in Magdala, where Rula had phoned ahead to expect 14 for lunch. When some members of our group found out the fish would be served with the head on, they decided to have schnitzel instead. Christy Schultz, who was particularly repulsed by those eyes staring off the plate, nearly wriggled out of her skin when she returned from the rest room to find someone had left the head from his lunch as a present for her. I know what you are thinking, but it was not I who did that.

After lunch we drove to Capernaum, the adopted home town of Jesus during his public ministry. It was no accident that Jesus chose a place along the busy commercial Via Maris corridor to make his headquarters. The hatred and rejection of Jesus by the rulers of the synagogues of Capernaum and two other cities of their time was so intense that he cursed them (Matthew 11)--and Jesus uses no idle words to curse something. These cities were obliterated so completely that it is only now, 2000 years later, that they have been found. A boat-shaped church stands today over the excavated foundations of a fifth century circular chapel built on top of an octagonal fourth century Christian gathering place, which in turn was built atop a multi-room house thought to be that of Peter, his wife and her mother. Nearby, the pillars and columns of a synagogue have been unearthed, beneath which lies the exposed mosaic floor of an even older synagogue which may have been the synagogue of Jairus (Luke 8) built by the centurion (Luke 7).

The other two cities cursed by Jesus were Korazim (the Chorazin of Matthew 11) and Bethsaida, home of Philip, Nathaniel and Andrew. This curse still prevails today, as they remain desolate and uninhabited. Excavations at both sites are progressing equally, so we would see only Korazim (besides, Bethsaida, as I found out later, is still laced with land mines left over from the Six Day War in 1967). We strolled among the partially standing walls of black basalt, an archway or two still intact, steps now leading to nowhere, and a miqvah, our first encounter with the small rectangular cavity of stone, sometimes with a ramp or steps leading into it, that served as a ritual bath in an ancient home. Only fresh rain water could be used to fill it, a precious commodity for a miqvah in the arid regions we would see tomorrow. Rula pointed out several Zizyphus spina christi trees to us, whose thorny branches are thought to be those used to weave the crown of thorns (Matthew 27). We were tempted to break off a twig from the live tree as a souvenir, but there were enough dead branches lying underneath the tree to provide a piece for each of us.

As we rounded the northeast coast of the Sea of Galilee, we came to the foothills of the Golan. Tensions with Syria and land mines would prevent us from venturing northward into the region of Caesarea Philippi and Mt. Hermon. This is also territory seized by Israel in 1967 and where Peter had expressed his steadfast conviction that Jesus is the Messiah (Mark 8). Whoever has control of the Golan Heights controls the water supply for Israel. The snows of Mt. Hermon in winter and rainfall in summer account for much of the annual tally, and this region produces the best cherries and apples of the land. We were now crossing the bridge over the Jordan River at its inlet to the Sea of Galilee. The Waters of Merom, a lagoon to the north seen on most Biblical maps, has been drained today for irrigation and fresh drinking water.

We turned south now along the east side of the Sea of Galilee and passed the "wilderness" of Tel-Hadar ("hill of glory") where Jesus fed 4000 people from seven loaves and a few small fish (Mark 8). We stopped at Kursi, the site of the Gadarene demoniac of Mark 5 and Luke 8 (Matthew 8 says there were two) who lived in the limestone caves among the tombs, terrorizing the townspeople. The ruins of a basilica rebuilt by the Crusaders lie here today, but halfway up the mountainside we could see the outlines of work underway to expand recent discoveries of the tombs. Because of the lower levels of the water now, the shoreline is probably less precipitous today than it was in the time of the ancient Gentiles mentioned in this account, but we could still envision the swine tumbling down these steep slopes into the Sea.

Continuing southward along the east coast, we came to the outlet of the Sea of Galilee into the Jordan River. For many years this was touted as the place where Jesus was baptized by John the Baptist. Scholars today, however, are fairly well agreed that this event more likely occurred as much as 50 or 60 kilometers south of here. The Jordanians, on whose land that probable spot rests, are taking advantage of its new significance with aggressive marketing to get the tourists to come over and take a look. Instead, we would be spending some time here at the traditional spot.

So many people come here to be baptized or consecrated that steps, ramps and handrails have been constructed which lead into the water. White robes can be rented, and changing rooms were available for a shekel. We observed two strong white-robed men in the water who pinched the nostrils of each member of one equally white-robed group as they tipped them quickly backwards under water. Pastor Paul consecrated any of us who wanted to reconfirm our faith, and I filled a small bottle with a sample of the water. It was the most inexpensive souvenir we brought home.

A short drive back to Tiberias completed our circle around the Sea of Galilee and it was dark as we trudged back to our room laden with memories. On our first evening here I had seen a place at the edge of the water called The Galilee Experience. The name sounded like a night club to me, and its appearance had a certain tell-tale dazzle that confirmed it, so I took little notice. I was more than surprised, therefore, to hear Rula ask if anyone was interested in accompanying her to Galilee Experience tonight after supper.

It turns out the place is a little theater that has a video about the area we are visiting and a live presentation by the Messianic Jews (a sect which accepts Jesus as the Messiah) who run it. The extensive gift shop located here had many items with an interesting admixture of Jewish and Christian themes, and the owner and his staff were more than willing to remain open for as long as we were willing to look around. We were rubbing shoulders in the aisles with another tour group led by one of their Messianics, and, while Sharlyn browsed around, I struck up a conversation with one of their members from Colorado, while his wife browsed around. Their tour must have paralleled ours, as I would be seeing him and their blue yomicha-wearing leader several more times in the next few days.

The next morning, Friday, November 9, I was awake at first light and decided to get some fresh air on a walk before breakfast. I wanted to take in some ordinary sights of the city, so I took our camera through the streets leading away from the direction we had already seen. Among the locksmith, nail salon, clothing and appliance shops I passed, I came across a restaurant with the unlikely name "El Gaucho." As if embarrassed by its own name, and as if hastily appended for clarification and reassurance, the word "kosher" was on the marquis as well.

Our last look at Galilee ever was poignant, as we now traveled highway 90, the longest in Israel, stretching from Metulla near the border with Lebanon to Eilat. Jerusalem is 150 kilometers south from Tiberias, so we would be on the bus quite a bit today, as we rode along the belvoir ("beautiful view") of the Jordan River. This fecund valley has a number of fish farms, besides farm after farm of its vegetables, citrus and grapes, as many workers of the kibbutzim and their families were visible harvesting and tilling. Rula even promised we would be seeing a raisin tree along here. It took a minute for that to sink in, as she winked that that was just a check to see if we were still awake.

The barbed and electrified fence along the east side of the highway was a reminder of the border with Jordan, and beyond it in many places was an "island of peace," the band of no-man's land serving as a buffer zone between the two countries. There is calm in Jordan today with its neighbor to the west, as the result of a series of peace agreements in recent years, but each side keeps a wary eye on the other, hoping the fragile tranquility will last. We passed the ruins of a fortress built by the Crusaders, and before long we reached our first stop at Bet-She'an ("house of rest").

A huge mound here telegraphed its historical and strategic significance. Like Megiddo, every nation and civilization had settled here, each building on top of its vanquished predecessor. It lies on the Kings Highway and represented to the ancients the focal point for control of the source of water from the mountains of Gilboa we could see in the distance. Once occupied by the Philistines, this was the Bethshan of I Samuel 31, where Saul's headless body was impaled on the wall as a trophy of victory after the battle of Gilboa.

Bet-She'an was also one of the Decapolis, the league of ten cities established by the Romans, as attested by the hippodrome that first greeted us as we drove up. The Romans usually built a wide arched avenue, called the cardo ("heart"), running north to south through the heart of their cities. Merchants would set up their bazaars along the cardo, and much of the commerce of the city stemmed from it. Much of the once beautiful cardo here has been unearthed now, and we marveled at the extent of the aqueducts, sewers, cisterns and public baths of their ancient water system. Huge columns and chiseled capitals litter the area, as evidence of the arcades and temples which once stood here.

Work is just beginning high up on the rest of the tel, and the steps leading to the top were beckoning for us to explore. I was curious what was up there, but frankly I was hoping the altitude would also offer some relief from the swarm of flies that plagued us from the first moment we stepped off the bus. It didn't. Renee Neddermeyer and her two daughters Ashley and Christy, as well as Tom and Mickey might have had the same idea, as we all scrambled up the stony path to the top of the mound. Sharlyn and Ellen Hooker, another member of our group, decided the loose rubble of the trail was too treacherous and waited below. Temperatures in Galilee had been very comfortably in the 70s most of the time, but as we approached the desert regions of the south, the thermometer was ratcheting its way into the 80s--and with that came these pests.

It wasn't that they were biting, but their persistence in landing on my neck and ear tips was most annoying. I finally pulled my cap over my ears raw from swatting and flicking and my collar up around my neck, but they still found my forehead, nose, cheeks and eyes just as much to their taste. After a quick look at the walls of many stone buildings and rooms just beginning to emerge from the top of the tel, I rejoined Sharlyn and Ellen for the long walk back to the gate. Here we found Pastor Paul, Sylvia and Rula sipping beer in the shade of the souvenir stand. Having seen it many times before, they took advantage of the chance to relax while the rest of us scrambled around the site.

We hadn't noticed it, but we were in a sensitive area--the famous West Bank, territory Israel had also seized in the 1967 war. The reason we hadn't noticed is that we had been in zone C, entirely occupied and controlled by the Israelis. Soon we came to a checkpoint, which marked our entry into zone B, jointly occupied by Israelis and Palestinians. The Israelis have military control of zone B but have agreed to give the Palestinians civil control. For the first time we started to see the white license plates of Palestinian cars among the yellow ones we had been seeing until now. Occasionally we noticed a red triangle warning of the active land mines which still lie buried along the border with Jordan. We tensed a bit whenever we saw a jeep or personnel carrier bearing the flag and markings of the UN pass our tour bus, but they were on routine maneuvers and represented no threat.

As we approached zone A, which is occupied and controlled militarily and civilly by the Palestinians, we had to tiptoe past the road leading to Jericho. This was a disappointment, but the road was barricaded, as contention there today would prevent us from seeing the phenomenal archaeological excavations of one of the oldest cities in the world. Jericho is actually three cities. The first was the Jericho of Joshua, whose marching around its fortifications at the direction of God in the account of Joshua 6 caused the massive stone walls to fall outward. If we had been able to see it, the tel would have revealed civilizations that occupied this site before Joshua arrived. Because the place was cursed by God, the second Jericho was built not on top, but beside the first.

Again and again the city is mentioned in both the Old and New Testaments. Often referred to as an oasis in the desert, Jericho is fed by springs which once were too bitter for drinking until they were miraculously sweetened with salt by Elisha (II Kings 2). As we pass Jericho, we think of Zacchaeus, Bartimaeus and the Good Samaritan. Local residents passing Jericho today are more likely to think of the Palestinian casino located here. Austria funded its construction in return for 10% of the profits. The sycamore Zacchaeus climbed is gone too. Nobody we asked could ever remember seeing one.

Eastward on our left were the mountains of Moab, among them Mt. Nebo, the peak from which Moses was allowed to view the promised land but not enter it. After passing the next checkpoint marking zone A, our route came to a T. I wish I had known it was coming, because I missed an opportunity to photograph what the locals would regard as something quite unremarkable. Where else on earth would I see a road sign in three languages pointing left to the Dead Sea and right to Jerusalem? Even worse, Sunday I would miss the one which had arrows pointing to Jerusalem, Jericho and the Dead Sea--all three on the same signpost! It's still there in memory, but, alas, not on film.

After traveling south all morning, we now turned west and began our long ascent toward Jerusalem. Our course along the Jordan had taken us close to the lowest point on earth, and now we were climbing from some 1200 feet below sea level to 2800 feet above. These were the hills of Judea so familiar to David. I didn't know the Valley of the Shadow of Death in his Psalm 23 was an actual place, but Rula pointed it out to us. We passed the encampments of Bedouins visible along the highway and off into the hills, distinctively characterized by small herds of camels or goats next to a dilapidated tent or other kind of shelter that could be quickly dismantled according to the vicissitudes of their ancient nomadic existence. Pastor Paul said a white flag seen waving from the doorway was a signal from the head of the house that he had a daughter who had reached puberty. Suitors scrutinized by him were each allowed to spend a night with her until she selected one to marry.

Although we were heading toward Jerusalem, we would be skirting the edge of the holy city to get to Bethlehem yet before lunch. If our tour had been two weeks or so earlier, Bethlehem would have been off limits, as tanks were rumbling through the streets to quell disorder there. As it was, tensions were high, and we would be improvising. Bethlehem is solidly in Palestinian hands, and Rula has a good Palestinian friend who owns the Bethlehem Souvenir Center just inside the boundary between Israeli and Palestinian territory south of Jerusalem. She had persuaded him to meet us at this checkpoint with vans to transport us to the relatively safe haven of his large store. The plan was to whisk us from there over to the Church of the Nativity some three or four kilometers away.

There was not a sound on the bus as we approached the checkpoint, but Ahmad said a word or two in Arabic through the window to the guards, and to our surprise they waved our bus through with a friendly greeting and a smile. Whoever had been praying for us back home got an answer in that moment. Not long ago Bethlehem was still a stronghold of Christianity in a land where Christians are a tiny minority, but in recent years many of them have been forced out, as their businesses are boycotted, permits are revoked, and civil rights become more and more elusive. Where they once numbered almost 100%, they have been overrun by Muslims now numbering about 70% of the population.

Rula had been advising us to hold off on souvenirs until we reach Bethlehem, and now the floodgates were opened to us. One incentive for us was the absence of the VAT (value added tax) here, for whatever reason. Mickey and Jane, who always came back to the bus at every rest stop with several bags from the souvenir shop, had a jamboree in this store. Sharlyn and I wanted a nice hand carved olive wood crèche as a gift for Thomas and found something close to what we had in mind, as well as gifts for Angela and Austin and token gifts for members of our carpool who would have to suffer through the tales of our exploits upon our return. As we tallied up our purchases in preparation for lunch at the sandwich shop next door, we were not prepared for what happened next.

Our arrival had not escaped the notice of several Palestinian street vendors. We had simply intended to leave our purchases on the bus, then pick up a sandwich at the little shop next door. But I was met at the door by one of these vendors, who laid a necklace of polished stones on my arm. "For you. Five dolla," he said. I politely refused. "Two for five dolla." Again I refused. "I give to you. Take." I wouldn't accept it. He tried again and again with different merchandise as I struggled to keep moving toward the bus. Sharlyn, who had been right behind me, got separated from me as she fought her own battle with another vendor. The vendors descended on each member of our group emerging from the building like the birds in Hitchcock's film.

As I finally reached the steps of the bus, Sharlyn was brushing past me, and I was relieved to see she made it safely aboard. But as I was disentangling myself from my antagonist, I was shocked to see her come back off the bus with a ten-dollar bill. She was about to hand it to her vendor when I said no. "She promise, she promise, she promise," her vendor yelled at me. She was buying the necklace of hematite my vendor was trying to sell me. When he saw she was buying it, my vendor, inches from my face, shouted, "Why you make trouble for me? You buy from him. You make trouble for me." Worse, as he tried to lay another necklace on my arm, I pulled away and the necklace fell to the ground. I was sure violence would ensue. As he bent to pick it up, I tossed a quick "sorry" over my shoulder as I leapt aboard the bus. I expected him to be at my heels, but he seemed to respect the bus as some kind of diplomatic territory and did not pursue. I wasn't sure whether I had created an international incident, so I was not about to move from my seat until I had a minute to think this through a bit. Each person from our group coming onto the bus was wearing at least two necklaces, waving a string of postcards, sporting a hat, or toting an armload of toys.

We managed to reach the sandwich shop, where we had our first experience with falafel. A favorite in Israel--or at least at the places the tourists frequent--falafel is made from chick peas ground into a paste and then deep fried. The falafel is then crumbled into pita bread with lettuce and other veggies and sold as a sandwich. If you prefer meat in your sandwich, you might order shawarma instead. Thin slices of veal or lamb are stacked and roasted, then small pieces of that loaf of meat are shaved off and put into the sandwich instead of or in addition to the falafel. To save cost, many merchants stack turkey with a piece of lamb fat on the top, then roast the stack vertically, so the lamb flavoring drips down through the turkey beneath. The topic of conversation over lunch was, naturally, those street vendors, and Pastor Paul seemed to think Sharlyn got a pretty good deal paying 10 dollars for a necklace which would probably fetch 40 or 50 dollars back home. He said that mineral is always found in the vicinity of gold--find a vein of hematite and you know gold is not far away.

Our drivers were ready, so we packed into two vans for the ride into shelled out Bethlehem and over to the Church of the Nativity a few kilometers away. We stopped at Manger Square and crossed the street to the place where tradition says the Savior of the world was born. Rula pointed out the familiar Jerusalem cross atop the ancient building we had already seen on television in America at Christmas. The church here today is the only Christian structure in the land left standing by the Persians in the 13th century, although the original grand archway that once served as the entrance is bricked shut today except for a low, narrow doorway. When the conquering Persians saw the icon of turbaned Wise Men, they mistakenly assumed this was a Persian building and left it intact. The purpose of the reduced opening was to prevent soldiers from entering on horseback.

The nave of the church is cross-shaped, with the altar at the top of the shape. The base section of the cross is owned by the Roman Catholics, the left wing by the Armenian Orthodox Church, and the right by the Greek Orthodox Church. As we entered, the Armenian monks were chanting and praying, so Rula walked over to whisper something to the old Greek Orthodox patriarch standing in the opposite wing. He handed her a key, and she motioned for us to follow her down to the crypts below the sanctuary. Incredibly, the bones of infants murdered by Herod and those of mothers who defended them to the death lay strewn about in small chambers just as they had been discovered. Not far away was the small stone cell where St. Jerome spent the last 30 years or so of his life, and beneath which he is buried.

When the Armenian service was finished, we were escorted down a few ancient stone steps to a highly stylized room purporting to be the location where Jesus was born. A 14-point star marks the spot, representing the 14 generations from Adam to Abraham, Abraham to David, and David to Christ. In the center of the star is a cavity through which one can reach the bedrock of the cave in which the birth probably took place. Thankfully, it isn't meant to mark the exact spot but merely symbolizes that the actual birth took place somewhere within the confines of this very cavern. Off to one side of the star is a small marble grotto which boasts the site of the manger. This is nonsense. In fact, it is so shrouded with decorative lattice work, we weren't sure what was supposed to be manger and what was mere display. We had just begun to look around and take pictures when a priest burst in, and, with urgency in his voice, asked us to clear a path. Soon a heavily robed and mitered patriarch swinging a censor strode ceremonially past, chanted a few words at the star, and again at the grotto, and then he was gone. All quite interesting, but it had a little too much hokie flavor for my taste.

I was not disappointed, however. It was awesome actually to be in the ancient city where David once lived and where without question the Savior was born, even if we couldn't be sure exactly what took place where. As we exited the church, I saw someone familiar. It took me a few seconds to register who it was--and then I saw the others. The vendors had followed us over here! Hawking posters of Bethlehem, postcard packets, scarves, and those ubiquitous necklaces, they were more aggressive than ever. Somehow in the jostling and cacophony, Ellen lost the postcards she had just bought. She was convinced the men sold them to her, then stole them back. Whether that was true or not, she discovered that her notebook was gone too. At every site we visited, I had noticed Ellen scribbling away furiously, making copious notes to capture every detail. It also was the log for her photos too, and now it was gone. I was heartbroken for her. We had piled back into our vans, and our drivers were nervously fidgeting to get moving, but to this minute I still regret I didn't insist we make a careful search that very moment for the notebook.

We had to run the gauntlet one more time as we dashed from the vans back to our bus, and we did not escape unscathed. I would be returning home with a cap reading "Bethlehem," and Sharlyn picked up a stuffed camel for little Rachel that plays music when you squeeze its tummy. Back on the bus now, we were leaving Palestinian territory and had to pass a checkpoint to enter Jerusalem. Did I really say that? Pinch me. Jerusalem, yes, we really were entering Jerusalem.

Israeli Jews live in east Jerusalem and Palestinian Muslims in west Jerusalem, a combined population of some 700,000. No Palestinian-licensed cars are allowed in Jerusalem; Palestinians who live there must register their cars with Israeli plates. We were approaching the old city from the south, and I was getting oriented as Rula pointed out the valley of Gehenna (or Hinnom, the word for the "valley of fire" Jesus used to refer to hell), ancient site of executions and the city dump, the famous gates of the walled city along the west side, the temple mount. We would be spending the night not far from Damascus Gate at the Novotel Jerusalem.

After we checked in, Sharlyn wrote a few postcards and wanted some stamps from the gift shop downstairs. As we approached the elevators down to the lobby, a young father was boarding with his son. He didn't refuse to let us on, but suggested we take a different elevator. Odd, I thought. At the front desk we were told the gift shop is closed until tomorrow at 6:00 p.m. Odd too. Then it hit me. This was Friday, and it was after sundown. On the Shabbat a special elevator stops at every floor, so Jewish guests need not expend any effort pressing buttons. The serenity of our meal in the dining room that evening was interrupted first by a cantor chanting solo, then by the whole table of men singing mournfully, then by several tables of men, women and children clapping and singing in unison. As the volume increased, I expressed my annoyance to Pastor Paul sitting at supper with us, who explained this was a kosher hotel, and it was unlikely that complaining would elicit much sympathy. It made me wonder how they would feel if all of us were to burst out with an impromptu cantata of Ein Feste Burg at the top of our lungs.

The next day, Saturday, November 10, we would spend right here in Jerusalem. As we boarded our bus, an old man was croaking out the wares he had for sale, when I thought he said something about "widow's mites." At the Caprice Diamond Center we had been shown silver denarius coins (the "penny" of Matthew 22 that represented a day's wage) and widow's mites (Mark 12 or Luke 21), each issued with a certificate of authenticity from the Ministry of Antiquities. Far too pricey at $160 for each denarius and $40 for mites, we had passed them up. Now he had widow's mites three for five dollars. To my eye they looked the same as the ones in Tiberias. Although I don't regret buying them, I did find out later how these modern fakes are made. Stamped from irregular chips of copper, they are fed to cattle to allow the digestive juices to provide the appearance of age and then sold to gullible tourists like me.

Soon we were passing the gates of the north wall of the old city on our way up Mt. Scopus (the present day site of Hebrew University, but the ancient site of Roman catapults) to the Mount of Olives on the east side. Our first stop was the traditional site of the Ascension, located in the center of a stone courtyard shared by a small minaret used by the Muslims several times a day to call the faithful to prayer. This site is venerable to them because one of their early leaders is buried near here. Christians are allowed to hold services in the courtyard once a year, Ascension Day. A dome has been erected over a depression in the stone which purports to be the footprint of Jesus as he left the earth. Utter nonsense that this is, we do know that the event took place, and we believe it happened somewhere on this very mountain.

Rula had warned us that the vendors we had already encountered at Bethlehem were nothing compared to the ones here on the Mount of Olives, notorious also for skillful pickpockets. A short distance away was a parapet on the hillside overlooking the Kidron Valley (also known in the Old Testament as the Valley of Jehoshaphat or Judgment Valley). We had a spectacular view of the Dome of the Rock, Golden Gate, even the Church of the Holy Sepulchre in the distance. The significance of this location as the perfect vantage point for an unobstructed photo of the city was not lost on these merchants who knew tourists would focus on it, so to speak. Belts, beads, key chains, postcards, and hats were thrust at us, but either we were prepared this time or they were not as vociferous as their Bethlehem counterparts. One of them tried to remove my cap in order to place an Arafat-style head scarf on me, but when I asked him politely not to touch me, he backed off immediately with an apology.

A camel was on hand to give rides to the tourists for two dollars. Mickey was the first to try it. She shrieked as two men unceremoniously hoisted her on, and again as the animal lurched to its feet. A third member of their crew walked closely behind with his pooper-scooper, in case it should be necessary, as Mickey was led a few steps along the walkway to show the rest of us how much fun it was. Several people lined up to take their turns, when a second camel appeared. Sharlyn was closest to it, and before I knew what was happening, she was handing me the camera. This one had a saddle with stirrups, which allowed her to mount with a little more dignity. The man handling the reins cried "hold on mama, hold on mama" as Sharlyn climbed on and rose high into the air. It was a ride of no more than a dozen steps, but in Sharlyn's memory it will go on for many years.

As we descended a pathway that could have been the route Jesus took to reach the home of Mary, Martha and Lazarus in Bethany, we passed the tombs of the prophets Haggai and Malachi. From here we could see the top of the church of Dominus Flevit ("Jesus wept"), with symbolic tear bottles as spires adorning its dome, marking the place where Jesus lamented the coming destruction of Jerusalem (Matthew 23-24). Most of the Mount of Olives today has been given over to graves. We stopped momentarily at the cemetery gate to stare in disbelief at the acres of Jewish tombs that stretch as far as the eye can see. We were curious about the piles of pebbles on each tomb. Rula explained that where we leave flowers at the graveside, which soon wither and decay, their loved ones leave something indestructible and immortal--stone. The Jews believe that the first to be quickened at resurrection will be the ones closest to the Golden Gate just across the valley, so they pay at least $25,000 for the privilege to be buried here. This seemed so typical. Just as we had seen them push their way to be first on the elevator, they even have to push their way to be first at resurrection!

Farther down the path we passed the magnificent gold turrets of the Russian Orthodox convent of St. Mary Magdalene, and before long we arrived at the Garden of Gethsemane ("olive press"). At the time of Jesus this beautiful place was much more expansive than it is today, but several massive olive trees that probably date from before the first century still stand in the small patch of the original property which preserves the place where some believe he anguished. A "stone's throw" away from where Peter, James and John might have slept while Jesus sweat, as it were, great drops of blood, is the rock where he prayed. Standing over the site is the Church of Agony, distinguished as one of only two buildings in the world (the Blue Mosque in Istanbul being the other) that has thin slices of alabaster for windows. This beautiful basilica is also called the Church of All Nations, with the crests of many nations painted in its ceiling. Outside, our solemn mood was broken when I saw a tiny face appear at the base of one of the hollow ancient trees. It was a newborn kitten who lived inside the tree, and soon two or three more emerged, followed by the mother, blinking at the light.

Soon it was time to board our bus for the short trip across the Kidron Valley for our first look inside the Old City. There are eight ancient gates through its walls, and we would be entering Lion's Gate on the northeast corner. We exited the bus quickly as Ahmad stopped at the red light on Sultan Suliman Street to drop us off. It was a short walk along the wall to the entrance, and we passed several women, veiled and heavily robed sitting along the stone pathway begging, some accompanied by very small children, barefoot and extending grimy hands for coins. Pastor Paul was ahead talking with Rula as they walked along, when from behind us we heard, "I know that voice." A woman in a tour group from Illinois, a regular listener to his radio program, asked us if that was really who it was. She ran excitedly ahead saying she just had to touch him. What a timely picture this was of the Galilean woman of Luke 8 who strained for a touch of just the corner of the robe of Jesus walking among the poor.

Lion's Gate on the east wall has at least three other names. The first Christian martyr, Stephen, was stoned just outside the wall here, so Christians referred to it thereafter as St. Stephen's Gate. It was the entrance nearest the road from Galilee, so it was sometimes called the Galilean Gate. As we passed through the massive archway we came to a stone plaza used by the shepherds of old as a parking lot for their flocks. When the shepherd returned, he would separate his sheep from the intermingled flock by calling them. At the time of Jesus the gate was called the Sheep Gate, and it was this metaphor that he uses in John 10 to describe his spiritual flock responding to his voice.

Our first stop along the stone street was the Basilica of St. Anne, mother of Mary, one of two possible sites considered the birthplace of Mary. Built by the Crusaders over the home of Anne, this stone structure has been called the most beautiful building in Israel--not for its elegance, but for its simplicity. Pastor Paul had been telling us to anticipate the sound we would hear in its interior--its incredible reverberation lasting at least seven seconds. To test its acoustics, we sang the Doxology with a long pause at the end of each phrase. Time seven seconds on your watch, and you will see how long it was before the last faint echo of our chorus died away.

Not far from the basilica were the excavated ruins of the Pool of Bethesda ("house of mercy"). We stood on a stone plaza at street level, and the pool itself was some thirty or forty feet down below. The fourth century church built over it had been destroyed by the Muslims and lay in ruins far below as well. In my mind I had picked out a route through the ancient steps and rubble to reach the pool down at the bottom where the angel of mercy had stirred the waters once a year (John 5), but as I was about to indulge my fancy to explore, I heard Avanti, and it was time to move on. That probably saved me from getting into some kind of trouble anyway.

Our route back from Bethesda took us past the St. Anne basilica again, and Pastor Paul noticed that another group of tourists had gone in. He couldn't resist the opportunity to join forces with them for one more chorus of the Doxology, and we all marveled once more at the rich aural treasure within.

We were back to the stone street that led from Lion's Gate, and a short distance away we stood at Ecce Homo Arch. This is a remnant of the original Antonia Fortress, the Roman garrison (named for Mark Anthony) of New Testament Jerusalem and home of Pontius Pilate. The arch is named for the Latin expression for "Behold the man" Pilate uttered (John 19) to elicit pity from the Jewish mob. Inside, we stood on the very same stone pavement ("Gabbatha") on which Jesus stood before Pilate (verse 13). The Sisters of Zion convent located here today where the Praetorium once stood calls this spot Lithostrotus, the first of 14 stops along the Via Dolorosa ("way of sorrows") the Roman Catholics recognize as the route Jesus took to the cross. In the first century this room must have been open to the outside air, as the pavement of the ancient street a few feet away bears striations chiseled into the stone to keep the hooves of the horses from slipping when it got wet.

While Rula led us through Lithostrotus, Pastor Paul intended to check out a lead he had been given about a so-called Prison of Christ near here, which purports to be the holding cell in which Jesus was confined awaiting his appearance before Pilate. He found the site padlocked and unattended, so he rejoined us back at Lithostrotus. Such a place is unlikely anyway, from the sequence of events in the Gospel accounts, but he was willing to approach the possibility with an open mind. Later on today, he promised, we would see another more credible cell.

The stone street we had been following now became the Via Dolorosa, and we continued along it westward away from Lion's Gate. Suddenly, merchants and merchandise increased dramatically, and Rula warned us over the clamor and din to be alert for pickpockets. Competition was keen as shopkeepers desperate for business barked out their bargains, and I was surprised to hear "come in and shop till you drop" and "over here we have blue light special" right here in the heart of Jerusalem. We struggled to stay together amidst the throngs in the narrow street, and soon our course came to a T, the street which Rula said marked the "cardo" of Jerusalem. One direction led to the Church of the Holy Sepulchre--the traditional site of the crucifixion--the other to a modern alternative site called the Garden Tomb. We would see the modern site another day, so we turned left.

Along the cardo now the noise and tumult increased. Ahead we could see why. An ambulance was trying to get through, as police and soldiers were shouting and physically pushing pedestrians out of the way. We pressed tight against an old building and drew in our breaths as the vehicle squeezed past us inches away. Inside we could see the victim, an old man under an oxygen mask. As long as we couldn't move anywhere anyway, Sharlyn decided to snap a picture of the stop of the Via Dolorosa we were standing near. It was difficult to form a group under these conditions, but we kept one eye on our leader some distance ahead and noticed that she was turning the corner to head west again.

Now the number of shops decreased again, noise levels became more tolerable, and the street widened into a stone plaza. We had arrived at the Church of the Holy Sepulchre. As Lutherans, we were partial to the Church of the Redeemer we could see nearby, but in a moment we would be entering one of the most revered places on earth. The Church of the Holy Sepulchre is really an arcade of churches representing at least six Christian denominations, including the Roman Catholics, Greek Orthodox, Armenians, Syrians, Coptics, and Abyssinians. The basilica stands over not just the tomb of Jesus, but over Calvary (in the original Hebrew "Golgotha"). However, if you expect to see anything today resembling the "place of a skull," you will look in vain. As we had seen at Bethlehem, separating decoration from substance was a challenge. The rock on which the cross would have stood looms 12 to 15 feet above the level of the plaza, forming a kind of balcony with a shrine built on it. Banistered marble steps lead up to the shrine, which features an ornate altar of brass, carved expensive hardwood, ivory, marble, gold and silver figurines. Beneath the altar is a small cylinder to reach through to touch the rock of Calvary, which is quite visible beside and around the altar.

The validity of this site (and many others as well) as the actual place of the crucifixion depends heavily on early tradition--the earlier its authenticity can be established the better. Many of the significant sites throughout Palestine were established in the fourth century, when Constantine became emperor of Rome. Christianity had operated underground for 250 years, and suddenly it became legal, even fashionable, to practice it. Constantine's mother Helena in particular became obsessed with primary sources, and, with money in hand, scoured the land for evidence of places and events of Scripture. As they were determined one by one, she had churches erected over the sites, which in many cases still have a high degree of credibility even today.

The authenticity of this spot as the real Calvary in particular is bolstered by the split in the rock that can be seen to the right of the altar and continuing down into the bedrock visible from the plaza below. We are told in Matthew's account of the crucifixion that the earth quaked and the rocks rent (Matthew 27). Nearby, Helena discovered a cave full of trash and debris from an earlier century, including beams used for crosses. Were they *the* crosses? Helena thought they were and had them brought to Rome, where pieces of them are retained by the Vatican to this day.

Everything we could say about Calvary we could also say for the tomb a few steps away inside the basilica. Do you have a mental picture of a cavity in a stone wall with a round stone that could be rolled into place to cover it? It was mine, so I was not prepared for the elaborately embellished walnut, gold and marble that stands here today. Unlike most of the other sites we had visited, this one had a long line. One tourist walked up to join her party some distance ahead of us. The old robed patriarch standing near the entrance to the chamber bellowed something at her, and I assumed he was scolding her for cutting into line. She looked confused too, so he motioned her over and without the benefit of English communicated to her with a great deal of commotion that her bare arms were indecent, and she would somehow have to cover her sleeveless top before being allowed to enter the tomb.

While the whole group of us waited in the queue, Pastor Paul took us two or three at a time around to the back side of the tomb. Here a tiny shrine belonging to the Armenian Orthodox Church had been built around the base of the rock from which the chamber had been cut, the only place today where the rock itself could be touched and seen unadorned by any gilt or glitter. Even more interesting nearby that was a series of other tombs standing open for inspection, still much as they were, except for the bones which had once lain in them, when they were discovered. Back in line for the main event, we found the Tomb itself was almost anticlimax. Its slab of marble over the resting place and its gilded and marble-clad walls, candelabras, silver and icons made it impossible to see any of the original tomb and difficult to reconcile with that picture in my mind as the place where the Resurrection took place.

At the time of Jesus the place where we now stood was not only outside, but part of a small garden or park with its own caretaker. A short distance to the north of the tomb is the Chapel of Mary Magdalene commemorating the beautiful place where the risen Lord appeared to her (John 20). In a niche inside this chapel (or possibly another of the several chapels inside this large basilica, I can't be sure) was the Column of Flagellation, a three-foot section of a pillar from the Praetorium to which Jesus was supposedly tied to be flogged. In the vestry nearby was the glass-encased sword of Sir Godfried, one of the most famous leaders of the Crusades.

It was time for lunch now, so we wandered back over to the cardo and found a little sandwich shop called the Everest Cafeteria (I have no idea how it acquired such a name) to pick up some falafel and shawarma.

Sharlyn and I shared some yogurt and a few slices of cheese we had brought along from the hotel, but she also spotted the lemon Fanta soda and ice cream bars for sale at the counter. As we sat there alfresco, the chairs became uncomfortably cool and a sprinkle of rain began. Everyone scrambled for cover. Sharlyn said nothing, but her dirty look said it all, as she had wanted to bring the umbrella along this morning and I had told her it was too much trouble to tote around. Fortunately for me, the duration of the rain was about a minute and a half.

Of course, no one could pass up an opportunity to shop around, so we spent a few minutes in one of the shops on the way to the next stop on our itinerary. The owner announced "everything 10% off" as we walked in. Before long "everything 20% off," as we browsed around. Sharlyn picked up a ceramic bowl depicting the mosaic at Tabgha, and by then "everything on that shelf 50% off." I hope he was as pleased as she was when she bought it. The cashier was having some difficulty operating the register, and I'm sure I did a double take when I heard the owner tell him to "shape up or ship out" as he came over to assist. It must have been in jest, because a grin immediately broke out on both faces. Outside, a vendor was selling panoramic posters of the Jerusalem skyline for a dollar. I didn't think I could go too far wrong at that price, so I picked one up.

We were working our way toward the south wall of the Old City. On a whim Pastor Paul had asked Rula if she knew where the Church of St. Mark is. It wasn't really planned, but it turned out to be one of the most memorable events of the day. We turned down an alley way and in a few minutes we were standing before the Syrian Orthodox Church of St. Mark's. Little known in the guidebooks and off the usual tour routes, this interesting landmark seems to have only relatively recently emerged in significance. From fourth century inscriptions found in the ancient walls below the building, this site is quite likely the home of John Mark.

The Syrian nun who answered our knock on the door seemed a little startled to see us, but kindly agreed to show us around. She referred to the "upper room" where the Last Supper took place (Mark 14) and related the story of the believers gathered in fear here also when Peter was imprisoned (Acts 12). I was a little confused at first when she promised a number of times to take us *down* to the "upper room," forgetting for a moment that the present day building would, of course, be built on top of it. Behind glass on the wall to one side was a very old dark painting of Mary and Jesus. Her credibility was marred somewhat by her claim that this icon was actually painted by Luke. Luke was a doctor, and I had my doubts he was also a painter. Before long she led us down the stone steps to where excavation has only begun to open up the treasure that lies beneath. The Syrian Christians are the only denomination to use Aramaic, the language Jesus spoke here on earth, so, at our request, she knelt before a small altar erected on the section of the floor exposed by the archaeologists and sang the Lord's Prayer in Aramaic. Before she finished, a young boy appeared out of nowhere on the steps behind us and sang the last few phrases with her. It was a lovely duet.

We were in the southwest quarter of the city now, the Armenian quarter, and from St. Mark's we walked toward the south wall of the Old City. We had started out in the Muslim quarter in the northeast and spent a good part of the day in the Christian quarter in the northwest. The Armenian quarter is the smallest--and getting smaller. Darren told me that whenever the Armenians want to initiate a civic project, the Jewish quarter blocks it unless they are willing to trade a piece of their property. As a result, the street lights go dark and the neighborhoods remain in constant disrepair because their attempts to get permits are perennially thwarted.

As we passed through Zion's Gate in the south wall, we could look out across the Hinnom Valley to see flat-topped Herodion, the man-made mountain Herod built for himself as a monument east of Bethlehem. The gate is also called David's Gate, because the "tomb of David" is located nearby. The real burial place of David is unknown, but the Jews revere this spot either as the supposed place or a commemorative place. Either way, it was sacred to them, and men had to have their heads covered to enter. I was a little surprised that the baseball cap I was wearing was not considered irreverent, but no one said anything to Tom (also wearing his) or me as we passed the scrutiny of the rabbi at the entrance. For those who needed them, paper yomichas were available, so Pastor Paul and Dick each put one on.

The traditional site for the Last Supper's "upper room" is the Cenacle a short distance south of David's Tomb. The room we see today was built by the Franciscans, but we could also see evidence that it had been in Muslim hands at some point in its history by the Arabic script in the icon in one of the windows. Not only is this definitely not the room from the first century in which Jesus sat with the Twelve for their last Passover meal, but it seems unlikely now that it is even the right location for it. However, early pilgrims reported a number of revered objects maintained in the original chapel built over this spot.

From here our bus took us around to the beautiful church we could see to the east across the valley. We were met at the door of the Church of St. Peter in Gallicantu by an affable Canadian priest who greeted us amiably and demystified the cryptic name Gallicantu for us--Galli for rooster and cantu for singing. Rooster, singing, rooster, singing. Oh, I get it--the "cock crow" that all four evangelists mention in the warning Jesus had given to Peter. Impressive as the magnificent brand new church we were entering was, we were more interested in what stood here at the time of Jesus. The temple weights and measures, which would have been only in the possession of the high priest, were discovered by archaeologists here in a sealed chamber on this site, so it is all but certain these were the walls of the house of Caiaphas. In the ruins here one of the pillars was found to have been cleanly cut at top and bottom, unlike its fellows lying broken off. It seems Helena had it transported to Rome, but, alas, it sank in the Mediterranean enroute.

It was here that Jesus was taken after Judas betrayed him in Gethsemane. The house of Annas was close by, where he was first taken as a token gesture, but the formalities would need to be conducted by the de facto high priest Caiaphas. After Jesus had been condemned by Caiaphas and the band of ruffians who arrested him, he would have to await the ratification of the full Sanhedrin at first light. After all, they wouldn't want to do anything which would defile them, like pass judgment in an illegal assembly during the night. We descended into the stone cistern used as the holding cell where he was imprisoned that night. The floor of this stone pit was easily large enough for a group our size. A lectern stood there with a book containing Psalm 88 in every language imaginable. Rula opened it to the page in English, where I read "...For my soul is full of troubles, and my life draweth nigh unto the grave. I am counted with them that go down into the pit....I am shut up and I cannot come forth."

It would have been in the courtyard outside where Peter had already denied his Lord and where Jesus "looked upon Peter" (Luke 22) after the cock crew. The path from Gethsemane led across the Kidron and up the steps out there to the palace of Caiaphas. When we stepped outside, there they were--the stone Hasmonean steps built in the second century B.C.--the very ones Jesus (and Peter) would have walked to the place where we now stood. As we descended and ascended those steps, we could say with certainty we had walked where Jesus had walked. Wow. That was the last stop on our itinerary for the day, and what an awesome end to it that was.

The next day, Sunday, November 11, we would spend in the desert, away from the cities. It didn't occur to me at the time, but that describes John the Baptist--and we would be in the same vicinity he frequented. Yesterday we had had an additional half hour to sleep, and today an additional half hour would be taken away. Up by 5:45, our whole group was standing outside the breakfast room of the hotel at 6:30--before the staff was even ready to open it for us. On the 40 km bus ride out of Jerusalem to the east and south, Pastor Paul conducted our church service. We were descending to the Dead Sea, and he used this as a metaphor for Christians in general--and Americans in particular. Although the Dead Sea is richer in minerals and deposits than any other place on earth, nothing lives in it because none of it can flow out. We too are dead if all the blessings and benefits flowing to us produce no fruits. A faith without works is dead (James 2).

Our first stop was Qumran, where the so-called Dead Sea scrolls were discovered in 1947. We didn't realize how efficient the air conditioning was until we stepped off the bus. It was hot. Worse, the flies were back. Were these the same ones from Bet-She'an who found us again or were we being targeted by their vexatious cousins? We heard again the oft-told tale of the Bedouin goatherder who chucked a rock into a cave to scare his goats out, when, hearing the sounds of breaking pottery, he discovered clay pots containing leather scrolls. The real hero in the story was the Bethlehem antiquities dealer who first realized their worth and electrified the world with news of discovery of the oldest manuscripts of the Old Testament known.

The question how the scrolls got here is not entirely settled, but none of the decaying fragments or surviving parchments are here any longer--we would see them tomorrow at the Israel Museum in Jerusalem. The theory advanced by most historians is that the scrolls were once the property of a right-wing Jewish sect known as the Essenes (Sons of Light). Forming a community of 600 here around 30 A.D., the breakaway Essenes had become disenchanted with the decadence and excesses of Jerusalem. Rainwater was precious, yet we saw the miqvah belonging to one ancient home, a cistern which would have been tightly sealed to prevent evaporation, and the stone foundations of the permanent settlement that have been uncovered here. Massacred by rival sects around the year 70, the Essenes disappeared.

As for the scrolls, it seems more than coincidence that cave number 4 in which they were discovered is in plain sight a short distance from the excavated remains of this Essene village. Whether they were being stored for safekeeping from advancing enemies or, considering the condition of some of the fragments, they had been ceremonially buried there is an open question, though we had seen the scriptorium where at least s7ome of the scrolls were probably copied. The whole corpus of 800 scrolls now recovered had extended into other caves nearby, so it is not at all unlikely that even more parchments could yet be discovered. This area is so remote and so desolate that there could actually be caves in these barren hills that no human eye has ever seen inside. Our attention was so focused on the caves to the west that we almost didn't notice the spectacular view to the east as we stood on the bluffs overlooking the fertile valley near the Dead Sea growing tomatoes and watermelons. Date palms are tolerant of salt water, and groves of them can be seen almost to the water's edge.

The souvenir shop here at Qumran featured a lemonade stand near the entrance. We had our ever-present bottled water with us, but the operator of the stand still convinced Sharlyn to buy an iced juice cocktail of orange, lemon, banana and I don't know what all. He also enticed us to sample the dates he had for sale. Sharlyn talked for the next two weeks about the wonderful flavor of those dates. At the time I underestimated the impression they made on her, or I would have paid the outrageous price of four dollars he wanted for a small container of them. As I sat in the shade waiting for her to return from the rest room, the flies were so bad it got me thinking this souvenir shop was missing out on a gold mine--fly swatters. It was a win-win situation. Just think, the shop is happy selling swatters, the tourists are happy swatting, and everyone is happy to be rid of the flies! As we boarded our air-conditioned bus again, Sylvia asked about Sharlyn's drink. When she told her it cost three dollars, Sylvia said, "Now you enjoy that." At that price I even used the leftover ice to cool my bottled water.

I already knew the Dead Sea is considerably larger than the Sea of Galilee, but I was still a little surprised how long we had been traveling along the shore and were still seeing it out our left window. The color of the water changes from blue in the north to green in the south. We had been seeing Ahava Cosmetics in the souvenir shops, but soon we passed the plant where they process mud directly from the Dead Sea to produce it. We would see a considerable number of other mining operations at the south end of the water, where the mineral deposits are the richest. Water levels have dropped so drastically, as mining and drought have combined to reduce volume, that a land bridge has formed at the natural constriction of the land where it pinches the Sea at its narrowest point, and a canal has been cut into it to keep south connected to north. It is below this southern tract of the Sea where the cities of Sodom and Gomorrah are thought to be buried on the bedrock 1200 feet below.

Rula had promised we would see a waterfall in the desert, difficult as that was to believe out here in the wilderness before us. But there would be a cost--in more than one sense of the word. First, it was not part of our scheduled tour, so we would have to pay the admission. She had her cell phone along, however, and we all cheered when she announced that TTI Travel had agreed to pick up that charge for us. Secondly, it would involve a considerable hike over rocky terrain and some steep trails--were we up for that challenge? We looked at each other and, despite the wide disparity in our ages and physical conditioning, decided to give it a go.

The focus of this transaction was now our next stop, the national park of Ein Gedi ("spring of the wild goats"). It is the En-gedi of I Samuel 23, where David hid out in caves when pursued by Saul. Rula said the park boasts three tigers, but I assume she probably meant mountain lions. We did not see either one, but there were a few ibex (wild goats) too shy to let us get within camera range. Although there were posted signs about them, Sharlyn was disappointed we didn't see any on or near the trails. Acacia trees, the wood from which Noah's ark was built, lined the stream, and after a quarter mile or so, sure enough, we came to a waterfall perhaps fifteen feet high. I thought this was it and snapped Sharlyn's picture from near the base of it.

Oh no, this is nothing, Rula said. The trail suddenly became more rugged, and some members of the group decided to reassess their limitations. Dick decided he would have to be content with his view of "little falls" here and waited there for our return. It was not easy for Ellen either, who was still suffering the effects of ankles broken in an auto accident not long ago, but she huffed along, determined to see what lay ahead. High on the cliffs we could clearly see caves of the kind where David and his men might have hidden out, and the serenity and wildlife of the brook trickling past us could easily have provided inspiration for the Psalms he wrote here. The ravens flapping around and nesting in the crags and tors above were reminiscent of the brook Cherith too where Elijah hid out from Ahab (I Kings 17). We rounded a turn in the path and suddenly there it was--the beautiful David's Falls, fifty or sixty feet high crashing into the pool underneath. Each of us found a rock near the base of the cascade on which to rest and contemplate for several minutes, and then we started the long hike back to the front gate.

On the way Rula pointed out a large 8-inch pipe that crossed our path. We had been drinking Ein Gedi brand bottled water, and this very pipe was the conduit transporting it from the spring upstream down the mountain to the plant somewhere below. Apparently the constancy of the minerals in this spring water was preferable to the uncertainty of the minerals in the tap water--at least we were not experiencing any diarrhea, and we could not argue with the way it was agreeing with our systems. We were almost back to our starting point when Mickey, while excitedly trying to video a tiny herd of ibex, tripped on a tree root sticking out and skinned her elbow. Tom and Sharlyn were quite concerned, but Mickey made light of it, bravely enduring hardship so as not to miss her photo op.

It was easily in the mid-90's, so it was refreshing to get back to the air conditioning on the bus. Our next stop was a place not mentioned in Scripture, yet a trip to Israel would not be complete without seeing the Hanging Palace of Herod the Great called Masada ("fortress"). Built as a refuge in the event of an attack from Egypt, Masada was used against Herod almost as soon as it was finished. A remnant of 1000 rebel Jews fled there from Jerusalem in 70 A.D. when the Romans leveled the city and took a stand against Caesar's best for three years. The fortress, situated high on a cliff overlooking the Dead Sea valley to the east, was so successfully siege-proof that it was almost impregnable--almost. The only military approach possible was from the west, and the massive ramp constructed to breach its thick stone walls stands quite visible today. The last line of defense was a heavy wooden wall, which the Romans burned with fire arrows--to find everyone dead except two old women and five children who survived to tell the tale. The others had been persuaded by their leader, Elezar Ben-Yoir, to take an oath of death rather than be taken alive as Roman slaves or gladiators. Each head of the household first killed his own family, then each killed another determined by lot until none remained. Their store of food had been burned to prove to the Romans they died in strength of their own volition and had not been beaten by siege.

Archaeologist Yigail Yashin rediscovered the site in the mid 20th century, and it was opened to the public in 1975. From the valley floor, some 1300 feet below sea level, there are today two ways up the 1400-foot cliff--cable car or the Snake Path, which provides access on foot up an ancient wadi. We hadn't had much exercise for several days, we had been eating far too well, and the little boy in me just felt like doing it, so I was inclined to walk up. But the cable car was leaving in a few minutes, and Rula had distributed tickets to all of us, so up we rode.

Up on top we saw the columns of the synagogue, huge cisterns, the spacious grain rooms, Roman bath, even a theater Herod had built for himself. Restoration is ongoing, and a black line has been painted at the point where 21st century stone has been laid on top of first century stone. Dizzyingly far below we could clearly see the stone perimeter of each of the strategically positioned Roman camps excavators have begun to uncover. To the west we studied the breach in the wall and peered down the long ramp that led to it. Smooth round boulders from the catapults had been piled up neatly there by somebody--either the archaeologists or the rebels themselves. A modern building flying an Israeli flag stands to the east, an outpost where Israeli military pilots come to take their oath of allegiance. As we made our way back to the east side of the mountain, we asked ourselves why. Was it really honorable to choose mass suicide? Wouldn't they be dead anyway if they had chosen to fight to the last man? Didn't they have enough faith at least to pray for a miracle and possibly live through it? Questions that will never be answered, that perhaps have no answer.

The cable car schedule was every hour or whenever there were forty passengers ready to board at either end. Since we would have about a 15 minute wait before the next car departed, my restlessness returned, and my inclination to walk down the Snake Path intensified. Casually I asked Rula to estimate how long it would take, and she said 25 minutes. Hmm, 15 minutes until the car leaves, 5 minutes for loading and the ride--that meant the group would only have to wait about 5 minutes for me at the other end. I felt like a kid begging his mother to go to the movies, but Rula good-naturedly said it would be OK. Several more minutes had elapsed while I thought about it, but it took only about 14 minutes to get down, so I was at the bottom to wave at my companions as they disembarked from the cable car. Whenever Jane or Tom saw a tee shirt after that reading "I climbed Masada," they teased me that I should buy it--but since I hadn't climbed up, I told them I hadn't earned the right to wear it. I didn't tell anyone, but my quadriceps were sore for two days.

We all needed a respite from the exertion at both Ein Gedi and Masada, so we made the Masada Oasis Restaurant here our lunch stop. We were by now so spoiled that a line of ten people was too long and I thought prices were a little out of line anyway, so we were content with the yogurt and cheese sandwiches we brought from breakfast. Sharlyn had a craving for the mango nectar she found in Galilee, but settled for a can of peach nectar here instead, in addition to the last of the oranges we had bought in Galilee. Half of the building was restaurant, and the other half was souvenir shop, so we browsed around, unimpressed with either the prices or the variety. Sylvia had been sampling perfume at each place we stopped, and now she was trying to interest me in the King Solomon's Cologne they had for sale here. To my nose the fragrance was exactly the same as the Queen of Sheba Cologne she tried on, but I was toying with the notion of buying some anyway, when from outside I heard Avanti and realized a credit card transaction at this late juncture was out of the question.

The last item on our agenda for today was a visit to a private beach on the Dead Sea. We would have an opportunity to swim in the saltiest body of water on earth. It would be impossible to sink, we were told. Moreover, anti-wrinkle cream and cosmetics were made from the mud here, and we would have a chance to smear ourselves with it. Then the other shoe dropped. Pastor Paul told us it was vital not to swallow any water. A young lady on one of his tours years ago had slipped getting into the water, accidentally ingesting some, and was in medical emergency. Rula had been counting hands to collect the bathhouse fee, and suddenly many hands were pulled back down. Sharlyn decided it was not worth the risk, but I had been hearing about the Dead Sea for a lifetime and was not going to miss my chance. We had been told the water would feel oily, and it wasn't until I had waded out 30 feet into it that I discovered why. I had just leaned into a back float when I could see the unmistakable rainbow pattern of an oil slick on the surface and realized I was swimming in "minerals." I also realized it was impossible to get back on my feet, so I back-stroked to the shore and decided that was enough Dead Sea for me.

While we swam, waded and smeared mud, Rula and Ahmad were renewing an old friendship with the energetic young lady who ran the souvenir shop here. They sat in the shade sipping cool drinks, chattering away. I don't know where it came from, but Ahmad started puffing on a Turkish pipe that somehow appeared next to their table. It had a large decorated pot from which a long hose extended, tipped by the mouthpiece from which he was drawing "hubbly-bubbly," as he called it. As I walked gingerly from the bathhouse to the water I could hear him chuckling, and while I was out on the water I became aware of his laughter getting louder and more frequent. After I changed and decided to investigate this merriment, others too had taken notice. The more he puffed, the happier he was getting. It was infectious, and soon we were all getting a little silly. Back on the bus

Rula assured us it was just harmless apple flavored tobacco Ahmad was using, and we all said "sure it is." The whole bus oohed again when the frisky souvenir shop lady bounded onto the bus just before the doors closed to present Ahmad with a little stuffed camel and a peck on the cheek. However, either Rula was right or whatever it was passed through his system very quickly, because the ride back to Jerusalem ran unerringly straight.

A few kilometers out of Jerusalem this morning, as we had descended through the Judean hills, I had noticed a camel along the side of the highway decked out with a bright orange saddle and a fancy tasseled bridle. Ever alert for tourist dollars, Bedouins were offering a photo opportunity next to the sign marking sea level (while sitting on their camel, of course). Before we left the beach now on our way back along there, I requested two brief photo stops--one of the signpost pointing to Dead Sea, Jericho and Jerusalem and the other of this sea level sign. But as I browsed around the gift shop, I spotted a post card of the "sea level camel" which I decided would suffice and canceled my request for that. As for the other stop, Rula said we would have to see--it would depend on traffic. She was busy planning details for tomorrow as we passed the first, then the second, then (oh no, there it goes) the third and final chance for the signpost I wanted. I groaned inwardly that it didn't work out, but when Rula apologized later, I pointed out that it was, after all, an unscheduled private request.

On the bus Rula had announced that the Israeli Ministry of Tourism was offering to pay eight of us 40 dollars each to be interviewed tonight about our visit to the Holy Land. Sounded great. But now she was telling us it was changed to tomorrow night instead. That meant Sharlyn and I would miss out. Our daughter Angela has a dear friend and former classmate named Maggie Duke living in Jerusalem until January, and we had already made plans to be with her family tomorrow night. Maggie's husband Darren is a Marine officer studying Hebraic and Arabic languages for a year at Hebrew University and absorbing as much of the culture and ideology here in Israel as possible.

Since the interview had been postponed, Pastor Paul asked if we might be interested in a night tour of new Jerusalem after supper. We had seen some of old Jerusalem, but not much of the modern city around it. For a few dollars from each of us Ahmad had offered to work overtime to show us around a bit, including a visit to Ben Yehuda Street for a little shopping and a peek at some of its night life. Our ears perked up when we heard shopping because Maggie had four small children, and we had been thinking it might be nice to have a few token presents for them tomorrow night.

At supper Pastor Paul pulled out a bottle of sabra he had picked up and offered a sample of it to anyone willing to throw in a small contribution towards the purchase--or even if they didn't. My taste was not up for hard spirits, but Sharlyn bravely sipped some. By eight o'clock we were back on the bus, whizzing past the ritzy King David Hotel, the not-so-ritzy Jerusalem YMCA, the big-business district, climaxing with a scenic panorama of the lights of the city looking north from high above Gehenna Valley. A short time later we were walking along Ben Yehuda Street.

Renee and her daughters Ashley and Christy found a place to sit outside in the cool of the evening to taste some Israeli beer, while the others went their separate directions investigating every shop that was open. Sharlyn and I found a novelty store that allowed us to pick up a few items for the kids and then joined up with Ellen and some of the others still browsing through knickknacks. On the way back to the bus we encountered two young Israeli policemen. Jane, a grandmother many times over but still quite attractive beyond her years, impulsively ran up and put her arm around one of them, posing for a picture. Never one to be outdone, Mickey ran over and did the same. The policemen were benevolently tolerant of the bizarre behavior of these wacky American tourists and continued on their way with a grin.

The next day, Monday, November 12, we returned to the Old City to see one of the most famous places in Jerusalem--the Western Wall, sometimes still called the Wailing Wall. We could see Absalom's Tomb in the Kidron Valley below as our bus approached the point along the south wall where we were dropped off near Dung Gate. Rula's explanation of its name was that it was the last of the gates to be reopened in the 16th century because of the trash and garbage accumulation against it. But the name has a Biblical origin as well (Nehemiah 3), and

I had always assumed it was the place ancient chamber pots were emptied. In any case it is also somewhat more tastefully referred to in Arabic as the Moroccan Gate. Another of the eight gates, Golden Gate (the Eastern Gate or Gate Beautiful) on the east wall, was sealed up with stone by Hadrian and is never to be reopened.

This is the Jewish quarter run by the Hassidim, and as soon as we passed through the gate we could see their influence. Ahead were separate turnstiles for men and women, each guarded by armed soldiers checking purses and parcels. But as we started to form two lines, the attendants waved women over to the men's line and vice versa--maybe because there were so few of us, I'm not sure. On the other side of the turnstiles we paused for a moment to get our bearings. We were standing on the southwest side of the temple mount. The corner we were looking at once supported Solomon's porch (mentioned in Acts 3, for instance), the pinnacle of which stood high above the Tyropean valley and was probably the place where Satan tempted Jesus to jump (Matthew 4 and Luke 4).

At the time of Abraham, before anything was built here, this was Mt. Moriah, where he was sent to sacrifice his only son Isaac (Genesis 22). It was Solomon who erected some 1200 arches around the peak of the mountain to form a large platform called the temple mount. Only the tip of the bedrock of Mt. Moriah protruded through, and it was on this tip that the Holy of Holies of the temple rested. Herod constructed the huge retaining wall we see today to reinforce and expand the temple mount to over 30 acres. In the 2000 years since then, the Tyropean valley (valley of the "cheese makers") which runs parallel to the western wall has been almost completely filled in with civilization, layer upon arched layer until the valley itself has disappeared. Only this one short section of the western wall at its south end remains exposed. But the whole south wall is completely exposed, as well as the east wall, so why is this remnant of the western wall so sacred? Because it is the closest point that a Jew can get to where the Holy of Holies once stood.

It is exactly on that identical point that the Dome of the Rock, the third most sacred site in the world to the Muslims, stands today on the tip of the bedrock, from where they believe Mohammed ascended to the seventh heaven. According to modern historians, the Holy of Holies was directly west of Golden Gate, and since the Dome is slightly south of that line, there is some technical dispute whether it stands precisely where the Holy of Holies was. But that is a distinction without a difference to the Hassidim, who are profoundly angered by this Muslim "sacrilege," and it seems all but inevitable that the boiling cauldron of religious fervor seething silently just below the surface in both camps will one day break out in full scale warfare. Until recently tourists were allowed into the Al Aqsa Mosque just south of the Dome on the same plaza, the fourth most sacred Muslim site, but some sort of conflagration just over a year ago closed its doors indefinitely.

The section of the western wall closest to the original temple is off limits to women, and it is considered a desecration even for men to approach it with an uncovered head. As we had seen at David's Tomb, paper yomichas were provided. Women are allowed to approach the parapet surrounding the sacred section, provided their arms are covered. A cornerstone thought to be from the temple, perhaps even from the Holy of Holies, is on display near the entrance. Hyssop, the "reed" that was used to pass a sponge filled with vinegar to Jesus on the cross (John 19), grows out of the cracks up high between the stones of the wall. Into the chinks down low are jammed thousands of scraps of paper on which the prayers of visitors have been written. The Hassadim, young and old, are seen facing the wall, scripture in hand, bobbing repeatedly toward the wall as they pray "with all their might." On Mondays and Wednesdays bar mitzvah ceremonies are conducted here, so we were present to witness the ritual for one phylacteried lad, hearing the husky incantations of six or seven white-robed men accompanied by one pitched an octave higher.

We took our pictures there and departed for what turned out to be one of the most fascinating highlights of our tour, with the most unlikely name--Holy Land Hotel. The hotel has turned over a sizable portion of its land for a 1:50 scale model of Jerusalem in the "second temple period," as they called it (the Jerusalem of the first century). It wasn't until I saw this model that I could comprehend how scraps of data we had been picking up fit together--the topographical layout of the Kidron, Hinnom and Tyropean valleys converging like the point of an arrow in the southeast, the proximity of the temple mount to the City of David, the bridge built across the Tyropean valley for the benefit of wealthy upper Jerusalem and the steps up from the valley for middle class lower Jerusalem. The series of temple courts can be problematical to sort out, but here they were, laid out to scale in relation to each other. I was trying to orient myself to find the Pool of Bethesda, when I remembered that the model is decidedly from the Jewish perspective, which probably would proscribe anything so "New Testament."

As we strolled around the perimeter listening to Rula's tutorial and admiring the workmanship of this model, a 70-something man in blue overalls I took to be a custodian came walking through. Rula interrupted herself in mid-sentence and introduced us to Haim Perez, the designer and creator of this marvelous masterpiece. He posed for pictures and chatted pleasantly with us, explaining that the model was started 20 years ago and is really still a work in progress, as he handed out souvenir pieces of the stone he uses in the project. An aerial view is possible from an observation deck nearby, but I did not have a wide angle lens which could take it all in, and to my great surprise and disappointment, the souvenir shop here had no pictures of the model.

After we finished looking around, Pastor Paul was making idle conversation with us about his younger days, when he was tall, thin and athletic (well over six feet tall, he approaches perhaps 300 pounds today). At that moment Sylvia returned from the rest room, and as she walked up, he put an arm on her shoulder and said, "I was good looking once--in fact Sylvia was the 31st girl I dated in college." Without missing a beat she put her arm around him and said, "and Paul was my 206th." He knew he had met his match and didn't say another word.

I'm not exactly sure which part of Jerusalem we were in here at the model (probably the west or southwest), but soon we were leaving the city limits to the west. We passed Har Herzl, a cemetery for notables of Israel, where prime ministers are buried. Along this four-lane highway we were on Rula also pointed out a hospital which has twelve stained glass windows of the apostles painted by celebrated artist Marc Chagall. A short distance later we arrived at Ein Karem (or En Kerem, "spring of the vineyard"). This was the town where Zacharias lived, the priest whose turn for temple duty came up as the events of the New Testament began to unfold. Priests in those days were well taken care of, so Zacharias had two houses--one here where John the Baptist was born and the other which would have been to the south across the highway, where Mary had visited her cousin Elizabeth in "a city of Juda." There is a legend here of an angel who appeared to Elizabeth with a warning to hide John behind a rock during Herod's slaughter of the infants.

The fourth century Church of St. John the Baptist which once stood here has been destroyed, but the present chapel, built in the 1960's, has glass panels in its floors which permit a glimpse of the mosaic floors and foundations of the original structure. Erected in the courtyard outside the church is a large signboard bearing the entire prophesy of Zacharias found in Luke 1. We stood together and read it aloud in unison, then, as had become our custom, entered the church to sing the Doxology. Inside we found another tour group of Korean men already occupying the pews. They sat politely while we stood at the front singing, then Pastor Paul turned to them and, not knowing whether they understood any English, gestured to them that we would like to hear them sing. One of their number stood up and said a few words to the rest in their own dialect, and in moments eight or ten strong male voices boomed out in unison the same chorus we had just sung--in Korean! We were moved to tears.

We rode a short distance again to Yad Va'shem ("a memorial" or "a name"), Israel's holocaust museum. Not many building projects enjoy the luxury of having more funding than they can find applications for it, but we were told that was the case here. Jews from all over the world have poured money into this memorial for the six million who were massacred, and construction was booming everywhere. We would not be spending much time here, but there were three of its buildings that were "must see."

First was the Children's Memorial, a gift in 1953 by the Spiegel family of California to honor the one and half million children killed in the Holocaust, including their son Uziel. The building is lighted by only six candles--multiplied by mirrors into one and a half million points of light. An awesome effect. Next was a stone path past the eternal flame in a somber, darkened Hall of Remembrance, with the ashes and personal effects of the victims from each of the twenty death camps strewn on top of six million black mosaic tiles. The last display we saw was a historical museum featuring a seemingly endless corridor meandering through hundreds of grisly photos depicting the horror and suffering of Hitler's mania. Outside were thousands of trees planted in memory of various individuals along an "Avenue of the Righteous among the Nations," Oskar Schindler among them. Sharlyn was interested in locating his tree, as was Mickey, so Rula directed us to where we could snap a picture of it. The effects of some of the other buildings on the grounds were duplicate memories in our minds of the graphic displays we had already seen in our own Holocaust Museum at home in Washington--an actual box car used to transport people as cattle, cannisters of poisonous gas, even a bar of human soap bearing the number of the victim from whom it was rendered.

Even though it was noon, no one felt like lunch after that, so we decided to buffer it with a visit to the Israel Museum's Shrine of the Book, where some of the Dead Sea scrolls are stored. We weren't sure at first whether this was a building or just a sculpture. A huge black wall the size of an outdoor theater screen stands on one side of a stark white marble plaza opposite an enormous white structure shaped like the top of a clay pot. The contrast is intentional, signifying Good and Evil, the Sons of Light and the Sons of Darkness. What looked like the lid of a clay jar is also intentional, as a reminder of the pottery in which the scrolls reposed for centuries and serving as the lid to the building below ground where the scrolls are housed today. It was a beautiful effect. Visible a quarter mile away to the northwest we could see from here the Knesset building, Israel's parliament, surrounded by the most expensive real estate in Jerusalem--renting for as much as $1000 a month. Renee whispered to me that her son's dorm room cost almost that much.

As the fountains came to life spraying water over the gigantic white lid, we entered the building and descended into the carefully controlled conditions of light, temperature and humidity inside. Some portion of every book of the Old Testament except Esther are represented in the fragments. However, the only scroll which is complete is the book of Isaiah, an exact copy of which is featured in the center of the room, completely unrolled and stretching around a lighted cylinder. Only one display case has an original fragment, about a yard long; the others are copies, widely varying in length, coloration and surviving condition. I found myself wishing I knew a little bit of Hebrew, amused to recognize some of the same script characters I had noticed on the hotel TV here on these ancient manuscripts. See, here is that upside-down 4 that seems to occur in nearly every word, and there is that little menorah. I was absorbed enough by the displays that I must have lost track of time.

Sharlyn had gone in search of a rest room, and by the time she returned, the others from our group had disappeared. We walked back to the main gate, but we didn't see our companions. Having passed the exit, we couldn't go back inside without paying the admission again, but our pink and lavender bus across the lot was hard to miss. Sharlyn couldn't pass up a peanut bar from a vendor nearby, so snack in hand we ambled toward the bus. We watched a gray-breasted crow land near a vehicle with its door open, and we were amused by the battle in its mind between curiosity and survival as it tried to decide if it should risk a quick hop inside that car. We waited on the bus for some time before the remainder of the group finally emerged through the gate. Nothing was said, but we felt a little shamed that they might have been trying to find us inside.

It was time for lunch in mid-afternoon now. On the way to the restaurant we came to a traffic circle. Ahmad was feeling capricious and whipped the bus around the circle a few times to get us dizzy and then continued on. Rula quipped that must have been a little present from Ahmad. We stopped at a souvenir store not far from our hotel called the Peaceland Bazaar. Upstairs was a lunch room with a few tables that hadn't been cleaned from the previous customers. From the black grime on the napkins we wiped them with ourselves, we wondered if they hadn't been cleaned from the previous century. The owner, a tall graying lanky man with a front tooth missing, took orders for sandwiches and bottled drinks. I didn't know it at the time, but Darren later told me he knows this man personally, having visited the store and even been invited to his house. Some sort of breach of protocol or faux pas had taken place, which apparently prevented them from visiting him again. Darren said the man had been so kind to them he felt bad that he would never know why the friendship ended.

At the bottom of the stairs was a wicker basket of perhaps 150 old Israeli coins no longer in circulation. I was casually interested in them and asked the owner how much for the whole basket. Expecting him to quote some bargain price, I was a little taken aback when he said, "Well, let's count them out and see, one, two, ...." I wasn't that interested. As we browsed around the store downstairs, I was overhearing snatches of negotiations between Pastor Paul and the owner. In conversation Pastor Paul had made reference to his interest in icons and other antiquities, but when I asked him what he was trying to acquire here, he changed the subject, and I took that as a cue not to pry. Soon we were on the bus for our last stop for the day, the Garden Tomb of General Gordon.

Gordon was looking out the window of his hotel room one day and couldn't believe his eyes. There in the distance was the wall of an ancient quarry of Solomon that looked like a skull. Next to it was a beautiful garden preserve with an empty tomb cut into the limestone nearby, complete with a track for a stone cover . He was astounded that he had in that moment discovered Calvary and convinced an association in London to purchase the land. Its physical features are a perfect fit for the picture most Christians have in their minds of the "place of a skull," the tomb of Joseph of Arimathea, and Mary Madgdalene in the garden. Besides the way this place suits the Gospel account, our veddy propah British guide was telling us, consider the following facts:

(1) Executions were traditionally carried out on the floor of a quarry, to where the condemned was thrown from above and stoned.

(2) An execution had to be done outside the city walls; the Holy Sepulchre site is inside the wall.

(3) Nowhere does it say in the Gospel accounts that the crucifixion was on a hill; the cross could have stood on this quarry floor.

(4) It would not have been possible for the crowd to spit upon Jesus if the cross were high on a hill.

(5) This grave has space for two, but only one cell was used and was found empty.

Impressive arguments. But they are based on 19th century tradition; the site at the Holy Sepulchre is based on fourth century tradition. Besides, not all of their premises are valid. I don't find in the accounts that anyone spit upon Jesus on the cross. There is also substantial evidence that at the time of Jesus the Holy Sepulchre site was outside the city wall (city walls were first built at the time of Nehemiah, then by Herod, then Agrippa in 66 A.D., and most recently by the Turks in the 16th century). The one used cell was determined from the bevel cut out for the feet of one body, but not the other--i.e., in carving out a grave, the rock was left uncut at the feet end until there was a body to measure how much to chisel out. But this could have any number of alternative explanations. However likely or unlikely this site is for authenticity, there are two things that can be said for it--first, it satiates the mental image in a way that the Holy Sepulchre never can and, second, we rejoice that both sites have an *empty* tomb!

Throughout our tour, and here at the Garden Tomb gift shop again, Sharlyn had been looking at lithographs by David Roberts, a 19th century artist of Holy Land scenes, but the right one that suited both her fancy and her purse never came along and still smolders on her wish list. Our tour here was over, and so was our itinerary for the day, so we had a short ride over to our hotel. As we stepped off the bus saying our customary thank yous and good evenings to Ahmad, we didn't realize it then, but it was the last time we would ever see him.

Pastor Paul had picked up a bottle of akra (I never saw the spelling of it) to share with the group over supper tonight, but we would not be joining them. Darren and Maggie Duke, with Rebekah, Joshua, Caleb and little Sarah Margaret picked us up at 6:30 for a drive out to the west of Jerusalem to Abu Ghosh for supper. The restaurant here was nice, but I didn't get the feeling it was posh, so I was a little surprised to learn that Bill Clinton had once come here on a visit to Israel.

The kids were delightful, familiar with all the traditional middle eastern appetizers we were being served. I usually carry three pens in my pocket, and soon all three were busy producing some of the finest artwork in Israel on the backs of the placemats. Delectable kabobs were brought out as the second course, but we had hardly made a dent in the appetizers, much less kabobs. Then Maggie announced that we would be going back to their house for the third course--cake and ice cream. On the way Darren gave us our second night tour of the city, including some of the same places we had seen with Ahmad last night. After a while we pulled into their underground garage and passed their bomb shelter (yes, a real bomb shelter) as we entered their townhouse. The real purpose of our visit, of course, was to see Bekah do handstands, Josh run his video game, Caleb play with his truck and Sarah Margaret get her jammies on. Our job was to pay attention to all of this, and each one made sure we were doing our job properly. Maggie's made-from-scratch pound cake was delicious, and before we knew it, it was time for Darren to run us back to our hotel. We pretended that our hugs were from Angela, they pretended that their hugs were for Angela, and just like that the evening was over.

When we walked into the hotel, Pastor Paul and Sylvia, Dick and Jane, Tom and Mickey, and Ellen were sitting in a circle in the lobby finishing the last of the akra over a post mortem of the Ministry of Tourism interviews. We got a little of the flavor of their evening and we gave them a little taste of ours. At a lull in the conversation Pastor Paul spontaneously suggested that he would tell a joke and then we should go around the circle, each telling one. This was excellent therapy for Ellen, who, we found out, lost her husband two years ago. When her turn came, she laughed so hard trying to tell her joke that the tears were running down her face as each word of her story came out one at a time between spells of doubling over nearly to the floor. I don't know which was funnier, the joke or the delivery, but she easily took first prize for the best entertainment.

The next day, Tuesday, November 13, was our last day in Israel. No tours had been scheduled, and we would not see Rula today. We were on our own. I wasn't sure that was such a good thing. Not that we were lacking in ideas, just organization. Renee and her girls wanted to check out the shopping malls. Pastor Paul and Sylvia had their own agenda, which did not include us. Tom and Mickey had sketched out a plan to see Hezekiah's tunnel, walk on top of the walls of the Old City, take the tour of the Rabbinical Tunnel along the base of the Western Wall, see Lazarus's tomb. When I mentioned this sketch to Darren, he raised some caveats. Some friends of theirs had paid to walk on the wall, only to be turned back by soldiers after traversing a very short distance. We would need flashlights for Hezekiah's tunnel, and one end of it is in Israeli hands, the other end in Palestinian. He told how he once had to scramble over the fence at the other end and was chased by some Palestinians demanding their fee. Flashlights would be a problem. We didn't have any. Darren offered to loan us his snakelight and worked out a plan where we could get it back to him before we left for the airport the next day.

Seven of us were standing outside the hotel deciding we would need two cabs to get over to Hezekiah's tunnel, when we were overheard by Hateem, one of the vendors who haunt the front doors of the hotels. He had a shop in the Old City and cab drivers at his disposal who would shuttle us around for the day for a fixed price. Should we trust him? Why not, we had been trusting people all week, so we decided to accept his offer. In minutes two of his cohorts pulled up and whisked us over to the Pool of Siloam.

Hezekiah's tunnel is obliquely mentioned in Scripture (II Kings 18 and II Chron. 32), without much elaboration on its construction details. As Sennacherib approached to besiege Jerusalem, Hezekiah rerouted the water source at the spring of Gihon outside the city wall to the Pool of Siloam inside the wall through this tunnel, then stopped up the spring. An engineering marvel for its day, it snakes its way under the City of David through solid granite in a giant S a yard wide, 20 feet high in places, and over 500 meters long. The mystery about how it could be dug from both directions and still meet in the middle is explained by an unauthorized ancient inscription left behind by one of the project overseers boasting of their accomplishment. The stonecutters simply followed the trickle seeping through a crack in the rock.

When Pastor Paul had recommended Hezekiah's tunnel as a site for today, he explained that we would be in ankle deep water and total darkness. Candlelight and bare feet would not do, as he could testify firsthand. Sharlyn and I had our flashlight and rubber thongs in hand as our group was met by two or three Palestinians at the gate. Unexpectedly, they offered to provide a guided tour--with suitable footwear and as many flashlights as we needed--for three dollars each. Such a deal! Our Muslim guide Naim took the lead as we lowered ourselves down a few stone steps into the channel. Since I was carrying the snakelight and extra batteries, Naim suggested I take the rear. Somehow I had the idea the water would be muddy or murky, but it was crystal clear--and cold.

As my feet touched the water, I was expecting to touch bottom a few inches farther. But I descended past the ankle, past the knee, too dark to see how much more. Ankle deep, my ... aah yeah, and it was getting wet too.

After a few feet the channel shallowed somewhat, and we splashed along, feeling as much as seeing our way. I was digging a trench once and remember clearly the claustrophobia I felt, so I was trying to chase those ghosts out of my mind. Everyone was in good spirits, Tom joking that Mickey and Jane had gone off into the gift shop, Jane accusing me of pinching her (from a distance of three people away), and Dick wondering where in here we could get lunch. Naim stopped to point out the depression in the rock left when the inscription had been removed to a museum for safekeeping. After about 20 minutes he stopped again, pointing up to a shaft which leads to the surface, and announced that the other end of the tunnel was closed and we would have to go back. His slight build allowed him to squeeze past everyone to my end and take the lead again back the other direction.

We were in at least knee-deep water most of the way, and I was now right behind Naim on the return trip. He seemed to be wading along pretty fast, and I was struggling so hard to keep up with him that I could imagine some of the others behind me were having difficulty as well. Like a man possessed he thrashed madly along, and soon I could see sunlight. We clambered up the stone steps, and I looked back, expecting to see at least someone not far behind. Ten minutes went by. Naim lit a cigarette. After twenty minutes we could hear voices, then a faint light, then, like miners coming back to the surface, finally we could see smiling faces. Everyone was exhilerated, as we found our street shoes again, and glad to be soaking up sunshine to warm up and dry out. We found out later that in fact the tunnel was not closed at the other end. Our Palestinian guides would have had to deal with the Israelis at Gihon and deceived us to save themselves the hassle.

The plan was to walk from here to Dung Gate and over to the Western Wall for a tour of the tunnel along its base. The distance was not that great, but the street leading from the Pool of Siloam over to there was pitched at a steep angle. I did not know at the time that Dick had had some heart trouble, so I probably seemed insensitive when I urged us to continue on after he announced he couldn't make it. The Palestinians at Siloam offered to take us over in a van, so we piled in for the short hop to the Gate.

It was about 10:30 now, so we had just enough time to take the tour. We had arranged to meet Hateem at the Church of the Holy Sepulchre at noon, and he would take us to his store for lunch to work out the details of the afternoon from there. It was working like clockwork--until we found out to our dismay that the next tour in English wasn't until 1:40. We had some time to kill. Tom was still talking about walking on top of the walls, but when I reminded him that was where snipers watching for trouble would be restricting our access, we decided to think again. Yesterday he had forgotten to leave the slip of paper on which Mickey had written a prayer for him to insert into the Wall, so this would give him a second chance to take care of that. But we still had over an hour.

The bazaars of Jerusalem along the cardo were close by, so of course Sharlyn, Mickey and Jane wanted to go there. We asked a passerby for the shortest route and he cordially offered to take us there. He introduced himself as Shlomo, and I was sure I knew why he was being so cooperative. But to my surprise, he refused any tip as he doffed his cap to us and went his way. I bought a map and a shrink-wrapped package of coins for which the dealer wanted five dollars, but with his arm around my shoulder it was "for you three dolla." With all our poking around in the shops, the time passed quickly. We got to the Holy Sepulchre early, so we even had a little time to retrace our steps through it before Hateem arrived. Unlike Saturday, when we had encountered some crowding and queues, the huge basilica was nearly empty.

Hateem cordoned off a corner of his store, the Dajani's Orient Bazaar, pulled out wicker stools for us to sit on, served us Turkish coffee, and even gave us the little porcelain demitasse beaker it came in as a souvenir. He didn't sell food, but we should feel free to pull out whatever we had along for lunch--and everything in the store was 20% discount, he announced. Sharlyn had been picking up mother-of-pearl pieces at the other shops and now found a nativity ornament she liked. Even with the discount it was nearly thirty dollars, but when Hateem saw her dazed look, he quickly assured her it was genuine mother-of-pearl from Italy, not plastic, as some other unscrupulous merchant might try to sell her.

Our plan now was to go over to Bethany to see the tomb of Lazarus after the Western Wall tunnel tour this afternoon. We estimated the tour would be finished by about 2:30, and Hateem pulled out his cell phone. His driver Akram would be waiting for us in a white stretch taxi at Lion's Gate at 2:30 sharp. Like the fairy godmother warning Cinderella, he then admonished us firmly that Akram would be able to wait there for us only ten minutes. It was a short walk back over to the Western Wall.

The Rabbinical Tunnel along the Western Wall is really not a tunnel at all. At the time of Herod it was the Tyropean Valley, open to the sky. The western side of his massive rectangular retaining wall extended down to the valley floor. In the years since, a series of stone arches were constructed perpendicular to the wall stretching across the valley floor, and eventually buildings took shape above that and above that until the valley was no longer a valley. We were now traversing that series of arches where the rubble along the base of the wall just to the north of the "Wailing Wall" has been excavated.

Our guide was telling us that some of the early inhabitants of the layer just above the arches discovered that if they broke through their floor, they had the use of a free basement (the space in which we were now standing within the arches). He said they could use it for storage, for a toilet or "just a place to hang out." "Hang out" sounded awfully American--an expression our college kids used. I decided to ask him where he was from. I wasn't surprised when he said he was a student from New York.

Imagine a stone building block 46 feet long and about 10 feet high. There before us was a single monstrous block that size sitting on the bedrock at the base of the wall--the largest in all four sides. I guessed incorrectly that the Holy of Holies must have been just above this point. No, that was a few feet farther along, a place he pointed out to us where an archway was today sealed up with stone. The archway is known as Warren's Gate (from its 16th century discoverer) and was the entrance to a small synagogue that had been built into the wall here. In the 20th century that synagogue came under threat so frequently that the decision was made to close it. An old rabbi, Yehuda Getz, so adamantly refused to allow this to happen that he made his office just outside the entrance and never left it until he died.

The tour continued northward, and before long we were ushered into a small auditorium. I looked at my watch. We needed to meet our driver at 2:30, and now it looked like we would be sitting here for a while. When I asked the guide whether he expected we would be finished by 2:30, he said, "Mmm, I doubt it." Mickey liked to ask questions at each site we visited, so I whispered to her that it looked doubtful we were going to meet Akram on time and suggested she might want to keep questions to a minimum. She nodded.

The auditorium had an excellent model of the Western Wall, with lights and switches to control movable sections of it to illustrate the phases of its development. It was impressive to see on the model how small the only section visible today, the Wailing Wall, is compared to the full length and height of the wall. As we moved farther along the wall again, our guide pointed out the mortised edges of each individual block--about three inches of each edge recessed to make the remainder of the block stand out in relief. At the place where we stood, the bedrock would have been below ground even in the first century, but a few more feet farther north from here the bedrock broke the surface and angled upward above ground. Herod ordered his men to chisel the exposed bedrock with the same mortising to make it appear seamless with the real block on top of it.

I was getting nervous about the time. 2:10, 2:14, 2:23.... We weren't going to make it. Our "tunnel" widened near here to a small plaza which in Roman times was an outdoor market selling fish, produce and merchandise. In order to control the flash flooding through the market place when it rained, the Romans built an aqueduct to funnel the runoff into a large pool. When we came to this pool, we saw a stone wall dividing it. We could see only about 1/3 of it; the other 2/3 was on the other side of that wall. It seems the 19th century archaeologist who discovered the pool decided to go for a dip--in the altogether. The Sisters of Zion in the convent above heard sounds of splashing through the stone floor below them that were not consistent with their meditations and decided to investigate. It wasn't long before their piece of the pool was walled off permanently.

Then suddenly we came to where the Western Wall is unfinished. Partially chiseled blocks lie haphazardly, chips and gravel strewn about in half-cleared rubble. The archaeologists found evidence everywhere of work abandoned hastily, stone-cutting tools lying exactly where they were dropped when workers fled. What happened? The what is fairly clear. Herod died. The why is not. Slaves may have seized an opportunity to escape, some political intrigue may have incited a skirmish, the workers may have been ordered to stop immediately or been needed on some new WPA project elsewhere. Speculation is rife. But here the progress would stop for a brief hiatus of some 2000 years.

We had run out of wall and tour at the same time, and that time was now 2:50. No chance of hooking up with Akram at this point--we had been warned. Or was there? I thought it might be worth a chance to catch him yet. I quickly climbed the stairs back to the surface and ran through the turnstile. At the exit I was trying to get my bearings, when I saw something familiar--Ecce Homo Arch. Oh, I know where I am, Lion's Gate is just down here.... As I ran along the stone street, I saw a man in the distance sitting glumly on some stone steps, his chin propped up with both hands. A long white taxi was parked nearby! Could it be? It was Akram. Where were we, he wanted to know.

The others came hustling along in a few minutes, and all of us were relieved that our coach had not turned into a pumpkin. In a few minutes we were on the highway that runs along the base of the Mount of Olives around to the east out of Jerusalem and over to Bethany. I was sitting in the front seat and on the way I wondered if our destination, the tomb of Lazarus, meant anything to our driver. "Are you Christian?" I asked him. No, Muslim. "Do you know what the tomb of Lazarus means to us?" I asked. "Well, I know who Jesus is," he replied. "He was a good man and a prophet." "But you reject him," I said. "Yes, god has no son," he countered, and launched from there into familiar territory. I was making Jane, sitting in the seat behind me, nervous. "We like you anyway," she kept saying.

He turned into a side street and a block or so farther we saw the sign, Lazarus Tomb. As soon as we stepped out of the taxi, two men, one of them permanently disabled on crutches, approached us. It would be three dollars admission for each us. We paid our money to the man on crutches and followed the other one. I thought the opening we could see from the street was the tomb, but he led us through the opening and down a long stone stairway to a chamber below large enough to accommodate all of our group standing together. Our guide explained that it was here that Jesus had stood when he called Lazarus to come forth (John 11). The wall in front of us had a hole about a yard wide and a foot high through which we could see the burial cell hollowed out behind it. Between us and that wall was a short stone passageway which descended underneath the wall into the cell. It was a bit tight, but quite possible to squeeze through that passageway into the burial cell, especially for someone my size. Fascinating. I don't know what the likelihood is that this site is genuine, but if it is not, someone has expended considerable effort to simulate authenticity. We know that Mary, Martha and Lazarus were wealthy, and only someone with considerable means would have a burial place this elaborate.

As we turned to take the stairs back to the top, our way was blocked by our guide. That would be three dollars from each of us. But we already paid up on top, we protested. No, this was for the tour and the explanation. What tour? What explanation? I shook my head, handed him a dollar and pushed past him. Sharlyn said she was with me and quickly made her way to the stairs too without paying another penny. Some paid to avoid an ugly scene, some didn't, but we were uniformly unimpressed with his little piece of chicanery--and relieved a second time to see our stretch taxi waiting for us at the street. Back on top we protested to the man on crutches that they should have been up front with us about the cost, but he shrugged and feigned ignorance. We decided a hasty departure was our best maneuver, so we didn't take the time to look inside the Church of St. Lazarus adjacent to the tomb. I mentioned this incident to Rula later, and she said if we had mentioned her name, they would not have dared to treat us this way. We didn't know.

On the ride back we came to a long line of cars at the checkpoint to reenter Jerusalem. To make conversation I turned to Akram and asked whether these checkpoints create problems for him. It was as if I had pushed the wrong button on the jukebox. He launched into a diatribe against the Israelis, which led to the plight of the Palestinians, which led to policy of the American government, which led to Islam, and his invective went on. The volume, the histrionics, and vituperation increased together. I was actually enjoying it somewhat, but Jane, nervous as before, kept saying, "We like you, but we like you." Tom attempted some verbal fire retardant with "we really all believe in the same god, don't we?" Then Akram mentioned something about visiting his brother in San Diego and I pounced on my chance to change the subject. "Have you ever been to Mexico?" "They speak Spanish there, you know." "Your English is very good, do you speak Spanish?" "When are you planning to visit him next?" By the time we arrived at our hotel, the decibels had descended to normal, and Jane could put the Pepto Bismal back into her purse. We paid him handsomely for waiting so patiently for us and shuttling us around town with such gusto. And with that, our tour of Israel came to an end.

Our flight tonight wasn't scheduled to depart until 11:55. This was a little awkward because we wouldn't be staying the night, yet our luggage would need to be somewhere throughout the day while we were out touring. The hotel graciously agreed they wouldn't make up our rooms until we actually left in the evening. But each of us discovered that the computerized card key no longer worked to open the door. I expected that to create complications, but the front desk simply punched in a code and soon we were back in to start our packing. By happenstance another tour group staying here in the same hotel would be on the same flight, and they had room on their bus for our small group. So their driver would be making the trip to Tel Aviv, and we would not see Ahmad. Rula, however, would see us through to the end, accompanying us to the airport.

We were getting a little choked up through supper, as Rula made a little speech and Pastor Paul had some kind words and a little gift for her. Too late some of us realized we should have picked up some flowers to accompany it. Darren and Maggie dropped in briefly, as we had arranged, to pick up their snakelight. We made introductions, as Darren chatted away in Arabic with Rula, and soon we boarded our bus to Tel Aviv. At the airport Rula had a hug for each of us, flashed her patented smile as she waved, and then this wonderful lady was gone.

The lines were agonizingly slow at the check-in. We had been randomly selected by the computer at Dulles to be checked thoroughly. Here at Tel Aviv it was Mickey. She was not taking it well as the attendants pawed through her carefully packed bric-a-brac, asking her endless questions about this book and that piece of jewelry. After we checked through, we saw someone familiar. It was the same man who had requested our return tickets last week when we arrived, now handing them back to us. Sharlyn said, "Is this Israel?" With a withering look I said, "What are you talking about? Of course, we're in Israel." "No, is this Israel?" she insisted. She had been paying attention when Rula told us that Israel, the TTI Travel agent here would be passing out our return tickets. We picked up some cash for the VAT we had paid at the Caprice Diamond Center, and after browsing through the shops along the airport concourse one last time, we were ready to go home.

The elevation on the screen of our 777 read 147 feet as we taxied out to runway 26. Our flight 91 lifted off just after midnight at 12:14 and over eleven hours (yes, *eleven*!) later landed at Newark at 4:28 a.m. The group didn't stay together very well as we passed customs, and by the time we got to the baggage claim, the only one I saw was Dick dragging his suitcase through the turnstile in the distance. It wasn't the farewell I envisioned. For some reason our luggage could not be checked all the way through to Washington Dulles, so we had to go through baggage recheck before we could leave the secure area of terminal B. At the top of the escalator we were surprised to see Pastor Paul, Sylvia, and Ellen waiting for the monorail over to terminal A. We were headed the opposite direction to terminal C, and our train was just pulling into the station. I waved to the three of them, but Sharlyn had a fondness for Sylvia and just had to run over to get a quick hug first. And just like that it was over.

Our connecting flight 1019 to Washington was anticlimactic, departing runway 22R at 7:04 and landing on runway 19R at Dulles more than a half hour early at 7:45. We hadn't slept much, but we were bounding along on adrenaline, exhilerated by the incredible experience we had just had. It was early in the day yet, but we would not be in the office today. There was plenty of unpacking, laundry, sorting through mail, and napping to do--and, of course, getting our "Rachel fix."

We wanted to get our thoughts on paper while memories were still fresh, so we don't yet have the luxury of reflection, but I doubt we will have many regrets. However, as we traveled from place to historic place, I found myself returning to the same wish that neither I nor anyone else can ever have--that we could see it as it was. As Christians, we were in a place unique. No other place on earth has the spiritual heritage for us as this patch of turf called Israel. But even if Abraham or David could return to their land today, they would not only not recognize it, they could not find it. The almost unparalleled cycle of upheaval and rebuilding of one tattered civilization after another reminds us of the words of Job 3: "With kings and counsellors of the earth, which built for themselves places lying in ruins."